HISTORY OF PHILOSOPHY

HISTORY OF PHILOSOPHY

BY

ALFRED WEBER

TRANSLATED BY

FRANK THILLY

PROFESSOR OF PHILOSOPHY, CORNELL UNIVERSITY

WITH

PHILOSOPHY SINCE 1860

BY

RALPH BARTON PERRY

PROFESSOR OF PHILOSOPHY, HARVARD UNIVERSITY

CHARLES SCRIBNER'S SONS

NEW YORK   CHICAGO   BOSTON   ATLANTA

SAN FRANCISCO   DALLAS

PREFACE TO REVISED EDITION

Weber's *History of Philosophy* has long been a standard work in which thoroughness of scholarship and vividness of style have been uniquely combined. The purpose of this edition is to make that text more useful without altering those essential features which have commended it to so many teachers of philosophy in English-speaking countries. The new material which I have added is designed to bring the account of modern philosophy down to the present. In writing these additional chapters (pages 458-594) I have been concerned to fill in the middle foreground rather than to deal with strictly contemporary thought. My aim has been to present only those recent philosophers whose doctrines have become a part of history. Among these are some who are still living, but whose earlier teachings are already a part of the European and American tradition. The omission or brief mention of contemporary thinkers does not imply an adverse estimate of their importance, but only the judgment that they are so much of the present that it is impossible to see them in historical perspective. At the same time I have endeavored in some measure to correct the provincialism which characterizes most histories of recent philosophy, and to direct the attention of English-speaking students to the philosophy of France, Germany, and Italy.

My colleague, Dr. Raphael Demos, has revised the references and bibliography of the entire book in order to simplify them and bring them up to date. Citations in foreign languages have in some cases been omitted, and wherever they remain they have been provided with translations. In this way the text will be suitable for students who are familiar with Greek, Latin, French, or German, but its use will not depend on the knowledge of any language other than English. Bibliographical references are reduced to such as are suitable to beginners rather than to advanced students.

In a word, this revision is designed to remove obsolete or unessential annotations, and to introduce the present-day student of philosophy to all the great philosophical doctrines and systems that have secured a permanent place in European and American thought.

RALPH BARTON PERRY.

CONTENTS

INTRODUCTION

I. GREEK PHILOSOPHY

FIRST PERIOD

AGE OF METAPHYSICS PROPER OR PHILOSOPHY OF NATURE

(B. C. 600–400)

A. *The Denial of Change*

B. *The Philosophy of Universal Flux*

C. *Explanation of Change*

vii

II. PHILOSOPHY OF THE MIDDLE AGES

FIRST PERIOD

REIGN OF PLATONIC-CHRISTIAN THEOLOGY

SECOND PERIOD

THE REIGN OF PERIPATETIC SCHOLASTICISM

A. Semi-Realistic Peripateticism

III. MODERN PHILOSOPHY

FIRST PERIOD

THE AGE OF INDEPENDENT METAPHYSICS

(FROM BRUNO TO LOCKE AND KANT)

SECOND PERIOD

AGE OF CRITICISM

THIRD PERIOD

METAPHYSICAL RECONSTRUCTION

FOURTH PERIOD

THE DEVELOPMENT OF EUROPEAN AND AMERICAN PHILOSOPHY SINCE 1860

A. Naturalism, Materialism, and Positivism

B. Spiritualism and Idealism

CONTENTS

HISTORY OF PHILOSOPHY

INTRODUCTION

§ 1. Philosophy, Metaphysics, and Science

Philosophy is the search for a comprehensive view of nature, an attempt at a universal explanation of things. It is both the summary of the sciences and their completion; both general science and a specialty distinguished from science proper; and, like its elder sisters, religion and poetry, forms a separate branch among the manifestations of the human mind.

The different sciences have special groups of facts for their subject-matter, and seek to discover the causes of these phenomena, or to formulate the laws according to which they are produced. In philosophy, on the other hand, the human mind endeavors to rise beyond such groups and their particular laws, and to explain the world as a whole, or *the universal fact or phenomenon*, by the cause of the causes, or the first cause. In other words, it attempts to answer the question, Why does this world exist, and how does it happen to be what it is?

But though philosophy has its own subject-matter and a separate sphere of its own, it is none the less connected with positive science by the closest of ties; and science cannot break these bonds without danger to itself. It is from the positive sciences, and particularly from psychology and allied branches, that philosophy derives its methods and the matter for its systems. The sciences, without philosophy, are an aggregate without unity, a body without a soul; philosophy, without the sciences, is a soul without a body, differing in nothing from poetry and its dreams. Science is the indispensable foundation and the matter, as it were, of philosophy; it is, to use an Aristotelian phrase, potential philosophy. Philosophy, in turn, is science in its full fruition, the most exalted function of the scholar, the supreme satisfaction of the scientific spirit and its natural tendency to comprehend everything into a unity.

Philosophy and science are intimately related, not only in essence and in interests, but also as to their origin and destiny. Animated by the same all-powerful instinct to discern the causes of things and to comprehend them into the unity of a first cause, the human mind no sooner reaches certain elementary truths in physics, mathematics, and morals, than it hastens to synthesize them, to form them into universal theories, into ontological and cosmological systems, i. e., to philosophize, to make metaphysics. It makes up for its ignorance of reality either by means of the imagination, or by that wonderful instinct of childhood and of genius which divines the truth without searching for it. This accounts for the aprioristic, idealistic, and fantastic character of the philosophy of the ancients, as well as for its incomparable grandeur. In proportion as our stock of positive knowledge is increased, as scientific labor is divided and consequently developed, philosophy becomes more and more differentiated from poetry; its methods are recognized, its theories gain in depth what the sciences acquire in scope. Every scientific movement gives rise to a philosophical movement; every new philosophy is a stimulus to science. Though this bond of union seems to have been ruptured during the Middle Ages, the breach is but an apparent one. Whatever hostility or indifference is manifested toward science, comes from the official philosophy of the School; it is never found among the independent philosophers, be they Christians, Jews, or Arabians. There may be as much opposition between science and a *certain* philosophy in the nineteenth century as there was in the times of Roger Bacon and Lord Verulam. True science and true philosophy have always been in perfect accord, and though there may be a semblance of rivalry, their relations are to-day as harmonious as they can be.[1]

---

[1] On the nature and import of philosophy, and its relation to other sciences, consult Paulsen, *Introduction to Philosophy*, New York, 1922; James, W., *Some Problems of Philosophy*, New York, 1911; Russell, *Some Problems of Philosophy* (Home University Library), New York; Fullerton, *Introduction to Philosophy*, New York, 1906.

§ 2. Division

To the Ionian Greeks belongs the honor of having created[1] European philosophy; to the Neo-Latins and the Germans, that of having given to it its modern development.

Hence there are, in the history to be outlined by us, two great and wholly distinct epochs, which are connected by the Middle Ages (period of transition).

I. In the development of Greek philosophy, we have two separate periods, — a period of spontaneous creation, and one of sceptical reflection and reproduction.

1. The problem which dominates the former is the problem of the origin of things: the problem of *becoming*. Among the Ionians, this philosophy assumes the form of materialistic pantheism; among the Italian philosophers, who are influenced by the Doric spirit, it is essentially spiritualistic pantheism. The systems produced by these two schools contain in germ all the doctrines of the future, especially the monistic and atomistic hypotheses, the two poles of modern scientific speculation. — From Thales to Protagoras, or from 600 to 440 B. C.

2. The age of critical reflection is inaugurated by the πάντων μέτρον ἄνθρωπος (man is the measure of all things) of the Sophists. This period evolves the important truth, foreshadowed by Zeno, Parmenides, and Anaxagoras, that the human

[1] By this word we do not mean to imply the absolute originality of Hellenic philosophy. The influence exercised upon its development by the Orient cannot be doubted. There is no trace of philosophy, properly so called, among the Greeks before they come in contact with Egypt, that is, before the reign of Psammetichus, who admits them into the country. Moreover, the fathers of Greek philosophy are *all* Ionians; from Asia Minor philosophy was imported, first into Italy, and at a comparatively recent period into Athens, that is, into Greece proper. But what is most important, we find in Ionian philosophy, and that too at its very outset, conceptions the boldness of which is in marked contrast with the comparative timidity of Attic philosophy, — conceptions which presuppose a long line of intellectual development. The influence of Egyptian and Chaldean science, which is, moreover, attested by Herodotus, may be compared to that exercised by the Arabian schools upon the development of Christian thought in the Middle Ages. Concerning the relation of Pythagoreanism and Platonism to Indian and Iranian speculation, and the part played by Babylon as the centre of intellectual exchange between the Orient and the Occident, see § 9.

understanding is a coefficient in the production of the phenomenon. To the problems of nature are added the problems
of the soul, to the cosmological questions, logical and critical
questions; to the speculations on the essence of things, investigations concerning the criterion of truth and the end of life.
Greek philosophy reaches its highest development in Plato,
as far as depth is concerned; in Aristotle and in the science of
Alexandria, as regards analysis and the extent of its inquiries.

II. Scientific progress, and consequently speculation, was
arrested by the invasion of the Northern races. The philosophical spirit was extinguished for want of something to
nourish it. Ten centuries of uninterrupted labor were followed
by ten centuries of sleep, — a sleep that was deep at first, and
then broken by bright dreams of the past (Plato and Aristotle)
and forecasts of the future. Although the logic of history is
less transparent during the Middle Ages than before and after
this period of transition, we notice two epochs that run parallel with those of Attic philosophy: one, Platonic, realistic,
turned towards the past (from St. Augustine to St. Anselm),
the other, Peripatetic, nominalistic, big with the future.

III. Modern philosophy dates from the scientific and literary revival in the fifteenth century. Its history presents,—

1. A period of expansion and ontological synthesis (Bruno,
Descartes, Spinoza, Leibniz), and,

2. A period of critical reflection and analysis (essays concerning the human understanding: Locke, Hume, Kant).

3. A period of metaphysical reconstruction (Fichte, Hegel,
Schopenhauer, etc.).

4. A period of varied critical and constructive tendencies.

§ 3. Brief Bibliography for the Student

General History of Philosophy: Rogers, *Students' History of
Philosophy*, New York, 1921; Webb, *History of Philosophy* (Home
University Library), London, 1915; Thilly, *History of Philosophy*,
New York, 1914; Windelband, *History of Philosophy*, tr. by Tufts,
New York, 1893; Ueberweg, *History of Philosophy*, New York,

1903; Calkins, *Persistent Problems of Philosophy*, New York, 1919.

Greek Philosophy: Benn, *The Greek Philosophers*, London, 1914; Appleton, *The Elements of Greek Philosophy*, London, 1922; Gomperz, *Greek Thinkers*, tr. by Berry, 4 vols., London, 1912; Taylor, M. E. J., *Greek Philosophy*, London, 1924; Zeller, *Outlines of the History of Greek Philosophy*, tr. by Alleyne & Abbott, New York, 1890; Burnet, *Early Greek Philosophy*, London, 1908; More, *Hellenistic Essays*, Princeton, 1923; Zimmerman, *The Greek Commonwealth*, Oxford, 1915; Dickinson, *The Greek View of Life*, London, 1896.

Mediæval Philosophy: De Wulf, *Mediæval Philosophy*, Cambridge, U. S. A., 1922; De Wulf, *Philosophy and Civilization in the Middle Ages*, Princeton, 1922; Taylor, *The Mediæval Mind*, 2 vols., London, 1911.

Modern Philosophy: Falckenberg, *History of Modern Philosophy*, tr. by Armstrong, New York, 1897; Hoffding, *Brief History of Modern Philosophy*, tr. by Sanders, New York, 1912; *Modern Classical Philosophers*, compiled by B. Rand, revised edition, Cambridge, U. S. A., 1924; Royce, *Spirit of Modern Philosophy*, New York, 1892; Lévy-Bruhl, *History of Modern Philosophy in France*, Chicago, 1899; Sorley, *History of English Philosophy*, Cambridge (Eng.), 1920; Riley, *American Thought*, New York, 1915.

I

GREEK PHILOSOPHY

FIRST PERIOD

AGE OF METAPHYSICS PROPER OR PHILOSOPHY OF NATURE
(B. C. 600–400)

§ 4. Origin of Greek Philosophy

The philosophy of the Hellenes emancipates itself from their religion in the form of theology and gnomic morality.[1] Aryan naturalism, modified by the national genius and the physical conditions under which it developed, forms its starting-point. This naturalism had passed the period of infancy long before the appearance of philosophy. The luminous Ether (Diaus-Zeus), the Sun and its fire (Apollo), the Storm-cloud and its thunderbolts (Pallas-Athene), were originally taken for the gods themselves. Just as the child transforms its surroundings into an enchanted world, and regards its doll and wooden horse as living beings, so the humanity-child makes nature after its own image. For the contemporaries of Homer and Hesiod, such objects are merely the sensible manifestations of the invisible divinity concealed behind them, a being that is similar to the human soul, but superior to it in power, and, like it, invested with immortality. The gods form a kind of idealized, transcendent humanity, whose vices as well as virtues are magnified. The world is their work, their empire, the theatre of their wishes, defeats, and triumphs. Man, whom they envy rather than love, exists for their pleasure. They are the highest personifications of the will-to-live, and are jealous

---

[1] Cf. on Greek religion and mythology, Harrison, *The Religion of Ancient Greece*, London, 1913; Cornford, *From Religion to Philosophy*, London, 1912.

of their unquestioned superiority; hence they deny him perfect happiness. The most assiduous worship, the richest sacrifices, the most perfect fidelity, cannot move them when our prosperity displeases them. Hence the melancholy which breathes in the gnomic poetry of a Solon or a Theognis, who prefer death to life, and esteem them happy who have never been born or who die young.

In the measure in which the moral conscience is developed and refined, religious ideas are transformed and spiritualized. The gods of Homer, who reflect the exuberant, versatile, and quarrelsome youth of the Hellenic nation, are succeeded by the just and wise gods, the creations of its riper manhood (Pindar, Æschylus, Sophocles). This *qualitative* transformation of the religious ideas is accompanied by a *quantitative* transformation. Polytheism aims at greater simplicity. The good, which the will perceives as its highest end, is synonymous with harmony, and harmony means unity in diversity. Religious and moral progress is, in consequence, a progress in the unitary and monotheistic direction.

The moral consciousness, which among the Greeks is identical with the sense of the beautiful, finds a powerful ally in reason and its natural tendency to unity. Guided by the monistic instinct, theology asks itself the question, Who is the oldest of the gods, and in what order do they spring from their common Father? and receives an answer in the theogonies of Hesiod, Pherecydes of Syros, and Orpheus. Here, for the first time, the philosophical spirit finds satisfaction; these fantastic conceptions are anticipations of the rational explanation of nature.

To conscience and reason a third factor, experience, is added. This, too, assists in the transformation of religious ideas by demonstrating, with increasing evidence, the impossibility of explaining all phenomena, without exception, by capricious wills. The facts of mathematics, because of their universality and necessity, especially defy theological interpretation; how indeed can we assume the fact that twice two is four or that the three angles of a triangle are equal to two right angles, to be the result of caprice and not of absolute necessity? In the same way the observation of astronomical and physical facts, and their constant regularity and periodicity, gives rise to the idea of a Will that is superior to the whims of the gods (μοῖρα), of an immutable Justice (δίκη), of a divine Law (θεῖος νόμος), of a supreme Intelligence (θεῖος λόγος). The pioneers of philosophy, men like Thales, Xenophanes, and Pythagoras, who were the first to protest against theological anthropomorphism, were likewise mathematicians, naturalists, and astronomers, if we may so designate men who had an elementary knowledge of the course of the stars, the properties of numbers, and the nature of bodies.

Philosophy dates her origin from the day when these *physicians*, as Aristotle terms them in distinction from their predecessors, the theologians, relegated the traditional gods to the domain of fable, and explained nature by principles and causes. Emerging as she did from the conflict between reason and religious authority, which sought revenge by systematically accusing her of atheism and treason, philosophy did not at once cast off the mythological garb. She loved to express herself in the rhythmical language of the poets; and even her conceptions retained the marks of the religious faith from which she sprang. The gods are not abolished; they are restored to their true nature, and regarded as *elements* (στοιχεῖα). Following the example of theology, philosophy begins to ask herself the question, What is the primitive element, the one that precedes the others in dignity and in time, and from which, consequently, the others have been *generated?* The theogonies become cosmogonies, and the only important question concerning which the first thinkers differ is the question as to what constitutes the primordial natural force, the *principle*.

§ 5. The School of Miletus. Thales, Anaximander, Anaximenes [1]

1. THALES, the head of what may be called the school of Miletus, and the father of all the Ionian schools, lived about 600 B. C. According to him, water is the first principle, the universal substratum, of which the other bodies are merely modifications; water envelops the earth on all sides; the earth floats upon this infinite ocean, and constantly derives from it the nourishment it needs.

This doctrine is the old Aryan myth of the heavenly Okeanos translated into scientific language: the water of the storm-cloud fructifies the earth and is the father of all living things. It is all we know positively of the philosophy of Thales. He is, moreover, represented to us by antiquity as the first geometrician, the first astronomer, and the first physicist among the Greeks. He is said to have predicted the eclipse of the 28th of May, 585, and to have been acquainted with the phenomenon of magnetism, as well as with the attractive property of polished amber.

2. According to ANAXIMANDER, a fellow-countryman and disciple of Thales, the author of a work *On Nature*, the first principle is not water, but the infinite atmosphere (τὸ ἄπειρον), from which it comes in order to fructify the earth. This infinite, indistinct matter is the mother of the heavens and the worlds which they encompass. Everything that exists owes its being to the first principle, and arises from it by separation; it is therefore just that everything render to it, at the hour appointed by Fate, the life which Fate has given it, in order that this life may circulate and pass to new beings. The opposites, warm and cold, dry and moist, which do not exist in the ἄπειρον (*apeiron* — infinite), the primitive chaos where every-

---

[1] For books on the pre-Socratics, in general, consult Fuller, *History of Greek Philosophy: From Thales to Democritus*, New York, 1923; Burnet, *Greek Philosophy*, Part I, *Thales to Plato*, London, 1914; Benn, *Early Greek Philosophy*, London, 1914.

thing is neutralized, are gradually parted off, and form nature, with its contraries, its opposite qualities, and separate elements. The first opposition is that between the warm and dry, on the one hand, and the cold and moist, on the other; the former occurring in the earth, the latter in the heavens which surround it. The earth is a cylindrical body, and floats freely in the infinite ether, being held in equilibrium because of its equal distance from all the other heavenly bodies. There are an infinite number of worlds which are alternately formed and destroyed. The first animals were produced in the water, and from them the more advanced species gradually arose. Man sprang from the fish. Individuals and species constantly change, but the substance whence they are derived, the *apeiron*, is indestructible, because it is uncreated. It envelops everything, produces everything, governs everything. It is the supreme divinity, possessing a perpetual vitality of its own.

3. ANAXIMENES of Miletus, the disciple of Anaximander and third representative of the Ionian philosophy, calls the generative principle of things air or breath (ἀήρ). His philosophy, which is a more exact formulation of Anaximander's doctrine, may be summarized in the following words: infinite matter, a perpetual motion of condensation and rarefaction that is something like a plastic principle, necessity directing the motion. Matter, motion, motive force, directing necessity: we find among the Ionians all the elements of the explanations of nature attempted afterwards. But their systems are like rudimentary organisms. The perfection of a living being depends upon the greater or less differentiation of its organs; the more its constitutive parts differ from each other and become specialized, the higher it rises in the scale of beings. Now, the Ionian philosophy is perfectly uniform. Thales regards water, Anaximenes air, as substratum, motive force, and fate, or the law of motion. Progress in science, as well as in nature, is made possible by the division of labor, by differentiation of the constitutive elements of being, by the multiplication and opposition of systems.

§ 6. The Problem of Change

1. The first question that arouses controversy is the problem of becoming. *Being* persists, *beings* constantly change; they are born and they pass away. How can being both persist and not persist? Reflection upon this problem, the metaphysical problem *par excellence*, since it lies at the root of all the sciences and dominates all questions, gives rise to three systems, the types of all European philosophies, — the Eleatic system; the system of Heraclitus; the atomistic system, which was proclaimed in the idealistic sense by the Pythagoreans, in the materialistic sense by Leucippus and Democritus, and with a dualistic turn by Anaxagoras. The first two are radical; each suppresses one of the terms of the antinomy; the third is a doctrine of conciliation. According to the Eleatic hypothesis, being is everything, change is an appearance; according to Heraclitus, change is everything, and being, or permanence, is but an illusion; according to the monadists and atomists, both permanence and change exist: permanence in *the beings*,[1] perpetual change *in their relations*. The Eleatics deny becoming; Heraclitus makes a god of it; the atomists explain it.

A. The Denial of Change

§ 7. Eleatic Philosophy. Xenophanes, Parmenides, Melissus, Zeno, Gorgias

At the time when Anaximander flourished in Miletus, another Ionian, Xenophanes of Colophon, immigrated into Magna Græcia, travelled through the cities as a philosopher and rhapsodist, and finally settled in Elea in Lucania, where he gained adherents. His theological innovations were developed and systematized by Parmenides of Elea and Melissus of Samos, who raised them to the dignity of a metaphysic. Zeno of Elea, the disciple of Parmenides, undertook to defend

---

[1] Considered by the Pythagoreans as ideal unities or numbers; by the atomists as real or material unities.

them by means of dialectics, thereby becoming the precursor
of the Sophists.

1. XENOPHANES is a decided opponent of the national
mythology, toward which he assumes a similar attitude to
that of the Hebrew prophets who raised their powerful voices
against polytheism and its empty conceptions. His written
and spoken words proclaim him as the real creator of philosophical monotheism, which he identifies with pantheism.
With an eloquence that is full of irony, his satires, some fragments of which are extant, combat the error of those who infinitely multiply the divine Being, who attribute to him a
human form (anthropomorphism) and human passions (an-
thropopathism). There is one God, he says, one only God,
comparable to the gods of Homer or to mortals neither in
form nor in thought. This God is all eye, all ear, all thought.
Being immutable and immovable, he has no need of going
about, now hither, now thither, in order to carry out his
wishes, but without toil he governs all things by his thought
alone. Mortals, of course, accept the authority of Homer and
Hesiod, and think that the gods are born as they are, and like
them have feeling, voice, and body; and they ascribe to the
gods all things that are a shame and disgrace among men, —
theft, adultery, and falsehood. They do as the oxen or lions
would do if they could paint: they would certainly represent
their gods in the form of lions or oxen. In place of these imaginary beings, let us adore the one infinite Being, who bears us
in his bosom, and in whom there is neither generation nor corruption, neither change nor origin.

2. PARMENIDES completes the teachings of his master, and
makes them the starting-point for a strictly monistic system.
Since there is no change in God, and since God is everything,
that which we call change is but an appearance, an illusion
(δόξα), and there is in reality neither origin nor decay. The
eternal being alone exists: this thesis forms the subject of a
philosophical poem, the fragments of which are the most ancient monument in our possession of metaphysical speculation
proper among the Greeks. In the first part, dedicated to

Truth, he demonstrates by means of specious arguments that our notions of change, plurality, and limitation contradict reason. In the second part, which deals with the merely illusory, he attempts to give an explanation of nature from the standpoint of illusion.

Starting out with the idea of being, he proves that that which is cannot have become what it is, nor can it cease to be, nor become something else; for if being has begun to exist, it has come either from being or non-being. Now, in the former case, it is its own product, it has created itself, which is equivalent to saying that it has not originated, — that it is eternal. The latter case supposes that something can come from nothing, which is absurd. For the same reasons, that which exists can neither change nor perish, for in death it would pass either into being or into non-being. If being is changed into being, then it does not change; and to assume that it becomes nothing is as impossible as to make it come from nothing. Consequently being is eternal. It is, moreover, immovable; for it could move only in space; now space is or is not; if space is, it is identical with being, and to say of being that it is moved in space is to say that being is moved in being, which means that it is at rest. If space is nothing, there cannot be any movement either, for movement is possible only in space. Hence, movement cannot be conceived in any way, and is but an appearance. Being is a continuous and indivisible whole. There is no void anywhere. There is no break between being and being; consequently these are no atoms. Let us suppose, for the sake of argument, that there existed a void, a break between the assumed parts of the universe. If this interval is something real, it is what being is, it *continues* being, instead of interrupting it; it unites the bodies instead of dividing them into parts. If the void does not exist, then it can no longer divide them. There is then no interval between being and being, and all beings constitute but one single being. Being (the universe) is absolute and self-sufficient; it has neither desires nor wants nor feelings of any kind. If it were relative, it could depend only on that which is or on that which is not. If being depends on being, it depends upon itself or is independent; if it depends on that which does not exist, it is still independent; which excludes from it all desire, all need, all feeling. When one is everything one has no desires. Finally, being is one; for a second being or a third being would be but a continuation of it, that is, itself. Hence, to sum up: Being can only be conceived as eternal, immutable, immovable, continuous, indivisible, infinite, unique. There is for the thinker but one single being, the All-One, in whom all individual differences are merged. The being that thinks and the being that is thought are the same thing.

In the second part of his poem, Parmenides deals with opinion (δόξα), which depends on the senses and is concerned with what is merely illusory. The universe, which reason conceives as an indivisible unity, is divided by the senses into two realms or rival elements: night or cold; and light, fire, or heat. The universe, which to reason is without beginning or end, has its apparent origin, its genesis; and this genesis is the successive victory of the principle of light over the principle of darkness. Night is the mother, the luminous principle is the father, of all forms (εἴδη). The world shows the traces of the two elements to which it owes its origin even in its smallest parts. The warm and the cold, the clear and the obscure, are universally combined in constant proportions. The universe is composed of a series of concentric spheres, in which the light and warm spheres alternate with the dark and cold spheres. The outermost sphere, which encloses all the rest, is solid, cold, and dark; beneath it lies the fiery sphere of the fixed stars. The central sphere is also solid and cold, but it is surrounded by a sphere of light and life. This fiery sphere which encircles the solid core of the earth is the source of movement (that is, of illusion[1]), the hearth of universal life, the seat of the Divinity, the Queen of the world, Justice, Necessity, the Mother of Love.

[1] Cf. the Maja of the Hindoos, the mother of illusions.

These doctrines, which partially reproduce Ionian and Pythagorean speculations, are not offered as the truth, but as hypotheses intended to orient us in the world of illusion. They have not for Parmenides the importance which they have for the Ionians. Inasmuch as he does not grant the existence of motion, but rejects as illusory that which constitutes the essence of nature, he accepts no other science than metaphysics, no other metaphysics than that of pure reasoning. On account of the opposition which he creates between the real and the intelligible, he is the chief forerunner of Platonic idealism, without, however, being a spiritualist in the modern sense. Spiritualism distinguishes between matter and mind; Eleatic metaphysics makes no such distinction. The being which it affirms is neither body nor soul, neither matter nor spirit; it is being, nothing but being; and everything else is merely an accident, an appearance, an illusion. Nay, if we interpret the word *matter* in the subtle metaphysical sense of *substance* or universal *substratum*, we may reckon Parmenides among the materialists, like his modern imitator Spinoza. But it would be a mistake to call him a materialist in the sense in which the term is applied to Democritus and the modern materialists; for materialism, properly so-called, exists only in opposition to spiritualism, which is later than Parmenides. The monism of Parmenides and Heraclitus is like the block of marble which may be formed into a basin or a Jupiter, or like the mother-cell from which, according to circumstances, a Socrates or an Erostratus may come; it is capable of being differentiated and developed into materialistic or spiritualistic monism.

3. Plato deduces idealism from it, while MELISSUS of Samos[1] (440) interprets it in an altogether materialistic sense. This philosopher, who was also a brave general and a clever politician, opposes the Ionian cosmogonies with the Eleatic doctrine of the eternity of the world. If becoming is impossible, it is henceforth useless and absurd to inquire into the manner

---

[1] The author of a book, περὶ τοῦ ὄντος (on being).

in which the universe originated. Being (τὸ ὄν) is infinite in time, and — which is contrary to the view of Parmenides, who conceived it as a sphere — infinite in space. This latter trait, which leaves no doubt as to the materialism of Melissus, gives his system a wholly modern stamp, and distinguishes it from most of the ancient systems, particularly from that of Aristotle. For the Greek, who judges of things artistically, regards the infinite as the imperfect, as without *limitation;* and the universe, which is the acme of perfection, is surely the perfect sphere, one-half of which is revealed to us by the sense of sight, and of which the earth is the centre.

4. ZENO, a pupil and follower of Parmenides, is the controversialist of the school, the inventor of the process of demonstration called *reductio ad absurdum,* the father of dialectics and sophistry. The One alone is conceivable; extension, magnitude, motion, and space, cannot be conceived. If there is such a thing as a (limited) magnitude, it must be infinitely great and infinitely small: infinitely great, because, being infinitely divisible, it is composed of an infinite number of parts; infinitely small, because unextended parts, even though multiplied by infinity, cannot produce extension or magnitude.

Movement cannot be conceived; for the line which separates its starting-point from its point of rest is composed of points, and, since the point has no extension, of an infinite number of points. Hence every distance, even the smallest, is infinite, and the stopping-point can never be reached. However near you may imagine the swift Achilles to be to the slow tortoise, he will never be able to overtake it, since, in order to do so, he would first have to pass over one-half of the distance, however small, which separates him from the tortoise, and, in order to pass over this half, he would first have to pass over the half of the half, and so on to infinity. The infinite divisibility of the line is for him an insurmountable obstacle. You have an idea that the arrow flies through space. But in order to reach its destination, it must pass over a series of points in space; hence it must successively occupy these different points.

Now, to occupy a point of space, at a given moment, means to be at rest: therefore the arrow is at rest and its movement is but illusory.

Furthermore, if movement takes place, it can take place only in space. Now, if space is a reality, it exists somewhere, that is, in a space, which in turn exists in another space, and so on. Motion is, therefore, impossible from every point of view, and we cannot suppose it to be real, unless we are willing to affirm an absurdity. Being alone exists, and this being is immutable matter.

5. GORGIAS of Leontinum, the rhetorician, a pupil of Zeno, who was sent by his country as an ambassador to Athens in 427, deduces the ultimate consequences from the Eleatic principle and ends in nihilism. He is not, like Zeno, content with denying motion and space; as his treatise "On Non-being or on Nature" shows, he negates being itself. Nothing exists, he says; for if a being existed, it would have to be eternal, as was proved by Parmenides. Now, an eternal being is infinite. But an infinite being cannot exist in space or in time without being limited by them. Hence it is nowhere, and that which is nowhere does not exist. And even if, assuming the impossible, something did exist, we could not know it; and even if we could, this knowledge could not in any wise be communicated to others.

Gorgias is the *enfant terrible* of the Eleatic school, whose extravagances turn the tide in favor of the Heraclitean principle: *Being is nothing, becoming is everything.* The *being* of Parmenides and Zeno, which is eternal and immutable, but devoid of all positive attributes, is, in fact, a mere abstraction. It resembles the garment of the king, the fine texture of which everybody pretended to admire, until, at last, a little child exclaimed, in the simplicity of its heart: "Why, the king is naked!"

B. The Philosophy of Universal Flux

§ 8. Heraclitus

HERACLITUS, who, on account of his love of paradox, was called the Obscure, flourished at Ephesus, near the end of the sixth century. He has left a deeper impress on Greek thought than any of the physicists of the first period, and more than one modern hypothesis is either foreshadowed or expressly formulated in the valuable fragments of his book *On Nature*.

Like the physicists of Miletus, Heraclitus considers all bodies as transformations of one and the same element. But this element is not, as with Anaximenes, the atmospheric air; it is a finer, more subtle substance, which he sometimes calls fire ($\pi\hat{v}\rho$), sometimes warm breath ($\psi v\chi\acute{\eta}$), and which resembles either what physics formerly called *caloric*, or the oxygen of modern chemistry. This original matter extends from the boundaries of the earth to the limits of the world. Everything that exists is derived from it, and strives to return to it; every being is transformed fire; and, conversely, every being may be, and, as a matter of fact, is, eventually changed into fire.[1] Atmospheric air and water are fire in process of extinction or in process of renewal; earth and solids are extinguished fire, and will be rekindled afresh at the hour fixed by Fate. According to an immutable law, the fire of the heavenly regions is successively transformed into vapor, water, and earth, only to return again, in the opposite direction, to its principle; then it thickens again, re-ascends into the heavens, and so on *ad infinitum*. The universe is, therefore, fire in the process of transformation, an ever-living fire, which is periodically kindled and extinguished. It is neither the work of a god nor of a man. It has had no beginning, and it will never end. There is an end of the world in the sense that all things ultimately return to fire; but the world eternally re-arises from its ashes.

---

[1] The physics of Heraclitus reminds one of the mechanical theory of heat taught by modern physics, which, like the sage of Ephesus, considers all organic life as a transformation of solar heat.

Universal life is an endless alternation of creation and destruction, — a game which Jupiter plays with himself. Rest, standstill, in a word, being, is an illusion of the senses. It is not possible to descend twice into the same stream[1]; nay, it is not even possible to descend into it once; we are and we are not in it; we make up our minds to plunge into the waves, and, behold! they are already far away from us. In the eternal whirl, the nothing constantly changes into being, and being is incessantly swallowed up in nothingness. Since non-being produces being, and *vice versa;* being and non-being, life and death, origin and decay, are the same. If they were not, they could not be transformed into each other.

The *perpetual flow* of things is not, as the expression might lead one to think, an easy process, like the gliding of a brook over a bed of polished stones. Becoming is a struggle between contrary forces, between opposing currents, one of which comes from above and strives to transform the celestial fire into solid matter; while the other re-ascends into the heavens, and strives to change earth into fire. It is this continuous battle between two contrary currents that produces all vegetable, animal, and intellectual life on the surface of the earth. Everything arises from the strife of opposites. Organic life is produced by the male and the female; musical harmony, by sharp and flat notes; it is sickness that makes us appreciate health; without exertion, there can be no sweet repose; without danger, no courage; without evil to overcome, no virtue. Just as fire *lives* the death of air, air, the death of fire, water, the death of air, earth, the death of water; so, too, the animal *lives* the death of the vegetable, man, the death of the animal, the gods, the death of man, virtue, the death of vice, and vice, the death of virtue. Hence, good is a destroyed evil, evil, a vanished good; and since evil does not exist without the good, nor the good without the evil, evil is a relative good, and good a relative evil. Like being and non-being, good and evil disappear in the universal harmony.

[1] Plato, *Cratylus,* p. 402 A.

The emphasis which Heraclitus lays on the perpetual flux and the absolute instability of things, on the vanity of all individual existence, the impossibility of good without evil, of pleasure without pain, of life without death, makes him the typical pessimist of antiquity, as opposed to the optimist, Democritus.[1] His negation of being likewise implies scepticism.[2] Inasmuch as truth is the same to-day, to-morrow, and forever, there can be no certain and final knowledge if everything perceived by the senses constantly changes. The senses, however, are not our only means of knowledge; in addition to them we have reason (λόγος, *logos*). The senses show us what passes away, and knowledge that is based on sensation alone is deceptive; reason reveals to us what is stable: the divine law, the only fixed point in the eternal flow of things. But the most enlightened human reason is still as far removed from divine reason as the ape is removed from human perfection. By distinguishing between the sensible phenomenon and the noumenon, as Heraclitus did, Ionian philosophy emerges from the state of innocence, as it were; it begins to suspect its methods, to distrust itself, to ask itself whether the ontological problem can really be solved at all; in a word, it foreshadows the critical question.

Anthropology cuts loose from general speculation and begins to form a prominent part in the system of Heraclitus. The soul is an emanation of the celestial fire, and can live only by remaining in contact with this source of life. It is constantly renewed by means of respiration and sensation. Generation is the transformation of the liquid seed into dry breath. Hence the latent fire of the earth passes through the liquid state and returns to its original condition in the human soul. The driest breath constitutes the wisest soul, but woe to the drunkard who prematurely causes his soul to pass back into the liquid state! In death the breath of life or the soul grad-

---

[1] See § 12.

[2] The school of Heraclitus, and particularly Cratylus, the best known of his disciples and one of the teachers of Plato, taught scepticism.

ually returns to earth. An individual's energy will depend upon his more or less constant communion with the celestial fire, the supremely intelligent and wise soul of the world.

Here we have the first feeble beginnings of physiological psychology, and they are naïvely materialistic. The philosophy of this period speaks of mind as popular chemistry speaks of spirits and essences; but though materialistic, it is so little aware of the fact that it does not even possess a technical term for matter. We are not conscious of ourselves except in opposition to what we are not.

To sum up: All things proceed from a dry and warm principle and eventually return to it; everything is in a state of perpetual change, and there is nothing immutable in the eternal process but the Law which governs it and which neither gods nor men can modify.

C. Explanation of Change

§ 9. The Pythagorean Speculation

Do the metaphysical doctrines of Pythagoreanism go back, in part at least, to Pythagoras himself? Are they the teachings of the members of the Pythagorean order, of men like Philolaus, who was exiled from Italy in the first half of the fifth century, and Archytas, who flourished at Tarentum during the second half of that century? The mystery in which the order was enshrouded from the very beginning makes it altogether impossible to answer this question. Aristotle himself seems to be in doubt in the matter; he never speaks of the teachings of Pythagoras, but only of the *Pythagoreans*. However that may be, one thing is certain: the first impetus towards arithmetical speculation known under the name of Pythagorean philosophy was given by the great mathematician of Samos, and even though direct and positive proofs are wanting, nothing can hinder us from proclaiming him as the originator of the doctrines set forth in this section.

Pythagoras, like Thales, of Ionian origin, was born at

Samos during the first half of the sixth century. He was at first the pupil of the theologian Pherecydes and perhaps also of Anaximander, the physicist. According to a tradition which, it must be confessed, has nothing to warrant it among the ancients, he visited Phœnicia, Egypt, and Babylon, where he was initiated into the Eastern theological speculations, and introduced to the study of geometry, which had already attained a high degree of perfection on its native soil. Returning to Greece about 520, he realized his ideals of religious, social, and philosophical reform at Crotona in Magna Græcia, by founding a kind of brotherhood, the members of which entertained the same opinions concerning morality, politics, and religion.[1]

Nothing certain is known of the end of the philosopher. His work prospered. The Pythagoreans were the possessors of all the sciences known in their time, — geometry, astronomy,

---

[1] When we compare the doctrines, aims, and organization of this brotherhood, as portrayed by the Neo-Platonic historians (especially Jamblichus), with Buddhistic monachism, we are almost tempted (with Alexander Polyhistor and Clement of Alexandria) to regard Pythagoras as the pupil of the Brahmans, nay, to identify him with Buddha himself. Indeed, not only do the names (Πύθων, Πυθαγόρας = *an inspired one, a soothsayer*, and Buddha = *enlightened*) bear such close resemblance to each other that even the most fastidious philologist can find no objection in translating Πυθαγόρειος by "preacher of Buddhism," but the Pythagorean and Buddhistic teachings are very much alike. Dualism, pessimism, metempsychosis, celibacy, a common life according to rigorous rules, frequent self-examinations, meditations, devotions, prohibitions against bloody sacrifices and animal nourishment, kindliness towards all men, truthfulness, fidelity, justice, — all these elements are common to both. The fact that most ancient authors and above all Aristotle himself have comparatively little to say concerning the person and life of Pythagoras, would tend to confirm the hypothesis of the identity of Pythagoreanism and Buddhism. However, the existence of Pythagoras, the mathematician, five centuries before the Christian era, is placed beyond doubt by the testimony of Heraclitus, Herodotus, etc. Furthermore, Buddhism in the form of Manichæism (that is to say, monachism) did not begin to spread westward before the third century of our era. We may perhaps explain everything satisfactorily by distinguishing between the Pythagoreanism of the Neo-Platonic historians and primitive and genuine Pythagoreanism. The biographers of Pythagoras were without exact and sufficient data regarding the life and work of the sage of Samos, and somewhat unscrupulous, besides, in the choice of their sources. They likewise allowed themselves to be misled by certain analogies; the essential features of their imaginary portrait are derived from Persian dualism and Hindoo pessimism.

music, and medicine,[1] — and consequently acquired an over-
powering influence among the Doric people, who were less advanced than the Ionians. They preponderated at Crotona, at
Tarentum, and in the Sicilian republics, until the middle of
the fifth century, when the victorious democracy partly ex-
pelled them. The exiles repaired to Thebes or to Athens. Here
their influence counteracted that of the Sophists, and brought
about the spiritualistic reaction of Socrates and Plato against
the materialism and scepticism which had, in the same epoch,
been imported from Sicily, Thrace, and Ionia.

Ionian metaphysics springs from physics; Pythagorean metaphysics is grafted on mathematics, and is consequently totally
different from the former at the very outset. What interests
the philosophers of Miletus is matter and its perpetual movement; what impresses Pythagoras and the Pythagoreans is
the immaterial in matter, the order which prevails in the
world, the unity, proportion, and harmony in its contrasts, the
mathematical relations underlying all things. In geometry, in
astronomy, and in music, everything is ultimately reduced to
number. Hence number is the principle and innermost essence
of the world; and things are sensible numbers. Every being
represents a number, and the final goal of science is to find for
each being the number for which it stands. The infinite series
of numbers, and consequently of things, is derived from unity.
As number is the essence of things, unity is the essence of
number. Pythagoreanism distinguishes two kinds of unities:
(1) the Unity from which the series of numbers (beings) is
derived, and which therefore contains and comprehends them
all; the absolute and unopposed unity, the Monad of monads,
the God of gods; and (2) the One, the first in the series of derived numbers which is opposed to the numbers *two*, *three*,
and every plurality, and consequently limited by the two, the

---

[1] These sciences, which constituted the subject-matter of Pythagorean instruction, were called μαθήματα, — the term from which the word *mathematics*
is derived. The original meaning of the word embraces the totality of human
knowledge.

three, and the plurality; it is a relative unity, a created monad. The opposition between the *one* and the *many* is the source of all the rest. All the contrasts of nature, the dry and the moist, the warm and the cold, the clear and the obscure, the male and the female, the good and the evil, the finite and the infinite, are but varieties of the one and the many, or of the odd and the even. Plurality as such is without consistency and may be divided into unities; the even number is reducible to the odd unit. The absolute unity is neither even nor odd; or rather, it is as yet both even and odd, singular and plural, God and the world. It is to Pythagoreanism what the *apeiron* is in the system of Anaximander: the neuter being that is superior and anterior to sexual contrasts, the absolute indifference which precedes and creates the dualism of forces and elements. But the Pythagoreans guard against calling it *apeiron*, since the *apeiron* is, according to them, opposed to the finite, as passivity to activity, or matter to the workman, or form, or plastic principle. Inasmuch as everything is, according to them, reduced to number, numerical relations, and ultimately to Idea, the matter and *motion* of the Ionians are, in their opinion, merely negative, the absence of ideal unity. Concerning the question of movement and origin, the conclusions of the Pythagoreans do not differ from the Eleatic doctrines. Movement and origin seem to be incompatible with their idealism. Although they have their own cosmogony, like the other schools of the period, they do not assume that the universe had a beginning in time, and consequently that there was a time when the universe did not exist. The world has existed from all eternity, and the cosmogony simply aims to explain the order, law, or series, according to which things *eternally* emanate from their principle.

Pythagorean physics therefore accommodates itself to human *sensualism*, just like the physics of Parmenides. It makes what is in itself immutable, variable. It places itself on the sensualistic standpoint held by the novices among its followers and represents the eternal unity as a sphere, as a compact sphere, in which the parts are not distinguished, and which floats in the infinite. The ideal opposition between the even and the odd, the one and the many, becomes the real opposition of the full and the void. At the origin of things, the full was without the void, or, at least, the void was external to it. The formation of the cosmos begins by the void breaking in upon the full. This process is like a perpetual breath which agitates the world. The void penetrates the sphere and establishes itself in it, thereby breaking it up into an infinite number of infinitesimal particles, reduced images of the sphere. Since, from the geometrical point of view, quality is reduced to quantity and form, these particles differ only in quantity and in figure. They form either cubes or pyramids (tetrahedrons) or octahedrons or icosahedrons or dodecahedrons. The unity reacts against this endless separation, and the particles are joined together again according to their geometric affinities and form elementary bodies: earth, fire, air, water, and ether. Fire is the element *par excellence*, being formed of tetrahedric particles. It is the symbol of the divine principle in nature and is concentrated into a central sun, the hearth of the universe and the abode of the Supreme God, around which revolve (1) the Ouranos, embracing the counter-earth and the earth; (2) the Cosmos proper, consisting of the moon, the sun (?), and the planets; (3) the Olympus with the fixed stars. Pythagoras substitutes for the earth a central fire (which is invisible because the earth keeps facing it with the part that is opposite to the one we inhabit), and makes the earth revolve around this centre. But this does not mean, of course, that he advanced the *heliocentric* theory; he merely foreshadowed the system which his school formulated during the following centuries without succeeding in having it accepted by the majority of scientists. The distances separating the spheres are proportional to the numbers which express the relations that exist between tones and the respective lengths of vibrating strings; and the result of their revolutions around the axis of the world is a divine harmony which the musical genius alone can perceive. This harmony is the soul of the universe. The different beings form an ascending scale according to the degree of perfection with which they reflect the universal harmony. The motion of the elementary being, the physical point, produces the line; the line moves and produces the plane; the plane produces the body, from which sensation, perception, and intelligence gradually arise (emanation).

The individual is mortal in so far as he springs from the temporary union of corporeal elements, according to a ratio that varies within certain limits. When these limits are passed, proportion becomes disproportion, an unequal struggle, disease, decay, and death. But the ideal contents of the broken vase are secure against destruction. The soul is a fixed number in the eternal scale of things, a portion of the world-soul, a spark of the celestial fire, a thought of God. In this respect it is immortal; at death it enters upon a state that is superior or inferior to our present life or like it, according as the soul has lived for God, for the world, or for itself (metempsychosis and palingenesis).

Although the Pythagoreans, like Parmenides and Heraclitus, accentuate one of the constitutive elements of reality and eventually negate concrete existence in order to exalt the Idea, they none the less introduce into Greek thought one of the most important factors in the solution of the Eleatic-Heraclitean problem: What is becoming or the process of perpetual change affirmed by the philosopher of Ephesus, and how can it be reconciled with the conception of the permanence and immutability of matter, which is advanced, no less authoritatively, by the school of Elea? We mean their theory of monads: the infinitesimal particles or physical points of which matter is made up. The subsequent systems all attempt to reconcile Elea and Ephesus by means of the physico-arithmetical theory of elementary units. Thought discovers in the atomistic hypothesis the middle term that unites Parmenides, who denies the great empirical fact of generation and change, and Heraclitus, who sacrifices being and its permanence to becoming, — thereby combining the two rival systems into a higher synthesis, — and lays the foundation for every rational explanation of the process of becoming. Henceforth philosophy no longer regards matter as a continuous mass, the essential properties of which are incessantly transformed. It breaks them up into parts that are in themselves immutable, but which continually change their relative positions. As a consequence, there can be both perpetual change in the aspects of matter (bodies) and permanence in the essence and properties of matter. All change is reduced to change of place: *mechanism.*

Empedocles, Anaxagoras, and Democritus, who hold this theory, differ from each other as Heraclitus, Pythagoras, and Anaximander differ among themselves; that is to say, the first makes motion, the second, the Idea ($\nu o \hat{\upsilon} s$), the third, matter, the keystone of his system.

§ 10. Empedocles

EMPEDOCLES, of Agrigentum, in Sicily (450), who in consequence of his knowledge of medicine, the cures which he effected, and the mystery with which he loved to surround himself, was regarded as a magician and a god, is the author of a grand philosophical poem, the fragments of which seem to place him in an intermediate position between the Eleatics and the Ionians.

He sides with the Eleatics in his denial of becoming, as Heraclitus understands it; and approaches the Ionians in assuming the reality of motion. Matter is immutable in its essence, but bodies are in a state of constant change; their constituent elements are combined and separated in different proportions. We cannot conceive how fire as such can become air, air, water, and so on; but it is conceivable that the thousand different combinations of these elements should produce an infinite variety of bodies. Hence we must abandon the notion of elementary unity; we must cease deriving air from ether, water

from air, earth from water, and consider these four elements
as equally original.

Have the *four elements* movement of their own, or have
they received it from a distinct principle, from a higher force?
It is hard to separate the thought of the philosopher from his
poetical phraseology, encumbered as it is by images and contradictions. We may, it seems, conclude from his poem that
he no longer assumes hylozoism (i. e., the view that all nature
is animated), the eternity of motion, and the original vitality
of matter in the same sense as the Ionian physicists. He appears to explain movement by an immaterial principle, or
rather, by two distinct immaterial principles, one of which
unites the elements, while the other separates them: Love or
the principle of union, and Discord, the principle of separation.[1] These two motive causes, which the imagination of the
poet interprets as opposing divinities, alternately rule the elements. Love first unites them and forms them into a single
spherical body. Discord ensues and divides them; as a result,
the earth, the ocean, the atmosphere, the heavenly ether, and
the stars arise. This period of primitive creation, which is the
work of Discord, is followed by an epoch of struggle between
Discord and Love, during which plants, animals, and men
originate. Discord has, in separating the elements, prepared
for each class of beings the habitation adapted to them, but
it could not form the organisms themselves, which are a mixture of the four elements and consequently the work of the
unifying principle, the product of Love reacting against the
exclusive sway of Antipathy. Although the two principles are
now at war with each other, Love will ultimately gain the victory, and the four spheres of the world, which are at present
separated, will, on the last day, be combined into a new chaos.
This alternation between periods of separation and periods of
union is a fatal necessity, and will go on forever.

Like Anaximander and Heraclitus before him, Empedocles

[1] Nowadays we should use the terms attraction and repulsion. The cosmogony
of Empedocles contains the germ of Kant's.

explains the origin of beings by the process of evolution, but he explains it in his own way. Their organs, he believes, first arose as shapeless and disconnected rudiments, then disappeared and reappeared, separated and reunited, until, at last, they were adapted to each other and joined together for good. The first formation of these beings was the result of chance; but their preservation, proficiency, and development were due to the fitness which they ultimately attained. Our philosopher also regards individual existence as a doubtful good. He is, therefore, the precursor of Schopenhauer as well as of Darwin. With Heraclitus and Hippasus, he identifies the soul with the fiery principle. Discord detached it from the spherical body, in which it originally existed, mixed with all the other beings. Like the rest, it will eventually return thither. Life is the expiation of the soul's desire for a separate existence. Passing through the stages of plant, animal, and man, it rises by degrees, and, by abstinences, fasts, and continent living, finally again becomes worthy of returning to God. The propagation of the human species is an evil, since it perpetuates the actual state of things and retards their return to the original unity.[1] Man is the image of the sphere. The four radical elements are represented in him: the earthly element, by the solid parts of the body; water, by its liquid parts; air, by the vital breath; fire, by the spirit. He is likewise affected by Love and Hate. His intellectual superiority follows from the fact that all the cosmical elements are concentrated in him. He perceives everything, because he *is* everything; he perceives solids because he is earth; liquids, because he is water; and so on. We have here a theory, or let us rather say the beginnings of a theory, of sensation that might be called homœopathic as distinguished from the allopathism of Anaxagoras. The latter

[1] The same views are held by Anaximander, who regards death as an expiation; by Plato, who despises the world of sense, and eagerly desires the return to the realm of pure ideas; by Plotinus of Lycopolis, who is ashamed of his body and the manner in which he entered into the world. The religious conceptions of the fall, of original sin and expiation are familiar to Aryan Europe as well as to Asia.

derives sensation from the coming-together of contraries; according to Empedocles, sensation results from the contact of similars. The blood, in which the four elements are most closely mingled, is the seat of sensation and of the soul. This is proved by the fact that when we withdraw all the blood from the body we deprive it of sensation, consciousness, life, — in a word, of soul. The health of a man depends on the composition of his blood. We are healthy and good when our blood is normally composed. The blood is sacred, and ought not to serve as nourishment. In these doctrines, which remind us of Egypt, Moses, Buddha, and Zoroaster, we see the dawn, as it were, of modern physiology.

In his theology, Empedocles conceals his naturalism under the traditional forms of mythology. He deifies — in name only, not actually, like popular belief — the four elements, which he calls Zeus, Hera, Orcus, and Nestis, and the two motive principles, Love and Discord. But we find in Empedocles, alongside of his theological atomism and naturalized polytheism, Eleatic monism and the tendency to reduce elements and principles to a higher unity, which is the only true God. Love is the principle of principles; the four elements are merely its agents, and Discord itself its indispensable accomplice: it is the ineffable, invisible, incorporeal God, flashing through the whole world with rapid thoughts.

The leading thought in the teaching of Empedocles, freed from its theological shell, meets us again in the system of the Ionian Anaxagoras. Anaxagoras is the founder of corpuscular physics, and, by his hypothesis of the ordering reason, anticipates the conception of purpose as the ruling principle of Nature, in the systems of Plato and Aristotle.

§ 11. Anaxagoras

ANAXAGORAS was born at Clazomenæ in Ionia, of an illustrious family. He seems to have emigrated to Athens about 460, and to have been, for thirty years, the central figure in this new intellectual centre of Greece. His friendship for Pericles, Euripides, and Protagoras, and his profound contempt for the official religion made it necessary for him to retire to Lampsacus towards the close of his life. Here he died about 429 B. C. Like the majority of the great physicists of antiquity, he left a book on Nature, a few fragments of which are still extant.

Anaxagoras opposes Heraclitus in two essential points:

1. He opposes his principle of change with a mechanical theory of nature.

2. He substitutes dualism for monism, assuming the existence of an unintelligent, inert substance and of an intelligent principle, the cause of motion.

1. THE MATERIALS OF THE COSMOGONY. — Matter cannot be reduced to a single element, to a homogeneous substance, like water, air, or fire, that may be transformed into other substances. It is inconceivable how a substance can become another substance. Hence there are several primitive elements, and not only four, as Empedocles teaches; nay, there is an infinite number of them. These germs of things are infinite in number and infinitely small, uncreated, indestructible, and absolutely unchangeable in essence. The quantity of these first principles is always the same; nothing can be destroyed or added; they change neither in quality nor in quantity. Nothing comes into being or passes away. Our usual notions of birth (coming-into-being) and death (passing-away) are absolutely wrong. Nothing is produced out of nothing, and nothing is lost; things are formed by the combination of pre-existing germs, and disappear by the disintegration of these germs, which still continue to exist. Hence it would be better to call *coming into being, mixture,* and *passing away* or *death, separation.* There is no other change except change of place and grouping, external metamorphosis, movement; the notion of change of essence or transubstantiation is a contradiction.

2. EFFICIENT AND FINAL CAUSES OF THE COSMOGONY. — Anaxagoras no longer regards the motion which produces and

destroys things as an original and eternal reality, inherent in the very nature of the elements. The latter are inert and incapable of moving by themselves. Hence they cannot account for the movement in the world and the order which rules it. In order to explain the cosmos, we must assume, in addition to the material, inert, and unintelligent elements, an element that possesses a force and intelligence of its own (νοῦς, *nous* — reason). This element of elements is absolutely simple and homogeneous; it is not mixed with the other elements, but is absolutely distinct from them. The latter are wholly passive; the *nous*, however, is endowed with spontaneous activity; it is perfectly free, and the source of all movement and life in the world. The inferior elements have no consciousness of their own; the mind knows all things past, present, and future; it has arranged and organized everything with design and according to its teleological fitness; it is the eternal governor of the universe, more powerful than all the other elements put together.

3. COSMOGONY. — In the beginning, the inert and unintelligent elements were all jumbled together. In this original chaos, everything was in everything: gold, silver, air, ether, all things which are now separated, formed an indeterminate and inert mass. The intelligent substance alone lived a distinct life of its own. Then it entered the chaos and disentangled it, making the cosmos out of it. The germs, being set in motion by the *nous*, were separated and mingled together again according to their inner affinities. From the point where movement is imparted to the chaos, the whirling motion gradually extends over a wider and wider space to all parts of the world; it continues, as is proved by the rotation of the heavens, and will continue without interruption until the mixture is completely separated. Our earth is a cylindrical body and is composed of the heaviest germs, which were carried towards the centre of the world by the original motion. The lighter corpuscles, which form water, were deposited upon this solid mass; higher up, the atmosphere is formed by the germs of

air: at last, in the heavenly regions, the most subtle elements, the fiery ether, are mixed together again. A second separation of elements takes place, and the original motion parts off from the earth the different solid, mineral, and other bodies which compose it; from the water it parts off the different liquids, and so on, until our central world receives the shape which it now has. The stars are solid masses, which were torn from the earth by the rotatory motion originally possessed by it in common with the rest of the universe, and which were ignited by coming in contact with the celestial ether. The sun is a fiery mass. The moon has mountains and valleys in it, and borrows its light from the sun.

The views which we have just expounded forecast the cosmogonic theories of Buffon, Kant, and Laplace. Anaxagoras also anticipates comparative physiology by advancing the principle of the continuity of beings, by pointing out the unity of purpose in the diverse vegetable and animal types. In spite of all that has been said, however, he is so far from being a spiritualist in the Cartesian sense of the term, that he conceives animals, and even plants, as sharing in the *nous*. If man is more intelligent than animals, it is, he believes, because his mind employs more developed organs. All living things, without exception, are endowed with mind.

How do living beings partake of mind? Does the intelligent principle of Anaxagoras exist outside of these beings, or is it but the sum of all the intelligences, all the purposes, and all the motive forces, whence movement in general results? Anaxagoras is so decided in his assumption that the *nous* is free and conscious of its action, that he regards the word Fate as devoid of meaning. Besides, the very term which he uses to designate the motive principle signifies reason, purpose. He seems to make a transcendent being of it, one that exists independently of other beings, and acts upon them in a purely mechanical way. He even seems to consider these beings, not as intelligent in the true sense of the word, but as automata which appear to be intelligent without really being so. On

the other hand, he speaks of the presence of the *nous* in living creatures as though he were a pantheist. The long and
short of it is, the thinkers of this remote age never broached
the questions of transcendency and immanency, personality
and impersonality, conscious intelligence and unconscious intelligence. Heraclitus found nothing objectionable in assuming a primitive substance and a perpetual state of change.
Similarly, we may suppose, Anaxagoras maintained both the
transcendency and the immanency of the *nous*, without even
suspecting that he was contradicting himself.

The same may be said in answer to the question whether
the *nous* of Anaxagoras is simply less material than other
substances, or whether it is an absolutely immaterial entity.
It is undoubtedly true, on the one hand, that the attributes
of the *nous* are altogether like those of the *spirit* of spiritualism, and that the *nous* seems to have nothing in common with
matter except existence. Yet, on the other hand, there seems
to be but a difference of degree between the *nous* and material substances: the *nous*, in fact, is the finest, the most mobile
thing of all; it is identical with the air of Anaximenes.[1] Hence,
it is merely the highest kind of matter and, consequently, not
absolutely opposed to it as in spiritualism proper. The dualistic conception is, as yet, only vaguely defined in the system of
Anaxagoras, who finds it hard to cut loose from the materialism of the physicists. This is evident from the fact that
Archelaus, his disciple, considers the *nous* as the finest kind
of matter. Moreover, Anaxagoras himself fails to apply the
notion of finality and his principle that the prime mover is an
intelligent being. Aristotle justly censures him for using mind
as a *deus ex machina* to account for the movement of matter,
and then wholly abandoning it for physical and mechanical
causes as soon as it has served his purpose in explaining the
origin of the first movement.[2]

---

[1] Thus Aristotle finds fault with Anaxagoras for identifying *nous* with ψυχή
(*psyche* — soul), though pretending to distinguish between them (*De anima*, I, 2).

[2] Aristotle, *Met.*, I, 4, 7. Cf. Plato, *Phædo*, 97 B.

Nevertheless, Anaxagoras went far enough in spiritualism to cause a reaction in Ionian physics, which became decidedly materialistic in consequence of this opposition.

§ 12. Diogenes of Apollonia, Archelaus, Leucippus, Democritus

1. DIOGENES of Apollonia rejects both the pluralism of elements and the dualism of unintelligent matter and immaterial intelligence. He is a disciple of Anaximenes, and assumes only one original element, air, which is the source of all life in nature, and the essence of all bodies. Mind, which Anaxagoras seems to regard as a separate principle, is wholly dependent on air. This is proved by the fact that the spirit leaves the body as soon as the breath is taken away. Hence we cannot say that air is the product of mind or thought; nay, the reverse is true, mind is the product of air. Without air there can be no life, no consciousness, no intelligence; hence air, that is, matter, is the only principle. Intelligence is not a distinct substance, but an attribute of air. It is obvious, says Diogenes, that the principle we assume is both great and mighty and eternal and undying and of great knowledge. It is the opinion of this physicist, whose views are closely akin to those of Melissus and the Eleatics, that dualism is the negation of the fundamental principle of science that everything originates from one substance. I believe, he goes on to say, that all things are differentiations of the same thing, and are the same thing; and this seems obvious to me. How, indeed, could the so-called elements, earth, water, air, etc., mix with one another, if they were not fundamentally the *same?* How could they help or harm each other? How could the earth produce plants, and plants animals? Let us therefore confess, with the ancient physicists, that all things arise from the same substance, and are destined to return to the same thing.

2. ARCHELAUS. — Archelaus of Athens, or, according to others, of Miletus, is a disciple of Anaxagoras. He adheres to

his teacher's atomism, but protests against the dualistic interpretation of his system. The *nous* is a separate thing like
water, gold, and iron. It differs from these substances as these
substances differ among themselves. Gold is not iron, but
iron and gold are both matter. So, too, mind, though neither
gold nor iron, is, nevertheless, material; it is the finest, the
most subtle, the most intangible substance, without, however,
being a simple thing. A simple substance is a substance that
is composed of nothing, and consequently does not exist.
Matter and substance are, therefore, synonymous terms.

3. THE ATOMISTS. — That is also, on the whole, the teaching of Leucippus and his disciple, Democritus of Abdera, in
Thrace, the most learned of the Ionian physicists and the
head of the ancient and modern materialistic[1] school (420 B. C.).
His numerous writings have been lost, but important fragments remain. Besides, direct sources being wanting, we may
refer to the exposition of atomistic principles in the poem of
Lucretius.[2]

The somewhat vague doctrines of Anaximenes, Diogenes,
and Anaxagoras, on the nature and organization of matter,
are clearly formulated by Democritus. With Anaximenes and
Diogenes, he affirms the homogeneity of all bodies; but, with
Anaxagoras, he conceives this indeterminate matter as divided
into an infinite number of infinitely small molecules, which
come together and separate. In that way bodies are formed
and destroyed. These molecules are infinite in number and
indivisible ($\check{a}\tau o\mu a$ — atoms), without, however, being mathematical points, for an unextended thing would be nothing.
They are identical in chemical quality, but differ in size and
form. They are endowed with perpetual motion, which they
do not receive from a transcendent principle, but which belongs to their essence. The force which moves them acts ac-

---

[1] We say *materialistic*, and not *atomistic*. For atomism is as old as Anaxagoras
and his theory of the infinitely varied elements, in fact if not in name.

[2] [*De natura rerum*, ed. by Lachmann (1850), Bernays (1852), Munro, with
Eng. tr. (1886). See Masson, *The Atomic Theory of Lucretius*, London, 1884.
— TR.]

cording to necessity, and not, as Anaxagoras seems to think, according to design and purpose. Democritus rejects all teleology, but denies chance also, though he sometimes employs the word τύχη (tyche) in the sense of necessity. According to him, the word "chance" merely expresses man's ignorance of the real causes of phenomena. Nothing in nature happens without cause; all things have their reason and necessity.

The Eleatics denied the void and consequently motion. To assume movement is equivalent to affirming the void. If there were no void, the atoms could not even be distinguished from one another; that is to say, they could not exist. Hence the void is the indispensable condition of their existence. It is also the condition of movement, and therefore as important in the formation of things as the full. The void is, as it were, a second principle, which is added to the *matter* of materialism, and gives the system of Democritus the dualistic turn which the most consistent monistic philosophies have not been able wholly to avoid. The void of Democritus meets us under the name of *apeiron* in Pythagoras; it is the non-being of Plato and Aristotle. Democritus regards it as the condition of motion and of matter; the idealists regard it as the condition of the dialectical movement of thought.

The perpetual motion produces a whirling movement among the atoms, in consequence of which they are combined according to their external affinities, — that is, according to size and form; for since they are all chemically the same, they neither attract nor repel each other. The heaviest atoms naturally move downward in infinite space, while the lightest form the atmosphere. Some atoms have uneven, rough, sharp, or hooked surfaces. These catch hold of each other and form acid or bitter substances; while atoms with smooth surfaces form substances which impress the senses agreeably. The soul consists of the finest, smoothest, and therefore most nimble atoms. When such atoms exist in isolation, or are mixed together in small quantities, the soul-atoms are insensible; when they are joined together in large masses, they acquire the faculty of sensation. They are scattered over the entire body, but gathered together more numerously in the sense-organs, where sensation is produced: in the brain, the seat of thought; in the heart, the seat of the affections; and in the liver, the seat of desire. Sensation and perception are explained as follows: Effluences go forth from all bodies and enter our organs of sense, where they excite sensation, and the brain, where they produce ideas or images of things.

Sensation is the only source of knowledge, and there is nothing in thought that has not passed through the channel of the senses. Our ideas represent our impressions, that is, the relations existing between ourselves and the external world; they are not direct reproductions of the objects themselves, the inner essence of which is concealed from us. We are self-conscious as long as the soul-atoms remain intact in the body; sleep ensues, and with it loss of consciousness, when a certain number of atoms escape; when nearly all of them escape, and but a few remain, we fall into a state of seeming death; and, finally, when all the psychical atoms are separated from the body at once, we die. Death cannot destroy these atoms, because the atom is indivisible and therefore indestructible; it destroys their temporary union in a body, and, consequently, the individuality formed by such a union. Since feeling does not belong to isolated atoms, but is produced only by a combination of atoms in the brain and in other organs, death puts an end to feeling and destroys the personality.

The gods are more powerful beings than man, but their immortality is not absolute. Since they are composed of atoms, like mortals, they eventually succumb to the common fate of all, though they live longer than human beings. In the eternal universe, no one has any absolute privileges. Since the gods are more powerful and wiser than ourselves, we should venerate them. We may assume that they come into relation with us, — in dreams, for example; but we should free ourselves from all superstitious fears concerning them, and not forget that above these beings, however powerful they may be, there is one still more powerful than they, — Necessity, the supreme, impersonal, and impartial law which governs the heavens and the earth. To this law, which nature imposes upon all beings alike, we must submit with joyous hearts. Our happiness depends upon it.

Atomistic materialism culminates in scepticism in Protagoras of Abdera, the philosophy of Heraclitus in Cratylus, and the Eleatic doctrine in Gorgias. This period forms a fruitful crisis in the history of Greek philosophy. Though temporarily discouraged by the examination of her resources for knowing the truth, philosophy emerged from the darkness, strengthened and exalted, conscious of her powers, and enriched by a series of studies that had, until then, never been pursued; I mean the intellectual and moral sciences.

SECOND PERIOD

AGE OF CRITICISM AND THE STUDY OF MAN

§ 13. Protagoras

PROTAGORAS, a fellow-countryman and friend of Democritus, acquired fame through the eloquent lectures which he delivered in Sicily and at Athens. He was no longer a philosopher but a sophist, that is, a teacher of philosophy who received pay for his lessons. His example was followed by a number of talented men, who undertook to acquaint the educated public with the conceptions of the philosophers, which had hitherto been restricted to the narrow confines of the schools. The laxness of their moral principles and their unbelief in polytheism caused these clever popularizers of knowledge to be stigmatized as *Sophists*. Their work, however, ranks in importance with that of the Humanists and Encyclopedists. Pampered as he was by the cultured, wealthy, and sceptical youths of the age, but detested by the common people, who remained passionately attached to the religion of their forefathers, Protagoras, like his contemporaries Anaxagoras and Socrates, fell a victim to the fanaticism of the masses and the hypocrisy of the great. He was banished, and his writings burned in the market-place (411). We may assign as the immediate cause of his condemnation, the doubts which he expressed concerning the existence of the gods in his book on them.

The scepticism of Protagoras represents the conclusion of a syllogism of which Heraclitus' doctrine of flux forms the major, and the sensualism of Democritus the minor, premise. The sensible world is a perpetual metamorphosis; the senses show only the things that pass away; they do not reveal the immutable, necessary, and universal. Hence, if we would know the truth, we must derive it from a better source than our deceptive senses; we must appeal to reflection, to reason. But, according to Democritus, reflection is simply the continuation of sensation, from which it does not essentially differ. Consequently, if sensation is changeable, uncertain, and illusory, and is at the same time the only source of knowledge, it necessarily follows that all knowledge is uncertain. No one knows anything but his own sensations. Things that are not given to us in sensation do not exist *for us*. Whatever we feel exists *for us*. Since the atoms of Democritus are not perceived by the senses, they are merely hypotheses without any real value, and the importance which the philosopher attaches to them is inconsistent with his doctrine. The same may be said of the *germs* of Anaxagoras, the *elements* of Empedocles, the *principles* of the school of Miletus; they are all purely hypothetical theories, and cannot be demonstrated. There is no truth for man except in what he perceives, feels, and experiences. And as sensations differ for different individuals, a thing seeming green to one and blue to another, large to one and small to another, it follows that there are as many *truths* as individuals; that the individual is the measure of the true and the false; that there are no universally valid truths or principles, or, at least, that we have no certain criterion by which to recognize the absolute truth of a metaphysical or moral proposition. The individual is the measure of the true and the good. An act that benefits one man harms another; it is good for the former, bad for the latter. Practical truth, like theoretical truth, is a relative thing, a matter of taste, temperament, and education. Metaphysical controversies are therefore utterly vain. It is not possible for us to prove anything but the particular fact of sensation; still more impossible is it to know the causes or ultimate conditions of reality, which escape all sense-perception.

Let man, therefore, occupy himself with the only really accessible object, with *himself!* Let him abandon his sterile speculations concerning ultimate causes, and concentrate his attention upon what is, after all, the only problem of importance, — the question concerning the conditions of happiness. Happiness consists in governing one's self and others; to govern one's self means to be virtuous; hence philosophy is the art of being virtuous. In order to govern others — in a society that is captivated by the beauties of language and always ready to sacrifice the matter to the form — it behooves one to be eloquent, that is, to think correctly and to speak correctly. Hence, philosophy is the art of thinking correctly and of speaking correctly. It consists of the following three branches: practical ethics, dialectics, and rhetoric.

These doctrines, in which the *subject* and the *object* are for the first time opposed to each other, exaggerate a highly important truth: the truth that reality is not something external to the thinking and feeling subject; that the feeling and thinking subject is a coefficient in the production of the phenomenon; in a word, that thought — whether it be transformed sensation or something else — is one of the principles of things, one of those primary conditions of reality for which philosophy has been seeking, a principle which it divined in the *logos* of Heraclitus, the One of Pythagoreanism, and the *nous* of Anaxagoras. Thought *not only strives* to reduce things to a unity, it *is* the unifying principle itself, that which unifies and measures reality; it is, indeed, the measure of all things. This maxim is no less epoch-making in the history of ancient philosophy than the γνῶθι σεαυτόν (*know thyself*) of Socrates. It demolishes the past in order to make room for new and sounder theories based upon the consciousness of self, and inaugurates the age of criticism.

The criticism of Protagoras and the Sophists yields many fruitful results.

It destroys the mental foundations of polytheism and prepares the way for the religion of Socrates, Plato, and the Stoics. In the second place, it destroys the naïve dogmatism of fantastic speculation; and its dialectical extravagances and sophistries compel thought to give an account of itself, its mechanism, its methods, and its laws. For several centuries, philosophy had used its reasoning powers without accounting for the nature and the forms of the syllogism; it had made its inferences and deductions without investigating the inductive and deductive methods. In this respect it resembled the millions of creatures who see and hear without having the slightest notion of the mechanism of sight and hearing. Sophisticism, even though it abuses the laws of thought, nay, let us say, precisely because it abuses them, makes the mind conscious of its laws and causes it to analyze them, and so becomes the forerunner of the science of logic, the development of which constitutes the glory of Aristotle. Simultaneously with the science of thought, it creates the science of its inseparable outer shell, language, — grammar, syntax, or philology in the broadest sense of the term. By laying so much stress on form, and showing such care in the use of words, the Sophists rendered the Greek language more flexible, and fashioned it into the wonderful instrument of thought which we admire in the dialogues of Plato.

The error of Protagoras and the subjectivistic Sophists consists in their interpreting man to mean, not man in general but the individual, not the human understanding but the understanding of each particular individual, and in assuming, in consequence, as many *measures* of the true and the false as there are individuals. Protagoras, like the majority of the Greek philosophers, exaggerates (1) the physiological and mental differences existing between individuals; (2) the illusions of sensation. He ignores the fact which science has since demonstrated, that the investigator may correct the data of the senses by means of each other, and his ignorance of this fact leads him to deny the existence of an objective criterion of truth. He fails to see that the human reason is essentially the same in all individuals. Men hinder him from seeing man.

It is this cardinal error in his philosophy which is rectified by Socrates.

§ 14. Socrates[1]

SOCRATES of Athens (469–399), once a sculptor like his father, was attracted to philosophy by the teachings of the Sophists, and, like them, devoted his life to the instruction and education of the youth. The brilliancy and spirituality of his conversation, which was Attic to a fault, the grandeur of his ideas, the boldness of his political paradoxes — everything about the man, except his outward form, was calculated to charm and attract. The martyrdom which he suffered only helped to raise the admiration of his many disciples to the highest pitch. Though an adversary of the Sophists, whose venality he condemned, he resembled them so much that he was mistaken for a Sophist. Like them, he expressed a contempt for metaphysics, natural science, which, he said, culminates in atheism, and mathematics, which, to his mind, consists of nothing but barren speculations. Like them and like the true Athenian that he was, he placed the study of the moral man and of the duties of the citizen in the very centre of education; like them, finally, he rated the formal culture of the mind much more highly than material instruction, without calculating the effect of intellectual freedom on the religion and the constitution of the State. Hence, he was, not without some show of reason, identified with the Sophists, and the hatred of the conservative democracy in its turn destroyed him. Aristophanes opened the battle against the reformer. He ridiculed him in the *Clouds* and at the same time aroused suspicion against his religious and political views. After the fall of the Thirty Tyrants, Socrates was accused "of not believing in the gods of the State, of proclaiming other gods, and of corrupting the youth," and condemned to drink the hemlock (399).

Although Socrates left no writings, we have a better knowl-

---

[1] *The Trial and Death of Socrates* (Golden Treasury Series), tr. by Church, London, 1912; *Socratic Discourses by Plato and Xenophon* (Everyman's Library Edition); Zeller, *Socrates and the Pre-Socratic Schools*, tr. by Reichel, London, 1885.

edge of him than of his predecessors. For this we are indebted
to two of his enthusiastic pupils, Xenophon and Plato. Their
accounts do not, by any means, agree with one another in all
respects. The Socrates of the *Memorabilia* is a moral philosopher and an apostle of natural religion rather than a metaphysician; the Socrates of the *Dialogues* of Plato is a keen and
profound thinker, the rival of Heraclitus, Parmenides, and
Anaxagoras. The simplest explanation of the difference is as
follows: Xenophon presents the teachings of the master according to his understanding of them; while Plato, whose
philosophical horizon is broader than that of Socrates, exaggerates the metaphysical import of his doctrine and uses
Socrates as a mask for his own ideas. Happily we have, besides
the very detailed but sometimes uncertain data of the two
disciples, the opinion of Aristotle to guide us, and he cannot,
to say the least, be accused of partiality.

The scepticism of Protagoras and the Sophists forms the
starting-point of the philosophy of Socrates. All he knows is
that he knows nothing; he is, furthermore, convinced that
certainty is impossible in the case of physical science. However, though he is a sceptic in cosmology, his scepticism does
not extend to the field of morals. He believes — and this conviction of his forms a new and positive element in the philosophy of his times — he believes that there is something in the
universe that can be known, and known absolutely; this, as
the words inscribed on the temple of Delphi, *Know thyself*,
indicate, is man. We can never know exactly what is the nature of the world, its origin, and its end, but we can know
what we ourselves ought to be, what is the meaning and aim
of life, the highest good of the soul; and this knowledge alone
is real and useful, because it is the only possible knowledge.
Outside of ethics there can be no serious philosophy.

By making man the real object of science, Socrates evidently did not intend to create a scientific anthropology, or
even to give us a psychology in the strict sense of the word.
Man means for him the soul as the seat of moral ideas. He

accepts no other science than ethics, of which Aristotle calls him the founder; but ethics is, in his opinion, a real, certain, and positive science resting on universal principles. Seemingly, indeed, Socrates does not get beyond the standpoint of Protagoras and his principle that man is the measure of all things. But the moral system of the great Sophist was not scientific, because it failed to recognize universal principles. By *man* as the measure of all things, Protagoras means the individual, and not human nature in general; he means the particular, accidental, changeable individual, and not the immutable and necessary moral element which is common to all. He did not believe in the existence of such a fundamental human nature. Moral ideas do not, in his opinion, possess objective and absolute value; goodness, justice, and truth depend upon individual taste, which is the sole and final judge. There are, therefore, as many *systems of ethics* as individuals, which amounts to saying that there is none. The Sophists were deceived by the diversity of opinions, judgments, and feelings which they discovered among men. This diversity is but apparent and on the surface. The moral ideas lie concealed and slumbering, as it were, beneath individual prejudices. We have only to remove this superficial layer by means of education, in order to discover in all the same ideas and the same aspirations towards goodness, beauty, justice, and truth.

Socrates' merit, therefore, consists in having attempted, at least in morals, to separate the general from the particular; in having advanced from the individual to the universal; in having again discovered, beneath the infinite variety of *men*, the one unchangeable *man*. Beneath the confused mass of *opinions* held by a demoralized century, he finds the true and immutable *opinion*, the conscience of the human race, the law of minds.[1] Hence Socrates not only rendered a service to ethics, he benefited metaphysics as well. In the midst of intellectual anarchy, he teaches thought how to infer and define, and helps to put an end to the confusion of ideas by giv-

---

[1] The universal reason of Heraclitus.

ing words their exact meaning. Thus, as long as there is no exact definition of the notion of God, a man has as much right to espouse atheism as theism: theism, if by God is meant the one indivisible Providence that governs the world; atheism, if we mean those anthropomorphic beings with whom the Greek imagination peopled the Olympus. The main thing, therefore, is to come to some agreement as to the terms; and to this end we must define them exactly, — an art in which Socrates excelled. He was, says Xenophon,[1] untiring in his efforts to examine and define goodness and wickedness, justice and injustice, wisdom and folly, courage and cowardice, the State and the citizen. He did not offer his definitions to his hearers ready-made. He differed from the sensualist Protagoras in his conviction that moral ideas are fundamental to humanity, that every human mind is *big with truth*, that education creates nothing that is not already there, but merely awakens and develops the latent germs of knowledge. He contented himself with being a *spiritual midwife*, and his chief delight lay in teaching his hearers how to discover the true definitions for themselves. A better teacher never lived. He practised his art, which he loved to compare with that of his mother, in the public places, on the walks, and in the work-shops; wherever he found an intelligent face before him. He was in the habit of plying those whom chance made his pupils with questions, — questions that were often trifling in their nature. He began by chiming in with their views. Then, by means of the most skilful questioning, he gradually forced them to confess that they knew little or nothing, and, finally, brought them to see the truth. The dialogues of Plato give us an insight into the famous *dialectical* method, which enabled Socrates to confound the learned pretensions of his interlocutors, and which has been called the *Socratic irony*.

Though Socrates sought to enlighten men, to teach them how to think correctly and to know the truth, his object was not to make them learned, but to make them happy and use-

[1] *Mem.* I, i, 16.

ful citizens. Ever since the days of Socrates, philosophy has regarded it as her prerogative to take the place of religion, morality, and positive faith, in the absence of a universally recognized official religion. This accounts for the peculiar character of the Socratic and post-Socratic schools, which are as much religious brotherhoods as learned schools. For Socrates, who is, to a certain extent, a national thinker, a full-fledged Athenian, and for whom actual life has greater charms than abstract theory, wisdom or knowledge is not the goal; it is the means, the indispensable means, of right living, as essential to the private individual as to the citizen and statesman. The intimate relation which exists between knowledge and will constitutes the fundamental principle and, in a measure, the very soul of his philosophy. The essential thought is that the more a man thinks and knows, the better will he act; that our moral value is directly proportional to our lights. From this principle the other characteristic propositions of his philosophy necessarily follow, namely: that virtue is teachable; that it is *one*, which means that we cannot be virtuous in one thing without being so in all things, or vicious in one without being so in all; finally, that no one is voluntarily bad, that evil is the fruit of ignorance.

The ethical system of Socrates is a mean between the idealism of Pythagoras and the realism that is inseparable from the sensationalistic and materialistic trend of the Ionian schools. It aims at the ideal, but it loves to express this ideal in sensible forms, to reflect moral beauty in physical beauty. Socrates is far from being an ascetic: he strives to subdue nature, to make it the instrument of intelligence, to rule over it as an absolute master; but he never dreams of suppressing it. He is a Grecian and an Athenian above everything else, and so sensitive to external charms and physical beauty that he feels himself obliged to wage constant war with the allurements of matter.

He agrees with his predecessors on religious matters in that he repudiates mythology and its fables, without, however, being a free-thinker in the modern sense. His spiritualistic faith is not even devoid of superstition. He believes in the supernatural, in superior beings or *demons* who watch over nations and inspire individuals. But he strongly emphasizes the universality of Providence, and thereby attacks the particularism of the Athenians, thus paving the way for the notion of the universal brotherhood of man, taught by Stoicism and Christianity.

Owing to his heroic death, his importance, though great, was overrated at the expense of that of his predecessors, who were philosophers of the highest order. But he is, nevertheless, one of those reformers whose sojourn on earth has been productive of lasting and fruitful results. His great work consists in having given to conscience the honored place which it deserves, in having reinstated the absolute, immutable, and universal. At a time when men publicly declared that good and evil are relative, and that the rule for judging an act is not the "changing" law of conscience, but its success, he had the courage to proclaim the authority of a conscience that merely varies in appearance, and the superiority of the moral law over individual caprice. Now, to maintain the absoluteness of morality meant the reform of philosophy as well as that of morals. For, in spite of what *independent* moralists may say, human thought cannot, without contradiction, affirm the absolute in practice and yet deny it in theory.

Of the many disciples of the new school, some, like Aristippus and Antisthenes, develop the ethical teachings of Socrates *in opposition* to the metaphysical speculations of the old schools; others, like Euclides and Plato, unite the Socratic conception of the highest good and the Eleatic notion of the absolute, the *end* of the moralists and the *first* cause of the metaphysicians, and thereby re-establish the union between the philosophy of morals and the philosophy of nature, which had been dissolved by scepticism.

§ 15. Aristippus and Hedonism. — Antisthenes and Cynicism. Euclides and the School of Megara

1. ARISTIPPUS of Cyrene was a sensualistic Sophist before joining the Socratics, and adhered to the theoretical teachings of that school. With Protagoras, he maintains that all our knowledge is subjective, and that we cannot know what things are in themselves. He sharply distinguishes between the object of knowledge and Kant's *thing-in-itself*, that is, the external and absolutely unknown cause of our sensations. His ethics, too, is more in accord with the principles of Protagoras than with those of Socrates. Pleasure (ἡδονή) is, according to him, the ultimate aim of life. Hence the name *hedonism* is applied to his doctrine, which must not, however, be interpreted as a coarse sensualism. He is a follower of Socrates and his moral principles on this important point, and demands, above all, moderation in indulgence, rational self-command in presence of the allurements of sense, and intelligent control of the vulgar instincts of our nature. We must, he said, remain masters of ourselves under all circumstances, so that we may say: ἔχω οὐκ ἔχομαι (I own, I am not owned).

Mental pleasures, friendship, paternal and filial love, art and literature, take precedence, in the scale of enjoyments, over fleeting sensuous feelings; and the wise man should particularly seek, not the pleasures of the moment, but lasting joys, a permanent state of moral content. Moreover, Aristippus and his adherents agree with the Sophists that all action has for its motive the desire to be happy, and for its end the pleasure which the act procures. They likewise agree with Protagoras in religion. The hedonists were outspoken freethinkers, and helped to demolish the remnants of the polytheistic faith among the educated classes. In a work entitled *The Gods*, Theodorus of Cyrene, called the Atheist,[1] openly espoused atheism; another hedonist, Euhemerus,[2] held, in a

---

[1] About 310 B. C.; a contemporary and *protégé* of Demetrius of Phalerus and of Ptolemy I.

[2] About 310 B. C.

sensational treatise (ἱερὰ ἀναγραφή, sacred history), that the gods were heroes, kings, and distinguished men who had been deified after their death. This theory proved very acceptable to a great number of Romans, and even Christians, who rejoiced at having paganism furnish them with such powerful weapons against itself. However narrow this view may seem, it has the merit of being one of the first attempts at a science which it has been left to our age to study and develop: I mean the philosophy of religion.

Hedonism passes through a process of evolution which may, at first sight, seem surprising, but which is no more than natural; it changes into pessimism in the philosophy of Hegesias,[1] called πεισιθάνατος ("persuader to die"). This evolution was the logical outcome of the hedonistic principle. The aim of life is, according to the Cyrenaic school, pleasure: the sensation of the moment, according to some; permanent pleasure or happiness, according to others. Now experience proves that life affords more pain than pleasure, and that unalloyed happiness is a dream. Hence the end of life is not and cannot be realized. Life, therefore, has no value. As a consequence, death is preferable to life; for death at least procures for us the only happiness possible to human beings, a negative happiness consisting in the absolute suppression of pain. This is the way in which Hegesias reasons, and all must reason who regard pleasure, joy, or happiness as the only end of life. Life has real value only for such as recognize a higher aim, namely, moral goodness, the performance of duty, virtue for virtue's sake; in other words, life has value only for him who considers it as a means and not as an end in itself, that is, in short, for the idealist. For him, virtue is the highest good. Now virtue can be realized only by living beings. Hence life itself, being the means and indispensable condition of virtue or of the highest good, is a relative good, and not the *summum bonum* (or highest good). Hence moral idealism necessarily excludes pessimism.

[1] A contemporary of Ptolemy I.

The hedonistic school, which again becomes optimistic in Anniceris of Cyrene,[1] is continued by the school of Epicurus,[2] who supplements the ethics of Aristippus with the physics of Democritus.

2. ANTISTHENES. — The idealistic teachings of Socrates are reproduced and exaggerated by Antisthenes of Athens, the founder of the Cynic school. The school was named after the gymnasium of *Kynosarges*, where Antisthenes delivered his lectures. Its motto is: Virtue for virtue's sake; virtue is the final and only goal of all our actions; virtue is the highest good. The Cynics, his successors, go so far in their enthusiasm as to proclaim the doctrine that pleasure is an evil; that man cannot be virtuous unless he renounces all material and even intellectual pleasures; they even reject mental culture and philosophy itself as evils. Despising, as they did, the pleasures of social life, they came to violate the simplest rules of politeness, and, in principle at least, rebelled against the laws themselves. For a life of refinement and civilization these "Rousseaus of antiquity" substitute the state of nature; cosmopolitanism takes the place of patriotism. The principle of individual autonomy, which had been proclaimed by the Sophists and by Socrates, passes from theory into practice. Not all the Cynics, however, are radicals. We must make allowances in the well-known history of Diogenes of Sinope, the disciple of Antisthenes, for popular malice, which naturally goes to extremes, and is apt to culminate in caricature. The moral idealism of Antisthenes, which was disfigured by the exaggerations of some of the Cynic philosophers, reappeared in a new and purer form in the doctrines of Zeno and the Stoics.

3. EUCLIDES, the founder of the school of Megara, made the first attempt to give the ethical system of the master a metaphysical support, which he finds in the philosophy of the Eleatics. He accepts the teaching of Parmenides that being is one, and the Socratic notion concerning the reality of the

---

[1] About 300 B. C. See Diog. L., II, 93 ff.　　　　[2] § 19.

nous and of moral principles. From these premises he boldly draws the conclusion that mind or goodness is being, the only absolutely existing being. All we know of Euclides is summed up in this sentence. But this alone assures him a distinguished place among the Attic philosophers; his system forms the connecting link between Socrates and Plato. The school of Megara, which Stilpo made famous, and that of Elis, which was founded by Phædo, the favorite pupil of Socrates, devoted themselves to the development of eristic dialectics, but soon found themselves eclipsed by the schools of Plato, Aristotle, Epicurus, and Zeno.

During the first period, philosophical interest was centred upon nature and the problem of becoming, while speculative Socraticism inaugurates the era of the philosophy of mind, which predominates in the second period, and culminates in the systems of Plato, Aristotle, the Epicureans, and the Stoics.

A. DENIAL OF MATTER. THE THEORY OF IDEAS

§ 16. Plato

PLATO of Athens was born of a noble family, about 427. He received his first instruction from Cratylus, the disciple of Heraclitus, then became a pupil of Socrates, and later of Euclides of Megara, who introduced him to the study of Parmenides. The mathematical speculations of the Pythagoreans also exerted a decided influence upon the development of his thought. From 385 to the close of his life (347) he taught philosophy in the Academy, a place which was presented to him by generous friends, and for centuries remained in possession of the Platonic school.

It is not a matter of indifference, says a great writer,[1] by which door we enter life. Socrates, the child of a family of artisans and himself an artisan during his younger days, took pleasure in mingling with the crowd whose follies he despised, and endeavored to instruct, elevate, and ennoble them. Plato,

[1] Goethe.

the descendant of Codrus and of Solon, was by birth predestined to become the author of the aristocratic *Republic*, the idealistic philosopher, for whom form is everything and matter a contamination, an obstacle, and a check; the poet-prophet who will have nothing to do with vulgar reality, and whose home is in the realms of the eternal, the absolute, and the ideal; the favorite teacher of the Fathers of the Church, the theosophists, and the mystics. Socrates exercises a somewhat prosy cautiousness in his thought. He is not willing to take any risks, he avoids hypothesis and the unknown. The philosophy of Plato is conspicuous for its bold imprudence, its love of adventure and mystery. His speculation is not like the Philistine whose life is spent in the market-place or in the workshop, and whose world is measured by the narrow boundaries of his native town; it is the lord of the manor, who retires to his mansion, after having seen the world, and turns his gaze towards the distant horizon; disdaining the noise of the cross-roads, he mingles only in the best society, where is heard the most elegant, the noblest, and the loftiest language that has ever been spoken in the home of the Muses.

Plato is the oldest Greek philosopher whose writings have been preserved, and the only one of whom we possess the complete works.[1] Of the treatises attributed to him by tradition some are surely spurious; others, like the *Parmenides*, the *Sophist*, the *Cratylus*, and the *Philebus*, are of doubtful origin. Criticism has also, but without just grounds, questioned the authorship of the *Apology* and the *Crito*. The writings whose genuineness is beyond doubt are nine in number, namely: (1) The *Phædrus*, which opposes the selfish rhetoric of the Sophists with the true eloquence of the philosopher, whose chief object

[1] *The Dialogues of Plato.* Translated into English with Analyses and Introductions, by B. Jowett, third edition, 5 vols., New York, 1892; *The Republic of Plato*, translated by Davies and Vaughan, The Home Library; Zeller, *Plato and the Older Academicians*, translated by Alleyne and Goodwin, London, 1888; Pater, *Plato and Platonism*, New York, 1902; More, *Platonism*, Princeton, 1917; Taylor, *Plato*, London, 1914; Nettleship, *Lectures on the Republic of Plato*, London, 1914; Bosanquet, *A Companion to Plato's Republic*, New York, 1895.

is the knowledge of the invisible world; (2) the *Protagoras*, or the Socratic doctrine of virtue; (3) the *Symposium*, or concerning the different manifestations of the *eros* (love), from sensual love to the philosophical love of beauty, truth, and goodness, as this was personified in Socrates; (4) the *Gorgias*, the true sage as opposed to the Sophist; (5) the *Republic*, or concerning the State which realizes the idea of justice; (6) the *Timæus*, or concerning the nature and origin of the world; (7) the *Theætetus*, or concerning knowledge and Ideas; (8) the *Phædo*, or concerning the immortality of the soul; (9) the *Laws*, a work which seems to be a partial retraction of the *Republic*. These treatises are dialogues. Socrates is the chief spokesman in the majority of them, and his speeches reflect the author's thought most faithfully. His use of the dialogue-form enables Plato to present us with his own philosophy as well as with the history of its origin, or the manner in which it arose among the Socratics. It is true, the dialogue-form may perhaps be objected to on the ground that it hinders us from obtaining a comprehensive view of the author's philosophy; indeed, the statement has been made that it is so difficult to systematize Plato's teachings because of his use of the dialogue. The reverse seems to be the case; in our opinion Plato employs this form precisely because he has no finished system. The dialogue might be regarded as an unsuitable method of exposition in case it concealed the philosopher's thoughts. But it hides nothing; form and content are here the same, and the dialogues of Plato present his philosophy in its psychological development.

A real difficulty, however, arises from the frequent use of myths and allegories. Plato employs them, either in order to assist his readers in understanding abstract truths, or in order to mislead the fanatical democracy as to his religious convictions,[1] or, finally, in order to hide the contradictions of his thought and to escape philosophical criticism by seeking refuge in the license of the poet. Most of the Platonic myths are

[1] *Timæus*, 28 C, 29 C–D.

mere allegories, which, as the author himself cautions us, must be taken for what they are worth. Some of them, however, seem to express the philosopher's real views. Hence the difficulty which we experience in the *Timæus* and the *Phædo*, of distinguishing clearly between the pedagogical element and the teaching itself, between the accidental and the essential, between the poetical symbol and the real meaning. Though Plato himself gives us an allegorical exposition of the drama of creation in his *Timæus*, does it therefore follow that the idea of Creation is absolutely foreign to his mind? When he speaks of a Creator and follows popular fancy in picturing him as a human workman, does that mean that theism is not the essential element of his thought? The *Phædo*, too, is full of mythological allegories, but who would have the boldness to declare, with Hegel, that Plato assumed pre-existence and immortality only for the world-soul and the divine *nous?* We must, in choosing between the idea and the form, — a delicate and rather difficult task, — avoid two contrary conceptions, both of which our historical sense would compel us to reject. In the first place, we must not be deceived by Plato's symbolism; we must not lay too much stress on what is but a literary form, and mistake mere figures of speech for the hidden meaning of things. But we must also abandon the notion that Plato was too great a man to be influenced in his reason by the imagination. We have no right to make him a Christian or a modern philosopher. It is undoubtedly true that Catholic mysticism borrows extensively from Platonic theology, and it is equally certain that Plato's dialectics contain the rudiments of the Hegelian system. But twenty centuries of development lie between the sowing of the seed and the full fruition, and we cannot identify the beginning and the end without anachronism. It is not enough to point out that the future is contained in the past; we must also indicate in what form it is found there, and show that this is not the final stage of evolution.

Plato is the product of Heraclitian, Socratic, and Italian

philosophy. With the school of Heraclitus he believes that the visible universe is in a state of perpetual change, that the senses are deceptive and cannot yield us truth, that the immutable does not exist in the world of sense, but in the world of ideas. From Socrates he learned that though we cannot know the ultimate principles of the universe, we can at least know ourselves, and that we can attain to a knowledge of the highest good through an infallible inner sense. But Socrates remained a sceptic as far as metaphysics was concerned. The Italic philosophy induced Plato to take a decisive step. In the Pythagorean and Eleatic systems he finds the inner sense (of Socrates) proclaimed, not only as the moral conscience and practical reason, but as theoretical reason, capable of revealing to us the absolute, eternal, and necessary essence of things. In mathematics and its self-evident axioms he discovers the most powerful weapon against the doctrine of the universal flux, in the sense in which Cratylus and the Sophists applied the principle. Geometry made a particularly deep impression upon him: the geometrical method served as a model for his metaphysics. Indeed, he even borrowed his philosophical vocabulary from this science. Geometry is based on *a priori*[1] intuitions: lines, triangles, circles, and spheres, are ideal figures or intelligible realities; their properties remain the same forever, and survive all the changes of the material world which reflects them. It is a rational science and has nothing to do with sense-perception, of which its truths are absolutely independent. Hence Plato's philosophy is, like *mathematics*, the only self-evident and necessary science, a science of *a priori* intuition and reasoning. Because of their resemblance to the principles of geometry, these *a priori* intuitions, upon which the system is grounded, are called *Ideas* (εἴδη, ἰδέαι), or unchangeable forms, or the eternal types of fleeting things, or noumena, the objects of true science as distinguished from phenomena, the objects of sense-perception and opinion. The

---

[1] The phrase *a priori* is used in philosophy to mean knowledge which is independent of experience.

philosophy of Plato is the science of *Ideas*. It is called *dialectics* after its new method. To this science of first principles, which is the fundamental and only science worthy of the name, is added the *theory of nature*. The latter, however, is of secondary importance, and does not deserve the name of science. *Ethics*, or the science of the highest good, is the last branch of dialectics and the crown of philosophy.

Hence we have to consider with Plato: (1) The Idea as such; (2) the Idea acting upon matter as a plastic principle, or nature; and (3) the Idea as the final goal of nature, or the highest good.

1. *The Idea*[1]

When we compare the mother who gives up her life for her child, the warrior who dies in defense of his country, and the philosopher who sacrifices himself for his convictions, we notice a similarity in their actions; they have the same common trait, and reproduce one and the same type, — the Idea of the good. When we compare a masterpiece of architecture or of sculpture with a tragedy of Sophocles and a beautiful human form, we discover in these apparently different objects a common trait, — beauty, or the Idea of the beautiful. When we compare the individuals of a species, say the human race, we find in them a number of qualities common to all, an identical type; these common characteristics, or the type which is reproduced in all, constitute man-in-himself, or the Idea of man. Finally, when we compare all the beings perceived by our senses, we notice that all have this in common: they exist or do not exist, they move or are at rest, they are identical or they differ from each other. Now, this *being*, shared by all, this *non-being*, or movement, or rest, or identity, or difference, is what Plato calls the Idea of being, the Idea of movement, etc. Hence he understands by the term *Ideas:* (1) what mod-

---

[1] For Plato's dialectics and ideology, see especially the *Theætetus* (151 ff.), the *Sophist* (218 ff.), the *Philebus* (15, 54, 58 ff.), the *Parmenides* (130 ff.), and the *Republic* (especially books VI and VII).

ern philosophy calls *laws* of thought, morality, or taste; (2) what Aristotle calls *categories*, or the general forms by means of which we conceive things, and which are embraced under the preceding class; (3) what natural science calls types, species, or, as Plato would say, Ideas. In short, he means by Ideas all possible generalizations; there are as many of them as there are common names. Every common name designates an Idea, as every proper name designates an individual. The senses reveal particulars, or natural objects; abstraction and generalization give us Ideas.

The great mission of Socrates was to form general ideas. But, like the sensationalistic school, which he opposed in other respects, Socrates simply regarded these ideas as thoughts or concepts of the mind. At this point Plato shows his originality. According to sensualism, our sense-perceptions alone represent real beings existing outside of us. According to Plato, general notions or concepts also represent realities, and these *realities*, these *objects* of our notions, which sensualism denies, he calls *Ideas*. Ideas are to our notions what natural objects are to our sense-perceptions: they are their objective causes. The objects which the deceptive and vulgar organs of sense present to us we regard as real objects; while the Ideas which we acquire through reason, the messenger of the gods, are looked upon by us as fleeting shadows that come and go with self-consciousness! If we consider sensible objects as real, how much greater reason have we to assume the reality of the objects of the intellect! The general Ideas, expressed by our concepts, Good, Being, Identity, Man, etc., are therefore *realities*. Hence the name *realism* was inaptly applied to mediæval Platonism, which is diametrically opposed to modern *realism*.

What! Shall we say, Ideas are real beings; the Idea of being, more real than being; the Idea of the sun as real and even more real than the sun which shines upon us from the heavens; the Idea of man as real, and even much more real than Socrates, Antisthenes, and Euclides! Common-sense rebels against such paradoxes. Socrates I see, but I do not see the man-type; I see beautiful men, beautiful statues, and beautiful paintings; I do not see the beautiful as such. I see moving bodies; I do not see motion as such, or the Idea of movement; I see living beings, but being or life in itself I cannot see anywhere. All these generalizations exist only in my mind, and have nothing real corresponding to them. Plato answers such objections by saying that when the sensualist sees beautiful objects and just acts, and fails to perceive beauty as such, or justice as such, it is because he has the sense for the former, while his sense for Ideas or his reason is at fault. If this were sufficiently developed, it would no longer see the real reality in material existence, but in the Ideas; it would look for reality, not in the world of sense, but in the intelligible world. We consider general Ideas as the mental copies of sensible beings, whose reality we assume. The reverse is true; the Ideas are the models or the originals, and the natural beings or the individuals are the copies. The Ideas are both *our* thoughts and the eternal objects of these thoughts; they are the *thoughts of God*, which no human intelligence can wholly reproduce, but which are none the less real, absolutely real.

Let us take the Idea of the beautiful, or beauty absolute (αὐτὸ τὸ καλόν). For the sensationalist, the beautiful, like the good and the just, is a quality which we abstract in thought from the sensible objects, and which does not exist apart from these objects. For Plato, the beautiful is a reality; it is not only real, but much more real than all the beautiful things put together. Whatever endures is more lasting and therefore more *real* than that which passes away. Now, every beautiful object, be it a man or a statue, an act or an individual, is doomed to destruction and oblivion; *beauty* in itself is imperishable. Hence it must be more real than all the things the sensationalist calls beautiful. So, too, the type of man is more real than the particular man, because it remains unchanged, while the individual passes away; the Idea of the tree or flower is more real than *a particular* tree or *a particular* flower, because it endures. The Idea *is* what it expresses; it is this *absolutely* and without qualification; all we can say of the sensible object is that it *has* something of what the Idea *is*, that it *partakes* of it, while the Idea is undivided being.

Let us again inquire into the beautiful, which is Plato's favorite Idea,[1] and which he loves to identify with the good. Its manifestations in the sensible world are only *relatively* beautiful, that is, as compared with ugly objects; they are not beautiful when we compare them with more beautiful things. They are fair to-day, foul to-morrow; fair at one place, or in one relation, or in one point of view, or to one person; foul under different circumstances and in the judgment of other persons. Hence everything in the world of phenomenal beauty is relative, fleeting, and uncertain. Ideal beauty is everlasting; without beginning and without end; without diminution and without decay; invariable, immutable, and absolute; it is beautiful in all its relations and from all points of view; it is beautiful at all times and in all places and for all persons; it is pure and clear and unalloyed, and therefore transcends the powers of the imagination. It is neither a mere notion nor purely individual knowledge, but an eternal reality.

What is true of the beautiful is true of the great and the small, and of all Ideas in general. Simmias is tall as compared with Socrates, but small by the side of Phædo. The Idea of the great is great in all points of view; it is absolutely great. Hence to sum up: (1) The Ideas are *real* beings; (2) the Ideas are *more real* than the objects of sense; (3) the Ideas are the *only* true realities; the objects of sense possess a merely borrowed existence, a reality which they receive from the Ideas. The Ideas are the eternal patterns after which the things of sense are made; the latter are the images, the imitations, the imperfect copies.[2] The entire sensible world is nothing but a symbol, an allegory, or a figure of speech. The meaning, the Idea expressed by the thing, alone concerns the philosopher. His interest in the sensible world is like our interest in the portrait of a friend of whose living presence we are deprived.

[1] *Symposium*, 211 ff.   [2] *Parmenides*, 132; *Timæus*, 48.

The world of sense is the copy of the world of Ideas; and conversely, the world of Ideas resembles its image; it forms a hierarchy. In our visible world there is a gradation of beings from the most imperfect creature to the perfect, sensible being, or the universe. The same holds true of the intelligible realm or the pattern of the world; the Ideas are joined together by means of other Ideas of a higher order; the latter, in turn, are embraced under others still more exalted, and so on; the Ideas constantly increase in generality and force, until we reach the top, the last, the highest, the most powerful Idea or the Good, which comprehends, contains, or summarizes the entire system, just as the visible universe, its copy, comprehends, contains, or summarizes all creatures. The relation existing between the Ideas and the highest Idea is analogous to that existing between objects of sense and Ideas. The objects, as we have said, *partake of* the Ideas which they express;[1] they exist, not in themselves, but as reflections of their Ideas; they have no reality other than that which they receive from these Ideas; they are, in short, to these Ideas what accidents are to substances. Similarly, the Ideas of a lower order exist by themselves and as substances, only as compared to their visible copies. As compared to the highest Ideas, they cease to be substances; they become modes of the only really *absolute* Idea, the Idea of the Good; in the presence of this sun of the intelligible world, their individuality passes away as the stars vanish at the coming of the orb of day.

Hence the Ideas are both individual or self-existent atoms and members of a higher unity. Plato himself emphasizes the principle of the unity and connection of Ideas at the expense of their individuality; his disciples, on the other hand, seem to lay more stress on the atomic and substantial character of the Ideas than on their unity.[2] The *clear and transparent* Ideas of the master are, to use a figure of speech, precipitated by the

---

[1] *Phædo*, 100.

[2] This substantialization of the Ideas is already noticeable in the *Sophist*, and has been regarded by some as an argument against the genuineness of the dialogue.

school, and the Lyceum consequently censures the Academy for adding to the material world another wholly useless material world. The Ideas of Plato form a unity or an organism; they live a common life; and it is utterly impossible to separate them from each other and to make distinct beings of them.[1] Indeed, they are independent of all time and space, that is, of the principle of separation and individualization. It is true, Plato speaks of the heavens as their abode, whither we must rise in order to contemplate them in their divine purity.[2] But this heaven is not a part of the physical universe. The home of the Ideas is not the same as that of the things; it is *sui generis*, a place suitable to the nature of the Ideas, an ideal, intelligible place; the home of the Ideas is mind, that is, the *Idea* as such. The Idea has no place outside of itself; it does not, like the atoms of Democritus, exist by virtue of empty space, but by itself. A prouder challenge could not be hurled at materialism: Space which you conceive as a condition of reality is quite the reverse; it is the cause of non-being and impotence. The Idea is real because it is *one* and *unextended*, and because unity is force, power, or reality. Now, that which is concentrated in the Idea as in a mathematical point, is distributed in space and time, scattered over a thousand places and a thousand different moments, and consequently enfeebled, impoverished, and relatively destroyed. Compared with the Idea, which you regard as a poor reflection of the real world, your supposed real world is itself but an Idea in the vulgar sense which you attach to the word, that is, a shadow, a nothing. The world is the relative; the Idea, the absolute.

If the Idea is the absolute, what is God, to whom Plato often refers, and, as it seems, refers in different senses, sometimes using the plural, sometimes the singular? In the *Timæus*,[3] the Creator is spoken of as the eternal God; his immediate creatures (the stars and the celestial spirits) are called gods; while the sensible universe is a god in process of becoming. Evi-

---

[1] *Meno*, 81.   [2] *Phædrus*, 247.   [3] *Timæus*, 28, 34, 41, *passim*.

dently, *the god who is to be* and the created divinities are accommodations to official polytheism, and the Creator is the only true God. But even this highest God does not seem to be absolute; in creating the universe he contemplates the eternal, which serves as his model. Now, the Idea or the Good is the eternal. Hence the Creator is *dependent* on the Idea as the copyist depends on the pattern which he follows. In order that the Creator may be the Supreme Being or the absolute, the model must be the Idea in itself or the Good personified. The assumption of an intermediate principle is apparently a necessary consequence of Plato's dualism between Idea and matter, while the conception of the Demiurge as a workman following a pattern forms a part of the mythical element in the narrative; the Creator and the pattern of creation are merged in the creative Idea, of which the Demiurge is the poetical personification. God and the Idea are so closely identified in Plato that it seems at times as though God depended on the Idea, at others, as though the Idea sprang from God, as the eternal source of all things. Since God is sometimes represented as below and sometimes as above the Idea, nothing is left to us but to take the middle ground and to say that the God of Plato is neither inferior nor superior to the Idea, but that he coincides with it, or that he is the Idea itself, considered as an active, plastic, and creative principle. That the Platonic school identified God with the absolute Idea may be readily inferred from the attributes which are ascribed to the Good and to the Supreme Being. A brief comparison will suffice to convince us of this fact. The absolute Idea (the Good, the One) is *the lord* of the spiritual world, as the sun is the lord of the visible world.[1] It even exceeds being and essence in dignity and power. It is the universal author of all things beautiful and right, parent of light and of the lord of light in this visible world, and the immediate source of reason and truth in the intellectual. On the other hand, the God of gods is represented to us as the eternal cause of the Good in the

[1] *Republic*, VI, 508 D.

world; as the supreme wisdom, by the side of which all human philosophy is imperfect; as the supreme justice, law-giver, and highest law, who rules the beginning, the end, and the middle of things; as the pure reason which has nothing to do with matter or with evil.[1] Hence, there cannot be the least doubt that the God of Plato is the absolute Idea of the Good. Does that mean that because his god is an Idea he is not a reality? On the contrary; because he is an Idea, and *nothing but an Idea*, he is the highest reality; for, from Plato's point of view, the Idea only is real.

Now the Idea does not exist in space proper, but in the intelligence which is its natural and, in a certain sense, its native abode. It cannot, therefore, come to us from without,[2] and it is a mistake to derive it from sensation. The absolute Idea, and with it all the other Ideas, are original endowments of the mind; they form its very essence. But they are at first latent in the mind, and we are not conscious of them. The senses show us their external copies, and, to a certain extent, *remind* us of the originals existing in us. Sensation *provokes* Ideas; it does not *produce* them. Its function consists in recalling to our minds the *a priori* Ideas which we possess without suspecting it. Moreover, the senses are deceptive; and instead of revealing the truth, they keep it from us. Reasoning is the only road to truth; and this springs from love. The love of truth is but a particular form of universal love. The home-sick soul, living in exile in the world of sense, fervently longs to be united with the absolute, to come face to face with the principle of light and truth. This pure and holy desire seeks for satisfaction in earthly emotions, in friendship and æsthetic

---

[1] *Republic*, VI, 506 ff.; VII, 517.

[2] Strictly speaking, it is not even correct to say: *it cannot come to us*, etc.; we should say: *the knowledge of the Idea, the notion* (λόγος) *cannot come to us*, etc.; for the Idea exists independently of the notions of our mind; it is "neither a notion nor a science" (p. 85); it neither comes nor goes; all that *comes* to the mind, or *becomes*, or is formed, or is developed, is simply our concepts, which, like the sensible things, are but shadowy copies of the eternal Ideas. — (*Allegory of the Cave, Rep.* VII.)

pleasure.[1] But the human embodiments of the Idea, or the material incorporations of the Idea in art, do not satisfy it. It has need of the pure Idea, and this it strives to contemplate directly or immediately by means of pure thought. The enthusiasm of the lover and the artist is but a feeble beginning of the enthusiasm felt by the philosopher in the presence of unveiled truth, ideal beauty, and absolute goodness. Moreover, the philosopher need not boast of having attained this ideal goal, for absolute truth is in God alone.[2] God, who *has* absolute truth because he *is* absolute truth, and the uncultured man, who does not even suspect its existence, do not search for truth; the love of truth ($\phi\iota\lambda o\sigma o\phi\iota a$) is peculiar to the man who is filled with light from on high.

In spite of its mystical character, Plato's method is rationalistic in the strict sense of the term. There is no contradiction between the terms mystical and rationalistic. Rationalism and mysticism are extremes that meet. In fact, rationalism invariably presupposes as its starting-point the immediate and *a priori* perception of an absolute principle, a perception which we call mystical, precisely because it is immediate and unanalyzable.

2. *Nature*

The transition from Idea to being, from metaphysics to physics, is not easy for Plato. If the Idea is self-sufficient, and if the intelligible world is a system of perfect *beings*, what is the use of a sensible reality, that must of necessity be imperfect, *alongside of* the Idea? What is the use of a material world that is inevitably doomed to evil? What is the use of copies by the side of the original, of copies that cannot reproduce it in its divine purity? The real world is evidently as great a source of trouble to Plato as it was to Parmenides. It cannot be explained by the Idea alone, but presupposes a second principle, which is no less real than mind: matter. Hence, when you assume the reality of the sensible world,

---

[1] *Phædrus*, 242 ff.   [2] *Phædrus*, 278.

you abandon the absolute monism of the Idea; you confess that the Idea constitutes only a part of reality, and make concessions to sensualism and materialism. And yet the sensible world exists; it is an undeniable and stubborn fact that has to be explained. Though full of imperfections, it is, after all, a sublime work of art, whose infinite harmonies inspire the idealist as well as the materialist with feelings of delight. The mind of man cannot wholly unravel the mysteries of the universe. Nevertheless, he should investigate it to the best of his ability, and untiringly search for a satisfactory solution of the problem. Plato finds the key to the answer in the conception of divine goodness; this enables his thought to pass from the ideal to the real.[1] The Idea is the absolute good; God is supreme goodness. Now the good or goodness cannot but create the good. God is life, and life must create life. Hence God must create; the Idea must reproduce itself.

Inasmuch as the Idea is the only reality, there is nothing outside of it but non-being. But, in so far as it is the highest reality, it is also the highest activity, the *being* that communicates itself to non-being. Hence, the Idea becomes a creator, a cause, a will, or a plastic principle in reference to non-being; so that non-being in turn becomes like being, and takes part in the absolute existence of the Idea. The non-being thus becomes the first matter out of which the Idea forms, after its own image, the most perfect, divine, and finished visible world possible: it becomes *matter* ($\H{\upsilon}\lambda\eta$), as Plato's successors would say. According to Plato, matter is nothing corporeal; it is something that may become so, through the plastic action of the Idea. The body is a determinate, limited, qualified, and qualifiable thing; matter, considered as such and apart from the forms which the Idea impresses upon it, is the unlimited itself; it is devoid of all positive attributes, and cannot therefore be designated by any positive term, since *every term determines;* it is the indefinable, the formless, the imperceptible. But though in itself indeterminate, formless, and imper-

[1] *Timæus*, 29 E.

ceptible, it may, through the plastic action of the Idea, receive all possible forms and determinations; it may become the mother of all sensible things, the universal recipient. It is identical with space and the place filled by bodies. It is not the product of the Idea, the creature of God, for: (1) Being cannot produce non-being, and matter is non-being; (2) creation is action; now, all action presupposes an object to be acted upon, or an object which suffers action; hence the divine activity presupposes matter, and does not create it. Matter is the condition of the creative activity of the Idea and therefore co-eternal with God. The eternity of matter does not detract from the supreme majesty of the Idea; the Idea continues to remain the highest being, while the eternal existence of matter is equivalent to eternal non-being.

But though eternal matter does not limit the Idea, which as such is absolute, it does, none the less, limit its operation in the universe. Matter is both the condition *sine qua non* of the action of the Idea and its eternal obstruction. It is both the indispensable auxiliary and the irreconcilable foe of the creative Idea. True, it is passive, but its passivity does not consist in absolute non-interference. Its co-operation is resistance. It is formless and unlimited, and therefore opposes and resists the form, limitation, and *finish* which the eternal artist desires to give it; this resistance manifests itself as inertia, weight, disproportion, ugliness, or stupidity. It is non-being or the perpetual negation of being, and consequently opposes and resists everything positive, stable, and immutable, and forever destroys the works of God. It is the primary cause of the imperfection of things, of physical and moral evil, as well as of their instability, their constant change, and of all that is uncertain, perishable, and mortal in them.

From the union of the ideal or paternal principle with the material or maternal principle springs the cosmos, the only son and image of the invisible Divinity, the god that is to be, the visible god, whose relative perfection reminds us of the Father of the Universe, the living animal, that reproduces, as faithfully as it can, the eternal ideal animal. This cosmos has (1) a body governed by necessity; (2) a rational content, a purpose, or a meaning, a final goal for which it was made, an end to realize (τέλος); and finally (3) a soul, the mysterious link which unites the contrary principles in the cosmos, and whose function it is to subordinate the material world to the Idea, or to subject brutal necessity to reason, to adapt it to the final purpose of the Creator. The body of the universe has the shape of a sphere, which is the most beautiful form imaginable, and makes the world the most faithful image of its intelligible archetype. It revolves upon its own axis and thus constantly returns to itself; hence it executes the most perfect movement, a movement which of all possible movements is most appropriate to the eternal repose of the Idea and best symbolizes its immutability. It is perfect and not liable to old age and disease; for it comprehends all the forces of nature, and nothing outside of it can hurt or destroy it. The universe cannot be eternal like the creative Idea; hence God makes it eternal, so far as this is possible; that is, he creates endless time. The mind of the universe, that is, the purpose revealed in its organization, or, in short, its final cause, is the most perfect possible reproduction (or as we should say nowadays, realization) of the Idea of the Good. Finally, the soul of the world consists of Number, which subjects chaotic matter to the laws of harmony and proportion.[1]

Atomistic materialism rejects final causes, and therefore opposes the view that the world has a meaning, or that it realizes an idea. Platonic idealism takes the *nous* of Anaxagoras seriously, and explains the creation of the world wholly from the teleological point of view. It acknowledges the existence of physical causes, but it subordinates them to final causes; the former are the means or involuntary instruments of the latter. Thus, the elements, in regard to which Plato follows Empedocles, are explained teleologically: fire, as a means of vision; earth, as a means of tactile perception. Two

[1] *Timæus*, 28 B, 31 C, 34 A, 39 D, 41 A, 92 B.

other elements are needed as intermediaries between these two extremes, that is, four in all, because the number four represents corporeality. We have seen how Plato (who, like all true Pythagoreans, is a geometrician above everything else) identifies matter and extension; he is therefore forced, with the Eleatics, to reject the void, which, according to Democritus, exists alongside of matter. Since matter is identical with space, and since space is universally the same, the substances composing it are not heterogeneous, as Anaxagoras claimed; the spaces, considered apart from their content, differ only in their outward form, or in figure. In this case Plato, who usually follows Pythagoras, involuntarily agrees with Leucippus and Democritus. Matter is divided into homogeneous corpuscles of different shapes. Only, these figures are not accidental, like the forms of the atoms; they are absolutely geometrical, that is, ideal, final, and providential. The solid element is composed of cubes; water, of icosahedrons; air, of octahedrons; and ether, of pyramids.

After fashioning the first matter with a view to its ultimate structure, the divine architect created the stars, first the fixed stars, then the planets, and then the earth; all these beings are created gods and therefore mortal in themselves; they were, however, endowed with immortality through the goodness of the Creator. At his command, these divinities, particularly the earth, the most venerable of all, produced organized beings, and, chief among these, man, the paragon of creation, for whom everything on earth was made. Plants were formed *in order to* nourish him, animals, *in order to* serve as a habitation for fallen human souls. Woman herself is a degeneration of man, the first-born son of Earth. Man is the epitome of the macrocosm; his soul is endowed with reason and then incorporated in a body. Everything in this body is arranged according to a fixed plan and for a rational end. The head is the seat of reason and therefore round; because this form is the most perfect of all and alone worthy of what is perfect. It is placed at the top of the body *in order to* direct the entire organism. The body has legs for locomotion, and arms with which to take hold of things. The breast is the seat of the noble passions; it is placed beneath the head *in order* that these passions may be under the rule of reason, but separated from the head by the neck, *so as* not to be identified with it. Finally, the coarser appetites reside in the abdomen and are separated from the noble passions by the diaphragm. *In order to*[1] subject them to the rule of reason and the nobler passions, nature placed in this region the liver, a smooth, bright organ, which resembles a mirror and is intended to reflect the images of thoughts. It is composed of bitter and sweet substances; by means of the former it restrains the disordered cravings, and discharges the latter when our desires conform to reason; at certain times it also acquires the power of divination. Finally, there is also a moral reason for the great length of the intestine which is coiled around itself; this hinders the food from passing through the body too quickly, and consequently keeps the soul from having a constant and immoderate desire for food, a desire which would stifle in it the love of wisdom and the voice of conscience. In short, the human body is, according to Platonism, a house of correction and education, constructed and organized with a view to the moral perfection of the soul.

The human soul, like the soul of the world from which it emanates, contains immortal elements and mortal elements; or rather, it combines them; it is the union of the two, or the proportion according to which these two kinds of elements (Idea and matter) are united in the individual. Intelligence or reason (τὸ λογιστικὸν μέρος) is the immortal part; sensuality (τὸ ἐπιθυμητικόν), the mortal part, because it essentially depends on corporeal life; will, energy, or courage (τὸ θυμοειδές), is the union of the two, and constitutes the soul

---

[1] All these data are taken from the *Timœus*. We have reproduced them here and italicized these *in order to's*, simply to give the reader a classical sample of the theory of final causes in its application to nature. Though the theory contains a spark of truth, it has for centuries impeded the progress of the physical sciences, by substituting the dreams of fancy for the observation of facts.

proper and its individuality. The immortality of the intelligent soul follows: (1) from its simplicity, which renders all
decomposition impossible; (2) from the goodness of the Creator; (3) from the fact that it is the very principle of life,
and a transition from being into non-being is impossible. The
immortality of the intelligent soul is also proved by the philosopher's desire to be freed from the body and its fetters,
and to come into direct communion with the intelligible world;
by the fact that life invariably and universally produces death,
and death, a new life; by the pre-existence of the soul, which
is demonstrated by the doctrine of recollection (if the soul has
existed before the body, why should it not exist after its decomposition?); by the relation existing between the soul and
the Ideas (it conceives the intelligible, and must therefore be
homogeneous with it and akin to it, that is, immortal, like its
object); and finally, by the fact that it controls the body,
which would be inconceivable if, as some Pythagoreans claim,
it were but the resultant of the bodily functions. Immortality,
however, is the prerogative of reason. The sensual part cannot lay claim to it, and the will itself, in so far as it is bound
to the organism, has no part in it.[1]

In so far as the problem of the soul borders upon physics,
it cannot be solved with absolute certainty. There is no science of passing things. The only certain science is the science
of Ideas; for Ideas alone are eternal and necessary. In the
domain of physics we must content ourselves with probabili-
ties; science being impossible here, we are reduced to faith.[2]

3. The Highest Good

Man is the end of nature, and the Idea the end of man.
Plato, like Antisthenes and the Cynics, finds the highest good,
not in pleasure but in man's most perfect likeness to God.
Now, since God is the Good or absolute Justice, we can resemble him only in justice. It is impossible, says Socrates-

---

[1] *Phædo*, 61–107.   [2] *Timæus*, 51, 52.

Plato,[1] that evils should pass away (for there must always remain something which is antagonistic to good). Having no place among the gods in heaven, of necessity they hover around the mortal nature and this earthly sphere. Wherefore we ought to fly away from earth to heaven as quickly as we can, and to fly away is to become like God, as far as this is possible. Now God is never in any way unrighteous; he is perfect righteousness; and he of us who is the most righteous is most like him.[2] Justice is the fundamental virtue, the mother of the virtues belonging to each of the *three souls*. For the intelligence it consists in the correctness of thought (σοφία, φιλοσοφία); for the will, in courage (ἀνδρία); for the sensibility, in temperance (σωφροσύνη). Wisdom is the justice of the mind; courage, the justice of the heart; temperance, the justice of the senses. Piety is justice in our relation with the Deity; it is synonymous with justice in general.

Man must be educated in order to attain justice and through it to become like God. He can never realize this virtue in isolation. Justice, or the final goal of things, is realized only in the collective man or in the State. Plato's ideal State, like the individual, embraces three parts or separate classes: (1) the philosophers, who constitute the legislative and executive power, the intelligence and the head of the State, or the ruling class; (2) the warriors, who are the heart of the State, or the militant class; (3) the merchants, artisans, agriculturists, and slaves, or the servant class, who correspond to the sensual soul, which is restricted to the lower parts of the human body. Wisdom belongs to the ruling class; courage to the military class; obedience to the two higher classes, who think and fight for them, belongs to the laboring, commercial, and serving classes. In order that the collective man or the State may form a real unity or an individual on the large scale, particular interests must be merged in the general interest, the family must be absorbed in the State, the individual must cease to be a proprietor. Henceforth the children belong to the State

[1] *Theætetus*, 176.　　　　　　　　[2] *Republic*, X, 613.

only, which forms one large family.[1] The State is the father of the children; the State also educates them. Up to the age of three, the education of the child consists solely in caring for the body. From three to six, its moral education is anticipated by the narration of myths. From seven to ten, gymnastics. From eleven to thirteen, reading and writing. From fourteen to sixteen, poetry and music. From sixteen to eighteen, mathematics. From eighteen to twenty, military exercises. When the twentieth year is reached, the State makes its first selection among the young people, choosing such as are fitted for the military career, and such as are qualified for the government. The latter make a thorough study of the different sciences until they are thirty years old. At the age of thirty, a second selection is made. The least distinguished enter upon the secondary positions of the administration; the others continue the study of dialectics for a number of years, and crown their education with ethics. After they have been introduced to the knowledge of the highest Good, they are capable of assuming the most exalted duties of the State. The latter is essentially a pedagogical institution, whose mission is to realize Goodness and Justice on our earth, and will not, therefore, tolerate art itself, except in so far as art is a means of education, and is employed in the service of the Good.[2]

These deductions, which are idealistic in the extreme, bring us back to the ontology of Plato. Reality, it must be remembered, does not, according to him, belong to sense-objects (or phenomena), but to the Ideas or types which these objects reproduce and which are perceived (conceived) by reason (the noumena). The phenomenon is real, only in so far as it partakes of the ideal type of which it is a *copy*. Now, the highest Idea, which is to the world of invisible realities what the sun

---

[1] This arrangement might seem strange to us, did we not remember that the Greek State simply consisted of the city. Furthermore, the communistic teachings of the *Republic* are not repeated in the *Laws*.

[2] Hence the theatre is not permitted in Plato's commonwealth; for it sets before us a world in which good and evil are necessarily intermingled. — (*Repub.*, III, 394–402).

is to the phenomenal universe, is the Good or absolute Goodness, the first and final cause of all being, and consequently superior and anterior to being itself, which it creates by natural radiation.

This ontology may be defined as the *monism of the good.* It is, undoubtedly, the sublimest and purest product of philosophical genius. Others may have advanced beyond it; no one has ever excelled it. The real object of science is the general, the universal, or the typical law of the particular facts. Thus, when the anthropologist occupies himself with Peter and Paul, his object is to know what *man* is; and the physicist's interest in the apple that falls from the tree, or in the snow-flake that floats in the air, or in the sinking avalanche, is occasioned by the fact that these particular phenomena serve to exemplify his theory of weight. The modern scientist, like Plato, regards the phenomenon as changing, the law as stable and therefore *more real* than the particulars. The mistake does not lie in exalting the universal over the particular; it consists in *separating* the former from the latter metaphysically, and in making a transcendent entity of the genus or type; it does not consist in exalting *nous* over perception, but in making two separate and even incompatible principles of them. In themselves, the type and the individual which realizes it, the law and the phenomenon which is its application, are but one and the same reality considered from different points of view; observation and reasoning are merely two stages of one and the same method. A physic, a physiology, or an anatomy that is the creation of pure reason is inconceivable. The universal must be derived from the particular, because it cannot be found anywhere else. Plato's failure to escape the illusion that the Idea is something separate, real, and transcendent, is in part due to the imperfect state of the philosophical terminology of his time. If, in place of form, he had used the word law, the term with which modern science has become so familiar, he would not easily have fallen into the error of the *separatistic* conception. But it is not merely the terminology that misleads him; it is the poet in Plato that impels the philosopher to *realize* the Idea. Aristotle, in a spirit of controversy, and a few sincere but unintelligent disciples of Plato, exaggerated the *realism* of the master, but the realism is there none the less,[1] and its consequences are only too apparent. The Idea is real in itself, and does not need to be realized. Then the cosmic process loses the reason for its existence; it no longer consists in the realization of an Idea; it is the fall of a god. Creation would be the overflowing of the Idea, as it were, and the generation of being, that is, according to Plato, of spiritual being, thought, or intelligence; for the being which comes from the Idea must "resemble" it as the son resembles his mother. *Being*, in the real and absolute sense of the term, and *being-mind* (thought) are one and the same thing, from this point of view. This explanation of the world, which, to tell the truth, is but a figure of speech, would perhaps suffice, if the world were actually a society of pure spirits, the abode of goodness, justice, and perfection. But it is a mixture of being and non-being, of spirituality and corporeality, of good and evil. Whence comes this second constitutive element of the phenomenon, this *non-being?* From the Idea? Impossible. The Idea can create nothing but *being*, intelligence, and goodness. Hence, a second principle that is co-eternal with the Idea has participated in the creation of the world; the monism of the good becomes a dualism of Idea and matter. By coming in contact with the latter, the Idea, or rather intelligence, its offspring, is polluted, diminished, and impoverished. Hence, intelligence must consider matter as its natural enemy, as the chief cause of its diminution, as the seat and the principle of evil; the mind will, of course, desire to be freed, as soon as possible, from the body which holds it in bondage, and from the visible world, which is a prison, a place of correction. The Utopian system of politics, which sacrifices nature to an abstract principle, asceticism, monachism, the horror of matter which we find among

[1] See especially *Repub.*, VI, 509.

the Neo-Platonists, the Gnostics, and even Catholics, all these elements are the logical consequences of a conception that makes the Idea a reality.

SPEUSIPPUS, the successor of Plato in the Academy (347-339), seems to see the need of combining the One (the Idea) and the many (matter) by means of a concrete principle that contains them both. He lays great weight on the Pythagorean notion of emanation, development, and series, which forms the very essence of Neo-Platonism, and teaches, in opposition to Plato, that perfection is to be found, not in the original and abstract unity, but in the developed, differentiated, and organized unity.[1] But his reverence for the name of Plato, and the position which he held as the scholarch of the school hindered him from subjecting the master's view to an impartial criticism. The same is true of Xenocrates, Polemo, Crantor, and Crates, who were succeeded by the sceptic Arcesilaus. It was left to Aristotle, the most distinguished among the pupils of Plato and the founder of a new school, to criticise and reform Academic idealism from the standpoint of concrete spiritualism.

§ 17. Aristotle[2]

ARISTOTLE was born at Stagira, not far from Mount Athos, in 385. His father, Nicomachus, the physician of King Amyntas of Macedon, came from a family of physicians. The blood of experimentalists and positive scientists flowed in his veins. In the year 367, he entered upon his course of study (as we should say nowadays) at Athens, where he became first a pupil and then the successful rival of the veteran Plato. From 343 to 340, he was the teacher of Alexander, the son of Philip. The friendship between him and Alexander proved advanta-

---

[1] Aristotle, *Met.*, XII, 7. Cf. § 65.

[2] *Works*, translated under the editorship of J. A. Smith and W. D. Ross, Oxford; *The Nicomachean Ethics*, translated by Welldon, New York, 1892; translated also by Williams, New York, 1876; Zeller, *Aristotle and the Earlier Peripatetics*, translated by Costelloe and Muirhead, New York, 1897; Grote, *Aristotle*, London, 1883; Wallace, *Outlines of the Philosophy of Aristotle*, Oxford, 1875; Taylor, *Aristotle*, London, 1919; Ross, *Aristotle*, New York, 1924.

geous to Aristotle, for it enabled him to accumulate vast collections, and contributed largely towards making him the father of natural science. In 334 he began to teach his philosophy in the walks of the Lyceum at Athens; hence the name applied to his school, and the epithet given to his disciples, — *Peripatetics*. After the death of Alexander, he was accused of Macedonianism and atheism, and compelled to retire to Chalchis, in the island of Eubœa, where he died in 322.

The writings attributed to Aristotle deal with almost all the sciences known to antiquity, that is, according to the philosopher's own classification,[1] with the *theoretical* sciences, which have truth for their object (mathematics, physics, and theology, or the first philosophy), with the *practical* sciences, which treat of the useful (ethics, politics, etc.), and with the *poetical* sciences, whose object is the beautiful. The *Categories*, the *De interpretatione*, the two *Analytics*, the *Topics*, etc., which have been collected under the name *Organon*, make Aristotle the real founder of logic. True, he was not the first to conceive all the principles of logic; the discussions of the Eleatics, the Sophists, and the Socratics, have shown us how reason gradually became conscious of the processes which it originally employed instinctively; thus the elementary axioms, such as the principle of contradiction, the principle of sufficient reason, the principle of excluded middle, the *dictum de omni et nullo*, and without doubt also the more special rules of the syllogism came to be formulated. But it required the genius of an Aristotle to co-ordinate these elements, to complete them, and to formulate them into the system of deductive logic, which constitutes his chief claim to fame. The physical and natural sciences are ably set forth in the *Physics*, the *De cœlo*, the *De generatione et corruptione*, the *Meteorology*, the *De anima*, the *Parva naturalia*, the *History of Animals*, the treatises *On the Parts of Animals*, *On the Progression of Animals*, *On the Generation of Animals*, etc. The problems of philosophy proper are discussed in a number of writings on first principles, which

[1] *Metaphysics*, VI, 1, 9.

a compiler collected into a single work comprising fourteen books, and placed *after the writings on physics* (μετὰ τὰ φυσικά): hence the name *metaphysics*, which has since been applied to philosophy proper, a term with which Aristotle himself was not acquainted. Ethics and politics are treated in the *Nicomachean Ethics*, in the *Magna Moralia*, in the *Eudemean Ethics*, in the eight books of the *Politics*. Rhetoric and poetry are discussed in the books known by those titles. Taken altogether, the works of Aristotle constitute a veritable encyclopedia of the knowledge possessed by the fourth century before Christ.

Philosophy is defined by Aristotle as the science of universals. Every real science is, or at least aims to be, a view of the whole, a general theory; hence the special sciences are partial *philosophies* as well as general theories concerning one or more groups of given facts, theories which are summarized and systematized by general philosophy. Conversely, philosophy proper or the first science is a separate science; it is coordinated with other sciences (second philosophy), and has a distinct subject-matter of its own: being as such, the absolute or God. But it is at the same time the universal science embracing all the specialties, because its object, God, embraces and contains the principles of all the sciences and the first causes of everything that exists.[1]

There was no doubt in Aristotle's mind as to the possibility of science, which had been denied by the Sophists and the Sceptics. Man is the only being who partakes of the active intellect, that is, of God himself, and through him of the knowledge of the absolute; man alone is endowed with speech. By means of language, we designate things as we conceive them; by reason, we conceive them as they are. The general ways of designating things, or the parts of discourse (the *categories* of language and of grammar), correspond to the different forms according to which we conceive them, or to the *categories* of the understanding (substance, quantity, quality, relation, place, time, position, mode of being, activity, passiv-

[1] *Met.*, I, 2, 14. Cf. I, 8; I, 10.

ity), and these categories of the understanding in their turn
signify the modes of being of the things themselves; that is,
the things are in reality either substances or quantities or relations, etc., and are not merely conceived as such.[1]

1. *First Philosophy*

The mathematical and physical sciences treat of the quantity, quality, and relations of things; the first philosophy has
as its object the queen of the categories, the category of substance, to which all the rest are related and on which they are
based. It inquires into the nature of being as such, regardless
of all relations of time, place, etc., that is, absolute and necessary being, the eternal essence of things as opposed to the
relative, contingent, and accidental.[2]

Hence Plato is right in regarding it as the science of real
being, as distinguished from that which *appears to be,* and is
in reality but a passing relation. He errs in conceiving the
Ideas as real beings existing apart from the individuals which
express them. In vain do we search in Plato's writings for the
proof that Ideas subsist apart from things. Moreover, it is
hard to see what this theory accomplishes. It does not solve
the metaphysical problem, but merely complicates it by adding to the real world a world of useless homonyms. The separate Ideas do not, in fact, contribute either towards the production, or the preservation, or the science of things. We are
at a loss to know what is the relation between things and
Ideas. The assertion that the Ideas are patterns and that the
things participate in them is to speak vain words, and to utter
poetic metaphors. Besides, if the general Idea is the substance
of the particulars or the essence of the things, how can it exist
apart from that of which it is the substance and the essence?
The general cannot exist outside of and alongside of the particular. Hence the Ideas or specific types, considered as such
and apart from the things, are not real beings or substances

---

[1] *Met.,* V, 7; VI, 4.
[2] *Met.,* VI, 1; XI, 4, 7.

(οὐσίαι), if we understand by substance that which exists by itself.[1] Aristotle does not, however, deny the objective existence of species. For him as well as for Plato, the general Idea is the essence of the particular, and may be called substance. What he denies is that Ideas exist apart from things. The Idea is inherent or immanent in the thing; it is its *form*, and cannot be separated from it except by abstraction. It is the essence of the particular and with it constitutes an indivisible whole. For the "one along with the many" we must substitute the "one among the many," cr "in the many."[2]

On the other hand, the materialistic theory is equally untenable. Matter has no reality apart from the form (that is, not only *the shape*, length, breadth, and height of the thing, but all of its properties). Matter without the Idea is as much of an abstraction as the Idea apart from the particular object which realizes it. Nor does movement exist by itself; it presupposes a substratum. Hence, neither the Idea nor matter nor movement has real or substantial existence; reality consists of all these taken as a whole, or of the particular. Reality is a concrete thing; it contains constitutive elements, which thought distinguishes, but which do not exist apart from each other. The most important of these elements is the Idea or the *form*, which Aristotle conceives as identical with essence or soul. Matter is merely its support, but it is an indispensable support.

The next question is, What are the generative causes of real being? All things which are produced either by nature or art have a material cause, a formal cause, an efficient or moving cause, and a final cause.[3] Thus, to take an example from art. A bed or a statue presupposes (1) matter: the wood or the marble or the brass of which the thing is made; (2) an idea (a plan or a pattern) according to which it is made; the idea of the statue exists in the mind of the sculptor, the idea of the bed, in the mind of the joiner; (3) arms, hands, and tools, as

---

[1] *Met.*, I, 9, 15, 16; V, 8, 14; XII, 10, 22; XIV, 3, 4, 9, 12.
[2] *Met.*, III, 4, 1; *Analyt. post.*, I, 11.   [3] *Met.*, I, 3. Cf. VII, 7, ff.

motive forces and efficient causes; (4) a purpose or motive that
sets these forces in action, and effects the transition from capacity or potentiality to actuality. The same is true of nature
and particularly of organic nature. A living organism, as, for
example, a man, is the product of the following four causes:
(1) the substance which forms the starting-point and substratum of the embryonic development; (2) the Idea or specific type according to which the embryo is developed, the
form which it tends to assume; (3) the act of generation; (4)
the (unconscious) purpose of this act, namely, the production
of a new man. There are, then, for every fact and for the universal fact itself (the world), four kinds of causes: matter, Idea,
force, and the final purpose. Through the co-operation of these
four principles, the real being, be it an object of art or a living
being, is produced. These principles, moreover, do not subsist as substances; they always inhere in a particular thing:
every natural product is preceded by an individual of the same
species, from which it is *generated*. Similarly, every phenomenon in art and ethics presupposes an actual cause. Each man
is educated by another educated man; the efficient cause is always a concrete being, and that which exists potentially becomes actual only through the instrumentality of some actual
thing.

Though philosophical reflection distinguishes four generative principles of things, three of them, the Idea, the motive
cause, and the final cause, are very often identified, and constitute but a single principle. Thus, in art, the Idea of Hermes
in the imagination of the sculptor, moves his nerves and muscles, and at the same time constitutes the end which he aims
to realize by means of matter. Take an illustration from nature. A man is to be produced. *Man* is the Idea which is realized by generation; a *man* realizes it, and he realizes it in order
to reproduce *man*.[1] In both cases the Idea is the formal cause,
the motive cause, and the final cause.

There are then, ultimately, only two principles of things,

[1] *Phys.*, II, 7.

— the *Idea* or *form* (εἶδος — *eidos*) which causes them and at which they aim, and the *matter* (ὕλη — *hyle*) of which they are made. The former is essential and the cause proper; the latter is of secondary importance and a mere condition. Since these two principles are the necessary antecedents of all becoming, they cannot have been produced themselves; for in that case they would have had to exist even *prior* to being, which is impossible. They necessarily precede all generation, since generation is possible only through them.[1] Both Aristotle and Plato regard matter and form as eternal; only, the Stagirite does not conceive the eternity of matter to mean absolute dualism. If matter and Idea are diametrically opposed to each other, as they seem to be in Plato, how can they ever be united, how can they co-operate and produce all things? Things that are diametrically opposed cannot be united.[2]

Plato's non-being or absolute privation and real matter are two entirely different things. Matter is accidental non-being, whereas privation is non-being as such. The conception of matter is one that is closely akin to the notion of substance; in certain respects matter is substance itself, while privation is nothing of the kind.[3] It is not the non-being, but the potential being, the possibility or capacity of being, the germ and the beginning of becoming. Concrete being, or the particular, represents the development of this germ, the realization of this possibility, the potential actualized. (Matter is the germ of the form, the potential form; the form, in turn, or rather the union of form and matter, which constitutes the particular thing, is matter in actuality.[4] Thus, in the technical field, wood, the matter of which the table is made, is a potential table; the finished table is the same wood in energy. Brass is a potential statue; the statue is the actualization of the brass. In nature, the egg is a bird in capacity; the bird is its ἐνέργεια (actuality). Matter is the beginning of all things;

[1] *Id.*, I, 10, 8.   [2] *Met.*, XII, 10, 7.
[2] *Phys.*, X, 10, 4.   [4] *Met.*, VIII, 6, 19.

the Idea (shape or form) is the goal for which it strives; matter is the rudimentary or imperfect state; the form is the perfection or completion (ἐντελέχεια). If matter were synonymous with privation, matter could not become anything, it could not be united with a form or assume those definite outlines which define the real being; for from nothing nothing can come. Instead of struggling against the form, it strives after it, it desires it, as the female desires the male.[1] (Matter and Idea or form are, therefore, correlative notions; instead of excluding each other, they presuppose and supplement each other; motion or evolution is the term which mediates between them; motion is the transition or transformation of the former into the latter. Hence the importance ascribed by Aristotle to the idea of movement;[2] it enables him, in a certain measure, to escape the dualism of Plato, which the latter himself had attempted to avoid by means of the conception of number or soul. His entire system is founded on the trinity of potentiality, movement, and actuality.[3] If matter is to form what capacity is to energy, the germ to the finished organism, then the opposition between the two principles is far from absolute, and all things are both potentiality and actuality, matter and form. Brass is form or energy in relation to the raw mineral, matter or potentiality in relation to the statue. The tree of which a bed is made is form, shape, or actuality in relation to the seed from which it grew, formless matter in relation to the bed. The youth is form in relation to the infant, formless matter in relation to the grown man.

The rule that every being is both form and substratum, idea and matter, soul and body, admits of but a single exception: the Supreme Being is pure form and without matter. According to Aristotle, matter invariably forms the starting-point for a process of development; it is the antecedent of a higher perfection. Now the Supreme Being is absolute perfection; hence he contains no *matter for a more* exalted being; in short,

[1] *Phys.*, I, 10, 7. [2] *Id.*, III, 1 ff.
[3] *Met.*, XII, 5, 6; 10, 21. Cf. XII, 2, 10.

he is immaterial. Aristotle here seems to contradict the nominalistic theory, on which his polemic against the *separate* Ideas of Plato is based, and, above all, refutes his own statement that everything is material.[1] But this difficulty partly disappears when we take into consideration his definition of the word *matter*. He means by it matter that has not yet been formed, the *provisional* as opposed to the final; it denotes imperfection, capacity, undeveloped germ. If this is what is meant by matter, then, evidently, every being in the universal scale of beings is idea or perfection, as compared to the lower stages, and matter or imperfection, as compared to higher beings; and the Supreme Being — but the Supreme Being only — is pure idea, pure form, or pure actuality. Aristotle also declares that the last matter (matter in the final stage of development) and the form are the same.[2] Hence we may conclude that he would not, perhaps, have objected to calling the Supreme Being *last matter* or the final stage of the universal evolution, though he would have denied that this higher phase of existence is in part material. But he does not accept the pantheistic conception of an absolute that develops, and is matter *before* being form, potentiality *before* being energy.[3] If the Supreme Being had first existed in germ and as potentiality, then it would have been necessary for an actual being to exist antecedent to God in order to energize this germ and to make God actual; for not only does all seed come from a pre-existent actual being, but no capacity ever becomes actual without the co-operation of an actual being. Not capacity but energy, not the potential but the actual, not the imperfect but the perfect, is the first principle anterior and superior to everything else.[4] This favorite conception of Aristotle really agrees with the Eleatic doctrine: *ex nihilo nihil;* its logical consequence is the negation of the chaos as the original form of existence, if we may apply the term "form" to the formless as such, or to the complete absence of all order. Since form or

---

[1] *Met.*, XII, 3, 8.   [2] *Id.*, VIII, 6, 19. Cf. VII, 10, 27; XII, 3, 8; 10, 8.
[3] *Id.*, XII, 7, 19–20. Cf. *Phys.*, II, 9, 6.   [4] *Ibid.*

absolute energy and matter are both eternal, it follows that
matter has never been without form, and that there never
was a state of chaos.[1]

The eternal actual Being is both the motive or generating
cause, the form, and the final goal of things.

It is the first mover and itself immovable. The existence of
this first mover is the necessary consequence of the principle
of causality. Every movement implies, in addition to the
thing moved, a moving principle, which, again, receives its
motion from a higher motive force. Now, since there can be
no infinite series of causes, we are obliged to stop at a first
mover. To deny this and at the same time to assume the
reality of motion, to assume with Leucippus, Democritus, and
others, an infinite series of effects and causes without a first
cause, is to violate one of the most fundamental laws of
thought. Moreover, the first cause acts forever, and the ensuing motion is likewise eternal. The universe has neither a beginning nor an end in time, although it has its limits in space.

Here a difficulty arises: How can that which is immovable
and remains so, move? How can the motive cause act without setting itself in motion? It must be assumed that God
acts as the beautiful and the desirable act. Thus, a masterpiece of art or nature moves and attracts us, and yet remains
completely at rest itself. Similarly, the ideal which I strive
to realize, or the goal at which I aim, sets me in motion without moving itself. So, too, matter is moved by the eternal
Idea without the slightest movement on the part of the absolute being. It has a desire for God, but God is the first cause
of this desire.[2]

Inasmuch as the Supreme Being is immaterial, it can have
no impressions, nor sensations, nor appetites, nor a will in the
sense of desire, nor feelings in the sense of passions; all these
things depend on matter, the passive or female principle, the
recipient of the form. God is pure intelligence. The human
understanding passes from a potential state through the stages

[1] *Met.*, XII, 6, 15.   [2] *Id.*, XII, 7, 3.

of sensation, perception, and comparison. The divine *nous* has an immediate intuitive knowledge of the intelligible essence of things. Our discursive thought pursues an object which is different from it and which cannot be attained except by gradual stages, while the absolute thought is identical with its object. [Since nothing is higher than God, and since the thought of God has the highest possible object, God is the object of his own thought.]God's life is free from all pain and imperfection, and therefore beyond desire and regret; it is supremely happy; human life with its emotions is but a feeble image of it. God enjoys what but few favored mortals enjoy, and then only for a limited period of time; his life consists in the pure contemplation of the intelligible truth.[1]

As the final cause of the universe and the highest good, God is both *in* the things or their immanent essence and *above* the things, apart from the world, or transcendent. Discipline exists both *in* an army and *outside* of it in the mind of the general. Similarly, God is both the law and the lawgiver, the order and the orderer of things.[2] Everything is organized, ordered, and harmonized by him and with a view to him; and since he is *one* (matter alone is manifold[3]), there can be but one single, eternal universe. Conversely, the unity which prevails in the world proves the unity of God.

On this principle of principles depend the heavens and nature.[4]

2. *Second Philosophy, or the Philosophy of Nature*

According to Aristotle, the sky is the perfect sphere, of which the earth is supposed to be the centre; nature is everything within this sphere that is subject to motion or to rest; or, more abstractly, it is motion itself, in so far as the latter emanates from the first mover and is continued by the secondary causes. Physics is a theory of motion.[5] It inquires into

---

[1] *Met.*, XII, 7, 11. [2] *Id.*, XII, 10, 1, 2. [3] *Id.*, VIII, 6, 21.
[4] *Met.*, XII, 7, 11. [5] *Phys.*, III, 1, 1.

the immovable principle (the divine), the imperishable moving power (the heaven), and the perishable world or sublunary nature.[1] There are as many kinds of movement as there are categories of being.[2] The principal ones are: (1) movement that affects the substance, or origin and decay; (2) movement that affects the quality, or change of quality, alteration; (3) movement that affects the quantity, or addition and subtraction; (4) local movement, or change of place.[3] The first (origin and decay), however, is not, strictly speaking, a movement, while, of the other three, change of place is regarded by all the physicists, and especially by Anaxagoras, as the most important, the most universal, and the most original form of motion.[4] Motion, change, energy, or *entelechy*, is the realization of the potential as such.[5] But it is not a substance, and does not exist apart from the things which it affects.

Space is more like a substance. It is, however, neither the material of which bodies are made, as Plato erroneously supposes in the *Timæus*,[6] nor their form, nor the interval which separates them, but the limit between the surrounding and the surrounded body,[7] between the contents and the container. This singular definition is intended by Aristotle as a disavowal of the conception that there is such a thing as empty space separating bodies from each other (the void of Democritus), a view which he regarded as erroneous. Movement, according to him, does not imply the existence of the void; it is invariably a change of place of different bodies. The condensation of a body presupposes the rarefaction of the surrounding body, and *vice versa*. Consequently, there is no void either in the bodies or outside of them.[8] Since space cannot be conceived without movement, the immovable (the divine) is not in space. Moreover, inasmuch as space is the boundary between the container and the contained, and since the universal is not contained in anything, but contains every-

[1] *Id.*, II, 7.　　[2] *Id.*, III, 1, 2.　　[3] *Id.*, III, 1, 7.
[4] *Id.*, VIII, 10.　　[5] *Id.*, III, 1, 7.　　[6] *Phys.*, IV, 1.
[7] *Id.*, IV, 6.　　[8] *Id.*, IV, 8.

thing, the universe or the All cannot occupy a particular place. Hence the universe, or the whole of things, does not, strictly speaking, move. Its parts alone suffer a change of place. Taken as a whole, however, it can only revolve upon itself. Indeed, certain portions of the heavens move, not upward and downward, but in a circle, and only the denser or lighter substances are carried downward and upward.[1]

Like space, time exists only as the condition of motion; it is the measure or number of motion. It is potentially infinite, like motion (whatever Plato may say of it), and this distinguishes it from space, which is limited. It is nonsense to speak of an actually infinite space. Infinity is merely potential and never actual; for the actual has form; it is determined or finite; the potential is not finite, but infinite. Conversely, infinity has potential existence only in the infinite multiplication of numbers and the infinite divisibility of magnitudes. Now, time is the measure of motion and consequently a number, and number presupposes a person who can count. Hence it follows that time presupposes a soul and cannot exist except for a numbering soul.[2]

We distinguished between several kinds of movement, the most important of which is called change of place. The latter, again, has different forms. The first and the most perfect of these is movement in a circle, which is the only motion that can be endless, simple, and uniform. Rectilinear motion cannot be constant, and is therefore less perfect than the other. It cannot be continued *ad infinitum*, because Aristotle's universe is limited; hence, in order to continue, it must return upon itself or become oscillatory; and there is bound to be a stop, however minimal it may be, at the point where the movement begins again to go in the opposite direction.

Circular movement and rectilinear movement upward and downward are the two great forms of motion in the physical world. The former, which is the most perfect, because it is simple and continuous, belongs to the highest heavens, the

[1] *Id.*, IV, 7, 5.   [2] *Phys.*, IV, 20, 4.

solid vault which supports the fixed stars;[1] the latter, which
is less perfect because it is not absolutely continuous, moves
the lower or central parts of the universe. The eternal revolution of the outermost heavens around the axis of the world is
immediately caused by the immovable first mover, who moves
the other parts of the world only indirectly and by means of
the highest heavens. Hence, the sphere of the fixed stars is in
the πρῶτον κινοῦν κινούμενον, the first moved mover, and
communicates its motion to the lower or planetary spheres.
These solid but transparent spheres, of which there are about
fifty, revolve around a common centre, the centre of the earth,
which is also the centre of the world. But their movement is
no longer a simple movement; they rotate from left to right,
like the outermost heaven, but they also move from right to
left. This complicated movement can only be explained on
the assumption that each sphere has, in addition to the first
moved mover, a particular, relatively independent mover.
Finally, the central sphere, that is, the earth and its inhabitants, its ocean, and its two atmospheres, is placed under the
direct guidance of the planets and under the indirect influence
of the fixed stars. It does not revolve around its own axis,
but executes complex movements, the fundamental form of
which is upward and downward movement.

Things that move downward from the universal circumference to the universal centre are called heavy; things that move
upward from the earth towards the sky are called light. The
opposition between heavy and light is the same as that between cold and warm; for experience shows that cold air falls
and warm air rises. On this double opposition depends the
differentiation of elements. Heavy and cold matter forms the

---

[1] The modern theory of heavenly bodies moving in space, a view which prevailed among the Ionians and the Pythagoreans, seems to be wholly foreign to
Aristotle. When he speaks of the heaven and its motion, he does not mean,
by metonymy, the motion of the stars enclosed in this space; his idea is that
the heaven itself, that is, the entire series of concentric spheres, which consist
of the same substance as their stars, moves. He also likens the motion of the
stars to the movement of a person seated in a chariot; the person is immovable
and yet advances as the chariot advances.

earthy or solid element; light and warm matter produces fire. Water and air, that is, moisture and dryness, form two intermediate elements, whose purpose is to reconcile the contrary extremes. Although Aristotle thus assumes the four elements of Empedocles, he maintains with Heraclitus and Democritus that these elements are homogeneous, and that they represent successive transformations of one and the same matter. In fact, experience shows him that solids pass into liquids, liquids into gases, gases into fire, and *vice versa*, that fire and gases are liquefied, and liquids solidified. Hence, he identifies the chemical notion of element with the physical notion of state.

The difference existing between the elements of sublunary matter depends essentially on the nature of the movement peculiar to the earth, and does not extend beyond our world. It is not found in the celestial spheres, which consist of pure ether. This ether is not a fifth element, as has been erroneously believed, but the original and neutral substance which Anaximander called the *apeiron*, and which is the substratum common to the four elements of the terrestrial sphere. There can be no dense liquid, gaseous, or fiery elements in the heavens, because there is no contrast between heavy and light, cold and warm, in that region; and this contrast does not exist in the heavenly spheres, because rectilinear and vertical motion is unknown there.

Removed as they are from the contrasts of our perishable world, and coming into direct communion with the first mover, who dwells in the outermost heaven,[1] the bright inhabitants of the skies enjoy happiness unalloyed, and are endowed with immortality. They of all beings most resemble the unmoved first mover. Their movements are not arbitrary; what seems to be an imperfection is in reality a divine prerogative. Even the free man is much more determined in his actions than the slave and the animal; for he obeys the established laws of the State, while they contribute but little to public affairs, and habitually act by chance.[2] The more reason

[1] *Phys.*, VIII, 14, 24.   [2] *Met.*, XII, 10, 4.

a being possesses, the more regular are its acts, and the less arbitrary is its behavior. Moreover, the more immovable the *secondary gods* are, the more they resemble him in whom there is neither movement nor change of any kind. As immovable beings, any number of them can exist in one and the same sphere. The planets, which are inferior in dignity to the fixed stars, are likewise immortal and uncreated beings endowed with life and activity.[1] The movers of the planets impart to their respective spheres movements that are opposed to the divine and perfect movement of the highest heavens, thereby declaring their independence of the Deity and their hostility towards the universal order. We have here the beginning of evil, but so small a beginning that the life of Mercury, Venus, Mars, Jupiter, Saturn, the Sun, and the Moon,[2] is, as compared with the life of the earth, a divine, perfect, and happy existence.

The operation of the four elements, and the perpetual change of bodies resulting from it (the universal flux of Heraclitus), are confined to the terrestrial and sublunary sphere. This is the sphere of becoming, birth, and death, and — in so far as φύσις (physis-nature) signifies production, generation, or becoming — the stage of *nature* proper as distinguished from the sky, which is the abode of the *supernatural*, that is, of the unchangeable and everlasting.[3] The opposition between earth and heaven, the Here and the Beyond, the natural and the supernatural, has not, it is true, the same meaning and import in Aristotle as in Catholicism; still it is certain that this dualism adds to his cosmology a tinge of Platonic mysticism that contrasts with his ontological principles. It was this dualistic conception of an earth placed in the centre of the world and a God placed at the periphery, as far from the earth as possible, that caused the Church to adopt the Aristotelian system, and led to its being forced upon the minds of men as revealed truth, even after the great majority of scientists had taken sides with Copernicus.

---

[1] *De cœlo*, 292.   [2] Both sun and moon are considered as planets.
[3] *Met.*, XI, 6, 12.

Aristotle's meteorology is more independent than his astronomical theories, which are based on the preconceptions of his age. The terrestrial atmosphere comprises two regions, one of which is moist and cold, and surrounds the earth and the ocean; while the other is formed of an element that is lighter and warmer than air, called fire by Heraclitus, and extends to the vault of the heavens.[1] In the highest atmosphere are situated the comets and the Milky-Way (!). The lower atmosphere produces winds, storms, rainbows, and other meteors, which are explained, in the same way as earthquakes and tides, by the reciprocal action between the upper and lower atmospheric strata and the waters of the earth. Aristotle's theory, or at least his explanation of aerial and ocean currents, contains, as we see, a shadow of the truth. But it is in the sphere of natural science proper that his genius bursts forth in all its grandeur.

The organic world is the real domain of final causes. Here, more than anywhere else, nature reveals herself as an artist of infinite capacity, universally choosing the simplest and the best means of arriving at her goal. What distinguishes nature from art is this: The goal at which the artist aims exists in his thought as a clearly conceived idea, while in nature it exists as an instinct. There is an end to be realized in the case of the bird which creates itself as well as in the case of the bed that is made by the joiner. In order to become a reality, the end *bed* needs the hands of the joiner; the end *bird* realizes itself; in both instances, however, final causes play an important part. But what of the objection that nature sometimes produces monsters? Well, mistakes may be made in her domain as well as in the domain of art. A grammarian may, in spite of his knowledge, make a mistake in spelling; a physician, though skilful, may administer the wrong medicine. So, too, errors can creep into the operations of nature, and monstrosities are merely deviations from a goal that is aimed at without success.[2] Nature desires the best without always being able

---

[1] *Meteorology*, 1, 3. [2] *Phys.*, II, 8, 9.

to achieve it.[1] Her mistakes must be charged to matter, not to the active idea.[2] Furthermore, it would be absurd to deny natural teleology simply because we do not see in nature a deliberating motive principle. Art does not deliberate, either; in the majority of cases there is no need of reflection. Art moves from without, nature from within. If the art of naval construction were in the wood, it would resemble nature in its action.[3] Hence nature acts teleologically as well as art.[4] *The end or purpose is the very principle that makes her act,*[5] *and pre-exists in principle in the organisms produced by her.*[6]

Organisms differ from inorganic bodies in that they are impelled by an inner principle, which employs a number of organs in order to realize its purposes. The vegetable kingdom is not an end in itself; the animal which lives on the plant is its end. Hence the soul of the plant simply performs the functions of assimilation and reproduction. The soul of the animal has, in addition, the faculty of feeling, to which is added, in higher animals, the capacity to retain sense-impressions. The sensations of sight, hearing, smell, taste, and touch, meet in a common sense, which synthesizes them and constitutes a rudimentary form of inner apperception. The soul of the animal is susceptible of pleasure and pain; hence it strives for what makes an agreeable impression upon it, and shuns the contrary (the active faculty or will). Hence the spontaneous movement of the animal. In addition to all these endowments of animal life, the human soul possesses the faculty of knowledge or reason. Owing to this, man is the masterpiece of nature, the most perfect organic being.[7] He is the final goal (τέλος) at which nature aims throughout the advancing forms of the animal kingdom. Her failure to attain this goal immediately is due to the resistance of matter; but, untiring in her efforts, she makes many attempts which come nearer and nearer to the final purpose for which she strives, until the end

---

[1] *Politics*, I, 2, 14, 19. [2] *Phys.*, II, 8, 8.
[3] This is what modern metaphysics calls the *immanent teleology* of nature.
[4] *Phys.*, II, 8, 15, 16. [5] *Id.*, II, 9, 4.
[6] *Met.*, IX, 8; *De part. anim.*, II, 1. [7] *Historia animalium*, IX, 1.

is finally realized. So, too, the young artist tries a thousand times before completely realizing his conception.

The organic world therefore forms an ascending scale. The organisms and their corresponding souls are perfected in the measure in which the ultimate purpose of the zoological development, the human species, penetrates and overcomes inorganic matter.[1] Corresponding to the elementary plant-soul we have an organism in which up and down are distinguishable, but in which there is no difference between front and back, right and left; the plant has its mouth below (the root) and its genital apparatus above (the flower); it has no back or chest. A body corresponds to the animal soul, in which is found the double opposition between up and down, right and left. In man, at last, the up and down coincides with the absolute up and down.

The animal kingdom is divided into two classes, one of which embraces sanguineous animals, viz., mammalians, birds, fishes, amphibia; while the other consists of insects, crustaceans, testaceans, and mollusks.[2] Warmth is inseparable from life, and the relative perfection of an animal directly depends upon the amount of heat in it. Aristotle believes in spontaneous generation on a grand scale, although he denies it in the case of higher animals. Owing to his ignorance of the facts established by modern geology in reference to the changes which the earth has undergone, he seems to assume the eternity of life and of species in the direction of the past as well as of the future.

The relation existing between the organized body and the soul, its vital principle, is the same as that existing between matter and form, potentiality and actuality, capacity and function. Because of this intimate correlation, the organized body exists and lives only for the sake of the soul, which is its final cause or the purpose for which it exists; but the soul, too, is a reality only in so far as it *animates* something, in so far

[1] The fundamental conception of comparative anatomy.
[2] *De partibus animalium*, I, 3.

as it is the soul of a body, the energy of an organism, the function of an instrument. Without the body the soul may, indeed, exist potentially, but not actually or in reality. It is, according to Aristotle, as impossible to feel, to desire, and to will, without the necessary corporeal organs, as it is to walk without feet or to make a statue out of nothing.[1] The soul is to the body what cutting is to the axe; the function of cutting would be the soul of the axe if the latter were a living being. Now, just as cutting is impossible without an axe, so, too, the constitutive functions of the soul are inseparable from the body.

From the relation obtaining between the organism and its vital principle, it necessarily follows, in the second place, that metempsychosis, or the doctrine according to which any soul may inhabit any body, is impossible. Since the soul is the function of the body, or rather the sum of its functions or the resultant of its forces, it is evident that its manifestations or acts (that is, in the last analysis, the soul itself, since it is essentially action and energy) are determined by the nature and special organization of the body which it animates. We cannot produce the tones of the flute by means of an anvil, nor the sound of an anvil by a flute. It is equally impossible to have a human soul in the body of a horse, and *vice versa*.

The body is potentiality or capacity, and the soul its energy or function. The latter, again, is potentiality or capacity, or rather a sum of capacities; it consists of the capacities of feeling, perceiving, and willing, of which sensation, perception, and volition are the actions or energies. Hence the soul is *the entelechy* or *primary function of an organized body*, and its manifestations or effects are the secondary functions or energies of this body.[2]

In so far as the soul is sensation, imagination, memory, and will, it suffers the fate of all earthly things; it is perishable.[3] The intellect itself has a mortal part in addition to its immor-

---

[1] *De generatione animalium*, II, 3. Cf. *Met.*, VII, 11, 11.
[2] *De anima*, II, 1.   [3] *De anima*, III, 5.

tal and divine element. The mortal part comprises the sum of our ideas in so far as these are determined by bodily impressions, that is, whatever the intellect receives, suffers, and does not create or bring forth. The entire passive side of the intelligence (νοῦς παθητικός) shares the fate of the body, without which it cannot be conceived. Only the active intellect (νοῦς ποιητικός), the pure reason, which conceives the universal and the divine, enjoys the privilege of immortality; for it alone cannot be explained as a function of the body; nay, it is essentially different and separable from this, while the other faculties cannot be separated from it.[1] The active intellect is not a capacity, but an actual being; it is not a product of nature, a result of the development of the soul, like sensibility, imagination, and memory; it is not a product, an effect, or a creature at all, but an absolute principle, that existed before the soul as well as before the body, and was united with it mechanically. This separate intellect is absolutely immaterial, impassive, imperishable, and eternal; without it the passive and perishable intellect cannot think.[2]

This seeming immortality,[3] with which Aristotle endows the soul, again disappears when we remember that not only does the active intellect not constitute the thinking individual, but that it does not even form a part of him, — that it comes from without, and is not bound to the *me* by any organic tie. It is hard to tell what Aristotle really means by this *active intellect*, and the majority of his many commentators have exhausted their wits in trying to explain it. The logic of the system demands that we identify it with God himself; for its definition agrees, in every respect, with that of the absolute *nous*.[4] Moreover, Aristotle cannot assume a plurality of separate intelligences without contradicting a principle of his metaphysics: *whatever is plural is material*.[5] The active intellect is declared to be absolutely immaterial. Hence it can only exist in the singular: it is unique, and resembles the immanent reason, the

[1] *De anima*, II, 9.   [2] *Id.*, III, 5. Cf. *De gener. et corrupt.*, II, 3.
[3] *Met.*, XII, 3, 10.   [4] *Ibid.*   [5] *Id.*, XIII, 6, 21.

world-soul, or the universal spirit of Stoic pantheism, of which the particular souls are temporary personifications. The transcendency of the God of Aristotle would not exclude such an interpretation, for the *Metaphysics* affirms both the transcendency of the Deity and his immanency in the universe as the physical and moral order of the world; but what excludes it is the very emphatic assertion that the active intellect is substantial.[1] Logically, this intellect can be nothing but the Supreme Being himself. When Aristotle allows himself to call the active intellect a part of the soul and its immortal part at that, we shall say that his logic is at fault. One thing, however, is certain: by affirming that the eternal intelligence alone is immortal, he positively denies individual immortality. On this point of the Peripatetic teaching there cannot be the slightest dispute.

The active intellect is by no means identical with the human intellect, and its immortality is of little or no use. Indeed, according to Aristotle's theory of knowledge, which is closely akin to the teachings of Democritus and sensationalism, the human understanding is not the creator or the father, but only the recipient or the mother of ideas. It is, by nature, devoid of all content, and resembles an empty tablet or a white page.[2] Peripatetic sensualism assumes, nevertheless, that ideas pre-exist in the mind, if not actually, potentially at least; in other words, it maintains that the mind originally possesses, not ready-made ideas, but the faculty of forming them.[3] The *ex nihilo nihil* is one of Aristotle's fundamental doctrines. Although he holds that the infant mind is an empty tablet, that experience is the source of our knowledge, that intelligence is developed and realized by sensation, he does not teach either an anti-philosophical dualism or a vulgar mechanism. On the contrary, dualism affirms one of the principles of knowledge to the exclusion of the other; it isolates thought and keeps it from having intercourse with nature, on the plea that any increase

---

[1] *De anima*, III, 5.   [2] *Id.*, III, 4.
[3] See the discussions of this subject by Locke and Leibniz (§§ 56 and 57).

produced through the senses would be a pollution. Plato teaches such a dualism. As far as Aristotle is concerned, the charge of dualism may with justice be brought against his theology, on the one hand, and his theory of the active intellect, on the other.

The presence of the *nous* makes the human soul an intermediate being between the animal and God. In sensibility, perception, and memory, it resembles the animal; in reason it is like God. This dual aspect constitutes its originality as a moral being. There can be no morality without the coexistence of animal and intellectual principles. The animal is not a moral being, because it is devoid of intellect. Nor can there be any question of morality in the case of God, who is pure thought. Hence morality is the distinguishing characteristic of human nature, and if the end of every being is the complete and perfect realization of its nature, the end of human life consists neither in the one-sided development of the animal functions nor in changing man into God (which would be foolish and impossible), but in the complete and harmonious expansion of our dual essence. For man the highest good consists in the happiness resulting from the harmonious co-operation of the intellect and the animal elements. Such a state of equilibrium constitutes virtue. The harmony between the active and passive intellect is called intellectual virtue; this manifests itself as wisdom in theory, and as prudence or common-sense in practice. The harmony between the intellect and the will is called ethical virtue, that is, courage, temperance, liberality, magnificence, magnanimity, gentleness, sincerity, and sociableness. Virtue is not the extreme opposite of vice (as Plato holds); it is the mean between two extremes. Courage, for example, is a virtue, and as such the mean between timidity and foolhardiness; liberality is the mean between avarice and prodigality.[1]

Inasmuch as man is by nature a political animal, individuals cannot make and change the State at will; on the contrary,

[1] *Nicomachean Ethics*, II, 5 ff.

the State forms the individuals. The family, property, and slavery are natural institutions. It is no truer that the same form of government is as suitable to all nations and circumstances than that the same garment fits everybody. The monarchy is the best form of government when the power is in the hands of a good prince; for in this case it is an image of the government of the universe: a perfect monarchy under a perfect monarch. But this form is the most odious of all when it becomes tyranny. The safety of the State consists in a just apportionment of powers, and depends essentially on the strength of the middle classes.[1]

Aristotle's ethics and politics, like his metaphysics, are decidedly antagonistic to the Utopian ideals of Plato. He is a realist and a positivist, a common-sense thinker, so to speak, and takes into special account the facts of experience; he is exceedingly careful not to set up an ideal goal which humanity can never reach. His entire philosophy is a doctrine of the golden mean, and as far removed from a coarse sensationalism as from an idealism that is out of harmony with real life. In his love of science for science's sake, the suppleness and versatility of his genius, his predilection for measure, proportion, and the harmony of the ideal and the real, Aristotle represents the climax of Greek thought. But he also marks its decline, and inaugurates a new epoch in the general evolution of humanity. He resembles a Semite or a Roman in the unremitting good sense which he displays, and in his sober positivism. His style is not, like that of his master, the work of the Muses. But his philosophy is even more realistic in matter than in form. His fundamental metaphysical teaching, which makes matter a necessary element of finite existence; the epistemological doctrine that the mind is an *empty tablet;* his monotheism, which is much more outspoken and absolute than Plato's; his morality of the golden mean; his monarchical tendencies, — everything about his system is a forecast of the

[1] *Politics,* IV, 9.

new world, the elements of which were prepared at Pella,
Rome, Alexandria, and Jersualem.

Among the most distinguished scholarchs who succeeded
him in the Lyceum are to be mentioned Theophrastus, Dicæ-
archus, Aristoxenus, and, above all, Strato of Lampsacus, the
teacher of Ptolemy Philadelphus. Aristoxenus denies the immortality of the intellect, and Strato the existence of God;
which proves, either that the master's doctrine of immortality
and the first mover was merely an accommodation, or that
his ancient followers were even less united than his mediæval
disciples. What distinguishes the pupils from the master, and
what characterizes post-Aristotelian philosophy as a whole, is
the gradual division of scientific labor which takes place after
Aristotle. The work of Aristotle the scientist was continued
in Sicily, Egypt, and the islands of the Mediterranean; while
Athens, and in Athens the Lyceum itself, merely retained a
philosophy of reasoning, dialectics, and eristics, which cared
less and less for the physical *cosmos*, and devoted its entire
attention to the soul.

What is the essence, the aim, the destiny of the human soul,
the favorite topic of Attic philosophy? Plato regards thought
as the essence and end of the soul, and Aristotle's theology is
at bottom simply an apotheosis of *nous*. Epicurus, however,
like Democritus, negates the thought-substance and teaches
a philosophy of pleasure. Between these two extremes we
have the concrete spiritualism of the Stoics.

B. MATTER THE ULTIMATE REALITY

§ 18. Epicurus

EPICURUS[1] was born about 340, at Gargettos, of Athenian
parents. Reflection on his mother's superstitious practices and
the study of Democritus made him sceptical, and convinced

---

[1] Hicks, *Stoic and Epicurean*, New York, 1910; Pater, *Marius the Epicurean*,
London, 1904; Lucretius, *On the Nature of Things*, translated by Munro (New
Universal Library).

him that our fear of the gods and the hereafter is the principal obstacle to the happiness of man; and it is the business of philosophy to make us happy by freeing us, through observation and reasoning, from the belief in the supernatural. In the society which he founded at Athens about 306, his personal influence seems to have been very great, and the maxims which he dictated to his disciples formed the permanent basis of the Epicurean teaching long after his death (270). But neither polytheism nor Christianity had any interest in preserving his numerous writings,[1] nearly all of which have been lost, and this combination of Socrates and Voltaire has been more bitterly attacked than any other founder of a school.

Unlike Aristotle, who loves science for science's sake, and considers the first philosophy as the best and most divine science, "although others may be more useful," [2] Epicurus makes science the servant of life, and is interested in theory only in so far as it is related to practice. The aim of philosophy, which he divides into the *canonic* (logic), physics, and ethics, is, according to him, to make human life tranquil and peaceful (ἀταραξία, ataraxy), and this aim he finds realized in the system of Democritus, with whom he agrees in almost every respect.

Matter is not *non-being*, as Plato holds, but the positive and only principle of things, the universal *substratum*, of which soul, mind, and thought are mere accidents. Outside of it, there is nothing but the void, the condition of movement. Matter is composed of innumerable, uncreated, and indestructible atoms in perpetual motion. According to Democritus, these corpuscles naturally and necessarily move downward. But inasmuch as they are joined together and form bodies, it must be assumed, according to Epicurus, that they deviated

---

[1] About three hundred, according to Diogenes Laertius. With the exception of the *Letters*, etc., preserved by this historian, we know nothing of the lost writings except what we can learn from the quotations found in various Greek authors, the valuable *résumé* presented by Lucretius in his *De rerum natura*, and the fragments of the work περὶ φύσεως, etc., discovered at Herculaneum.

[2] *Met.*, I, 2, 19–25.

from the perpendicular line. Such a deviation could only have been the result of chance. Epicurus is not, therefore, an absolute determinist, for he assumes chance, that is, the possibility of an effect without a cause. This view allows him to recognize in ethics the freedom of indifference, or causes without effects.[1]

But though, by an inconsistency that does more credit to his imagination than to his logic, he differs from Democritus on the subject of causality, he agrees with him regarding the eternity of the universe. The absolute creation and absolute destruction of the world are out of the question. Creation in the proper sense of the term is impossible. In order to convince ourselves that the world is not the work of the gods, we have simply to consider the nature of its alleged creators, on the one hand, and its imperfections, on the other. Why should such perfect and supremely happy beings, who are self-sufficient and have no need of anything, burden themselves with creating the world? Why should they undertake the difficult task of governing the universe? Let us, however, suppose for a moment that the world is their product. If they have created it, they have created it either eternally or in time; in the former case, the world is eternal; in the latter, we have two possibilities: Either creation is a condition of divine happiness, and then the gods were not supremely happy for an entire eternity, inasmuch as they did not create the world until after the lapse of an eternity of inaction; or, it is not, and in that case, they have acted contrary to their innermost essence. Moreover, what could have been their purpose in making it? Did they desire a habitation? That would be equivalent to saying that they had no dwelling-place for a whole eternity, or at least, none worthy of them. Did they create it for the sake of man? If they made it for the few sages whom this world contains, their work was not worth the trouble; if they did it in order to create wicked men, then they are cruel beings. Hence it is absolutely impossible to hold that creation is the work of the gods.

[1] Lucretius, *De rerum natura*, II, 216 ff.; Diog. L., X, 133–134.

Let us examine the matter from the standpoint of the world. How can we assume that a world full of evils is the creation of the gods? What have we? Barren deserts, arid mountains, deadly marshes, uninhabitable arctic zones, regions scorched by the southern sun, briers and thorns, tempests, hail-storms and hurricanes, ferocious beasts, diseases, premature deaths; do they not all abundantly prove that the Deity has no hand in the governance of things? Empty space, atoms, and weight, in short, mechanical causes, suffice to explain the world; and it is not necessary for metaphysics to have recourse to the theory of final causes. It is possible, nay, it is certain that gods exist: all the nations of the earth agree to that. But these supremely happy beings who are free from passion, favoritism, and all human weaknesses, enjoy absolute repose. In their far-off home they are unmoved by the miseries of humanity; nor can they exert any influence on the life of man. There can be no magic, divination, or miracles, nor any kind of intercourse between them and us.

We should cease to fear the punishments of Tartarus. The soul is material, and shares the fate of the body. What proves it to be matter — exceedingly fine matter, of course — is the influence exercised upon it by the body in fainting, anæsthesia, and delirium, in cases of injury and disease, and, above all, the fact that the advance and the decline of the soul correspond to analogous bodily conditions. The intellectual faculties are weak in the period of childhood; they grow strong in youth, and gradually decay in old age. Sickness causes a serious reaction upon the soul; without the body the soul has no power to manifest itself. Nay, more than that; the dying man does not feel his soul gradually withdrawing from one organ to another, and then finally making its escape with its powers unimpaired; he experiences a gradual diminution of his mental faculties. If the soul retained full consciousness at death, and if, as certain Platonists maintain, death were the transition of the soul to a higher life, then, instead of fearing death, man would rejoice at it, which is not the case. Moreover, our fear of death is not caused by our dread of non-existence; what makes us regard it with such terror is the fact that we involuntarily combine with the idea of nothingness an idea of life, that is, the notion of feeling this nothingness; we imagine that the dead man is conscious of his gradual destruction, that he feels himself burning, or devoured by the worms, that the soul continues to exist and to feel. If only we could succeed in wholly separating the idea of life from its opposite, and bravely relinquish all thought of immortality, death would lose its terrors. We should say to ourselves: Death is not an evil; neither for him who is dead, for he has no feeling; nor for the living, for him death does not yet exist. As long as we are alive, death does not exist for us, and when death appears we no longer exist. Hence we can never come in contact with death; we never feel its icy touch, which we dread so much.

Consequently, we should not be hindered by foolish fears from attaining the goal of our existence, happiness. Pleasure is the highest good; not the pleasure accompanying a passing sensation, but pleasure as a permanent state, — that state of deep peace and perfect contentment in which we feel secure against the storms of life. The pleasures of the mind are preferable to voluptuousness, for they endure; while sensations vanish away like the moment which procures them for us. We should avoid excess in everything, lest it engender its opposite, the permanent pain resulting from exhaustion. On the other hand, we must consider such painful feelings as, for example, painful operations, as good, because they procure health and pleasure. Virtue is the tact which impels the wise man to do whatever contributes to his welfare, and makes him avoid the contrary. Virtue is not the highest good, but the true and only means of realizing it.

Owing to its simplicity, its anti-mystical character, and its easy application, the Epicurean system became a formidable rival of Platonism, Peripateticism, and Stoicism. Italy received it with especial favor, and reckoned among its disciples, the poet Lucretius, who wrote the *De rerum natura*, T. Cassius,

L. Torquatus, T. Pomponius Atticus, Cæsar, Horace, and Pliny the Younger. During the reign of the Cæsars, Stoicism was represented by the republican opposition, while Epicureanism gathered around its standard the partisans of the new order of things, who were fortunate in being able to realize the ideals of the master under the auspices of a great and peaceful power. Protected as it was by the Emperors,[1] the school destroyed what remained of the crumbling edifice of polytheism, and at the same time attacked the new religion and the supernatural Christian.

C. Apotheosis of Will

§ 19. Stoicism[2]

The founder of the Stoic school, Zeno of Citium in Cyprus, was the son of a family of merchants of Phœnician origin. Upon losing his fortune through shipwreck, he decided to indulge his taste for study. He was alternately the disciple of Crates, the Cynic, of Stilpo, the Megarian, and of the Academicians, Xenocrates and Polemo. Thereupon he taught philosophy in the Στοὰ ποικίλη (porch or corridor) at Athens. Convinced of the rightness of suicide, he put an end to his life about 260, leaving a great reputation and a large number of disciples behind. The school was continued by Cleanthes, a native of the Troad, the supposed author of the so-called hymn of Cleanthes, and after the voluntary death of the lat-

---

[1] A Latin and Greek inscription recently discovered in the excavations of the Archæological Society at Athens and dating from the time of Hadrian, wholly confirms what we already know as to the special protection accorded to the school of Epicurus by the Emperors. Owing to this, it exerted the preponderating influence during the first centuries of our era, and aroused great jealousy among the Platonic, Peripatetic, and Stoic schools. The inscription also gives us some information, at least indirectly, concerning matters hitherto little known, as, for example, the organization of the school during the imperial period, its mode of appointing scholarchs, etc.

[2] Murray, *The Stoic Philosophy*, New York, 1915; Stock, *Stoicism*, London, 1908; Zeller, *Stoics and Epicureans*, translated by Reichel, London, 1892; Marcus Aurelius, *Meditations* (Everyman's Library); Epictetus, *Moral Discourses* (Everyman's Library).

ter, by Chrysippus of Tarsus (according to others, of Soli) in Cilicia (280–210), in whose numerous polemical writings against the Academy the teachings of the school received their final form.

In order to form a correct conception of Stoicism we must remember (1) that it is not merely a philosophy and a system of ethics, but a religion raised upon the ruins of popular polytheism; (2) that its founder and its most ardent disciples trace their origin either to Semitic Asia or to Roman Italy; (3) that it is not the work of a single individual, but a collection of doctrines from different sources which meet in one and the same channel like the tributaries of a river. Hence its conservatism in religion and its dogmatism in metaphysics. Hence also its practical turn, and, finally, the complex and wholly eclectic nature of its teachings.

Like Epicurus, Zeno and the Stoics pursue science for the sake of life; truth, in so far as it is good and useful; the search for the *first* cause of being, in order to discover the *final* goal of life. Wisdom, i. e., theoretical and practical virtue, is the goal. Theoretical virtue consists in thinking correctly and in having correct notions of the nature of things; but practical virtue, which consists in right living and in acting according to reason, is the highest type of virtue, the goal aimed at by theoretical virtue, which is but a means. Whatever does not tend to make us better, and has no influence on our impulses and actions, is indifferent or bad. Logic, metaphysics, and the sciences have no justification except in so far as they are of practical value. They introduce us to the study of ethics, and this gives them their importance in the teachings of the school.

Conformably with its anti-dualistic tendencies, Stoicism rejects Plato's *separate Idea*, even more emphatically than Aristotle. Ideas or universals have no objective existence; they exist neither outside of things, as Plato teaches, nor in things, as Aristotle holds; they are mere abstractions of thought, to which nothing corresponds in reality. Moreover, the soul has no innate ideas; it is an empty tablet, and all its concepts come to it from without. The sensible impression is, according to Cleanthes, like an impression made upon a material object, like the mark of a seal upon wax. Chrysippus defines it as a modification of the soul. Sensation is the common source of all our ideas. The latter are divided into four categories, according as they express: substantiality, quality, mode of being, or relation. An idea is true when it is an exact reproduction of its object. The criterion of the truth of an idea is its clearness, its self-evidence. There are, according to Zeno, four degrees of knowledge: presentation, assent, comprehension, and understanding. In order to illustrate the highest degree of knowledge, which the philosopher alone attains, Zeno, it is said, used to place his left hand upon his clenched right. Following the example of Aristotle, the Stoics regarded grammar and rhetoric as integral parts of logic. They are worthy successors of the great logician in this field; indeed, the majority of our technical terms in grammar and syntax are of Stoic origin.

The Stoic metaphysic is, like their theory of knowledge, even more realistic than the system of Aristotle. It is concrete spiritualism pure and simple. Mind and body are two aspects of one and the same reality. In the real being, mind is the active element; matter, the passive element. There is no such thing as pure spirit. Whatever Aristotle may think of him, God has a body, and the world constitutes this body. The universe is a living being, of which God is the soul, the governing intelligence, the sovereign law, the motive principle, the animating warmth.

The Stoic theology is a kind of compromise between pantheism and theism. God is identical with the universe, but this universe is a real being, a living God who has a knowledge of things, who governs our destinies, who loves us, and desires our good, without, however, participating in human passions. The Stoics ascribe providential love to the Infinite Being; hence their teaching differs essentially from that of the Peripatetics and Epicureans. Their pantheism, which does not exclude the notion of Providence, is essentially religious. They have a pious respect for the religious forms of paganism; they grant the existence of gods who are inferior to Jupiter, and who are revealed either in the stars or in the forces of nature; but they declare these gods to be mortal, and ascribe immortality to the Supreme Being alone.[1]

The Stoic system of physics is like that of Heraclitus; it adopts the view that heat is the principle of life, the theory of the periodical conflagration and renewal of the world, and shows what an important part the struggle for existence plays in nature. Inasmuch as the world is the body of the Deity, it is necessarily a perfect organism and immaculately beautiful. Conversely, the perfection of the universe proves that it envelopes an infinite Intelligence, which is not, it is true, a transcendent principle, like the God of Aristotle, who moves only the Empyrean, but an omnipresent being like the human soul, which is present in all parts of the body. The evil in the world cannot shake the Stoic's faith in God; for just as a false note may contribute to the general harmony, and as, in a picture, the shadows tend to relieve the light and the colors, so, too, the evil contributes to the realization of the good. In the struggle with injustice, cowardice, and intemperance, justice, courage, and moderation shine with a brighter light. Instead of shaking the faith of the Stoic in Providence, evil confirms it, for evil adds to the universal harmony. The details alone are imperfect; the whole of things is supremely perfect.

Man is to the God-universe what the spark is to the flame, the drop to the ocean. Our body is a fragment of universal matter; our soul, a warm breath emanating from the soul of the world. Since, from the Stoic point of view, reality is synonymous with corporeality, the soul too is matter. If it were not so, the reciprocal action between it and the body would

---

[1] The Stoics of the different periods differ widely as to religion. The ancient Stoics are unenlightened enough to combat the heliocentric system in the name of religion, while the Roman Stoics are much more liberal, but not less accommodating. They look upon myths as allegories, the hidden meaning of which must be unravelled. Jupiter is the soul, but the intelligent soul, of the world.

be inconceivable. The incorporeal cannot act upon a body. The decomposition of the body does not necessarily involve the destruction of the soul; and even if there be no hereafter for all men, the soul of the sage at least, which is more vigorous than that of common mortals, survives death. But though it may exist beyond the grave, say for centuries, even the philosopher's soul is not immortal in the absolute sense; for on the last day it will, like everything else in the world, disappear in the universal conflagration. Absolute immortality belongs to God alone. The fate which awaits the soul is not, however, a destruction of its substance; it will return to the infinite ocean whence it came.

The Stoics had no fixed dogmas concerning theoretical questions like the above; one might believe in immortality or not, without ceasing to be a disciple of the Stoa.[1] What constituted the Stoic and united all the members of the school was the moral idealism which had been taught long before the times of Zeno by men like Socrates, Plato, and Antisthenes; and their motto was *virtue for virtue's sake*. The highest good, according to Stoicism, is to practise virtue for its own sake, to do your duty because it is your duty; everything else, health, fortune, honors, pleasures, are indifferent, and even bad, when they are the sole object of your strivings. Virtue alone makes us happy, provided we seek it in a disinterested manner. It does not consist merely in the outward performance of the good but in an habitual disposition of the soul. It is *one;* you cannot be virtuous in one respect and vicious in another. It is the common source of what we call *the virtues*, i. e., wisdom, courage, temperance, and justice. To possess one of these cardinal virtues is to possess them all in principle; not to have one of them means to have none. A man is good in all things or bad in all. There is no mean between virtue and vice. Theoretically, there are but two classes of men, the good and the bad, although in reality there seem to be shades, transitions, and compromises between good and evil. Happy

---

[1] Thus the school of Rhodes, a branch of the Athenian school, rejected the doctrine of final conflagration.

is the sage, who, versed in the secrets of nature, knows himself and others; whom this knowledge frees from the guardianship of men, the times, social prejudices, and the laws themselves, in so far as they are the products of human caprice and not of reason. He alone is truly free; he has overcome the world as well as his own passions. Nothing can affect him nor make him falter; neither the happenings of the world nor the storms in his own heart. Let come what come may, he is resigned; for everything is decreed by Nature and Fate; and Nature and Fate are synonymous with Reason, Providence, and good Will. Hence, the supreme rule which he observes in all things: *sequi naturam*, to follow nature, that is, the law which nature enjoins upon conscience, and which is identical with the law that governs the world.

It would be an easy task to point out the contradictions in the theories which we have just outlined, to contrast the moral idealism of the Stoics with the thorough-going realism of their ontology. But, as was said, we have in Stoicism not the system of a single individual but a collection of doctrines advanced by one and the same sect, a religion for the educated classes, who desired to bring their "new faith" into harmony with the old, a kind of *union between virtue* and the polytheistic Church, embracing the most diverse elements, but inspired with the same ideals. Panætius of Rhodes and Posidonius of Apamea, the teacher of Cicero and Pompey, introduced the teachings of Stoicism into the Roman world. Owing to the close affinity existing between these teachings and the Latin and Semitic spirit, the Stoics were not long in gaining adherents. Those especially who, on the decline of the Republic, battled unsuccessfully against the growing despotism of the Cæsars, men like Cicero, Cato, and Brutus, found in this philosophy a deep source of encouragement and consolation. To Stoicism we owe Cicero's *De finibus bonorum et malorum*, Seneca's[1] *Moral Letters*, the noble teachings of Epictetus which

---

[1] The theory has long ago been abandoned that Seneca and the Apostle St. Paul were on terms of friendship with each other. The best the extreme advocates of the view that a relationship exists between Stoicism and Paulinism can

Flavius Arrianus preserved in his *Encheiridion*, and the twelve books *Ad se ipsum* of the Emperor Marcus Aurelius, one of the most admirable products of ancient ethics. Nevertheless, its influence cannot be compared with that of Christianity. It was confined to the world of letters and hardly penetrated the masses. Stoicism has nothing to make it popular; it pursues the paths of science and of meditation; it, too, shuns "the vulgar crowd" and is identified, in practice, with Epicureanism.

§ 20.　Sceptical Reaction.　Pyrrhonism[1]

Aristotle was both a zealous theorist and an earnest dogmatist. Although Zeno and Epicurus cared very little for abstract science, they recognized its importance for life. According to the Stoics, who differ from the Cynics in this respect, science teaches us to recognize Providence in nature and in history, to respect its authority, and to follow its inspirations; according to the Epicureans, it frees us from superstition and the spiritualistic prejudices which destroy our happiness. Both schools agree that there is a criterion of truth. Peripatetic dogmatism is opposed by the sceptical reaction which had been inaugurated by Democritus and Protagoras. PYRRHO of Elis,[2] a contemporary of Aristotle and a friend of Alexander the Great, represents this movement. He, too, like the Socratics and Epicurus and Zeno, his younger contemporaries, desires *ataraxy;* but he does not believe that metaphysics can obtain it for us. There are, as a matter of fact, no two schools of philosophy that agree upon the essential problems. Hence, instead of procuring peace, the source of true happiness, speculation brings us trouble and uncertainty, and involves us in endless contradictions. It is useless, because it causes

do, is to appeal to the fact that Chrysippus, the chief founder of Stoicism, and the Apostle St. Paul (who was, however, educated at Jerusalem) were born in the same province and perhaps in the same town.

[1] Maccoll, *The Greek Sceptics*, London, 1869; Patrick, *Sextus Empiricus and Greek Scepticism*, 1899.

[2] Born about 365 B. C.

disputes without end; impossible, because we can, in every case, prove both the affirmative and the negative side. The essence of things is incomprehensible. Pyrrho's sage refrains from making dogmatic statements on either side; he suspends his judgment as much as possible, and refrains from taking part in heated discussions. He avoids absolute negation as well as categorical affirmation, and therefore differs from the dogmatists, who affirm knowledge, and the Sophists, who demonstrate its impossibility.

The physician TIMON, an admirer and friend of Pyrrho of Elis, published, among other sceptical writings, a satirical poem (Οἱ Σίλλοι), in which he emphasizes the contradictions of the metaphysicians from Thales to the Academician Arcesilaus. Eusebius has preserved the fragments of this work in his *Præparatio evangelica*. His doctrine may be summarized in three paragraphs: (1) The dogmatic philosophers cannot prove their starting-point, which therefore is merely hypothetical; (2) it is impossible to have an objective knowledge of things: we know how they affect us, we shall never know what they are apart from our intelligence and our senses; (3) hence, in order to be happy, we must abandon barren speculations, and unreservedly obey the law of nature.

Pyrrhonism reminded the philosophers, in a pointed way, that the problem of certitude is a fundamental one. In consequence of the rivalry existing between the Academy and the younger dogmatic Stoic school, the sceptics soon found themselves established in the chair of Plato. The first appearance of the critical problem inaugurated the age of reason in Greece, its reappearance after the death of Aristotle marks the period of decline in Hellenic philosophy.

§ 21. Academic Scepticism

The scepticism of the Academy is simply an exaggeration of the underlying principle of this school, and, in a measure, a return to the original sources. Scepticism, as we know, formed the starting-point of Socrates and Plato. The names of Arcesilaus and Carneades, the founders of the Middle and the New Academy, are connected with this movement. ARCESILAUS of Pitane, the successor of the scholarch Crates, returns to the Socratic method. He does not set up a system of his own, but confines his efforts to developing the minds of his hearers; he teaches them how to think for themselves, to investigate, to separate truth from error. His only dogma is: to assume nothing unconditionally. He was at first a critical philosopher, but the dogmatic opposition of Zeno drove him into the arms of extreme scepticism. Zeno makes clear ideas the criterion of truth. Arcesilaus, however, calls attention to the many illusions in which the senses involve us. Socrates had said: One thing alone I know, and that is that I know nothing. Arcesilaus exaggerates his scepticism and declares: I do not even know that with certainty. He does not, however, deduce the final consequences of his principle. Certainty cannot be reached in metaphysics, but it is possible in the domain of ethics, in which he agrees with the Stoics. But his successors are logically compelled to extend their scepticism to ethics.

The most consistent among them is CARNEADES, who differs in nothing from the Sophists of the fifth century. He is an opponent of the Stoics in ethics and religion as well as in ontology and criticism. With wonderful dialectical skill he brings out the contradictions involved in the Stoic theology. The God of the Porch is the soul of the world; like the soul, he possesses feeling. Now a sensation is a modification. Hence the Stoic God may be modified. But whatever is changeable may be changed for the worse; it can perish and die. Hence the God of the Stoics is not eternal, their sensational God is not God. Moreover, as a sensible being the God of the Stoa is corporeal, which suffices to make him mutable. If God exists, Carneades goes on to state, he is either a finite or an infinite being. If he is finite, he forms a *part* of the whole of things, he is a part of the All and not the complete, total, and perfect being. If he is infinite, he is immutable, immovable, and without modification or sensation; which means that he is not a living and real being. Hence, God cannot be conceived either as a finite or an infinite being. If he exists, he is either incorporeal or corporeal. If he has no body, he is insensible; if he has a body, he is not eternal. God is virtuous or without virtue; and what is a virtuous God but a God who recognizes the good as a law that is superior to his will, i. e., a god who is not the Supreme Being? And, on the other hand, would not a god without virtue be inferior to man? The notion of God is therefore a contradictory one, however you may conceive it.

Carneades handles the conceptions of right, duty, and responsibility in the same way. Upon being sent to Rome on a political mission, he delivered two sensational speeches, one in favor of justice on the first day, another against it, the next. There is no absolute certitude in morals any more than in metaphysics. In the absence of evidence, we must content ourselves with probability (τὸ πιθανόν) in theory as well as in practice.

Neo-Academic scepticism was superseded among the scholarchs who succeeded Carneades by a somewhat ingenious form of critical eclecticism, and then by a syncretism that indiscriminately combined the doctrines of Plato, Aristotle, Zeno, Epicurus, and Arcesilaus.

§ 22. Sensationalistic Scepticism

Idealistic scepticism, which traces its origin to the Eleatics, was opposed by sensationalistic scepticism. This form of scepticism, which had been taught by Protagoras, Aristippus, and Timon, was continued by a number of thinkers who were for the most part physicians. The invariable result of their investigations is that we have no criterion of truth, no knowledge of things-in-themselves. Arcesilaus and Carneades base their arguments upon dialectics and the inevitable contradic-

tions involved in it; while empiristic scepticism, the type of
modern positivism, appeals also to a series of physiological
and experimental facts. In his eight books on *Pyrrhonism*,
valuable fragments of which have been preserved by Sextus,[1]
one of these doubters, Ænesidemus of Cnossus,[2] develops the
reasons which influenced Pyrrho and induced the author himself to call in question the possibility of certain knowledge.
These reasons are as follows: —

(1) The differences in the organization of sensible beings,
and the resulting different and sometimes contradictory impressions produced by the same objects. All things seem yellow to a man suffering from the jaundice. Similarly, the same
object may be seen in different colors and in different proportions by each particular animal.

(2) The differences in the organization of human beings. If
all things were perceived by us in the same way, we should
all have the same impressions, the same ideas, the same emotions, the same desires; which is not the case.

(3) The differences in the different senses of the same individual. The same object may produce contrary impressions
upon two different senses. A picture may impress the eye
agreeably, the touch disagreeably; a bird may please the sense
of sight and have an unpleasant effect upon the hearing. Besides, every sensible object appears to us as a combination of
diverse elements: an apple, for example, is smooth, fragrant,
sweet, yellow or red. Now, there are two possibilities. The
fruit in question may be a simple object, which as such has
neither smoothness nor sweetness nor color, but occasions an
impression *sui generis* in each particular sense depending upon
the particular nature of the sense-organ. But it is also possible that the apple is quite the reverse of simple; it may be still
more complex than it appears to us; possibly it contains an

---

[1] Sext. Emp., *Hyp. Pyrrh.*, I, Diog. L., IX; Ritter and Preller, pp. 481 ff.; V.
Brochard, *op. cit.*

[2] Born in Cnossus in Crete. Ænesidemus (Αἰνησίδημος) probably lived in
Alexandria at the beginning of the Christian era. [See Saisset, *Le Scepticisme.
Ænésidème, Pascal, Kant*, 2d ed., Paris, 1867; Natorp, *op. cit.* — Tr.]

infinite number of other very essential elements, of which we have no knowledge whatever, because the corresponding senses may be lacking.

(4) The circumstances in which the sensible subject is placed produce infinite differences in his impressions. During our waking states things appear otherwise than in sleep; in youth they affect us otherwise than in old age, in health otherwise than in sickness, in the normal state of the brain otherwise than in drunkenness.

(5) The uncertainty of knowledge resulting from the position, distance, and general topical relations of objects. A vessel seen at a distance seems stationary; a light burning in broad daylight is invisible; an elephant looks enormous near at hand, small at a certain distance; the neck of a pigeon changes its color according to the observer's point of vision. Phenomena are, therefore, always determined by the relative position of the object and its distance; and since the objects which we observe are necessarily in a *certain* position and at a *certain* distance, we may, indeed, say what they are in *such and such* positions and at *such and such* distances, but not what they are independently of these relations. Experience never gives us anything but relative knowledge.

(6) No sensation is pure; foreign elements coming either from the external world or from ourselves are mixed with each. Sounds, for example, are different, according as the air is dense or rare. Spices emit a stronger odor in a room and when it is warm than in the open air and in the cold. Bodies are lighter in water than in air. We must also take into account what our own bodies and minds add to the sensation. We must note the influence exercised on sensation by the eye, its tissues and its humors: an object that is green to my neighbor seems blue to me. Finally, we must take into consideration the influence of our understanding, the changes it may produce in the data furnished by the senses in order to convert them into ideas and notions.

(7) Qualities differ according to quantities. The horn of a

goat (the whole) is black; the detached fragments (the parts) are whitish. Wine taken in small quantities has a strengthening effect; taken in large doses it weakens. Certain poisons are fatal when taken alone; in mixture with other substances they cure.

(8) We perceive only phenomena and relations; we never perceive the things themselves. We know what they are in relation to other things and ourselves; we are absolutely ignorant of what they are *in relation* to themselves.

(9) A final and one of the strongest reasons for doubt is the influence of habit, education, and social and religious environment. We are accustomed to seeing the sun and are therefore indifferent to it; comets, however, are exceptional phenomena and consequently produce the most vivid impressions in us. We esteem what is rare; we despise the common things, although the latter may have more real value than the former. For the Jew educated in the worship of Jehovah, Jupiter is but an idol; for the Greek, who has been taught to worship Jupiter, Jehovah is the false God. Had the Jew been born a Greek, and the Greek descended from the race of Abraham, the reverse would be true. The Jew abstains from bloody sacrifices, because his religion commands it; the Greek has no scruples whatever against the practice, because his priests find nothing objectionable therein. Different countries, different customs! It seems as though we shall never be able to say what God is in himself and independently of human notions, or to know right and wrong as such and apart from our conceptions.

The same philosopher subjects the notion of *causality* to a critique[1] the essential features of which are reproduced by David Hume. The causal relation is, according to Ænesidemus, inconceivable for the corporeal as well as for the incorporeal world. Nor can it exist between bodies and minds. The efficient cause of a body cannot be a body; in fact, we cannot conceive how two can be derived from the unit, three

[1] Sextus Empiricus, *Adv. math.*, IX, 220 ff.

from two, and so on. For the same reason, the efficient cause cannot be an immaterial entity. Besides, an immaterial being can neither touch matter nor be touched by it, neither act upon it nor be acted upon by it. The material cannot produce the immaterial, and *vice versa*, since the effect is necessarily of the same nature as the cause; a horse never produces a man, and *vice versa*. Now, with regard to objects which we call causes, it must be said that only bodies and immaterial beings exist. Hence, there are no causes in the proper sense of the term.

We reach the same conclusion in reference to motion and rest. Rest cannot produce motion, nor motion, rest. Similarly, rest cannot produce rest, nor motion, motion.

The cause is either simultaneous with, or antecedent to, or consequent upon, its effect. In the first case, the effect may be the cause, and the cause the effect; in the second, there is no effect as long as the cause acts, and there is no longer an acting cause as soon as the effect is produced. The third case is an absurd hypothesis.

What we call a cause must act by itself or through the mediation of something else. On the first hypothesis the cause would have to act always and in all cases, which is disproved by experience; on the second, the intermediate cause may be the cause as well as the so-called cause.

The supposed cause possesses a single property or it possesses several. In the former case, the supposed cause must always act in the same manner under all circumstances; which is not true. The sun, for example, sometimes burns, sometimes warms without burning, and sometimes illuminates the object without burning or warming it; it hardens clay, tans the skin, and reddens fruits. Hence the sun has diverse properties. But, on the other hand, we cannot conceive how it can have them, because, if it had them, it would at once burn, and melt, and harden everything.

The objection that the effect produced by it depends on the nature of the object exposed to its rays makes for scepticism. It is equivalent to a confession that the hardened clay and the melted wax are as much *causes* as the sun; hence, that the *real cause* is the contact between the solar rays and the object acted upon. But the contact is exactly what we cannot conceive. For it is either indirect or immediate. If indirect, there is no real contact; if direct, there is no contact either, but the two objects are united, fused, identified.

Passive action is as incomprehensible as efficient action. To be passive or to suffer means to be diminished, to be deprived of being in a certain measure. In so far as I am passive, I am non-existent. Hence, to be passive means to be and not to be at the same time; which is contradictory. Furthermore, the idea of becoming involves an evident contradiction; it is absurd to say that clay *becomes* hard or wax *becomes* soft, for it is assuming that clay is hard and soft, or wax soft and hard, at the same moment; it amounts to saying that what is not, is, and what is, is not. Hence, no becoming. Hence, also, no causality. The impossibility of causality means that becoming is impossible.

Agrippa, another sceptic, about a century later than Ænesidemus, also emphasizes the relative and subjective character of our conceptions, the discord among philosophers, their predilection for theories, their reasonings in a circle,[1] and the fact that the syllogism cannot give us certain knowledge, inasmuch as every major premise is the conclusion of a preceding syllogism, and so on *ad infinitum*.

The last and boldest of the Greek sceptics is SEXTUS EMPIRICUS, a physician of vast learning, who lived at Alexandria about the year 300 A. D., and of whom we have two valuable works: the *Pyrrhonic Hypotyposes* and the treatise *Against the Mathematicians*. He turns his attention to science, which, in consequence of its self-evident principles, offers a final refuge to dogmatism and metaphysics, and maintains the uncertainty, not only of grammar, rhetoric, music, astronomy, and

---

[1] The Stoics, for example, proved the existence of God by the perfection of the world, and the perfection of the world by the existence of God.

the philosophical sciences proper, but also of arithmetic and geometry, in which he discovers the fundamental contradiction that the line is both extended and composed of inextended points. Hence no science is certain; everything is vague, doubtful, and contradictory, both in theory and in method; in mathematics as well as in physics, in logic as well as in ethics. True scepticism, like Pyrrho's, does not even grant unconditionally that all sciences are uncertain. The categorical assertion that metaphysics in the Peripatetic sense, i. e., knowledge of things-in-themselves, is impossible, stamps one as a dogmatist and metaphysician. This is, according to the Pyrrhonians, the error in the scepticism of the New Academy, which is but a negative dogmatism. The true sceptic refrains from making any absolute judgment whatsoever. His perfect neutrality ($\epsilon\pi o\chi\acute{\eta}$) enables him to realize, if not a state of absolute apathy, at least that repose and moral equilibrium in which true happiness consists. The sceptic, like the Stoic and Epicurean, pursues a practical end above everything else, but the way to reach it is to abstain from ontology. His system consists in not having a system; and should the fancy seize him to advance a dogma, it would be to doubt his own scepticism.

But by doubting its own conclusions, radical scepticism abdicated in favor of Academic probabilism.

§ 23. The Scientific Movement

While philosophy was degenerating into barren scepticism, the sciences, which had one by one cut loose from the parent science, $\sigma o\phi\acute{\iota}a$ (wisdom), made wonderful strides in the Greek islands of the Mediterranean and in Egypt. Mathematics flourished in Egypt at a time when Greece was still steeped in barbarism. Experimental science, it is true, advanced but very slowly. It was, like philosophy, paralyzed by the insane delusion that the senses are deceptive and that reason is incapable of rectifying them. Besides, the natural impatience

of the Greeks inclined them to reasoning and *a priori* speculation rather than to the detailed and painstaking labor involved
in observation and experience. But the sciences in which
reasoning plays the chief part, mathematics and mathematical physics, the exact sciences, in a word, made rapid strides.
They alone escaped the destroying touch of universal scepticism. In spite of the attacks of empiricism, there could be no
reasonable doubt of the truth that twice two are four, and
that the three angles of a triangle are equal to two right
angles.

In Sicily, where Pythagorean traditions had been perpetuated, Hicetas and Archimedes of Syracuse taught a system of
astronomy (as early as the third century B. C.) that closely resembled the Copernican system. Archimedes gave to physics
the method of determining specific weights, invented the sun-
glass and the endless screw, and created the science of mechanics by his theory of the lever. At the same time, a fellow-
countryman of Pythagoras, Aristarchus of Samos, proposed
that the distance between the earth and the sun be measured
by the dichotomy of the moon, and, what is more important,
— for this method has proved to be impracticable, — attempted to substitute for the geocentric system of Aristotle
the hypothesis that the earth revolves around the sun. This
theory was accepted and developed by Seleucus of Seleucia
in Babylonia, but stamped as impious by the Stoics, and rejected by Ptolemy himself, the most celebrated if not the
greatest among the astronomers of Alexandria. It did not
succeed in supplanting the old conception until the dawn of
modern times, when it was advanced by Copernicus, Kepler,
and Galileo.

On the opposite shore of the Mediterranean arose the city
of Alexandria, which was founded in the second half of the
fourth century by the conqueror who gave it his name. Under
the Ptolemies this became the educational as well as commercial centre of the world. Here rather than at the schools of
Athens are to be found the legitimate spiritual descendants of

Plato and Aristotle. Athens had banished the king of science, and its star went down forever. The spirit of the Stagirite descended upon his pupil, and from Alexander to Ptolemy and his successors. The Museum which they founded in the new capital of Egypt was a wonderful institution. Nothing in ancient or modern times can be compared to this attempt to organize science. Here scholars from every nation were entertained at public expense; thousands of students flocked hither from all the surrounding countries. Here the naturalists found a botanical garden, a vast zoological collection, and an anatomical building; the astronomers, an observatory; the *littérateurs*, grammarians, and philologists, a splendid library, which contained, during the first centuries of our era, 700,000 volumes. Here Euclid wrote (about 290) his *Elements of Geometry*, his treatises on *Harmony, Optics*, and *Catoptrics;* here Eratosthenes, the royal librarian under Ptolemy Philadelphus, pursued his remarkable astronomical, geographical, and historical labors; here Apollonius of Perga published his treatises on *Conic Sections;* here Arystillus and Timocharus made the observations which led to the discovery of the precession of the equinoxes by the astronomer Hipparchus; here Ptolemy write the *Almagest*, which remained the authoritative system of astronomy until the time of Copernicus, and his *Geography*, which was used in the schools of Europe for fourteen centuries. Ever since this epoch, the conceptions of the sphericity of the earth, its poles, its axis, the equator, the arctic and antarctic circles, the equinoctial points, the solstices, the inequality of climate on the earth's surface, have been current notions among scientists. The mechanism of the lunar phases was perfectly understood, and careful though not wholly successful calculations were made of intersidereal distances.

On the other hand, literature and art flourished under the careful protection of the Court. Literature and its history, philology and criticism, became sciences. The Hebrew Bible and other books of Oriental origin were translated into Greek. Buddhists and Jews, Greeks and Egyptians, mingled together, bringing with them the most diverse forms of religion. These conditions led to the development of comparative theology, on the one hand, and to the fusion of beliefs or a kind of religious eclecticism, on the other, and paved the way for Catholic unity.

§ 24. Eclecticism

The scientific movement of Alexandria was suddenly checked in the second century by the centralizing power of Rome. From that time on, the Greek genius showed unmistakable signs of decay. Literature and art declined rapidly. Philosophy was suffering from the incurable disease of scepticism. Torn from its native soil, it went to seed. The physical sciences remained stationary after the days of Galen, the physician, and the astronomer Ptolemy. The religion of the fathers became an object of scandal and derision; while ethics, which ought to have taken the place of religion, wavered between the trivialities of Epicureanism and the Utopias of the Stoa; the nearer it seemed to approach its ideal, *ataraxy*, the more the latter seemed to elude its grasp. In this state of senile prostration, Greek thought looked back with longing to the days of its creative force; it cultivated a taste for history and archæology, in a word, for the past. Sceptical even of scepticism and yet unable to produce anything original, it became eclectic and lived on its memories. The ancient schools, each of which but recently possessed a separate principle, a distinguishing characteristic, and an individuality of its own, the Academy, the Lyceum, and the Stoa, after a struggle of three centuries, gradually became reconciled with each other and were eventually fused into a colorless syncretism.

It was, however, not impotence alone that led to such a fusion of elements. As long as Judaism retained its national and exclusive form, it proved ineffective. But when Philo of Alexandria[1] attempted to reconcile the teachings of Moses and

[1] A Jewish theologian, a contemporary of Jesus. Many of his writings are still extant; the majority of them are commentaries on the Old Testament. In order to reconcile Scripture with the philosophy of his century he had recourse

Plato, and Jesus and his apostle, Paul of Tarsus, divested Judaism of its national garb, there was no further obstacle to its progress in the Græco-Roman world. Public opinion had long ago inclined towards monotheism. Peripateticism and Roman Stoicism boldly advanced it, but their teachings reached the educated classes alone. Christianity was a religion in the true sense of the term. Eminently popular, it showed a preference for the uncultured, the poor, and the lowly, for all such as desired the coming of a better world. Hence it became a formidable adversary, before whom it was necessary to close the ranks and firmly reunite the scattered parts of ancient philosophy.

Pythagoras and Plato were invoked against Biblical revelation; the God of Xenophanes, Socrates, and Aristotle, against the God of the Jews and the Christians. The Stoic example was followed, and the attempt made to reconcile traditional polytheism with monotheism by means of the pantheistic conception of a supreme and unique principle, embodying itself in a number of secondary divinities. This conception passed into monotheism and found expression in the *eons* of the Christian Gnostics, the *sephiroth* of the Jewish cabalists, and the *hypostases* of Catholic theology. In conformity with the Greek spirit and in opposition to Christian tendencies, the times continued to identify the beautiful and the good, the ugly and the bad, metaphysical evil and moral evil. Good was ascribed to spirit, the formal or ideal principle, evil to matter struggling against the dominion of the Idea. Some conceived God as a neutral principle, superior both to mind and matter, and yet the cause of both; others identified him with the spiritual or ideal principle, meaning thereby not the unity of contraries but the antithesis of matter. Henceforth matter is not his product or creation, but a rival principle co-eternal with him and equal in power. Here we have a more

to allegory, like the Stoics. His theory of the λόγος (the Word, as the revelation of God, the Son of God, the second God) has passed into Christianity (*The Gospel according to St. John*, chap. I).

or less pronounced dualism, which exercises an influence on its adversaries and is reflected in the gnostic heresies. If God alone, it is held, is without sin, it is because he alone is without matter; and if matter is the source of evil, then every corporeal being is sinful. Hence follow the necessity of sin and the obligation on the part of the sage to mortify the body by ascetic practices and abstinences. The Christian belief in the resurrection of the flesh is opposed by the Platonic dogma of the immortality of the soul apart from the body; creation *ex nihilo*, by the conception of the pre-existence of souls and the eternity of matter.

Nevertheless, the greatest concessions were made to the enemy. Provided he consented to place Orpheus, Pythagoras, and Plato in the same category with Moses, Isaiah, and St. Paul, and recognized the thinkers of ancient Greece as the organs of the eternal *logos*, he was offered the hand of friendship. All religions were held to be akin to each other, and conceived as products of a primitive revelation modified in various ways by differences in nationality. The most liberal thinkers, men like Moderatus, Nicomachus, and Numenius, loved to call Moses the Jewish Plato, and Plato the Attic Moses. But with the exception of a few Christian doctors, most of the adversaries rejected the compromise offered by eclecticism. Although disposed to recognize the scattered truths in Plato, they called in question Plato's originality and alleged that he had drawn them from the Bible.

Greek philosophy found itself obliged to change its old methods of controversy in dealing with the arguments of Christianity. With the exception of a few Fathers of the Church, who were as tolerant as they were learned, the Christians, following the example of Judaism, recognized no other philosophy than Biblical exegesis, no other criterion of the truth of a doctrine than its agreement with revelation, as set forth in Scripture. Hence it was necessary to appeal to the texts or to lower one's colors to Christianity; arguments drawn from pure reason and discussions not based on the texts were no longer accepted. Hence also the unusual ardor with which the philosophers of the period studied the texts of their predecessors, particularly those of Plato and Aristotle. Indeed, their enthusiasm degenerated into a veritable fetichism of the letter, which proved to be no less extreme than the letter worship of their adversaries.[1] The writings of the great Attic philosophers became a kind of Bible, a kind of supernatural revelation, in contents as well as in form. They were regarded as inimitable masterpieces and so greatly admired that every phrase and every word was considered inspired. The philologists, grammarians, and critics vied with each other in their efforts to analyze, purify, establish, and explain the texts. They loved to imitate not only the mode of thought but the style of Plato; indeed these form-loving Greeks valued the latter almost as highly as the contents. Alcinous and Atticus wrote commentaries on Plato; Alexander of Aphrodisias — to mention only the most distinguished among the commentators — devoted his learning and ingenuity to the interpretation of Aristotle.

Among some, literalism gave rise to the strangest superstitions. Plutarch of Chæronea and Apuleius, mistaking the form for the contents, the allegorical meaning for the real meaning, looked upon Plato as an apostle of the most vulgar polytheism. But, on the other hand, Ammonius Saccas, the founder (though otherwise little known) of the Neo-Platonic school of Alexandria, Longinus, the supposed author of the treatise *On the Sublime*, Erennius, the successor of Ammonius, and above all Plotinus of Lycopolis, penetrated more deeply into the spirit of the illustrious Athenian and gave his conceptions the systematic and definitive form which they had hitherto lacked. In Neo-Platonism and particularly in the philosophy of Plotinus, the Greek mind seems to make a final serious attempt to formulate the result of ten centuries of reflection and to

[1] The genuine writings of the ancient philosophers did not suffice, hence the *Orphics*, the *Books of Hermes*, the *Chaldean Oracles*, etc., were manufactured. This is the golden age of apocryphal literature.

express its final convictions concerning God, the world, and
the human soul.

§ 25.   Plotinus and Neo-Platonism[1]

PLOTINUS of Lycopolis in Egypt, a disciple of Ammonius
Saccas of Alexandria, came to Rome about 244, and taught
philosophy for twenty-five years. The school which he founded
in that city included men from every country and every sta-
tion in life: physicians, rhetoricians, poets, senators, nay, even
an emperor and an empress, Gallienus and Salonina. It became the centre of what remained of Pagan philosophy, science, and literature. Countless commentaries were written
on the Attic philosophers; they were even worshipped as
Jesus, the apostles, and the martyrs were worshipped by the
Christian community, which had in the meanwhile become
large and influential. Plotinus, who wrote nothing until he
was fifty years old, left fifty-four treatises at the time of his
death (270). These his disciple Porphyry published in six
Enneads or series of nine writings each.

The fundamental conception of this important work is ema-
natistic pantheism. It looks upon the world as an *overflow*,
as a diffusion of the divine life, and upon its *re-absorption* in
God as the final goal of existence. The stages in the overflow
are: spirituality, animality, and corporeality; of re-absorption:
sensible perception, reasoning, mystical intuition. Let us consider, with the author, (1) the principle, and (2) the three
stages in the hierarchy of beings.

I.   GOD. — Every being is composed of matter and form.
God (the One, the Form) and matter ($\H{v}\lambda\eta$) are the constitutive
principles, and, as it were, the two poles of the universe. God
is the power which produces everything, the active power;
matter, the power which suffers everything, becomes everything, and is infinitely modified; it is the opposite of the absolute actuality. However, though matter takes on form, it

---

[1] Taylor, *Select Works of Plotinus* (Bohn's Philosophical Library), New York,
1909; Inge, *The Philosophy of Plotinus*, 2 vols., New York, 1918.

does not, according to Plotinus, constitute an absolute antithesis; there is, in the last analysis, but one supreme principle: Form, Unity, or God.

Divine unity is not a numerical unity. The unity of number presupposes the two, the three, and so on, while the divine unity is equal to infinity and contains everything. It is not divisible like the numerical unity with its endless fractions; it transcends our conception; it is the miracle of miracles. It produces all things and is produced by none; it is the source of all beauty, without being beautiful itself, the source of all form, without having any form itself, the source of all thought and intelligence, without being a thinking and intelligent being itself, the principle, the measure, and the end of all things, without itself being a thing in the proper sense of the term. It is pure thought, the source of every concrete thought, the pure light which makes us see all things, and which consequently we do not, ordinarily, distinguish from the things themselves; it is the principle of goodness, the highest good, without being *good*, like a creature participating in goodness. It *has* neither goodness nor beauty nor intelligence, but *is* goodness, beauty, and thought itself. To attribute inner perception to God and to make an individual being of him, means to diminish him. Self-consciousness has value for us; it would have none *for* God. What is obscure seeks for light by means of vision; but has light itself any need of sight? Not that the Supreme Being is unconscious or blind like a stone or plant; he transcends the unconscious as well as the conscious; the opposition between the conscious and unconscious does not exist for God. Nor has he a will in the human sense of the term; he does not strive for any good; he does not desire anything but himself, because there is nothing desirable outside of him; he is peace, rest, and supreme content. He is neither free, as souls are, nor determined, like bodies; he is superior to free-will, which wavers between opposing notions, and to corporeal beings, which are impelled by a foreign power. Inasmuch as every quality assigned to him limits him, we must refrain from giving him attributes; he is both everything and nothing imaginable. To attribute or to *give* to him anything whatever, means to deprive him of it.

Hence Plotinus is obliged to confess that the attributes which he himself had ascribed to God (the One, the Good, pure Thought, pure Actuality) are inadequate. All we can say of God is that he transcends everything that can be conceived and said. Strictly speaking, we cannot even affirm that he *exists*, for he transcends existence itself. He is the highest abstraction, and we cannot reach him except by means of an absolute and radical abstraction. We cannot even conceive Ideas without abstracting from the sensible data; now, since God is as far superior to Ideas as these are to sensible things, we must, in order to reach God, abstract from all Ideas. After thought has arrived at this height, it must push away the ladder which helped it rise, and abandon itself to meditation; it becomes contemplation or adoration. To attempt to define God either in thought or in language means to lose him.

Plato's God is superior to being,[1] but not to the Idea; he is the king of Ideas and the Idea as such; he is accessible to reason. The God of Neo-Platonism is superior even to the Idea,[2] and therefore eludes thought. Consequently, there is an undeniable difference between the two systems. We have no right, however, to exaggerate this difference and to bring Plotinus the mystic in opposition with Plato the rationalist. The human mind can, according to Plotinus, be united with the absolute, only after it has performed diligent intellectual labor and has previously passed through all the intervening stages between vulgar opinion and philosophical knowledge.

---

[1] *Repub.*, VI, 509.

[2] Plotinus, it must be added, is not always consistent. Like his modern imitator, Schelling, he regards God, sometimes as the unity which is superior to all contrasts and therefore to the contrast between matter and mind, sometimes as spirit in opposition to body. The latter conception dominates his moral system. Asceticism and the *nirvana* are the natural consequences of the view.

Although he holds that thought cannot penetrate into the
sanctuary, he considers it as an indispensable means of carrying us to the threshold of the temple; and though he discharges
his guide upon arriving at the goal, it is not because he dis-
dains him. On the other hand, as we have seen, Plato's philosophy contains all the elements of what has been called Alexandrian mysticism: intellectual love, enthusiasm, the sage's
delight in the world of ideas.

The universe emanates from the absolute as light emanates
from the sun; as heat, from fire; the conclusion, from the
axiom. God is goodness, the Father who desires that all things
should exist. But there is a vague or conscious desire in all
things that emanate from him to return to him. Everything
is attracted to him and desires to approach him. Individuality
is not the final form of existence; it is merely the passage from
God, the principle of things, to God, their ideal goal; from
God, the infinite power, to God, the absolute actuality. If
the world is a system of harmony, it is because all things converge towards the same absolute. The *return* of being to its
divine source is made possible through thought, contemplation, intuition, which alone gives the soul the supreme satisfaction which it demands. To perceive, to see, to contemplate,
is the goal of all action, of all striving, of all movement. Each
man seeks for the absolute in his own manner. There are
meditative natures and practical natures; but the former are,
according to Plotinus, superior to the latter. Both aspire to
the same goal. The former, however, seek to reach it by the
most direct way, i. e., by thought; the latter, by endless mean-
derings; for action is an aberration of thought and denotes a
relative weakness of the understanding. Contemplation is not
only the final goal of life, but life itself. Animals, plants, nay,
everything in existence, are endowed with perception. Since
all life is ultimately reduced to thought, and since God is the
creator of all things, we may say with Aristotle (qualifying
the statement as above), that God is pure thought, having no
other object than himself, the principle of intelligence, or the

power of intuition which makes us see all things without seeing itself.

II. THE THREE STAGES OF BEING. 1. *Intelligence.* — Intelligence is the first divine emanation and therefore the greatest thing in the world; the succeeding emanations are more and more imperfect. Creation is a fall, a progressive degeneration of the divine. In the intelligence, the absolute unity of God splits up into intelligence proper and the intelligible world, subject and object (to use the modern expressions). However, the intelligence is, as compared to bodies, almost an absolute unity; at any rate, the intelligible world and the reason contemplating it are not, as yet, separated either in time or in space; the *nous* and the intelligible world are *in each other.* The Ideas are immanent in the intellect which conceives them; the intellect is inseparable from the Ideas.

The passage of the divine unity into this first duality, the *how* of the emanation, is as much of a mystery as God himself. Whatever rational explanation might be given, it would still be insufficient. If the dyad, it has been said, comes from the monad, then the latter contains the former in germ. But that would make the monad a dyad and not a monad in the absolute sense. Others identify the One and the All. But if God is only the sum of existing things, then he is a mere word used to designate the result of an addition, and not the supremely real principle from which the things are derived. God is anterior to the All, in dignity if not in time. Still, we may call him the All, in so far as he is the essence of everything in existence. An attempt has been made to explain emanation by calling it a partition of the original unity. But the divine unity, which is not a numerical unity, is indivisible. It has been compared with the gleaming of a bright body, with the radiation of the sun, with a cup that eternally overflows, because its contents are infinite and cannot be held in it. However beautiful these figures may be, they are taken from the material world and cannot explain the immaterial. Hence, emanation is in reality a miracle, like God himself.

There are two kinds of Ideas: (1) genera, or general forms of all existing things, viz., being, identity, difference, rest, motion, and (2) specific types of individual beings. We may conceive all genera as modifications of the only being, and all specific types as comprehended in a single being: the universal Type, or the Idea of the universe. Everything that exists in the visible world has its corresponding Idea or prototype in the intelligible world. Not only the Idea of man, but Ideas of Socrates, Plato, and so on, exist; that is to say, there are as many Ideas as individuals. Each one of us realizes a distinct Idea. Hence the Idea is not the species resolving itself into a number of passing individuals; it is the individual considered as eternal. From the fact that there are as many Ideas as individuals, it does not follow that the number of Ideas is unlimited. Though the number of existing individuals is in-finite for our imagination, it is not actually infinite; if it were so, the universe would not be a perfect being, i. e., perfect in the Greek sense. So, too, a fixed and unchangeable number of Ideas or types of individuals exist in the intelligence, the creation of God.

2. *The Soul.* — The intelligence, too, is creative, like the absolute whence it emanates, but its productive power is less. Its emanation or radiation is the soul, which is like the *nous* but inferior to it. The fact is, reason finds its Ideas in itself; they are its immanent possession and substance, while the soul must search for them or ascend to them by reflection, and therefore reaches, not the Ideas themselves, but their more or less adequate images, the simple notions. The soul is not, like the intellect, endowed with immediate and com-plete intuition; it is restricted to discursive thought, or analysis.

It is subordinate to the intellect, and therefore strives towards it as reason itself strives towards God. Its mission is to *become* what the intellect *is a priori;* that is, intelligent. Just as there is but *one* absolute, *one* reason, and *one* intelligi-ble world, so there is, at the bottom of all individual souls, but

one single soul manifesting itself in infinitely different forms:
the soul of the world. Like the *nous*, which contemplates the
absolute and also produces the soul, the soul has two functions, one of which is to contemplate and look inward, where
it finds the Ideas and the absolute, while the other is expansive and creative. Its emanation, which is less perfect than
itself, is the body.

3. *The Body*. — Though the body is far removed from the
source of all things (God is the One, the body, the greatest
plurality), it bears the stamp of the absolute. The intellect
has its Ideas; the soul, its notions; the body, its forms.
Through these the body still belongs to the higher spheres of
being; they are to the body what perceptions are to the soul,
what Ideas are to reason: a reflection of the absolute, a trace
of the divine. The form of bodies represents what reality they
have; their matter, what they lack of reality; their form is
their being; their matter their non-being. Corporeal nature
fluctuates between being and non-being; it is eternal becoming, and everything in it is in perpetual change.

After the world of bodies comes pure matter, or non-being,
an obscure and bottomless abyss, as it were, into which the
ideal world projects its rays. Matter is not body, for every
body is composed of matter and form; it is but the substratum,
the principle of its inertia; it has neither form, nor dimension,
nor color, nor anything that characterizes the body; all these
qualities proceed from the formal principle, the absolute; it
has no other attribute than privation. Since all force and life
have their source in the intellect and in God, matter is impotence, boundless indigence, the negation of unity, the cause of
the infinite multitude of bodies, incoherence, diffusion, the
absolute absence of form, i. e., ugliness itself; the absence of
the good, i. e., evil itself. From the standpoint of Plotinus as
well as of Hellenism in general, unity, form, intelligence,
beauty, and goodness are synonymous terms, as are also, on
the other hand, plurality, matter, ugliness, and evil.

It must not be understood that he considers matter and evil

as non-existent. To assume that he denies the existence of matter and of evil would be equivalent to making him say that poverty is the absence of wealth and therefore nothing, that it does not exist, and, consequently, that charity is useless. Matter is so great a reality that its influence is exercised, not only upon the corporeal sphere, but also upon the soul and upon reason itself. We have seen that the body still, though vaguely, resembles the mind, because of the form which it assumes and which is nothing but an embodied Idea. Conversely, we shall say, however superior the mind may be to corporeal nature, it is not *absolutely* immaterial. Matter exists in the mind, though in another form than in nature; i. e., as the *notion* of matter, intelligibly, in the conceptual state, not corporeally. But more than that; not only is matter in the mind in so far as the mind conceives it; it is mingled with every one of its thoughts, indissolubly connected with all its conceptions. Without matter, the mind would not be distinct from the absolute. In fact, God alone is unity in the absolute sense; the intellect is not unity in the same sense; in it unity expands into a plurality of Ideas, which are distinct from one another, although they are perceived by one and the same intellectual intuition. It is true, the Ideas in our mind are not separated corporeally; but it is also certain that the mind contains them as pluralities. Now, matter is the very principle of plurality. Hence it lies at the very basis of the intellect, which, without it, would be swallowed up in the absolute unity of God.

In order to understand this paradox, which is essentially Platonic, it must be remembered that the *matter* of Plato, Aristotle, and Plotinus, is not the matter of the materialists; it is not body, but the *transcendent substratum*, the *principle* of corporeality, that which makes the body a body, but is itself an incorporeal thing like the mind. It even transcends the intelligence; it rises above it like an impenetrable mystery that defies the reason even of the gods. Moreover, Plotinus does not place matter among the *genera;* he places it beyond the world of Ideas in the supra-intelligible realm which reason cannot reach, although we may recognize the Idea of matter in the Ideas of *otherness* and movement. If we call what can be the object of intelligence, what the intelligence can define, comprehend, or embrace under an exact formula, "intelligible," then matter is evidently not intelligible; for it is the opposite of form; it resists all limitation and consequently all comprehension. To comprehend matter is to see darkness; to see darkness is to see nothing; hence, to comprehend matter is to comprehend nothing.

Is matter a second absolute? One is sometimes tempted to regard Plotinus as a decided dualist; his system of ethics, especially, lays itself open to the charge of dualism. But the metaphysician cannot assume two absolutes. Plotinus, therefore, recalling the statement of Aristotle that the first matter and the first form are identical, conceives the supra-intelligent matter, or, in other terms, the first cause of bodies, as identical with God. Matter, which Platonism loves to call the infinite, is, in the last analysis, nothing but infinite potentiality, unlimited productivity, the creative power of God. The highest actuality is also the highest power. How is that possible? The question is the same as the one raised above: How can plurality emanate from divine unity? How can we explain emanation, creation? That is a mystery.

III. ETHICS. — The soul, which is intermediate between the intellect and the body, contains elements of both, and is an epitome of the universe. It is, as it were, the meeting-place of all cosmical powers. Logical necessity reigns in the intellectual sphere; physical necessity, in the world of bodies. The soul is the seat of the free-will. It is subject to the allurements of the body and those of the intellect. It may therefore turn towards reason and live a purely intellectual life, but it may also turn towards matter, fall, and become embodied in a low and earthly body. Hence, there are three kinds of souls: (1) souls which live for reason and for God, or divine souls; (2) souls which waver between mind and body, heaven and earth: demons, or geniuses which are partly good and partly bad; (3) souls which dwell in matter and inhabit base bodies. The heavenly souls, like the soul of the world itself, are supremely happy. Their happiness consists in their *apathy*, in their obedience to divine reason, and in the contemplation of the absolute. Their bodies consist wholly of light, and have nothing material in them, using this term in the sense of *terrestrial*. Eternally perfect and always the same, they have neither memory nor prevision, neither hope nor regret; for only such beings have memory and hope as change their conditions, be it for better or for worse. They are not even, like the human soul, conscious of themselves; they are absorbed in the contemplation of Ideas and of the absolute. It is this unconsciousness, this exclusive apperception of divine things, which constitutes their supreme happiness.

Human souls were not always enclosed in base bodies; they were at first heavenly souls, conscious of God alone and not of themselves; but they separated their lives from the universal life, in order to become selfish individuals and to assume vulgar bodies, which isolate them from each other. The assumption of an earthly body is a fall for which the miseries of our present existence are the just punishment. It was a free act, in so far as no power outside of us forced us to do it; a necessary act, in so far as our own nature determined it. Every man is the author of his fate, and, conversely, his fate depends upon his individual character. True, we choose only the fate which we *can* choose, but we choose this simply because we do not *desire* anything else.

Moreover (and here we note a difference between Neo-Platonism and modern pessimism in favor of the former), incarnation is but a relative misfortune and even a blessing, provided the soul descends into matter merely in order to transform it, and ascends heavenwards as soon as possible. Nay, the soul profits by its contact with the body, for it thereby not only learns to recognize evil but also to exercise its hidden powers, to produce works which it would otherwise not have been able to accomplish. Furthermore, though closely connected with the body, it remains separate from it. This is proved by the fact that, instead of assisting our aspirations towards the ideal world, the body opposes them, and that the philosopher welcomes death. The human soul is like the Olympus whose summit is steeped in azure while its sides are beaten by the storm; it is not confounded with the body, but escapes its bondage by means of the intelligence, its better part.

The ethical system of Plotinus reminds us of Plato and Stoicism. The end of human life is the purification of the soul and its gradual assimilation with the divinity. Three roads lead to God: music (art), love, and philosophy; three paths, or rather a single one with three stages. The artist seeks for the Idea in its sensible manifestations; the lover seeks for it in the human soul; the philosopher, finally, seeks for it in the sphere in which it dwells without alloy, — in the intelligible world and in God. The man who has tasted the delights of meditation and contemplation foregoes both art and love. The traveller who has beheld and admired a royal palace forgets the beauty of the apartments when he perceives the sovereign. For the philosopher, beauty in art, nay, living beauty itself, is but a pale reflection of absolute beauty. He despises the body and its pleasures in order to concentrate all his thoughts upon the only thing that endures forever. The joys of the philosopher are unspeakable. These joys make him forget, not only the earth, but his own individuality; he is lost in the pure intuition of the absolute. His rapture is a union of the human soul with the divine intellect, an ecstasy, a flight of the soul to its heavenly home. As long as he lives in the body, the philosopher enjoys this *vision* of God only for certain short moments, — Plotinus had four such transports, — but what is the exception in this life will be the rule and the normal state of the soul in the life to come. Death, it is true, is not a direct passage to a state of perfection. The soul which is purified by philosophy here below, continues to be purified beyond the grave until it is divested of individuality itself, the last vestige of its earthly bondage.

§ 26.   The Last Neo-Platonic Polytheists.   Porphyry, Jamblichus, Proclus

1. Plotinus was succeeded in the Neo-Platonic school at Rome by his friend Malchus or PORPHYRY,[1] a native Phœnician, who published the *Enneads*. Porphyry is still more convinced than his master of the identity of the doctrines of the Academy and the Lyceum. Although much inferior to Plotinus, on whom his teachings essentially depend, he, nevertheless, exercised an influence on the progress of philosophy during the following centuries, because of the clearness with which he set forth the problem of universals in his *Introduction to the Categories of Aristotle*. Indeed, the question whether genera and species are realities apart from the thought which conceives them, forms the chief topic of interest during the Middle Ages.

Neo-Platonism changes in character towards the end of the fourth century without essentially modifying its principles. Plotinus and Porphyry, who antedate the reign of Constantine and the ultimate triumph of Christianity, are outspoken opponents of superstition, like all the great thinkers since the days of Xenophanes. But among their successors the search for truth is gradually subordinated to the interests of religion and apologetics. After ten centuries of opposition against traditional religion, philosophy became alarmed at its work of destruction; it came to the conclusion that its stubborn opposition had simply advanced the cause of a religion that was foreign to the Greek spirit and hostile to classic culture, and that its official representatives would be a thousand times more intolerant than the Greek and Roman priesthood. Thus it happened that philosophy, the sworn enemy of the popular faith, became the palladium of the persecuted gods; she became *ancilla Panthei* (servant of the Pantheon), prior to be-

[1] Died at Rome, 301.

coming *ancilla Ecclesiæ* (servant of the Church). To promote polytheism, to promote it at all hazards: such was the desperate task undertaken by her. Henceforth she regards everything in paganism as good; she not only excuses and tolerates the strangest superstitions, the exorcism of spirits, the practices of sorcery, magic, and theurgy, but even commands them and practises them with feverish zeal. The Greek mind literally lapses into its second childhood.

The death-struggle is, however, broken by lucid moments. Among the few surviving defenders of the dying polytheistic faith we must mention two men who, though compromising with paganism and pompously assuming the title of hierophants, bring the history of ancient philosophy to a brilliant close. I mean Jamblichus of Chalcis in Cœlesyria (died about 330), the most distinguished champion of what we call Syrian Neo-Platonism (in order to distinguish this ultra-mystical movement from the philosophy of Plotinus, which is still profoundly Greek), and Proclus of Byzantium (412–485), who taught at Athens and occupied a position between the school of Rome and Jamblichus, of whom he was an enthusiastic admirer.

2. JAMBLICHUS draws his inspiration from the speculations of non-Christian literature, from Pythagoras, Plato, the religious traditions of the Orient and Egypt, and especially from his sacred triple ternary. His mathematical genius and brilliant imagination enable him to undertake a philosophical reconstruction of the pagan Pantheon. The gods emanate from the depths of the unspeakable unity in ternary series, and form a triple halo, as it were, around the Monad of monads. He opposes the Christian conception of the God-man and exaggerates the theological spiritualism of Plotinus by declaring the absolute to be *non-communicable*. The Supreme God is not only divested of all intelligence, but of all qualities whatsoever. Hence the real beings do not participate in the absolute unity but in the secondary unities emanating from it. These beings are also transcendent, but plural. This hierarchy

of derived gods is divided into three stages: intellectual gods, supramundane gods, and the immanent gods of the world. We come into communication only with these gods (the Ideas of Plato, the Numbers of Pythagoras, the substantial Forms of Aristotle); they are our Providence. The absolute has no share in the governance of things.

3. PROCLUS derives the priestly characteristics of his philosophy from Jamblichus, and his systematic and scholastic tendencies from Plotinus. He bases his system on the triple triad of Jamblichus, and deduces from the absolute and non-communicable unity: first, being, i. e., the *infinite*, the *end* or form, and their unity, the finite: secondly, *life*, i. e., potentiality, existence, and their unity, intelligible life; thirdly, intelligence, i. e., static thought, thought in motion or perception, and their unity, reflective thought. Each of these three triads[1] reveals to those initiated into philosophy one of the aspects of the first and supra-intelligible cause: first, his unspeakable unity; secondly, his inexhaustible fertility; thirdly, his infinite perfection. These are the emanations of the absolute. The absolute in itself is superior to being and even to thought, as the principle is superior to its consequence and the cause to its effect, and therefore forever unknowable. Whatever is supernatural in its essence can be reached only by supernatural means; theurgy[2] alone can reveal it to the initiated. Knowledge is confined to the intelligible sphere and needs the realities of religion in order to attain to the supra-intelligible.

This is, in language freed from senile pedantry, the last word of Neo-Platonic metaphysics, "the last will and testament" of antique thought. From the ontological point of view and compared with primitive Platonism, Neo-Platonism would be an advance in the monistic direction, if it had been content to subordinate the Idea to a higher principle containing both being and thought.[3] But its opposition to Christianity, the

---

[1] Cf. the triple triad in the system of Hegel.
[2] Θεουργία, ἔργον τοῦ θεοῦ, manifestation of the divine power.
[3] The *will* of concrete spiritualism.

fundamental dogma[1] of which assumes the *communicability* of the divine, impelled it wantonly to exaggerate the transcendency of this supreme principle; which was precisely the chief defect of Platonism. And how much inferior it is to Platonism from the ethical and religious point of view! Proclus looks upon the *practice* of magic as the essence of religion; for Plato religion means the *practice* of justice. There is as great a difference between these two conceptions as between mature, enlightened, and vigorous manhood and decrepit and superstitious old age.

In 529 the last refuge of polytheistic Neo-Platonism, the school at Athens where Proclus had taught,[2] was closed by order of the Emperor Justinian. The public manifested such indifference towards these ruins of the past, that the edict was scarcely noticed. Christianity had taken possession of the empire two centuries ago; the concrete and thrilling questions of religion, which is a product of the will, and the troubles caused by the invasions of the barbarians, superseded the serene and peaceful θεωρία (contemplation).

[1] The dogma of the *incarnation*.

[2] The last scholarchs are: Marinus of Flavia Neapolis in Palestine, the successor of Proclus, Isidore of Alexandria, and Zenodotus and Damascius of Damas (*Quæstiones de primis principiis*, ed. Kopp, Francf., 1826). The school was closed while the latter was at its head. With the school of Athens is connected the name of the Cilician Simplicius, the excellent commentator of Epictetus and Aristotle (*Categories, De anima, De cælo,* and *Physics*), who was a fellow-student and afterwards a pupil and companion in exile of Damascius.

II

PHILOSOPHY OF THE MIDDLE AGES

FIRST PERIOD

REIGN OF PLATONIC–CHRISTIAN THEOLOGY

§ 27. Christian Platonism

The breath of expiring Hellenism passed into Christianity. The doctrines of Plato and his latest interpreters continued to influence the ablest thinkers among the followers of the Gospel, and the philosophy of the Church during the entire Middle Ages merely re-echoes the teachings of the great Athenian philosophers.

In the cosmopolitan city of Alexandria, where the Greek mind came in contact with the Semitic genius, there was formed, at the beginning of the third century, a kind of Christian Neo-Platonic school. The Latin Fathers, Tertullian,[1] Arnobius, and Lactantius, rejected philosophy as a heathen product, contact with which must be avoided. The Greek and Egyptian Fathers, however, never ceased to cultivate it. Indeed, the attacks directed against the Gospel by philosophy itself compelled them to study it. Owing to the successful pressure thus exerted, the Christian faith was reduced to dogma; it was formulated and systematized. The authors of the dogmas had to *philosophize* in spite of themselves and in self-defense, so to speak. Some of them went so far as to regard the teachings of the heathen sages as divine revelations similar to the Gospel. Plato was the only philosopher

---

[1] Tertull., *De præscript. hær.*, c. 7; *Apol.*, c. 47; *Adv. Marcion.*, V, 19. The *Credo quia absurdum* of Tertullian is to be taken literally. If reason has become deceptive in consequence of the Fall, it is evident that a doctrine contradicting it (an absurd doctrine) has more chances of being true than one conforming to it. Nothing is more *logical* than the challenge which this distinguished theologian hurls at reason.

who received serious consideration. The school of Alexandria taught an essentially religious philosophy, differing in this respect from the other schools, which were, for the most part, sceptical. One could not but recognize certain similarities between Plato and Christianity; but how was this relationship, which sometimes amounted to identity, to be explained? Some — and they were in the majority — believed that Plato had drawn from the writings of the Old Testament. The enlightened minority concluded that the philosophers worthy of the name must have been inspired by the same divine reason which revealed itself in Jesus of Nazareth. Still others had recourse to both hypotheses. Justin the Martyr, the author of an *Apology* of Christianity, assumes that the *logos* is universal in its operation, and claims eternal happiness for Socrates, Heraclitus, and, in general, for those among the heathen, who, though not knowing Jesus, lived according to Reason. Athenagoras, the author of the treatise *On the Resurrection of the Dead*, Tatian the Apologist, St. Clement of Alexandria, and his disciple Origen, all express Neo-Platonic conceptions in their writings. The apostles, says Origen, have set forth the fundamental doctrines of the faith in a manner capable of being understood by the ignorant and the learned alike, leaving it to such among their successors as were endowed with the Spirit to discover the reasons for their assertions. Origen consequently makes a distinction between the popular and the scientific manner of expressing the Christian faith, between the form it assumes in the writings of the apostles and the form in which it must be conceived by the Christian philosopher: a distinction which forms the basis of Scholastic rationalism. Finally, Athanasius, Basil the Great, Gregory of Nyssa, Gregory of Nazianzus, and among the Latin Fathers (most of whom were hostile to philosophy), Augustine, were directly or indirectly influenced by Academic and Alexandrian teachings.

It would be impossible to enter upon a detailed study of the Patristic doctrines without encroaching upon the domain of pure theology; hence it will be enough for our special purpose to explain the philosophy of Augustine, whose writings form the connecting link between Greek thought and Scholastic speculation.

§ 28. St. Augustine[1]

After a youth of dissipation, the rhetorician AURELIUS AUGUSTINUS of Thagaste, Africa (354–430), embraced the religion of his mother. He united in his soul a deep love of Christ and an ardent zeal for philosophy, although, after becoming Bishop of Hippo, he gradually favored an absolute submission to the religious authority represented by him. His writings, the most important of which are the *Confessions* and the *City of God*, have left a deep impress upon the doctrines and the entire literature of the Roman Church.

For him as for Plato, science means a purer, clearer, more exalted life, the life of the thinker.[2] Reason is *capable* of comprehending God; for God has given it to us in order that we may know all things and consequently God.[3] To philosophize is to *see* truth directly and without the intervention of the eyes of the body. Reason is the eye of the soul. Wisdom is the highest truth after which we should strive. Now, what is wisdom but God? To have wisdom means to have God. True philosophy is therefore identical with true religion:[4] both have the same strivings for the eternal. Why should God despise Reason, his first-born Son, — Reason, which is God himself! He gave it to us in order to make us more perfect than other beings. Nay, faith, which some oppose to reason, is possible only to a being endowed with reason. Chronologically, faith precedes intelligence: in order to understand a thing we must first believe it. However, though faith is a condition of knowledge, it is nevertheless a provisional state, inferior to knowledge, and ultimately resolves itself into it.

---

[1] *Confessions of St. Augustine*, tr. by Pusey, London, 1909; McCabe, *St. Augustine and His Age.*
[2] *De libero arbitrio*, I, 7. [3] *Id.*, II, 3, 6. [4] *De vera religione*, 5.

The theodicy of St. Augustine is essentially Platonic, and at times even approaches the boldest conceptions of the school of Alexandria. God is the being beyond whom, outside of whom, and without whom, nothing exists; he is the being below whom, in and through whom, everything exists that has reality; he is the beginning, the middle, and the end of all things. Goodness, justice, and wisdom are not accidental attributes of God, but his innermost essence. The same is true of his metaphysical attributes. Omnipotence, omnipresence, and eternity are not mere accidents of the Divine Being, but his divine essence. God is substantially omnipresent, without, however, being everything; everything is in him, though he is not the All. He is good and yet without quality; he is great, without being a quantity; he is the creator of intelligence and yet superior to it; he is present everywhere, without being bound to any place; he exists and yet is nowhere; he lives eternally and yet is not in time; he is the principle of all change and yet immutable. In speculating about God, reason is necessarily involved in a series of antinomies; it states what he is not, without arriving at any definite conclusion as to his nature; it conceives him, — in this sense it is capable of him, — but it cannot comprehend him in the fulness of his perfection. The important point is to distinguish carefully between God and the world. St. Augustine, whose conceptions closely border upon pantheism, as the preceding shows, escapes it by his doctrine of creation *ex nihilo*. If the universe has emanated from God, then it is itself of divine essence and identical with God. Hence, it is not an *emanation* but was *created* by an act of divine freedom. God is not the soul of the world; the world is not the body of God, as the Stoics held. The immanency of God in the world would be contrary to the divine majesty.

Some falsely interpret the doctrine of the Trinity in the tritheistic or polytheistic sense. Here lies another danger. The three hypostases, although distinct, constitute but one and the same God, just as reason, will, and the emotions form

but one and the same human being. St. Augustine's criticisms
on Arianism are very profound. What do you mean, he demands of the Arians, by assuming that the Son created the
world at the command of the Father? Do you not thereby
assert that God the Father did not create the world, but
simply ordered a demiurge to create it? What is the Son if
not the *word* of God, and what is a command if not an act of
speech? Hence, God commanded *the Son through the Son* to
create the world. What a strange and absurd conclusion!
Arianism errs in that it desires to *picture* the Trinity to itself;
it imagines two beings placed very near to each other; each
one, however, occupying his particular place; and one of them
commands, while the other obeys. Arianism should have seen
that the command by means of which God created the world
out of nothing simply means the creative Word itself. God
is a spirit, and we should not and cannot form an image of the
immaterial.

Inasmuch as God created the world by an act of freedom,
we must assume that the world had a beginning; for eternal
creation, the conception of Origen and the Neo-Platonists, is
synonymous with emanation. Philosophers raise the objection that creation in time would imply an eternity of inaction
on the part of the Creator; but they are wrong. Their error
consists in considering the eternity which *preceded* creation as
an infinitely long duration. Duration is time. Now, outside
of creation there is neither space, nor time, nor, consequently,
duration. Time or duration is the measure of motion; where
there is no movement there is no duration. Since there is no
movement in eternity and in God, there is no duration in him,
and time, as Plato aptly remarks, begins only with movement,
that is, with the existence of finite things. Hence, it is incorrect to say that the God of the Christians did not create things
until after an infinite series of infinitely long periods of absolute inaction. Moreover, St. Augustine recognizes the difficulty of conceiving God without the universe. On this point,
as well as on many others, Augustine the philosopher conflicts

with Augustine the Christian. This constant discord between his faith and his reason leads to numerous inconsistencies and contradictions. God, for example, created the world by an act of his free-will, and yet creation is not the result of caprice but of an eternal and immutable decree. It is immaterial whether the immutable will of God compels him to create the world at a fixed period of time or whether it eternally compels him to do it; in either case we have absolute determination. St. Augustine realizes this, and eventually unreservedly declares that divine freedom is the principle and supreme norm of things. Since the divine will is the ultimate principle, than which there is nothing higher, it is useless and absurd to inquire into the final cause of creation.[1] God called other beings than himself into existence, because he willed to do so. Human reason has no right to go farther than that. All it may do is to ask itself the question: Why did God make things so different from each other and so unequal? St. Augustine answers, with Plato, that the diversity of the parts is the condition of the unity of the whole.

The existence of the soul is proved by thought, consciousness, and memory. You are in doubt about your existence, are you? But to doubt means to think, does it not? and to think is to exist, is it not?[2] It is more difficult to say what the soul is. According to some, it is fire or fine air or the fifth element, possessing the property of thought, understanding, and memory; others identify it with the brain or the blood, and make thought an effect of the organization of the body. But these are mere hypotheses, disproved by the simple fact that we are not conscious of any of these substances constituting the soul. If we were made of fire or of air or of any other material, we should know it by an immediate perception which would be inseparable from our self-consciousness. The

---

[1] *Quæst. div., quæst.,* 28. The same views are held by the pantheist Spinoza, the atheist Schopenhauer (*Welt als Wille,* II, *Epiphilosophie*), and Claude Bernard (quoted by the *Revue chrétienne,* March, 1869, p. 138).

[2] This is the *cogito ergo sum* of Descartes.

soul is a substance differing from all known matter as well as from matter in general; for it contains notions of the point, the line, length, breadth, and other conceptions, all of which are absolutely incorporeal.[1]

Granting this, what shall we say of the origin of the soul? There are thinkers, even among the Christians, who conceive it as emanating from God. That, however, does it too much honor. It is a creature of God, and has had a beginning, like every other creature.[2] However, even among those who on principle assume that the soul is a creature, opinions differ as to the mode of its creation. Some hold that God directly created only the soul of Adam and that the souls of other men are produced by descent from Adam. This theory (which undoubtedly favors St. Augustine's doctrine concerning the transmission of Adam's sin to his descendants) is materialistic, for it considers the soul as capable of being communicated and divided. Others maintain that souls were created, but existed before bodies; they were not introduced into them until after the Fall; the object of their captivity being the expiation of the errors of a previous life. This doctrine, which Plato holds, is disproved by the fact that we have not the slightest recollection of any such state of pre-existence. Plato finds that even illiterate persons will, upon proper questioning, assert great mathematical truths, and concludes therefrom that such persons existed prior to the present, and that the ideas aroused in their minds by our inquiries are but reminiscences. But his hypothesis loses its force when we remember that such ideas may be developed by the Socratic method in all minds endowed with common-sense. If they are reminiscences, it would have to be assumed that all men were geometricians and mathematicians in their pre-existent state; which, judging from the small number of transcendental mathematicians among the human race, seems very improbable. Plato's argument in favor of pre-existence would perhaps have more weight in case great mathematical truths could be extracted

---

[1] *De quantitate animæ*, 13.   [2] *Epistle* 157.

only from a few minds. Finally, there is a third conception, according to which souls are created as soon as bodies are created. This theory is more in line with spiritualistic principles, although it is not so good a support for the dogma of original sin as the others.

The immortality of the soul necessarily follows from its rational nature. Reason brings the soul into immediate communion with eternal truth; indeed, the soul and truth constitute but one and the same substance, as it were. The death of the soul would mean its utter separation from truth; but what finite being would be powerful enough to produce such a violent rupture? and why should God, who is truth personified, produce it? Are not thought, meditation, and the contemplation of divine things independent of the senses, independent of the body and of matter? Hence, when the body turns into dust, why should that which is independent of it perish with it?

In rejecting the notion of pre-existence, St. Augustine also abandons the theory of innate ideas, or rather, he modifies it. He assumes, with Plato, that when God formed the human soul, he endowed it with eternal ideas, the principles and norms of reason and will. Thus interpreted, St. Augustine accepts the doctrine of innate ideas. He denies, however, that these ideas are reminiscences or survivals of a pre-existent state, and he does so on the ground that if such a theory were true, we would not be creatures, but gods. He rejects the doctrine of pre-existence because it implies an existence that has no beginning. He also becomes more and more suspicious of the theory of innate ideas, because the theory might lead one to conclude that ideas existed *originally* in the human soul and were not implanted by a being outside of the soul. St. Augustine's chief aim is to elevate God by debasing man; to represent the latter as a wholly passive being who owes nothing to himself and everything to God. In the words of the Apostle: "What hast thou that thou didst not receive? Now, if thou didst receive it, why dost thou glory as if thou hadst not received it?" Man as such is the personification of impotence and nothingness. Whatever he possesses, he has received from others.

The human soul is passive, receptive, contemplative, and nothing more. It *receives* its knowledge of sensible things through the senses; it *receives* its moral and religious notions through the instrumentality of the Spirit. It owes its conception of the external world to the terrestrial light surrounding its body, and its knowledge of celestial things to the heavenly light which forms its spiritual environment. However, this interior light, which is nothing but God himself, is not outside of us; if it were, God would be an extended and material being; it is in us without being identical with us. In it and through it we perceive the eternal forms of things, or as Plato calls them, the Ideas, the immutable essences of passing realities. God himself is the form of all things, that is, the eternal law of their origin, development, and existence. He is the Idea of the ideas, and, consequently, the true reality, for reality dwells not in the visible but in the invisible; it is not found in matter but in the Idea.

St. Augustine's idealism, which comes from Plato and anticipates Malebranche's *vision in God* and Schelling's *intellectual intuition*, was, like his philosophy in general, subjected to the influence of the theological system championed by him during the latter part of his life. The inner light, which reveals to the thinker God and the eternal types of things, seems to him to grow dimmer and dimmer, the more convinced he becomes of the fall and radical corruption of human nature. Reason, which, before the Fall, was the organ of God and the infallible revealer of celestial things, is obscured by sin; the inner light changes into darkness. Had it remained pure, God would not have had to incarnate himself in Jesus Christ in order to reveal himself to humanity. Reason would have wholly sufficed to reclaim the lost human race. But the word was made flesh, and, the inner light being obscured, the Father of light appealed to our senses in order to transmit through them what reason was no longer able to give us. In this way, Augustine the theologian transforms the idealism of Augustine the philosopher into sensualism.

The moral ideas of St. Augustine suffer the same changes. His conceptions rise far beyond the general level of Patristic ethics, when Plato inspires his thought. In his polemic against moral philosophy, Lactantius had declared in true Epicurean fashion: "Virtue is not to be sought, as they maintain, on account of itself, but on account of the happy life which supervenes upon virtue,"[1] and Tertullian had written the words: "Good and best is that which God teaches. I consider it rash to dispute the good teachings of God. For it is not because it is good that we have to attend to it, but because God teaches it."[2] St. Augustine's reply to Lactantius is, that virtue and not happiness constitutes the highest goal of free activity, or the sovereign good. He opposes to eudæmonism ethical idealism. Against the indeterminism of Tertullian he raises the objection that the moral law does not depend on any one, but that it is itself the absolute. The divine will does not make goodness, beauty, and truth; absolute goodness, absolute beauty, and absolute truth constitute the will of God. Is the moral law good because God is the highest law-giver? No. We regard him who has given us the moral law as the highest law-giver, because it is good. A thing is not bad because God forbids it; God forbids it because it is bad. St. Jerome and St. Chrysostom condoned and even authorized official falsehood. Permit falsehood, and you permit sin! answers the Bishop of Hippo. St. Augustine is perfectly aware of the insoluble difficulties which the problem of human freedom considered in its relations to divine prescience, and the question of the origin of evil, present. If God foresees our actions, these lose their fortuitous character and become necessary. Then how are we to explain free-will, responsibility, and sin? If God is the source of all things, must we not also assume that evil proceeds from his will? And even if evil were only privation, the absence of

---

[1] *Inst. Div.*, III, 12.   [2] *De penitentia*, IV.

good, would not this lack of virtue be caused by the refusal of the divine will to enlighten the soul and to turn it in the direction of the good?

The philosophical reasons inclining St. Augustine towards determinism are supplemented by religious reasons. He feels that he is a sinner and incapable of being saved through his own efforts. The natural man is the *slave* of evil, and divine grace alone can make him free. Now, divine grace cannot be brought about by man; it is entirely dependent on God's freedom. God saves man because he desires it, but he does not save all men. He chooses among them, and destines a certain number for salvation. This *election* is an eternal act on his part, antecedent to the creation of man. That is, some men are *predestined* for salvation, others are not. St. Augustine ignores the question of predestination for damnation, as far as he can, but it is logically impossible for him to escape this necessary consequence of his premise.

However superior his teaching may be to that of Pelagius, his adversary, it is plain that, as soon as his thought enters upon the path of theological fatalism, it gradually sinks to the level of the ethics of Lactantius and Tertullian. The determinism in which his metaphysical speculations culminate is absolute, embracing man and God in its scope; while the determinism postulated by his religious consciousness applies only to man and leaves God absolutely undetermined. For Augustine the thinker, absolute goodness constitutes the essence of the divine will; for Augustine the champion of predestination, good and evil are dependent on God's will. The God of the Platonic thinker manifests himself to the world in Jesus Christ by virtue of an inner necessity; according to the doctor of the Church, the incarnation is but one of the thousand means which God might have employed to realize his aims. The philosopher admires and respects the ancient virtues; the theologian sees in them nothing but vices in disguise.

St. Augustine excellently exemplifies the intellectual and

moral crisis that forms the boundary between the classical epoch and the Middle Ages.

§ 29. The Death Struggles of the Roman World. — Barbarism. — The First Symptoms of a New Philosophy

When St. Augustine expired, the Western Empire lay at the point of death. From every side the Northern hordes broke through the frontiers. Gaul and Spain were in their hands, and Italy menaced. With the collapse of the State, the entire Græco-Roman civilization sank into ruins. The Church alone of all the old institutions had a chance of weathering the storm. She opened the gates of a better world to the naïve believers of the North as well as to the *blasé* Græco-Latin sceptics, and closed them upon the unworthy. This *power of the keys* she received directly from God, and it gave her a powerful hold on both Romans and barbarians. Moreover, the Church not only represented the ancient ideals, which the future had to develop or transform; she also proclaimed the essentially new and fruitful principle of the equality of nations and individuals before God, the doctrine of the unity and solidarity of the human race; in a word, the idea of humanity. And so it happened that, when the catastrophe arrived, the Church remained stable and inherited the empire. As the heir of classical culture and the depositary of the instruments of salvation, she henceforth bestows the gifts of education upon the barbarians, and the bread of Heaven upon all. She establishes new nations; and under her fostering care the Neo-Latin and Germanic civilization shows the first signs of life.

However, centuries passed before the death struggles of antiquity ended, and a new world was born. The literary traditions of Greece and Rome were kept alive in parts of Italy and the Eastern Empire. While the last thinkers of paganism were consuming their strength in weak efforts to revive the religion of the past, a Christian, hiding his identity beneath the pseudonym of Dionysius the Areopagite, advanced beyond the timid speculations of the Greek Fathers, and christianized the Neo-Platonic system, thereby sowing the seed in Christian thought which sprang up in Maximus the Confessor, Scotus Erigena, Hugo and Richard of St. Victor, Eckhart, Böhme, and Bruno. Marcianus Capella (about 450) wrote an encyclopedia of the sciences. John Philoponus, a contemporary of the Neo-Platonist Simplicius, published commentaries on the works of Aristotle and defended the teachings of Christianity. At about the same period, the Roman Boethius[1] translated Plato and Aristotle, and wrote his delightful treatise *De consolatione philosophiæ*, which breathes the spirit of Epictetus and Marcus Aurelius; Cassiodorus, another Italian (died 575), published the treatise *De artibus ac disciplinis liberalium litterarum*, which with the Encyclopedia of Marcianus Capella, the commentaries of Boethius, and the *Isagoge* of Porphyry, formed the basis of mediæval instruction.[2] Let us also mention Isidore of Seville and his twenty books of *Etymologies;* St. John of Damas, a celebrated theologian and scholar; and Photius, the Patriarch of Constantinople, the author of the *Bibliotheca* or *Myriobiblion*, a kind of philosophical anthology.

It is evident, literature gradually retires within the confines of the Church. In the West, especially, all intellectual activity centred in it. But the smouldering spark of learned culture was with difficulty kept alive in the hearts of a clergy for the most part recruited from the barbarians. The times were steeped in ignorance. The Latin language, which the Church continued to use, formed the only bond of union between the classical world and the new generation. At a time when brutal passions raged, when the secular clergy themselves were addicted to a vulgar realism and showed an absolute indifference to spiritual things, the convents became the refuge of thought and study. Here, the mind, elsewhere distracted by external

---

[1] A statesman who was executed in the reign of Theodoric, 525. *Opera* [Venice, 1491].

[2] According to this scheme of instruction, there are seven liberal arts, three of which, grammar, rhetoric, and dialectics, form the *trivium;* while the other four, music, arithmetic, geometry, and astronomy, constitute the *quadrivium.* There is a threefold and a fourfold path leading to the highest science, theology.

things, found ample opportunity and leisure moments to contemplate itself and its real treasures. Unable as yet to produce original works of their own, the monks spent their time in copying manuscripts, and to their zealous activity we owe our knowledge of quite a number of ancient masterpieces.

But they did more; they founded schools and instructed the youth. The monastic schools rivalled the cathedral schools. Great Britain possessed model monasteries, which produced such men as the Venerable Bede, Alcuin, a pupil of the school of York, who became the counsellor and friend of Charlemagne, and helped to found the Palatine Academy and a great number of cathedral and monastic schools, finally and above all, Scotus Erigena, the first and, on the whole, most profound philosopher of the Christian Middle Ages, the founder of Scholasticism.

The fatherland of Scotus, Occam, and the two Bacons, has every reason to boast of being the Ionia of modern philosophy.

§ 30. Scholasticism

As the sole legatee of the Roman Empire, the Church is the predominant power of the Middle Ages. Outside of the Church there can be no salvation and no science. The dogmas formulated by her represent the truth. Hence, the problem no longer is to *search* for it. The Church has no place for philosophy, if we mean by philosophy the pursuit of truth. From the mediæval point of view, to philosophize means to explain the dogma, to deduce its consequences, and to demonstrate its truth. Hence, philosophy is identical with positive theology; when it fails to be that, it becomes heretical. Christian thought hemmed in by the law of the Church resembles a river confined between two steep banks; the narrower the bed, the deeper the stream. Being unable to escape from the dogma encompassing it, it endeavors to penetrate it, and eventually undermines it.

Thus the philosophy of the Christian School, Scholasticism,

arises and gradually gains a foothold. Scotus Erigena is its founder; St. Anselmus, Abelard, St. Thomas, and Duns Scotus are its most distinguished representatives. Scholasticism is modern science in embryo; the philosophy of the European nations developing within the mother Church in the form of theology. It is not, like the speculation of the Church Fathers, a child of classical antiquity, from which the fall of the Roman world separates it. It springs from the healthy soil of the Germanic and Neo-Latin world, and is the product of other races and a new civilization. France, England, Spain, Germany: Western Europe, in a word, is its home. It has its period of youth, maturity, and decline. Scholastic philosophy is at first influenced by Platonism through the mediation of St. Augustine; from the thirteenth century on, it gradually suffers the influence of Aristotle's philosophy. Hence, we notice two great periods in the history of Scholasticism: the Platonic period and the Peripatetic period. The latter divides into two sub-periods, of which the first interprets Aristotle in the realistic sense, while the second conceives him as a nominalist. From the fourteenth century on, Scholasticism is engaged in the struggle between the *realists* and *nominalists*, and towards the middle of the fifteenth century, it succumbs to the secular and liberal reaction inaugurated by the Renaissance. After that it ceases to be a great intellectual power, and seeks refuge, body and soul, within the pale of the Church, of which it is, to this day, the official philosophy.[1]

What is its ruling thought, its fundamental doctrine? The "last of the Scholastics," though passing over the Middle Ages with "seven-leagued boots,"[2] formulates it most aptly in the following words: "Philosophy and theology have the same contents, the same aim, and the same interests. . . . In explaining religion, philosophy simply explains itself, and in

---

[1] The most distinguished among its post-Renaissance representatives is Francis Suarez of Granada (1548–1617), a follower of Thomas of Aquin and author of the *Disputationes metaphysicæ* (Paris, 1619), etc.

[2] Hegel, *Vorlesungen über die Geschichte der Philosophie*, vol. III, p. 99. [Engl. translation by Haldane, vol. III, p. 1.]

explaining itself it explains religion." [1] Indeed, this principle lies at the root of all its systems. The distinguishing characteristic of the period upon which we are now entering is, that it reconciles elements previously and subsequently in conflict with each other. An alliance is formed between philosophy and theology, faith and reason, "grace" and "nature." The Latin Fathers, as well as the free-thinkers by whom modern philosophy was founded, considered these two spheres as antagonistic. The Fathers took sides with "grace"; the philosophers, with "nature"; while in the judgment of the Schoolmen, at least those of the first period, there can be no contradiction between the revealed dogma and natural reason. But inasmuch as doctrines seemed to contradict each other on many points, the problem became to *reconcile* them, to *demonstrate* the truth of the dogma, and to prove that ecclesiastical Christianity is a rational religion. To render the dogma acceptable to reason, says an eminent follower of the philosopher just quoted,[2] that is the programme of Scholasticism. The dogma affirms: *Deus homo* (God-man); Scholasticism asks: *Cur Deus homo?* (Why is God man?). In order to answer this question, theology forms an alliance with philosophy; faith, with science. This alliance constitutes the very essence of Scholasticism. The latter is a compromise between philosophy and faith. Indeed, Scholasticism declines as soon as the nominalistic doctors, on the one hand, and the humanists, on the other, recognize the necessity of separating the two domains.

§ 31. Scotus Erigena

The first great Schoolman, JOHN SCOTUS ERIGENA, a native of Ireland, was invited to take charge of the Palatine Academy by Charles the Bald, about the middle of the ninth century. His treatise, *De divina prædestinatione*, which he wrote against the heresy of Gottschalk, and his Latin translation of

---

[1] *Vorlesungen über die Philosophie der Religion*, vol. I, p. 5 [vol. XI, *Complete Works*].

[2] K. Fischer, *op. cit.*, vol. I, 1, ch. IV.

Dionysius the Areopagite, which he failed to submit to the Pope for approval, alienated from him the sympathies of the Church. He continued to enjoy, however, the protection of the Emperor. The date of his death is as uncertain as the date of his birth.

Scotus resembles Origen in breadth of mind, and is much superior to his times. He suffered the same fate: the disfavor of the Church, which failed to canonize him. His learning, however, rises far beyond the scientific level of the Carlovingian epoch. Besides Latin, he knew Greek and perhaps also Arabic. In addition to his knowledge of the Greek Fathers and Neo-Platonism, he possessed wonderful powers of speculation and boldness of judgment. He stands out like a high volcano on a perfectly level plane. His philosophy, as set forth in the *De divisione naturæ*, is not, indeed, an innovation on the Neo-Platonic doctrines. Like the Pseudo-Dionysius, the Areopagite, it reproduces the system of emanation of the Alexandrine school in Christian form. But it was almost a miracle for any one living in the ninth century and on this side of the Pyrenees to understand Plotinus and Proclus.

The object of philosophy is, according to Scotus, identical with that of religion. Philosophy is the science of the faith, the understanding of the dogma. Speculation and religion have the same divine content and differ in form only. Religion worships and adores, while philosophy studies, discusses, and with the aid of reason explains the object which religion adores: God or uncreated and creative Nature.

In its broadest sense, the word *nature* comprises all beings, both uncreated and created things. Nature thus interpreted embraces four categories of existence: (1) that which is uncreated and creates; (2) that which is created and creates; (3) that which is created and does not create; (4) that which is uncreated and does not create. Existence is possible only in these four forms.

This classification may, however, be simplified. The first class is, in fact, the same as the fourth, for both of them con-

tain that which is uncreated, and consequently correspond to
the only being existing in the absolute sense of the word, to
God. The first class embraces God in so far as he is the creative principle, the beginning or the source of things; the fourth
also contains God, but only in so far as he is the end, the con-
summation, and the highest perfection of things. We also
find, upon comparing the second and the third classes, that
they form a single class containing all created things, or the
universe, in so far as this is distinct from God. The Idea-
types, which are realized in individuals, are productive created
beings (the second class). Individuals are created and non-
productive things; for types or species, not individuals, possess the power of reproduction. Hence, we have left two
classes in place of the four original ones: God and the universe.

But these two categories or modes of existence are also
identical. In fact, the world is in God, and God is in it as its
essence, its soul, its life. Whatever living force, light, and intelligence the world contains, is God, who is immanent in the
cosmos; and the latter exists only in so far as it participates
in the divine being. God is the sum-total of being without
division, limit, or measure; the world is divided and limited
being. God is unexplicated being; the world is explicated, revealed, manifested being; God and the universe are one and
the same being, two different modes or forms of the only infinite being; or rather, the world alone is a mode of being, a
modification, and limitation of being, while God is being without mode of being or any determination.[1]

Scotus derives the word θεός (*theos*, God) either from θεωρῶ,
video, or from θέω, *curro*.[2] According to the former etymology,
it means absolute vision or intelligence; according to the latter, eternal movement. But both meanings are merely figurative. For, since God is the being by the side of whom or

---

[1] *De divisione naturæ*, III, 10: God is everything, and everything is God; III,
17–18: Hence we should not consider God and the creature as a duality, but
as one and the same being; cf. 22–23.

[2] *Id.*, I, 14.

in whom there is no other being, we cannot, strictly speaking, say that God sees or comprehends anything. And as far as divine movement is concerned, we may say that it in no wise resembles the locomotion peculiar to creatures; it proceeds *from* God, *in* God, *towards* God; that is, it is synonymous with absolute rest. Since God is superior to all differences and all contrasts, he cannot be designated by any term implying an opposite. We call him good, but incorrectly, since the difference between good and evil does not exist in him. We call him God, but we have just seen that the expression is inadequate. We call him Truth; but truth is opposed to error, and there is no such antithesis in the Infinite Being. We call him the Eternal One, Life, Light; but since the difference between eternity and time, life and death, light and its opposite, does not exist in God, these terms are inexact. No term, not even the term *being*, will do him justice, for being is opposed to non-being. Hence God is indefinable as well as incomprehensible. He is higher than goodness, higher than truth, higher than eternity; he is more than life, more than light, more than God, more than being itself. None of the categories of Aristotle can comprehend him, and inasmuch as to comprehend means to bring an object under a class, God himself cannot be comprehended. He is the absolute nothing, the eternal Mystery.

The innermost essence of the human soul is as mysterious and impenetrable as God, since this essence is God himself. All that we know of it is that it is movement and life, and that this movement, this life, has three degrees: sensation, intelligence, and reason: the human image of the divine Trinity. The body was created with the soul; but it has fallen from its ideal beauty in consequence of sin. This beauty, which is latent in the actual organism, will not manifest itself in its purity except in the life to come. Man is an epitome of all terrestrial and celestial creatures. He is the world in miniature, and as such the lord of creation. He differs from the angels only in sin, and raises himself to the level of divine

being by penitence. Sin belongs to the corporeal nature of
man; it is the necessary effect of the preponderance of the
senses over the intellectual life in process of development.

The fall of man is not only the consequence, but also the
cause of his corporeal existence. The imperfections and the
diseases of his actual body, his dull materiality, the antagonism between the flesh and the spirit, the difference of the
sexes, all these things in themselves constitute sin, fall, separation from God, the dismemberment of the universal unity.
On the other hand, since there is no real being outside of God,
what we call separation from God, fall or sin, is but a negative
reality, a defect or privation. Evil has no substantial existence. A thing has real existence only in so far as it is good,
and its excellence is the measure of its reality. Perfection and
reality are synonyms. Hence absolute imperfection is synonymous with absolute non-reality; which implies the impossibility of the existence of a personal Devil, that is, an *absolutely*
wicked being. Evil is the absence of good, life, and being.
Deprive a being of everything good in it, and you annihilate
it.

Creation is an eternal and continuous act, an act without
beginning or end. God precedes the world in dignity, not in
time. God is absolutely eternal; the world is relatively so.
It emanates from God as the light emanates from the sun, or
heat from fire. In the case of God, to think is to create, and
his creative activity is, like his thought, without beginning.
Every creature is virtually eternal; our entire being is rooted
in eternity; we have all pre-existed from eternity in the infinite series of causes which have produced us. God alone is
eternal actuality; he alone never existed as a simple germ.
The nothingness from which the world is derived, according
to Scripture, is not equal to o; it is the ineffable and incomprehensible beauty of the divine nature, the supra-essential
and supernatural essence of God, inaccessible to thought and
unknown even to the angels.

The genera, species, and individuals are evolved in succession from the Infinite Being. Creation consists in this eternal analysis of the general. Being is the highest generality. From being, which is common to all creatures, life, which belongs only to organized beings, is separated as a special principle. Reason springs from life and embraces a still narrower class of beings (men and angels); finally, from reason are derived wisdom and science, which belong to the smallest number. Creation is a harmonious sum of concentric circles; we have constant crossings between the divine essence, which overflows, expands, and unfolds, and the world or the periphery, which strives to return to God and to be merged in him. The aim of human science is to know exactly how things spring from the first causes, and how they are divided and subdivided into species and genera. Science in this sense is called dialectics, and may be divided into physics and ethics. True dialectics is not, like that of the Sophists, the product of human imagination or capricious reason; the author of all sciences and all arts has grounded it on the very nature of things. Through knowledge and wisdom, its culmination, the human soul rises above nature and becomes identified with God. This return to God is effected, for nature in general, in man; for man, in Christ and the Christian; for the Christian, in his supernatural and essential union with God through the spirit of wisdom and science. Just as everything comes from God, everything is destined to return to God. Scotus teaches predestination, i. e., universal predestination for salvation. All fallen angels, all fallen men, all beings, in a word, will return to God. The punishments of hell are purely spiritual. There is no other recompense for virtue than the *vision* or immediate knowledge of God, no other pain for sin than remorse. Punishments have nothing arbitrary in them; they are the natural consequences of the acts condemned by the divine law.

§ 32. St. Anselm

Scotus Erigena went out like a meteor on a dark night. While the Arabian schools[1] were continuing the philosophical and scientific traditions of Greece and the Orient with credit to themselves, the alliance between reason and faith had only a few isolated representatives in Christian Europe during the tenth and eleventh centuries, viz.: Gerbert[2] (Sylvester II), who is indebted for his knowledge to the Arabians; Berengar of Tours;[3] Lanfranc;[4] and Hildebert of Lavardin, Bishop of Tours, the author of a treatise on morals.[5] The great questions which occupied the mind of Scotus no longer interested them. These subtle reasoners spent their time in discussing the most trivial subjects and the most childish problems: Can a prostitute again become a virgin through the divine omnipotence? Does the mouse that eats the consecrated host eat the body of the Lord? Christian philosophy is still in its infancy, and therefore delights in such childish sports. But these sports are significant preludes to the combats which the future has in store.

[1] The most celebrated schools in the Orient were: Bagdad, Bassora, Bokhara, Koufa; in Spain: Cordova, Granada, Toledo, Sevilla, Murcia, Valencia, Almeria, etc. The Arabians are apt pupils of the Greeks, Persians, and Hindoos in science. Their philosophy is the continuation of Peripateticism and Neo-Platonism. It is more learned than original, and consists mainly of exegesis, particularly of the exegesis of Aristotle's system, the strict monotheism of which recommended it to the disciples of Islam. The leaders of Arabian thought are, in Asia: Alkendi of Bassora, a contemporary of Scotus Erigena; Alfarabi of Bagdad (same century), among other things the author of an *Encyclopedia*, which the Christian Schoolmen valued very highly; Avicenna (Ibn-Sina died at Ispahan, 1036), celebrated in Europe as a physician and learned interpreter of Aristotle; Algazel of Bagdad (died 1111), a sceptical philosopher and orthodox Mussulman; in Spain: Avempace (Ibn-Badja) of Saragossa, died 1138, Ibn-Tophaïl of Cadiz (1100–1185), Averroes (Ibn-Roschd) of Cordova, the "commentator of commentators" (1126–1198), all of them learned physicians, mathematicians, philosophers, and fruitful writers. After the days of Averroes, Arabian philosophy rapidly declined, never to rise again, but it left its impress on Jewish thought (Avicebron or Ibn-Gebirol, eleventh century, the author of the *Fountain of Life;* Moses Maimonides, 1135–1204, the still more noted author of the *Guide to the Misguided*, etc.), and through the latter on Christian thought.

[2] Died 1003.   [3] Died 1088. *De sacra cœna adversus Lanfr.*, Berlin, 1844.

[4] Died 1089. *Opera*, ed. Giles, Oxford, 1854.

[5] Died 1134. *Opera*, ed. Beaugendre.

The first really speculative thinker after Scotus is St. Anselm, the disciple of Lanfranc. He was born at Aosta (1033),
entered the monastery of Bec in Normandy (1060), succeeded
Lanfranc as Abbot (1078), and as Archbishop of Canterbury
(1093). He died in 1109. He left a great number of writings,
the most important of which are: the *Dialogus de grammatico*,
the *Monologium de divinitatis essentia sive Exemplum de ratione
fidei*, the *Proslogium sive Fides quærens intellectum*, the *De
veritate*, the *De fide trinitatis*, and the *Cur Deus homo?*

The second Augustine, as St. Anselm has been called, starts
out from the same principle as the first; he holds that faith
precedes all reflection and all discussion concerning religious
things. The unbelievers, he says,[1] strive to understand because they do not believe; we, on the contrary, strive to understand because we believe. *They and we have the same object
in view;* but inasmuch as they do not believe, they cannot
arrive at their goal, which is to understand the dogma. The
unbeliever will never understand. In religion faith plays the
part played by experience in the understanding of the things
of this world. The blind man cannot see the light, and therefore does not understand it; the deaf-mute, who has never
perceived sound, cannot have a clear idea of sound. Similarly,
not to believe means not to perceive, and not to perceive means
not to understand. Hence, we do not reflect in order that we
may believe; on the contrary, we believe in order that we may
arrive at knowledge. A Christian ought never to doubt the
beliefs and teachings of the Holy Catholic Church. All he can
do is to strive, as humbly as possible, to understand her teachings by believing them, to love them, and resolutely to observe
them in his daily life. Should he succeed in understanding
the Christian doctrine, let him render thanks to God, the
source of all intelligence! In case he fails, that is no reason
why he should obstinately attack the dogma, but a reason
why he should bow his head in worship. Faith ought not
merely to be the starting-point, — the Christian's aim is not

---

[1] *Cur Deus homo?* I, 2.

to *depart* from faith but to remain in it, — but also the fixed rule and goal of thought, the beginning, the middle, and the end of all philosophy.[1]

The above almost literal quotations might give one the impression that St. Anselm belongs exclusively to the history of theology. Such is not the case, however. This fervent Catholic is more independent, more of an investigator and philosopher than he himself imagines. He is a typical scholastic doctor and a fine exponent of the alliance between reason and faith which forms the characteristic trait of mediæval philosophy. He assumes, *a priori*, that revelation and reason are in perfect accord. These two manifestations of one and the same Supreme Intelligence cannot possibly contradict each other. Hence, his point of view is diametrically opposed to the *credo quia absurdum* (I believe because it is absurd). Moreover, he too had been besieged by doubt. Indeed, the extreme ardor which impels him to search everywhere for arguments favorable to the dogma, is a confession on his part that the dogma needs support, that it is debatable, that it lacks self-evidence, the criterion of truth. Even as a monk, it was his chief concern to find a simple and conclusive argument in support of the existence of God and of all the doctrines of the Church concerning the Supreme Being. Mere affirmation did not satisfy him; he demanded proofs. This thought was continually before his mind; it caused him to forget his meals, and pursued him even during the solemn moments of worship. He comes to the conclusion that it is a temptation of Satan, and seeks deliverance from it. But in vain. After a night spent in meditation, he at last discovers what he has been seeking for years: the incontrovertible argument in favor of the Christian dogma, and he regards himself as fortunate in having found, not only the proof of the existence of God, but his peace of soul. His demonstrations are like the premises of modern rationalism.

Everything that exists, he says, has its cause, and this cause may be one or many. If it is one, then we have what

[1] *De fide trinitatis;* cf. *Monologium,* Preface.

we are looking for: God, the unitary being to whom all other beings owe their origin. If it is manifold, there are three possibilities: (1) The manifold may depend on unity as its cause; or (2) Each thing composing the manifold may be self-caused; or (3) Each thing may owe its existence to all the other things. The first case is identical with the hypothesis that everything proceeds from a single cause; for to depend on several causes, all of which depend on a single cause, means to depend on this single cause. In the second case, we must assume that there is a power, force, or faculty of self-existence common to all the particular causes assumed by the hypothesis; a power in which all participate and are comprised. But that would give us what we had in the first case, an absolute unitary cause. The third supposition, which makes each of the "first causes" depend on all the rest, is absurd; for we cannot hold that a thing has for its cause and condition of existence a thing of which it is itself the cause and condition. Hence we are compelled to believe in a being which is the cause of every existing thing, without being caused by anything itself, and which for that very reason is infinitely more perfect than anything else: it is the most real (*ens realissimum*), most powerful, and best being. Since it does not depend on any being or on any condition of existence other than itself, it is *a se* and *per se* (by itself and through itself); it exists, not because something else exists, but it exists because it exists: that is, it exists necessarily, it is necessary being.

It would be an easy matter to deduce pantheism from the arguments of the *Monologium*. Anselm, it is true, protests against such an interpretation of his theology. With St. Augustine he assumes that the world is created from nothing. But though accepting this teaching, he modifies it. Before the creation, he says, things did not exist *by themselves*, independently of God; hence we say they were derived from nonbeing. But they existed eternally *for God* and in God, as ideas; they existed before their creation, in the sense that the Creator foresaw them and predestined them for existence.

The existence of God, the unitary and absolute cause of the world, being proved, the question is to determine his nature and attributes. God's perfections are like human perfections; with this difference, however, that they are essential to him, which is not the case with us. Man has received a share of certain perfections, but there is no necessary correlation between him and these perfections; it would have been possible for him not to receive them; he could have existed without them. God, on the contrary, does not get his perfections from without; he has not received them, and we cannot say that he *has* them; he *is* and must be everything that these perfections imply; his attributes are identical with his essence. Justice, an attribute of God, and God are not two separate things. We cannot say of God that he has justice or goodness; we cannot even say that he is just; for to be just is to participate in justice after the manner of creatures. God is justice as such, goodness as such, wisdom as such, happiness as such, truth as such, being as such. Moreover, all of God's attributes constitute but a single attribute, by virtue of the unity of his essence.

All this is pure Platonism. But, not content with spiritualizing theism, Anselm really discredits it when, like a new Carneades, he enumerates the difficulties which he finds in the conception. God is a simple being and at the same time eternal, that is, diffused over infinite points of time; he is omnipresent, that is, distributed over all points of space. Shall we say that God is omnipresent and eternal? This proposition contradicts the notion of the simplicity of the divine essence. Shall we say that he is nowhere in space and nowhere in time? But that would be equivalent to denying his existence. Let us therefore reconcile these two extremes and say that God is omnipresent and eternal, without being limited by space or time. The following is an equally serious difficulty: In God there is no change and consequently nothing accidental. Now, there is no substance without accidents. Hence God is not a substance; he transcends all substance. Anselm is alarmed at these dangerous consequences of his logic, and he therefore prudently adds that, though the term "substance" may be incorrect, it is, nevertheless, the best we can apply to God, and that to avoid or condemn it might perhaps jeopardize our faith in the reality of the Divine Being.

The most formidable theological antinomy is the doctrine of the trinity of persons in the unity of the divine essence. The Word is the object of eternal thought; it is God in so far as he is thought, conceived, or comprehended by himself. The Holy Spirit is the love of God for the Word, and of the Word for God, the love which God bears himself. But is this explanation satisfactory? And does it not sacrifice the dogma which it professes to explain to the conception of unity? St. Anselm sees in the Trinity and the notion of God insurmountable difficulties and contradictions, which the human mind cannot reconcile. In his discouragement he is obliged to confess, with Scotus Erigena, St. Augustine, and the Neo-Platonists, that no human word can adequately express the essence of the All-High. Even the words "wisdom" (*sapientia*) and "being" (*essentia*) are but imperfect expressions of what he imagines to be the essence of God. All theological phrases are analogies, figures of speech, and mere approximations.

The *Proslogium sive Fides quærens intellectum* has the same aim as the *Monologium:* to prove the existence of God. Our author draws the elements of his argument from St. Augustine and Platonism. He sets out from the idea of a perfect being, from which he infers the existence of such a being. We have in ourselves, he says, the idea of an absolutely perfect being. Now, perfection implies existence. Hence God exists. This argument, which has been termed the *ontological argument*, found an opponent worthy of Anselm in Gaunilo, a monk of Marmoutiers in Touraine.[1] Gaunilo emphasizes the difference between thought and being, and points out the fact that we

---

[1] Gaunilo's refutation of the ontological proof is found in the works of Anselm under the title: *Liber uno insipiente adversus S. Anselmi in Proslogio ratiocinationem.*

may conceive and imagine a being, and yet that being may not exist. We have as much right to conclude from our idea of an enchanted island in the middle of the ocean that such an island actually exists. The criticism is just. Indeed, the ontological argument would be conclusive, only in case the idea of God and the existence of God in the human mind were identical. If our idea of God is God himself, it is evident that this idea is the immediate and incontrovertible proof of the existence of God. But what the theologian aims to prove is not the existence of the God-Idea of Plato and Hegel, but the existence of the personal God. However that may be, we hardly know what to admire most, — St. Anselm's broad and deep conception, or the sagacity of his opponent who, in the seclusion of his cell, anticipates the Transcendental Dialectic of Kant.

The rationalistic tendency which we have just noticed in the *Monologium* and the *Proslogium* meets us again in the *Cur Deus homo?* Why did God become man? The first word of the title sufficiently indicates the philosophical trend of the treatise. The object is to search for the *causes* of the incarnation. The incarnation, according to St. Anselm, necessarily follows from the necessity of redemption. Sin is an offense against the majesty of God. In spite of his goodness, God cannot pardon sin without compounding with honor and justice. On the other hand, he cannot revenge himself on man for his offended honor; for sin is an offense of infinite degree, and therefore demands infinite satisfaction; which means that he must either destroy humanity or inflict upon it the eternal punishments of hell. Now, in either case, the goal of creation, the happiness of his creatures, would be missed and the honor of the Creator compromised. There is but one way for God to escape this dilemma without affecting his honor, and that is to arrange for some kind of *satisfaction*. He must have infinite satisfaction, because the offense is immeasurable. Now, in so far as man is a finite being and incapable of satisfying divine justice in an infinite measure, the infinite being himself must take the matter in charge; he must have recourse to *substitution*. Hence, the necessity of the *incarnation*. God becomes man in Christ; Christ suffers and dies in our stead; thus he acquires an infinite merit and the right to an equivalent recompense. But since the world belongs to the Creator, and nothing can be added to its treasures, the recompense which by right belongs to Christ falls to the lot of the human race in which he is incorporated: humanity is pardoned, forgiven, and saved.

Theological criticism has repudiated Anselm's theory, which bears the stamp of the spirit of chivalry and of feudal customs. But, notwithstanding the attacks of a superficial rationalism, there is an abiding element of truth in it: over and above each personal and variable will there is an absolute, immutable, and incorruptible will, called justice, honor, and duty, in conformity with the customs of the times.

We have now to speak of the part the great Schoolman played in the discussion that arose after his promotion to the Archbishopric of Canterbury: I mean the controversy between the *realists* and the *nominalists*, or let me rather say, between the idealists and the materialists, — for this "monkish quarrel" was in reality a conflict between metaphysical principles.[1]

§ 33. Realism and Nominalism

The Catholic or *universal* Church does not merely aim to be an aggregation of particular Christian communities and of the believers composing them; she regards herself as a superior power, as a reality distinct from and independent of the individuals belonging to the fold. If the *Idea*, that is, the general or universal, were not a *reality*, "the Church" would be a mere collective *term*, and the particular churches, or rather the individuals composing them, would be the only *realities*. Hence,

---

[1] We should say *realists* instead of "materialists," were it not for the fact that the former term was, during the Middle Ages, applied to the opposite side. We mean the party which unduly emphasizes the real or material principle, and which in the history of mediæval philosophy represents Ionianism and Peripateticism, as distinguished from Academic idealism.

the Church must be realistic,[1] and declare with the Academy: Universals are real. Catholicism is synonymous with realism. Common-sense, on the other hand, tends to regard universals as mere notions of the mind, as signs designating a collection of individuals, as abstractions having no objective reality. According to it, individuals alone are real, and its motto is: Universals are names or symbols; it is nominalistic, individualistic.

The latter view was advanced and developed about 1090 by ROSCELLINUS, a canon of Compiègne. According to him, universals are mere names, *vocis flatus*, and only particular things have real existence. Though this thesis seemed quite harmless, it was, nevertheless, full of heresies. If the individual alone is real, the Church is but a *flatus vocis*, and the individuals composing it are the only realities. If the individual alone is real, Catholicism is no more than a collection of individual convictions, and there is nothing real, solid, and positive, but the personal faith of the Christian. If the individual alone is real, original sin is a mere phrase, and individual and personal sin alone is real. If the individual alone is real, there is nothing real in God except the three persons, — the Father, the Son, and the Holy Ghost; and the common essence which, according to the ·Church, unites them into one God, is a mere word, a *flatus vocis*. Roscellinus, who is especially emphatic on the latter point, is not content with defending his tritheistic heresy; he takes the offensive and accuses his adversaries of heresy. To hold that the Eternal Father himself became man in Christ in order to suffer and die on Calvary, is a heresy condemned by the Church as Patripassianism. Now, if the Father, the Son, and the Holy Ghost have the same essence,

---

[1] Let me remind the reader that in the Middle Ages the term *realist* meant *idealist*, that is, the direct opposite of what it means now. The same is true of the words *objective* and *subjective*. What we call *objective*, Scholastic philosophy calls *subjective* (viz., that which exists as a subject, substance, or reality independent of my thought); while what we call *subjective* is called *objective* (viz., that which exists merely as an *object* of thought and not as a real subject). This terminology, the converse of ours, is still found in Descartes and Spinoza.

and if this essence is an objective reality, it follows that the essence of the Father or the Father himself became man in Christ: a statement which is explicitly contradicted by Scripture and the Church herself.

Roscellinus had pointed out a difficulty in the dogma, — an offense for which the Church never forgave him. The Council of Soissons condemned his heresy and forced him to retract (1092). Nominalism thus anathematized held its peace for more than two centuries, and did not reappear until about 1320, in the doctrine of Occam.

The most ardent champions of realism in the controversy aroused by the canon of Compiègne were St. Anselm and William of Champeaux, a professor at Paris and afterwards Bishop of Châlons.[1] St. Anselm combated not only the dogmatic heresy but also the philosophical heresy, namely, the negation of Platonic idealism, the antithesis of speculative philosophy. "Reason," he says,[2] "is so confused with corporeal ideas in their souls (he is speaking of the nominalists), that they find it impossible to get rid of them and to separate from such material ideas that which ought to be considered in itself and independently of all corporeal intermixture. . . . They cannot understand that *man is something more than an individual*."

WILLIAM OF CHAMPEAUX deduces the extreme consequences of realism. According to him, nothing is real but the universal; individuals are mere names. From the anthropological point of view, for example, there is in reality, according to Champeaux, but *one* man, the universal man, the man-type, the genus man. All individuals are fundamentally the same, and differ only in the accidental modifications of their common essence. Champeaux is but a step removed from pure pantheism, and yet he is the defender of orthodoxy, the passionate adversary of the heresy of Roscellinus! What a strange confusion of ideas and interests! What an intellectual chaos,

[1] Died 1121.
[2] *De fide trin.*, c. 2. We were, therefore, justified in translating *nominalism* by the word *materialism*, p. 171.

out of which the Catholic theology of our day is with difficulty beginning to bring order!

Between extreme nominalism, which says: *Universale post rem* (the universal after the particular), and extreme realism, which has for its motto: *Universale ante rem* (the universal before the particular), there was room for a doctrine of mediation, which may be summarized as follows: The universal is neither before nor after the particular but in the particular. This we get in the *conceptualism* of Abelard.

§ 34. Abelard

PIERRE ABELARD, or Abailard, was born in Palais, near Nantes, 1079, and studied at Paris under William of Champeaux, the most skilful controversialist of the period. Quarrelling with his teacher, who was jealous of his pupil's brilliant talents, Abelard, though only twenty-two years of age, opens a school at Melun, then at Corbeil. His reconciliation with Champeaux brings him back to Paris, where he meets with unparalleled success as a teacher. Falling a victim to the vindictiveness of the canon Fulbert, whose niece he had seduced, he retires to the Abbey of St. Denis, while Heloise takes the veil at Argenteuil. In his retirement he writes the treatise *De trinitate*, a work which brings down upon his head the wrath of the Church. The Council of Soissons condemns him to deliver his book to the flames (1122). At Nogent-sur-Seine he founds an Oratory, which he dedicates to the Trinity, and particularly to the Paraclete. This he afterwards surrenders to Heloise, in order to enter upon his duties as Abbot of St. Gildas de Ruys. Denounced as a heretic by St. Bernard of Clairvaux, he is again condemned, this time to imprisonment (1140); but he finds an unexpected refuge in the Abbey of Clugny, and a noble protector in Peter the Venerable, through whose efforts St. Bernard is finally moved to forgiveness. These troubles undermine his health, and cause his death in 1142. In addition to his *De trinitate*, we have to mention his *Letters*, his *Introduc-*

tio ad theologiam, and his *Theologia christiana*, his *Ethics* (*Nosce te ipsum*), the *Dialogue between a Philosopher, a Christian, and a Jew*, published by Reinwald (Berlin, 1831), and the treatise *Sic et non*, published by V. Cousin in the *Ouvrages inédits d'Abélard* (Paris, 1836).

Abelard is too speculative a thinker to accept the notions of Roscellinus, and too positivistic to subscribe to the theory of William of Champeaux. According to him, the universal exists in the individual; outside of the individual it exists only in the form of a *concept*. Moreover, though it exists in the individual as a reality, it exists there not *as an essence* but *as an individual*. If it existed in it essentially, or, in other terms, if it exhausted the essence of the individual, what would be the difference between Peter and Paul? Although Abelard's theory is not identical with nominalism, it comes very near it. It is to the ultra-idealistic doctrine of Champeaux what the concrete idealism of Aristotle is to the abstract idealism of Plato. Abelard, who was not acquainted with Aristotle's *Metaphysics*, divines its contents from the few hints he gets from the *Organon*. That alone would assure him a high place among the doctors of the Middle Ages.

Abelard is, moreover, the most independent, the most courageous, and the most relentless among the Schoolmen. Though respectful towards the Church, he is not afraid of incurring its displeasure, when occasion demands it. He agrees with the author of the *Cur Deus homo?* that revealed truth and rational truth are identical, but he does not, like Anselmus, accept St. Augustine's *credo ut intelligam* (I believe in order that I may understand). It is surprising with what frankness his *Introductio* condemns *the presumptuous credulity of those who indiscriminately and hastily accept any doctrine whatsoever before considering its merits and whether it is worthy of belief*. He is an enthusiastic admirer of Greek philosophy, which, however, as he himself confesses, he knows only from the works of St. Augustine.[1] He finds all the essential doctrines of Christian-

---

[1] *Theologia christiana*, Book II.

ity, its conception of God, the Trinity, and the incarnation, in the great thinkers of antiquity, and the distance between Paganism and the Gospel does not seem so great to him as that between the Old and the New Testaments. It is especially from the ethical point of view, he believes, that Greek philosophy has the advantage over the teachings of the sacred books of Israel. Hence, why should we deny the pagan thinkers eternal happiness because they did not know Christ? What is the Gospel but a reform of the natural moral law? Shall we people hell with men *whose lives and teachings are truly evangelical and apostolic in their perfection, and differ in nothing or very little from the Christian religion?* [1]

How does Abelard manage to find such doctrines as the Trinity in Greek philosophy? The *three persons* are reduced to three attributes of the Divine Being: power, wisdom, and goodness. Taken separately, he says, these three properties: power, knowledge, and will, are nothing; but united they constitute the highest perfection. The Trinity is the Being who can do what he wills, and who wills what he knows to be the best. From the theological stand-point, this is monarchism, a heresy opposed to the tritheism of Roscellinus. Metaphysically, it is concrete spiritualism, which denies that force and thought are separate entities, and holds that they are united in the *will*.

In times of religious fervor, morality is identified with piety, ethics with theology, while enlightened and sceptical periods tend to separate them. The first appearance of a system of ethics independent of dogmatics is therefore an important symptom. Such a work is Hildebert of Lavardin's popular treatise on ethics, *Moralis philosophia*,[2] an imitation of Cicero and of Seneca; such is, above all, the much profounder and more scientific treatise of Abelard: *Nosce te ipsum* (know thyself).

Not that Abelard dreams of separating ethics from ontology, as our independent moralists do. But the reality on which he

---

[1] *Theologia christiana*, II.   [2] See § 32.

bases the moral law is not the divine free-will of the Latin
Fathers. Since God is the best and most perfect Being, all his
acts are necessary. For, if it be right that a thing be done, it
is wrong not to do it; and whoever fails to do what reason
demands is no less at fault than he who does what it prohibits.
And just as God's conduct is determined by reason, we, his
creatures, are, in turn, determined by the divine will. Inasmuch as God is the absolute cause, the Being in whom we
live, move, and have our being, and who is therefore the source
of our power and will, it follows that God is, in a certain sense,
also the author of whatever acts we may perform, and that he
does what he makes us do.

The tendency to evil is not sin, but the condition of virtue,
for virtue is a struggle, and all struggle presupposes opposition.
Nor is the act as such the *matter* of the sin; the act as such is
indifferent. The sin lies in the *form* of the act, that is, in the
will which dictates it. Neither the tendency to evil nor the
act in itself is sin, but the *intention*, though arrested, of satisfying an evil desire or indulging a passion. It follows that the
man who has consented to an evil action and is hindered in
its accomplishment by some circumstance or other, is as cul-
pable as though he had performed it. The intention deserves
punishment as much as the act, and he who consents to do evil
has already done evil. The Supreme Judge does not judge
appearances and the outside, but the spirit. By distinguishing
between the desire and the intention to surrender one's self
to it, between the natural craving and the will to follow it,
Abelard repudiates that exaggerated form of pessimism which
regards the life of man as one perpetual sin; by characterizing
the external act as indifferent, he attacks the growing formalism of Catholic morality. As was pointed out, the conceptualistic theory shows the first signs of the influence exerted by
Aristotle on the Middle Ages. The ethics of Abelard reminds
us of Aristotle and his ethics of the golden mean.

The influence of Abelard was considerable. We observe it
in Bernard of Chartres called *Sylvestris*, in William of Conches,

the learned professor of Paris, who, in his *Philosophia minor*, protests against ecclesiastical intolerance, in Gilbert de la Porrée, Bishop of Poitiers,[1] in John of Salisbury, Bishop of Chartres,[2] and even in his adversary, Hugo of St. Victor. Gilbert is branded as an atheist by St. Bernard because he distinguishes between God and the Deity, between the person and the essence of the Supreme Being. "The divine Spirit," says John of Salisbury in his *Polycraticus*,[3] "the creator and giver of life, replenishes not only the human soul but every creature in the universe. . . . For outside of God there is no substantial creature, and things exist only in so far as they share in the divine essence. By his omnipresence God envelops his creatures, penetrates them and fills them full of himself. . . . All things, even the most insignificant, reveal God, but each reveals him in its own way. Just as the sunlight is different in the sapphire, the hyacinth, and the topaz, so, too, God reveals himself in an infinite variety of forms in different orders of creation."

The same freedom of form and the same monistic tendency as regards the matter, joined with the deepest and purest religious feeling, we find in Hugo of St. Victor, the first great mystic of the Middle Ages.

§ 35.   Hugo of St. Victor

We observe a most striking difference between HUGO of Blankenburg, a monk of St. Victor at Paris (1096–1140), and his illustrious contemporary. Abelard is a Frenchman: he has a perfect mania for clearness, precision, and form; his faith is a matter of knowledge; logic is his "god." Hugo is of German origin. His tastes as well as his duties exclude him from the brilliant scenes in which the genius of Abelard unfolds itself. In the solitude of his cell he devotes himself to study, meditation, and contemplation. He is no less independent than Abelard, but with him it is all a matter of feeling rather than of reflection. He is a skilful dialectician, but opposed to the

---

[1] Died 1154.   [2] Died 1180.   [3] *Polycraticus*, I, 1, 5; III, 1; VII, 17.

formalistic rationalism of the School. Although his liberalism differs very much from that of Abelard, he arrives at similar results. Rationalism and mysticism both tend towards monism. Hence mysticism exercises a no less harmful influence upon the dogma than rational criticism, during the Middle Ages; hence, also, mysticism and pantheism are synonymous in France.

Hugo's views, especially as set forth in his work, *De sacramentis christianæ fidei*, are surprisingly bold. An absolute orthodoxy does not seem to him to be essential to salvation, or even possible. We may, according to him, be thoroughly convinced of the truth of the dogmas without agreeing on their interpretation; unity of faith by no means implies identity of opinions concerning the faith. It is impossible to have uniform notions of God, because God transcends all human conception. This is a characteristic trait of mysticism, and essentially distinguishes it from the rationalism of Abelard and Anselm. Although assuming with the latter that the Trinity is simply supreme power (the Father), supreme intelligence (the Son or the Revealer), and supreme goodness (the Holy Ghost), Hugo teaches that the infinite Being is absolutely incomprehensible.

God is not only supra-intelligible; nay, we cannot even conceive him by analogy. What, indeed, is analogous to God? The earth? The heaven? The spirit? The soul? None of all these is God. You say: I know that these things are not God; but they bear some resemblance to him, and may therefore serve to define him. You might as well show me a body in order to give me an idea of mind. Your example would surely be inappropriate, and yet the distance from mind to body is less than that between God and mind. The most opposite creatures differ less among themselves than the Creator differs from the creature. Hence it is impossible to understand God, who exists only for faith. For Abelard, the pure dialectician, an incomprehensible God is an impossible God; for Hugo, the intuitionist and mystic metaphysician, he is the highest reality.

Hugo was the first, after St. Augustine, to pay serious attention to psychology. He is an earnest champion of animism in this field. Body and soul are, in his opinion, separate substances, without being absolutely opposed to each other; for there is a double bond of union between them: the imagination, which is, so to speak, the corporeal element of the soul, and sensibility, which is, as it were, the spiritual element of the body. The soul possesses three fundamental forces: natural force, vital force, and animal force. The natural force has its seat in the liver, where it prepares the blood and the humors which are distributed through the veins over the entire body. It is alternately appetitive, retentive, expulsive, and distributive, and is common to all animals. The vital force, which resides in the heart, manifests itself in the function of respiration. It purifies the blood by means of inhaled air, and causes it to circulate through the arteries. It also produces vital heat.[1] The animal or psychic force, which is situated in the brain, produces sensation, movement, and thought. Each of these manifestations of the soul employs a different region of the brain. Sensation is connected with the anterior portion, movement with the posterior portion, and thought with the middle portion of this organ. We have not two different souls: a sensitive soul, the principle of corporeal life, and an intelligent soul, the principle of thought. The soul (*anima*) and the spirit (*animus sive spiritus*) are one and the same principle. The spirit is this principle considered in itself and independently of the body: the soul is this same principle in so far as it animates the body.

There is a genuineness about these lines of the *De anima* that contrasts with the fruitless quibblings of dualistic spiritualism; and when in the *Libri didascalici* Hugo of St. Victor traces the successive stages of psychical life from the plant to man, he seems to anticipate evolution and comparative psychology.

---

[1] Hugo has a vague idea of the circulation of the blood and the difference between venous and arterial blood. He also seems to regard the liver as the chief organ for the preparation of the vital fluid.

§ 36. The Progress of Free Thought [1]

The disciple of Hugo, the Scotchman RICHARD,[2] Prior of St.
Victor, outlines a system of religious philosophy in his *De
trinitate* that breathes the same spirit of free investigation as
the writings of his master. This may be seen from the following characteristic lines: "I have often read," he says, "that
there is but one God, that this God is *one* as to substance,
three as to persons; that the divine persons are distinguished
from each other by a characteristic property; that these three
persons are not three gods, but one only God. We frequently
hear and read such statements, but I do not remember ever
having read how they are proved. There is an abundance of
authorities on these questions, but an extreme dearth of arguments, proofs, and reasons. Hence, the problem is to find a
firm, immovable, and certain basis on which to erect the system." [3]

Richard finds such a basis for the dogma of the Trinity in
the idea of divine love, which necessarily creates an object for
itself. But this proof he does not regard as sufficient. While
his *De trinitate* is conceived in the spirit of Abelard, his *De
contemplatione* openly espouses Hugo's views. Richard abandons the attempt to reach God by the reasoning powers, and
substitutes feeling for reflection. He distinguishes six stages
in the mystical ascension of the soul towards God. In the
higher stages the soul is expanded, raised above itself, delivered from itself. However, whether you call him a mystic or
a rationalist, Richard teaches a kind of Neo-Platonic emanation and the identity of nature and of grace.

ALANUS OF LISLE,[4] though an orthodox churchman, tries to
construct a system of dogmatics by means of a strictly mathematical method, and concludes that everything is in God and
God in everything.

---

[1] Read Haskins, *Studies in the History of Mediæval Science*, Cambridge
(U. S. A.), 1924.

[2] Died 1174.   [3] I, ch. 5–6.

[4] Alanus ab insulis, professor at Paris, died 1203.

ROBERT OF MELUN[1] distinguishes — a serious symptom! — between events which take place according to Nature and events which take place according to the power of God which is above Nature. He is, however, truly devoted to the Church and its doctrines, defending it against the heresies which begin to threaten it. There are people, he says, who deny the miraculous conception of Christ on the ground that such a phenomenon would be contrary to the natural course of events. But is not God, the author of nature, above nature, and has he not the power to change the regular course of nature? How are these doubters going to explain the origin of Adam and Eve? Just as the protoplasts could originate without an earthly mother, Jesus was able to come into the world without a human father.

In addition to these attempts at Christian philosophy we have the *Eight Books of Sentences* by the Englishman, ROBERT PULLEYN,[2] and the *Four Books of Sentences* by Peter of Novaro, or the Lombard (*Magister sententiarum*).[3] PETER THE LOMBARD's work, the success of which soon eclipsed Pulleyn's, forms a complete system of dogmatics. It considers a whole host of questions which betray the barrenness of Scholastic discussions, but which also show what progress has been made by thought in its opposition to the guardianship of the Church: How can we reconcile divine prescience with free creation? (If God foresaw that he would create, then he had to create, and creation is not an act of freedom. If God did not foresee it, what becomes of his omniscience?) Where was God before creation? (He could not have been in heaven, for heaven too was created.) Could God have made things better than he has made them? Where were the angels before the creation of heaven? Can angels sin? Have they a body? In what form do God and the angels appear to men? How do demons enter into men? What was Adam's form before his appearance on earth? Why was Eve taken from a side and not from some other part of Adam's body? Why was she

---

[1] Died 1173.   [2] Died about 1154.   [3] Died 1164, Bishop of Paris.

created while Adam was asleep? Would man be immortal if
he had never sinned? And in that case how would men have
multiplied? Would children have come into the world as full-
grown men? Why did the Son become man? Could not the
Father and the Holy Ghost have become man? Could God
have become incarnate in woman as easily as in man? These
how's and *why's*, multiplied without end, betray the naïve
curiosity and the charming indiscretion peculiar to the child,
but they are at the same time unmistakable symptoms of the
coming maturity and freedom of thought.

The *Sentences* intensified the pious mystics' dislike for the
subtleties of dialectics. Gradually abandoning systematic
theology, mysticism turns its attention to practical Christianity, to preaching and the composition of devotional books;
and while the *Master of the Sentences* professes to serve the
Church with no less zeal than Robert of Melun, Walter of St.
Victor, who died about 1180, denounces the Lombard, his
pupil Pierre of Poitiers, Gilbert of Porrée, and Abelard, as the
four labyrinths of France in which we must take care not to
lose ourselves. But this opposition merely helped to develop
heresy. A distinction is made not only between the effects of
the divine will and the effects of nature, but between philosophical truth and religious truth. The view begins to prevail
that a thing may be true in philosophy without being true in
religion, and *vice versa*. A vague suspicion arises that the
Church is fallible, and that a breach between faith and science,
theology and philosophy, is not impossible.

A number of critical thinkers, influenced by Arabian pantheism, were bold enough to defend the philosophy of immanency. They regarded the three persons of the Trinity either
as three successive manifestations of the Divine Being, or as
three different stages in the development of the human conception of God. The Father is the God of the Old Testament,
God dwelling in heaven; the Son is the God of the New Testament, God bridging the chasm and coming nearer to man;
the Holy Ghost is the God of the future, the true God con-

ceived as the universal and omnipresent Being. God is everything and produces everything in all things. He is, therefore, not only present in the consecrated host, but also in the daily bread. His spirit manifested itself in the great men of Greece as well as in the Prophets, Apostles, and Fathers. There is no other heaven than a good conscience, no other hell than remorse; and the worship of saints is idolatry.

These doctrines, which were ably taught by Simon of Tournay, Amalric of Bena, and David of Dinant, spread rapidly among the clergy and the laity. About the year 1200 they formed a formidable though secret opposition to the supreme authority of tradition. The Church, seriously threatened in its unity, averted the danger by burning a great number of heretics at the stake and anathematizing the physics of Aristotle, from which David of Dinant was accused of having drawn his heresies (1209).

SECOND PERIOD

THE REIGN OF PERIPATETIC SCHOLASTICISM

A. Semi-Realistic Peripateticism

§ 37. Growing Influence of the Philosophy of Aristotle

We have pointed out the relation existing between Platonic *realism* and the Catholic system. In Catholicism as in Platonism, in the Church as in Plato's State, the universal is superior to the particular; the whole precedes, rules, and absorbs the parts; the Idea is the true reality, the power superior to all individual existences. The philosophy of a period reflects the spirit peculiar to that period. The heroic age of Catholicism, the age of faith which produced the Crusades and built the Gothic cathedrals, could not but have an essentially idealistic, Platonic, and Augustinian philosophy. Scotus Erigena and St. Anselm were the great representatives of this epoch. But even in the writings of these men, and still more so in those of their successors, we discover, beneath the seeming harmony of their philosophy and theology, contrasts, disparities, and contradictions. Erigena culminates in monism; William of Champeaux, in the philosophy of identity; Abelard, in determinism; Alanus, Gilbert, and Amalric of Bena, in pantheism. The Schoolmen of the period, if we may believe them, are convinced that reason and the dogma agree; and their philosophy merely aims to prove the agreement and to justify the faith. But it is certain that from 1200 on this conviction was gradually shaken. As soon as Scholasticism discriminated between philosophical truth and religious truth, it divided into the disparate elements which it professed to unite, and sealed its doom. Scholasticism had not reached the climax of its development before it began to show symptoms of decay. It needed a powerful stimulus to keep it alive; new life and vigor had to be infused into it from without; this it received from Aristotle.

At the beginning of the thirteenth century, Christian Europe knew nothing of Aristotle's writings except a part of the *Organon* in the Latin translation ascribed to Boethius. From this time on, things rapidly change. About 1250, Robert, Bishop of Lincoln, translates the *Nicomachean Ethics* into Latin. The Dominicans Albert of Bollstädt and St. Thomas of Aquin write valuable commentaries on the Stagirite, and in every way encourage the translation of his works. But it is particularly to the Arabians[1] that the Christian Middle Ages owe their knowledge of his treatises on physics and ontology. During the eleventh and twelfth centuries, Avicenna in Persia and Averroes in Spain publish commentaries on them, and either by oral teaching or by their written works intensify the interest for Peripatetic philosophy. Two royal friends of letters, Roger II of Sicily and the Emperor Frederick II, surround themselves with Arabian scholars, under whose direction Latin translations of Aristotle and his commentators are made. These translations are presented to the universities of Bologna, Paris, and Oxford. In this way thousands of students become acquainted with the doctrines of the great Greek. Prior to this time, only Aristotle the logician had been studied, and that, too, rather superficially. Henceforth, Aristotle the moralist, the physicist, and the metaphysician, becomes an object of study.

The Aristotelian system was an innovation, and consequently the conservative Church had to combat it. For was not its author both a heathen and a favorite of the disciples of the false prophet, and, therefore, the incarnation of all anti-Christian tendencies? Was he not, in a certain measure, the source of the heresies of David of Dinant and his consorts? The Church condemned Aristotle's treatises on physics in 1209, and his *Metaphysics* in 1215. But she soon saw the error of her ways. From 1250 on, she allowed public lectures on

[1] See p. 164, note 1.

Aristotle to be delivered at Paris; and fifty years later the Stagirite became her official philosopher, whom one could not contradict without being accused of heresy; he is the precursor of Christ in the order of Nature, as John the Baptist was in the order of Grace. This reaction was no more than natural. True, Aristotle was a pagan philosopher, and consequently an opponent of the faith; but if, in spite of that, his doctrine should be found to agree with the Gospel, it would add all the more to the glory of Christ. Aristotle taught the existence of a God apart from the universe, and that alone ought to have won him the sympathies of the Church threatened by the pantheistic heresy, which appealed to Plato for aid.

More than that; Aristotle offered the Church a system which she had the greatest interest in appropriating, with certain limitations. The times had already become familiar with the conception of *nature*. They spoke of nature and its course as opposed to God and the effects of his will. Christian thought could not help returning to this fundamental conception of science, in the course of its development, while the Church could no more oppose it than she could hinder the formation of the European States. She could not destroy these States, and therefore made them subject to herself; she was unable to extirpate the conception of nature, and therefore drew it into her service. Now, the metaphysics of Aristotle was admirably fitted for such a purpose. For, does not Aristotle regard nature as a hierarchical system of which God — and consequently the Church — is both the basis and the summit? With the admirable tact which seldom failed her, Catholicism recognized Aristotle in order to make capital out of him.

But the chief advantage resulting from an alliance with Peripatetic philosophy was the following: As soon as Aristotle's system received recognition as the only authentic expression of human reason, its authority naturally transcended that of free thought. Hence Peripateticism gave the Church a still better means of regulating Scholastic philosophy than she already possessed. During the Platonic period thought enjoyed a relative independence; its object was to prove the agreement between the dogma and natural reason; and, as we have seen, it was quite rationalistic in the performance of this task. Henceforth the question no longer is to prove the agreement between the dogma and natural reason, but its agreement with the letter of Aristotle's writings. The proof of this agreement makes Aristotle the highest authority and his system the official criterion of a philosopher's orthodoxy. Aristotle still stands for reason, but reason now is disciplined and reduced to a fixed code. Left to itself, reason is a changeable authority, and its agreement with faith not necessarily a settled fact. What to St. Anselm seemed agreement, Abelard, Gilbert, Amalric, and David regarded as contradictory. The mind is mobile, revolutionary; the letter is eminently conservative. By adopting the philosophy of Aristotle, the Church made use of the most illustrious thinker in order to enslave thought.

The advantages arising from this alliance with Peripatetic philosophy were, it is true, accompanied by disadvantages that became serious dangers in the sequel. In the first place, the truth of the dogma was proved by its agreement with Aristotle; this raised the authority of Aristotle and philosophy above the authority of the Church. Then the influence of the Stagirite necessarily introduced into Scholasticism a new element, not very favorable to the spiritual omnipotence of the Church: the taste for science and the spirit of analysis.

§ 38. The Peripatetics of the Thirteenth Century

The Church was converted to Peripateticism by a number of eminent thinkers who were less original than St. Anselm and Abelard, but, owing to the more abundant material at their disposal, more learned than their predecessors. At their head stands the Englishman ALEXANDER OF HALES,[1] professor of theology at Paris, whose commentaries on the *Sentences* of

[1] Died 1245.

Peter the Lombard and the *De anima* of Aristotle won for him the title *doctor irrefragabilis*.

WILLIAM OF AUVERGNE, Bishop of Paris,[1] whose learning equalled that of Alexander, wrote a series of treatises inspired by Aristotle, and a voluminous work, *De universo*, a kind of metaphysics, the wonderful erudition of which proves that the author was thoroughly acquainted with the Arabian commentaries on the Stagirite. His Peripatetic leanings, however, did not hinder him from denying the eternity of the world, nor from believing in creation, Providence, and the immortality of the soul.

The Dominican VINCENT OF BEAUVAIS,[2] the teacher of the sons of St. Louis, gathers the treasures of learning and of Peripatetic speculation in his fourfold speculation: natural, doctrinal, moral, and historical. He cites almost all the writings of Aristotle, and already speaks triumphantly of the new logic as opposed to the old logic. He is an open adherent of the Lyceum on the subject of universals, which still forms the chief topic of discussion among the Schoolmen, and declares with Abelard: Universals in things. Universals are real, even more real than particulars, without, however, existing independently of particulars. As in the system of Abelard, universals and particulars are no longer abstractly and mechanically juxtaposed in the metaphysics of Vincent, but are joined together by the principle of individuation. A new terminology is used by this Schoolman to express Aristotelian conceptions. The $\tau\acute{\iota}$ $\acute{\epsilon}\sigma\tau\iota$ ("what") of Aristotle, for example, becomes the *quidditas* (or essence). The philosophical vocabulary is developed and enriched at the expense of Ciceronian Latin, which the Renaissance afterwards undertakes to rescue from the neglect of the School.

Though a realist, in so far as he regards the universal as a reality, Vincent makes an important advance towards nominalism by distinguishing between the metaphysical universal and the logical universal, i. e., between the specific type which

[1] Died 1249.　　　　　　　　　　　　　　[2] Died 1264.

really exists in the individuals composing the species and the general notion which corresponds to this type, and is but an abstraction of thought. This distinction is a nominalistic deviation from realism, for the pure realism of Champeaux and Anselm absolutely identifies the specific type and the general idea. It is, however, far from being pure nominalism, for nominalism is the absolute negation of the metaphysical universal as an objective reality.

Another Dominican, who has already been mentioned,[1] ALBERT OF BOLLSTÄDT,[2] wrote commentaries on most of Aristotle's works, and labored with untiring zeal for the propagation of the Peripatetic philosophy. He manifests a remarkable taste for natural science, in which respect he anticipates Roger Bacon, Raymundus Lullus, and the scientific Renaissance. We see how dangerous the Peripatetic alliance proved to the Church !

The Franciscan John of Fidanza, known as ST. BONAVENTURA,[3] is less learned and less interested in nature, but more speculative than Albert. He admires both Aristotle and Plato, rational philosophy and contemplative mysticism, piety and knowledge, thus uniting in his person two elements which were growing farther and farther apart. The Church recognized his services by canonizing him, and the School bestowed upon him the title of *doctor seraphicus*.

Finally, two illustrious rivals complete the Peripatetic galaxy of the thirteenth century and finish the work of conciliation between the Church and the Lyceum: the Dominican St. Thomas of Aquin and the Franciscan Duns Scotus.

§ 39.   St. Thomas of Aquin

THOMAS OF AQUIN[4] (Aquino), the son of a noble family in the kingdom of Naples, preferring the peaceful pleasures of

---

[1] § 37.   [2] Albertus Magnus, died at Cologne in 1280.

[3] Died 1274. Author of a *Commentary on the Sentences of the Lombard*, of an *Itinerarium mentis in Deum*, conceived in the spirit of the mystics of St. Victor, etc. Edition of Strasburg, 1482, Rome, 1588, ff., etc.

[4] De Wulf, *Mediæval Philosophy*, illustrated from the system of Thomas Aquinas, Cambridge (U. S. A.), 1922.

study to the adventurous life of a feudal lord, entered the
order of St. Dominic, in spite of the formal protests of his
father. On the eve of his departure from Italy to Paris, he was
kidnapped by his brothers and imprisoned in the paternal
castle, from which he managed to escape two years later.
Taking up his abode at Cologne, he became an enthusiastic
disciple of Albert the Great and a profound student of Aristotle. Henceforth all his efforts were directed towards ac-
quainting the Christian Occident with the Aristotelian philosophy as set forth in the Greek text, particularly with the
Physics and *Metaphysics*, of which only Latin translations
made from Arabian translations were known. He afterwards
returned to the Peninsula, where he died in 1274, scarcely fifty
years of age.

Philosophy is indebted to him for a series of treatises bear-
ing on the metaphysics of Aristotle (*Opuscula de materiæ
natura, de ente et essentia, de principiis naturæ, de principio in-
dividuationis, de universalibus*, etc.). His *Summa theologiæ*,
which gradually eclipsed the *Sentences* of Peter the Lombard,
forms the basis of the dogmatic teachings of the Church

The philosophy of St. Thomas has no other aim than the
faithful reproduction of the principles of the Lyceum. We are
therefore interested, not so much in the contents, as in the
Neo-Latin form in which the ideas of the Stagirite are expressed. Our modern philosophical vocabulary is in part derived from the system of St. Thomas.

Philosophy proper or the first philosophy has for its object
being as such. There are two kinds of beings: objective, real,
essential beings, and beings that are mere abstractions of
thought or negations, such, for example, as poverty, blindness,
and imperfection in general. Poverty, blindness, and privation exist; they are entities, but not essences.[1] Essences, substances, or beings properly so called are, in turn, divided into
simple or pure essences, and essences composed of form and
matter. There is but *one* simple essence or pure form: God.
All the rest are composed of matter and form.

[1] *Opusculum de ente et essentia.*

Matter and form are both beings; they differ from each other in that form is actualized, while matter is as yet merely potential. In a general sense, matter is everything that can be, everything that exists in possibility. According as the possible thing is a substance or an accident, metaphysics distinguishes between potential, substantial being (example: the human seed is a potential man) and potential accident (example: man is a potentiality of intelligence). Potentiality by itself does not exist; potentiality for something exists as a relatively independent subject. The form is what gives being to a thing.[1] According as this thing is a substance or an accident, we have to deal with a substantial form or an accidental form. The union of matter and form is generation, which is, in turn, substantial generation or accidental generation. All forms, God excepted, are united with matter and individualized by it, constituting genera, species, and individuals.[2]

Only the form of forms remains immaterial and is subject neither to generation nor decay. The more imperfect a form is, the more it tends to increase the number of individuals realizing it; the more perfect a form is, the less it multiplies its individuals. The form of forms is no longer a species composed of separate individuals, but a single being within which all differences of person are constantly merged in the unity of essence. Since God alone is pure form, without matter and consequently without imperfection (matter being that which does not yet exist, or the lack of being), God alone is the perfect and complete knowledge of things.[3] He possesses absolute truth because he *is* absolute truth. Truth is the agreement of thought with its object. In man, there is more or less agreement between thoughts and objects; they are, however, never identical. God's ideas not only exactly reproduce the things, they *are* the things themselves. Things first *exist*, and then man thinks them: in God, thought precedes the things, which exist only *because* and *as* he thinks them. Hence there is no

---

[1] *Opusc. de principiis naturæ.*   [2] *Id.*, c. 3.

[3] *Summa theologiæ*, I, question 4.

difference in him between thought and being; and, since this identity of knowledge and its object constitutes truth, God *is* truth itself.

The demonstration of the existence of God is the first and principal task of philosophy. Philosophy could not, however, perform this task, or even have a conception of God, had not the Creator first revealed himself to man in Jesus Christ. In order that the human mind might direct its efforts towards its real goal, it was necessary for God to point it out, that is, to reveal himself to humanity at the very beginning. No philosophy is legitimate that does not take revelation for its starting-point and return to it as its final goal: it is true only when it is *ancilla ecclesiæ* (servant of the Church), and, in so far as Aristotle is the precursor of Christ in the scientific sphere, *ancilla Aristotelis* (servant of Aristotle). The Church of God is the goal towards which all things tend here below.

Nature is a hierarchy in which each stage is the *form* of the lower stage and the *matter* of the higher stage. The hierarchy of bodies is completed in the natural life of man, and this life, in turn, becomes the foundation, and, in a certain measure, the material for a higher life, the spiritual life, which is developed in the shadow of the Church and nourished by its Word and its sacraments, as the natural life is nourished by the bread of the earth. The realm of nature is therefore to the realm of grace, the natural man to the Christian, philosophy to theology, matter to the sacrament, the State to the Church, and the Emperor to the Pope, what the means are to the end, the plan to the execution, the potency to the actuality.

The universe, which consists of the two realms of nature and of grace, is the best possible world. For God in his infinite wisdom conceived the best of worlds; he could not have created a less perfect world without detracting from his wisdom. To say that God conceived perfection and realized an imperfect world would presuppose an opposition between knowledge and will, between the ideal principle and the real principle of things, which contradicts thought as well as faith. Hence the

divine will is not a will of indifference, and the freedom of
God, far from being synonymous with caprice and chance, is
identical with necessity.

In spite of seeming contradictions, the same is true of the
human will. Just as the intellect has a principle (reason) which
it cannot discard without ceasing to be itself, the will has a
principle from which it cannot deviate without ceasing to be
free: the good. The will *necessarily* tends to the good; but
sensuality tends to evil and thus paralyzes the efforts of the
will. Hence sin arises, which has its source, not in the freedom
of indifference or of choice, but in sensuality.[1] There is moral
predestination, but not arbitrary predestination, for the divine
will itself is subordinated to reason. Determinism extended to
God loses the offensive character which it had in the theology
of St. Augustine.

The system of St. Thomas marks both the climax of the
development of Catholic metaphysics and the beginning of its
fall. Before the days of St. Thomas, Scholastic philosophy
had shown symptoms of decline; in him it shines with a light
before which the most illustrious names pale. His devotion
to the Church and its interests, his philosophical talents, which
he employs in the service of Catholicism, and his faith in the
perfect harmony between the dogma and philosophical truth
as set forth in Aristotle, make him the most typical doctor of
the Church after St. Augustine and St. Anselm. But his faith,
ardent though it be, does not possess the strength of an unshakable conviction; it is rather a willed faith, an energetic
will constantly struggling against the thousand difficulties
which reflection throws in its way. From St. Thomas downward, reason and Catholic faith, official theology and philosophy, are differentiated and become more or less clearly conscious of their respective principles and interests. Metaphysics continued, for a long time, to be subject to theology; but
though dependent, it henceforth had a separate existence, a
sphere of activity of its own.

[1] *Summa theologiæ*, question 82; *Contra gentiles*, III.

Philosophy proper receives its official sanction, as it were, by the organization of the four Parisian faculties, an event which occurred during the lifetime of St. Thomas. This period marks the decline of Scholasticism. The theologians themselves, with John Duns Scotus at their head, do all they can do to hasten it.

§ 40. Duns Scotus

JOHN DUNS SCOTUS of Dunston (Northumberland), a monk of the order of St. Francis, professor of philosophy and theology at Oxford and Paris, was the most industrious among the Schoolmen. Although he died at the age of thirty-four (1308), his writings fill a dozen volumes.

We have just seen how philosophy was officially recognized as a science distinct from theology. During the times of Duns Scotus, i. e., about the end of the thirteenth century, philosophy formed an independent science by the side of theology, and even dared to oppose the latter. The philosophers, said Duns Scotus, differ from the theologians as to whether man has any need of acquiring, by supernatural means, knowledge which his reason cannot attain by natural means. This statement not only shows the existence of a philosophy that is independent of theology, but the disagreement which has existed between philosophers and theologians ever since.

Duns Scotus, like a genuine Schoolman, occupies a position between the two camps. With the theologians he recognizes the need of revelation; but he agrees with the philosophers that St. Augustine is wrong in assuming that man can know *absolutely* nothing of God without supernatural revelation. With the theologians he declares that the Bible and the teachings of the Church are the supreme norms of philosophic thought; but he is, on the other hand, a philosopher and a rationalist to the extent of believing in the authority of the Bible and of ecclesiastical tradition, only because *the doctrines of the Bible and the Church conform to reason.* Hence reason is, in his eyes, the highest authority, and the sacred texts have for him but a derived, conditional, and relative authority. With this as his guiding principle, he does what no Schoolman had done before him: he attempts to prove the credibility of Holy Writ, and, in choosing his arguments, he evidently gives the preference to the internal proofs.

The more familiar we become with Scholastic literature, the less apt are we to exaggerate the progress of free thought from the thirteenth to the nineteenth centuries. The historians who endeavor to trace all modern negations to the Reformation ignore, or affect to ignore, the fact that in the ninth century the Catholic Scotus Erigena denied eternal punishment; that in the twelfth, the Catholic Abelard declared the teachings of the Greek philosophers to be superior to those of the Old Testament; that in the thirteenth, a great number of Catholics refused to believe in the miraculous conception and in the resurrection of Christ; that in the same century, or two hundred years before the Reformation, and at a time when the power of the Holy See was at its height, St. Thomas and Duns Scotus found themselves obliged to prove, with all the arts of logic, the need of revelation and the credibility of the Divine Word; finally, that these submissive, devoted, and orthodox doctors of the Church combined with their Christian convictions a freedom of thought, the like of which is but rarely met with in the Protestant theology of the seventeenth century.

The Thomistic system borders on pantheism, while the philosophy of Duns Scotus is decidedly Pelagian; the illustrious Dominican sacrifices the freedom of the individual to the great glory of God; while the Franciscan doctor believes that he is rendering God a no less signal service by exalting the individual and free-will at the expense of grace.

Duns Scotus serves the order to which he belongs as faithfully as his God and the Church. The great mediæval orders are the forerunners of the theological parties of Protestantism. They are, at present, merged in the indivisible unity of the Roman orthodoxy; during the period of which we are speaking, they were real parties, opposed to each other, not only on practical questions, but on points of doctrine which do not, even now, strike us as secondary. The rivalry between these two orders often infused new life into Scholasticism. The contest between Duns Scotus and the Scotists against Thomism really represents a struggle for Church supremacy between two powerful orders. The glory reflected upon the Franciscan order by St. Bonaventura was dimmed by the fame of the Dominicans, Albert the Great and Thomas of Aquin. Jealous of the good name of his order, Duns Scotus endeavors to expose and refute what he calls the errors of Thomism. Thomas remaining true to the dogmatic and didactic tenets of his order, is the apostle of faith and grace. Duns Scotus, whose heart is also filled with the spirit of his order, — a spirit of living and practical piety, — becomes the apostle of action, meritorious works, and human freedom. With an acumen that is wholly in keeping with his title, *doctor subtilis*, he undertakes the criticism of St. Thomas.

Thomistic determinism, assuming as it does the superiority of the intellect over the will, has the true ring of Catholic philosophy. By bending the will beneath the yoke of an absolute principle, it humiliates the self-love of the individual, destroys his confidence in his own powers, and makes him conscious of his insignificance. But when the foundations of the system are laid bare they are found to be very weak. Thus, on the one hand, it makes God himself a relative being, whose will is the slave of his intelligence. On the other hand, it does more than humiliate the individual: it discourages him and drives him to despair or moral indifference. Should the Church adopt this system, it would without fail soon cease to be the sanctuary of virtue and the mother of saints. Hence the *primacy* of the intelligence must be opposed by that of the will,[1] and for determinism we must substitute the true philosophy

[1] The *voluntarism* of Duns Scotus is to the *intellectualism* of Thomas what the Kant of the *Critique of Practical Reason* is to the Kant of the *Critique of Pure Reason*, and what the *panthelism* of Schopenhauer is to the *panlogism* of Hegel.

and the real thought of Aristotle: the doctrine of divine and human liberty.

If we would not confuse the true God with the Fate or the *natura naturans* (nature as a principle or cause) of the Neo-Platonists, we cannot hold, with the Thomists, that the world is the necessary product of his essence, his intelligence, or his will. God created the world by an act of freedom. It would have been possible for him not to create it. His will was not inclined that way by any higher principle, for it is itself the highest principle of divine acts. The existence of the world, far from being necessary, is the free effect of the free-will of God. Abelard is therefore wrong in assuming that God could create only what he created, and that what he created he created necessarily; and Thomas is in error when he teaches that the world is necessarily the best possible world. God does not create all that he can create; he creates only what he desires to call into existence.

The first cause of things, the divine will, is consequently also the supreme law of created spirits. Goodness, justice, and the moral law are absolute, only in so far as they are willed by God; if they were absolute independently of the divine will, God's power would be limited by a law not depending on him, and he would no longer be the highest freedom or, consequently, the Supreme Being. In reality, the good is therefore the good, only because it is God's pleasure that it should be so. God could, by virtue of his supreme liberty, supersede the moral law which now governs us by a new law, as he superseded the Mosaic law by that of the Gospel; above all, he could — and who knows but what he really does in many cases? — exempt us from doing good without our ceasing, on that account, to be good. In the creation as in the government of the world, God knows no other law, no other rule, no other principle, than his own freedom. And it is because he is free to exempt us, in case he so desires, from carrying out any particular law of the moral code that the Church in turn has the right to grant dispensations. If God is not absolutely free in this matter, as he is in all things; if he is, as Thomas of Aquin claims, a being absolutely determined in his will by his supreme wisdom, what becomes of the right of indulgences? Like God, man is free; the Fall did not deprive him of free-will; he has *formal* freedom, i. e., he may will or not will; and he has *material* freedom, i. e., he can will A or will B (freedom of choice or indifference).

These doctrines, though diametrically opposed to St. Augustine's, could not be disagreeable to the Church, the Pelagian tendencies of which they reflected and encouraged. But they concealed a danger, and the Church, which failed to canonize Duns Scotus, seems to have appreciated it. By his emphatic affirmation of individual liberty, the subtle doctor proclaimed a new principle, an anti-authoritative power, which grew from century to century, and finally led to the emancipation of the religious conscience and the downfall of ecclesiastical tradition as the supreme authority in matters of faith and conscience. So, too, on the subject of universals, Duns Scotus approaches nominalism and empiricism, though striving to remain true to the realistic and rationalistic system upheld by the Church. All his sympathies are, at bottom, for the individual; for the will is his principle; and though reason is common to all, the will is what characterizes the individual. The question of individuation is his favorite problem. His contemporary, Henry Goethals,[1] following the example of William of Champeaux, regarded the principle of individuation as a mere negation; while St. Thomas based it on matter (the non-being). Duns Scotus, however, declares it to be a positive principle, and gives it the name of *hæcceitas*, or individuality. The individual is, according to him, the sum of two equally positive and real principles: the *quidditas* (the universal, or the type common to the individuals of one and the same species) and the *hæcceitas*, the principle of the individuality or of the difference of individuals. The universal has no reality apart from the individual, nor the individual apart

[1] 1217–1293.

from the universal. Reality is found in the union of the two principles, of the ideal and the real, that is, in the individual.

By his doctrines of individual liberty and individuality Duns Scotus paves the way for the nominalism of his disciple Occam. His doctrine of accidental creation hastens the rupture between science and the authoritative rationalism of the Church, and the advent of modern empiricism; for if the laws of nature and the moral law itself are contingent, all science and morality itself depend on experience as their only basis. To place the will in the first rank in metaphysics and reason in the second, means to subordinate reasoning to the methods of observation and experience. Duns Scotus not only hastens the breach between science and dogma; but the breach seems to be already made when, in his *Quæstiones subtilissimæ*, he rejects innate ideas, and declares the proof of the immortality of the soul and of the existence of God to be impossible from the standpoint of science.

B. Nominalistic Peripateticism

§ 41. Reappearance of Nominalism. Durand, Occam, Buridan, D'Ailly

The distance from the conceptualism of Vincent of Beauvais, Thomas of Aquin, and Duns Scotus to nominalism is not great. Indeed, the semi-realism of Duns Scotus resembles the doctrine of Roscellinus more closely than that of Champeaux. WILLIAM DURAND of Saint-Pourçain,[1] first a disciple of St. Thomas, then influenced by the doctrines of Scotus, comes still nearer to nominalism in formulating the following thesis: *To exist means to be an individual.* Finally, the Franciscan WILLIAM OF OCCAM,[2] the precursor and fellow-countryman of John Locke, openly antagonizes realism as an absurd system. According to the realists, he says, the universal exists in several things at once; now the same thing cannot exist simultaneously in several different things; hence the universal

[1] Born in Auvergne, died 1332, Bishop of Meaux.   [2] Died 1343.

is not a thing, a reality, but a mere sign that serves to designate several similar things, a word; and there is nothing real except the individual.

Scepticism is the necessary consequence of nominalism, which has already been outlined in § 33. Science has for its object the general, the universal, the necessary. The science of man, let us say in the spirit of Plato, does not deal with Peter for the sake of Peter, or with Paul for the sake of Paul; it studies Peter and Paul in order to know what man is. It is the universal man, the species man, whom it seeks in the individual. The same is true of all sciences. Now, if the universal is a mere word having no objective reality, and if the individual alone is real, then there can be no anthropology, nor any science. We can know and tell what both Peter and Paul are; we can study each particular plant and animal; but the universal man, plant, and animal can never become objects of science, because they nowhere exist. Hence, nominalism is sceptical of science; its motto agrees with that of Protagoras: *The individual is the measure of all things*.

The highest science, theology, does not escape William's sceptical criticisms. He accepts the teaching of his master, and declares that it is impossible to demonstrate the existence and unity of God. The ontological and cosmological arguments are equally weak, in his judgment, and the necessity for the existence of a first cause seems to him to be a purely hypothetical necessity. Indeed, reason may invariably oppose the no less probable theory of the infinite causal series. Hence, there can be no rational or scientific theology; and if the science pursued by such thinkers as Origen, Augustine, Anselmus, and Thomas is impossible, then Scholasticism itself becomes a mere heap of barren hypotheses. Science belongs to God, faith to man.

Let the doctors of the Church recognize the futility of their speculations, and become interpreters of practical truth and propagators of the faith! Let the Church abandon this empty, terrestrial science! Let her cast off all the worldly elements with which she has been tainted by her contact with the world; let her reform and return to the simplicity, purity, and holiness of the Apostolic times! Though Occam sided with the King in the quarrel between Philip the Fair and the Holy See; and though he fled from France and offered his services to Louis of Bavaria,[1] who was also at loggerheads with the Vicar of Christ, he was neither hostile nor indifferent to the Church. On the contrary, like all true followers of St. Francis, he felt a deep love for his spiritual mother. And because he loved her, he desired to see her great and holy and removed from the harmful influences of the world; he could not approve of the Pope's interference with the temporal affairs of the European States. It was his devotion to the Church that forced him to make common cause with the enemies of the Holy Father.

Nominalism not only weakens the alliance between faith and science; it also attempts to sever the bond which had for centuries united the Church with the world. Its reappearance not only marks the decline of Scholasticism; simultaneously with it, we notice the first symptoms of the decadence of the Papal power, to which the European monarchs henceforth offer a successful resistance. The nominalism of Occam, though sincere in its desire to promote the welfare of the Church, nevertheless resembles all philosophy; it mirrors the ruling purpose of the age, i. e., the necessity on the part of the secular powers, the states, the nations, the languages, intellectual culture, the arts, the sciences, and philosophy, to shake off the yoke of Christian Rome. From the reappearance of nominalism we date the first beginnings of national life and modern languages, and the opposition to the political, religious, and literary centralization, to which the heir of Cæsarean traditions had subjected Europe. Nominalism therefore conceals beneath its seeming devotion to the Church and its pious con-

---

[1] He is said to have addressed the following remark to Louis: *Tu me defendas gladio, ego te defendam calamo* (You defend me with the sword, I defend you with a pen).

tempt for science, a mass of tendencies hostile to Catholicism. And the Church gives it the same reception which she had given Aristotle a century before: she condemns it. But the heresy had taken deep root this time; it satisfied the political, intellectual, and religious strivings of the epoch too well to be suppressed.

The doctrines of Durand and Occam gave the signal for the struggle between the realists and nominalists. The conflict raged during the fourteenth and fifteenth centuries, it transformed the universities into veritable fields of battle — the expression is not a metaphor — and continued down to the Renaissance and Reformation. Realism had distinguished followers during the fourteenth century, e. g., WALTER BUR-LEIGH, who defended it in the name of science and philosophy; THOMAS OF BRADWARDINE,[1] Archbishop of Canterbury, who upheld it in the name of the faith, and accused Occam of Pelagianism; THOMAS OF STRASBURG,[2] and MARSILIUS OF INGHEN,[3] the first rector of the University of Heidelberg, who tried to reconcile the opposing doctrines. But even in its conceptualistic form, it attracted only the most speculative minds; the clear and well-defined conceptions of nominalism appealed more and more to what is called common-sense. In spite of the obstinate resistance of the realistic party and of the government which this party had succeeded in interesting in its behalf, the teachings of Occam eventually made their way into the Sorbonne, where they were ably reproduced by JOHN BURIDAN,[4] and more or less modified in the dogmatic sense, by PIERRE D'AILLY,[5] *the eagle of France.*

Nominalism represented the reformatory tendencies of the times, and could not but triumph.

---

[1] Died 1349.   [2] Died 1357.   [3] Died 1396.

[4] Died about 1360. He wrote *Summa dialect.*, Paris, 1487; *Comp. log.*, Venice, 1480; and a series of commentaries on Aristotle, published in Paris and Oxford.

[5] Died 1425. *Quæstiones super quatuor l. sent.*, Strasburg, 1490; *Tractatus et sermones*, 1490.

§ 42. Downfall of Scholasticism. Revival of the Interest in Nature and Experimental Science. Roger Bacon. Mysticism

In vain did the nominalist Pierre d'Ailly struggle against the conclusions of Occam, and attempt to defend Scholasticism against the claims of scepticism. The alliance between the essential elements of Scholasticism had been seriously weakened. It is true, Occam, Durand, Buridan, and Gabriel Biel,[1] are sceptics only in metaphysics; still by holding that we can *know* nothing of God, Providence, the Fall, Redemption, Resurrection, and Judgment, and that we must be content with *believing* all these doctrines, they make them uncertain and problematical, and involuntarily advance the cause of heterodoxy. They themselves give up science for faith; others, who are less devoted to the Church, gradually abandon faith and become free-thinkers. Thus in 1347, JOHN OF MERCURIA, a member of the Cistercian order, was condemned for having taught: (1) that everything that happens in the world, the evil as well as the good, is effected by the divine will; (2) that sin is a good rather than an evil; (3) that he who succumbs to an irresistible temptation does not sin. Thus also in 1348, a bachelor of theology, NICOLAS OF AUTRICURIA, had the boldness to present the following theses to the Sorbonne: (1) We shall easily and quickly reach certain knowledge, if we abandon Aristotle and his commentaries, and devote ourselves to the study of nature itself. (2) It is true, we conceive God as the most real being, but we cannot know whether such a being exists or not. (3) The universe is infinite and eternal; for a passage from non-being to being is inconceivable. — Such expressions of free thought were as yet uncommon, but for that very reason all the more remarkable.

Speculative philosophy and its anti-scholastic strivings received a powerful ally in the experimental sciences, which were revived by the study of Aristotle's works on physics and

[1] Professor at Tübingen, died 1495.

by the influence of the Arabian schools of Spain; to these we owe our system of numerals, the elementary principles of algebra and chemistry, and our knowledge of the astronomical traditions of the Orient. The instruction offered in Christian schools was purely dialectical and formal; it trained the mind for discussion, but left it an utter blank. As early as the thirteenth century, the Franciscan monk ROGER BACON,[1] a professor at Oxford, recognized the serious imperfections in the system, and conceived the plan of reforming it by the introduction of the sciences. His three works, *Opus majus*, *Opus minus*, and *Opus tertium*, the fruit of twenty years' investigation, to which he devoted his entire fortune, constitute the most remarkable scientific monument of the Middle Ages. Not only does he call attention to the barrenness of the scholastic *logomachies*, the necessity of observing nature and of studying the languages, but he recognizes, even more clearly than his namesake of the sixteenth century, the capital importance of mathematical deduction as an auxiliary to the experimental method. Nay, more than that; he enriches science, and especially optics, with new and fruitful theories. But his scientific reforms were premature in the year 1267, which marks the appearance of his *Opus majus*. His plan was submitted to the court of Rome, but owing to the intrigues of the obscurantist party, it fell flat, and procured for Roger twelve years of confinement. The seed sown by this most clear-sighted thinker of the Middle Ages upon the barren soil of Scholasticism did not spring up until three centuries later.

Albert the Great (§ 38), though not attaining to Bacon's eminence, shows a marked preference for the study of nature, which he himself, like his age, confused with magic. During the same epoch, Don RAYMOND LULLUS[2] of Palma, a curious mixture of theologian and naturalist, missionary and troubadour, endeavored to popularize the science of the Ara-

---

[1] *Doctor mirabilis*, 1214–1294. Bridges, *The Life and Work of Roger Bacon*, London, 1914.

[2] 1234–1315.

bians by means of a universal method, which he called *ars magna*. His teachings, which were recorded in numerous writings, gained for him, during the succeeding centuries, enthusiastic followers, whose chief concern was to discover the philosopher's stone and to make gold. Assisted by such trifles, the human mind gradually returned to the observation of reality, and came to regard nature as an object of study no less important than Aristotle. About 1400, the physician RAYMOND OF SABUNDE,[1] a professor at Toulouse, had the boldness to prefer to books made by human hands the *book of nature, which being the work of God is intelligible to all.*

The official philosophy, with its barren formalism, its ignorance of reality, and its hopeless indolence, had arrayed against it thought chafing under the yoke of the ecclesiastical Aristotle and yearning for progress and freedom, and natural science, which foreshadowed its future grandeur in the rudimentary form of magic. Finally, it also gave offense to religious feeling and mystical piety because of its inability to supply the soul with substantial nourishment and to inspire the Christian life with an ardent love for goodness. Mysticism had for centuries been the ally of Scholastic speculation; in Scotus Erigena, the sages of St. Victor, and St. Bonaventura, it tempered the cold reasonings of the School with its glowing warmth, and descended upon their barren logic like a refreshing dew. It widened the narrow circle of an intolerant orthodoxy by laying greater stress upon faith itself as a subjective phenomenon and the animating principle of the soul, than upon the object of faith. But the more deeply Scholasticism became absorbed in formal disputes and childish discussions, the more distasteful and antagonistic it became to the religious spirit which longed for a life in God and was stifled by the categories of Aristotle.

Some mystics, like ST. BERNARD[2] and Walter of St. Victor, inveigh against logic because they consider it dangerous to the dogmas of the Church. Others, who are less scrupulous in

---

[1] Died 1436.   [2] 1091-1158.

this respect, but equally anxious to possess God, are carried away by the ardor of their religious sentiments to the extreme conclusions of pantheistic speculation. According to them, dialectics is a labyrinth in which the soul, instead of reaching God, is farther and farther removed from him, and finally loses him altogether. Feeling, they believe, brings us directly into communion with God; with one bound we overcome the obstacles of discursive thought and are carried to the centre of things and the source of being, where self-consciousness is merged in the consciousness of God. According to some, feeling alone will transport the soul by enchantment to the summit of existence and the source of life. So ECKHART,[1] the Dominican provincial of Cologne and a typical pantheistic mystic. Others, though seeking to be united with God, do not expect to reach their goal except after long and wearisome trials; hence, to the love of God they add the love of goodness and moral struggle as indispensable conditions of the Christian *nirvana* to which they aspire. To this class belong JOHN TAULER,[2] a Dominican preacher of Cologne and Strasburg, JOHN WESSEL,[3] and THOMAS À KEMPIS,[4] the supposed author of the *Imitation of Christ;* all of these are indebted for the new element in their teachings to the wholly Pelagian influence of nominalism. This influence is still more pronounced in the Frenchman JOHN GERSON,[5] the chancellor, and Nicolas of Clemanges,[6] the rector of the University of Paris, whose mysticism is nothing but moral asceticism, and differs essentially from its German namesake. But beneath these different forms lurks one and the same anti-scholastic tendency, one and the same spirit of reform.

§ 43. The Revival of Letters [7]

Corresponding to each of the elements of progress just mentioned, we notice a group of highly important historical facts,

---

[1] Died about 1300.   [2] Died 1361.   [3] Died 1489.
[4] Died 1471.   [5] Died 1429.   [6] Died 1440.

[7] See Hudson, "The Story of the Renaissance," *Cambridge Modern History*, vol. I; Symonds, *The Renaissance in Italy;* Burckhardt, *The Culture of the Renaissance,* tr. by Middleman.

which give a decided impetus to these tendencies. Free thought eagerly seizes upon the literary masterpieces of antiquity, which are made known by Greek emigrants, and which the timely invention of printing helps to render accessible to all. The scientific spirit of the age and its naturalistic bent, admirably assisted by the invention of the compass and the telescope, triumphs in the discovery of America and of the Solar System. The contemplation of these new and infinite worlds arouses feelings of enthusiasm and confidence which become more and more dangerous to Scholasticism and the authoritative system of the Church. At the same time, the religious spirit receives encouragement from the great reform movement of the sixteenth century, inaugurated by the literary awakening in the fifteenth.

Under the auspices of the Byzantine government, which survived the ruin of the ancient world, the Hellenic peninsula preserved, in antiquated and pedantic form, the literary and philosophical traditions of antiquity, its taste for classical learning, and its love for the great philosophers, Plato and Aristotle. Here the writings of these thinkers were studied in the original at a time when Greek was not only a dead language but absolutely unknown in the Occident. A kind of worship grew up around them, and the more impossible it seemed to surpass them, the greater admiration they inspired. As long as such stars and their satellites shone in the heavens of Byzantium and Athens, the taste for learned studies and free speculation could not disappear from Grecian soil, and even the theological pedantry of the Emperors could not destroy it. In the main, therefore, the Orient exerted a wholesome and liberalizing influence on the Occident.

In a certain sense, this influence goes back to the period of the Crusades. By an "irony of fate," not infrequent in history, the Catholic Church failed to reap the expected fruits of these expeditions. The Orient had been invaded in the name of the Roman faith, and the Crusaders brought back nothing but heresies. The futile efforts made by the Western

Church, during the first half of the fifteenth century, to bring about a reconciliation with the Eastern Church resulted similarly. The influence of the Greek Orient was beneficial to the Occident, but injurious to the hierarchical tendencies of Catholicism. Some centuries before, the Calabrians, Barlaam and Leontius Pilatus, and, after them, Dante, Petrarch, and Boccaccio had cultivated a taste for Greek literature in Italy; but the Orient did not exercise a direct and lasting influence upon Europe until after 1438, when the Byzantine Church sent her scholars to Florence. The object of their mission was the reconciliation of the two churches; but they became the missionaries of classical civilization from the Orient to the Empire of the Popes.

Greek scholars flocked to Italy in still greater numbers, causing a veritable migration from the Orient, when Byzantium and the last remains of the Eastern Empire fell into the hands of the Turks (1453). This event raised Italy to the position which she had occupied in literature, art, and philosophy two thousand years before; she again became *Magna Græcia*. In the year 1440, the Greek scholar GEORGIUS GEMISTUS PLETHO, an ambassador to the Council of Florence, whom the munificence of Cosmo dei Medici had succeeded in detaining in Italy, founded a Platonic Academy in Florence. His fellow-countryman BESSARION succeeded him in the government of the School and in the work of propaganda. He defended the Academy against his compatriots Gennadius, Theodorus Gaza, and Georgius of Trebizond, followers of the Lyceum, and gained a large number of Italian adherents for Plato, notwithstanding the opposition of the Peripatetics and their orthodox supporters.

The fellow-countrymen of Dante were completely fascinated with the Greek language. It was studied with the passionate ardor peculiar to the Italian people. Philosophy became the all-important science. The Venetian HERMOLAUS BARBARUS, LAURENTIUS VALLA of Rome, and ANGELUS POLITIANUS were zealous disciples of the exiles of Byzantium. The love of ancient literature and the dislike for the language of the School extended even to the leaders of the Church. The Cardinal NICOLAS OF CUSA (Kuss[1]), who possessed the qualities of a Bruno and a Descartes, had the courage openly to criticise the errors of Scholasticism, and recommended the philosophy of Plato, which he identified with the Pythagorean theory of numbers, as in every way preferable to the reigning system. The wave of classicism even reached the throne of St. Peter; and it is a well-known fact that Leo X and his secretary Bembo greatly preferred Cicero to the Vulgate. The religion of Virgil and Homer superseded the religion of Christ in the hearts of the high dignitaries of the Church and the secular scholars, poets, and artists; the joyful Olympus was exchanged for the severe Golgotha; Jehovah, Jesus, and Mary became Jupiter, Apollo, and Venus; the saints of the Church were identified with the gods of Greece and Rome, — in a word, the times returned to paganism.

MARSILIUS FICINUS,[2] a pupil of the Florentine Academy, continues the struggle begun by Bessarion in behalf of Plato. For him, Platonism is the quintessence of human wisdom, the key to Christianity, and the only efficient means of rejuvenating and spiritualizing the Catholic doctrine. As the editor, translator, and commentator of Plato and the Alexandrians, Marsilius Ficinus is one of the fathers of modern classical philology as well as of the philosophical Renaissance. An equally distinguished person is the Count John PICO OF MIRANDOLA

---

[1] Diocese of Treves. Cusanus, whose real name was Krebs, died in 1464. His *Works* appeared in three folio volumes, Paris, 1514 [German transl. of his most important writings, by F. A. Scharpff, Freiburg, 1862]. The best known of his treatises, *De docta ignorantia*, is found in the first volume. The second, which contains his treatises on astronomy and mathematics, makes him the forerunner of Copernicus and of the reform of the calendar. He anticipates Bruno by his doctrine of the absolute unity-God, and Schelling and Hegel by his conception of the *coincidence of contradictories*.

[2] A Florentine, 1433–1499. Florence and the century of the literary renaissance also produced the great politician and Italian patriot, Nicolo Macchiavelli (1469–1527), the author of *Il principe*, etc. [works translated by C. E. Detmold, Boston, 1883], whose system is based on the principle that *the end justifies the means* (separation of politics from morals).

(1463–1494). Pico recommends Hebrew in addition to the study of the Greek language and literature; believing, as he does, that the Jewish Cabala is as important a source of wisdom as Plato and the New Testament. He bequeaths his love of philology and his Cabalistic prejudices to his nephew, John Francis Pico of Mirandola, a less talented but more pious man than his uncle, and to the German REUCHLIN, who, upon returning to the Empire, becomes the founder of classical and Hebrew philology in his country, and by combating Hochstraten and the obscurantists paves the way for the spiritual deliverance of his native land.

§ 44. Neo-Platonism. Theosophy. Magic

The mixture of new ideas and old superstitions gives rise to a number of curious theories, partially modelled after Neo-Platonic doctrines, which represent the stages, as it were, by which the philosophical and scientific mind gains its independence. They may be classed under the title *theosophy*. Theosophy shares theology's belief in the supernatural and philosophy's faith in nature. It forms an intermediate stage, a kind of transition, between theology and pure philosophy. It does not attain to the dignity of modern experimental science; for it rests upon an inner revelation, which is superior to sensible experience and reasoning. It does not study nature for nature's sake, but in order to discover the traces of the mysterious Being which nature hides as well as reveals. Now, in order to discover it, theosophy needs a key of Sesame, a no less mysterious instrument than the object of its studies. It therefore enters upon a search for secret doctrines, and greedily seizes and utilizes whatever is offered in this line. Hence the enthusiasm which the teachings of the Jewish Cabala and of Neo-Platonism arouse in Pico of Mirandola, who compares them with those of the Bible, and in Reuchlin, who exalts them in his *De verbo mirifico*[1] and his *De arte cabalistica*.[2]

Theosophy is not content with fathoming the great mystery;

---

[1] Bâle, 1494.   [2] Hagenau, 1517.

it does not regard it as enough to know nature; it desires what Francis Bacon afterwards desired: to rule over it, to master it, to control it. And just as it claims to reach a knowledge of things by means of secret doctrines, it boasts of being able to control them by secret arts, by formulas and mysterious practices. That is to say, it necessarily becomes magic.[1] Magic is based upon the Neo-Platonic principle that the world is a hierarchy of divine forces, a system of agencies forming an ascending and descending scale, in which the higher agencies command and the lower ones obey. Hence, in order to govern nature and to change it according to his wishes, the theosophist must be united with the higher forces on which the sublunary sphere depends; and since, according to Aristotle and Ptolemy, the heavenly powers or the sidereal agencies are such higher forces, astrology plays an important part in the lucubrations of the theosophist.

This union of Platonism, or rather Pythagoreanism, with magic is best exemplified in Reuchlin's disciple, AGRIPPA of Nettesheim,[2] the author of a treatise, *De vanitate scientiarum*, directed against scholastic dogmatism; in Jerome CARDANUS,[3] a noted physician and mathematician, whose teachings, a singular mixture of astrological superstitions and liberal ideas, are stamped as anti-Christian by the orthodoxy of the period; in the learned Swiss physician Theophrastus of Hohenheim, called PARACELSUS,[4] who shares the belief of Pico, Reuchlin, and Agrippa in the inner light "that is much superior to bestial reason," and their love for the Cabala, whose doctrines his system identifies with those of Christianity. From the *Adam cadmon*, who is none other than Christ, spring, according to Paracelsus, the soul of the world and the many spirits governed by it, the Sylvans, Undines, Gnomes, and Salaman-

---

[1] Cf. §§ 25 and 26.　　[2] Born at Cologne, 1487; died at Grenoble, 1535.

[3] Of Pavia, 1501–1576. Cardanus is remembered in the history of mathematics by his rule for the solution of equations of the third degree (*Ars magna sive de regulis algebraicis*, published 1543, the date of the appearance of Copernicus's *Celestial Revolutions*).

[4] 1493–1541.

ders, and whoever, through absolute obedience to the divine will, is united with the *Adam cadmon* and with the heavenly intelligences, is the best physician, and possesses the universal panacea, — the philosopher's stone. With a great deal of superstition and a little charlatanism, the precursors of the scientific reformation combine a keen love of nature and a profound aversion to Scholasticism, which their opposition largely assists in overthrowing.

§ 45. Aristotle versus Aristotle, or the Liberal Peripatetics. Stoics. Epicureans. Sceptics

While Pletho and Bessarion were preaching Plato, Genna-dius, Georgius of Trebizond, and Theodorus Gaza, ardent Peripatetics and adversaries of the Academy of Florence, introduced the learned Italian public to the study of the texts of Aristotle. The better they became acquainted with the words of the great philosopher, the more they recognized the notable differences between the real Aristotle and the Aristotle of Scholasticism; and while Plato, Plotinus, and Proclus attracted the more imaginative minds, the positive thinkers, who were no less hostile to traditional philosophy than the Academicians of Florence, appealed from Aristotle misinterpreted to the authentic Aristotle of the Greek texts. The result was noteworthy. The system which had been regarded as the strongest support of the Church was found to disagree with her on several essential points. A liberal Peripatetic school, chiefly composed of laymen, was formed in opposition to official Peripateticism. Although maintaining a prudent reserve towards the Church, these liberal Peripatetics assisted in undermining her authoritative system by laying bare, one after another, the heresies of the philosopher whom she shielded with blind tenderness. To convict an author of heresy whom the Church had declared infallible, was to make the Church fallible; was to attack her supreme authority in the field of thought; was to respond to the emancipation of conscience, taking place beyond the mountains, with the emancipation of the intellect.

In his treatise *On the Immortality of the Soul*, the leader of the new school,[1] PETRUS POMPONATIUS (Pomponazzi[2]), boldly raises the question whether immortality is a corollary of Aristotle's principles, and, with Alexander of Aphrodisias,[3] answers it in the negative. He thereby, on the one hand, ignores the authority of St. Thomas, who had declared that the philosophy of the Stagirite was favorable to this fundamental dogma of religion; and, on the other, denies the doctrine itself; for both Pomponatius as well as the Church regarded the philosophy of Aristotle, not as a system among other systems, but as the true philosophy. Pomponatius, who had to make his peace with Leo X in order to escape the anathemas of the Church, declares that he personally believes in immortality, because he accepts the authority of the Church in matters of religion; but it is evident from the manner in which he refutes the objections raised against the opposite view that he does not believe in it.

Say what you will, he writes, it cannot be held that all men achieve intellectual perfection; while moral perfection does not consist in an ideal that cannot be realized on earth, but in the conscientious performance of the duties imposed upon each individual by his special task. The conscientious and upright magistrate attains the perfection in his sphere of which he is capable and for which he is destined; the industrious farmer, the merchant, the honest and active artisan, realize, each according to his means, the relative perfection of which nature has furnished them the elements. Absolute perfection belongs to the absolute Being alone.

The argument which infers the immortality of the soul from

---

[1] Called the school of Padua, in honor of the city in which Pomponatius taught.

[2] Born at Mantua, 1462; died 1525; professor at Padua.

[3] See on the Alexandrists and the Averroists, Marsilius Ficinus, *Preface to the Translation of Plotinus*. Some interpreted Aristotle, as did Averroes, in the pantheistic sense; others agreed with Alexander of Aphrodisias, and interpreted him in the deistic sense. All rejected individual immortality and miracles.

the necessity of an eternal reward of virtue, and an eternal punishment of crime, is based upon a false, or at least imperfect and vulgar, conception of virtue and vice, reward and punishment. Virtue which is exercised merely for the sake of a reward other than itself, is not virtue. This is proved by the fact that everybody regards an act performed in a wholly disinterested manner, and without the hope of some material advantage, as more meritorious than an act performed for an advantage or to satisfy an interest. We must distinguish between the *essential* reward and the *accidental* remuneration of virtue. The essential recompense, which is inherent in virtue and consequently never lacking, is virtue itself and the inseparable joy connected with it; and the same may be said of vice, which carries its own punishment with it, even though it is not followed by external and accidental pains. It is an incontrovertible fact that men practise righteousness for the sake of the reward beyond the grave, and that they abstain from crime on account of their fear of hell; but this proves that their moral ideas are still rudimentary, and that they have need of rattles and bugbears where the philosopher acts solely from principle.

But if the soul is not immortal, all religions are in error, and the whole world is deceived! Well, does not Plato say that all men are in many respects deluded by the same prejudice? And does he not therefore hold of little worth arguments based on universal consent? Finally, as regards apparitions of the dead, resurrections, and ghosts: such proofs in favor of a hereafter do not prove anything but the marvellous power of the imagination influenced by faith. If, as Aristotle explicitly teaches, the soul is the *function* of the body, it is evident that there can be no soul without a body. And what, then, becomes of sorcery and the exorcism of spirits? What becomes of the supernatural?

In his treatise *On Magic*, Pomponatius openly avows his disbelief in miracles as the suspension of the natural order of things; and though he admits the miracles of Jesus and Moses in order to mislead the Inquisition, he explains them naturally, that is, he denies them indirectly. And he rejects them, on the authority of the man whom the Church considered as the stanchest supporter of the supernaturalistic Christian, — on the authority of Aristotle.

Finally, in his treatise *On Fate*, he dwells, with apparent satisfaction, on the contradictions involved in the doctrines of divine prescience and providence, predestination and moral freedom. If God ordains everything in advance, and foresees everything, then we are not free; if man is free, then God does not foresee his acts, and his knowledge is dependent on his creatures. Aristotle himself, — Pomponatius does not dare to say so openly, so great is the authority of the philosopher of the Church, — Aristotle contradicts himself on this important question, the solution of which seems to transcend the capacity of human reason. However that may be, determinism has all the logic on its side, and Pomponatius is in sympathy with it. In that case God is the source of evil! Scholastic nominalism interposes. Our philosopher is forced to admit this; but he consoles himself with the thought that if *there were not so much evil in the world, there would not be so much good in it.*

PORTA,[1] SCALIGER,[2] CREMONINI,[3] ZABARELLA,[4] continue the liberal Peripateticism of Pomponatius during the sixteenth century, and advocate his theory of the soul. They also practise his prudent reserve, as the following motto recommended by Cremonini shows: *Intus ut libet, foris ut moris est* (inwardly as you please, outwardly in conformity to custom). The Church, however, kept a close watch upon them, and suspected them of atheism. A product of this school, LUCILIO VANINI,[5]

---

[1] Died 1555.   [2] 1484–1558.
[3] 1552–1631. Professor at Ferrara and Padua.
[4] 1533–1589. Professor at Padua.
[5] His real name was Pompeio Lucilio Vanini. In his works he calls himself Julius Cæsar Vaninus. He was born at Tauresano, near Naples, in 1584, and burnt alive at Toulouse on the 9th of February, 1619, after having had his tongue cut off. He left two works: *Amphitheatrum æternæ providentiæ*, Lyons, 1615, and *De admirandis naturæ arcanis*, Paris, 1616 (best known by the title *Dialogues on Nature*, transl. into French by Cousin).

a restless and extremely vain soul, was burnt by the Inquisition, in spite, or perhaps because of, his declaration "that he would state his opinions concerning the immortality of the soul only in case he were old, rich, and a German." These Peripatetics of the left no longer swear by the words of the master like the orthodox Peripatetics. They venerate Aristotle as the highest type of the philosophical mind; but their Peripateticism does not consist in a servile obedience to the letter of his writings, from which they frequently deviate.

Some, impressed by the similarity between the real teachings of Aristotle and the Platonic and Alexandrine doctrines, approximate the Florentine Academy, though still following the standard of the Lyceum; while the Platonists, on the other hand, whom a careful study of Aristotle had initiated into the secrets of his metaphysics, consent to a compromise between Platonism and Peripateticism. On the Platonic side we have John Pico of Mirandola, whose work on the agreement between Plato and Aristotle remained unfinished; on the Neo-Peripatetic side, we have ANDREAS CÆSALPINUS,[1] a learned naturalist, who anticipated Harvey's discovery, and created an artificial system of botany. The universe, according to Cæsalpinus, is a living unity, a perfect organism. The "first mover" is the innermost substance of the world, — the substance of which the particular things are the modes or determinations. He is both absolute thought and absolute being. Though a mode of the divine substance, the human soul is none the less immortal, since its essence, thought, is independent of the body.

Still others, like BERNARDINO TELESIO of Cosenza (1508–1588), the founder of the *Academia Telesiana* or *Cosentina* of Naples, and FRANCESCO PATRIZZI (1527–1597), who were trained in the humanities as well as in the secret science of Paracelsus and Cardanus, approximate the naturalistic systems of the Ionian school in their cosmological conceptions. In connection with Telesio, we must mention the illustrious

---

[1] 1519–1603. Physician of Clement VIII.

names of Giordano Bruno (§ 49) and Francis Bacon (§ 51), both of whom knew his writings and were influenced by them.

While the speculative genius of Southern Italy was revealing to the world the real Aristotle, Plato, Parmenides, and Empedocles, the French and Flemish thinkers on the other side of the mountains, took a deeper interest in moral philosophy and positive science than in metaphysical speculation. Pyrrhonism was revived in the *Essays* of MICHEL DE MONTAIGNE (1533–1592) and in the writings of PIERRE CHARRON (1541–1603), SANCHEZ (died at Toulouse, 1632), LAMOTHE-LEVAYER (1586–1672); Stoicism, by JUSTUS LIPSIUS (1547–1606); Epicureanism, by the learned physicist GASSENDI, the opponent of Cartesian intellectualism (1596–1655). Although these freethinkers, with the exception of Gassendi, whose teachings were again taken up by the eighteenth century, do not contribute directly to the reform of philosophy, they at least exert an indirect influence by discrediting the still powerful metaphysics of the School, by exposing the uselessness of its formulas and the barrenness of its disputes. Humanists and naturalists, dogmatists and sceptics, Italians and Frenchmen, are united in the common desire for emancipation, reform, and progress. *Nature* is their watchword; here, as in Greece, the theological age is followed by the era of the *physicists*.

§ 46.   The Religious Reform[1]

Ideas enlighten humanity on its onward march, but the will or the instinctive passions impel it onward.[2] The Humanists demolished, piece by piece, the system which had been so carefully constructed by the doctors of the Church; but their excessive prudence or their indifference hindered them from attacking the Church herself, towards whom they affected an attitude of respectful submission. Pomponatius, Scaliger,

[1] See Lindsay, *History of the Reformation*, New York, 1907; Creighton, *History of the Papacy*, New York, 1899; Beard, *Martin Luther and the Reform in Germany*, London, 1883; Smith, *Life and Letters of Martin Luther*, New York, 1911; Smith, *Erasmus*, New York, 1924.

[2] § 4.

Erasmus, and Montaigne were more liberal than the leaders of the Reformation; but their liberalism is exactly what rendered them indifferent to religion and unfitted them for the grand work of the emancipation of conscience. The Church was so tolerant of pagan antiquity, so fond of classical studies! The Popes themselves were so cultured, so liberal, and so worldly! Yet, the spiritual omnipotence of Rome formed one of the chief obstacles in the way of philosophical reform, and it took a more powerful force to shake the colossus than the love of letters or the taste for free thought. Such a force was the religious conscience of Luther and the Reformers. In the name of the inner power that controlled them and impelled them onward, they attacked, not the philosophical system patronized by the Church, but the Church herself and the principle of her supreme authority.

As we have seen, the mediæval Church is both church and school, the depositary of the means of salvation and the dispenser of profane instruction. As long as the people continued in a state of barbarism, the power which she exercised in this double capacity was beneficent, legitimate, and necessary. But after the pupil becomes of age, the best of guardians acts as a hindrance from which he seeks deliverance. The Renaissance had actually destroyed the claim, which the Church advanced, of being the sole and privileged school, but it acknowledged the Church as the highest religious and moral authority. The Reformation finishes the work of the fifteenth century by emancipating the conscience. The sale of indulgences formed the immediate occasion for the outbreak. This shameful traffic had been legalized by the Catholic system. Since the Church is God's representative on earth, whatever she commands agrees with God's own will. Hence if she demands money from the faithful and couples with the contribution the promise of the pardon of sins, the faithful can do nothing but submit to her authority. The procedure may perhaps shock the moral sense a little. But what are our individual feelings against the revelation which the Church receives from

God? Are God's ways our ways, and is not the divine folly wiser than the wisdom of men? Was not the revealed truth an offense to the children of the age from the very beginning? . . . Luther's conscience rebelled against such sophistry. By protesting against these scandalous indulgences he revolted against the dogma sanctioning them, and against the spiritual power which recommended them. For the authority of so evil-minded a church he substitutes the supreme authority of Scripture; against the Catholic principle of meritorious works he opposes the doctrine of justification by faith.

The principle proclaimed by Luther, and soon after by Zwingli, Calvin, and Farel, quickly penetrated and powerfully influenced all spheres of human action. As soon as it was acknowledged as a truth that salvation comes through faith alone and not by works, the dispensations conferred by the Church lost their value. If grace is everything and merit nothing, then, it must be confessed, God cannot be thankful to us for renouncing family, society, and the joys and duties of life. Even Luther, who is by no means a lover of philosophy, but who has a very lively appreciation of nature, really advances the humanitarian and modern cause by repudiating, in principle at least, the dualism of the spiritual and the temporal, of priests and laymen, of heaven and earth. Melancthon, who is both a disciple of the Renaissance and a champion of the Reformation, plainly recognizes the community of interests existing between the literary and the religious revival. The two currents ultimately meet in Ulrich Zwingli, who was both an earnest Christian and a profound thinker, and whose theology is an energetic protest against the antithesis of a godless nature and a God antagonistic to nature.

§ 47. Scholasticism and Theosophy in the Protestant Countries. Jacob Böhme

Zwingli's progressive tendencies, however, made little headway, during the sixteenth and seventeenth centuries, against the doctrinary zeal of the theologians of the North. The authority of the Church and of the Pope was superseded, among the Protestants by the symbolism of the Reformation. It was impossible to pass immediately from the rule of authority to absolute freedom. The religious conscience, which had been violently agitated by a sudden revolution, needed a capable guide in place of the one just lost. Theology, again, could not, in its struggle with Catholicism, do without an external, visible, and standard authority in matters of science and religion. Hence the Reformation produced no immediate change in philosophy. In spite of the efforts of NICOLAS TAURELLUS, of Mömpelgard (1547–1606) and PIERRE DE LA RAMÉE or Ramus (1515–1572), who bitterly opposed the routine methods and the system of Aristotle, as then understood, the Universities continued to teach traditional Peripateticism in the form adapted by Melancthon to the needs of the Protestant dogma.

The anti-scholastic opposition of Reuchlin, Agrippa, and Paracelsus was continued by the Saxon pastor VALENTINE WEIGEL (1533–1593), the two VAN HELMONTS, the Englishman ROBERT FLUDD (died 1637), who, like a true Protestant, bases his cosmology on Genesis, the learned COMENIUS (died 1671), whose trinity of matter, light, and spirit calls to mind the three stages of being in Plotinus and the three Peripatetic principles of matter, movement, and action; finally, by JACOB BÖHME the theosophist of Görlitz (1575–1624).

Böhme was born of poor parents and apprenticed to a shoemaker at an early age. He received absolutely no instruction, and knew only the Bible and the writings of Weigel. But these sufficed to develop the latent capacities of this child of the people. He divines that *the visible things conceal a great mystery*, and he experiences a deep desire to unravel it. An earnest Christian, he studies the Scriptures, entreating God to enlighten him with his Spirit, and to reveal to him what no mortal man can discover through his own efforts; and his prayers are answered. In three successive revelations, God shows him the *inner centre of mysterious nature* and helps him to penetrate the *innermost heart of creatures at a single rapid glance*. Yielding to the urgent wishes of some of his friends, he decides to record his vision in a treatise called *Aurora*, which procures him the title the *German philosopher*. This book, like his other works, is written in German, the only language with which Böhme was familiar, and for that reason, if for no other, belongs to the modern world. It contains heresies of which the author has not the slightest notion, but which are vigorously condemned by the ecclesiastical authorities of Görlitz and cause him to be placed under strict surveillance for the rest of his days.

Indeed, from the Preface on, the sincerest orthodoxy is mingled with the most advanced conceptions of ancient and modern speculation. If you desire to be a philosopher and to fathom the nature of God and the nature of things, first pray to God for the Holy Ghost, who is in God and in nature. Aided by the Holy Spirit, you can penetrate even into the *body of God, who is nature*, and into the essence of the holy Trinity: for the Divine Spirit dwells in the whole of nature as the human spirit dwells in the body of man.

Enlightened by this Spirit, what does Böhme find at the very source of things? A constant duality, which he calls gentleness and sternness, sweetness and bitterness, good and evil. Everything that lives contains these contraries. Indifferent things, — things, that is, neither sweet nor bitter, neither warm nor cold, neither good nor bad, — are dead. Böhme sees this conflict, this struggle between two opposing principles, which become reconciled in death, in all beings, without exception, — in terrestrial beings, in angels, and in God, who constitutes the essence of all beings. God without the Son is a *will* that desires nothing because it is everything and has everything, — a will without a motive, a love without an object, a powerless power, an unsubstantial shadow, a blind essence without intelligence and without life, a centre without a circumference, a light without brightness, a sun without rays, a night without stars, a chaos without light, color, or form: a bottomless abyss, eternal death, nothingness. God the Father and the Son is the living God, the absolute or concrete spirit, the perfect being. The Son is the self-centred infinity, the heart of the Father; the torch that illuminates the boundlessness of the Divine Being, as the sun sheds its light into the immeasurable space; the eternal circle which God describes around himself; the *body of God*, having the stars as its organs, and their orbits as its eternally throbbing arteries; the totality of the forms contained in heaven and earth; the mysterious nature that lives, and feels, and suffers, and dies, and is again revived in us. But the opposition which constitutes the essence of God and of all beings is not the primordial being: it comes from Unity; the Son comes from the Father and is a secondary being. First nature, then mind; first will without an object or self-consciousness, then conscious will.

Although we may without difficulty extract the characteristic conceptions of concrete spiritualism from these metaphors, they assume a purely theological form in Böhme. This pioneer of German philosophy is a seer, a prophet who does not seem to understand himself, so imbued is he with the traditional view of things. Thought has simply changed masters in the Protestant world; it is what it was before, a servant of theology. It owes its final deliverance to the discoveries of Columbus, Magellan, Copernicus, Kepler, and Galileo, who refute the accepted notions concerning the earth, the sun, and the heavens, and thereby destroy the prejudice which makes the Scripture what it neither is nor claims to be: an infallible text-book of physical science.

§ 48. The Scientific Movement

From the middle of the fifteenth century on, Western Europe experienced a series of surprises. Led by the Greek scholars who settled in Italy, she entered directly into the promised land, which the Arabians of Spain had in part revealed to her: I mean, antiquity with its literature, philosophy, and art. The historical horizon of our fathers, which originally bounded

the Catholic era, grows larger and extends far beyond the beginnings of Christianity. The Catholic Church, outside of
which nothing but darkness and barbarism seemed to prevail,
was now regarded simply as the daughter and heir of an older,
richer, more diversified civilization, of a civilization more in
accord with the genius of the Western races. The Romance
and Germanic nations of Europe feel closely akin to these
Greeks and Romans whom the Church excluded from her pale,
but who were, in so many respects, superior to the Christians
of the fifteenth century in all the spheres of human activity.
The Catholic prejudice, according to which there can be
neither salvation nor real civilization nor religion nor morality
beyond the confines of the Church, gradually disappears. Men
cease to be exclusive Catholics and become *men*, humanists,
and philanthropists in the broadest sense of the term. Not
merely a few stray glimpses of the past, but the whole history
of Aryan Europe with its countless political, literary, philological, archæological, and geographical problems are unrolled
before the astonished gaze of our ancestors. Henceforth the
historical sciences, which received but little attention during
antiquity, and were almost unknown to the Middle Ages, constituted an important branch of study, and finally occupied
the centre of interest.

Scarcely had man discovered humanity when he was made
acquainted with the real form of his earthly habitation, of
which he had hitherto seen but one of the façades. The Catholic universe consisted of the world known to the Romans, i. e.,
of the Mediterranean valley and the Southwestern part of
Asia, with Northern Europe added. But now Columbus discovers the New World. Vasco da Gama sails around the Cape
of Good Hope and finds the sea-route to India; above all, Magellan succeeds in making the tour of the earth. These discoveries verify an hypothesis with which the ancients had
long been familiar, — the hypothesis that our earth is a globe,
isolated and suspended in space. What could be more natural
than to infer that the stars too float in space without being

attached to anything, and that the spheres of Aristotle are mere illusions?

The earth is now conceived as a globe, but everybody still regards it as the immovable centre around which the heavenly spheres revolve. TYCHO BRAHE directs the first attack against the traditional and popular cosmography by placing the sun in the centre of the planetary system; but he still believes that this solar system revolves around the earth. COPERNICUS takes the decisive step by placing the earth among the planets and the sun in the centre of the system. This theory, which had already been advanced by several of the ancients,[1] and which Copernicus presents merely as an hypothesis, is confirmed by the splendid labors of KEPLER, who discovers the form of the planetary orbits and the laws of their motion; and of GALILEO, who teaches that the earth has a double motion, and, with a telescope of his own construction, discovers the satellites of Jupiter and the law of their revolution.

The heliocentric theory arouses great alarm in both Churches. Kepler is persecuted; Galileo is forced to retract. The stubborn conservatives maintain that the acceptance of the Copernican system would destroy the very foundations of Christianity. If the sun is the centre of the planetary orbits, if the earth moves, then, so they hold, Joshua did not perform his miracle, then the Bible is in error, and the Church fallible. If the earth is a planet, then it moves *in heaven*, and is no longer the antithesis of heaven; then heaven and earth are no longer opposed, as tradition assumed, but form one indivisible universe. Moreover, to affirm, in defiance of Aristotle, that the world is infinite, is to deny the existence of a heaven *apart* from the universe, of a supernatural order of things, of a God *on high*. That is the way the Church reasoned; she identified faith with doctrines of faith, God with our ideas of God, and stamped the adherents of Copernicus as atheists.

But in spite of the efforts of the Church, the new theories spread, the discoveries and inventions multiplied. First came

[1] § 22.

the invention of printing, then the compass, and then the telescope. Before Newton completed the new cosmology by his theory of universal attraction, and transformed what, until then, had been a mere hypothesis into an axiom, the sciences had shaken off the yoke of Scholasticism, and slowly but surely advanced. LEONARDO DA VINCI and his fellow-countryman FRACASTOR continue the labors of Archimedes and the scholars of Alexandria in physics, optics, and mechanics. The Frenchman VIÈTE extends the limits of algebra and applies it to geometry; and the Englishman NEPER (Lord John Napier) invents the logarithms. In biology, the Belgian VÉSALE, by his *De corporis humani fabrica* (1553), lays the foundation of the science of human anatomy; and the Englishman HARVEY, in a work published 1628, proves the theory of the circulation of the blood, previously advanced by the Spaniard Michel Servet,[1] and the Italians Realdo Colombo[2] and Andreas Cæsalpinus.[3]

Of all the modern discoveries, the Copernican theory proved to be the most influential. The appearance of the *Celestial Revolutions* is the most important event, the greatest *epoch*, in the intellectual history of Europe. It marks the beginning of the modern world. By revealing to us the *infinite*, which antiquity conceived as a mere negation, it did not, indeed, shake our faith in things invisible, — nay, it revived and strengthened the same, — but it seriously modified our ideas concerning their relation to the world. For transcendentalism, or the doctrine of the aloofness of God from things mundane, the ruling notion of the Middle Ages, it definitively substituted the modern principle of *divine immanency*.[4]

---

[1] Pulmonary circuiation is taught in a passage of the *Christianismi restitutio*, begun as early as 1546.

[2] 1494–1559; Vésale's successor at Padua (1544), and the author of *De re anatomica* (1558).

[3] In his *Quæstiones medicæ*, 1598.

[4] Hegel (*o. c.*), who recognizes in *immanency* the ruling thought of the modern world, though dating it from the Lutheran Reformation, characterizes the transition from the Middle Ages to our own epoch as follows: "It seemed to mankind as though God had just created sun, moon, stars, plants, and animals;

This conception had as its necessary consequence the philosophical reform, which was inaugurated by the free-thinkers of the fifteenth and sixteenth centuries and continued, about the year 1600, by a number of bold innovators (Bruno in Italy, Bacon in England, Descartes in France).

as if the laws of nature had just been established. Now, for the first time, they became interested in all these things, recognizing their own reason in the universal reason. War was declared, in the name of the natural laws, against the great superstition of the period, and against the prevailing notions regarding the formidable and remote powers, which, as was thought, could not be overcome except by magic. In the battle which ensued, Catholics and Protestants fought side by side."

III

MODERN PHILOSOPHY

FIRST PERIOD

THE AGE OF INDEPENDENT METAPHYSICS

(FROM BRUNO TO LOCKE AND KANT)

§ 49. Giordano Bruno[1]

GIORDANO BRUNO was born at Nola, near Naples, in 1548.
While still a young man, he entered the Dominican order, but
the influence exercised upon him by the writings of Nicolas
Cusanus, Raymond Lullus, Telesio, and his profound love of
nature, soon turned him against the monastic life and Catholicism. He visited Geneva, where he met with bitter disap-
pointments, Paris, London, and Germany, journeying from
Wittenberg to Prague, from Helmstaedt to Frankfort. But
Protestantism proved no more satisfactory to him than the
religion of his fathers. Upon his return to Italy he was arrested
at Venice by order of the Inquisition, imprisoned for two years,
and then burnt at the stake in Rome (1600). His adventurous life did not hinder him from writing numerous treatises,
the most remarkable of which are the following: *Della causa,
principio ed uno* (Venice, 1584); *Del infinito universo e dei
mondi* (*id.*, 1584); *De triplici minimo et mensura* (Frankfort,
1591); *De monade, numero et figura* (*id.*, 1591); *De immenso
et innumerabilibus s. de universo et mundis* (*id.*, 1591).

Bruno was the first metaphysician of the sixteenth century
who unreservedly accepted the heliocentric system. Aristotle's
spheres and divisions of the world he regarded as purely imaginary. Space, he held, has no such limits, no insurmountable

---

[1] See McIntyre, *Giordano Bruno*, London, 1903; Frith, *Life of Bruno*, London,
1887.

barriers separating our world from an extra-mundane region reserved for pure spirits, angels, and the supreme Being. Heaven is the infinite universe. The fixed stars are so many suns, surrounded by planets, which, in turn, are accompanied by satellites. The earth is a mere planet, and does not occupy a central and privileged place in the heavens. The same may be said of our sun, for the universe is a system of solar systems.

If the universe is infinite, we must necessarily reason as follows: There cannot be two infinities; now the existence of the world cannot be denied; hence God and the universe are but one and the same being. In order to escape the charge of atheism, Bruno distinguishes between the universe and the world: God, the infinite Being, or the *Universe*, is the principle or the eternal cause of the *world : natura naturans* (nature as source); the world is the totality of his effects or phenomena: *natura naturata* (nature as effect). It would, he thinks, be atheism to identify God with the *world*, for the world is merely the sum of individual beings, and a sum is not a being, but a mere phrase. But to identify God with the *universe* is not to deny him; on the contrary, it is to magnify him; it is to extend the idea of the supreme Being far beyond the limits assigned to him by those who conceive him as a being *by the side* of other beings, i. e., as a finite being. Hence Bruno loved to call himself *Philotheos*, or lover of the divine, in order to distinguish clearly between his conception and atheism. This proved to be a useless precaution, and did not succeed in misleading his judges.

As a matter of fact, the God of Bruno is neither the creator nor even the first mover, but the *soul* of the world; he is not the transcendent and temporary cause, but, as Spinoza would say, the *immanent* cause, i. e., the inner and permanent cause of things; he is both the material and formal principle which produces, organizes, and governs them *from within outwardly :* in a word, their eternal substance. The beings which Bruno distinguishes by the words "universe" and "world" really constitute but one and the same thing, considered sometimes from the realistic standpoint (in the mediæval sense), sometimes from the nominalistic standpoint. The universe, which contains and produces all things, has neither beginning nor end; the world (that is, the beings which it contains and produces) has a beginning and an end. The conception of nature and of necessary production takes the place of the notion of a creator and free creation. Freedom and necessity are synonymous; being, power, and will constitute in God but one and the same indivisible act.

The creation of the world does not in any way modify the God-universe, the eternally identical, immutable, incommensurable, and incomparable Being. By unfolding himself, the infinite Being produces a countless number of genera, species, and individuals, and an infinite variety of cosmical laws and relations (which constitute the life of the universe and the phenomenal world), without himself becoming a genus, species, individual, or substance, or subjecting himself to any law, or entering into any relations. He is an absolute and indivisible unity, having nothing in common with numerical unity; he is in all things, and all things are in him. In him every existing thing lives, moves, and has its being. He is present in the blade of grass, in the grain of sand, in the atom that floats in the sunbeam, as well as in the boundless All, — that is, he is omnipresent, because he is indivisible. The substantial and natural omnipresence of the infinite Being both explains and destroys the dogma of his supernatural presence in the consecrated host, which the ex-Dominican regards as the corner-stone of Christianity. Because of this real all-presence of the infinite One, everything in nature is alive; nothing can be destroyed; death itself is but a transformation of life. The merit of the Stoics consists in their having recognized the world as a living being; that of the Pythagoreans, in having recognized the mathematical necessity and immutability of the laws governing eternal creation.

Bruno sometimes calls the Infinite, the Universe, or God, *matter*. Matter is not the non-being of Greek idealism and the

Schoolmen. It is inextended, i. e., immaterial in its essence, and does not receive its being from a positive principle outside of itself (the form); it is, on the contrary, the real source of all forms; it contains them all in germ, and produces them in succession. What was first a seed becomes a stalk, then an ear of corn, then bread, then chyle, then blood, then animal semen, then an embryo, then a man, then a corpse, and then returns to earth or stone or some other material, only to pass through the same stages again. Thus we have here something that is changed into all things, and yet remains substantially the same. Hence, matter alone seems to be stable and eternal, and deserves to be called a principle. Being absolute, it includes all forms and all dimensions, and evolves out of itself the infinite variety of forms in which it appears. When we say a thing dies, we mean that a new thing has been produced; the dissolution of a combination means the formation of a new one.

The human soul is the highest evolution of cosmical life. It springs from the substance of all things through the action of the same force that produces an ear from a grain of wheat. All beings whatsoever are both body and soul: all are living *monads*, reproducing, in a particular form, the Monad of monads, or the God-universe. Corporeality is the effect of an outward movement or the expansive force of the monad; in thought the movement of the monad returns upon itself. This double movement of expansion and concentration constitutes the life of the monad. The latter lasts as long as the backward and forward motion producing it, and dies as soon as this ceases; but it disappears only to arise again, in a new form, soon after. The evolution of the living being may be described as the expansion of a vital centre; life, as the duration of the sphere; death, as the contraction of the sphere and its return to the vital centre whence it sprang.

All these conceptions, especially the evolutionism of Bruno, we shall meet again in the systems of Leibniz, Bonnet, Diderot, and Hegel, which his philosophy contains in germ and in the undifferentiated state, as it were. As the synthesis of monism and atomism, idealism and materialism, speculation and observation, it is the common source of modern ontological doctrines.

§ 50. Tommaso Campanella

Another Southern Italian and Dominican, TOMMASO CAMPANELLA,[1] anticipated the English and German *essays* concerning human understanding, i. e., modern criticism. This doughty champion of philosophical reform and Italian liberty was born near Stilo in Calabria, 1568, and died at Paris, 1639, after spending twenty-seven years in a Neapolitan dungeon on the charge of having conspired against the Spanish rule.

Campanella is a disciple of the Greek sceptics. This school taught him that metaphysics is built on sand unless it rests on a theory of knowledge. His philosophy consequently first discusses the formal question.[2]

Our knowledge springs from two sources: sensible experience and reasoning; it is empirical or speculative.

Is the knowledge acquired by sensation certain? Most of the ancients are of the opinion that the testimony of the senses must be ignored, and the sceptics sum up their doubts in the following argument: The object perceived by the senses is nothing but a modification of the subject, and the facts which, the senses tell us, are taking place outside of us, are in reality merely taking place in us. The senses are *my* senses; they are a part of myself; sensation is a fact produced in me, a fact which I explain by an external cause; whereas the thinking subject might be its determining but unconscious cause as easily as any *object*. In that event, how can we reach a cer-

---

[1] *Opere di Tommaso Campanella* ed. by A. d'Ancona, Turin, 1854 (*Campanellæ Philosophia sensibus demonstrata*, Naples, 1590; *Philos. rationalis et realis partes V.*, Paris, 1638; *Universalis philosophiæ sive metaphysicarum rerum juxta propria dogmata partes III, id.*, 1638; *Atheismus triumphatus*, Rome, 1631; *De gentilismo non retinendo*, Paris, 1836, etc.).

[2] For Campanella's theory of knowledge, see especially the *Introduction* to his *Universal Philosophy or Metaphysics*.

tain knowledge of the existence and nature of external things? If the object which I perceive is merely my sensation, how can I prove that it exists outside of me? By the inner sense, Campanella answers. Sense-perception must derive the character of certitude, which it does not possess in itself, from reason; reason transforms it into knowledge. Though the metaphysician may doubt the veracity of the senses, he cannot suspect the inner sense. Now, the latter reveals to me my existence immediately, and in such a way as to exclude even the shadow of a doubt; it reveals me to myself as a being that exists, and acts, and knows, and wills; as a being, furthermore, that is far from doing and knowing everything. In other words, the inner sense reveals to me both my existence and its limitations. Hence I necessarily conclude that there is a being that limits me, an objective world different from myself, or a non-ego; and thus I demonstrate by the *a posteriori* method a truth that is instinctive, or *a priori*, or prior to all reflection: the existence of the non-ego is the cause of the sensible perception in me.

Does this argument refute scepticism? To tell the truth, it only half refutes it, and our philosopher has no thought of claiming the victory. Indeed, it does not necessarily follow that because the senses are veridical in showing us objects, they show us the latter *as they are*. The agreement which, dogmatism assumes, exists between our mode of conceiving things and their mode of being, is, according to Campanella, a consequence of the analogy of beings, and this, in turn, is the consequence of an indemonstrable truth: their unitary origin. Besides, he will not grant that the human mind has an absolute knowledge of things. Our knowledge may be correct without ever being complete. Compared with God's knowledge, our knowledge is insignificant and as nothing. We should know things as they are, if knowledge were a pure act (if to perceive were to create). In order to know the things in themselves, or absolutely, we should have to be the absolute as such, i. e., the Creator himself. But though absolute knowledge is an ideal which man cannot realize, — an evident proof that this world is not his real home, — the thinker ought to engage in metaphysical research.

Considering its subject-matter, universal philosophy or metaphysics is the science of the principles or first conditions of existence. Considering its sources, means, and methods, it is the science of reason, and more certain and authoritative than experimental science.

To exist means to proceed from a principle and to return to it. What is the principle, or rather, what are these principles? for an abstract unity is barren. In other words: What is essential to a being's existence? Answer: (1) That this being *be able* to exist. (2) That there be in nature an *Idea*, of which this being is the realization (for without knowledge nature would never produce anything). (3) That there be a *tendency*,[1] or desire for realizing it. Power, knowledge, and will, — such are the principles of relative being. The sum of these principles, or rather, the supreme unity which contains them, is God. God is absolute power, absolute knowledge, and absolute will or love. The created beings, too, have power, perception, and will, corresponding to their propinquity to the source of things. The universe is a hierarchy comprising the mental, angelic, or metaphysical world (angels, dominations, world-soul, immortal souls), the eternal or mathematical world, and the temporal or corporeal world. All these worlds, even the corporeal world itself, participate in the absolute, and reproduce its three essential elements: power, knowledge, and will. So true is this that even inert nature is not dead; nay, feeling, intelligence, and will exist, in different degrees, in all beings, not even excepting inorganic matter.

Every being proceeds from the absolute Being, and strives to return thither as to its principle. In this sense all finite beings whatsoever *love* God, all are religious, all strive to live

[1] By thus categorically affirming the will as the principle of essence, Campanella differs both from the materialists and the pure idealists. No one before Leibniz more clearly conceived the fundamental conception of concrete spiri-tualism.

the infinite life of the Creator, all have a horror of non-being, and in so far as all bear within themselves non-being as well as being, all love God more than themselves. Religion is a universal phenomenon and has its source in the dependence of all things on the absolute Being. Religious science or theology is so much higher than philosophy, as God is greater than man.

In spite of these concessions to Catholicism, in spite of his *Triumphant Atheism*, and his dream of a universal monarchy for the Holy Father, Campanella's attempted reforms were suspected by the Church, and miscarried. Philosophy could not hope to make any advance in Italy; henceforth she takes up her abode in countries enlightened or emancipated by the religious reformation: in England and on both banks of the Rhine.[1]

§ 51. Francis Bacon

In England the philosophical reform receives the impress of the Anglo-Saxon character, and takes quite a different turn from the Italian movement. The sober and positive English mind distrusts the traditions of Scholasticism as well as the hasty deductions of independent metaphysics. It prefers the slow and gradual ascent along the path of experience to Italian speculation, which quickly reaches the summit, and then, unable to maintain itself, becomes discouraged and falls back into scepticism. It is impressed with the fact that the School and its methods had no share in the recent progress of the sciences; that these intellectual conquests were made outside of the School, nay, in spite of it. The sciences owe their success neither to Aristotle nor to any other traditional authority,

[1] The most distinguished among the Italian philosophers of the seventeenth and eighteenth centuries is Giovanni Battista Vico, who died in 1744. He is noted for his *Scienza nuova* (Naples, 1725), one of the first attempts at a philosophy of history. The attempt has been made by able modern thinkers like Gallupi, Rosmini, Gioberti, Mamiani, Ferrari, etc. (§ 71), to restore to Italy the philosophical prestige enjoyed by that country during the period of the Renaissance (see Raphael Mariano, *La philosophie contemporaine en Italie*, Paris, 1868). [On Vico see Professor Flint's book in *Blackwood's Phil. Classics.* — Tr.]

but to the direct contemplation of nature and the immediate influence of common-sense and reality. True, the bold investigators of science reasoned no less skilfully than the logicians of the School, but their reasonings were based on the observation of facts. Conversely, when they started from an *a priori* conception, or hypothesis, they verified it by experience, as Columbus did, and refused to recognize its truth until it had received this indispensable sanction. Thus we have, on the one hand, an utterly powerless and barren official philosophy; on the other, a surprising advance in the positive sciences. The conclusion which forced itself upon English common-sense was the necessity of abandoning *a priori* speculation and the abused syllogism in favor of observation and induction.

This conviction, which had been expressed by Roger Bacon as early as the thirteenth century, is proclaimed in the writings of his namesake FRANCIS BACON, Baron of Verulam, Lord Chancellor of England (1561–1626): *The Dignity and Advancement of Learning;*[1] *Novum organum scientiarum,*[2] etc.[3]

The problem is, to begin the whole labor of the mind again, to raise science upon an absolutely new basis (*instauratio magna*). If we would ascertain the hidden nature of things, we must not look for it in books, in the authorities of the School, in preconceived notions and *a priori* speculations. Above all, we must give up imitating the ancients, whose influence has retarded the progress of knowledge. With the exception of Democritus and a few positivists, the Greek philosophers observed but little and superficially. Scholasticism followed in the footsteps of antiquity. It seems as though the Schoolmen had lost their sense of the real. Our knowledge is full of prejudices. We have our whims, our preferences, our idols (i. e., idols of the tribe, of the cave, of the forum, of the theatre), and we project them into nature. Because the circle is a regular line and affords us pleasure, we infer that the

---

[1] Appeared in English, 1605.

[2] First published under the title *Cogitata et visa* in 1612.

[3] See Spedding, *Life and Times of Francis Bacon*, 2 vols., London, 1879; Fowler, *Bacon*, London, 1881; Steeves, *Francis Bacon*, London, 1910

planetary orbits are perfect circles. We do not observe at all, or we observe but poorly. We infer that because persons have escaped a great misfortune five times, some supernatural agencies have been at work; and we fail to take account of the equally numerous cases when they did not escape. One may truly say with the philosopher who was shown, in a temple, the votive tablets suspended by such as had escaped the peril of shipwreck: "But where are the portraits of those who have perished in spite of their vows?" We assume final causes, and apply them to science, thereby carrying into nature what exists only in our imagination. Instead of understanding *things*, we dispute about *words*, which each man interprets to suit himself. We continually confuse the objects of science with those of religion, — a procedure which results in a superstitious philosophy and a heretical theology. "Natural philosophy is not yet to be found unadulterated, but is impure and corrupted, — by logic in the school of Aristotle; by natural theology in that of Plato; by mathematics in the second school of Plato (that of Proclus and others), which ought rather to terminate natural philosophy than to generate or create it."

Philosophy's only hope in this chaos of opinions and *a priori* systems is to break entirely with Greek and scholastic traditions, and to accept the inductive method. What traditional philosophy calls induction proceeds by simple enumeration, leads to uncertain conclusions, and is exposed to danger from one contradictory instance, deciding generally from too small a number of facts. Genuine induction, the method of modern science, does not hurry on rapidly from a few isolated and uncertain phenomena to the most general axioms, but patiently and carefully studies the facts, and ascends to the laws continually and gradually. In forming our general law "we must examine and try whether it be only fitted and calculated for the particular instances from which it is deduced or whether it be more extensive and general. If the latter, we must observe whether it confirm its own extent and generality by giving surety, as it were, in pointing out new particulars, so that we may neither stop at actual discoveries, nor with careless grasp catch at shadows and abstract forms." [1]

It is an exaggeration of Bacon's merit to regard him as the creator of the experimental method and of modern science. On the contrary, Bacon was the product of the scientific revival of the sixteenth century, and his manifesto is but the conclusion, or as we might say the moral, which English common-sense draws from the scientific movement. But, though he cannot be said to have originated the experimental method, we must at least concede to him the honor of having raised it from the low condition to which scholastic prejudice had consigned it, and of having insured it a legal existence, so to say, by the most eloquent plea ever made in its favor. It is no small matter to speak out what many think and no one dares to confess even to himself.

Nay, more. Though experimental *science* and its methods originated long before the time of the great chancellor, Bacon is none the less the founder of experimental *philosophy*, the father of modern positivistic philosophy, in so far as he was the first to affirm, in clear and eloquent words, that true philosophy and science have common interests, and that a *separate* metaphysics is futile. An outspoken adversary of the metaphysical spirit, he expressly begs his readers "not to suppose that we are ambitious of founding any philosophical sect, like the ancient Greeks or some moderns; for neither is this our intention, *nor do we think that peculiar abstract opinions on nature and the principles of things are of much importance to men's fortunes.*" [2] Hence he not only opposes Aristotle, but "every abstract opinion on nature," i. e., all metaphysics not based on science.

He distinguishes, moreover, between *primary philosophy* and *metaphysics*. Primary philosophy treats of the notions and

---

[1] *Novum organum*, B. I, §§ 1, 2, 3, 14, 15, 19, 26, 31, 38–68, 71, 77, 79, 82, 89, 96, 100 ff. [Translations taken from Devey's ed. of Bacon's works in Bohn's Library. — Tr.]

[2] *Novum organum*, I, 116.

general propositions common to the special sciences, viz. (according to Bacon's strange division, "that is derived from the three different faculties of the soul," memory, imagination, and reason): *history*, which includes *civil history* and *natural history; poesy;* and *philosophy*, which he divides into *natural theology, natural philosophy*, and *human philosophy*. Metaphysics is the speculative part of natural philosophy; it deals with forms (in the scholastic sense) and final causes, whereas the *practical* part of natural philosophy, or physics proper, deals only with efficient causes and substances. But Bacon does not value metaphysics very highly, and it sounds like irony when, after having called final causes barren virgins, he assigns them to this science. As regards natural theology, its sole aim is "the confutation of atheism." Dogmas are objects of faith, and not of knowledge.[1]

This method of distinguishing between science and theology, philosophy and faith, reason and revelation, is diametrically opposed to the ways of the School. The old realistic Scholasticism identified philosophy with theology. Bacon, like the nominalists, cannot keep them far enough apart. He justifies himself for being a naturalist in science and a supernaturalist in theology on the ground of this absolute distinction, and a number of English thinkers follow his example. But the distance is not great between the exclusion of the invisible from the domain of science and its complete denial. Thomas Hobbes, a friend of Bacon, teaches a form of materialism which his political conservatism scarcely succeeds in disguising.

§ 52. Thomas Hobbes

THOMAS HOBBES (1588–1679), the son of a clergyman, born at Malmesbury, in Wiltshire, was the tutor of Lord Cavendish, and, owing to the latter's influence, a loyal friend of the Stuarts. Returning to his country after an absence of thirteen years in France, he devoted himself exclusively to literary

[1] *De dignitate et augm. sc.*, III.

labors.[1] Hobbes's fame as a political writer and moralist has somewhat obscured his merit as an ontologist and psychologist. And unjustly so; for he is the forerunner of materialism, criticism, and modern positivism.

Philosophy is defined by Hobbes as the reasoned knowledge of effects from causes, and causes from effects.[2] To philosophize means to think correctly; now, to think is "to compound and resolve conceptions," i. e., to add or subtract, to compute, or to reckon; hence, to think correctly means to combine what ought to be combined, and to separate what ought to be separated. Hence it follows that philosophy can have no other object than *composable* and *decomposable* things, or bodies.[3] Pure spirits, angels, ghosts, and God, cannot be *thought*. They are objects of faith, and belong to theology, — not objects of science falling within the scope of philosophy. Corresponding to the division of bodies into natural and artificial, moral and social bodies, we have: natural philosophy (logic, ontology, mathematics, physics) and political philosophy (morals and politics). Physics and moral philosophy are both empirical sciences, having bodies as their objects, and outer and inner sense as their respective organs. Outside of the science of observation, there is no real knowledge.[4]

From these premises follows a wholly materialistic theory of perception. Inner perception, the primary condition and basis of intellectual life, is merely our feeling of brain action. To think, therefore, is to feel. Knowledge consists in the addition of sensations. Sensation, again, is but a modification, a movement taking place in the sensible body. Memory, the indispensable auxiliary of thought, is simply the duration of

---

[1] *Elementa philosophica de cive*, 1642 and 1647; *Human Nature, or the Fundamental Elements of Policy*, London, 1650; *Leviathan sive de materia, forma et potestate civitatis ecclesiasticæ et civilis*, 1651; 1670 (in Latin); *De corpore*, 1655; *De homine*, 1658. His complete works (English and Latin), collected and edited by J. Molesworth, 16 vols., 8vo, London, 1839–1845; Calkins, *Metaphysical System of Hobbes: Selections from His Writings*, Open Court Series, Chicago, 1905; Stephen, *Hobbes*, New York, 1904; Taylor, *Hobbes (Philosophies Ancient and Modern)*, London, 1908; Robertson, *Hobbes*, London, 1886.

[2] *De corpore*, p. 2.   [3] *Id.*, p. 6.   [4] *De corpore*.

sensation: to remember is to feel what one has felt. Sensations cannot be explained, in the manner suggested by some of the ancients, as effluences emanating from bodies, and similar to them. These images of things, or, in the terminology of the Schoolmen, *sensible and intelligible species*, are, according to Hobbes, as bad as the *occult qualities* and other hypotheses of the Middle Ages. Instead, we must say: The simple motion which the objects produce in surrounding matter is communicated to the brain by the mediation of the nerves.

Hobbes here states a truth already known to Democritus, Protagoras, and Aristippus: the highly important truth of the wholly subjective character of perception. What we perceive — light, for example — is never an external object, but a motion, a modification taking place in the cerebral substance.[1] We need no further proof of this than the fact that light is perceived when the eye receives a more or less powerful blow; the sensation is merely the effect of the excitement produced in the optic nerve. And what holds for light in general may be said of each particular color, which is but a modification of light. The senses therefore deceive us in so far as they make us believe that sound, light, and colors exist outside of us. The objectivity of the phenomenon is an illusion. The qualities of things are accidents of our own being, and there is nothing objective except the motion of bodies, which arouses these accidents in us. Hobbes reasons as Berkeley afterwards reasoned; but the latter carries out his argument to the very end; proceeding from sensualistic premises, he finally denies the existence of bodies, and culminates in subjective idealism. Hobbes only goes half way: the reality of matter is, in his opinion, an unimpeachable dogma.

Soul or spirit he defines sometimes as brain action, sometimes as nervous substance. By spirit, he says, I understand a physical body refined enough to escape the observation of

[1] *Human Nature*, p. 6: *The image or colour is but an apparition unto us of the motion, agitation, or alteration which the object works in the brain or spirits, or some internal substance of the head.*

the senses. An incorporeal spirit does not exist. The Bible itself makes no mention of such a being. Animals and man differ in degree only; both being corporeal beings. We possess no real advantage over brutes except speech. We are no more endowed with free-will than the lower beings. Like them, we are governed by irresistible appetites. Reason without passion, moral principles without a material attraction, exert no influence on the human will; it is impelled by the expectations of the imagination, the passions, and the emotions: love, hatred, fear, and hope. "A voluntary action is that which proceedeth from the will"; but the volition itself is not voluntary; it is not our deed; we are not the masters of it. Every act has its sufficient reason. According to the indeterminists, a free or voluntary act is one which, though there be a sufficient reason for its performance, is not necessary. The absurdity of this definition is obvious. If an occurrence or an act does not happen, it is because there is no sufficient reason for its happening. Sufficient reason is synonymous with necessity. Man, like all creatures, is subject to the law of necessity, to fate, or, if we choose, to the will of God. Good and evil are relative ideas. The former is identical with the agreeable; the latter with the disagreeable. Interest is the supreme judge in morals as in everything else. Absolute good, absolute evil, absolute justice, absolute morality, are so many chimeras, gratuitous inventions of the theological mind and metaphysics.

Hobbes's system of politics is consistent with these ontological premises. Liberty he considers as impossible in politics as in metaphysics and ethics. In the State as well as in nature might makes right. The natural state of man consists in the war of all against all (*bellum omnium contra omnes*). The State is the indispensable means of putting an end to this conflict. It protects the life and property of individuals at the cost of a passive and absolute obedience on their part. What it commands is good; what it prohibits is bad. Its will is the supreme law.

We shall not dwell on this absolutistic theory, the logical

consequence of materialism. Let us note in what two important respects Thomas Hobbes differs from Bacon. First, Hobbes teaches a system of metaphysics, — the materialistic metaphysics; secondly, his definition of philosophy places a higher value on the syllogism than the author of the *Novum organum* sets upon it. The latter had, in proclaiming induction as the universal method, overlooked (1) the part deduction plays in mathematics, and (2) the part played by the mathematical element and *a priori* speculation in the discoveries of the fifteenth century. Hence Hobbes occupies a position between pure empiricism and Cartesian rationalism.

§ 53. Descartes and the Method of Doubt

RENÉ DES CARTES,[1] born 1596 at La Haye in Touraine, and educated by the Jesuits of La Flèche, spent the greater part of his life abroad. In Germany he fought as a lieutenant in the Imperial army; in Holland he published his *Philosophical Essays*, comprising the *Discourse on Method* (1637), the *Meditations* (1641), the *Principles of Philosophy* (1644). His admirer Queen Christina invited him to Sweden, where he died 1650, the same year in which his *Traité des passions de l'âme* appeared at Amsterdam. Besides the above, we must mention the following characteristic works: *Le monde ou traité de la lumière*, and the *Traité de l'homme ou de la formation du fœtus*, which were published after the death of the author.

In order to understand Descartes the philosopher, we must remember that he was an emulator of Gassendi, Galileo, Pascal, and Newton, the successor of Viète, and one of the founders of analytical geometry. Descartes was a mathematician above everything else; a geometrician with a taste for metaphysics rather than a philosopher with a leaning for geometry and algebra. Indeed, his philosophy simply aims to be a gen-

[1] Haldane & Ross, *The Philosophical Works of Descartes*, two vols., Cambridge (England), 1912; *Descartes' Meditations and Other Selections*, Open Court Edition, Chicago, 1912; Fischer, *Descartes and His School*, London, 1887; Smith, *Studies in the Cartesian Philosophy*, London, 1902; Haldane, *Descartes, His Life and Times*, London, 1905.

eralization of mathematics; it is his ambition to apply the geometric method to universal science, to make it the method of metaphysics. The *Discourse on Method* does not leave us in doubt on this point: "Above all," he says, "I was delighted with the mathematics on account of the certainty and evidence of their demonstrations, but *I had not as yet found out their true use*, and although I supposed that they were of service only in the mechanic arts, I was surprised that upon foundations so solid and stable no loftier structure had been raised." [1] And again: "Those long chains of reasoning, quite simple and easy, which geometers are wont to employ in the accomplishment of their most difficult demonstrations, led me to think that *everything which might fall under the cognizance of the human mind might be connected together in the same manner*, and that, provided only one should take care not to receive anything as true which was not so, and if one were always careful to preserve the order necessary for deducing one truth from another, there would be none so remote at which he might not at last arrive, nor so concealed which he might not discover."

These passages and many others make it quite plain that the Cartesian method consists in mathematical deduction generalized. How, then, did Descartes come to be called the inventor of inner observation or the psychological method? Descartes needed first principles from which to proceed in his deductions, and self-observation furnished him with such principles, from which he deduced all the rest in the geometrical manner (*more geometrico*). Hence, those who regard Descartes as the author of the psychological method are right, in so far as observation is one of the phases and the preparatory stage, as it were, in the Cartesian method; but they err in so far as they regard it as more than an introduction, or kind of provisional scaffolding for deductive reasoning, which undoubtedly constitutes the soul of the *Cartesianism of Descartes*. Let us add that Descartes not only uses inner observation; he is a

[1] *Discours de la méthode* (Torrey's translation), Part I, § 10.

learned anatomist and physiologist (so far as that was possible in the seventeenth century), and as such appreciates the great value of experience. He loves to study *the great book of the world;* and for any one to oppose him to Bacon on this point is sheer ignorance. The most recent historians of Cartesianism justly insist that it is impossible to separate Descartes the philosopher from Descartes the scientist; and French positivism, too, is right in reckoning among its ancestors a man who tried to make philosophy an *exact* science. Descartes's failing, a failing which he shares with very many metaphysicians, and which is the result of his scholastic training, consists in his impatient desire to conclude and systematize; which hinders him from distinguishing sufficiently between the method of scientific investigation and the method of exposition.

The application of the geometrical method to metaphysics for the purpose of making it an exact science· that is the leading thought in Cartesianism. The geometer starts out from a small number of axioms and definitions, and, by means of deduction, reaches wonderful results. Descartes follows this method. He needs, first, axioms and definitions; the first part of our exposition will show us how inner observation, aided by reasoning, supplies them. From these definitions he then deduces a series of consequences, which will form the subject of the second part.

1. Observing that all he knows or thinks he knows he has received through the senses and from tradition, and that the senses often deceive us, Descartes resolves to doubt everything: to traditional science he opposes a *radical doubt.* But he does not doubt merely for the sake of doubting. His scepticism, though radical, is provisional, and has for its object the creation of certain and self-acquired knowledge. He differs both from the philosophers of the Church and the sceptics properly so called. The Schoolmen had said: Believe in order to understand; he however says: Doubt in order to understand. Pyrrho, Sextus, and Montaigne had doubted before him, but

they did not succeed in mastering their doubts; they were tired of seeking for the truth, and so made doubt an end in itself, a definitive and hopeless system. For Descartes doubt is but a means which he hastens to abandon as soon as he has discovered a certain, primary truth. This, rather than his scepticism, the fact, namely, that he adds to his negation a positive and eminently fruitful principle, makes him the father of modern rationalistic philosophy.

What is this principle, and how does Descartes discover it? His very doubts reveal it to him. I doubt, says he: that is absolutely certain. Now, to doubt is to think. Hence it is certain that I think. To think is to exist. Hence it is certain that I exist. I think, therefore I exist. *Cogito, ergo sum.* Though Descartes derives the substance of his argument from St. Augustine, he formulates it differently; he presents it in such an attractive and precise form as to impress the mind and to gain its immediate approval. To the classical formula, *cogito ergo sum*, Cartesian philosophy owes a large share of its success. Descartes's motto is not, however, an inference, and he does not wish us to regard it as such. As an inference it would be a vicious circle; for the conclusion is really identical with the major premise. It is a simple analytical judgment, a self-evident proposition.

Here then we have a certain basis, on which to construct a system of no less certainty than its fundamental principle; for it is evident that all the propositions following necessarily from an axiom must be as true as the axiom itself.

Thus far, then, I merely know that I exist. I cannot advance and extend the circle of my knowledge without exercising the greatest care; I must remember constantly *that self-evidence, and that alone, is needed to make me certain of anything.* It is evident that I think and that I exist, but it is not evident that the object of my thought exists outside of me, for the nature which deceives me by making me believe in the rising and the setting of the sun, may also delude me by making me assume the reality of sensible things. My ideas may be merely the product of my own imagination. Heat, cold, and even disease, may be hallucinations. We should have to abandon all attempts to prove the contrary, we should forever remain confined within the narrow circle of certitude described by the *sum quia cogito* (I exist because I think) and doubt everything else, did we not find among our ideas one whose foreign origin is self-evident: the idea of God or of the infinite and perfect Being.

This idea cannot be the product of my thought, for my thought is finite, limited, and imperfect, and it is *self-evident* that a finite cause cannot produce an infinite effect. Shall we say that the idea of the infinite is purely negative? On the contrary, it is the most positive idea of all, the one which precedes all the others, and without which the idea of the finite would not be possible. Shall we raise the objection that the human ego, though *actually* imperfect, may be *potentially* infinite, because it strives for perfection, and can therefore produce the idea of God? But the idea of God is not the idea of a potentially perfect being, it is the idea of the actually infinite being. We do not attribute to God an acquired perfection. Our knowledge increases and grows more perfect little by little, perhaps indefinitely; but nothing can be added to God, the eternally absolute and perfect being. Hence, if the idea of God cannot come from us, it must necessarily come from God, and God necessarily *exists*.

Moreover, the existence of God follows from the very idea of the perfect being, for existence is an essential element of perfection; without it, God would be the most imperfect of beings. This argument, advanced by St. Anselmus, apparently makes the existence of God *depend* on our idea of the perfect being. Such, however, is not Descartes's meaning. We should not say, God exists because my mind conceives him; but, My reason conceives God, because God exists. The true foundation of our faith in God is not our own conception of him, — that would be a subjective and weak basis, — but God himself, who reveals himself to us in the innate idea of infinity.

The objection that the existence of a mountain or a valley, for example, does not follow from the intimate and necessary correlation existing between the idea of a mountain and the idea of a valley, is a sophism. From the fact that I cannot conceive a mountain without a valley, nor a valley without a mountain, it does not follow that a mountain or a valley exists, but that the two ideas are inseparable from each other. Similarly, from the fact that I cannot conceive God except as existent, it follows that the idea of God implies the existence of the perfect Being.[1]

I know, then, (1) *that I exist;* and, (2) *that God exists.* The certainty of God's existence is a matter of the greatest importance; on it depend all truth, all certitude, all positive knowledge. Without it I could not advance beyond the *cogito, ergo sum;* I should know myself and never know the not-me. It enables me to destroy the barrier erected by doubt between thought and external things. It teaches me (3) that *the corporeal world exists.* God, and God alone, vouchsafes the reality of my ideas; the idea of God which he has implanted in me is the perpetual refutation of scepticism. In short, as long as I leave out of account the idea of God, I may suppose that the sensible world is an illusion caused by some evil demon, or by the nature of my own mind. But the existence of God as the author of all things being proved, it becomes evident that my instinctive belief in the existence of the world is well founded; for I receive it from a perfect being, that is, from a being incapable of deceiving me. Henceforth, doubt is impossible, and whatever trace of scepticism I may have retained is superseded by an unshakable confidence in reason.[2]

---

[1] In reality, the ontological argument is no more of an inference than the *cogito, ergo sum.* It is an axiom, a truth which the soul perceives immediately and prior to all reflection.

[2] *Meditation,* V, 8: "But after I have recognized the existence of a God, and because I have at the same time recognized the fact that all things depend upon him, and that he is no deceiver, and in consequence of that I have judged that all that I conceive clearly and distinctly cannot fail to be true . . . no opposing reason can be brought against me which should make me ever call it in question; and thus I have a true and certain knowledge of it. And this same

The three realities whose existence has been proved, — God, the ego, and the corporeal world, — may be defined as follows: God is the infinite substance, on which everything depends and which itself depends on nothing; the soul is a substance that thinks; the body is an extended substance. By "substance" we can understand nothing else than a thing which so exists that it needs no other thing in order to exist.

2. Observation and reasoning form the basis of the Cartesian system. *A priori* deduction completes the structure.

And here we find, at the very outset, a syllogism which contains the elements of the Spinozistic system. If substance is a thing which needs no other thing in order to exist, it follows that *God alone is a substance in the real sense of the term.* Now, by substance we can conceive nothing else than a thing which so exists as to need nothing except itself in order to exist. There may be some obscurity in the phrase: "to need nothing except itself"; for, *strictly speaking, God alone is such a being,* and no created thing can exist a single moment without being sustained and preserved by his power. Accordingly, the School is right in saying that the term "substance" does not apply to God and the creatures *univocally.* Hence, creatures are not substances in the proper sense. Some are substances as compared with others; they are not substances as compared with God, for they depend on him.

Descartes, therefore, understands by *relative and finite sub-*

knowledge extends also to all the other things which I recollect having formerly demonstrated, as the truths of geometry and others like them; for what is there which can be objected to oblige me to call them in question? Will it be that my nature is such that I am very liable to be mistaken? But I know already that I cannot deceive myself in judgments the reasons for which I clearly perceive. Will it be that I have formerly regarded many things as true and certain which afterwards I have discovered to be false? . . . Will it be that perhaps I am asleep? . . . But even if I am asleep, all that presents itself to my mind with evidence is absolutely true. And thus I recognize very clearly that the certainty and the truth of all knowledge depend on the knowledge alone of the true God: so that before I knew him I could not perfectly know anything else. And now that I know him, I have the means of acquiring a perfect knowledge of an infinitude of things, not only of those which are in him, but also of those which belong to corporeal nature. . . ."

stance a thing which needs nothing but God in order to exist; by *mode*, that which cannot exist or be conceived without something else which is its substance; by *attribute*, the essential quality of the substance, from which we cannot abstract without at the same time destroying the substance itself.

Minds and bodies are (relative) substances. Thought constitutes the attribute, i. e., the essence of mind;[1] extension, the attribute, i. e., the essence of body.

From the fact that extension constitutes the essence of body, it follows: (1) That there can be no extension in the universe without body, i. e., no empty space; nor bodies without extension, i. e., atoms; (2) That the corporeal world is illimitable, since extension cannot be conceived as having limits (here Descartes contradicts Aristotle and agrees with Bruno); (3) That body has, strictly speaking, no centre, that its form is naturally eccentric and its motion centrifugal; for the centre is a mathematical point, and the mathematical point, inextended.

The properties of extension are divisibility, figurability, and mobility. But divisibility is merely a movement of separation and of union. Hence, the properties of extension, and consequently of matter, consist in motion.

There is no other motion than motion in extension, local motion or change of place.

Furthermore, motion cannot originate in the bodies themselves: they cannot be said to *move themselves*, to set themselves in motion and to persist in it of themselves; for bodies are extended, extended only, even in their smallest parts, and absolutely devoid of the inner principle, the centre of action and impulsion which we call soul or ego. They are entirely passive; they do not *move themselves* at all, but *are moved* by external causes. We cannot even say that they are heavy, if we understand by weight a *tendency* of the body to fall towards

---

[1] *Id.*, I, 9: By the word *thought* I understand everything that so takes place in us that we of ourselves immediately perceive it; hence, not only to understand, to will, to imagine, but even to feel, are the same as to think.

the centre of the earth, i. e., a kind of spontaneous activity in matter. The material world knows no other law than the law of necessity. The particles of matter, to which the Creator originally imparted rectilinear motion, are distributed in vortices (*tourbillons*), forming stars, then planets, which are extinguished stars, and finally other heavenly bodies. The science of the world is a problem of mechanics. The material world is a machine, an indefinite — not infinite — chain of movements, the origin of which is in God.

However, we must not mix theology with our interpretation of nature; and physics should entirely abandon the search for final causes, which has hitherto impeded the progress of this science.

Minds are diametrically opposed to bodies: i. e., they are essentially active and free; and just as there is nothing inextended in body, mind contains nothing that is not thought, inextended, and immaterial. Body is everything that mind is not; mind is the absolute negation of everything that body is. The two substances entirely exclude each other, they are entirely opposed to each other: body is absolutely soulless; the soul, absolutely immaterial (dualism of substances, dualistic spiritualism).[1]

Like soul and body, the science of soul and the science of body have nothing in common. Physics should confine itself wholly to mechanical interpretation, while the soul should be explained only in terms of itself.

Although sensation seems to be an action of the body upon the soul, voluntary motion, an action of the soul upon the body, this is not actually the case; for there can be no reciprocal action between substances whose attributes exclude each

---

[1] *Meditation*, VI. Here we notice a striking difference between Descartes and Leibniz, between dualistic spiritualism and concrete spiritualism. Descartes goes so far as to deny *force* (*tendance*) to body; while Leibniz attributes to it (i. e., to the monads constituting it) not only *force*, but also *perception:* it contains the *idea* which it desires to *realize*, without, however, being conscious of it. The characteristic trait of mind as compared with body is not *perception* but *apperception*, not the tendency itself, but the consciousness of the goal aimed at.

other. Man is a composite being, a combination of soul and body. The soul derives its sensible ideas from its own nature on occasion of the corresponding excitations; the body, on the other hand, is an automaton, whose movements are occasioned by the volitions of the soul. The body and the soul lead separate lives; the body is subject to necessity, the soul endowed with free-will; being independent of the body, it survives its destruction. The two parts composing the human being are so exclusive as to make a real *union between soul and body absolutely impossible.* "Those who never philosophize," Descartes[1] writes to Princess Elizabeth, "and employ their senses only, do not doubt that the soul moves the body, and that the body acts upon the soul. But they regard them both as one and the same thing, i. e., they conceive them to be united; for to *conceive things as united is to conceive them as one and the same thing.*" And when she objects that the reciprocal action between soul and body is a self-evident fact, and that it is easier to attribute extension to the soul than to contradict this evidence, Descartes replies: "I pray your highness kindly to attribute matter and extension to the soul, or, in other words, to conceive it as united to the body; and after you have so conceived it and have tested the notion in your own case, it will not be difficult to see that the matter attributed to thought is not thought itself, and that the extension of this matter is quite different from the extension of thought: the former is bound to a certain place from which it wholly excludes the extension of the body, which is not the case with the latter, and your highness will find no trouble in understanding the distinction between body and soul in spite of the fact that your highness has conceived them as united."

The theory, however, does not hinder Descartes from speaking of the reciprocal action between soul and body, as though this action were real and direct. His anthropology, particularly as formulated in the *Traité des passions,*[2] everywhere

---

[1] *A Madame Élizabeth, Princesse Palatine* (Letter XIX, Vol. III, ed. Garnier).
[2] Amsterdam, 1650.

assumes what his metaphysics denies. In contradiction to the very explicit statements which have just been quoted, Descartes holds that the soul is united to all parts of the body; that it exercises its functions more especially in the pineal gland; that the soul and the body act upon each other through the medium of this gland and the animal spirits. However, he never goes so far as to identify the "two substances." The *Traité de l'homme et de la formation du fœtus*[1] points out the distinction which he draws between them: the body walks, eats, and breathes; the soul enjoys, suffers, desires, hungers and thirsts, loves, hopes, fears; perceives the ideas of sound, light, smell, taste, and resistance; wakes, dreams, and faints. But all these phenomena are consequences — consequences and not effects — of movements caused in the pores of the brain, the seat of the soul, by the entrance and the exit of the animal spirits. *Without the body, and particularly without the brain, all these phenomena, as well as the memory in which they are retained, would disappear,* and nothing would be left to the soul except the conception of pure ideas of substance, thought, space, and infinity, — ideas which are wholly independent of sensation. Moreover, *the ideas* which need the co-operation of the senses, and consequently of the brain, *are entirely different from the objects which we suppose them to represent.* The idea is immaterial; the object, material; the idea is therefore the opposite of the object, even though it be its faithful image. Our ideas of material qualities no more resemble the objects than pain resembles the needle causing it, or the tickling resembles the feather which occasions it.

We see, the founder of French philosophy, though a rationalist and spiritualist in principle, really approximates empiricism and materialism. His animal-machine anticipates the *Man a Machine* of La Mettrie. Though dogmatic in his belief that extension is a reality, he is the precursor of Locke, Hume, and Kant, in that he makes a clear and absolute distinction between our ideas of material qualities and their external causes.

[1] Paris, 1664 (published by Clerselier).

§ 54. The Cartesian School [1]

The philosophy of Descartes clearly and accurately expressed the ideals of its age: the downfall of traditional authorities in matters of knowledge, and the autonomy of reason. It met with immense success. Though accused of neologism and atheism by the Jesuits of France and the severe Calvinists of Holland, though attacked in the name of empiricism by THOMAS HOBBES and PIERRE GASSENDI, and in the name of scepticism by HUET, Bishop of Avranches,[2] and PIERRE BAYLE,[3] it gathered around its standard men like CLERSELIER,[4] DE LA FORGE,[5] SYLVAIN RÉGIS,[6] CLAUBERG,[7] ARNAULD,[8] NICOLE,[9] MALEBRANCHE, GEULINCX, BALTHAZAR BEKKER, and SPINOZA. Even the leaders of militant Catholicism. BOSSUET and FÉNELON, felt its irresistible influence.[10]

Two great problems dominate the speculations of the new school. What is the relation between soul and body, mind and matter? That is the ontological question, with which the question regarding the origin of ideas and the certainty of knowledge, or the critical problem, is closely allied. What is the relation between the soul and God, — between human

---

[1] F. Bouillier, *Histoire de la philosophie cartésienne.*

[2] 1630–1721. *Censura philosophiæ cartesianæ*, Paris, 1669, etc. The sceptical free-thinker Huet differs from Bayle, and resembles Pascal in that he teaches theological scepticism, i. e., a form of scepticism which serves as a stepping-stone for religious faith.

[3] 1647–1706. Author of the celebrated *Dictionnaire historique et critique* (Rotterdam, 1697 ff.), and precursor of the religious criticists of the eighteenth and nineteenth centuries.

[4] Died 1686. Publisher of *Opera posthuma Descartis.*

[5] *Tractatus de mente humana, ejus facultatibus et functionibus*, Amsterdam, 1669.

[6] 1632–1707. *Cours entier de la philosophie*, 3 vols., Paris, 1690; Amst., 1691.

[7] 1625–1665. *Initiatio philosophi s. dubitatio cartesiana*, 1655; *Logica vetus et nova; ontosophia; de cognitione Dei et nostri*, Duisburg, 1656; *Opera philosophica*, Amst., 1691.

[8] Died 1694. *Works*, Lausanne, 45 vols., 4to, 1775–1783.

[9] Died 1695. Philosophical works published by Jourdain, 1845.

[10] The former, in his *Traité de la connaisance de Dieu et de soi-même;* the latter, in his *Traité de l'existence et des attributs de Dieu*, and his *Lettres sur la métaphysique.*

liberty, on the one hand, and divine omnipotence, on the other? That is the moral question, which is closely connected with the preceding.

In order to solve the former, reasoning and experience must be reconciled. If we consult the facts only, sensation is evidently the body's action upon the soul, the action of matter on mind. And evidently, voluntary movement is the action of the mind on the body. We are acted upon by matter, and react upon it. Hence a relation, a very intimate relation, obtains between the two substances. But when they compare the results of observation with the dualistic metaphysics of the master, the Cartesians become involved in insoluble difficulties, and are confronted by mysteries on every side. The mind is a thinking substance and without extension; the body, an extended and unconscious substance. The mind is nothing but thought; matter, nothing but extension. Now, though we may conceive that an extended substance receives an impulse from another extended substance, and then communicates this to a third substance, likewise extended, the aforesaid extended substance cannot possibly be moved by something absolutely inextended; nor, conversely, can an absolutely inextended thing transmit any movement whatever to such an extended substance. We can conceive of mutual action between similar substances, but not between opposite substances. Hence we cannot assume that a real influence (*influxus physicus*) is exercised by the body upon the soul, or *vice versa*.

According to Arnold Geulincx,[1] of Antwerp, and Nicholas Malebranche,[2] a member of the Oratory of Jesus, the most illustrious representatives of the Cartesian school, the "ap-

---

[1] 1625–1669. Arnoldi Geulincx, *Logica fundamentis suis, a quibus hactenus collapsa fuerat, restituta*, Leyden, 1662; *Metaphysica vera et ad mentem peripateticam*, Amsterdam, 1691; Γνῶθι σεαυτόν *sive Ethica*, 2d ed., with notes, Leyden, 1675 ff.; *Physica vera*, 1688; etc. *Philosophical Works* of Geulincx, ed. by J. P. N. Land, 3 vols., The Hague, 1891–1893.

[2] 1638–1715. *De la recherche de la vérité, où l'on traite de la nature, de l'esprit de l'homme et de l'usage qu'il doit faire pour éviter l'erreur dans les sciences*, Paris, 1675; 1712 [new ed., with an introduction by F. Bouillier, Paris, 1880; Engl. tr. by Taylor, London, 1700, 1720]; *Conversations métaphysiques et chrétiennes*, 1677;

parent" action between soul and body can be explained only by the supernatural concourse of God. God intervenes *on occasion* of every volition, in order to excite in our bodies the movement which the soul cannot communicate to it of itself, and *on occasion* of each corporeal excitation, in order to produce the corresponding perception in the soul. Our volitions are the *occasional causes*, God the efficient cause of our movements; the sense-objects are the occasional causes, God the efficient cause of our perceptions.

Occasionalism concealed the boldest negations beneath its seeming naïveness. For, in the first place, if there is no direct influence between mind and body; if God, that is, infinite wisdom and goodness, is the necessary and only mediator between matter and soul, we must conclude, with the Dutch Cartesian Balthasar Bekker,[1] that sorcery, magic, or spiritism, in every shape or form, is a detestable and ridiculous superstition.

Nay, more. If God is the efficient author of all my perceptions and movements, I am nothing but a nominal, apparent, and fictitious subject, and God is the real subject of my actions and thoughts: it is he who acts in me; it is he who thinks in me. The former consequence of occasionalism (God acts in me) was drawn by Geulincx, the latter (God thinks in me) by Malebranche. According to Geulincx, we are not, strictly speaking, minds, but *modes* of mind. Take away the mode, and God alone remains.[2] According to Malebranche, God is the abode of spirits, as space is the abode of bodies. He is to the soul what light is to the eye. Just as this organ dwells in the light, so the mind is in God, thinks in God, sees in God. We do not perceive the material things themselves, but the idea-types of the things, their ideal substance as it exists in

---

Traité de la nature et de la grâce, Amsterdam, 1680 [Engl. tr., London, 1695]; *Traité de morale*, Rotterdam, 1684 [new ed. by H. Joly, Paris, 1882]; *Méditations métaphysiques et chrétiennes*, 1684; *Entretiens sur la métaphysique et sur la religion*, 1688; *Traité de l'amour de Dieu*, 1697; etc.

[1] 1634–1698.   [2] *Metaphysica*, p. 56.

God. Indeed, how could the eye of the mind see material things? To see an object means to assimilate it, to make it our own, does it not? And how can substances which exclude each other by their very essence, how can mind and matter, penetrate each other? How can the spiritual eye assimilate what is foreign to its nature? Mind can *see* nothing except mind.

Cartesianism, though at first theistic, ultimately changed into a kind of pantheism in the systems of Geulincx and Malebranche, which naturally led to absolute determinism in ethics; for it made God the universal agent, so to speak. This element particularly impressed the Dutch Calvinists and the Catholics who accepted Jansen's and St. Augustine's teachings on predestination and prevenient grace (Arnauld, Nicole, Lancelot, etc.). These thinkers combined extreme rationalism with the mysticism of PASCAL.[1] But the system had only to be divested of its theological shell to become Spinozistic naturalism.

[1] 1623–1662. Engl. transl. of Pascal's *Thoughts* by C. Kegan Paul, London, 1885; of *Provincial Letters*, 1889. As a physicist and mathematician, and especially as a writer, the author of the *Pensées* and *Lettres provinciales* ranks with Descartes. As a philosopher he was at first equally attracted by Cartesian dogmatism, which appealed to his "geometric mind," and the new Pyrrhonism of Montaigne. Then, owing to the influence of Port-Royal and the occurrence of an event which produced in him an entire change of heart, he became an enthusiastic adherent of Augustinian Christianity. His *Pensées* form the raw material, so to speak, of what he intended to be an apology of his new faith. Reason revealed itself to him in all its weakness, and made him a sceptic; nature appeared to him in all her ugliness, and made him pessimistic. It was the "heart" — we should say, the conscience — that revealed to him the real God, the living and personal God of the Gospel. For philosophy he henceforth had nothing but contempt. — Among the modern writers who have made a study of Pascal, Vinet possesses the merit of having presented him in his true light, i. e., as the forerunner of Schopenhauer and Schleiermacher. Cousin saw in Pascal nothing but the sceptical and maniacal element. Though not ignoring the pathological element in his mysticism, we, for our part, discover three truths in his philosophy: first, reason and experience, without conscience, cannot yield us real truth; secondly, experience without conscience necessarily leads to pessimism; and finally, the will — for that is what Pascal means by the words *heart* (*cœur*) and *feeling* (*sentiment*) — takes precedence of reason, and subjects it to its laws.

§ 55.　Spinoza

Baruch (Benedict) SPINOZA,[1] Spinosa, or Despinoza, was born at Amsterdam, in 1632, of Portuguese Jewish parents, who were, it seems, in good circumstances. In accordance with the wishes of his father he studied theology, but soon showed a decided preference for free philosophical speculation. After being excommunicated by the synagogue, which made unsuccessful attempts to bring him back to the faith of his fathers, he repaired to Rhynsburg, then to Voorburg, and finally to The Hague, where he died, a poor and persecuted man, in 1677. His love of independence led him to decline the Heidelberg professorship of philosophy offered him by Karl Ludwig, the Elector Palatine. He wrote his principal works at The Hague between the years 1660 and 1677. In 1663 he published the treatise entitled: *Renati Descartes principiorum philosophiæ Pars I et II more geometrico demonstratæ*, and in 1670, the anonymous work: *Tractatus theologico-politicus*, in which he discusses and gives rationalistic solutions of such problems as inspiration, prophecy, miracles, and free investigation. His chief work, *Ethica more geometrico demonstrata*, and several other less important treatises, were issued after his death under the care of his friend Ludwig Meyer. His *Tractatus de Deo, homine, ejusque felicitate* was unknown to the philosophical public until 1852.

Spinozism, as set forth in the *Ethics*, is the logical consequence of the Cartesian definition of substance, and the consistent application of the method of the French philosopher.[2]

---

[1] Elwes, *Works of Spinoza*, 2 vols., London, 1883; *Ethics of Spinoza*, Everyman's Library Edition; Wolf: *God, Man and His Wellbeing*, London, 1910; Pollock, *Spinoza, His Life and Philosophy*, London, 1880; Martineau, *A Study of Spinoza*, London, 1882; Caird, J., *Spinoza*, Edinburgh, 1888; Joachim, *A Study of the Ethics of Spinoza*, Oxford, 1901.

[2] We do not at all wish to be understood as denying the influence which the Jewish theology of the Middle Ages exercised on Spinoza's intellectual development. This influence is apparent, and it would be ridiculous to call it in question. It was owing to it that Spinoza found what he did find in Descartes; he was already a pantheist when he took up the study of the French philosopher. Still, we must maintain that his leading thought, and particularly his method, are the logical outcome of the Cartesian system.

Our author is not content with developing his doctrines by pure deductive reasoning, but also presents them in the geometrical manner. From a certain number of definitions he deduces a system whose parts are logically connected with each other. This method of exposition is not an arbitrary form or a provisional framework: it is of a piece with the system, and, one might say, constitutes its permanent skeleton. When Spinoza treats of the world, of man and his passions, as Euclid in his *Elements* treats of lines, planes, and angles, it is because, in principle and in fact, he sets as great a value upon these objects of philosophy as the geometer upon his. Just as the conclusions of geometry inevitably follow from their axioms, so the moral and physical facts which the philosopher considers follow with absolute necessity from the nature of things, expressed by their definitions; and he no more inquires into their final causes than the geometer asks to what end the three angles of a given triangle are equal to two right angles. It is not his method that leads him to mathematical determinism; on the contrary, he employs it because, from the very outset, he views the world from the geometrical, i. e., deterministic standpoint. He agrees with Descartes, Plato, and Pythagoras that philosophy is the generalization of *mathematics*.

I. Definitions

The fundamental notions of Spinoza's system are substance, attribute, and mode. "By *substance*," he says, "I understand that which exists in itself, and is conceived by itself, i. e., that which does not need the conception of any other thing in order to be conceived." [1] "By *attribute* I understand that which the intellect perceives as constituting the essence of the substance." [2] "By *mode* I understand the modifications of the substance, i. e., that which exists in and is conceived by something other than itself." [3]

[1] *Ethics*, I, Def. 3. [2] *Eth.*, I, Def. 4. [3] *Eth.*, I, Def. 5.

II. Deductions

1. *Theory of Substance*

From the definition of substance it follows: (1) that substance is its own cause; otherwise it would be produced by something other than itself, in which case it would not be a substance; (2) that it is infinite (if it were finite, it would be limited by other substances, and consequently depend on them); (3) that it is the only substance; for if there were two substances, they would limit each other and cease to be independent, i. e., they would cease to be substances. Hence there can be only one substance, which depends on nothing, and on which everything depends.[1] At this point Spinoza deviates from the Cartesian philosophy; but he deviates from it because the system itself invites him to do so. Descartes himself had intimated by his definition of substance that in reality God alone is substance, and that the word *substance* when applied to creatures has not the same meaning as when applied to the infinite Being. But instead of removing the ambiguity, he continued to call finite things *substances;* and in order to distinguish them from God, *created substances*, as though his definition could make a created, relative, and finite substance anything but a substance that is not a substance. Hence we must refrain from applying the term "substance" to things which do not exist by themselves; the term must be reserved for the being which exists in itself and is conceived by itself, i. e., for God. God alone is substance, and substance is God.

Substance being the only being, and not dependent on anything, is absolutely free in the sense that it is determined solely by itself. Its liberty is synonymous with *necessity*, but not with *constraint*. To act necessarily means to determine one's

---

[1] *Monotheism* here becomes *monism*. According to monotheism, God is the only God but not the only being; according to monism or pantheism, he is the only being and the only substance: he is the only existing being (*Eth.*, I, Prop. 14; *Letter* XLI).

self; to act under constraint means to be determined, in spite of one's self, by an external cause. That God should act, and act as he does, is as necessary as it is that the circle should have equal radii. Because a circle is a circle, its radii are equal; because substance is substance, it has modes, but it is free because its own nature and no extraneous cause compels it to modify itself. Absolute freedom excludes both constraint and caprice.

Substance is eternal and necessary; or, in the language of the School, its essence implies existence. It cannot be an individual or a person, like the God of religions; for, in that case, it would be a determined being, and all determination is relative negation. It is the common source of all personal existences, without being limited by any of them. *It has neither intellect nor will:* for both presuppose personality. Not being intelligent, it does not act with an end in view; it is the efficient cause of things. "I confess," says Spinoza, "that the view which subjects all things to the indifferent will of God, and makes them all depend on his caprice (Descartes, the Jesuits, and the Scotists), comes nearer the truth than the view of those who maintain that God acts in all things with a view to the good. For these latter persons — Plato, for example — seem to set up something outside of God, which does not depend on God, but to which God, in acting, looks as a model, or at which he aims as a goal. This surely is only another way of subjecting God to fate, and is a most absurd view of God, whom we have shown to be the first and only free cause of the essence and the existence of all things."

Though Spinoza calls God the cause of the universe, he takes the word "cause" in a very different sense from its usual meaning. His idea of cause is identical with his notion of substance; his conception of effect, with that of accident, mode, modification. God, according to him, is the cause of the universe as the apple is the cause of its red color, as milk is the cause of whiteness, sweetness, and liquidness, and not as the father is the cause of the child's existence, or even as the sun is the cause of heat. The father is the external and transient cause of his son, who has a separate existence of his own. So, too, heat, though connected with the sun, has an existence apart from the star producing it: it exists alongside of and outside of the sun. The case is not the same with God as related to the world; he is not its transcendent and transient cause, but the *immanent* cause; i. e., if we understand Spinoza correctly, God is not the cause of the world in the proper and usual sense of the term, a cause acting from without and creating it once for all, but the permanent substratum of things, the innermost substance of the universe.[1] God is neither the temporal creator of the world, as dualism and Christianity conceive him, nor even its *father*, as Cabalistic and Gnostic speculation assumes; *he is the universe itself, considered* SUB SPECIE ÆTERNITATIS (under the aspect of eternity), the eternal universe. The words *God* and *universe* designate one and the same thing: Nature, which is both the source of all beings and the totality of these beings considered as its effects.

In short, Spinoza is neither an acosmist nor an atheist, but a cosmotheist or pantheist in the strict sense of the word; that is to say, his cosmos is God himself, and his God the cosmical substance.

2. *Theory of Attributes*

Substance consists of infinite attributes, each of which expresses in its way the essence of God. The human intellect knows two of these: extension and thought. The cosmic substance is an extended and thinking thing; it forms both the substance of all bodies, or matter, and the substance of all minds. Matter and mind are not two opposite substances, as in Cartesianism; they are two different ways of conceiving one and the same substance, two different names for one and the same thing. Each of the attributes of the substance is *rela-*

---

[1] Hence, the Spinozistic conception of immanency implies both permanency and, if we may use the term, *interiority;* that is to say, the immanent God is both the inner and the permanent cause of the universe.

tively infinite. The substance is *absolutely* infinite in the sense that there is nothing beyond it: the attribute is only relatively infinite, that is, after its kind. Extension is infinite as such, and thought is infinite as such; but neither extension nor thought is absolutely infinite, for alongside of extension there is thought, and alongside of thought there is extension, not counting such attributes of substance as are unknown to us. Substance as such is the sum of all existing things; extension, though infinite as extension, does not contain all existences in itself, since there are, in addition to it, infinite thought and the minds constituted by it; nor does thought embrace the totality of beings, since there are, besides, extension and bodies.

It seems difficult, at first sight, to reconcile the theory of substance with the theory of attributes. According to the former, substance is absolutely undetermined being; according to the latter, it has attributes and even an infinity of attributes. Hence, Spinoza's God seems to be both an unqualified being and an infinitely qualified being. It has been suggested that Spinoza, like the Neo-Platonic philosophers and the Jewish theologians who do not apply attributes to God, may have meant by attributes, not qualities inherent in God, the suprarational, incomprehensible, and indefinable being, but the different ways according to which the understanding conceives God, i. e., purely subjective and human ways of thinking and speaking. An attribute would then mean: what the human understanding *attributes*, ascribes, and, as it were, adds to God, and not what is really and objectively (or as Spinoza would say, formally) in God; and substance would be conceived as an extended and thinking thing, without really being so. Spinoza's definition of attribute (*id quod intellectus de substantia percipit* TANQUAM *ejusdem essentiam constituens*) is more favorable to this interpretation than one would suppose. In our opinion it signifies: that which the intellect perceives of substance *as constituting* the essence of it; but it might also mean: that which the intellect perceives of substance *as though it constituted* its essence.[1] However, if the second interpretation were the correct one, Spinoza could not have said that the substance *is* an extended and thinking thing, nor, above all, that we have an adequate idea of it. Besides, it is wholly unnecessary to translate the passage in the subjectivistic and "non-attributistic" sense, simply in order to reconcile the seemingly contradictory theses of Spinoza. In fact, the contradiction is purely imaginary and arises from a misconception. The celebrated *determinatio negatio est* does not signify: determination is negation, but: *limitation* is negation. By calling God an absolutely undetermined being, Spinoza does not mean to say that God is an absolutely indeterminate being, or non-being, or negative being, but, on the contrary, that he has absolutely *unlimited* attributes, or absolutely *infinite* perfections, — that he is a positive, concrete, most real being, the being who unites in himself all possible attributes and possesses them without limitation.

Spinoza evidently intended to forestall the objections of the non-attributists[2] by ascribing to God *infinita attributa*, which seems to mean both *infinite attributes* and an *infinity of attributes*. God is therefore no longer conceived as having separate attributes, which would make him a *particular being;* he is the being who combines in himself all possible attributes, or the totality of being. Now each divine attribute constitutes a world: extension, the material world; thought, the spiritual world. Hence, we must conclude from the infinite number of divine attributes that there exists an infinite number of worlds besides the two worlds known to us, — worlds which are

[1] [The difference between the two interpretations may be more clearly stated as follows: Some construe the participle *constituens* as agreeing with *quod*, while others refer it to *intellectus*. According to the latter (*formalistic*) view, which is accepted by Hegel and Ed. Erdmann, the attributes are mere modes of human thinking, they are merely *in intellectu*, not *extra intellectum*, not *realities* in God. According to the former (*realistic*) explanation given by K. Fischer and others, the attributes are not merely modes or forms of thought, but expressions of God's nature. They are not merely in the human mind but in God. God is equal to all his attributes.]

[2] Who maintain that to give attributes to God means to limit him.

neither material nor spiritual, and have no relation to space or time, but depend on other conditions of existence absolutely inaccessible to the human understanding. This conception opens an immense field to the imagination, without being absolutely contrary to reason. However, it must be added, strictly speaking: *infinita attributa* are boundless attributes rather than innumerable attributes. Had Spinoza been decided on the question as to whether the absolute has attributes other than extension and thought, he would evidently not have employed an ambiguous expression. In fact, his *substance* has extension and thought only, but it has them in infinite degree.

Let us point out another difficulty. Spinoza holds that God has neither intelligence nor will; yet he attributes thought to him, and speaks of the *infinite intelligence* of God. These two assertions seem to contradict each other flatly. But we must remember that according to Jewish and Catholic theology (and Descartes himself), God has not discursive understanding, which needs reasoning and analysis in order to arrive at its ends; they attribute to him intuitive understanding, the active reason of Aristotle. We must remember, above all, that Spinoza's God is not the "author of nature," but nature itself. Now there is indeed reason in nature, but it is unconscious. The spider weaves its web without the slightest notion of geometry; the animal organism develops without having the faintest conception of physiology and anatomy. Nature thinks without thinking that it thinks; its thought is unconscious, an instinct, a wonderful foresight which is superior to intelligence, but not intelligence proper. By distinguishing between *cogitatio* and *intellectus*, Spinoza foreshadows the Leibnizian distinction between perception and *apperception*, or conscious perception.

As compared with Cartesianism, Spinozistic metaphysics has the merit of having realized that thought and extension do not necessarily presuppose two opposite substances. Its fruitful notion of their consubstantiality anticipates the concrete spiritualism of Leibniz. The assertion that one and the same substance may be both the subject of thought and the subject of extension is, as Leibniz aptly says, neither materialism nor idealism in the narrow sense of these terms; it combines the truths contained in these extreme theories into a higher synthesis. It is not materialism; for Spinoza does not hold that thought is an *effect* of movement, or to use his own terminology, a "mode of extension." Each attribute, being infinite and absolute after its kind, can be explained by itself alone. Hence, thought cannot be explained by matter and movement (by this thesis he wards off materialism); nor can extension and movement, i. e., matter, be the product of thought (by this thesis he wards off the idealism of Malebranche). But though thought and extension exclude each other in so far as they are attributes, they belong to the same substance; conceived thus, mind and matter are the same thing. These "attributes of substance" are not dependent on each other; matter is not superior and anterior to mind, nor does thought in any way excel extension; one has as much worth as the other, since each is, in the last analysis, the substance itself. This identity of substance, unrecognized by Descartes, explains the agreement between the movements of the body and the "movements" of the soul in man and in animals. Since one and the same substance and, what is still more important, one and the same being manifests itself in the physical order and in the intellectual order, this substance, this being, manifests itself in both spheres according to the same laws, and the two realms are parallel.

3. *Theory of Modes*

The modifications of extension are motion and rest; the modifications of thought are intellect and will. Movement, intellect, and will, i. e., the entire relative world (*natura naturata*) are modes or modifications of substance, or, what amounts to the same, of its attributes. These modes are infinite, like the attributes which they modify. Movement, intellect, and will, the physical universe and the intellectual universe, have neither beginning nor end. Each one of the infinite modes constitutes an infinite series of finite modes. Movement, i. e., infinitely modified extension, produces the infinitude of finite modes which we call bodies; intellect and will, becoming infinitely diversified, produce particular and finite minds, intellects, and wills. Bodies and minds (ideas) are neither relative substances, which would be a contradiction in terms, nor infinite modes, but changing modes or modifications of the cosmical substance, or, what amounts to the same, of its attributes.

By distinguishing between infinite modes and finite modes, Spinoza means to say that motion is eternal, while the corporeal forms which it constitutes originate and decay, — that intellects and wills have existed for eternities, but that each particular intellect has a limited duration. Bodies or limited extensions are to infinite extension, particular intellects to the infinite intellect, and the particular wills to the eternal will, what our thoughts are to our soul. Just as these exist only for the soul, of which they are temporary modifications, so, too, this soul, like the body, exists only for the substance, of which it is a momentary modification. Compared with God, souls and bodies are no more substances than our ideas are beings apart from ourselves. In strictly philosophical language, there is only one substantive; everything else is but an adjective. The substance is the absolute, eternal, and necessary cause of itself; the mode is contingent, passing, relative, and merely possible. The substance is necessary, i. e., it exists because it exists; the mode is contingent and merely possible, i. e., it exists because something else exists, and it may be conceived as not existing.

In view of this opposition between *immutable* substance and *modes*, we may ask ourselves the question: How much reality do modes possess in Spinoza's system? A mode is inconceivable without a subject or a substance that is modified. Now, the substance is unchangeable, it cannot be modified; hence the mode is nothing; movement, change, the cosmic process,

particular beings, individuals, bodies, souls, the whole of derived nature, in a word, have no real existence. Still this conclusion, which Parmenides and Zeno drew, is not Spinoza's.
On the contrary, he declares with Heraclitus that motion is
co-eternal with substance; he makes an *infinite mode* of it.
Unmindful of the principle of contradiction, but supported by
experience, he affirms both the immutability and the perpetual
change of being. In this conflict between reasoning and the
evidence of facts, which is as old as metaphysics, he deserves
credit for not sacrificing thought to reality, or experience to
reason. But he tries to smooth over the difficulty; he does not
perceive, or does not wish to perceive, the antinomy, leaving
it to modern speculation to point it out and to resolve it.

The human soul, like all intellectual modes, is a modification of infinite thought, the human body a modification of infinite extension. Since the intellectual or ideal order and the
real or corporeal order are parallel, every soul corresponds to
a body, and every body corresponds to an idea. The mind is
therefore the conscious image of the body. Not that the mind
is the body becoming conscious of itself; the body cannot be
the conscious subject, for thought cannot come from extension, nor extension from thought. Spinoza, like Descartes,
regards body as merely extended, and soul as merely thought.
But the body is the *object* of thought or of soul, and there can
be no thought, apperception, or soul, without a body. The
mind does not know itself, it is not an idea of the mind except
in so far as it is an idea of the body or, rather, an idea of a
bodily affection.

Sensation is a bodily phenomenon; it is a prerogative of animal and human bodies, and results from the superior organization of these bodies. Perception, on the other hand, is a mental fact: simultaneously as the body is affected by an excitation the mind creates an image or idea of this excitation. The
simultaneity of these two states is explained, as we have said,
by the identity of the mental and bodily substance. The mind
is always what the body is, and a well-formed soul necessarily

corresponds to a well-organized brain. By the same law (the identity of the ideal and the real orders), intellectual development runs parallel with physical development. Bodily sensations are at first confused and uncertain; to these confused modifications of the imperfect organism correspond confused and *inadequate* ideas of the *imagination*, the source of prejudice, illusion, and error: this makes us believe in general ideas existing independently of individuals, in final causes presiding over the creation of things, in incorporeal spirits, in a divinity with human form and human passions, in free-will and other idols.

It is characteristic of *reason* to conceive *adequate* and perfect ideas, that is to say, such as embrace both the object and its causes. The criterion of truth is truth itself and the evidence peculiar to it. He who has a true idea, at the same time knows that he has a true idea, and cannot doubt it. To the objection that fanaticism too is convinced of its truth and excludes uncertainty and doubt, Spinoza answers that the absence of doubt is not, as yet, positive certainty. Truth is true in itself; it does not depend on any argument for its truth; if it did, it would be subject to that; it is its own standard. Even as light reveals both itself and darkness, so is truth the criterion both of itself and of error.

The imagination represents things as they are in relation to us; reason conceives them from the standpoint of the whole in which they are produced, and in their relation to the universe. The imagination makes man the centre of the world, and what is human the measure of all things: reason rises beyond the self; it contemplates the universal and eternal, and refers all things to God. All ideas are true in so far as they are referred to God, that is, whose objects are conceived as modes of the infinite Being. It is also characteristic of reason that it rejects the notion of contingency, and conceives the concatenation of things as necessary. The idea of contingency, like so many other inadequate ideas, is a product of the imagination, and is entertained by such as are ignorant of the real causes and the necessary connection of facts. Necessity is the first postulate of reason, the watchword of true science. The imagination loses itself in the details of phenomena; reason grasps their unity; unity and consubstantiality, — that is the second postulate of reason. Finally, it rejects, as products of the imagination, final causes and *universals* considered as realities.

The only *universal* that *really* exists and is at the same time the highest object of reason, is God, or the infinite and necessary substance of which everything else is but an accident. According to Spinoza, reason can form an adequate idea of him, but not the imagination.

The will or active faculty is not essentially different from the understanding. It is nothing but a tendency of reason to retain ideas agreeable to it, and to reject such as are distasteful. A volition is an idea that affirms or negates itself.

Will and intellect being identical in their essence, it follows that the development of the one runs parallel with that of the other. Corresponding to the imagination, which represents things according to our impressions, we have, in the practical sphere, passion, or the instinctive movement which impels us towards an object or makes us shrink from it. When what the imagination shows us is of such a nature as to give our physical and moral life a greater intensity; or, in other words, when a thing is agreeable and we strive for it, this wholly elementary form of willing is called desire, love, joy, or pleasure. In the opposite case it is called aversion, hatred, fear, or grief.

To the higher understanding corresponds, in the practical sphere, the will proper, that is, the will enlightened by reason, and determined, not by what is agreeable, but by what is true. Not until it reaches this stage can the will, which is quite passive in the state of instinct, be called an active faculty. We act, in the philosophical sense, when anything happens either within us or outside of us, of which we are the adequate cause (*adæquata*), that is, when anything follows from our nature within us or outside of us, which can be clearly and distinctly understood through our nature alone. On the other hand, we are passive when something happens within us or follows from our nature, of which we are but the partial cause. To be passive or to be acted upon does not, therefore, mean not to act at all, but to be limited in one's activity. We are passive in so far as we are a part of the universe, or modes of the divine being. God or the universe, by the very fact that he is unlimited, cannot be passive. He is pure action, absolute activity.

However active man may seem in his passions, he is really passive in the proper and primary sense of the term: i. e., limited, impotent, or the slave of things. He can be made free and become active only through the understanding. To under-stand the universe is to be delivered from it. To understand everything is to be absolutely free. Passion ceases to be a passion as soon as we form a clear idea of it. Hence, freedom is found in thought and in thought alone. Thought, too, is relatively passive in so far as it is limited by the imagination, but it can free itself from this yoke by sustained application and persistent effort. Since freedom is found only in thought, our knowledge of things is the measure of our morality. That is morally good which is conducive to the understanding; that is bad which hinders and diminishes it.

Virtue is the power of the understanding; or, still better, it is man's nature in so far as this has the power of producing certain effects which can be explained by the laws of that nature alone. To be virtuous is to be strong, or to act; to be vicious is to be weak, or passive. From this point of view, not only hatred, anger, and envy, but also fear, hope, and even pity and repentance, must be reckoned among the vices. Hope is accompanied by a feeling of fear, pity and sympathy, by a feeling of pain, that is to say, by a diminution of our being, by a weakening of our energy. Repentance is doubly bad; for he who regrets is weak and is conscious of his weakness. The man who orders his life according to the dictates of reason will therefore labor with all his might to rise above pity and vain regrets. He will help his neighbor as well as improve himself, but he will do it in the name of reason. Thus will he be truly active, truly brave, and truly virtuous (in the original sense of the Latin word). He will be brave, for he will not let himself be conquered either by human miseries or his own mistakes, and he will not let himself be vanquished, because he knows that all things follow from the necessity of God's nature.

For the philosopher, who is convinced of the necessity of human actions, nothing merits hatred, derision, contempt, or pity. From his absolute standpoint of reason, even the crimes of a Nero are neither good nor bad, but simply necessary acts. Determinism makes the philosopher optimistic, and raises him, by gradual stages of perfection, to that disinterested love of nature which gives everything its value in the whole of things, to that *amor intellectualis Dei*, or philosophical love of nature, which is the summit of virtue. This sentiment differs essentially from the love of God of positive religions. The latter has for its object a fictitious being, and corresponds to the elementary stage of understanding called opinion or imagination. Since the God of the imagination is an individual, a person like ourselves, and like every living and real person, possesses feelings of love, anger, and jealousy, our love for him is a particularistic feeling, a mixture of love and fear, of happiness and restless jealousy; and the happiness which it procures for us is still far removed from the perfect blessedness to which we aspire.

The philosophical love of God, on the other hand, is an absolutely disinterested feeling; its object is not an individual who acts arbitrarily and from whom we expect favors, but a being superior to love and to hate. This God does not love like men; for to love is to feel pleasure, and to feel pleasure is to pass from less to greater perfection; now the infinitely perfect being cannot be augmented. Hatred likewise is foreign to him, since to hate is to be passive, and to be passive is to be diminished in one's being, which cannot be the case with God. Conversely, the hatred which some men entertain towards God, and their complaints against him, are possible only from the standpoint of the imagination, which conceives God as a person acting arbitrarily. We hate persons only; we cannot therefore really hate God, conceived as the necessary order of things, as the eternal and involuntary cause of everything that exists. The philosopher cannot help loving God; at least, he cannot but feel perfectly contented, peaceful, and resigned in contemplating him. This complete acquiescence of the thinker in the supreme law, this reconciliation of the soul with the necessities of life, this entire devotion to the nature of things, — is what Spinoza, by accommodation, without doubt, calls the intellectual love of God, the source of eternal happiness.

In this peculiar feeling, the difference between God and the soul, or substance and mode, is obliterated; the loved object becomes the loving subject, and conversely. The intellectual love of man towards God is identical with the love of God towards himself. Owing to this "transformation of natures," the human soul, which is perishable in so far as its functions are connected with the life of the body, is immortal in its divine part, the intellect. By the immortality of the soul we mean, not so much the infinite duration of the person as the consciousness that its substance is eternal. The certainty that the substance of our personality is imperishable, because it is God, banishes from the soul of the philosopher all fear of death, and fills him with an unmixed joy.

Let us sum up. Substance is that which exists by itself and by itself alone. Hence neither bodies nor minds can be called substances; for both exist by virtue of the divine activity. God alone exists by himself and by himself alone: hence there is but one absolutely infinite substance. This substance or God has two relatively infinite attributes: extension and thought. Extension is modified, and forms bodies; thought is infinitely diversified, and forms minds. Such is the metaphysics of Spinoza. Necessity and joyful resignation: these two words sum up his ethical teachings.

We have shown in what respect Spinozism advances beyond the Cartesian philosophy. By making mind and matter, soul and body, manifestations of a common principle, it destroys the dualism of a physical universe, absolutely divested of all ideal content, and an exclusively intellectual order of things, a world of abstract, incorporeal entities, which are as different from the real cosmos as the latter is supposed to be from the realm of pure thought. The universe is one. True, it contains two elements that are eternally distinct and cannot be explained in terms of each other: matter and thought; but these two elements, although distinct, are inseparable because they are not substances, but attributes of one and the same substance. Every movement, or, in other words, every modification of infinite extension, has an idea, i. e., a modification of infinite thought, corresponding to it; and *vice versa :* every idea has as its necessary accompaniment a corresponding fact in the physiological order. Thought is not without matter, nor matter without thought. Spinozism points out the intimate correlation between the two elements of being, but guards against identifying them, as materialism and idealism do, from opposite points of view.

But this gain is counterbalanced by a difficulty which seems to make for Cartesian dualism. Spinoza holds that one and the same thing (substance) is both *extended* and thinking, that is, *inextended ;* hence, he flagrantly violates the law of contradiction. True, he anticipates this objection by declaring, in opposition to Descartes, that corporeal substance is no more *divisible,* in so far as it is substance, than spiritual substance; and so prepares the way for the Leibnizian solution. But, on the other hand, he goes right on calling corporeal substance *extended (res extensa).* Now, indivisible extension is a contradiction in terms.

It was left to Leibniz to prove that there is nothing contradictory in the assumption that one and the same thing can be both the principle of thought and the principle of corporeal existence. He proclaimed the truth which is now accepted as a fundamental principle in physics, that the essence of matter does not consist in extension, but in *force,* and thereby turned the scales in favor of concrete spiritualism. It is a contradiction to hold that the same thing is both extended and inextended; it is not a contradiction to say that the same thing is force and thought, perception and tendency.

§ 56. Leibniz

The life of GOTTFRIED WILHELM LEIBNIZ, like his doctrine, forms the counterpart of Spinoza's. The illustrious Jew of Amsterdam was poor, neglected, and persecuted even to his dying day, while Leibniz knew only the bright side of life. Most liberally endowed with all the gifts of nature and of fortune, and as eager for titles and honors as for knowledge and truth, he had a brilliant career as a jurist, diplomat, and universal savant. His remarkable success is reflected in the motto of his theodicy: *Everything is for the best in the best of possible worlds.* He was born at Leipsic in 1646, and died on the 14th of November, 1716, as Librarian and Court Counsellor of the Duke of Hanover, Privy Counsellor, Imperial Baron, etc., etc.

His principal philosophical writings are: *Meditationes de cognitione, veritate et ideis* (1684); *Discours de la Métaphysique* (1685); *Lettres sur la question si l'essence du corps consiste dans l'étendue* (in the *Journal des savants,* 1691); *Nouveaux essais sur l'entendement humain* (in reply to Locke's *Essay*); *Essais de Théodicée sur la bonté de Dieu, la liberté de l'homme et l'origine du mal* (1710), dedicated to Queen Sophia Charlotte of Prussia; *La monadologie* (1714); *Principes de la nature et de la grâce, fondés en raison* (1714); finally, his *Correspondence.*[1]

[1] Engl. translation of important philosophical writings by G. M. Duncan, New Haven, 1890; of the *New Essays,* by A. G. Langley, London and New York, 1893; see also translation by Latta, *Monadology and Other Essays,* Oxford, 1898; by Montgomery, *Discourse on Metaphysics,* etc., Open Court Edition, Chicago, 1920; Dewey, *Leibniz's New Essays,* Chicago, 1888; Russell, *The Philosophy of Leibniz,* Cambridge (England), 1900; Conturat, *La Logique de Leibniz,* Paris, 1901.

Leibniz opposes to the dualism of extended or unconscious substance and inextended or conscious substance his theory of *monads* or inextended and *more or less* conscious substances. It seems that he derived the expression and the conception from Bruno's *De monade* and *De triplici minimo*[1] (1591).

Both the physical and mental realms contain a series of phenomena which do not depend exclusively either on thought or on extension. If the mind is conscious thought and nothing but that, how shall we explain the countless *minute perceptions* (*perceptions petites*) which baffle all analysis, those vague and confused feelings which cannot be classified, in short, everything in the soul of which we are not conscious? The soul has states during which its perceptions are not distinct, as in a profound, dreamless sleep, or in a swoon. During these states the soul either does not exist at all, or it exists in a manner analogous to the body, that is, without consciousness of self. Hence there is in the soul something other than conscious thought: it contains an unconscious element, which forms a connecting link between the soul and the physical world.

Moreover, what are attraction, repulsion, heat, and light, if matter is inert extension, and *nothing but that?* Cartesianism can neither deny nor explain these facts. Consistency demands that it boldly deny, on the one hand, the existence of order and life in the corporeal world, on the other, the presence in the soul of all ideas, sensations, and volitions which temporarily sink below the threshold of consciousness and attention, and reappear at the slightest inner or outer solicitation. It must unhesitatingly affirm that there is nothing inextended in the material world, and nothing unconscious in the spiritual world. But that would be to fly in the face of facts, and to assert an absurdity. No; extension, as the Cartesians conceive it, cannot of itself explain sensible phenomena. It is synonymous with passivity, inertia, and death, while everything in nature is action, movement, and life. Hence,

---

[1] [According to L. Stein (*Leibniz und Spinoza*), from F. Mercurius van Helmont. — Tr.]

unless we propose to explain life by death, and being by non-being, we must of necessity suppose that the essence of body consists of something different from extension.

And, indeed, does not the state of extension, which constitutes the nature of body, presuppose an *effort* or force that extends itself, a power both of resistance and expansion? Matter is essentially resistance, and resistance means activity. Behind the (extended) state there is the *act* which constantly produces it, renews it (extension). A large body moves with more difficulty than a small body; this is because the larger body has greater power of resistance. What seems to be inertia, or a lack of power, is in reality more intense action, a more considerable effort. Hence, the essence of corporeality is not extension, but the force of extension, or active force. Cartesian physics deals with inert masses and lifeless bodies only, and is therefore identical with mechanics and geometry; but nature can be explained only by a metaphysical notion that is higher than a purely mathematical and mechanical notion; and even the principles of mechanics, that is, the first laws of motion, have a higher origin than that of pure mathematics. This higher notion is the idea of FORCE. It is this power of resistance that constitutes the essence of matter. As to extension, it is nothing but an abstraction; it presupposes something that *is extended, expanded, and continued*. Extension is the diffusion of this "something." Milk, for example, is an extension or diffusion of whiteness; the diamond, an extension or diffusion of hardness; body in general, the extension of materiality. Hence, it is plain that there is something in the body anterior to extension (the force of extension). True metaphysics does not recognize the useless and inactive masses of which the Cartesians speak. *There is action everywhere. No body without movement, no substance without effort.*

Only the effects of force are perceptible; in itself it is an insensible and immaterial thing. Now force constitutes the essence of matter; hence matter is in reality immaterial in its essence. This paradox, which is also found in Leibniz, Bruno, and Plotinus, in principle overcomes the dualism of the physical and mental worlds. Though force forms the essence of that which is extended, it is itself inextended; it is therefore indivisible and simple; it is original; for composite things alone are derived and have become what they are; finally, it is indestructible, for a simple substance cannot be decomposed. A miracle alone could destroy it.

Thus far Leibniz speaks of force as Spinoza speaks of substance, and there seems to be merely a verbal difference between him and his predecessor. But here their paths diverge. Spinoza's "substance" is infinite and unique; Leibniz's "force" is neither one nor the other. If there were but one single substance in the world, this one substance would also be the only force; it alone would be able to act by itself, and everything else would be inert, powerless, passive, or, rather, would not exist at all. Now, the reverse is actually true. We find that minds act by themselves, with the consciousness of their individual responsibility; we likewise find that every body resists all other bodies, and consequently constitutes a separate force. Shall we say, in favor of Spinozism, that the indwelling forces of things are so many parts of the one force? But that cannot be, since force is essentially indivisible. By denying the infinite diversity of individual forces, the abstract monism of Spinoza *reverses the very nature of things, and becomes a pernicious doctrine.* Where there is action there is active force; now there is action in all things; each constitutes a separate centre of activity; hence there are as many simple, indivisible, and original forces as there are things.

These original forces or *monads* may be compared to physical points or to mathematical points; but they differ from the former in that they have no extension, and from the latter, in that they are objective realities. Leibniz calls them *metaphysical points* or *points of substance* (they are both exact, like mathematical points, and real, like physical points), *formal points, formal atoms, substantial forms* (in scholastic language), to indicate that each constitutes an individual, independent of all the other monads, acting of itself and depending only on itself in form, character, and entire mode of life.

Whatever happens in the monad comes from it alone; no external cause can produce modifications in it. Since it is endowed with spontaneous activity, and receives no influence from without, it differs from all other monads, and differs from them *forever*. It cannot be identified with anything; it eternally remains what it is. *It has no windows by which anything can enter or pass out.*[1] Since each monad differs from and excludes all the rest, it is "like a separate world, self-sufficient, independent of every other creature, embracing the infinite, expressing the universe."[2] It follows that two individual things cannot be perfectly alike in the world.

But here a serious objection arises. If each monad constitutes a separate world, independent of all other beings; if none has "windows" by which anything can enter or depart; if there is not the slightest reciprocal action between individuals, — what becomes of the universe and its unity? Spinoza sacrificed the reality of individuals to the principle of unity; does not Leibniz go to the other extreme? Are there not, according to his assumption, as many universes as there are atoms? This difficulty, which necessarily confronts all atomistic theories, Leibniz circumvents rather than solves. He has broken up, shattered, and pulverized the monolithic universe of Spinoza: how will he be able to cement these infinitesimal fragments together again, to reconstruct the one and the all?

He finds the synthetic principle in the *analogy* of monads and in the notion of *pre-established harmony*. Though each monad differs from all the rest, there is an analogy and a family resemblance, so to speak, between them. They resemble each other in that all are endowed with *perception* and *desire* or *appetition*, — Schopenhauer would say, *will*. Those on the lower stages in the scale of things, as well as the high-

---

[1] § 7.
[2] *Nouveau système de la nature*, § 16. [I have in many instances used Duncan's translations, making such changes as I deemed proper. — Tr.]

est and most perfect monads, are forces, entelechies, and *souls*. *Souls alone exist*, and that which we call extension or body is nothing but a confused perception, a phenomenon, a sensible manifestation of effort, that is to say, of the immaterial. Thus the dualism of soulless matter and *denaturized* mind is forever overcome. "Whatever there is of good in the hypotheses of Epicurus and of Plato, of the greatest materialists and the greatest idealists, is here combined."[1] Matter signifies a relation, a negative relation; it does not express a mode of the monad's positive being, as the negative expression *impenetrable* very well indicates; thought (perception) and tendency (appetition) are positive attributes, permanent modes of being, not only of the higher monads but of all without exception. Leibniz emphatically maintains that perception is universal, and answers the objection that beings inferior to man do not *think*, by the statement that "there are infinite degrees of perception, and perception is not necessarily sensation."[2] The more the Cartesians persisted in denying all analogy between human thought and the mental phenomena in animals, the more he inclined towards this paradoxical conception. The perceptions of lower beings are infinitely minute, confused, and unconscious; those of man are clear and conscious: that is the entire difference between soul and *mind*, perception and *apperception*.

The perceptions of the monad do not, it is true, extend beyond itself. Having no "windows by which anything can enter or depart," it can only perceive itself. We ourselves, the higher monads, do not perceive anything except our own being, and that alone we know immediately. The real world is wholly inaccessible to us, and the so-called world is merely the involuntary projection of what takes place within ourselves. If, notwithstanding, we know what takes place outside of us, if we have an (indirect) perception of the external world, it is because we are, like all monads, representatives of the universe, and because, consequently, that which takes place

[1] *Réplique aux réflexions de Bayle*, p. 186.　　[2] *Lettre à M. des Maizeaux*.

in us is the reproduction in miniature of that which takes place on the large scale in the macrocosm. Since the monad directly perceives itself alone and its own contents, it follows that the more adequate an image it is itself, the more complete will its perception of the universe be. The better a monad represents the universe, the better it represents *itself*. If the human soul *has* a clear and distinct idea of the world, it is because it *is* a more exact and more faithful image (*idea*) of the universe than the soul of the animal and the soul of the plant.

All monads represent and perceive, or, in a word, reproduce the universe, but they reproduce it in different degrees, and each in its own way. In other terms, there is a gradation in the perfection of the monads. In the hierarchy thus formed, the most perfect monads rule, the less perfect ones obey. Accordingly, we must distinguish between physical individuals, such as nature offers, and the metaphysical individuals or monads composing them. A plant or an animal is not a monad and individual in the metaphysical sense, but a combination of monads, of which one rules and the others obey. The central monad is what is called the soul of the plant, animal, or man; the subordinate monads grouped around it form what we call body. "Each living being," as Leibniz expressly states,[1] "has a ruling entelechy, which is the soul in the animal, but the members of this living body are full of other living beings, — plants, animals, — each of which has also its entelechy or governing soul." "Each monad," he also says,[2] "is a mirror of the universe, from its point of view, and accompanied by a multitude of other monads composing its organic body, of which it is the ruling monad." [3]

However, by virtue of the autonomy of the monads, this dominating influence of the central monad is purely ideal; the latter does not really act upon the governed monads. The obedience of the governed monads is, in turn, quite spontaneous. They do not subordinate themselves to the ruling

---

[1] *Monadologie*, § 70.   [2] *Lettre à M. Dangicourt*, p. 746.
[3] *Extrait d'une lettre à M. Dangicourt*, p. 746; *Monadologie*, § 70.

monad because this forces them to do so, but because *their
own nature compels them to do it*.[1] In the formation of organisms, the lower monads group themselves around the more
perfect monads, which, in turn, spontaneously group themselves around the central monad. This process might be compared to the construction of a temple in which the columns
spontaneously put themselves in the desired place, with the
capital pointing upward and the pedestal at the bottom. An
inorganic body, a rock, or a liquid mass is likewise an aggregation of monads, but without a ruling monad. Such bodies are
not inanimate; for each of the monads composing them is
both soul and body; but they seem inanimate because their
constitutive monads, being of like nature, do not obey a governing monad, but hold themselves in equilibrium, so to speak.

After these preliminaries, we expect Leibniz to solve the
problem of the reciprocal action of soul and body in the simplest and easiest manner. Thought and extension are not
substances which repel and exclude each other, but different
attributes of one and the same substance. Hence, nothing
seems more natural than to assume a direct connection between intellectual phenomena and the facts of the physiological world. That is not the case, however, and the metaphysics
of Leibniz finds itself as powerless as Cartesianism before this
important problem. The connection just mentioned would be
perfectly apparent if the human individual were a single monad, having as its immaterial essence the soul, and as its sensible manifestation, the body. If by body we meant the material element inhering in the central monad (for it must be
remembered that each monad, and consequently also the central monad or the highest soul, is both soul and body), nothing
would be more proper than to speak of a mutual action between soul and body. But, as we have just shown, the physical individual is not an isolated monad, but a central monad
surrounded by other monads, and it is the latter, or this group
of subordinate souls, which, strictly speaking, constitute the

---

[1] *Ad Des Bosses Epist. XXX.*

body of the individual. Now, the monads have no windows; within one and the same monad, the ruling monad, for example, there may and must be a causal relation between its successive states; such a relation, however, is impossible between two different monads.

Hence a real and direct action of the dominant monad upon the subordinate monad, or of soul upon body, is as impossible in Leibniz's system as in that of Descartes. This action is merely apparent. In sensation the soul seems to suffer the influence of the body, and the parts of the body, in turn, move as though their movements were determined by the volitions of the soul. As a matter of fact, neither one nor the other is affected by something external to it. No soul state, no volition, for example, can "penetrate" the monads constituting the body; hence the soul does not act directly upon the body; our arms are not moved by an act of will. Nothing in the body can "penetrate" the dominant monad: hence, no impressions enter the soul through the senses, but all our ideas are innate. Body and soul seem to act on each other; the former moves when the latter wills it, the latter perceives and conceives when the former receives a physical impression, and this is due to a *pre-established harmony*, owing to which the monads constituting the body and the ruling monad necessarily agree, just as two perfectly regulated clocks always show the same time.

The theory of pre-established harmony differs from the occasionalistic system in an important point. The latter assumes a special divine intervention every time the soul and the physical organism are to agree. God regulates the soul by the body or the body by the volitions of the soul, as a watchmaker constantly regulates one clock by the other. According to Leibniz, the harmony between the movements of the body and the states of the soul is the effect of the Creator's perfect work, as the perpetual agreement between two well-constructed watches results from the skill of the mechanic who has constructed them. Those who assume that the Cre-

ator constantly intervenes in his work, regard God as an un-
skilful watchmaker, who cannot make a perfect machine, but
must continually repair what he has made. Not only does
God not intervene at every moment, but he never intervenes.
"Mr. Newton and his followers," says Leibniz,[1] "have a curious opinion of God and his work. According to them, God
must wind up his watch from time to time; otherwise it would
cease to move. He had not sufficient insight to make it run
forever. Nay, God's machine is so imperfect, according to
them, that he is obliged to clean it, from time to time, by an
extraordinary concourse, and even to repair it as a watchmaker repairs his work; the oftener he is obliged to mend it
and to set it right, the poorer a mechanic he is." . . . "According to my system, bodies act as if there were no souls,
and souls act as if there were no bodies, and both act as if each
influenced the other." [2]

Perhaps,[3] from the theological point of view, Leibniz's theory of pre-established harmony is preferable to the hypothesis of the assistance or perpetual concourse of God, but it
does not satisfy the *curiosity* of the philosopher any more than
does the Cartesian theory. To say that body and soul agree
in their respective states by virtue of a pre-established harmony is to say that a thing is because it is. Leibniz conceals
his ignorance behind a science that rises above all the theories
of the past. When we consider how extravagantly Leibniz's
friends and Leibniz himself eulogized his system, we hardly
know what to wonder at most, the delusion of our philosopher
or the simplicity of his admirers.

We have found, with Leibniz, that monads reflect the universe in different degrees; that some monads reflect it better

---

[1] *Lettre à Clarke*, p. 746.   [2] *Monadologie*, § 81.

[3] We say *perhaps;* for the objection may be urged against Leibniz that the
perpetual miracle of the Cartesians is not a miracle in the sense that the natural
course of things is violently interrupted, and that it is not a miracle precisely
because it is perpetual. From this point of view, pre-established harmony, a
miracle performed once for all, at the beginning of things, is a conception
philosophically inferior to the Cartesian hypothesis.

than others. This pre-supposes the existence of a lowest monad, which reproduces the universe in the most elementary
manner possible, and a highest monad, which expresses it in
a perfect manner: a positive and a superlative. Between these
two extremes we have an infinite chain of intermediate monads. Each intermediate monad forms a different *point*, and,
consequently, a different *point of view*, on the line connecting
the extremes; each, as such, differs from all the rest. But the
monads are infinite in number. Hence we have on the ideal
line between the lowest and the highest monad, i. e., on a line
that is limited on all sides and is *not infinite*, an infinity of different points of view. From this it follows that the distances
separating these points of view are infinitely small, that the
difference between two adjacent monads is imperceptible (*dis-
crimen indiscernibile*).

The principle of *continuity* removes the gaps which are supposed to exist between the mineral and vegetable kingdoms,
and the vegetable and animal kingdoms. There are no gaps,
no absolute oppositions in nature; rest is an infinitely minute
movement; darkness, infinitely little light; the parabola, an
ellipse one of whose foci is infinitely distant; perception in the
plant, an infinitely confused thought. This conception bridges
the chasm which the Cartesians made between brutes and
man. Brutes are merely imperfect men, plants imperfect animals. Leibniz does not, however, regard man as a product of
evolution. Far from it. Each monad remains eternally what
it is, and the soul of the plant cannot therefore be transformed
into an animal soul, nor an animal soul into a human soul.
But his doctrine of the pre-existence of monads, and his teaching that they develop indefinitely, logically culminate in the
theory of transformation. "I recognize," he writes[1] to Des
Maizeaux,[2] "that not only the souls of brutes, but all monads
or simple substances from which the composite phenomena
are derived are as old as the world"; and a few lines above he

[1] Erdmann's edition, p. 676.
[2] The biographer of Bayle and editor of his *Dictionnaire historique et critique*.

says: "I believe that the souls of men have pre-existed, *not as reasonable souls but as merely sensitive souls*, which did not reach the superior stage of reason until the man whom the soul was to animate was conceived." The view that man pre-existed in the animal could not be stated with greater clearness. It even seems as though Leibniz's "souls" pre-exist in the inorganic world, like so many germs. In its state of pre-existence, he says, in substance, the monad which is to become a soul is *absolutely naked*,[1] or without a body; that is to say, it is not surrounded by that group of subordinate monads which will form its organs, and, consequently, exists in a kind of unconscious state. Hence, the monads destined to become either animal or human souls wholly resemble inanimate bodies, from the beginning of the world until they are incorporated.

The passage of the monads into bodies (incarnation) cannot be conceived as a metempsychosis or a metasomatosis, if we mean by these two terms the introduction of the soul into a body formed without its assistance. Nor can future life be considered in such a light. By virtue of the law of pre-established harmony, the development of the soul runs parallel with that of the body, and although there is no real and immediate communion between the central monad and the subordinate monads constituting its body, there is an ideal correlation between the latter and the soul. With the reservation made above,[2] it is correct to call the soul the architect of the body. A soul cannot give itself any body whatsoever, nor can any body serve as its organ.[3] Each soul has its body. But though there is no metempsychosis, i. e., no passage of souls into bodies already formed, there is *metamorphosis*, and perpetual metamorphosis. The soul changes its body only gradually and by degrees. Owing to the principle of continuity, nature never makes leaps, but there are insensible transitions everywhere and in everything.

---

[1] *Monadologie*, § 24.   [2] P. 282.

[3] This expression can only be used in a figurative sense by Leibniz, for there is no actual relation between body and soul.

Future life cannot be incorporeal. Human souls and all other souls are never without bodies; God alone, being pure action, is wholly without body. Since the central monad is "primitive" like all monads, it cannot be created *ex nihilo* upon its entrance into actual life, nor annihilated at its departure. "What we call generation is development or increase; what we call death is envelopment and diminution. Strictly speaking, there is neither generation nor death, and it may be said, that not only is the soul indestructible, but also the animal itself, although its machine is often partially destroyed."[1] As regards rational souls, it may be assumed that they will pass "to a grander scene of action" at the close of their present life. Moreover, their immortality is not the result of a particular divine favor or a privilege of human nature, but a metaphysical necessity, a universal phenomenon embracing all the realms of nature. Just as each monad is as old as the world, so, too, each one "is as durable, as stable, and as absolute as the universe of creatures itself."[2] The plant and the grub are no less eternal than man, the angels, and the archangels. Death is but a turning-point in the eternal life, a stage in the never-ending development of the monad.

In the system of Leibniz we again find Spinoza's extended and thinking substance; but here it appears as the force of extension and perception, and is multiplied infinitely. We likewise meet his notion of *mode* and his determinism, but this is softened by the doctrine of the substantiality of individuals. In spite of its absolute identity, the monad develops continually. Our author takes it "for granted that every being, and consequently the created monad also, is subject to change, and even that this change is continual in each."[3] The soul, like the body, is in a state of change, tendency, and appetition. This perpetual change is called life. Each of these states composing it is the logical consequence of the preceding state and the source of the following state. "As every present state

[1] *Id.*, §§ 73, 77.   [2] *Nouveau système de la nature*, § 16.
[3] *Monadologie*, § 10.

of a simple substance is naturally a consequence of its preceding state, so its present is big with the future." [1]

Hence, freedom of indifference is out of the question in the human soul. In the system of Leibniz, each substance or monad is free in the same sense as Spinoza's unitary substance; i. e., it is not determined by any power outside of itself. But though not determined from without, it is not on that account independent of its own nature, free in reference to itself. The determinism of Leibniz is to that of Spinoza what the determinism of St. Thomas is to the predestination of St. Augustine. It allows each spirit to be "as it were, a little divinity in its own department," and so softens the element in fatalism which is objectionable to the moral sense, without, however, ceasing to apply the law of causality and the principle of sufficient reason to both the physical and moral realms. "I am very far removed," he says, "from accepting the views of Bradwardine, Wiclif, Hobbes, and Spinoza, but we must always bear witness to the truth," [2] and this truth is autonomous determinism: nothing determines the acts of the soul except the soul itself and its preceding acts.

If each monad is, "as it were, a *little* divinity in its own department," if each is a little absolute, what is the highest Divinity, the real absolute? If we were to judge from what we now know of the theory of monads, we should reply: Leibniz substitutes for the monotheism of Descartes and the pantheism of Spinoza a kind of polytheism, for the monarchical conception of the universe, a kind of cosmical republic governed by the law of harmony. But, though that may be his secret thought, it is not his exoteric doctrine. The harmony which governs the universe is a harmony *pre-established by God:* it is not itself the absolute. The monads, which "are the true atoms of nature and the elements of things," [3] are none the less created. They are indestructible, but a miracle can destroy them. That is to say, they are neither absolutely primitive and eternal, nor, in a word, the absolute; but they

---

[1] *Id.*, § 22.   [2] *Théodicée*, II.   [3] *Monadologie*, § 3.

depend on a divinity, "the primitive unity or the original simple substance, of which all monads, created or derived, are the products, and are born, so to speak, from moment to moment, by continual fulgurations of the Divinity." [1] Hence, we have created monads on the one hand, and an uncreated monad, the Monad of monads, on the other; the former are finite and relative; the latter is infinite and absolute.

This Monad of monads is not, like Bruno's, the universe itself considered as infinite; it is a real God, that is, a God distinct from the universe. Leibniz proves his existence by the principle of sufficient reason. "This sufficient reason for the existence of the universe cannot be found in the succession of contingent things, that is, of bodies and their representations in souls; because matter being indifferent in itself to motion and to rest, and to this or that motion, we cannot find the reason of motion in it, and still less of a particular motion. And although the present motion which is in matter comes from the preceding motion, and this, in turn, from one preceding it, we do not advance one step though we go ever so far; for the same question always remains. Thus, it is necessary that the sufficient reason, which has no further need of another reason, be outside of this series of contingent things, and be found in a substance which is their cause, or which is a necessary being, having the reason of its existence in itself, otherwise we should still have no sufficient reason at which to stop. And this ultimate reason of things is called God. This simple primitive substance must contain in itself eminently the perfections contained in the derivative substances which are its effects; hence it will have perfect power, knowledge, and will, that is, it will have omnipotence, omniscience, and supreme goodness." [2] Although Leibniz protests against anthropomorphism, he speaks of God as having "*chosen* the best possible plan in creating the universe, . . . and, above all, the laws of movement best adjusted and most conformable to abstract or metaphysical reasons. . . ." Such, for ex-

---

[1] *Id.*, § 47.　　　　[2] *Principes de la nature et de la grâce*, §§ 8, 9.

ample, by virtue of which "the same quantity of total and absolute force is always preserved in it," and that other law by virtue of which "action and reaction are always equal." [1]

The difficulty confronting the Leibnizian theology is the same as that which meets Descartes. The latter had to confess that the word "substance" when applied to God has not the same meaning as when applied to the creature, and, consequently, that the creature is not a substance in the true sense: a statement which occasioned the system of Spinoza. Leibniz's theology, too, seems to be caught on the horns of a dilemma: Either God is a monad, and in that case finite beings are not monads in the strict sense of the term (which overthrows the monadology); or, created beings are monads, and then we cannot call God a monad unless we identify him with his creatures. But the pliant and cautious genius of a Leibniz turns to account even his defeats. Though the idea of God is confused and contradictory for our intelligence, it is not so in itself. The fact that we are confronted with insoluble difficulties in contemplating the absolute, simply proves that the human soul is not the Monad of monads, — that it occupies a distinguished but not the highest place in the scale of substances. Hence, it must follow from the very nature of things that we can have only a confused notion of the Supreme Being. Just as the plant has a confused perception of the animal, and the animal a confused perception of man, so, too, man has only an indistinct perception and a faint inkling of higher beings and the Supreme Being. In order to have an adequate notion of God, one would have to be God, and the fact that we have no such notion finds its natural explanation in the transcendency of the Supreme Being. God is supernatural or transcendent in relation to man, as man is a supernatural being with respect to animals, the animal a supernatural being with respect to plants, and so on. If we mean by reason the human understanding, God is also supra-rational in so far as he surpasses human nature (or is supernatural); that is, he

[1] *Id.*, §§ 10, 11. Cf. *Théodicée*, III, § 345.

transcends human intelligence as much as his perfection surpasses ours.

We see with what skill the philosopher of universal conciliation acquits himself of his task as a mediator between science and Christianity. Unlike the English philosophers, his contemporaries, who in true nominalistic fashion endeavor to separate religion and philosophy, he begins the work of St. Anselm and St. Thomas all over again on a different plan. His highest ambition is to form an alliance between philosophy and faith, and, if possible, between Lutheranism and Catholicism. He adopts the motto of the Schoolmen: Absolute agreement between the dogmas of the Church and human reason.[1] He antagonizes those who distinguish between philosophical truth and religious truth, — a distinction which saved the free-thinkers of the Renaissance from anathema, — and he finds fault with Descartes for having cleverly evaded the discussion of the mysteries of faith, as though one could hold a philosophy that is irreconcilable with religion, or as though a religion could be true that contradicts truths otherwise proved.

Behind his seeming orthodoxy, however, we may easily detect the traces of his rationalism. When he proclaims theism he does so in the name of philosophy; when he affirms the supernatural he does it in the name of reason, and, to a certain extent, by means of rationalism. He is so far removed from assuming the absolute transcendency of the divine being, as to hold that what transcends human reason cannot contradict reason. Like the ancient Schoolmen before him, he continues to remind us that whatever is above reason is not therefore *against* reason, that whatever is decidedly contradictory to reason cannot be true in religion. By virtue of the law of universal analogy, there must be an analogy, an agreement, a harmony, between divine reason and human reason; and a

---

[1] Nothing better characterizes the essentially scholastic tendency of Leibniz than the following title of one of his last compositions: *The Principles of Nature and of Grace, Founded on Reason* (1714), and this other title: *Discourse on the Conformity of Faith with Reason* (Introduction to the *Theodicy*).

radical opposition between the Creator and the creature is not conceivable. Owing to this agreement, man *naturally* possesses faith in God and in the immortality of the soul, these two central doctrines of all religion; and revelation simply helps to bring out the truths which have been implanted in the human mind by the Creator. Christianity is evidently reduced to the narrow proportions of deism in the system of Leibniz, and revelation becomes a mere sanction of the principles of natural religion.

But, how could a thinker who held that souls have "no windows through which anything can enter or pass out" do otherwise than favor theological rationalism; how could he seriously declare that the soul is enlightened by a supernatural revelation? How could the man who laughed at Newton and the Cartesians for assuming that God interferes with the world, really assume a special intervention of God in history? If we believe in revelation, we must also assume that God has given or can give to the soul the means of communicating with the external world, or windows, to use Leibniz's expression. Now, if God can give windows to the intelligent monad, then it is not contrary to its nature to have them, — then it *can* have them. This means that it can cease to be an absolutely spontaneous force or an absolute ruler in its domain; it means, in a word, that it ceases to be a monad. Leibniz must choose between two alternatives: he must either accept the theory of monads and pre-established harmony, which, according to his explicit declaration,[1] excludes all special divine intervention, or abandon his system in favor of the faith of the Church.

The author of the *Theodicy*, like St. Thomas, subordinates the will of God to the divine reason and its eternal laws. This is a characteristic trait of Leibnizian rationalism, and contrary to the doctrines of Descartes and his teachers, the Scotists and the Jesuits, according to whom not only metaphysical and moral truths, but even mathematical axioms, depend on

[1] *Principes de la nature et de la grâce*, § 13.

the divine will. "It must not be imagined," he says,[1] "as is sometimes done, that the eternal truths which are dependent on God are arbitrary and depend on his will, as Descartes and afterwards M. Poiret[2] seem to have believed. . . . Nothing could be more unreasonable. . . . For if the establishment of justice (for example) happened arbitrarily and without reason, if God hit upon it haphazard, as we draw lots, then his goodness and wisdom are not revealed in it, and it does not bind him. And if he established or made what we call justice and goodness by a purely arbitrary decree and without reason, *he can unmake them and change their nature*, so that we have no reason to suppose that he will observe them always. . . . It is no more contrary to reason and piety to say (with Spinoza) that God acts without knowledge, than to claim that his knowledge does not find the *eternal rules of goodness and of justice* among its objects; or finally, that he has a will which has no regard for these rules."[3]

Hence, the God of Leibniz is not like an Oriental monarch; he is a sovereign bound by laws which he cannot unmake, a kind of constitutional king and chief executive of the universe, rather than the all-powerful autocrat of Tertullian and Duns Scotus. He resembles the God of Montesquieu, who "has his laws," rather than the God of the indeterministic theologians. The supreme power is not the will of God *taken by itself*, but his will governed by the eternal laws of his intelligence, laws which determine his conduct without constraining him, since they constitute the very essence of his nature. Instead of *the nature of God*, Spinoza simply said *nature*. According to Leibniz, the Supreme Being is nature manifesting itself through the medium of a personal will; according to Spinoza, he is nature acting without such a me-

---

[1] *Monadologie*, § 46.

[2] A pastor at Hamburg, a native of Metz (1646–1719). Against the theory of *innate* ideas of his sometime teacher Descartes, and Locke's theory of *acquired* ideas, he sets up his mystical theory of *infused* ideas, that is, ideas communicated by an inspiration from on high (*Œconomie divine*, 7 vols., Amsterdam, 1687; etc.).

[3] *Théodicée*, II, 176–177.

dium; or, if we choose, an unconscious will. Hence, both thinkers are determinists, however violently Leibniz may protest against the teachings of the Jew of Amsterdam.

In creating things, God was determined by his infinite reason, and necessarily created the best possible world. Evil exists only in the details, and serves to enhance the glory of the good: the whole is supremely perfect. The *Theodicy* deals with the question of physical, metaphysical, and moral evil, and aims to refute those who regard the existence of evil as an argument against Providence. It is a popular rather than a scientific book. It is surprising with what familiarity the author speaks of God, just as though God had initiated him into the innermost secrets of his nature. How can Leibniz, who has such certain knowledge that God is not the free author of the natural and moral laws, that his will depends on his intelligence, that he necessarily created the best possible world, maintain that God is supra-rational? What a strange procedure! First he relegates the Being of Beings to the domain of mystery, like so many theologians, and then he defines him, describes him, and makes out a complete inventory of his attributes, as though he were describing a plant or a mineral. For this reason as well as on account of his attitude towards empiricism, Leibniz, whose monadology is so great, so original, and so modern, still belongs to the tribe of the Schoolmen.

But the time had now come for subjecting ontology to the critical sifting process. The controversy between Leibniz and the Englishman Locke concerning the origin of ideas formed the prelude to an important epoch in the history of modern philosophy.

In view of his principle "that the monad has no windows," Leibniz cannot grant that our knowledge has any other source than the soul itself. Nothing can enter it; hence, strictly speaking, the direct observation of external facts or experience is impossible. Experience through the medium of the senses is an illusion; it is, in reality, nothing but confused thought.

He repeatedly declares that the soul, and the soul alone, is both the subject and the object of sensation. We never perceive and experience anything but ourselves. Everything in the mind is spontaneous production, thought, or speculation. Whether we shall regard our thought as the result of an impression from without, or as the product of the mind itself, will depend on its degree of clearness or confusion. Thought, however, though autonomous, is not arbitrary and free from law. It obeys the sovereign laws of contradiction and sufficient reason. But it does not depend on anything external to the thinking monad, around which the *principle of distinction* rises like an impassable wall. Leibniz also declares, in answer to Locke's denial of innate ideas, that nothing is inborn in the understanding *except the understanding itself*, and, consequently, the germ of all our ideas.

The difference between Leibniz and Locke seems very slight: Locke by no means denies the innate power of the mind to form ideas, while Leibniz grants that ideas do not pre-exist in the mind *actually;* they exist in it virtually, as the veins in a block of marble might mark the outlines of a statue to be made from it. Now, then, either the expression, virtual or potential existence of ideas in the mind, has no meaning, or it is synonymous with power (*potentia, virtus*), or mental faculty of forming ideas, a faculty which Locke is perfectly willing to admit. But this seemingly insignificant controversy really represented the opposition between the Middle Ages and modern philosophy, between the speculative method, which passes from conceptions to facts, and the positive method, which passes from facts to conceptions. Locke does not merely combat the idealistic principle; what he especially antagonizes is the idealistic prejudice that *a priori* reasoning relieves the philosopher of the duty of directly observing facts. By declaring himself against the author of the *Essay concerning Human Understanding*, Leibniz, who was otherwise more profound and more speculative than his opponent, sided with the School, that is, with the past against the future.

All that was necessary was to present his doctrines in scholastic form. This the mathematician CHRISTIAN WOLFF[1] proceeded to do. The Leibnizian system contained a precious gem: the conception of active force, which had superseded the dualism of thought and extension, and this treasure was lost in the labored attempts of the professor of Halle to remodel the system. This clear and systematic but narrow-minded thinker revived the extended and thinking substances of Cartesianism, without even suspecting that he was thereby destroying the central and really fruitful notion of the *Monadology*. Thus altered and divided into rational ontology, psychology, cosmology, and theology, the Leibniz-Wolffian metaphysics dominated the German schools until the advent of Kantianism.[2]

[1] 1679–1754. Professor at the University of Halle, from which the influence of the Pietists succeeded in removing him. He was recalled by Frederick II. Latin works: *Oratio de Sinarum philosophia*, Halle, 1726; *Philosophia rationalis sive logica methodo scientifica pertracta*, Frankfort and Leipsic, 1728; *Philosophia prima s. ontologia, id.*, 1730; *Cosmologia generalis, id.*, 1731; *Psychologia empirica, id.*, 1732; *Psychologia rationalis, id.*, 1734; *Theologia naturalis*, 1736–1737; *Jus naturæ*, 1740; *Philosophia moralis sive ethica*, Halle, 1750; *Philosophia civilis sive politica, id.*, 1746; *Jus gentium*, 1750; and a large number of treatises in the German language.

[2] The principal disciples of the Leibniz-Wolffian school are: Ludovici (*Ausführlicher Entwurf einer vollständigen Historie der wolffischen Philosophie*, 3 vols., Leipsic, 1736–1738); Bilfinger (1693–1750), author of numerous and lucid commentaries on the philosophy of Leibniz and Wolff; Thümming (*Institutiones philosophiæ Wolffianæ, etc.*); Baumgarten (1714–1762), who, in his *Æsthetica* (2 vols., 1750–1758), adds the theory of the beautiful in art, or *æsthetics*, to the philosophical sciences, etc. Kant himself was a disciple of Wolff before he became his adversary, and the numerous representatives of the German *Aufklärung*, which preceded the appearance of the *Critiques*, were related to Wolff (Reimarus, Moses Mendelssohn, Lessing, Nicolaï, etc.).

SECOND PERIOD

AGE OF CRITICISM

§ 57. John Locke. Experience as the Source of Knowledge

The author of the work criticised by Leibniz, JOHN LOCKE,[1] was born at Wrington in Somersetshire. A fellow-countryman of Occam and the two Bacons, he shows the anti-mystical and positivistic tendencies common to English philosophy. The study of medicine revealed to him the barrenness of scholastic learning. What, in his opinion, perpetuated the traditions of *a priori* speculation and the ignorance of reality, was the Platonic doctrine of innate metaphysical, moral, and religious truths, teachings which RALPH CUDWORTH[2] and Descartes himself had undertaken to defend. The fact is, if truth is native to the mind, it is useless to search for it outside by observation and experimentation. Then we may, by means of *a priori* speculation, meditation, and reasoning, evolve it from our own inner consciousness, as the spider spins its web out of itself. This hypothesis Descartes consistently carries out when he "closes his eyes and stops his ears," and abstracts from everything acquired by the senses; but he ceases to be consistent when he assiduously devotes himself to the study

---

[1] 1632–1704. Complete works, London, 1714 ff.; 9 vols., *id.*, 1853; philosophical works, ed. by St. John, 2 vols., London, 1854. Next to his *Essay concerning Human Understanding*, his most important work is *Thoughts on Education*, London, 1693; in French, Amsterdam, 1705. Lord King, *Life of Locke*, London, 1829; Th. Fowler, *Locke* (*English Men of Letters*), London, 1880; A. C. Fraser, *Locke* (*Blackwood's Philosophical Classics*), Edinburgh, 1890; Alexander, *Locke* (*Philosophies Ancient and Modern*), London, 1908; Gibson, *Locke's Theory of Knowledge*, Cambridge (Eng.), 1917. See also Green, *Introduction to Hume*.

[2] 1617–1688. In his chief work, *The True Intellectual System of the Universe* (London, 1678), he combats the materialistic conclusions of Thomas Hobbes with the system of Christianized Platonism, which also influenced men like Malebranche, Leibniz, Bonnet, and Herder. [See C. E. Lowrey, *The Philosophy of Ralph Cudworth*, New York, 1885.]

of anatomy and physiology. Indeed, the favorite method of
the metaphysics of the monasteries and universities was to
close one's eyes, to stop one's ears, and to ignore the real
world. This method prevailed as long as the conviction existed that our ideas have their source within us. Hence, it was
necessary, in order to make the philosophers "open their eyes
to the real world," to prove to them that all our ideas come
to us from without, through the medium of sensation: it was
necessary to demonstrate that our ideas are not innate but
acquired.

This Locke undertook to do in his *Essay concerning Human
Understanding* (London, 1690), which, with important additions by the author, was translated into French by Coste
(1700). This great work marks the beginning of a series of
investigations which were completed by Kant's *Critique*.
Locke's aim is: (1) to discover what is the origin of our ideas;
(2) to show what is the certainty, the evidence, and the extent
of our knowledge; (3) to compel philosophy to abandon what
surpasses human comprehension *by clearly marking the limits
of its capacity*.[1]

We have no innate knowledge: such is his revolutionary doctrine against idealism.

As it is evident that new-born children, idiots, and even the
great part of illiterate men, have not the least apprehension
of the axioms alleged to be innate, the advocates of innate
ideas are obliged to assume that the mind can have ideas without being conscious of them.[2] But to say a notion is imprinted
on the mind, and at the same time to maintain that the mind
is ignorant of it, is to make this impression nothing. If these
words, *to be in the understanding*, have any positive meaning,
they signify *to be perceived and to be understood by the under-*

---

[1] *Essay*, Book I, ch. I, Introduction.

[2] Thus Leibniz speaks of unconscious perception, and Leibniz is right, notwithstanding the English philosopher's objections. His only mistake consists
in his failure to recognize that the unconscious perceptions need some external
solicitation in order to become conscious, which, however, his preconceptions
will not allow him to assume.

standing: hence, if any one asserts that a thing is in the understanding, and that it is not understood by the understanding, and that it is in the mind without being perceived by the mind, it amounts to saying that *a thing is and is not in the understanding.*

The knowledge of some ideas, it is true, is very early in the mind. But if we will observe, we shall find that these kinds of truths are made up of acquired and not of innate truths. It is by degrees that we acquire ideas, that we learn the terms which are employed to express them, and that we come to understand their true connection. The universal consent of mankind to certain truths does not prove that these are innate; for nobody knows these truths till he hears them from others. For, if they were innate, "what need they be proposed to gain assent?" An innate and unknown truth is a contradiction in terms.

The principles of morals are no more innate than the rest, unless we so call the desire for happiness and the aversion to misery, which are, indeed, innate tendencies, but which are not the expressions of some truth engraven on the understanding. In this field universal consent cannot be invoked in any case; for moral ideas vary from nation to nation, from religion to religion. The keeping of contracts, for example, is without dispute one of the most undeniable duties in morality. But, if you ask a Christian, who believes in rewards and punishments after this life, why a man should keep his word, he will give this as a reason: Because God, who has the power of eternal life and death, requires it of us. But if a Hobbist be asked why, he will answer, Because the public requires it, and the Leviathan will punish you if you do not. Finally, a pagan philosopher would have answered that the violation of a promise was dishonest, unworthy of the excellence of man, and contrary to his vocation, which is perfect virtue.

The fact is urged against Locke that conscience reproaches us for the breach of the rules of morality. But conscience is nothing else but *our own opinion of our own actions,* and if conscience were a proof of the existence of innate principles, these principles could be contrary to each other, since some persons do, for conscience's sake, what others avoid for the same reason. Do not the savages practise enormities without the slightest remorse? The breaking of a moral rule is undoubtedly no argument that it is unknown. But it is impossible to conceive that a whole nation of men should all publicly reject what every one of them certainly and infallibly knew to be a moral law. No practical rule which is anywhere transgressed *by general consent* can be regarded as innate. To hold that the practical principles are innate is to declare all moral education impossible.

That does not mean that there are only positive laws. There is a great deal of difference between an innate law and a law of nature, between a truth originally imprinted on our minds and a truth which we are ignorant of, but may attain to the knowledge of by the use and due application of our natural faculties. Furthermore, consider the origin of a host of doctrines which pass as indubitable axioms: though derived from no other source than the superstition of a nurse or the authority of an old woman, they often grow up, by length of time and consent of neighbors, to the dignity of principles in religion and morality. The mind of the child receives the impressions which we desire to give it, like white paper on which you write any characters you choose. When children so instructed reach the age of reason and come to reflect on themselves, they cannot find anything more ancient in their minds than those opinions, and therefore imagine that those *propositions of whose knowledge they can find in themselves no original, are the impress of God and nature, and not things taught them by any one else.*[1]

Moreover, how can a truth, that is, a proposition, be innate, if the ideas which make up that truth are not? In order that a proposition be innate, certain ideas must be innate; but, excepting perhaps some faint ideas of hunger, warmth, and

[1] C. III, 23.

pains, which they may have felt in the mother's womb, there is not the least appearance that new-born children have any settled ideas. Even the idea of God is not innate; for besides the individuals who are called atheists and who are really atheists, there are whole nations who have no notion of God nor any term to express it. Moreover, this notion varies infinitely from coarse anthropomorphism to the deism of the philosophers. And even if it were universal and everywhere the same, it would not, on that account, be more innate than the idea of fire; for there is no one who has any idea of God who has not also the idea of fire.

The soul is originally an *empty tablet*. Experience is the source of all our ideas, the foundation of all our knowledge, that is, the observations which we make about external sensible objects or about the internal operations of our minds. *Sensation* is the source of our knowledge of external objects, *reflection*, of our knowledge of internal facts. There is not in the mind a single idea that is not derived from one or both of these principles. The first ideas of the child come from sensation, and it is only at a more advanced age that he seriously reflects on what takes place within him. The study of languages may be cited in support of this thesis. In fact, all the words which we employ depend on sensible ideas, and those which are made use of to stand for actions and notions quite removed from sense have their rise from thence, and from obvious sensible ideas are transferred to more abstruse significations. Thus, for example, to imagine, apprehend, comprehend, adhere, conceive, instil, disgust, disturbance, tranquillity, etc., are all words taken from the operations of sensible things and applied to certain modes of thinking. Spirit, in its primary signification, is breath; angel, a messenger. If we could trace all these words to their sources, we should certainly find in all languages the names which stand for things that fall not under our senses to have had their first rise from sensible ideas.[1] Follow a child from its birth

[1] B. III, chap. I, 5.

and observe the alterations that time makes, and you shall find, as the mind by the senses comes more and more to be furnished with ideas, it comes to be more and more awake, and thinks more, the more it has matter to think on.

Locke answers the question, When do we begin to think? as follows: As soon as sensation furnishes us with the materials. We do not think before we have sensations. Nothing is in the intellect which has not already been in experience. (*Nihil est in intellectu quod non antea fuerit in sensu.*) According to the idealist, thought is the essence of the soul, and it is not possible for the soul not to think; it thinks antecedent to and independently of sensation; it always thinks even though it is not conscious of it. But experience, which alone can settle the question, by no means proves it, and *it is not any more necessary for the soul always to think than it is for the body always to move.*[1] The absolute continuity of thought is one of those hypotheses which have no fact of experience to bear them out. A man cannot think without perceiving that he thinks. With as much reason might we claim that a man is always hungry, but that he does not always feel it. Thought depends entirely on sensation. In its sublimest ideas and in its highest speculations it does not stir beyond those ideas which sense or reflection has offered for its contemplation. In this part the understanding is purely passive. The objects of our senses obtrude their particular ideas upon our minds whether we will or not. These simple ideas, when offered to the mind, the understanding can no more refuse to have, nor alter, nor blot them out, than a mirror can refuse, alter, or obliterate the images of the objects placed before it.

There are two kinds of ideas, some *simple* and some *complex*. These simple ideas, the materials of all our knowledge, are suggested to the mind only by those two ways above mentioned, viz., sensation and reflection. The mind, though passive in the formation of simple ideas, is active in the formation of complex ideas. It *receives* the former, it *makes* the latter.

[1] B. II, chap. I, 10.

When it has once received the simple ideas it has the power to repeat, compare, and unite them, even to an almost infinite variety, and so can make new complex ideas. But it is not in the power of the most fruitful mind to form a single new simple idea, not taken in by the way of sensation and reflection. The dominion of man, in this little world of his own understanding, is the same as it is in the great world of visible things, wherein his power, however managed by art and skill, reaches no farther than to compound and divide the materials that are made to his hand; *but can do nothing towards the making the least particle of new matter, or destroying one atom of what is already in being.*[1]

The simple ideas come into our minds by one sense only, or by more senses than one, or from reflection only, or, finally, by all the ways of sensation and reflection.

Among the ideas which come to us only through one sense (colors, sounds, tastes, smells, etc.), there is none which we receive more constantly than the idea of *solidity* or impenetrability. We receive this idea from touch. This, of all simple ideas, is the idea most intimately connected with and essential to body. Solidity is neither space — with which the Cartesians erroneously identify it — nor hardness. It differs from space as resistance differs from non-resistance. A body is solid in so far as it fills the space which it occupies to the absolute exclusion of every other body; it is hard, in so far as it does not easily change its figure. It is not properly a definition of solidity that Locke pretends to give us. If we ask him to give us a clearer explanation of solidity, he sends us to our senses to inform us. The simple ideas we have are such as experience teaches us; but if, beyond that, we endeavor to make them clearer in the mind, we shall succeed no better.

The ideas which come to the mind by more than one sense (sight and touch) are those of space or extension, figure, rest, and motion. By reflection we get the ideas of perception or the power of thinking, and the ideas of volition or the power

[1] B. II, chap. II, 2.

to act. Finally, the ideas of pleasure, pain, power, existence, and unity come to us by sensation and reflection.

Some of the external causes of our sensations are real and positive, others are only privations in the objects from whence our senses derive those ideas, like those, for example, which produce the ideas of cold, darkness, and rest. When the understanding perceives these ideas, it considers them as distinct and as positive as the others, without taking notice of the causes that produce them, which is an inquiry not belonging to the idea, as it is in the understanding, but to the nature of the things existing without us. Now these are two very different things, and carefully to be distinguished; we must not think that our ideas are exactly the images and resemblances of something inherent in the object which produces them; *for most of the ideas of sensation which are in our minds are no more the likeness of something existing without us than the names that stand for them are the likeness of our ideas*, although these names are apt to excite ideas in us as soon as we hear them.[1]

Different things should have different names; hence, whatsoever the mind perceives in itself, every perception that is in the mind when it thinks, Locke calls *idea*, and the power or faculty to produce any idea in our mind he calls the *quality* of the subject (we should say: of the object).

That being established, Locke, like Hobbes, distinguishes two kinds of qualities.[2] Some, such as solidity, extension, figure, and mobility, are inseparable from the body, in what state soever it be: such as it constantly keeps in all the alterations it suffers. These are the *original* or *primary* or real qualities of body. Others, like colors, sounds, tastes, etc., do not belong to the bodies themselves, and are nothing but the power which they have to produce various sensations *in us* by

---

[1] B. II, chap. VIII, 1 ff. Here we have the fundamental principle of *criticism* which, as we have seen, was advanced by Aristippus, Pyrrho, Ænesidemus, Hobbes, and Descartes. The eighth chapter of the second book of the *Essay*, of which the above is a summary, and especially § 7 of this chapter, is the classical expression of the philosophy to which Kant gives its real name.

[2] *Id.*, 9.

their primary qualities, that is, by the bulk, figure, texture, and motion of their insensible parts. Locke calls them *secondary qualities: qualities*, in order to comply with the common way of speaking, which considers white, red, and sweet as something inherent in the bodies; *secondary*, in order to distinguish them from those which are real qualities.

Whatever reality we may by mistake attribute to them, colors, smells, sounds, and tastes are nothing but sensations produced *in us* by the primary or real qualities of bodies, — sensations which in no way resemble the qualities which exist *in the objects*. What is sweet, blue, or warm in idea is nothing but a certain bulk, figure, and motion of the insensible parts in the bodies themselves which we call so. Take away the sensation which we have of these qualities; let not the eyes see light or colors, nor the ears hear sounds; let the palate not taste, nor the nose smell; and all colors, tastes, odors, and sounds will vanish and cease to exist. In the opposite hypothesis, the result will be the same. Suppose man were endowed with senses sufficiently fine to discern the small particles of bodies and the real constitution on which their sensible qualities depend, and they will produce in him quite different ideas. The effects of the microscope prove it; blood, for example, seems quite red to us, but by means of this instrument, which discovers to us its smallest particles, we see nothing but a very small number of red globules; and we do not know how these red globules would appear if we could find glasses with a magnifying power that is a thousand or ten thousand times greater.

The formation of ideas presupposes the following faculties in the understanding: (1) *perception*, which is the first step and degree towards knowledge, and the inlet of all the materials of it; (2) *retention*, which keeps the ideas brought into the mind, for some time actually in view (contemplation), and revives again those which after imprinting have disappeared from it (memory); (3) *discernment*, or the faculty of clearly distinguishing between the different ideas; (4) *comparison*, which forms that large tribe of ideas comprehended under relations; (5) *composition*, whereby the mind joins together several simple ideas which it has received from sensation and reflection, and combines them into complex ones; finally (6) *abstraction*.[1] If every particular idea that we take in should have a distinct name, the number of words would be endless. To prevent this, the mind makes the particular ideas received from particular objects, general; it separates them (*abstrahere*) from all the circumstances which make these ideas represent particular and actually existent beings, as time, place, and other *concomitant* ideas. This operation of the mind is called *abstraction*. It is the prerogative of the human mind, whereas the preceding faculties are common to man and brutes.

The mind is passive in perception proper, but becomes more and more active in the following steps; comparison, the composition of complex ideas, and abstraction, are the three great acts of the mind. But, however active the mind may be in the formation of complex ideas, these are in the last analysis but modes or modifications of the materials which it passively receives from sensation and reflection.

Thus the ideas of place, figure, distance, and immensity are modifications or modes of the simple idea of space, which is acquired by sight and touch; the ideas of periods, hours, days, years, time, eternity, are modifications of the idea of duration or succession, which we acquire by observing the constant train of ideas which succeed one another in our minds; the idea of finite and infinite, modifications of the idea of quantity.

If it be objected that the ideas of infinity, eternity, and immensity cannot have the same source as the others, since the objects which surround us have no affinity nor any proportion with an infinite extension or duration, Locke answers that these ideas are merely negative, that we do not *actually* have in the mind any positive idea of an infinite space or an endless duration (Aristotle). All our positive ideas are always lim-

[1] B. II, chaps. IX ff.

ited. The negative idea of an infinite space and duration comes from the power which the mind has of extending its ideas of space and duration by an endless number of new additions.

We get the idea of active and passive power (receptivity) when we observe, on the one hand, the continual alteration in things, and, on the other, the constant change of our ideas, which is sometimes caused by the impression of outward objects on our senses, and sometimes by the determination of our own will.

When we reflect on the power which the mind has to command the presence or the absence of any particular idea, or to prefer the motion of any part of the body to its rest, and *vice versa*, we acquire the idea of will. *Will* is not opposed to *necessity*, but to *restraint*. Liberty is not an attribute of the will. Will is a power or ability, and freedom another power or ability; so that to ask a man whether his will be free is to ask whether one power has another power, one ability another ability. To speak of a free will is like speaking of swift sleep or square virtue. We are not free to will. We are not free to will or not to will a thing which is in our power, when once we give our attention to it. The will is determined by the mind, and the mind is determined by the desire for happiness. On this point Locke, Leibniz, and Spinoza are in perfect accord, and unanimously opposed to Cartesian indeterminism.

The notions which we have just analyzed are combinations of simple ideas of the same kind (*simple modes*). Others, like obligation, friendship, falsehood, and hypocrisy, are composed of simple ideas of different kinds (*mixed modes*). Thus, the mixed mode which the word *lie* stands for is made of these simple ideas: (1) articulate sounds; (2) certain ideas in the mind of the speaker; (3) words which are the signs of those ideas; (4) those signs put together by affirmation or negation, otherwise than as the ideas they stand for are in the mind of the speaker.

We get the idea of these mixed modes as follows: (1) By ex-

perience and observation of things themselves. Thus, by seeing two men wrestle or fence we get the idea of wrestling or
fencing. (2) By invention, or voluntary putting together of
several simple ideas in our own minds: so he that first invented
printing or etching had an idea of it in his mind before it ever
existed. (3) By explaining the names of actions we never
saw, or notions we cannot see. The several fashions, customs,
and manners of a nation give rise to several combinations of
ideas which are familiar and necessary to that nation, but
which another people have never had any occasion to make.
Special names come to be annexed to such special combinations of a people, to avoid long periphrases in things of daily
conversation (*ostracism* among the Greeks, *proscription* among
the Romans), and so there are in every language particular
terms which cannot be literally translated into any other.

So much for the complex ideas that express modes.

The complex ideas of *substances* (man, horse, tree) are
formed as follows: The mind observes that a certain number
of simple ideas, conveyed in by the different senses, constantly
go together, and accustoms itself to regard such a complication of ideas as one object, and designates it by one name.
Hence, a substance is nothing but a combination of a certain
number of simple ideas, considered as united in one thing.
Thus the substance called *sun* is nothing but the aggregate of
the ideas of light, heat, roundness, and constant, regular motion. By substance, the philosophy of the School, and afterwards Descartes, imagined an unknown object, which they
assumed to be the support (*substratum*) of such qualities as
are capable of producing simple ideas in us, which qualities
are commonly called accidents. But this substance considered
as *anything else* but the combination of these qualities, as
something hidden behind them, is a mere phantom of the
imagination. We have no distinct idea of such a substratum
without qualities. If any one should be asked wherein color
or weight inheres, "he would have nothing to say, but the
solid extended parts; and if he were demanded *what is it that*

solidity and extension adhere in, he would not be in a much better case than the Indian before mentioned, who, saying that the world was supported by a great elephant, was asked what the elephant rested on; to which his answer was, — a great tortoise; but being again pressed to know what gave support to the broad-backed tortoise, replied, — something, he knew not what." [1] Our knowledge does not extend beyond the assumed *accidents*, that is, beyond our simple ideas, and whenever metaphysics attempts to proceed beyond them it is confronted with insurmountable difficulties.

The third class of complex ideas express *relation*. The most comprehensive relation wherein all things are concerned is the relation of cause and effect. We get the idea of this by noticing, by means of the senses, the constant vicissitude of things, and by observing that they owe their existence to the action of some other being. Locke does not analyze the idea of cause as thoroughly as his successor Hume. We shall see that the latter regards it as no less illusory than the idea of substance, or substratum.

In passing from the study of ideas to the problem of knowledge and certitude, Locke enters upon a philological discussion, which we have partly reproduced above, and which stamps him as one of the founders of the philosophy of language.

All things that exist are particulars. The far greatest part of words (with the exception of proper names) are general terms; which has not been the effect of neglect or chance, but of reason and necessity. In what do the *species* and *genera* consist, and how do they come to be formed? Our ideas are at first particular. The ideas which the children have of their nurse and their mother represent only those individuals. The names which they first gave to them are confined to these individuals and designate only them. Afterwards, when time and a larger acquaintance with the world have made them observe that there are a great many other things that resem-

[1] B. II, chap. XXIII, 2.

ble their father and mother and those persons they have been used to, they frame an idea, which they find those many particulars do partake in; and to that they give, with others, the name *man*. And thus they come to have a general name, and a general idea; wherein they make nothing new, but only leave out of the complex idea they had of Peter and James, Mary and Jane, that which is peculiar to each, and retain only what is common to all. In the same way they acquire all general ideas. This process of abstraction and generalization is a necessity; for it would be impossible for each thing to have a particular name. It is beyond the power of human capacity to frame and retain distinct ideas of all the particular things we meet with, — of every tree, of every plant, of every beast, that affected the senses. Still less possible would it be to retain their names. But even if it could be done, it would not be of any great use for the improvement of knowledge; for although our knowledge is founded on particular observations, it enlarges itself by general views, which can only be formed by reducing the things to certain *species* under general names.

General notions (*universalia*) are nothing but abstract and partial ideas of more complex ones, taken from particular existences. They are simple products of our minds. *General and universal belong not to the real existence of things; but are the inventions and creatures of the understanding.*[1] It is true that nature, in the production of things, makes several of them alike; there is nothing more obvious, especially in the races of animals, and all things propagated by seed. But the reduction of these things to *species* is the workmanship of the understanding. Owing to its lack of a thorough knowledge of nature, the Platonic doctrine, which regarded universals as the ingenerable and incorruptible essences of things, disregarded this fact of experience that *all things that exist, besides their author, are liable to change;* thus, that which was grass to-day is to-morrow the flesh of a sheep, and within a few days after becomes part of a man. In the organic world, as elsewhere,

[1] B. III, chap. III, 11.

the genera, species, essences, and substantial forms, dreamt of by the metaphysicians, far from being things regularly and constantly made by nature and having a real existence in things themselves (Aristotle) or apart from them (Plato), "appear, upon a more wary survey, to be nothing else but an artifice of the understanding, for the easier signifying such collections of ideas as it should often have occasion to communicate by one general term." Notice, moreover, how doubtful is the signification of the word "species," and how difficult it is to define organic beings. So uncertain are the boundaries of animal species that none of the definitions of the word "man" which we yet have, nor descriptions of that sort of animal, are so perfect and exact as to satisfy a considerate inquisitive person. We may find that learned men multiply species too much, but we may also hold the opposite. Why, for example, are not a shock and a hound as distinct species as a spaniel and an elephant? Any one who carefully observes the individuals ranked under one and the same general name can hardly doubt that many of them are as different, one from another, as several of those which are ranked under different specific names.

We may remark, in passing, that the modern theory of the transmutation of species is nothing but an application of Locke's teaching that species have no objective reality. Let us also note the important fact that this extreme nominalism closely approximates extreme realism. Scholastic nominalism denies the reality of species, and absolutely affirms the reality of individuals to the exclusion of everything else. In this sense Leibniz is a nominalist. English nominalism, from which the theory of transformation takes its rise, denies not only the existence of species, but also the stability of the individuals themselves. All things, says Locke, besides their author, are liable to change. Now this is exactly what Spinoza teaches. He is not content with repudiating universals for the sake of the one universal Being, but considers the individuals themselves as passing modes of what he calls substance, what the materialists call matter, and Locke and the positivists call the great unknown.

Hence, species, genera, and universals are mere words (*flatus vocis*). The traditional error of the metaphysicians consists *in taking words for things*.[1] The disciples of the Peripatetic philosophy are persuaded that the *ten categories* of Aristotle, *substantial forms*, *vegetative souls*, *abhorrence of a vacuum*, are something real. The Platonists have their *soul of the world*, and the Epicureans their *endeavor towards motion in their atoms*. All this is gibberish, which, in the weakness of the human understanding, serves to palliate our ignorance and cover our errors. We must be content; there are limits to our knowledge that cannot be crossed.

Well, then, what is knowledge?

It is nothing but the perception of the connection and agreement, or disagreement and repugnancy, of any of our ideas. From this definition it follows that our knowledge does not reach further than our ideas; nay, it is even much narrower than these, because the connection between most of our simple ideas is unknown. Hence we may affirm that, although our knowledge may be carried much further than it has hitherto been, it will never reach to all we might desire to know concerning those ideas we have, nor be able to resolve all the questions that might arise concerning any of them. Thus, we have the ideas of matter and thinking, but *possibly shall never be able to know whether any mere material thing thinks or no; it being impossible for us to discover whether Omnipotency has not given to some systems of matter fitly disposed, a power to perceive and think*.[2] We are perfectly conscious of the existence of our soul, without knowing exactly what it is; and he who will take the trouble to consider freely the difficulties contained in both the spiritualistic and the materialistic hypotheses, will *scarce find his reason able to determine him fixedly for or against the soul's materiality*. Just as we are absolutely ignorant whether there is any opposition or connection between

---

[1] B. III, chap. X, 14.　　　　　[2] B. IV, chap. III, 6.

extension and thought, matter and perception, so too it is impossible for us to know anything of the union or incompatibility between the secondary qualities of an object (between its color, taste, and smell), on the one hand, and between any secondary quality and those primary qualities on which it depends, on the other.

Though our knowledge does not reach further than our ideas and the perception of their agreement or disagreement, *and though we have no knowledge of what the things they represent are in themselves*, it does not follow that all our knowledge is illusory and chimerical.

We have an intuitive and immediate knowledge of our own existence, even if we are ignorant of the metaphysical essence of the soul. We have a demonstrative knowledge of God, although our understanding cannot comprehend the immensity of his attributes. Finally, we know the other things by sensation. It is true, we do not know them immediately, and consequently our knowledge is real only so far as there is a conformity between our ideas and the reality of things. But we are not absolutely without a criterion for knowing whether our ideas agree with the things themselves. It is certain that our simple ideas correspond to external realities; for since the mind can by no means make them to itself without the intervention of the senses (as witness men born blind), it follows that they are not fictions of the imagination, but the natural and regular productions of things without us, really operating upon us. The reality of external things is further proved by the fact that there is a very great difference between an idea that comes from an actual sensation and one that is revived in memory, and that the pleasure or pain which follows upon an actual sensation does not accompany the return of these ideas when the external objects are absent. Finally, our senses bear witness to the truth of each other's report concerning the existence of sensible things without us. He that *sees* a fire may, if he doubt whether it be anything more than a bare fancy, *feel* it too, and be convinced by putting his hand in it, which certainly could never be put into such exquisite pain by a bare idea or phantom.

Let us sum up. There are no innate ideas; no innate truths, maxims, or principles; no other sources of knowledge but sensation for external things, and reflection for what takes place within us. Consequently, it is impossible to know anything outside of what experience, be it external or internal, furnishes us. Philosophy must abandon the transcendent problems of substance, essence, and the inner constitution of things, as well as all methods except observation, induction, and experience. The soul exists, but we cannot know whether its essence is material or immaterial. The freedom of indifference is denied. God exists, but we know nothing of his nature. Outside of us exist solidity, extension, figure, and motion, as primary qualities, or such as inhere in the bodies themselves. The substance of bodies is identical with the sum of these qualities. These qualities are distinguished from secondary qualities (colors, sounds, tastes, smells, etc.), which are merely sensations of the soul produced by the primary qualities of bodies, and do not exist as such in the objects themselves. Finally, the reality of species is absolutely denied.

These doctrines are the culmination of the nominalistic movement which was inaugurated by Roscellinus and renewed by Occam; they likewise form the beginning of modern scientific philosophy. As the preceding paragraphs show, the teachings of Descartes and Bacon greatly resemble each other in many respects, particularly in the matter of final causes. A no less noteworthy fact, one that may serve as an argument against the scepticism which bases itself solely on the constant disagreement among philosophers, is the harmony existing between Locke and Spinoza, that is to say, between empiricism and rationalism. Locke agrees with his contemporary at Amsterdam not only in his repudiation of species, but in his denial of the liberty of indifference, and in his view that ethics is as susceptible of demonstration as mathematics.

The name of the most illustrious scientist of the seventeenth century is connected with Locke's empiricism supplemented by mathematical speculation. I mean ISAAC NEWTON (1642–1727), the founder of celestial mechanics, whose *Mathematical Principles of Natural Philosophy* is, next to the *Celestial Revolutions* of Copernicus, the grandest monument of modern science. His calculus of fluxions, which anticipated, or at least was discovered independently of, Leibniz's integral and differential calculus, his analysis of light, and, above all, his theory of universal gravitation, according to which bodies are attracted to each other in direct proportion to their masses and in inverse ratio to the squares of their distances, have exercised an incalculable influence upon what he calls natural philosophy.

Locke's philosophy, with its principles of observation and analysis, also formed the nucleus of a distinguished school of English moralists. We might mention the names of: SHAFTESBURY,[1] CLARKE,[2] HUTCHESON,[3] FERGUSON,[4] ADAM SMITH,[5] and many others.[6] The *free-thinkers*,[7] who flourished in Great Britain and on the Continent at the end of this period, and the philosophers proper whom we have still to consider, are like-

---

[1] 1671–1713. [*Characteristics of Men, Manners, Opinions, and Times*, 1711; ed. by W. Hatch, 3 vols., London, 1869.]

[2] 1675–1729. Works, 4 folio vols., London, 1738–1742.

[3] 1694–1747. [*Inquiry into the Original of our Ideas of Beauty and Virtue*, London, 1725 ff.; *Philosophiæ moralis institutio*, Glasgow, 1745; *A System of Moral Philosophy*, id., 1755. See Fowler and Albee. — TR.]

[4] 1724–1816. [*Institution of Moral Philosophy*, London, 1769; tr. into German by Garve, Leipsic, 1772. — TR.]

[5] 1723–1790. [*Theory of Moral Sentiments*, London, 1759. Cf. Farrer, *Adam Smith (English Philosophers Series)*, London, 1880. — TR.]

[6] [Cumberland, *De legibus naturæ*, London, 1672; Engl. tr. by Jean Maxwell, id., 1727. Cf. Ernest Albee, *The Ethical System of Richard Cumberland (Phil. Review*, 1895). Joseph Butler, *Sermons upon Human Nature*, London, 1726. Cf. W. Collins, *Butler (Phil. Classics)*, Edinburgh and London, 1889. Home, *Essays on the Principles of Morality and Natural Religion*, 1751. Paley, *Principles of Moral and Political Philosophy*, London, 1785. J. Bentham, *Principles of Morals and Legislation*, 1789.]

[7] [John Toland, *Christianity not Mysterious*, London, 1696. A. Collins, *A Discourse of Freethinking*, London, 1713. M. Tindal, *Christianity as Old as the Creation*, London, 1730. Thomas Chubb, *A Discourse concerning Reason with Regard to Religion*, London, 1730. T. Morgan, *The Moral Philosopher*, London, 1737 ff. Lord Bolingbroke, Works ed. by D. Mollet, 5 vols., 1753–1754.]

wise descendants of Locke. English philosophy is, to this day, almost as empirical and positivistic as in the times of Bacon and Locke. We may even claim, in general, that England, though rich in thinkers of the highest order, has never had but a single school of philosophy, or, rather, that it has never had any, for its philosophy is a perpetual protest against Scholasticism.

§ 58. Berkeley and Subjective Idealism

After what has been said of the agreement existing between Locke and Spinoza, it will hardly surprise us to see a disciple of the English philosopher offering the hand of friendship to Leibniz and Malebranche, the champions of intellectualism and innate ideas across the sea. Although Locke and his opponents differ on several essential points, they reach practically the same conclusions concerning the world of sense. Malebranche and Leibniz spiritualize matter; they explain it as a confused idea, and ultimately assume a principle endowed with desire and perception, that is, mind. Locke's criticism, on the other hand, does not wholly reject the material world; one-half of it is retained. Extension, form, and motion exist outside of us; but neither colors, nor sounds, nor tastes, nor smells exist independently of our sensations. Moreover, Locke attacks the traditional notion of substance, or substratum, and defines real substance as a combination of qualities. Indeed, he goes so far as to say that *the idea of corporeal substance or matter is as remote from our conceptions and apprehensions as that of spiritual substance or spirit!* [1] Hence, all that was needed to arrive at the negation of matter or absolute spiritualism was to efface the distinction which he had drawn between primary and secondary qualities, and to call all sensible qualities, without exception, *secondary*.

This is done by GEORGE BERKELEY, who thus enters upon a course against which Locke had advised in vain. Berkeley was born in Ireland, 1685, of English ancestors, became Bishop

[1] *Essay concerning Human Understanding*, II, ch. XXIII, 5.

of Cloyne, 1734, and died at Oxford, 1753. The following are his most important works: *Essay towards a New Theory of Vision, Treatise on the Principles of Human Knowledge, Three Dialogues between Hylas and Philonous, Alciphron, or the Minute Philosopher.*[1]

Locke recognizes, with Descartes and Hobbes, that color is nothing apart from the sensation of the person seeing it, that sound exists only for the hearing, that taste and smell are mere sensations, and do not inhere in the things themselves. But in addition to such secondary qualities, which do not inhere in the objects but in the perceiving subject, he assumes primary qualities existing without the mind and belonging to an unthinking substance: extension, figure, and motion. And that is where he is wrong. Just as color, smell, and taste exist only for the person perceiving them, so extension, form, and motion exist only in a mind that perceives them. Take away the perceiving subject, and you take away the sensible world. Existence consists in perceiving or being perceived. That which is not perceived and does not perceive does not exist. The *objects* do not exist apart from the *subjects* perceiving them. According to the common view, these objects — houses, mountains, and rivers — have an existence, natural or real, distinct from their being perceived by the understanding, and our ideas of them are copies or resemblances of all these things without us. Now, says Berkeley, either those external objects or originals of our ideas are perceivable, or they are not perceivable. If they are, then they are ideas (for an idea = something perceived). In that case, there is no difference between objects assumed to be without us and our ideas of them; and "we have gained our point." "If you say they are not, I appeal to any one whether it be sense to assert a color is like something which is invisible; hard or soft, like something which

[1] Fraser, *Selections from Berkeley*, 1891; *Theory of Vision, Principles of Human Knowledge, Three Dialogues*, in Everyman's Library; *Principles of Human Knowledge*, Open Court Edition, Chicago, 1920; Fraser, *Berkeley and Spiritual Realism*, London, 1908; Johnston, *The Development of Berkeley's Philosophy*, London, 1923.

is intangible; and so of the rest." Hence, there is no real difference between things and our ideas of them. The words *sensible thing* and *idea* are synonymous.

Our ideas, or the things which we perceive, are visibly inactive. It is impossible for an idea to do anything, or to be the cause of anything. Hence, spirit or thinking substance alone can be the cause of ideas (sensible things). A spirit is one simple, undivided, active being, — as it perceives ideas, it is called the *understanding*, and as it produces or otherwise operates about them, it is called *will*. Now all ideas (perceived things) being essentially passive, and spirit eminently active, it follows that we cannot, strictly speaking, have an *idea* of spirit, will, or soul; at any rate, we cannot form as clear an idea of it as of a triangle, for example. Inasmuch as the idea is absolutely passive and spirit the very essence of activity, *the idea of spirit* is a contradiction in terms, and no more like spirit than night is like the day.[1]

In so far as mind perceives ideas it *produces* things; and these are not two distinct operations: to perceive signifies to produce, and *the ideas are the things themselves*. Nevertheless, the objects which I perceive have not a like dependence on my will. Nay, very many of them do not depend on it at all. "When in broad daylight I open my eyes, it is not in my power to choose whether I shall see or no, or to determine what particular objects shall present themselves to my view." There is therefore — thus Berkeley proves the existence of God — some other will that produces them, a more powerful spirit that imprints them upon us. "Now the set rules or established methods wherein the Mind we depend on excites in us the ideas of sense, are called the *laws of nature;* and these we learn by experience. . . . The ideas imprinted on the senses by the Author of nature are commonly called *real things;* and

---

[1] Berkeley repeatedly points out the impossibility of forming an adequate idea of spiritual things, such as spirit, soul, or will, and he explains this by the radical difference existing between spirit, the essentially active thing, and idea, the essentially passive thing (*Principles of Human Knowledge*, §§ 27, 89, 135). He likewise insists on the necessity of clearly distinguishing between *spirit* and *idea*, thus contradicting Spinoza, who regards them as synonyms (*id.*, § 139).

those excited in the imagination being less regular, vivid, and constant, are more properly termed *ideas* or *images of things*. The ideas of sense are allowed to have more in them, that is, to be more strong, orderly, and coherent, than the creatures of the mind; but this is no argument that they exist without the mind."

To the objection that this makes the sensible world, with its sun, stars, mountains, and rivers, a chimera or an illusion, Berkeley answers that he does not in the least doubt the existence of things. He is even willing to accept the term *corporeal substance* if we mean by it a combination of sensible qualities, such as extension, solidity, weight, and the like. But he utterly repudiates the scholastic notion which conceives matter as a *substratum* or support of accidents or qualities without the mind perceiving them, as *a stupid, thoughtless somewhat*, which can neither perceive nor be perceived, existing alongside of, and independent of, the thinking substance.[1] The objection that, according to his principles, we eat and drink ideas, and are clothed with ideas, is not more serious than the preceding one. It overlooks the fact that he employs the word *idea*, not in its usual signification, but in the sense of perceived thing. But it is certain that our victuals and our apparel are things which we perceive immediately by our senses, that is, ideas. Finally, it is held that, according to his teaching, the sun, moon, and trees exist only when they are perceived, and are annihilated when we no longer perceive them. They would undoubtedly cease to exist if there were no one to perceive them; for existence consists in being perceived or in perceiving. But if our mind cannot perceive them, another spirit can perceive them or continue their existence, so to speak; for though Berkeley denies the objective existence of bodies, he assumes a plurality of spiritual beings.

It is true, mankind and even philosophers steadfastly assume the existence of matter. The explanation is simple. They are conscious that they are not the authors of their own sensations. and evidently know that they are imprinted from

[1] *Principles of Human Knowledge*, § 75.

without. They have recourse to the hypothesis of matter as the external origin of their ideas, instead of deriving them directly from the Creative Spirit which alone can produce them, (1) because they are not aware of the contradiction involved "in supposing things like unto our ideas existing without; (2) because the Supreme Spirit, which excites those ideas in our minds, is not marked out and limited to our view by any particular finite collection of sensible ideas, as human agents are by their size, complexion, limbs, and motions; and (3) because his operations are regular and uniform. Whenever the course of nature is interrupted by a miracle, men are ready to own the presence of a superior agent. But when we see things go on in the ordinary course they do not excite in us any reflection."

The negation of matter as a substance without the mind silences a number of difficult and obscure questions: Can a corporeal substance think? Is matter infinitely divisible? How does it operate on spirit? These and the like inquiries are entirely banished from philosophy. The division of sciences is simplified, and human knowledge reduced to two great classes: knowledge of ideas and knowledge of spirits.[1] Moreover, this philosophy is alone capable of overcoming scepticism. If we assume, with the ancient schools, that a substance exists without the mind, and that our ideas are images of it, then scepticism is inevitable. On that hypothesis, we see only the appearances, and not the real qualities of things. What may be the extension, figure, or motion of anything really and absolutely, or *in itself*, it is impossible for us to know; we know only the relations which things bear to our senses. All we see, hear, and feel is but a phantom. All these doubts are inevitable as soon as we distinguish between ideas and things.[2]

---

[1] *Principles of Human Knowledge*, § 86. Berkeley afterwards (§ 89) adds a third group of knowledge: that of relations existing either between things or ideas (physical sciences and mathematical sciences).

[2] Kant's conclusions fully confirm these profound remarks of Berkeley (*Principles*, §§ 85 ff.). It was because the *Critique of Pure Reason* asserted the dogma combated by the Irish philosopher (the *thing-in-itself* considered as existing independently of the phenomenon) that it became involved in scepticism.

The absolute spiritualism of Berkeley is a unitary, homogeneous system, unquestionably superior to the hybrid philosophies of Descartes and Wolff. Nay, it is, in my opinion, the only metaphysic that may be successfully opposed to materialism, for it alone takes into consideration the partial truth of its objections. It overcomes the dualism of substances, and thus satisfies the most fundamental demand of the philosophical spirit, — the demand for unity. In this respect it has all the advantages of radical materialism without being hampered by its difficulties. It greatly resembles the system of Leibniz, but excels it in clearness, consistency, boldness, and decision. Leibniz's opinions on matter, space, and time are undecided, conciliatory, and even obscure. Berkeley shows no sign of hesitation. An earnest and profoundly honest thinker, he tells us, in a straightforward manner, that the existence of matter is an illusion; that time is nothing, abstracted from the succession of ideas in our minds; that space cannot exist without the mind; that minds alone exist; and that these perceive ideas either by themselves or through the action of the all-powerful Spirit on which they depend.

But besides these advantages, his philosophy also possesses disadvantages. We need not repeat the petty objection of his supposed adversaries, who make him say that we eat and drink ideas and are clothed with ideas. We may, however, ask, What, on his theory, becomes of the vegetable and animal kingdoms, which the more realistic Leibniz regards as having objective existence? If it be true that unperceiving and unperceived things do not exist, what becomes of the soul in deep sleep? If the picture opposite to my bed exists only because I see it, what minds perceive it after I have gone to sleep, and thus hinder it from ceasing to exist? How shall we picture to ourselves a plurality of human individuals, if space exists in the mind only? How does Berkeley know that there are other minds than his own? How, moreover, does the creative Spirit produce sensible ideas *in us?* All these points and many others remain unexplained; for his *deus ex machina* ex-

plains nothing, and his theory of intervention is of no more
avail than occasionalism and pre-established harmony. He is
both a thorough-going theologian and a philosopher; his interests are both scientific and religious, and he attacks materialism[1] not only as a theoretical error but as the source of the
most serious heresies.[2]

§ 59. Condillac

The philosophy of Locke was introduced into France by
Voltaire.[3] Here it found an original follower in the abbot
Étienne Bonnot de CONDILLAC,[4] the founder of absolute sen-
sationalism.

Locke distinguishes two sources of ideas: sensation and reflection, while Condillac, in his *Traité des sensations* recognizes
but one, making reflection a product of sensibility. His proof
is ingenious. He imagines a statue, which is organized and
alive, like ourselves, but hindered by its marble exterior from
having sensations. Its intellectual and moral life advances as
the various parts of this covering are removed.

---

[1] By materialism Berkeley understands not only the negation of spiritual substance, but the view that there exists, independently of the mind, a substance,
or substratum, of sensible qualities, which it perceives. To assume the reality
of matter is enough to stamp one as a materialist in the Berkeleyan sense.

[2] §§ 133 ff. — A system wholly similar to that of Berkeley was taught by his
contemporary and colleague, the churchman Arthur Collier (1680–1732), a disciple of Malebranche and author of *Clavis universalis, or a New Inquiry after
Truth, Being a Demonstration of the Non-existence or Impossibility of an External
World*, London, 1713.

[3] 1694–1778. *Lettres sur les Anglais*, 1728; *Éléments de la philosophie de Newton, mis à la portée de tout le monde*, Amsterdam, 1738; *La métaphysique de Newton ou parallèle des sentiments de Newton et de Leibniz*, Amsterdam, 1740; *Can-
dide ou sur l'optimisme*, 1757; *Le philosophe ignorant*, 1767. Simultaneously with
these writings of Voltaire, the *Entretiens sur la pluralité des mondes* of Fontenelle
(1657–1757) and the works of Maupertuis (1698–1759) made known to the
French the labors of Copernicus and Newton, which were continued by Lagrange
and Laplace.

[4] Born at Grenoble, 1715; tutor of the Prince of Parma; abbot of Mureaux;
died 1780. Besides the *Traité des sensations* (1754), he produced the following
works: *Essai sur l'origine des connaissances humaines* (1746); *Traité des sys-
tèmes* (1749); *Traité des animaux*, 1755; *Logique* (posthumous, 1781); *Langue
des animaux* (posthumous). Complete works, Paris, 1798; 1803, 32 vols. in
12mo. F. Réthoré, *Condillac ou l'empirisme et le rationalisme*, Paris, 1864.

Let us first remove the marble covering its olfactory organs. Now the statue has only the sense of smell, and cannot, as yet, perceive anything but odors. It cannot acquire any idea of extension, form, sound, or color. A rose is placed before it. From the impression produced by it, a sensation of smell arises. Henceforth it is, from our point of view, a statue that smells a rose; in reality, however, it is nothing but the *odor* of this flower. The statue does not and cannot, as yet, possess the slightest notion of an *object;* it does not know itself as the subject of sensation; its consciousness, its "me," is nothing but the scent of the rose. or, rather, what *we* call the scent of the rose.

Since this impression and the resulting sensation is the only thing with which our statue is occupied, that single sensation becomes *attention.*

We take away the rose. Our statue retains a trace, or an echo, as it were, of the odor perceived. This trace or echo is *memory.*

We place a violet, a jasmine, and some asafœtida before the statue. Its first sensation, the odor of the rose, was neither agreeable nor disagreeable, there being nothing to compare it with. But now other impressions and other sensations arise. These it compares with its memory images. It finds some agreeable, others disagreeable. Henceforth the statue desires the former and rejects the latter. Towards these it entertains feelings of aversion, hatred, and fear, towards those, feelings of sympathy, affection, and hope. That is to say, from the sensations experienced by it, and their comparison, arise the passions, desires, and *volitions. I will* signifies *I desire.* The will is not a new faculty added to sensibility; it is a transformation of sensation; sensation becomes desire and impulse after having been attention, memory, comparison, pleasure, and pain.

From comparison, that is, from the multiplication of sensations, arise, on the other hand, judgment, reflection, reasoning, abstraction, in a word, the *understanding.* Our statue per-

ceives disagreeable odors, and at the same time recalls other
odors which gave it pleasure; these past sensations reappear
in opposition to the present sensation, not as immediate sensations, but as copies or images of these sensations, that is, as
ideas. It directs the attention to two different ideas and compares them. When there is double attention, there is comparison; for to be attentive to two ideas, and to compare
them, is the same thing. Now, the statue cannot compare
two ideas without perceiving some difference or resemblance
between them: to perceive such relations is *to judge*. The acts
of comparison and judgment are therefore merely attention;
it is thus that sensation becomes successively attention, comparison, and judgment.

Some odors, that is, some of the states experienced by the
statue, yielded pleasure, others yielded pain. Hence it will
retain in memory the ideas of pleasure and pain common to
several states or sensations. Pleasure is a quality common to
the rose-sensation, the violet-sensation, and the jasmine-sen-
sation; pain is a quality common to the odor of asafœtida,
decaying matter, etc. These common characteristics are distinguished, separated, *abstracted*, from the particular sensations with which they are associated, and thus arise the abstract *notions* of pleasure, pain, number, duration, etc. These
are *general ideas*, being common to several states or modes of
being of the statue. We do not need a special faculty to explain them. Abstraction itself, the highest function of the
understanding, is a modification of sensation, which, consequently, embraces all the faculties of the soul. The *inner perception*, or the *me*, is merely *the sum of the sensations we now
have, and those which we have had*.

Condillac endows his statue with a single sense, — the sense
of smell, — and then evolves all mental faculties out of sensation.[1] Any one of the five senses would have served his purpose equally well.

---

[1] Condillac's object in choosing the least important of the five senses is plain.
If the sense of smell suffices to make a complete soul, then, *a fortiori*, the combination of all five senses, or the total sensibility, will suffice.

If now, we join to smell: taste, hearing, and sight, by taking away one marble covering after another, then tastes, sounds, and colors will be added to the odors perceived by the statue, and its intellectual life will become so much richer, more manifold, and complex.

There is, however, an essential idea which neither smell, nor taste, nor hearing, nor *even sight*, can yield, and that is the idea of an *object*, the idea of an *external world*. Colors, sounds, odors, and tastes are mere sensations or states, not, as yet, referred to external objects. Before external causes can be substituted for its sensations, the statue must be endowed with the most important of all senses: the sense of touch. Touch alone can reveal to us the objective world, by giving us the ideas of extension, form, solidity, and body. Even sight cannot suggest them. Persons born blind cannot, upon receiving their sight, distinguish between a ball and a block, a cube and a sphere, until they *touch* these objects.[1] Only after having touched things do we refer the impressions received by our other senses, such as colors, sounds, tastes, and smells, to objects existing outside of us. Hence, touch is the highest sense, and the guide of the other senses; it is touch which teaches the eye to distribute colors in nature.

Conclusion and summary: All our ideas, without exception, are derived from the senses, and *especially from touch*.

Though Condillac is a sensationalist, and a sensationalist in the strict sense of the term, he is not, on that account, a materialist.[2] He differs from Locke, who grants that matter can think, and agrees with the Cartesians that compounds cannot think, and consequently that the subject of sensation cannot be corporeal in its nature. The movements of the body are, according to him, merely occasional causes of mental

---

[1] Allusion to Cheselden's celebrated operation.

[2] Sensationalism is usually, but erroneously, confused with materialism. Sensationalism is a theory concerning the origin of our ideas, an explanation of the phenomenon of mind — a theory of knowledge — while materialism is an ontology, a system of metaphysics. Sensationalism and materialism are undoubtedly closely related, for materialism is necessarily sensational. But the reverse is not true.

phenomena. Moreover, it is not certain that the body is an extended substance, as Descartes claims. But *even if there were no real extension, that would not be a sufficient reason for denying the existence of bodies*. Hence the negation of extension as such does not, according to Condillac, involve the acceptance of the immaterialism of Berkeley. He agrees with Leibniz that bodies might really exist and yet not be extended in themselves, that their essence might consist of something other than extension, and that this might be merely a subjective phenomenon, or a mode of perceiving them. At all events, there is something other than ourselves; that cannot be doubted. But what may be the nature of this "other thing," the statue does not know, nor do we know. That is, Condillac, the consistent disciple of Locke, is a sceptic in metaphysics, but his scepticism does not, as we have just seen, call in question the existence of matter, nor, consequently, materialism, using the term in the Berkeleyan sense. If to assume the reality of matter is to be a materialist, then, of course, he is a materialist. But in that case, Descartes is also a materialist. Moreover, he too, like Descartes, curries favor with the Church, which, in his capacity as a priest, he dare not openly antagonize. True, the human soul is merely the recipient of sense-impressions, and devoid of all faculties of knowledge except sensation; it is nothing but a prolonged and infinitely modified sensation. But that does not mean, he intimates, that it has *always* been restricted to sensation as the source of truth: its present nature dates from the Fall. Perhaps it was endowed with a higher faculty before the Fall. All we can say is that this is no longer the case.

It is hard to take these restrictions of the abbé of Mureaux seriously.

§ 60. Progress of Materialism

The empirical school's contempt for metaphysics refers only to the dualistic metaphysics, and not to the system of Hobbes, Gassendi, and Democritus. Philosophy gradually abandoned dualism. It might have adopted the immaterialism of Berkeley and Collier; but this hypothesis, though satisfying the monistic instinct, had against it the evidence of facts and the native realism of the French and English minds. Hence, philosophy continued, in spite of Berkeley, to concede *primary* qualities to bodies. True, tastes, smells, colors, sounds, and temperature are nothing but sensations of the subject which perceives them, and do not exist, as such, in the things themselves and outside of us. But extension, impenetrability, figure, motion, etc., are primary qualities, i. e., inherent in a reality external to and independent of our perception, and of these qualities bodies, or matter, are composed. Hence, the latter has objective reality, and does not owe its existence to our sensation, i. e., to the mind, as Berkeley claimed.

The belief in the objective and absolute existence of bodies persisted. Hobbes's assertion that *all substances are bodies*, and the hypothesis of Locke, according to which matter can think, seemed less presumptuous when Leibniz, repudiating the Cartesian teaching, substituted for extended matter, matter endowed with force, a kind of intermediate reality, or connecting link between brutal matter and pure spirit. This conception made it possible for one to assume a real and physical action of body on mind, without fear of materializing spirit. Experience, moreover, on whose territory the new philosophy had firmly established itself for all time to come, advanced the cause of materialism by its emphatic declaration that body acts on mind, and that the mental world depends on the physical world.

JOHN TOLAND (1670–1721), a fellow-countryman of Berkeley, whose genius, character, and fate remind one of Bruno and Vanini, becomes the champion of materialism in his *Letters to Serena*[1] and his *Pantheisticon* (1710). Matter is

---

[1] *Letters to Serena* (Serena is Queen Sophia Charlotte of Prussia, the friend of Leibniz, at whose court Toland lived from 1701–1702), followed by a *Refutation of Spinoza*, and a treatise on movement as the essential property of matter (London, 1704).

not, according to him, the "extended substance" of Descartes, an inert, lifeless mass that receives its motion from a transcendent deity; it is an *active* substance, that is, *force.* Extension, impenetrability, and action are three distinct notions, but not three different *things;* they are simply three different modes of conceiving one and the same matter. Matter is originally and necessarily active, and hence does not receive its motion from without; motion is its essential and inseparable property, — as essential and inseparable as extension and impenetrability. Since matter as such is force, motion, and life, we do not need either a soul of the world, in order to explain universal life, or an individual soul as the source of psychical life and the vital principle of the organic body. The hylozoistic and vitalistic hypothesis is based on the erroneous conception that matter is inert, that it is merely the theatre and the means, and never the source, of action. The abandonment of this false view will result in the collapse of the dualistic theory. Body ceases to be a substance that cannot think, and soul or mind is simply one of its functions. Furthermore, thought does not belong to substance in general, as Spinoza assumes; matter, though active, is unconscious in itself, and becomes conscious only in the brain (a view already held by Democritus). There can be no thought without a brain; *thought is the function of this organ, as taste is a function of the tongue.*

Less bold in form but the same in substance are the conclusions of the *Observations on Man,*[1] the work of the physician and naturalist DAVID HARTLEY (1704–1757). There can be no thought without a brain. The brain is not the thinking subject; the soul is the thinking subject. But though the soul is entirely distinct from the body, it cannot be regarded as essentially different from corporeal substance. The action of the brain on thought is established by the facts, and proves conclusively that matter and mind differ in degree and not in essence, for there can be no reciprocal action between two es-

---

[1] *Observations on Man, his Frame, his Duty, and his Expectations,* London, 1749; 6th ed., 1834.

sentially different substances. The so-called material world represents an ascending scale of substances, or rather forces; these become more and more refined and spiritualized, as we pass from mineral masses to light. The distance from the stone to the luminous agent is so great that one is tempted to oppose the latter to the former as spiritual substances are opposed to material substances. And yet no serious thinker would dream of removing optical phenomena from the domain of physics. The infinitely subtile, refined, and intangible substance called light is none the less matter. Why, then, should we not assume that the above-mentioned series continues beyond ether, and finally ends in thought or soul? This mental agent is so far removed from light, in fineness and mobility, as the latter is from the stone and wood, *without on that account ceasing to be matter.*

The white medullary substance of the brain and the spinal marrow constitute the seat of sensation and the source of voluntary motion. Every modification of this substance is accompanied by a corresponding modification in our soul-life. The modifications of the cerebral and nervous substance, corresponding to those of the soul, are vibrations or "tremblings" produced by external excitations and transmitted through the sensory nerves to the central portion of the brain. The nervous substance, which may be perceived by our senses and experimented on, most probably contains an infinitely subtile and mobile fluid, which might be identified with electricity and ether. The vibrations of this fluid or ether cause sensations. When these vibrations are reproduced a certain number of times, they leave *traces;* these traces are our *ideas.* Our soul-life depends entirely on the *association* of these ideas, which, in turn, depends on the association of sensations, i. e., vibrations of ether or nervous fluid. True, these vibrations are not, as yet, sensations; they affect the body, and sensations affect the soul; they belong to the domain of physiology, and sensations belong to the domain of psychology. But the fact that the latter are effects of the former conclusively proves that corporeal substance is analogous, if not identical, with thinking substance.

JOSEPH PRIESTLEY (1733–1804), theologian, philosopher, and naturalist, to whom we are indebted for the discovery of oxygen,[1] considers, in his *Disquisitions relating to Matter and Spirit*,[2] the proofs of his predecessors, ancient as well as modern, in favor of the materiality of the soul, and adds some arguments of his own:

1. If the soul is an inextended substance, it does not really exist in space; for to be in space is to occupy a portion of it, be it never so small. Hence the soul is not in the body: such is the absurd conclusion which Cartesian spiritualism compels us to draw.

2. *Principia non sunt multiplicanda præter necessitatem.* (Principles must not be multiplied unnecessarily.) Now, there is no need of assuming for thought a new and essentially different principle from the principles by which science explains the phenomena of light, electricity, etc., which show striking similarities with psychical phenomena.

3. The development of the soul runs parallel with that of the body, on which it wholly depends.

4. There is not a single idea of which the mind is possessed but what may be proved to have come to it from the bodily senses, or to have been consequent upon the perceptions of sense.

5. Our ideas of external objects, — the idea of a tree, for example, — consist of parts, like their objects. How is it possible that such ideas should exist in an indivisible and absolutely simple soul?

6. The soul ripens and declines. How can an absolutely simple being without parts be increased, modified, or diminished?

7. If man has an immaterial soul, every animal, which feels,

[1] Thus named by Lavoisier, who recognized it as one of the essential elements of atmospheric air.

[2] London, 1777. [*The Doctrine of Philosophical Necessity*, London, 1777; *Free Discussions of the Doctrines of Materialism*, London, 1778. — TR.]

perceives, remembers, combines, and judges, must have one also.

8. What is the use of the body, and why is the soul associated with it, if it can feel, think, and act independently of it?

9. Spiritualism claims that an extended being cannot think. But is it not still more inconceivable that an inextended entity — a simple mathematical point — should contain an infinite number of ideas, feelings, and volitions, as the human soul does? The soul is a reality no less manifold than the universe which it reflects.

10. The will is determined by motives, reasons, and arguments. Hence, spiritualism objects, if the soul is material, matter is moved by motives, reasons, and arguments. But the matter which materialism invests with the faculty of thinking is not the gross and inert mass which it is at first supposed to be; it is the ether, that mysterious agent which we know only by its manifestations, but which we assume to be the basis of intellectual phenomena as well as of extension, impenetrability, and movement. Besides, it may be said, in answer to the spiritualists, that if the theory of "matter influenced by motives" is objectionable to them, their "simple substance influenced by an extended substance" (in sensation and perception) is no less objectionable to the materialistic thinker.

11. If the soul, says spiritualism, is composed of parts, atoms (or, as we should say nowadays, of living cells of gray cortical substance), how can it be felt as a unity? How does it become conscious of the *me*?[1] This feeling, this perception of the unity which is called the *ego*, is conceivable only in a real individual, in a unity, monad, or atom, and not in a *sum* of monads, atoms, or individuals, not in the whole nervous system. For a sum or whole is merely an idea, a mental being; its parts alone have *real* existence (nominalism). Hence these (the monads, atoms, or individuals making up the nervous system) can feel

---

[1] In a word: How can the *one* arise from the many?

themselves, each for itself and separately, as unities or I's; but the nervous system, the whole, cannot, for the whole is not an individual, an objective and existing reality. Priestley declares that he cannot explain the difficulty, but that, if it really is a difficulty, it exists for spiritualism as well. Psychological consciousness is nothing but plurality reduced to unity, or unity derived from plurality, or, in a word, the synthesis of the one and the many, i. e., an inexplicable mystery. Spiritualism is as unable to tell how a multitude of ideas, feelings, and volitions can constitute the unity of self, as materialism is powerless to explain how a multitude of atoms can form a unity. Hence, spiritualism has no advantage over its adversary in this respect.

12. It is objected that the soul wars against the body, that it is possessed of a self-moving power, while the body needs a foreign mechanical impulse, that the body alone becomes weary and never the soul; finally, that, if the human soul is material, God himself ceases to be a pure spirit. Priestley replies that there are also conflicts between the different tendencies of the soul, and yet that spiritualism does not dream of referring each of these tendencies to a principle or a different substance; that the body is not inert, as was believed before the days of Leibniz, and that no substance is without force; that thought fags and exhausts the brain, which is refreshed in sleep; finally, that we cannot extend our reasonings concerning finite beings to the infinite, but that the "materiality" of God is more consistent with the dogma of omnipresence than the opposite view.

Priestley appeals to the Bible, and believes that his system can be reconciled with Christianity and even with Calvinism.[1] French materialism, however, does not share these illusions. In the *Testament de Jean Meslier*,[2] which Voltaire made

[1] There is, indeed, a connecting link between Priestley's system and the reformed dogma: we mean their common opposition to *indeterminism*. Indeterministic and Pelagian Catholicism offers materialism no such support.

[2] A *curé* of Étrépigny in Champagne, died 1733. *Testament de J. Meslier*, published in 3 vols., with a preface and a biographical introduction, by R. Charles, Amsterdam, 1865.

public, we find the bold utterances of Toland repeated. The same may be said of the writings of the physician, Julien Offroy DE LA METTRIE [1] (1709–1751), who was one of the first outspoken materialists in France. Curiously enough, this leader of the opponents of spiritualism is a disciple, not of Toland, but of the man whom French spiritualism recognizes as its head: Descartes. We must remember that Descartes was not only the author of the *Meditations* and the dualistic hypothesis, but that he wrote the *Treatise on the Passions of the Soul*, and founded the modern mechanical theory. Descartes not only proved the existence of God and the spirituality of the soul,[2] but also showed "*how all the limbs can be moved by the objects of the senses and by the spirits* WITHOUT THE AID OF THE SOUL"; [3] that it resides in the pineal gland; that memory presupposes cerebral impressions; that animals are machines; that the intellectual phenomena which we discover in them can and must be mechanically explained. The advance from the *animal-machine* of Descartes to the *homme-machine* is slight; and La Mettrie makes it. If the animal can feel, perceive, remember, compare, and judge, without the aid of an immaterial soul, simply by means of its nervous and cerebral organization, there is no reason why we should concede a soul to man, whose sensibility, will, and understanding are merely more highly developed animal functions. Man is not an exception; he does not form a separate and privileged caste in universal nature. The laws of nature are the same for all. There can be no difference in this respect between men, brutes, plants, and animals. Man is a machine, but a more complicated machine than the animal: "he is to the ape or the most intelligent animals, what Huyghens's planetary pendulum is to a watch made by Julien Leroy."

---

[1] *Histoire naturelle de l'âme*, The Hague (Paris), 1745; *L'Homme-machine*, Leyden, 1748; *L'Homme-plante*, Paris, 1748. Works of La Mettrie, London (Berlin), 1751. [Cf. Lange, *History of Materialism*.]

[2] These "errors" are, in La Mettrie's opinio n, nothing but "a trick to make the theologians swallow the poison of mechanism. The *animal-machine* is Descartes's grandest discovery."

[3] *Passions de l'âme*, I, Art. 16.

This developed animal did not fall from the clouds, nor did it arise, ready-made, from the bowels of the earth. It is not the work of a supernatural creator, the realization of an idea: it owes its origin to a natural *evolution* which gradually evolves more and more perfect forms from the elementary organisms. The human species is no more a separate creation than the other animal and vegetable species; its present form has been evolved from lower animal forms, slowly and by progressive stages. The evolutionistic and transformistic conception, familiar to ancient philosophy,[1] reappears, in various forms, but wholly conscious of its aims, in the *Pensées sur l'interprétation de la nature* of DENIS DIDEROT,[2] in the work, *De la nature*, of ROBINET,[3] in the *Palingénésie philosophique* of CHARLES DE BONNET,[4] precursors of Lamarck and Darwin. According to Diderot, the entire universe is an endless fermentation, a ceaseless interchange of substances, a perpetual circulation of life. Nothing lasts, everything changes, — *species as well as individuals*. Animals have not always been what they are now. In the animal and vegetable kingdoms, individuals arise, grow, decline, and die. Can we not say the same for entire species? Now, there is an affinity, and perhaps identity, between kingdoms, just as between species. Thus, who can ever exactly determine the boundaries between plants and animals? Plants and animals are defined in the same way. We speak of three kingdoms, but why should not one emanate from the other, and why should not the animal and vegetable

---

[1] We found it in Anaximander, Empedocles, Anaxagoras, and Democritus.

[2] Born at Paris, 1713; died 1784. The founder of the *Encyclopédie* (*Dictionnaire raisonné des arts, des sciences et des métiers. Par une société de gens de lettres, mis en ordre et publié par M. Diderot*, Paris, 1751–1763). His most important philosophical writings are: *Pensées sur l'interprétation de la nature*, Paris, 1754; *Rêve de D'Alembert; Lettre sur les aveugles; Éléments de physiologie*. M. Assézat has edited the *Complete Works* of Diderot from the original editions. He includes what has been published at different periods, and the unpublished manuscripts preserved in the Hermitage library (Paris, 1875). [On Diderot see the works of K. Rosenkranz (1866) and John Morley (1878, 1886).]

[3] 1723–1789. *De la nature*, 4 vols., 8vo, Amsterdam, 1763–1768.

[4] A Genevan, 1720–1793. *La palingénésie philosophique ou idées sur l'état passé et sur l'état futur des êtres vivants*, Geneva, 1769.

kingdoms *emanate from universal heterogeneous matter?* The evolution is wholly mechanical. Nature, with its five or six essential properties, such as potential and active force, length, breadth, depth, impenetrability, and *sensibility, which exists potentially in the inert molecule*, and matter, suffices to explain the world. We should not search for *designs (intentions)* where there are only accidental facts. The spiritualists say: Look at man, that living proof of final causes! What do they mean? The real man or the ideal man? Surely not the real man, for there is not a perfectly constituted, perfectly sound man on the entire surface of the earth. The human species consists of an aggregation of more or less deformed and unhealthy individuals. Now, why should that make us sound the praises of the alleged creator? Praises, indeed! We have nothing but apologies to offer for him. And there is not a single animal, a single plant, a single mineral, of which we cannot say what has just been said of man. Of what use are the phalanges in the cloven foot of the hog? Of what use are the mammæ in males? The actual world is as a day-fly to the millions of real or possible worlds of the past and future; it is what the insect of Hypanis is to man, who sees it live and die in the passing of a day. The day of a world lasts a little longer, that is all.

These conceptions of the world and man are shared by HELVÉTIUS,[1] who, like Thomas Hobbes and Mandeville,[2] considers egoism and self-interest as the true and sole motive of our acts; by the mathematician D'ALEMBERT,[3] whose philosophy reveals a delicate tinge of scepticism, which distinguishes it favorably from its environment, and brings it

[1] Claude Adrien, 1715–1771. *De l'esprit*, Paris, 1758 (anonymous); *De l'homme, de ses facultés et de son éducation*, London (Amsterdam), 1772 (anonymous); *Les progrès de la raison dans la recherche de la vérité*, London, 1775. Complete works, Amsterdam, 1776; Zweibrücken, 1784; Paris, 1794; 1796 (this last edition in 10 vols., 12°).

[2] Bernard de Mandeville, 1670–1733. *The Fable of the Bees, or Private Vices made Public Benefits*, London, 1714, 1719.

[3] 1717–1783. Author of the masterly *Discours préliminaire* of the *Encyclopedia*, which he helped to found. *Mélanges de littérature, d'histoire et de philosophie*, 5 vols., Paris, 1752.

nearer to criticism; by the political economists TURGOT [1] and CONDORCET,[2] who construct a positive philosophy of history, based on the necessity of human actions and the law of continued progress; by the Baron d'HOLBACH,[3] whose *Système de la nature*, published at London, 1770, under the pseudonym of Mirabaud, is a complete theory of ontological and psychological materialism. Matter and motion: these two words sum up everything. Matter and motion are eternal. The universe is neither governed by a God nor by chance, but by immutable and necessary laws. These laws do not depend on a personal power capable of modifying them; nor do they form a brutal necessity, a Fate hovering above things, a yoke imposed upon them from without: they are merely the *properties* of things, the expression of their innermost nature. The universe is neither an absolute monarchy *à la* Duns Scotus, nor a constitutional monarchy *à la* Leibniz, but a republic. Theism is the sworn enemy of science. Pantheism is merely a shamefaced theism, or atheism in disguise. The mechanical theory sufficiently explains all things. There is no finality in nature. Eyes were not made *for* seeing, nor feet *for* walking, but seeing and walking are the effects of a certain arrangement of atoms, which, if different, would produce different phenomena. There is no soul apart from nervous substance. Thought is a function of the brain. Matter alone is immortal; individuals are not. The free-will of the indeterminists is a denial of the universal order. There are not two separate realms and two series of laws, — physical laws and moral laws, — but one undivided and indivisible universe, subject, in all its parts and at all periods, to the same necessity.

Finally, on the eve of the Revolution, the physician CABANIS (1757–1808), in his *Considérations générales sur l'étude de l'homme et sur les rapports de son organisation physique avec*

---

[1] *Discours sur les progrès de l'esprit humain*, etc. [Complete works by Dupont de Nemours, 4 vols., Paris, 1808–1811.]

[2] *Esquisse d'un tableau historique des progrès de l'esprit humain* (posthumous work), 1794.

[3] 1723–1789.

ses facultés intellectuelles et morales,[1] formulated the principles of psychological materialism with such frankness and vigor as have never been excelled. Body and mind are not only most intimately connected; they are one and the same thing. The soul is body endowed with feeling. The body or matter thinks, feels, and wills. Physiology and psychology are one and the same science. Man is simply a bundle of nerves. Thought is the function of the brain, as digestion is the function of the stomach, and the secretion of bile the function of the liver. The impressions reaching the brain cause it to act, just as the food introduced into the stomach sets that organ in motion. It is the business of the brain to produce an image of each particular impression, to arrange these images, and to compare them with each other for the sake of forming judgments and ideas, as it is the function of the stomach to react upon food in order to digest it. Intellectual and moral phenomena are, *like all others*, necessary consequences of the properties of matter and the laws which govern beings.[2]

On this latter point, *philosophers*, be they conservative or radical, dogmatic or sceptical, jurists and *littérateurs*, naturalists and physicians, agree. By subjecting the Deity himself to laws, MONTESQUIEU simply denies God as an absolute personal power. His God is the *nature of things*, in which are grounded the *necessary relations* which we call laws. VOLTAIRE is a deist, but he assumes, with Locke, that matter can think.[3] J. J. ROUSSEAU is a spiritualist in his way, but *nature, which we have abandoned and to which we must return*, is his God also.[4] The

---

[1] In the *Mémoires de l'Institut*, years IV and VI (1796 and 1798); reprinted, Paris, 1802.

[2] Closely related to the system of Cabanis is the intellectual or cerebral physiology (known by the name of *phrenology*) of Gall, Spurzheim, and Broussais.

[3] See page 322, note 3.

[4] 1712–1778. *Discours sur l'origine et les fondements de l'inégalité parmi les hommes*, Paris, 1753; *Le contrat social*, 1762; *Émile ou de l'éducation*, 1762. [*Œuvres*, Paris, 1764; 1818–1820; 1868. L. Moreau, *J. J. Rousseau et le siècle philosophique*, Paris, 1870; John Morley, *Rousseau*, 2 vols., London, 1873. — TR.]

pioneers of German literature, Lessing, Herder, and Goethe, combine with the highest idealism the same naturalistic and monistic, if not materialistic, tendency. What united these different thinkers was their outspoken or secret opposition to Cartesian dualism, which set up a separate order of things, called free spiritual substances, not subject to the laws of nature, a kind of caste or privileged aristocracy. Equality before the law of nature, and (in view of the failure of sense-perception and speculation to establish the freedom of indifference) determinism *for all*, without excepting even the Supreme Being: these were the watchwords of the philosophers until they became the watchwords of the Revolution in 1789.

§ 61. David Hume.[1] The Culmination of Empiricism in Scepticism

"There are no bodies," the idealists dogmatically declared; "there is no spiritual substance," was the equally dogmatic assertion of the materialists. The Scotchman, DAVID HUME (1711–1776), an acute thinker and classical historian of England,[2] opposes to each of these schools the doubts of Protagoras and Locke: Can the human mind solve the onto-

---

[1] [*Treatise on Human Nature*, 3 vols., London, 1739–1740. Hume afterwards worked over the three books of the *Treatise*, and published them under the following titles: *An Enquiry concerning Human Understanding*, 1748; *A Dissertation on the Passions;* and *An Enquiry concerning the Principles of Morals*, 1751. *Essays, Moral, Political, and Literary*, 1741. *The Natural History of Religion*, 1755. *Dialogues concerning Natural Religion* appeared after Hume's death. The *Autobiography* was published by Adam Smith, London, 1777. The essays on *Suicide* and the *Immortality of the Soul* appeared 1783. See Hume's *Treatise of Human Nature* in two vols., in Everyman's Library; and his *Enquiry concerning Human Understanding* in the Open Court Edition, Chicago. Works on Hume: Huxley, *Hume*, London, 1901; Knight, *Hume*, London, 1886; Green, *Introduction* to ed. of Hume's works.]

[2] *History of England from the Invasion of Julius Cæsar*, etc., 6 vols., London, 1754–1763. Hume's historical work made a greater impression on his age than his philosophical works. He himself was especially proud of his achievements as a historian (see *Letters of David Hume to William Strahan*. Now first edited by G. Birkbeck Hill, Oxford, 1888). Our age, however, has reversed this opinion. Hume, the spiritual father of Kant, now takes precedence over Hume, the rival of Robertson and Gibbon.

logical problem? Is metaphysics, considered as the science of the immanent essence and primary causes of things, possible? In his *Essays*, which are inimitable masterpieces of acumen and clearness, modern philosophy enters upon the path marked out by English empiricism. The human mind begins to reflect upon its resources with a view to ascertaining the pre-conditions of knowledge, the origin of metaphysical ideas, and the limits of its capacity. Philosophy becomes decidedly critical and positivistic.

For the old metaphysics, i. e., the alleged science of the essence of things, *"that abstruse philosophy and metaphysical jargon, which, being mixed up with popular superstition, renders it in a manner impenetrable to careless reasoners, and gives it the air of science and wisdom,"* [1] we must, according to Hume, substitute *criticism*. In other words, we must *inquire seriously into the nature of human understanding*, and show, from an exact analysis of its powers and capacity, that it is by no means fitted for such remote and abstruse subjects as traditional metaphysics busies itself with. We must submit to this fatigue, in order to live at ease ever after; *and must cultivate true metaphysics with some care, in order to destroy the false and adulterate.*

Though criticism is more modest in its pretensions than ontology, it is no inconsiderable part of science to know the different operations of the mind, to separate them from each other, to class them under their proper heads, and to correct all that seeming disorder in which they lie involved, when made the object of reflection and inquiry. This science has the immense advantage over metaphysics of being certain. *Nor can there remain any suspicion that this science is uncertain and chimerical; unless we should entertain such a scepticism as is entirely subversive of all speculation, and even action.* [2] *To throw up all at once all pretensions of this kind may justly be deemed more rash, precipitate, and dogmatical than even the*

---

[1] *An Enquiry concerning Human Understanding*, sect. I.
[2] *An Enquiry concerning Human Understanding*, sect. I, p. 10.

boldest and most affirmative philosophy.[1] We esteem it worthy of the labor of a philosopher to give us a true system of the planets, and adjust the position and order of those remote bodies. How much more highly should we value those who, with so much success, delineate the parts of the mind, in which we are so intimately concerned! We have succeeded in determining the laws by which the revolutions of the planets are governed. And there is no reason to despair of equal success in our inquiries concerning the mental powers and economy. All we have to do is to enter upon the enterprise with thorough care and attention.

Hume loves to call himself a sceptic, and he is a sceptic as regards dogmatic metaphysics. But from the above explicit statements and many other like assertions, it would seem that his philosophy is nothing but criticism. It is not his purpose to renounce philosophy or even metaphysics, but to give it a different direction and a different object, to turn it from fruitless speculation, and to establish it on the firm and certain foundation of experience. Had Hume been an absolute sceptic he could never have produced an Immanuel Kant. Now, whatever difference there may be between the results of these two thinkers, one thing is certain: The spirit of their theoretical philosophy, the fundamental conception of their investigations, and the goal at which they aim, are perfectly identical. Theirs is the critical spirit, and positive knowledge the goal at which they aim. To claim for Kant the sole honor of having founded criticism is an error which a closer study of British philosophy tends to refute.

The following is the substance of Hume's inquiries concerning human understanding: —

All our perceptions may be divided into two classes: *ideas* or *thoughts* and *impressions*. Ideas are the less lively perceptions, of which we are conscious when we reflect on our sensations. By the term "impression" Hume means all our more lively perceptions, when we hear, or see, or feel, or love, or hate, or

[1] *Id.*, p. 12.

desire, or will.[1] Nothing, at first view, he says, seems more unbounded than thought; but a nearer examination shows that it is really confined within very narrow limits, and that it amounts to no more than the faculty of compounding, transposing, augmenting, or diminishing the materials afforded us by the senses and experience. *All the materials of our thinking are derived either from our outward or inward sentiment; the mixture and composition of these belongs alone to the mind and will.*[2] Or, in other terms, *all our ideas or more feeble perceptions are copies of our impressions or more lively ones.* Even the idea of God arises from reflecting on the operations of our own mind, and augmenting, without limit, those qualities of goodness and wisdom which we observe in ourselves. We may prosecute this inquiry to what length we please; we shall always find that every idea which we examine is copied from a similar impression. A blind man can form no notion of colors; a deaf man of sounds. Moreover, all ideas, compared to sensations, are naturally faint and obscure.

After having proved that all our ideas are derived from sensation, Hume shows that they succeed each other in a certain order, and that there is a certain connection between them. This order and this connection presuppose certain principles of connection, according to which our thoughts succeed each other. They are: *Resemblance, contiguity in time or place,* and *causality.* The question here presents itself: Are these principles, especially causality, the most important of all notions, *a priori,* innate, anterior to all impressions, as idealism claims, or are they ideas in the sense which sensationalism attaches to the term, i. e., faint sensations, copies of similar impressions? Kant answers the first question in the affirmative; Hume, the latter. He devotes all the efforts of

---

[1] *An Enquiry concerning Human Understanding,* sect. II, p. 14.

[2] *Id.,* p. 14. We have here, word for word, the teaching of Kant, who, however, adds that this mixture and composition depends on *a priori* forms, inherent in the mind. Hume also assumes that it depends on principles; but, absolute sensationalist that he is, derives the principles themselves from sensation, experience, and habit.

his criticism to the notion of causality, force, power, or necessary connection, and the explanation of its origin. This idea,
like all others, arises from sensation. Experience teaches us
that one billiard-ball communicates motion to another upon
impulse, and that the latter moves in a certain direction. We
have no *a priori* knowledge either of the movement or of the
direction of the movement. Between what we call the cause
and what we call the effect there is no necessary connection
that could ever be discovered *a priori*. The effect is totally
different from the cause, and consequently can never be discovered in it. The mind can never possibly find the effect in
the supposed cause, by the most accurate scrutiny and examination; and wherever experience shows us that a particular
effect succeeds a particular cause, there are always many other
effects which, to reason, must seem fully as consistent and
natural. In vain, therefore, should we pretend to determine
any single event, or infer any cause or effect, without the
assistance of observation and experience. In a word, the idea
of cause is no exception to the rule according to which all our
ideas arise from sensation.

It remains to be seen how it is derived, what is the impression
from which it comes?

Let us first observe — and here the sensationalistic explanation strikes a difficulty which Hume fully appreciated — let
us observe that what we call power, force, energy, or necessary
connection can never be perceived. One object follows another
in an uninterrupted succession; that is all we see; but the
power or force which actuates the whole machine is entirely
concealed from us. We know that, in fact, heat is a constant
attendant of flame; but what is the connection between them
we cannot conjecture or even imagine. Since external objects
give us no such idea, let us see whether this idea be derived
from reflection on the operations of our own minds. It may be
said that we are every moment conscious of internal power;
while we feel that, by the simple command of our will, we can
move the organs of our body, or direct the faculties of our

mind. But the influence of volition over the organs of the body is a fact which, like all other natural events, can be known only by experience. The motion of our body follows upon the command of our will. Of this we are every moment conscious. But the means by which this is effected; of this we are so far from being conscious that it must forever escape our most diligent inquiry. A man suddenly struck with a palsy in the leg or arm, or who had newly lost those members, frequently endeavors, at first, to move them, and employ them in their usual offices. Here he is as much conscious of power to command such limbs as a man in perfect health. But consciousness never deceives. Consequently, neither in the one case nor in the other, are we ever conscious of any power. We learn the influence of our will from experience alone. And experience only teaches us how one event constantly follows another, without instructing us in the secret connection which binds them together and renders them inseparable.

The idea which we are examining is not derived from any consciousness within ourselves. Nor do we get it through the senses. Then how does it originate? As we can have no idea of anything which never appeared to our outward sense or inward sentiment, the necessary conclusion seems to be that we have no idea of power or connection at all, and that these words are absolutely without meaning, when employed either in philosophical reasonings or common life.

But there still remains one method of avoiding this conclusion; it is to explain the idea of cause by *custom* or habit. We are accustomed to seeing certain events in constant conjunction. When any natural object or event is presented, it is impossible for us, by any sagacity or penetration, to discover or even conjecture, without experience, what event will result from it, or to carry our foresight beyond that object which is immediately present to the memory and senses. But when one particular species of event has always, in all instances, been conjoined with another, we make no longer any scruple of foretelling one upon the appearance of the other. We observe, for example, that there is a constant connection between heat and flame, between solidity and weight, and we are accustomed to infer the existence of one from the existence of the other. We then call the one object, *cause*, the other, *effect*. We suppose that there is some connection between them, some power in the one by which it infallibly produces the other, and operates with the greatest certainty and strongest necessity.

Hence the idea of cause does not arise from any single impression, from the perception of a particular object; it springs from our habit of seeing several impressions and several objects follow each other in regular order. This connection, therefore, which we feel in the mind, this customary transition of the imagination from one object to its usual attendant, is the sentiment or impression from which we form the idea of power or necessary connection.

To recapitulate: Every idea is copied from some preceding impression or sentiment; and where we cannot find any impression, we may be certain that there is no idea. In all single instances of the operation of bodies or minds, there is nothing that produces any impression, nor consequently can suggest, any idea of power or necessary connection. But when many uniform instances appear, and the same object is always followed by the same event, we then begin to entertain the notion of cause and connection. We then feel a new sentiment or impression, to wit, a customary connection in the thought or imagination between one object and its usual attendant; and this sentiment is the original of that idea which we seek for.

Hume, whose criticism aims to overthrow the principle of causality on the ground that it is neither an *a priori* possession, nor derived from any particular experience, is nevertheless a thorough-going determinist in morals and in history. Indeed, he is, with Hobbes and Spinoza, one of the founders of *positive* historical science, which is based on the principle of necessary human action. "It is universally acknowledged," he says,[1] "that there is a great uniformity among the actions of men,

[1] *An Enquiry concerning Human Understanding*, sect. VIII, p. 68.

in all nations and ages, and that human nature remains still
the same, in its principles and operations. The same motives
always produce the same actions; the same events follow from
the same causes. Ambition, avarice, self-love, vanity, friendship, generosity, public spirit; these passions, mixed in various
degrees, and distributed through society, have been, from the
beginning of the world, and still are, the source of all the actions
and enterprises which have ever been observed among mankind. Would you know the sentiments, inclinations, and
course of life of the Greeks and Romans? Study well the
temper and actions of the French and English; you cannot be
much mistaken in transferring to the former most of the
observations which you have made with regard to the latter.
Mankind are so much the same, in all times and places, that
history informs us of nothing new or strange in this particular.
*Its chief use is only to discover the constant and universal prin-
ciples of human nature."*

"Were there no uniformity in human actions, and were
every experiment which we could form of this kind irregu-
lar and anomalous, it were impossible to collect any general
observations concerning mankind. . . . The vulgar, who
take things according to their first appearance, attribute the
uncertainty of events to such an uncertainty in the causes
as makes the latter often fail of their usual operation, though
they meet with no impediment in their operation. But
philosophers, observing that almost in every part of nature,
there is contained a vast variety of springs and principles,
which are hid by their minuteness or remoteness, find that it
is at least possible the contrariety of events may not proceed
from any contingency in the cause, but from the secret operation of contrary causes. *This possibility is converted into certainty* by farther observation, when they remark that, upon
an exact scrutiny, a contrariety of effects always betrays a
contrariety of causes, and proceeds from their mutual opposition. A peasant can give no better reason for the stopping of
any clock or watch than to say that it does not commonly go

right, but an artist easily perceives that the same force in the spring or pendulum has always the same influence on the wheels, but fails of its usual effect, perhaps by reason of a grain of dust, which puts a stop to the whole movement. From the observation of several parallel instances, philosophers form a maxim *that the connection between all causes and effects is equally necessary, and that its seeming uncertainty in some instances proceeds from the secret opposition of contrary causes.*" The human will is governed by laws which are no less steady than those which govern the winds, rain, and clouds (Spinoza); the conjunction between motives and voluntary actions is as regular and uniform as that between the cause and effect in any part of nature.[1]

This truth has been universally acknowledged among mankind; it is the source of all the inferences which we form concerning human actions, the basis of all our inferences concerning the future. Physical necessity and moral necessity are two *different names*, but their nature is the same. Natural evidence and moral evidence are derived from the same principle. In spite of the reluctance which men have to acknowledge the doctrine of necessity in words, they all tacitly profess it. "Necessity, according to the sense in which it is here taken, has never yet been rejected, nor can ever, I think, be rejected by any philosopher. . . . By liberty, then, we can only mean a power of acting or not acting, according to the determinations of the will (Locke). . . . It is universally allowed that nothing exists without a cause of its existence, and that chance, when strictly examined, is a mere negative word, but it is pretended that some causes are necessary, some not necessary. Here then is the advantage of definitions. Let any one define a cause, without comprehending, as a part of the definition, a *necessary connection* with its effect. Whoever attempts to do that will be obliged either to employ unintelligible terms, or such as are synonymous to the term which he endeavors to define, and if the definition above mentioned

[1] *An Enquiry concerning Human Understanding*, sect. VIII, pp. 71 f.

be admitted, liberty when opposed to necessity, not to constraint, is the same thing with chance, which is universally allowed to have no existence."

Experience refutes the dualism of will and physical agencies; it also destroys the dualism of reason and instinct. Animals, as well as men, learn many things from experience, and infer that the same events will always follow the same causes. By this principle they become acquainted with the more obvious properties of external objects, and gradually, from their birth, treasure up a knowledge of the nature of fire, water, earth, stones, heights, depths, etc., and of the effects which result from their operation. The ignorance and inexperience of the young are here plainly distinguishable from the cunning and sagacity of the old, who have learned, from long observation, to avoid what hurt them, and to pursue what gave ease or pleasure. A horse that has been accustomed to the field becomes acquainted with the proper height which he can leap, and will never attempt what exceeds his force and ability. An old greyhound will trust the more fatiguing part of the chase to the younger, and will place himself so as to meet the hare in her doubles; *nor are the conjectures which he forms on this occasion founded in anything but his observation and experience.* Animals, therefore, are not guided in these inferences by reasoning, neither are children, neither are the generality of mankind, in their ordinary actions and conclusions; neither are the philosophers themselves. Animals undoubtedly owe a large part of their knowledge to what we call instinct. *But the experimental reasoning itself, which we possess in common with beasts, is nothing but a species of instinct or mechanical power that acts in us unknown to ourselves.*[1]

The universal propensity to form an idea of God, if not an original instinct, is at least "a general attendant of human nature."[2] This proposition contains the gist of Hume's theology. He is an outspoken opponent of all positive religions, and

---

[1] *An Enquiry concerning Human Understanding*, sect. IX, pp. 85 ff.
[2] *The Natural History of Religion*, sect. XV, p. 362.

finds it hard to regard them as "anything but sick men's dreams," or "the playsome whimsies of monkeys in human shape." [1] The doctrine of immortality is "a riddle, an enigma, an inexplicable mystery." He opposes the following arguments to miracles: There is not to be found in all history any miracle attested by a sufficient number of men, of such unquestioned good sense, education, and learning, as to secure us against all delusion in themselves; of such undoubted integrity, as to place them beyond all suspicion of any design to deceive others; of such credit and reputation in the eyes of mankind, as to have a great deal to lose in case of their being detected in any falsehood; and at the same time attesting facts performed in such a public manner, and in so celebrated a part of the world, as to render the detection unavoidable. The passion of surprise and wonder gives a sensible tendency towards the belief of those events from which it is derived. Supernatural relations abound among ignorant and barbarous nations; or if a civilized people has ever given admission to any of them, that people will be found to have received them from ignorant and barbarous ancestors, who transmitted them with that inviolable sanction and authority which always attend received opinions. It is a general maxim that no testimony is sufficient to establish a miracle, unless the testimony be of such a kind that its falsehood would be more miraculous than the fact which it endeavors to establish.[2]

Although Hume's conclusions in theology, as well as in ethics and psychology, wholly agree, on the one hand, with the doctrines of the rationalist Spinoza, and on the other, with those of the French materialists, the Scotch philosopher nevertheless maintains to the end his scepticism, as he loves to call it, or criticism, or positivism, as we designate it nowadays, in order to distinguish it from the scepticism of the ancients. True scepticism, as he conceives it, does not consist in perpetually doubting all things, but in limiting "our enquiries to such subjects as are best adapted to the narrow capacity of

[1] *Id.*, p. 362.   [2] *Essay concerning Human Understanding*, sect. X, p. 94.

human understanding.[1] . . . This narrow limitation, indeed, of our enquiries, is, in every respect, so reasonable, that it suffices to make the slightest examination into the natural powers of the human mind, and to compare them with their objects, in order to recommend it to us." [2]

The most salient feature of this scepticism, as compared either with metaphysical dogmatism, or the naïve objectivism of *common-sense*, is that it distinguishes between things as they are and things as they appear to us. Without any reasoning, says Hume,[3] we always suppose an external universe, which depends not on our perception, but would exist, though we and every sensible creature were absent or annihilated. This very table, which we see white, and which we feel hard, is believed to exist, independent of our perception, and to be something external to our mind, which perceives it. Our presence bestows not being on it; our absence does not annihilate it. It preserves its existence uniform and entire, independent of the situation of intelligent beings, who perceive or contemplate it. But this universal and primary opinion of all men is soon destroyed by the slightest philosophy. And no man who reflects ever doubted that the existences which we consider, when we say, *this house* and *that tree*, are nothing but perceptions in the mind, and fleeting copies or representations of other existences which remain uniform and independent. Even the *primary* qualities of extension and solidity are perceptions of the mind. — (Berkeley.)

Are these perceptions produced by external objects resembling them? Here experience, which alone can answer this question of fact, is and must be entirely silent. Do external objects at least exist? Experience is equally silent on this point. However, to doubt the existence of bodies is an excessive scepticism, which action and employment, and the common occupations of life, subvert. This excessive scepticism, or Pyrrhonism, true scepticism rejects as barren. Every time it attempts to reappear, nature puts it to flight. Nevertheless,

[1] *Id.*, XII, p. 133.   [2] *Id.*   [3] *Id.*, p. 124.

the existence of bodies, being a matter of fact, is incapable of demonstration. The only objects of *real knowledge* and demonstration are quantity and number. Experience decides concerning all matters of fact and existence, and experience never goes beyond probability.[1] — (Carneades.)

Hume's teachings were violently opposed, in the name of *common-sense* and morality, by THOMAS REID,[2] the founder of the so-called Scottish school, and by his disciples, OSWALD,[3] BEATTIE,[4] and DUGALD STEWART.[5] All of these men were psychologists of merit, but, with the exception of Reid, mediocre metaphysicians. In order to refute Hume it was necessary to put one's self in his position, — the critical position, — to use his own weapons, to renew the inquiry into the human understanding, and, if possible, to make it more thorough and complete. Kant, the most illustrious continuer and the most acute critic of the Scotch philosopher, saw that very clearly. "Common-sense," he says, "is a precious gift of God. But we must prove it by its acts, by deliberate and rational thought and speech, and not appeal to it as to an oracle, whenever reasons fail us. It is one of the subtle devices of our times to appeal to common-sense when our knowledge gives out, and the shallowest fool confidently measures his strength with the profoundest thinker's. . . . And what is this appeal to common-sense but a bid for the applause of the rabble, which cannot but bring the blush to the cheek of the philosopher? I

---

[1] In excluding physics from the sphere of pure knowledge, the idealist Plato advances the same opinion.

[2] 1710–1796. Professor at Glasgow. *Inquiry into the Human Mind on the Principles of Common-sense*, London, 1764 ff. Complete works, ed. by W. Hamilton, Edinburgh, 1895. Fraser, Thomas Reid (Famous Scots Series), London.

[3] *Appeal to Common Sense in Behalf of Religion*, Edinburgh, 1766.

[4] 1735–1803. Professor at Edinburgh. *Essay on the Nature and Immutability of Truth in Opposition to Sophistry and Scepticism*, Edinburgh, 1770; *Theory of Language*, London, 1778; *Elements of the Science of Morals*, 1790–1793.

[5] 1753–1828. *Elements of the Philosophy of the Human Mind*, 3 vols., London, 1792–1827; *Outlines of Moral Philosophy*, 1793 [ed. with critical notes by J. McCosh, London, 1863. Collected works, ed. by W. Hamilton, 10 vols., Edinburgh, 1854–1858. Thomas Brown (1778–1820), a pupil of Stewart, approximates Hume (*Inquiry into the Relation of Cause and Effect*, Edinb., 1803 ff.) — TR.].

cannot help thinking that Hume had as much good sense as Beattie." Reason can be corrected by reason alone.[1]

It is true, Hume's philosophy was not unassailable. There were breaks in his criticism; difficulties were eluded rather than solved. If experience is the sole source of knowledge, whence arises the exceptional character of absolute certainty which Hume himself concedes to mathematics? If there is nothing in the intellect which was not previously in the senses, how shall we explain the ideas of cause, necessary connection, and necessity? As was seen, the Scotch criticist explains the idea of necessary connection by the principle of habit. After the constant conjunction of two objects, we are determined by custom alone to expect the one from the appearance of the other. But this explanation does not suffice. The idea of necessity cannot come from experience alone, for the widest experience supplies us only with a limited number of cases; it never tells us what happens *in all cases*, and consequently does not yield necessary truth. Besides, it is not true that the notion of causality is that of necessary contiguity in time.[2] Causality signifies connection, and therefore contains an element not included in the notion of contiguity. Now, Hume expressly states that *one event follows another, but that we can never observe any tie between them. They seem conjoined, but never connected.* Hence, if experience *never shows us a cause*, but only a *succession* of events (for that is what Hume means by the ill-chosen term *conjunction*, which is synonymous with

[1] *Prolegomena zu einer jeden künftigen Metaphysik*, Preface, vol. III (Rosen-kranz), p. 8.

[2] What succession, as Thomas Reid aptly remarks, is older and more regularly observed than that of day and night? Now, it never occurs to any one to consider night as an *effect* of day, and day as the *cause* of night. Moreover, there is this peculiarity about the truths of experience that the certainty we get from them is susceptible of increase and diminution. After a second success-ful test, the physician is more convinced of the virtue of his medicine than after the first, and so on, until a long line of authentic cases changes into certainty what was at first a mere presumption and surmise. The case is quite different with a truth like the following: Nothing happens without a cause. The child, whose experience has just begun, believes in it with the same instinctive force as the adult and the old man, and experiences multiplied by the myriads can neither increase nor diminish its certainty.

connection), must we not either negate the idea of causation, or infer a different origin for it?

At this point Hume's criticism is corrected and completed by that of Kant.

§ 62. Kant.[1] The Doctrine of Criticism

IMMANUEL KANT, born in Königsberg, Prussia, 1724, was the son of plain people. His paternal grandparents emigrated to Germany from the fatherland of Hume. After pursuing his studies at the University of his native city (1740–1746), Kant became a private tutor, then a *Privatdocent* in the University of Königsberg (1755), where he taught logic, ethics, metaphysics, mathematics, cosmography, and geography. He was made full Professor in 1770, and continued his lectures until 1797. In 1804 he died, rich in honors and in years. Kant never left his native province, and never married. He enjoyed good health, was absolutely regular in his daily habits, free from the cares of family-life, and, for three-quarters of a century, devoted to science and intellectual pleasures. Thus he realized, in a certain measure, the ideal of the philosophers of Athens and Rome; but his cheerful temperament and sociable disposition softened the harshness in the character of the Stoic sage. When we remember, besides, that he was a reformer in philosophy, it will hardly surprise us to hear that history likens him to Socrates.

His philosophical writings may be divided into two separate classes. Those of his dogmatic period[2] betray the disciple

[1] *Critique of Pure Reason*, tr. by Max Müller, New York, 1922; *Prolegomena to Any Future Metaphysics*, Open Court Edition, Chicago; *Critique of Practical Reason*, and other works on the Theory of Ethics, tr. by Abbott, New York, 1923; *Critique of Judgment*, tr. by Bernard, New York, 1892; Selections (from *Critique of Pure Reason*, *Critique of Judgment*, and ethical writings) by Watson, New York, 1888.   Works on Kant: E. Caird, *The Philosophy of Kant*, London, 1876; Paulsen, *Kant* (tr. by Creighton and Lefevre), New York, 1916; Prichard, *Kant's Theory of Knowledge;* Oxford, 1909; Wenley, *Kant and his Philosophical Revolution*, Edinburgh, 1910; Smith, *Commentary to Kant's Critique of Pure Reason*, London, 1918; Ward, *A Study of Kant*, Cambridge (Eng.), 1922.

[2] To the first period belongs his *Allgemeine Naturgeschichte und Theorie des Himmels*, one of the masterpieces of general physics.

of Leibniz and Wolff; though anticipating, especially his *Dreams of a Spirit Seer* (1766), the teachings of his maturer years. Those of his second period (1770–1804), during which the influence of Hume led him to break with dogmatism, present a new philosophy. Chief among them are: *De mundi sensibilis atque intelligibilis forma et principiis* (1770); *Critique of Pure Reason* (1781; 2d edition, revised, 1787): his masterwork, which forms the basis of the following: *Prolegomena to Any Future Metaphysics* (1783); *Foundation of the Metaphysics of Ethics* (1785); *Metaphysical Foundations of Natural Science* (1786); *Critique of Practical Reason* (1788); *Critique of Judgment* (1790); *Religion within the Bounds of Pure Reason* (1793).

Our age, as Kant often says, is the age of *criticism;* and by that word he understands the philosophy which, before affirming, weighs, and, before assuming to know, inquires into the conditions of knowledge. Not only is the philosophy of Kant criticism in this general sense; it is also criticism in the special sense of being a theory of ideas; it is *critical*, as distinguished from the extreme theories of Leibniz and Locke, in that it discriminates (κρίνειν, *discernere*), in the formation of ideas, between the product of sensation and the product of the spontaneous activity of pure reason. It acknowledges with sensationalism that the *matter* of our ideas is furnished by the senses; with idealism it claims that their *form* is the work of reason, — that reason, by its own laws, transforms into ideas the given manifold of sensation. Criticism neither aims to be sensationalistic nor intellectualistic in the extreme sense of these terms, but *transcendental;* i. e., going beyond (*transcendens*) the sensationalistic and idealistic doctrines, it succeeds in reaching a higher standpoint, which enables it to appreciate the relative truth and falsehood in the theories of dogmatism. It is a method rather than a system, an introduction to philosophy rather than a finished system. Its motto is the "know thyself" of Socrates, which it interprets to mean: Before constructing any system whatever, reason must inquire into its resources for constructing it.

In its examination of reason, criticism carefully separates the different elements of this faculty, and, true to the critical spirit whence it springs, *distinguishes* between the theoretical order, the practical order, and the æsthetical order. Reason resembles a queen, who, under three different names, governs three separate states, each having its own laws, customs, and tendencies. In the theoretical sphere, it manifests itself as the faculty of knowing, or the sense of *truth;* in the practical sphere, as the active faculty, or the sense of *goodness;* in the æsthetical sphere, as the sense of *beauty* and teleological fitness. The Kantian philosophy gives each of these three spheres its due, examining one after another, without prejudice or dogmatic prepossessions.

I. CRITIQUE OF PURE REASON

And, first of all, it asks: What is knowledge?

An idea taken by itself (man, earth, heat) is not knowledge; in order to become knowledge, the ideas of man, earth, and heat must be combined with other ideas; there must be a subject and a predicate, i. e., a judgment. Examples: Man is a responsible being; the earth is a planet; heat expands bodies. Hence, all knowledge is formulated into propositions; all knowledge is judgment, but not every judgment is knowledge.

There are *analytic* judgments and *synthetic* judgments. The former merely analyze an idea, without adding anything new to it. Example: Bodies are extended. The predicate *extended* adds nothing to the subject that is not already contained in it. This judgment tells me nothing new; it does not increase my knowledge. When, on the other hand, I say: The earth is a planet, I make a synthetic judgment, i. e., I join to the idea of the earth a new predicate, the idea of a planet, which cannot be said to be inseparable from the idea of the earth; nay, it has taken man thousands of years to connect it with the latter. Hence, synthetic judgments enrich, extend, and increase my knowledge, and alone constitute knowledge; which is not the case with analytic judgments.

But here Kant makes an important reservation. Not every synthetic judgment is necessarily *scientific* knowledge. In order to constitute real scientific knowledge, with which alone we are here concerned, a judgment must be true in all cases; the union which it establishes between subject and predicate should not be accidental, but necessary. "It is warm," is undoubtedly a synthetic judgment, but it is accidental and contingent, for it may be cold to-morrow; hence it is not a scientific proposition. Whenever, however, you say: Heat expands, you state a fact which will be as true to-morrow and a thousand years from now as it is to-day; you state a necessary proposition and a concept properly so called.

But what right have I to affirm that this proposition is necessary, universal, true in every instance? Does experience reveal to me all cases, and are there no possible cases, beyond our observation, in which heat does not expand the bodies which it usually expands? Hume is right on this point. Since experience always furnishes only a limited number of cases, it cannot yield necessity and universality. Hence, a judgment *a posteriori*, i. e., one based solely on experience, cannot constitute scientific knowledge. In order to be necessary, or scientific, a judgment must rest on a rational basis; it must be rooted in reason as well as in observation; it must be a judgment *a priori*. Now, mathematics, physics, and metaphysics consist of synthetic judgments *a priori*.[1] Hence, to sum up: Knowledge may be defined as *synthetic judgment a priori*. This is Kant's answer to his preliminary question: What is knowledge?

How can we form synthetic judgments *a priori?* In other terms: Under what conditions is knowledge possible? This is the fundamental problem which Kantian criticism undertakes to solve.

It is possible, Kant answers, provided the senses furnish the materials for a judgment, and reason the cement needed to unite them. Take the proposition already cited: Heat expands bodies. This proposition contains two distinct elements:

[1] Before Kant's time, mathematical propositions were regarded as analytic.

(1) the elements furnished by sensation: heat, expansion, bodies; (2) an element not given by sensation, but derived solely from the intellect: the causal relation which the sentence in question establishes between heat and the expansion of bodies. What is true of our example is true of every scientific judgment. Every scientific judgment necessarily contains sensible elements and pure or rational elements. In denying the former, idealism ignores the fact that persons born blind have no idea of color, and, consequently, no notion of light; in denying the rational, innate, *a priori* element, sensationalism forgets that the most refined senses of the idiot are incapable of suggesting a scientific notion to him. The critical philosophy occupies a place between these two extreme theories, and recognizes both the rôle of sensibility and that of pure reason in the formation of our judgments.

But we must make a more penetrating analysis of the faculty of knowledge. As we have just seen, it is divided into two subfaculties, one of which furnishes the materials of our knowledge, while the other fashions them, or makes concepts of them. Hence, our examination of reason, in the broad sense of faculty of knowledge, will take up: (1) the sensibility (intuitive reason) and (2) the understanding proper.

1. *Critique of Sensibility, or Transcendental Æsthetic*

We now know in a general way that knowledge is the common product of sensibility and the understanding. But what are the conditions of sense-perception, or, to use Kant's language, intuition (*Anschauung*)?

Sensibility, we said, furnishes the understanding with the materials of its knowledge. But the materials themselves, of which the garment is to be made, already have a certain shape; they are no longer absolutely raw materials: the latter have been subjected to the preliminary processes of spinning and weaving. Or, in other words, our sensibility is not purely passive; it does not turn over to the understanding the materials which the latter needs, without adding something of its own; it impresses its stamp, its own forms, upon things; or, as one might say, it marks the perceived object just as the outline of our hands is traced upon a handful of snow. It is in particular what the faculty of knowledge is in general: both receptive and active; it *receives* a mysterious substance from without, and *makes* an intuition of it. Hence, there are, in every intuition, two elements: a *pure* or *a priori* element and an *a posteriori* element, form and matter, something that reason produces spontaneously and something, I know not what, derived elsewhere.

What is this form? What are the *a priori* elements which our sensibility does not receive, but draws from its own nature and adds to each of its intuitions, just as the digestive apparatus adds its juices to the swallowed food, in order to transform it into chyle? These *a priori* intuitions, which sensationalism denies, and whose existence the *Critique of Pure Reason* proves, are *space*, the form of the outer sense, and *time*, the form of the inner sense. *Space and time are original intuitions of reason, prior to all experience :* this is the immortal discovery of Kant, and one of the fundamental teachings of the critical philosophy.

The following proofs may be offered in support of the view that space and time come from reason and not from experience: (1) Although the infant has no accurate notion of distance, it tends to withdraw from disagreeable objects and to approach such as give it pleasure. Hence it knows *a priori* that such objects are in front of it, by the side of it, beyond it, etc. Prior to all other intuitions, it has the idea of *before, beside, beyond,* i. e., the idea of space, of which these are but particular applications. The same is true of time. Prior to all perception, the child has a feeling of *before* and *after*, without which its perceptions would be a confused, disordered, disconnected mass. That is, prior or *a priori* to every other intuition, it has the idea of time.

(2) Another proof that space and time are *a priori* intuitions: Thought may abstract from everything that fills space and time; in no case can it abstract from space and time themselves.

This proves that these intuitions, instead of coming from without, are, so to say, of a piece with reason; that they are, in the inaccurate language of dogmatic philosophy, *innate*, that they are, in the last analysis, identical with reason.

(3) But the decisive proof of the a-priority of the ideas of space and time is furnished by mathematics. Arithmetic is the science of duration, the successive moments of which constitute number. Geometry is the science of space. Now arithmetical and geometrical truths possess the character of absolute necessity. No one would seriously maintain: My previous experience teaches me that three times three are nine, or that the three angles of a triangle are equal to two right angles, etc., for everybody knows that such truths are independent of experience. Experience, being restricted to a limited number of cases, cannot give a truth the absolute and unquestionable character possessed by the axioms of mathematics; these truths do not spring from experience but from reason: hence the sovereign authority which characterizes them, and the impossibility of doubting them for a single instant. But such truths are concerned with space and time. Hence, space and time are intuitions *a priori*.

Shall we call them general ideas formed by comparison and abstraction? But an idea thus formed necessarily contains fewer characteristics than the particular idea; the idea of man is infinitely less comprehensive and poorer than the particular idea of Socrates, Plato, or Aristotle. Now, who would be bold enough to assert that universal space contains less than a particular space, or, infinite time, less than a fixed period of time? The ideas of space and time are, therefore, not the results of an intellectual operation, of the comparison of different spaces, from which the general idea of space is derived; or of a comparison of moments of duration, whence arises the general idea of time. They are not results, but principles, conditions *a priori* and *sine quibus non* of perception. The common man imagines that he *perceives* space and time, that space and time are, just like their contents, *objects* of perception. But as a matter of fact, it is as impossible for them to be perceived as it is for the eye to see itself (its image in the mirror is not the eye itself). We see all things *in* space, but we cannot see space itself, nor perceive duration independently of its content. All perception presupposes the ideas of space and time; and unless we had these ideas *a priori*, unless reason created them prior to all its intuitions, unless they pre-existed as original and in-alienable forms, sense-perception could never take place.

We now know the conditions under which sense-perception operates. It depends on the *a priori* ideas of space and time, which are, as it were, the prehensile organs of sensibility. These ideas are not images corresponding to external objects. There is no object called space, nor an object called time. Time and space are not *objects* of perception, but *modes of perceiving objects*, instinctive habits, inhering in the thinking subject.

The *transcendental ideality* of space and time: such is the important conclusion reached by the critical examination of sensibility, the *mene thekel* of dogmatism. Let us see what this conclusion implies. If neither space nor time exists independently of reason and its intuitive activity, then things, considered in themselves and independently of the reason which thinks them, have no existence in time or space. Hence, if sensibility, in consequence of an instinctive and inevitable habit, shows us things in time and space, it does not show them as they are in themselves, but as they appear to it through its spectacles, one of whose glasses is called time; the other, space. As they appear to it! which means that sensibility gives us appearances, or phenomena, and that it is incapable of giving us the *thing-in-itself*, the noumenon. And since the understanding obtains the materials which it needs exclusively from the senses, since there is no other channel through which the materials can come, it is evident that it always and necessarily operates upon phenomena, and that the mystery concealed beneath the phenomenon forever baffles it, as it forever baffles the senses.

2. *Critique of the Understanding, or Transcendental Logic*

Kant distinguishes, in the general faculty of knowledge, between sensibility, which produces intuitions or sensible ideas, and the understanding, which elaborates them. In the understanding he again distinguishes between the faculty of judgment, i. e., the faculty of connecting the intuitions with each other according to certain *a priori* laws (*Verstand*), and the faculty of arranging our judgments under a series of universal Ideas (*Vernunft*, reason, in the narrowest sense of the word). The inquiry concerning the understanding is therefore subdivided into the critique of the faculty of judgment (*Verstand*) and the critique of reason proper (*Vernunft*), or, to use Kant's own language, into the *Transcendental Analytic* and the *Transcendental Dialectic*.

A. Transcendental Analytic

Just as the intuitive faculty perceives all things in time and space, reason moulds its judgments according to certain forms or general concepts, which, in philosophy, have been called categories, ever since the days of Aristotle. Kant agrees with Hume that the highest category, the idea of *cause*, conceived as the necessary relation between two phenomena, is not derived from experience. Hume, however, regards it as the result of our habit of seeing certain facts constantly conjoined together, and consequently considers it as a prejudice useful to science, but without metaphysical value. Kant, on the other hand, defends its validity; and from the impossibility of deriving it from experience, infers that it is innate. The idea of cause and all other categories are, according to him, *a priori* functions of the understanding, *means of knowledge and not objects of knowledge*, just as time and space are, according to the same philosopher, *modes of seeing* (*intuendi*) *and not objects of intuition*.

Not content with proving, against empiricism, that the categories are innate, Kant attempts to make out an inventory of them, and to deduce them from a principle. He gives us a complete list; indeed, far too complete a list. His love of symmetry impels him to add a category of limitation (which Schopenhauer ingeniously calls a false window), and a category of being and non-being (*Dasein und Nichtsein*), which he erroneously distinguishes from the concepts of reality and negation. As far as the logical deduction of *a priori* ideas is concerned, we must confess that it is merely a pious wish; no one before Hegel has really made a serious attempt to solve this problem.

The theory of judgment which Kant finds in traditional logic, serves as his guide in the discovery and classification of the categories. Indeed, he says, the judgment is the highest function of the understanding. Now the categories are the forms according to which we judge. Hence there are as many categories as there are kinds of judgments. Logic enumerates twelve of them: (1) the universal judgment (All men are mortal); (2) the particular judgment (Some men are philosophers); (3) the singular judgment (Peter is a mathematician); (4) the affirmative judgment (Man is mortal); (5) the negative judgment (The soul is not mortal); (6) the limiting judgment (The soul is immortal); (7) the categorical judgment (God is just); (8) the hypothetical judgment (If God is just, he will punish the wicked); (9) the disjunctive judgment (Either the Greeks or the Romans are the leading nation of antiquity); (10) the problematical judgment (The planets are, perhaps, inhabited); (11) the assertory judgment (The earth is round); (12) the apodictic judgment (God must be just). The first three express totality, plurality, and unity, i. e., in a word, the idea of *quantity;* the fourth, fifth, and sixth express reality, negation, and limitation, or, the idea of *quality;* the seventh, eighth, and ninth express substantiality and inherence, causality and dependence, and reciprocity, or, in short, *relation;* finally, the tenth, eleventh, and twelfth express possibility and impossibility, being and non-being, necessity and contingency, i. e., the idea of *modality.*

There are, therefore, twelve categories, arranged in threes, under four groups or fundamental categories: quantity, quality, relation, and modality. One of these, *relation*, governs and embraces all the rest. It is the highest category, since every judgment, whatever it may be, expresses a relation.

From these four cardinal categories four rules or principles necessarily follow, which are, therefore, also *a priori:*

(1) From the standpoint of quantity, every phenomenon, i. e., everything presented by the intuitive faculty as existing in space and in time, is a quantity, i. e., a fixed extent and a fixed duration. This principle excludes the hypothesis of *atoms*.

(2) From the standpoint of quality, every phenomenon has a certain content, a certain degree of intensity. This principle excludes the hypothesis of *the void*.

(3) From the standpoint of relation, all phenomena are united by the tie of causality; which excludes the hypothesis of *chance;* there is, moreover, a reciprocal action between the effects and their causes; which excludes the idea of fate.

(4) From the standpoint of modality, every phenomenon is *possible* that conforms to the laws of space and time, and every phenomenon is *necessary*, the absence of which would imply the suspension of these laws; which excludes *miracles*.

The first and second of these principles constitute the law of *continuity;* the third and fourth, the law of *causality*.

These categories and the principles which follow from them form the *pure*, innate, *a priori* element, and, as it were, the patrimony of the understanding (*Verstand*). The latter does not receive them; it draws them from its own inner nature; it does not find them in the phenomenal world; *it imposes them upon it*. These conclusions of the transcendental logic are of the highest importance. But, before we develop them, we must, in a few words, explain what Kant means by the *schematism of pure reason*.

The analysis of the faculty of knowledge has outlined the boundaries between sensibility and the intellect (sensibility receives the impressions, co-ordinates them, and makes intuitions of them; the intellect synthesizes the intuitions, i. e., judges and reasons). We discriminated, in sensibility, between *a posteriori* intuitions and the *a priori* intuitions of space and time; in the understanding we discovered a number of *a priori* concepts, which are so many compartments, as it were, in which reason stores and elaborates the products of experience. But though containing many elements, the faculty of knowledge is, nevertheless, *a unity*. This essential unity of reason in the diversity of its operations is the *ego*, the feeling or apperception of which accompanies all intellectual phenomena, and constitutes their common bond, so to speak. Kant is not satisfied with a mere analysis; not only does he take apart the knowledge-machine, as we might say, he also attempts to explain how it works, and to show how the parts fit into each other. He, therefore, imagines the categories of limitation, reciprocity or concurrence, and reality, as connecting links between affirmation and negation, substantiality and causality, possibility and necessity: fictions which gave rise to the triads of Fichte and Hegel (thesis, antithesis, and synthesis). It is owing to the same demand for synthesis that he raises the question: How can reason act upon the data of sensibility; by what means, by what arm, as it were, does it lay hold of sensible intuitions and make notions of them?

This operation is, in his opinion, effected by means of the idea of time, the natural intermediary between intuitions and concepts. Though time, like space, belongs to the domain of sensible things, it is less material than space, and partakes more of the entirely abstract nature of the categories. Owing to its resemblance to the categories, the idea of time serves as an image or symbol to express the *a priori* notions in terms of sense, and becomes a kind of interpreter between the intuitive faculty and the understanding, which, without it, cannot assist in the formation of the judgment.

Considered as a series of moments, or as number, time expresses the idea of quantity: The image of universality is the totality of moments of time; the particular is expressed by a certain number of moments; the singular, by *one* moment. The content of time symbolizes the idea of quality (reality is expressed by a time filled with events; negation, by a time in which nothing happens). Time likewise symbolizes the idea of relation: Permanence in time represents the idea of substance; succession of moments, the idea of cause and effect; simultaneity, the idea of reciprocity and concurrence. Finally, time is the image of the categories of modality: That which corresponds to the conditions of time is possible; that which exists at a definite time is real or actual; that which is eternal is necessary. Hence, the idea of time serves as a scheme for the *a priori* concepts of the understanding; it is a framework, so to speak, of the ideal constructions, for which the senses furnish the stones, and reason the mortar. Reason uses the idea of time as an interpreter between itself and sensibility; and this operation is called, in the pedantic language of criticism, the schematism of pure reason.

The conclusion of the critique of the intellect merely corroborates the sceptical and subjectivistic results of the *Transcendental Æsthetic*.

The critique of the intuitive faculty has demonstrated that we see things through colored glasses (space and time), i. e., otherwise than they are in themselves. The examination of the understanding shows that we communicate with them through an entire system of glasses. Sensibility perceives them, but in doing this, it impresses its forms upon them, i. e., it transforms them. We do not perceive them as they are, but as they appear to us, that is, *as we make them*. When we perceive them, they have already been stamped; indeed, they are perceived by the very forms inhering in sensibility (space and time). They are no longer things; they are nothing but *phenomena*. Hence the phenomenon may be defined as the thing transformed by the mould of the intuitive faculty. What constitutes it is, on the one hand, the thing which impresses the senses, but above everything else, the sensibility itself, or reason in the broad sense of the term: it is ourselves; it is the *I*,

the perceiving and thinking subject, *that makes the phenomenon.*
The phenomenon is the product of reason; it does not exist outside
of us, but in us; it does not exist beyond the limits of intuitive
reason.[1]

Now, while the *Æsthetic* brings us to the tnreshold of subjective idealism, the *Transcendental Logic* carries us right into
it, in spite of Kant's protests against our confounding him
with Berkeley. Not only, he tells us, does reason, as an intuition, constitute, produce, or create the phenomenon, but
reason, in the form of the understanding, also determines the
reciprocal relations of sensible phenomena. Reason makes
them *a priori* quantities, qualities, causes, and effects, and
thus impresses upon them the seal of its legislative power; it is
through reason that the things become quantities, qualities,
effects, and causes, which they are not in themselves. Hence
we may say without exaggeration that it is *reason which pre-*
scribes its laws to the sensible universe : it is reason which makes
the cosmos.

Such are Kant's own words,[2] and we emphasize these memorable theses because they form the immediate basis of the
systems of Fichte, Schelling, and Hegel. And yet the latter
are called the apostates of criticism, whom Kant himself
repudiates! Nevertheless, the man who said that reason, —
and human reason, *nota bene,* — prescribes its laws to the
universe, is the father of Hegelian panlogism. But, we must
add, he is so, in spite of himself; the bent of his philosophy is
essentially different from that of his successors. Instead of
deifying the human understanding, he claims to limit it, — to
force the overflowing river into its natural channel, the phenomenal world, and to exclude forever the sphere of the absolute.
When Kant says that reason creates the universe, or at least
assists in its creation, he means the phenomenal universe, the
totality of phenomena, and he very candidly admits that there
may be, beyond the phenomenal world, a world of noumena
or realities which cannot be perceived, which are inaccessible

---

[1] *Kritik,* p. 389; *Prolegomena,* pp. 44, 51.   [2] *Prolegomena,* p. 85.

and consequently superior to reason.[1] Kant is far from being a panlogist in the Hegelian sense of the term; nay, the very object of the entire second part of his critique of the understanding, the *Transcendental Dialectic*, is to demonstrate the incompetence of theoretical reason beyond the domain of experience, and the futility of metaphysics considered as the science of the absolute.

B. Transcendental Dialectic

From the faculty of judgment (*Verstand*) Kant distinguishes that of embracing the totality of our judgments under certain general points of view, which he calls *Ideas*. This faculty, the highest of all in the intellectual sphere, is reason in the narrow sense of the term, the νοῦς of the ancients. The concepts of "reason," or Ideas,[2] are: the *thing-in-itself*, or the *absolute*, the *universe*, the *soul*, and *God*. Their function is similar to that of the *a priori* intuitions (space and time), and that of the categories. Just as the former arrange the impressions of sense, and the latter, the intuitions, so the Ideas arrange the infinite mass of judgments and reduce them to a system. Hence "reason," which fashions them, is the highest synthetic faculty, the systematic and scientific faculty. Thus, from the co-operation of sensibility, judgment, and "reason" arise the sciences. For example: The outer sense, by means of its *a priori* intuitions of space and time, furnishes us with a series of phenomena; the understanding, with the help of its categories, makes concepts, judgments, and scientific propositions of them; finally, "reason" embraces these *disjecta membra* under the Idea of the cosmos, and makes a science of them. So, too, the inner sense furnishes us with a series of facts; the understanding makes concepts of them; and "reason" combines these concepts into the Idea of the soul, and produces the

---

[1] The absolute rationalism of his successors, on the other hand, does not admit any kind of transcendency.

[2] The term is derived from Platonism, but the Ideas of Kant are not, like those of Plato, *realities* existing apart from our thought.

science of psychology. By viewing the totality of phenomena from the standpoint of the absolute or of God, reason creates *theology*.

The "Ideas" and "reason," as a separate faculty of the understanding, seem to be superfluities in the Kantian system. The Idea of the cosmos is nothing but the category of totality; the Idea of the soul and the Idea of God are the categories of substance and cause, applied to inner facts (soul) and to the sum-total of phenomena (God). "Reason," consequently, is not a faculty distinct from the understanding; it is merely its complete development. But we shall not insist on this critical detail. Let us rather hasten to discuss the most important topic of the *Dialectic*: the doctrine of the a-priority of the Ideas.

Just as space and time are not perceived *objects*, but *modes* of perceiving objects; just as the categories of quantity, quality, and relation are *means*, not *objects*, of knowledge, so, too, the universe, the soul, and God are *a priori* syntheses of reason and not beings existing independently of the thinking subject. At least, it is impossible for reason to demonstrate their objective existence. Reason, as Kant insists, really knows nothing but phenomena, and receives the *matter* of all its operations from sensibility alone. Now the universe, as absolute totality, the soul, and God are not phenomena; the Ideas — in this, says Kant, they differ from the categories — do not receive any content from sensibility; they are supreme norms, regulative points of view, no more, no less. Old metaphysics erred in regarding them as anything else.

Dogmatism deludes itself when it claims to know the absolute. It resembles the child that sees the sky touching the horizon, and imagines that it can reach the sky by moving towards the seeming line of intersection. The sky is the thing-in-itself, the absolute, which, by a kind of optical illusion, seems to us to be an object that can be studied and experienced; the horizon, which recedes as the child advances, is experience, which seems to attain the absolute, and which, in reality, cannot approach it; the child itself is the dogmatic metaphysician. Let us say, to be just, that the illusion is common to all intellects, just as the illusion that the heaven bounds the earth is shared by all. But there is this difference between the dogmatic philosopher and the critical philosopher. The former, like the child, is the dupe of his illusion, while the latter explains it and takes it for what it is worth. Kant might have summed up his entire critique as follows: Knowledge is relative; a known absolute signifies a relative absolute; which is contradictory.

What is true of traditional ontology is true of psychology, cosmology, and theology.

Rational psychology, as Descartes, Leibniz, and Wolff conceived it, rests on a paralogism. "I think," says Descartes, "therefore I am" — and mentally adds: a substance. Now, that is just what he has no right to do. *I think*, means: I am the logical subject of my thought. But have I the right to infer from this that I am a substance in the sense which Cartesian metaphysics attaches to the term? A logical subject is one thing, a metaphysical subject is quite another. When I express the judgment: The earth is a planet, the logical subject of this proposition is the *ego* that formulates it; while the earth is the real subject. The celebrated thesis of Descartes is a paralogism, because it confuses the *I*, the logical subject, with the *I*, the real subject. Metaphysically, I do not know the *ego*, and I shall never know it, except as the logical subject, as an Idea inseparable from my judgments, as the premise and necessary concomitant of all my intellectual operations. I shall never know more. As soon as I make a substance of it, I make it the object of a judgment, which is, according to Kant, as absurd as though I pretended to *see* space and time. Space and time are *a priori* ideas which serve as a framework for sensible ideas, without being objects of the senses themselves. So, too, the *cogito* is an *a priori* judgment, preceding all other judgments as an absolute condition, without, however, in any way anticipating the nature of the *ego*. I cannot judge metaphysically concerning the ego, because it is I who am judging:

one cannot be both judge and litigant, as they say in law; or subject of the discourse and the real subject, as they say in logic.

If it is not possible to prove that the ego exists as a substance, the doctrines of the simplicity, immateriality, and immortality of the human soul cannot stand.

From the existence of simple ideas it does not necessarily follow that the soul is a simple substance, for there are also collective ideas. To conclude from the simplicity of ideas the simplicity of the "spiritual substance" would be equivalent to inferring the simplicity of the cosmical substance from the simplicity of weight, or the unity of motive force from the simplicity of what mechanics calls the resultant.

Suppose, however, the soul were a simple substance; simplicity is not immortality. We must remember that, from Kant's point of view, bodies are phenomena, i. e., facts produced by sensibility, the sensible subject or the ego, with the co-operation of an absolutely unknown cause. The phenomenon — we must always return to this fundamental thesis of criticism — the phenomenon is nothing external to the sensible subject; heat, light, and color, although called forth by an external, wholly mysterious, solicitation, are products of sensibility, inner facts, — in short, ideas.

Kant, it is true, seeks to draw a line of demarcation between the phenomenon and the intuition or idea, between what happens at the boundary of the ego and the non-ego, and what is entirely subjective; but with indifferent success. The phenomenon takes place in us and is consequently identical with the idea. Hence, in so far as they are phenomena, *bodies are ideas.* Why, then, should not the bodies, on the one hand, and the intuitions properly so called, the categories, and the judgments, on the other, have a common substance? Why should not that which we call matter be an immaterial thing, and what we call mind or soul, be a material thing?

Immortality, therefore, likewise ceases to be a self-evident doctrine. According to the supporters of this dogma, the soul is not only an indestructible substance, but preserves, in death, the consciousness of self. Now, we discover, in inner perception, infinite degrees of intensity, and may conceive a descending scale that culminates in complete destruction.

By showing us the possibility of what dogmatism had previously affirmed in Spinoza, viz., the identity of spiritual substance and material substance, criticism does away with the hypotheses of *influxus*, divine assistance, and pre-established harmony. These theories lose their *raison d'être* as soon as it is proved that the "substances" of Descartes and the "monads" of Leibniz are nothing but phenomena, derived, *perhaps*, from a common source. The problem is no longer to explain the reciprocal action of soul and body, but to ascertain how the same reason, the same ego, can produce phenomena as diametrically opposed as material facts and intellectual facts, extension and thought. In this new form, the question retains all its importance and mysterious fascination for Kant. He touched upon it, as we saw, in connection with the idea of time and its function as an intermediary between the intuitions and the categories, but he could not penetrate more deeply into the subject without contradicting his premises. To attempt to solve it meant to state what sensibility is *in itself*, what the understanding is *in itself;* it meant to make the thing-in-itself an object of metaphysical knowledge.

After overthrowing rational psychology, Kant undertakes to demolish rational cosmology in the Wolffian sense. Instead of confining itself to the domain of experience, this alleged science makes an Idea, the cosmos, the object of its speculations. When it considers this Idea from the standpoint of quantity, quality, relation, and modality, it necessarily becomes involved in antinomies. Antinomies are theories which contradict each other, each one, at the same time, being as capable of demonstration as the other.

ANTINOMY OF QUANTITY

We can demonstrate, with the same show of reason, that the universe is a limited quantity, and that it is unlimited in space and time, i. e., infinite and eternal.

(1) *The universe is limited in time and in space.* Let us assume, for the sake of argument, that it is not. The universe, as a whole, is composed of parts which exist simultaneously. Now, I cannot conceive it as a whole except by a mental addition, a successive synthesis of its parts. But, by hypothesis, these parts are infinite in number. Hence their successive addition requires an infinite time. Consequently, the idea of the universe, the result of this addition, presupposes that an *infinite time* has elapsed to form it. But *elapsed* time is not infinite time. To reach a sum, the number of parts to be added must be limited: we cannot add an infinite number of parts. Now, the idea of the universe is a synthesis, the result of an addition. Hence, the universe has a limited extent (Aristotle). Let us likewise assume that it has no limit in time, that it has no beginning. On this hypothesis, an infinite number of moments have elapsed up to a given time. But an infinite lapse (i. e., finitude) of time is a contradiction in terms. The universe, therefore, is limited in space and in time (Plato).

(2) *The universe is unlimited in space and in time.* Otherwise, there would be, beyond its limits, an infinite space (for the idea of space does not admit of limits); hence there would be space *by the side of* things, and we might speak of a relation between the universe and the infinite space surrounding it, i. e., of a relation between objects and something which is not an object; for we now know that space is not an object. But a relation between an object and something that is not an object is impossible; a relation may obtain between things in space; there can be none between things and the space in which they exist. Hence the universe is unlimited. — If it had had a beginning, it would have been preceded by time without content, i. e., by *nothing*, for time without content is equal to nothing. Now from nothing nothing can arise. Hence the universe is eternal (Parmenides, Aristotle).

ANTINOMY OF QUALITY

Considered from the standpoint of quality (i. e., of its inner nature), is cosmical matter composed of atoms or elements which are, in turn, composite? Both the thesis and the antithesis may be proved with equally cogent reasons.

Thesis: *Matter is composed of simple elements, or atoms.* Let us assume that the opposite theory is true, and that matter is composed of parts, in turn composed of parts divisible into parts, and so on to infinity. If, in this hypothesis, we abstract from the idea of composition and decomposition, nothing whatever is left; now, out of nothing nothing can be composed. Every composite thing presupposes simple constitutive elements. Hence, matter is composed of indivisible elementary substances, monads, or atoms.

The antithesis, according to which *matter is infinitely divisible*, is equally easy of proof. In so far as the assumed atoms are material, they are extended. Now, that which is extended is divisible. Inextended particles are no longer matter. Hence, there are no simple material elements.

ANTINOMY OF RELATION

Does the universe, considered as an order of things, embrace free causes, or is it governed, without exception, by necessity? Metaphysicians have demonstrated both the thesis and the antithesis.

The thesis, which affirms that *there are free causes*, is proved as follows: Let us suppose that all things are connected with each other by a necessary nexus. If, on this hypothesis, we desire to pass from an effect to its first cause, it will be found that this first cause does not exist, or at least that the cause which seems to be the *first* is not really the first, but merely a link in the infinite chain of events. Now, according to the principle of sufficient reason, in order that an event be produced, all the causes necessary to its production must exist, and all the conditions which it presupposes must be satisfied. If one of these conditions is absent, the event cannot be produced. But, on the hypothesis of an infinite chain, there is no first cause or condition of a given event. If this cause is lacking, the occurrence cannot take place. Now, it does take place;

hence, there is a first cause, that is, a cause that is not again the necessarily predetermined effect of a previous cause, or, finally, a free cause. Hence, there are in the world, besides necessary occurrences, free occurrences and free causes.

According to the antithesis, *everything is necessary connection*, and liberty is merely an illusion. Let us assume a free cause. This cause necessarily exists prior to its effects, and, moreover, it pre-exists in a different state from that which it assumes when the effect is produced; first, it exists as a virgin, then, when the effect is produced, as a mother, so to speak. Thus we have, in the cause in question, two successive states without a causal tie, which is contrary to the principle recognized by the critique, that every phenomenon is an effect. Hence, liberty in the indeterministic sense is impossible.

ANTINOMY OF MODALITY

According to the thesis, *there exists either in the world or beyond it, a necessary being, an absolute cause of the universe.* The demonstration is similar to the proof of the existence of free causes. The world is a series of effects. Each effect, to be produced, presupposes a determined series of causes or conditions, and, consequently, a first cause or condition, an existence that is no longer contingent but necessary.

According to the antithesis, *there is no necessary being, either in the universe as an integral part of the cosmos, or beyond it, as the cause of the world.*

Now, if there is, *in the world and as part of it*, something necessary, this can only be conceived in two ways: (1) it exists at the beginning of the world; or (2) it coincides with the whole series of phenomena constituting it. Now, every beginning is a moment of time. Hence, an absolute beginning would be a moment of time without a preceding moment; which is inconceivable, for the idea of time admits of no limits. Hence, there is no necessary being *at the origin of things*. But it is also incorrect to say with Spinoza and the pantheists, that the whole of things and the totality of the moments of time, i. e., the universe, is necessary and absolute being. For, however immeasurable it may be, a totality of relative and contingent beings will no more constitute an absolute and necessary being than a hundred thousand idiots will constitute one intelligent man. Hence, there is nothing necessary *in the world*.

Nor is there anything necessary *beyond the universe*. For if the necessary being exists outside of the world, it exists outside of time and space. Now it is, by hypothesis, the principle, the source, the beginning of things. As their beginning, it constitutes a moment of time. But it is outside of time. That is to say, the necessary being cannot be conceived either in the form of immanency or in that of transcendency.

The fourth antinomy is not so much concerned with cosmology as with rational theology, the futility of which it shows in advance. Nevertheless, Kant devotes eighty-eight pages to the critique of the theodicy and the proofs of the existence of God.

The ontological proof (Anselm, Descartes) concludes from the idea of God the objective existence of a supreme being, and has no more value than the following reasoning of a poor man: I have the idea of a hundred thalers, hence these hundred thalers exist — in my purse. This is the same objection which Gaunilo of Marmoutiers had urged against St. Anselm.

The cosmological argument (from the contingency of the world) falsely assumes that there can be no infinite series of causes and effects without a first cause.[1] By connecting the series of contingent things with a first and necessary cause, it imagines that it closes the series, while, in reality, there still remains, between this alleged first cause and the following cause, the yawning chasm which separates the necessary from the contingent, and the absolute from the relative. But even granting the cogency of the proof, it would not follow that the necessary being, whose existence it claims to establish, is the personal being which theology calls God.

[1] See the fourth antinomy.

The teleological or physico-theological proof infers from the finality revealed in nature the existence of an intelligent creator. This argument has the advantage that it makes a deep impression on the mind, and the preacher is free to use it in preference to all other reasonings. But from the scientific point of view it has no value; for (1) it passes from sensible data to something that does not fall within the scope of the senses; (2) it professes to establish the existence of a God who is the creator of matter; (3) with what right, moreover, does it compare the universe to a clock or a house? Is the world necessarily *a work* presupposing a workman? Why, instead of being a machine begun at a given time, could it not be an eternal reality? (4) Besides, what is finality? Is it inherent in the things themselves? or is it not rather our own caprice which confers upon them their teleological character, according as they please us or displease us (Spinoza)?

The moral proof, which is based on the purposiveness in the moral order, on the existence of the moral law, on the phenomenon of moral conscience and the feeling of responsibility, is peremptory from the standpoint of practical reason, but from the standpoint of pure theory it shares the weakness of the teleological proof, of which it is, at bottom, merely a variation.[1]

In short, the critique of the faculty of knowledge does not culminate in atheism, but neither does it lead to theism; it does not lead to materialism, nor does it infer the spirituality of the soul and freedom; that is to say, its last word is the ἐποχή (withdrawal) in matters of metaphysics. Enclosed within the magic circle of our intuitions, our concepts, our *a priori* Ideas, we perceive, we judge, we know, but we know phenomena merely, i. e., relations existing between an object absolutely unknown in itself and a thinking subject, which we know only by its phenomena, and whose essence is shrouded in eternal

---

[1] The critique of monotheism, polytheism, and pantheism, is the same as that of theism. Theism erroneously subsumes an Idea of reason under a category, being; the error of monotheism, polytheism, and pantheism consists in applying to the same Idea the categories of quantity: unity, plurality, and totality.

mystery. What we call the world is not the world in itself; it is the world remodelled and transformed by sensibility and thought; it is the result of the combined functions of our intellectual faculties and a something, we know not what, which arouses them; it is the relation of two unknowns, the hypothesis of an hypothesis, the "dream of a dream."

II. CRITIQUE OF PRACTICAL REASON

Although the *Critique of Pure Reason* reduces us to a scepticism which is all the more absolute because it is reasoned, proved, scientifically established, and legitimized, it would be a grave mistake to consider the sage of Königsberg as a sceptic in the traditional sense, and to impute to him a weakness for the materialism of his age. Scepticism is the upshot of the *Critique of Pure Reason;* it is not, however, the ultimatum of Kantianism. To assert the contrary is completely to misunderstand the spirit of the philosophy of Kant and the final purpose of his critique. This is by no means hostile to the moral faith and its transcendent object, but wholly in its favor. It is, undoubtedly, not Kant's intention to "humiliate" reason, as Tertullian and Pascal had desired to do, but to assign to it its proper place among all our faculties, its true rôle in the complicated play of our spiritual life. Now, this place is, according to Kant, a subordinate one; this function is *regulative* and modifying, not *constitutive* and creative. *The* WILL, *and not reason, forms the basis of our faculties and of things :* that is the leading thought of Kantian philosophy. While reason becomes entangled in inevitable antinomies and involves us in doubts, the will is the ally of faith, the source, and, therefore, the natural guardian of our moral and religious beliefs. Observe that Kant in no wise denies the existence of the thing-in-itself, of the soul, and of God, but only the possibility of proving the reality of these Ideas, by means of reasoning. True, he combats spiritualistic dogmatism, but the same blow that brings it down overthrows materialism; and though he attacks theism, he likewise demolishes the dogmatic pretensions of the atheists. What he combats to the utmost and pitilessly destroys is the dogmatism of *theoretical* reason, under whatever form it may present itself, whether as theism or atheism, spiritualism or materialism; is its assumption of authority in the system of our faculties; is the prejudice which attributes metaphysical capacity to the understanding, *isolated from the will and depending on its own resources.* By way of retaliation — and here he reveals the depth of his philosophic faith — he concedes a certain metaphysical capacity to *practical reason,* i. e., to *will.*

Like the understanding, the will has its own character, its original forms, its particular legislation, a legislation which Kant calls "practical reason." In this new domain, the problems raised by the *Critique of Pure Reason* change in aspect; doubts are dissipated, and uncertainties give way to practical certainty. The moral law differs essentially from physical law, as conceived by theoretical reason. Physical law is irresistible and inexorable; the moral law does not compel, but bind; *hence it implies freedom.* Though freedom cannot be proved theoretically, it is not in the least doubtful to the will: it is a *postulate* of practical reason, an immediate fact of the moral consciousness.

Here arises one of the great difficulties with which philosophy is confronted: How can we reconcile the postulate of practical reason with the axiom of pure reason that every occurrence in the phenomenal order is a necessary effect, that the phenomenal world is governed by an absolute determinism? Kant, whose belief in free-will is no less ardent than his love of truth, cannot admit an absolute incompatibility between natural necessity and moral liberty. The conflict of reason and conscience, regarding freedom, can only be a seeming one; it must be possible to resolve the antinomy without violating the rights of the intelligence or those of the will.

The solution would, undoubtedly, be impossible, if the *Critique of Pure Reason* absolutely denied liberty, but the fact is, it excludes freedom from the phenomenal sphere only, and not from the intelligible and transcendent world, which exists behind the phenomenon, though it is unknowable. Theoretical reason declares: Freedom, though impossible in the phenomenal world, is possible in the absolute order; it is conceived as a noumenon; it is intelligible; and practical reason adds: it is certain. Hence, there is no real contradiction between the faculty of knowledge and of will. Our acts are determined, in so far as they occur in time and in space, indetermined and free, in so far as the source whence they spring, our *intelligible character*, is independent of these two forms of sensibility.

This would not be a solution if time and space were objective realities, as dogmatic philosophy conceives them. *From that point of view*, Spinoza is right in denying freedom. However, as soon as we agree with criticism, that space and, above all, time are modes of seeing things, and do not affect the things themselves, determinism is reduced to a mere theory or general conception of things, a theory or conception which reason cannot repudiate without abdicating, but which by no means expresses their real essence.

The Kantian solution of the problem of freedom at first sight provokes a very serious objection. If the soul, as intelligible character, does not exist *in time*, if it is not a phenomenon, we can no longer subsume it under the category of causality, since the categories apply only to phenomena and not to "noumena." Hence it ceases to be a cause and a free cause. Nor can we apply to it the category of unity. Hence it ceases to be an individual apart from other individuals: it is identified with the universal, the eternal, and the infinite. Fichte, therefore, consistently deduces his doctrine of the absolute ego from Kantian premises. Our philosopher, however, does not seem to have the slightest suspicion that this is the logical conclusion of his theory. Nay, he postulates, always in the name of practical reason, individual immortality as a necessary condition of the solution of the moral problem, and the existence of a God apart from the intelligible ego, as the highest guaranty of the moral order and the ultimate triumph of the good. It is true, Kant's theology is merely an appendix to his ethics, and is not to be taken very seriously. It is no longer, as in the Middle Ages, the queen of the sciences, but the humble servant of independent ethics. This personal God, afterwards postulated by the *Critique of Practical Reason*, forcibly reminds us of the celebrated epigram of a contemporary of our philosopher: "If there were no God, we should have to invent one."

The real God of Kant is Freedom in the service of the ideal, or the good Will (*der gute Wille*).

His conviction in this matter is most clearly expressed by the doctrine of the *primacy of practical reason*, i. e., of the *will*. Theoretical reason and practical reason, though not directly contradicting each other, are slightly at variance as to the most important questions of ethics and religion, the former tending to conceive liberty, God, and the absolute as ideals having no demonstrable objective existence, the latter affirming the reality of the autonomous soul, responsibility, immortality, and the Supreme Being. The consequences of this dualism would be disastrous if theoretical reason and practical reason were of equal rank; and they would be still more disastrous, were the latter subordinated to the former. But the authority of practical reason is superior to that of theoretical reason, and in real life the former predominates. Hence we should, in any case, act *as if it were proved* that we are free, that the soul is immortal, that there is a supreme judge and rewarder.

In certain respects, the dualism of understanding and will is a happy circumstance. If the realities of religion, God, freedom, and the immortality of the soul, were self-evident truths, or capable of theoretical proof, we should do the good for the sake of future reward, our will would cease to be autonomous, our acts would no longer be strictly moral; for every other motive except the *categorical imperative* of conscience and the respect which it inspires, be it friendship or even the love of God, renders the will *heteronomous*, and deprives its acts of their ethical character. Moreover, religion is true only when completely identical with morality. Religion within the bounds of reason consists in morality, nothing more nor less. The essence of Christianity is eternal morality; the goal of the church is the triumph of right in humanity. When the church aims at a different goal, it loses its *raison d'être*.[1]

III.   Critique of Judgment

While the *Critique of Practical Reason*, with its categorical imperative, its primacy of the conscience, and its absolute independence of morality, satisfies Kant's moral feeling and his great love of liberty, which had been shaken by the conclusions of the *Critique of Pure Reason*, the philosophical instinct re-asserts itself in his æsthetics and teleology, which form the subject-matter of his *Critique of Judgment*. We have seen how, in the *Critique of Pure Reason*, he universally combines syn-thesis with analysis, how he solders together the heterogeneous parts of the cognitive apparatus: between the functions of sensibility and those of reason he discovers the intermediate function of the idea of time, which is half intuition, half cate-gory; between *a priori* concepts which are diametrically op-posed, he inserts intermediary categories. The same synthetic impulse leads him, in his *Critique of Judgment*, to bridge over the chasm which separates theoretical reason and the conscience.

The æsthetical and teleological sense is an intermediate faculty, a connecting link between the understanding and the will. Truth is the object of the understanding, nature and natural necessity its subject-matter. The will strives for the good; it deals with freedom. The æsthetical and teleological sense (or judgment in the narrow sense of the term) is con-cerned with what lies between the true and the good, between nature and liberty: we mean the beautiful and the purposive. Kant calls it judgment because of the analogy between its

---

[1] The *independent morality* of the socialist P. J. Proudhon (1809–1865) is grounded on these principles. It is based on the following proposition: "Morality must cease to lean on theology for support, it must free itself from all so-called revealed dogmas, and base itself solely on conscience and the innate principle of justice, without requiring the support of the belief in God and the immortality of the soul."

manifestations and what is called judgment in logic; like the judgment, the sense of the beautiful and the teleological establishes a relation between two things which as such have nothing in common: between what ought to be and what is, between freedom and natural necessity.

1. *Æsthetics.* — The æsthetical sense differs both from the understanding and the will. It is neither theoretical nor practical in character; it is a phenomenon *sui generis.* But it has this in common with reason and will, that it rests on an essentially subjective basis. Just as reason constitutes the true, and will the good, so the æsthetical sense makes the beautiful. Beauty does not inhere in objects; it does not exist apart from the æsthetical sense; it is the *product* of this sense, as time and space are the products of the theoretical sense. That is beautiful which pleases (quality), which pleases all (quantity), which pleases without interest and without a concept (relation), and pleases necessarily (modality).

What characterizes the beautiful and distinguishes it from the sublime, is the feeling of peace, tranquillity, or harmony which it arouses in us, in consequence of the perfect agreement between the understanding and the imagination. The sublime, on the other hand, disturbs us, agitates us, transports us. Beauty dwells in the form; the sublime, in the disproportion between the form and the content. The beautiful calms and pacifies us; the sublime brings disorder into our faculties; it produces discord between the reason, which conceives the infinite, and the imagination, which has its fixed limits. The emotion caused in us by the starry heavens, the storm, and the raging sea springs from the conflict aroused by these different phenomena between our reason, which can *measure* the forces of nature and the heavenly distances without being overwhelmed by the enormous figures, and our imagination, which cannot follow reason into the depths of infinity. Man has a feeling of grandeur, because he himself is grand through reason. The animal remains passive in the presence of the grand spectacles of nature, because its intelligence does not rise beyond the level of its imagination. Hence we aptly say, the sublime elevates the soul (*das Erhabene ist erhebend*). In the feeling of the sublime, man reveals himself as a being infinite in reason, finite in imagination. Both infinite and finite: how is that possible? Kant cannot fathom this mystery without surpassing the limits which he has prescribed to knowledge.

2. *Teleology.* — There are two kinds of purposiveness. The one arouses in us, immediately and without the aid of any concept, a feeling of pleasure, satisfaction, and inner harmony: this is subjective finality, which constitutes the beautiful. The other also arouses pleasure, but mediately, in consequence of an experience or an intermediate process of reasoning: this is objective finality, which constitutes the suitable (*das Zweckmässige*). Thus, a flower may be both the object of an æsthetical judgment in the artist, and of a teleological judgment in the naturalist, who has tested its value as a remedy. Only, the judgment which stamps it as beautiful is immediate and spontaneous, while that of the naturalist depends on previous experience.

The *Critique of Pure Reason* regards every phenomenon as a necessary effect, and therefore excludes purposiveness from the phenomenal world. Physics merely enumerates an infinite series of causes and effects. Teleology introduces between the cause and the effect, considered as the end or goal, the means, the instrumental cause. Theoretically, teleology is valueless. However, we cannot avoid it so long as we apply our teleological sense to the study of nature. Unless we abandon one of our faculties, which is as real and inevitable as reason and will, we cannot help recognizing purposiveness in the structure of the eye, the ear, and the organism in general. Though mechanism fully explains the inorganic world, the teleological view forces itself upon us when we come to consider anatomy, physiology, and biology.

The antinomy of mechanism, affirmed by the theoretical reason, and teleology, claimed by the teleological sense, is no more insoluble than that of necessity and freedom. Teleology is nothing but a theory concerning phenomena. It no more expresses the essence of things than mechanism. This essence is as unknowable for the *Critique of Judgment* as for the *Critique of Pure Reason.* Things-in-themselves are not in time; they have no succession, no duration. According to mechanism, the cause and its effect, according to teleology, the free cause, the means, and the goal at which it aims, follow each other, i. e., they are separated in time. But time is merely an *a priori* form of intuition, a mode of conceiving things; *as such* and apart from my thought or my theory, the cause and the effect of the mechanist, the creative agent, the means, and the goal of the teleologist, are in each other, inseparable, simultaneous. Imagine an understanding which is not bound to the *a priori* forms of space and time like ours, a free and absolute intellectual intuition: such an understanding would perceive the cause, the means, and the end at one glance; it would identify the end and the principle; the end would not follow the efficient cause, but would be immanent in it and identical with it. *Immanent teleology*, which identifies the ends of nature with the acting causes, is the natural solution of the antinomy of mechanism and purposiveness.

We see that the subjectivity of time and space is the most original and, on the whole, the most fruitful of Kant's teach-ings. There is no question so subtle, no problem so obscure, as not to be illuminated by it. Space and time are the eyes of the mind, the organs which reveal to it its inexhaustible content. These organs are at the same time the boundaries of its knowledge. But in spite of this insurmountable barrier, it feels free, immortal, and divine; and it declares its independence in the field of action. It is the mind which prescribes its laws to the phenomenal world; it is the mind from which the moral law proceeds; it is the mind and its judgment which make the beautiful beautiful. In short, the three *Critiques* culminate in absolute spiritualism. Kant compared his work to that of Copernicus: just as the author of the *Celestial Revolutions* puts the sun in the place of the earth in our planetary system, so the author of the *Critique* places the mind in the centre of the phenomenal world and makes the latter dependent upon it. Kant's philosophy is, undoubtedly, the most remarkable and most fruitful product of modern thought. With a single exception, perhaps,[1] the greatest systems which our century has produced are continuations of Kantianism. Even those — and their number has grown during the last thirty years — who have again taken up the Anglo-French philosophy of the eighteenth century, revere the illustrious name of Immanuel Kant.

[1] We mean the system of Comte, which is closely related to the French philosophy of the eighteenth century. Comte himself says, in a letter to Gustave d'Eichthal, dated December 10th, 1824: "I have always considered Kant not only as a very powerful thinker, but also as the metaphysician who most closely approximates the positive philosophy."

THIRD PERIOD

METAPHYSICAL RECONSTRUCTION

§ 63. Kant and German Idealism

The dogmatic Leibniz-Wolffian school,[1] the sceptic G. E. SCHULZE,[2] the eclectic HERDER,[3] JACOBI[4] and HAMANN,[5] the exponents of religious faith, accept the challenge which Kant had hurled at all traditions. Some "independents" (Salomon MAIMON,[6] BARDILI,[7] etc.) take exception to his teachings or protest against them, although they, too, feel his influence. But the Kantian philosophy was eagerly welcomed, though not wholly understood, by numerous disciples, some of them (BOUTERWEK,[8] KRUG,[9] FRIES,[10] etc.) being original thinkers.

[1] Eberhard (1738–1809), professor at Halle, was its chief representative.

[2] 1761–1833. Author of *Ænesidemus*, 1792. [If the categories cannot be applied to things-in-themselves, how can we know whether these exist or do not exist? "We can have no absolutely certain and universally valid knowledge, in philosophy, either of the existence or non-existence of things-in-themselves and their properties, or of the limits of human knowledge." Kant's critique logically culminates in scepticism. — TR.]

[3] 1744–1803. The theologian Herder, one of the stars of German literature, teaches a kind of Christianized Spinozism, in which he anticipates the philosophy of Schelling and Schleiermacher. To the *Critique* of Kant he opposes his *Meta-kritik, etc.*, Leipsic, 1799. He also wrote: *Ideen zur Philosophie der Geschichte der Menschheit*, Riga, 1784–1791.

[4] 1743–1819. Complete works, 6 vols., Leipsic, 1812–1825.

[5] 1730–1788

[6] 1754–1800. Maimon rejects the Kantian notion of the *thing-in-itself*, and approaches Fichte.

[7] 1761–1808. Bardili's *rational realism* anticipates Hegel's logic.

[8] 1766–1828. Professor at Göttingen, known especially by his *Aesthetik*, Leipsic, 1806.

[9] 1770–1842. Kant's successor at Königsberg, 1805, then (1809), professor at Leipsic. *Entwurf eines neuen Organon der Philosophie*, Meissen, 1801; *Fundamentalphilosophie*, 2d ed., 1819; *Das System der theoretischen Philosophie*, 3 vols., 2d ed., Königsberg, 1819–1823; *System der practischen Philosophie*, 3 vols., *id.*, 1817–1819; *Handbuch der Philosophie*, 2 vols., Leipsic, 1820–1821; *Das allgemeine Handbuch der philosophischen Wissenschaften*, 2d ed., 5 vols., Leipsic, 1832–1838. — Krug, who holds that an original *a priori* synthesis, not further to be explained, takes place within us between *being* and *knowledge*, calls his system: *transcendental synthetism*.

[10] 1773–1843. Professor at Heidelberg and Jena. Fries refers criticism to the domain of psychology, and bases it on inner observation. His philosophy is a

Its chief apostles were: SCHILLER,[1] the national poet of Germany, REINHOLD,[2] and FICHTE. The University of Jena became the brilliant centre of the new movement, the crucible, as it were, in which the new views were soon transformed.

The original and genuine criticism occupied a position between the sensationalism of Locke, Hume, and Condillac, and the intellectualism of Leibniz. Sensationalism had declared: All ideas and consequently all truths, to whatever order they may belong, are derived from the senses (and reflection); reason does not create them, it receives them. Intellectualism, on the other hand, had asserted: All our ideas and consequently all truths whatsoever are the product of reason. So-called outer perception is merely an elementary speculation; the thinking subject is wholly active, and even in cases where it imagines that it receives, it creates. Criticism agrees with sensationalism in holding that our ideas, without exception, are *given* by sensation; but, it adds, their *matter* or *material* alone is given, their *form* is the product of reason: in this respect intellectualism has the right on its side. In other words, it distinguishes, in every idea, a *material* element, which is furnished *a posteriori* by the senses, and a *formal* element, furnished *a priori* by thought. Every science, therefore, or philosophy, consists of two parts: a *pure*, rational, or speculative part, and an empirical part. Hence, criticism recognizes the partial truth of two systems and two methods; and conse-

---

connecting link between Kantianism and the Scotch school. We mention the following writings: *System der Philosophie als evidenter Wissenschaft*, Leipsic, 1804; *Wissen, Glaube und Ahndung*, Jena, 1805, 3d ed., 1837 [his best-known work: *Neue Kritik der Vernunft*, 3 vols., Heidelberg, 1807, 2d ed., 1828–1831]; and many highly prized text-books. He had numerous disciples; among them: the philosopher Apelt, the naturalist Schleiden, and the theologian De Wette.

[1] (1759–1805.) *Briefe über aesthetische Erziehung*, 1793–1795 [*Ueber Anmuth und Würde*, 1793; *Ueber naive und sentimentale Dichtung*, 1795–1796, Engl. tr. in Bohn's Library].

[2] 1758–1823. *Versuch einer neuen Theorie des menschlichen Vorstellungsvermögens*, Jena, 1789 [*Das Fundament des philosophischen Wissens*, 1791]. Reinhold's so-called *elementary* theory derives the *a priori* and *a posteriori* elements of knowledge from a common principle: the faculty of representation (*Vorstellungsvermögen*). It anticipates the subjective idealism of Fichte, which calls this common principle the *ego*.

quently repudiates the pretentious claim of either side to possess absolute truth and to employ the only possible method. It is both idealistic and realistic, and yet, strictly speaking, neither one nor the other.

But this state of equilibrium did not last long. Reinhold soon disturbed it with his *elementary theory*,[1] and Kant lived to see the triumph of absolute intellectualism, which, by way of reaction, led to the restoration of pure sensationalism. He protested, as loudly as he could, against this condition of things; yet it must be acknowledged that his *Critique of Pure Reason*, as well as his other two *Critiques*, contained the germs of the idealistic theories of the nineteenth century. Under the influence of the Spinozistic system which Lessing and Herder had recently introduced into Germany, these germs soon sprouted.

Kant had intimated that the mysterious unknown concealed behind the phenomena of sense might possibly be identical with the unknown in ourselves. This simple thought, which, however, he failed to carry out, contained the philosophy of Fichte.

But even if he had never advanced the hypothesis of the identity of the ego and the non-ego, his criticism would still bear a very pronounced idealistic stamp. Although it establishes an independent order of things apart from reason, a transcendent object, which impresses our senses and furnishes the material for our ideas, it assigns to pure reason the highest rôle imaginable. Reason, the thinking subject, *creates* space and time; reason, with the materials supplied by the senses, makes, constructs, or constitutes the phenomenon. The phenomenon is its work, if not its creation. Reason applies to phenomena the categories of relation and connects them by the tie of causality; through the legislative power of reason, phenomena become effects and causes; and if we mean by *nature*, not the totality of the things themselves, but only the sum of sensible and inner phenomena considered in their regular con

[1] See p. 386, note 2.

nections, then reason *makes or produces nature,* for reason prescribes to nature its laws. From reason, finally, are derived the
Ideas of the world, God, and the absolute.

If reason makes time and space, if reason determines and
regulates the phenomenon, if reason constitutes nature and
the universal order, what becomes of that which, according to
empiricism, is *given* to reason? The raw material of the phenomenon, or, what amounts to the same, of intuition and
thought, the unknown quantity which occasions the difference
between sound, light, smell, taste, temperature, pleasure, and
pain, "something, I-know-not-what," which brings it about
that a person born blind, though he may be an excellent
mathematician and perfectly able to understand the laws of
optics, cannot form a correct notion of light, — that is all that
is given to us, everything else being our own creation. Given
by whom? Given by what? By something, I-know-not-what,
which is called *the thing-in-itself,* a transcendent object, which,
consequently, cannot be *known,* a mysterious agent, which calls
forth sensations, and co-operates in the formation of ideas, but
in regard to which I have no right to affirm or to deny anything.

But how, then, can you affirm that it is an *agent,* that it
provokes sensations?[1] The transcendent object of intuition
(the thing-in-itself) is neither in space nor in time. Space and
time contain phenomena only, i. e., that which appears; and
the thing-in-itself does not appear. We cannot apply to it any
of the forms of the understanding; we cannot conceive it, as
Kant explicitly states,[2] either as magnitude, *reality*, or substance. Hence we cannot conceive it as the *cause* of our impressions, although Kant flatly contradicts himself and regards
it as such.[3] But if the thing-in-itself cannot be conceived either
as a quantity, or as a cause, or as a *reality*, it cannot be con-

---

[1] This contradiction was especially pointed out by J. Sigismund Beck (1761–
1840), who did not, however, succeed in eliminating it from Kantianism. [Beck
(*Einzig möglicher Standpunkt aus welchem die kritische Philosophie beurtheilt
werden muss*, Riga, 1796) rejects the thing-in-itself, and interprets the *Critique*
in the idealistic sense. — Tr.]

[2] *Kritik der reinen Vernunft*, p. 234.   [3] *Id.*

sidered as *anything;* it is nothing, or rather it exists only in the thinking subject; like space, time, and the categories, it is *identical* with the subject which conceives it.[1] The *matter* of our ideas, the transcendent substratum of the phenomena of sense, is the same as the substratum of the inner phenomena, the soul, or ego, or reason giving to itself not only the *form* but also the *matter* of its ideas. Reason not merely assists in the production of the phenomenon, it is the creator — the sole creator — of the phenomenal world. Hence it is, in the last analysis, an inconsistency of the Kantian philosophy to concede the existence of a thing-in-itself outside of and *by the side* of reason, so to speak. The *true* consequence of the *Critique of Pure Reason* is the monism of the ego, or absolute idealism.

But though the *Critique of Pure Reason* takes us to the threshold of panlogism, with its system and method, does not the result of the *Critique of Practical Reason,* the dualism of the "two reasons," absolutely hinder us from crossing it? The speculative Kantians, with Fichte at their head, do not regard this teaching as an obstacle to their interpretation of criticism, but consider it as an additional argument in its favor.

To begin with, by subordinating the theoretical reason to the practical reason, and affirming the primacy of the moral consciousness, Kant not only proclaims the dualism of the "two reasons," but also the monism of the practical reason, of which theoretical reason and the teleological judgment are mere modes or dependencies. He could not have affirmed this primacy, had he discovered absolute contradictions or insoluble antinomies between practical reason and theoretical reason. But such is not the case. There is a connecting link between theoretical reason and practical reason, and this connecting link is the *thing-in-itself,* the noumenon, the intelligible order, supposed by theoretical reason, postulated and openly affirmed by the conscience.

The "two reasons" would contradict each other, if one denied what the other affirms: the invisible, the ideal, the abso-

---

[1] Hence the name, *philosophy of identity.*

lute. In reality, the theoretical reason does not reject the absolute; it simply recognizes its inability to know it and to demonstrate its existence. The same may be said of freedom, which is synonymous with the absolute. What the *Critique of Pure Reason* does deny is liberty in the phenomenal world. It recognizes *in nature* nothing but the law of causality, mechanism, the determinism of facts, but it conceives liberty as a prerogative of the *thing-in-itself*, while maintaining the impossibility of a theoretical demonstration. The thing-in-itself *may* be considered as free. Now, practical reason categorically affirms the liberty of the acting subject, the freedom of the ego. Hence, the *Critique of Practical Reason*, instead of contradicting the idealistic conclusions, confirms them: the ego itself is the thing-in-itself (the free thing); the *object* which seems to determine us from without, is merely the *subject* acting within ourselves; object and subject, being and thought, nature and mind, are identical. If the *I* were determined by an object-*in-itself*, the "two reasons" would absolutely contradict each other; the ego would henceforth be a slave in theory and in practice, and moral freedom would be an inexplicable illusion. But the thing-in-itself, the thing which determines us "from without," being in reality the soul-*in-itself*, the self-determining subject; the ego, though determined, is free and autonomous, since it determines itself in the form of an external object.

Instead of making against idealistic monism, Kant's ethics culminates in it. True, it postulates the immortality of the soul and the existence of a personal God apart from the ego. But this double affirmation is a mere accident in the system: essential to it is the affirmation of the absolute freedom of the ego, the doctrine of the practical absolute of the ego. Now, the ego which Kant holds to be absolutely free is not the empirical ego, the phenomenal self, the self which exists in time, but the noumenal ego, i. e., the ego raised above space and time. To speak of the immortality of an ego that does not exist in time, for which, therefore, there is no *before* or *after*, is an inconsistency similar to the doctrine that the thing-in-itself is distinct from the personal subject, an inconsistency which has no organic connection with the essence of the system. The same holds for the theistic teaching. God is undoubtedly distinct from the empirical and phenomenal ego, but he cannot be anything but the absolute ego or the intelligible ego; otherwise there would be two *absolutes*.

The *Critique of Judgment* opened up a still wider field than the other two *Critiques* to the most illustrious disciples of Kant. They discovered in it not only a certain general tendency towards pantheism, foreign to the other writings of the master, but also theories which could not fail to culminate in pantheism. We mean his theory of the sublime, his *immanent teleology*, and especially his hypothesis of an intellect capable of an immediate and comprehensive intuition of things. The first makes a God-man of man; the second substitutes for the notion of creation that of evolution; the third makes a serious, though indirect, concession to dogmatic rationalism. True, Kant does not concede *intellectual intuition* to the human intellect, but he does not deny it to the intellect in general, and Schelling had only to generalize the Kantian hypothesis to convert the intellectual intuition into a philosophical method.

Such is the relation between Kantianism and the systems of Fichte, Schelling, and Hegel. Though these three philosophies, or, rather, these three phases of one and the same teaching, all proceed from criticism, they really make against it in so far as they occupy themselves particularly with what Kant had declared "forbidden fruit," i. e., the absolute. Their common aim is to re-establish the old metaphysics, but to re-establish it upon the basis of criticism. In almost the same way the monarchies which emerged from the ruins of the Revolution restored the past upon the basis of the principles of 1789. Kant and Fichte, in his first phase, are the philosophers of the Revolution; Schelling and Hegel are the philosophers of the Restoration.

§ 64. Fichte[1]

English sensationalism and the philosophy of relativity were founded by a student of medicine and a layman. German idealism and the philosophy of the absolute come from theology. JOHANN GOTTLIEB FICHTE (1765–1814), its founder, like Schelling and Hegel, first studied for the ministry. His *Criticism of All Revelation* (1792) won for him a professorship in Jena (1793). In 1794 he published his chief work: *Groundwork of All Scientific Knowledge*, which was afterwards revised and republished under different titles; and in 1796 his *Foundations of Natural Rights*. Accused of atheism, he resigned his chair (1799), and for ten years he and his young family suffered the trials attendant upon a more or less nomadic life. He died as a professor of the University of Berlin, founded in 1809. Besides the works which established his fame, we mention the following: *The Vocation of Man* (1800); *The Nature of the Scholar* (1805); *The Doctrine of Religion* (1806); *Speeches to the German Nation* (1808); etc. The German uprising against Napoleon was largely due to his influence.

Though his thought, like that of so many contemporary Germans of the Republic and the Empire, showed two distinct phases: one, rationalistic, humanitarian, and in sympathy with the Revolution; the other, mystical, pantheistic, and patriotic; the central notion of his system remained the same. This conception, or, let us rather say, this truth, the most exalted and at the same time the most paradoxical ever formulated by philosophy, is the *monism of the moral will*.[2]

Fichte is to Kant what Euclid-Plato is to Socrates, and to

---

[1] *Fichte's Popular Works*, tr. by Smith, London, 1889; *The Science of Knowledge, The Science of Rights*, and *The Science of Ethics*, tr. by Kroeger, London, 1889, 1889, 1897; Adamson, *Fichte*, London, 1881; Everett, *Fichte's Science of Knowledge*, Chicago, 1884.

[2] Although we recognize the truth of the central thought of Fichte's philosophy, we cannot accept his theory of the *absolute ego*, which Schelling refuted, nor, particularly, his method of *a priori* construction, which rests on a confusion of the will and the understanding, common to most of the thinkers prior to Schopenhauer.

Spinoza what Euclid-Plato is to Parmenides. With Kant he affirms the moral ideal, and with Spinoza, the unity of the "two worlds." Hence his philosophy is a synthesis, unique in its kind for modern times, of what seemed forever irreconcilable: monism and liberty. Identity of the ethical principle and the metaphysical principle: that is the fundamental dogma of his system. The *real* reality is, according to Fichte, the Good, active Reason, pure Will, the moral Ego. What the common mind regards as real is nothing but a phenomenon, a manifestation, a faithful or imperfect translation, a portrait or a caricature. The ultimate and highest principle from which we come and towards which we strive is not *being* but *duty;* it is an ideal which *is* not, but which *ought* to be. Being as such has no value, and does not, strictly speaking, exist. The stability or immobility of what we call substance, substratum, or matter, is a mere appearance (Heraclitus and Plato). It is all movement, tendency, and *will*. The universe is the manifestation of pure Will, the symbol of the moral Idea, which is the real *thing-in-itself*, the real absolute. To philosophize is to convince one's self that *being is nothing*, that *duty is everything;* it is to recognize the inanity of the phenomenal world apart from its intelligible essence; it is to regard the objective world, not as the effect of causes foreign to our practical reason, but as the product of the ego, as the objectified ego. There is no science except the science of the ego or *consciousness*. Knowledge is neither in whole (Hume, Condillac) nor in part (Kant) the product of sensation; it is the exclusive work, the *creation*, of the ego. There is no philosophy but idealism, no method but the *a priori* method. Philosophy does not discover ready-made truths, or establish facts that already exist. To philosophize, or to know, is to *produce* such facts, to *create* such truths.

Speculative thought does not begin with a *fact*, with something received or suffered by the ego, but with a spontaneous *act* of its creative energy. Its theses result from a regular succession of intellectual acts, which follow the law of opposition and reconciliation, foreshadowed by Kant in his threefold division of the categories (affirmation, negation, and limitation). The original act of the understanding, and every intellectual act in general, is threefold: (1) The ego posits itself; this is the act by which the ego takes possession of itself, or, rather, the act by which it *creates itself* (for to take possession would presuppose an ego existing prior to the ego, or a *given* fact); (2) A non-ego is opposed to the ego, or the ego is negated; (3) The ego and the non-ego reciprocally limit each other.

As the essential elements of one and the same concrete reality, these three original acts (*thesis* of the ego, *antithesis* of the non-ego, and *synthesis* of the ego and non-ego) form but a single act. By affirming itself as a subject, the ego distinguishes itself from an object which is not the ego; in producing itself, it at the same time produces its opposite, its limitation: the objective world. The latter is not, as "common-sense" and empiricism claim, an obstacle which the ego *encounters;* it is a limitation which it *gives* to itself. The sensible world has the appearance of something existing outside of the perceiving and thinking subject. It is an illusion which Kant himself could not wholly destroy. The limitation of the ego, the objective world, exists, but it owes its existence to the activity of the subject. *Suppress the* Ego, *and you suppress the world.* Creation is reason limiting itself; it is the will or pure thought, limiting, determining, or making a person of itself.

However, Fichte is obliged to confess, the ego limits itself by an inner necessity, which it cannot escape through thought alone: for it cannot think without thinking an object; it cannot perceive without affirming the existence of something which is not itself. Fichte recognizes with Kant, that the *thing-in-itself* cannot actually be reduced to thought, but he nevertheless maintains, in principle, that the *thing-in-itself* is merely the thinking principle itself. The dualism of the thinking subject and the thought object is an inevitable illusion of theoretical reason, from which, considering the infirmity of thought, action can and must free us. Hence, practical activity is the real triumph of reason, the affirmation of its omnipotence. True, in reality, the will is no more successful than the understanding in completely conquering the resistance of matter; in the phenomenal world, in which thought holds us captive, we cannot entirely escape the determinism of facts, or fatalism. The absolute autonomy of reason is an ideal which the ego pursues, but never attains. But this very conflict between the empirical and ideal reality proves that we are destined for an immortal lot: it is the source of our progress, the moving principle in history.

Fichte thus confirms the "primacy of practical reason," proclaimed by Kant. Moreover, he endeavors to insert this essential doctrine, which had been mechanically added to the Kantian system, into the very body of his philosophy.

Freedom is the highest principle, the essence of things. It is even superior to truth, considered from the purely theoretical standpoint, or, rather, it is the highest Truth. For that very reason it is not an abstraction, but the supreme reality. But this reality, the source of all other realities, precisely because it is freedom, cannot be an empirical *datum*, an immediate, brutal, and fatal *fact*. If freedom were given, or made, or produced, as the facts of the physical order are produced, it would not be freedom. True freedom is the freedom which *creates itself*, or *realizes itself*. Self-realization means self-development in a series of stages, or entrance into the conditions of duration and time. Now time, like space, is an *a priori* intuition of theoretical reason, a form of the understanding; time is the intuitive faculty itself, or the understanding exercising its elementary and original function. And since it is, as we have just seen, the necessary instrument of freedom, we conclude that the understanding, the theoretical reason, the faculty which divides the ego into subject and object, is the auxiliary of practical reason, the organ of the will, the servant of freedom.

Again: Freedom realizes itself in time; time is its means, its indispensable auxiliary. But time is the intuitive faculty itself, the theoretical reason perceiving things *successively*. Theoretical reason, or the understanding, is therefore the means, the organ, which practical reason employs to realize itself. Instead of being, as Kant seemed to conceive it, a power foreign and therefore hostile to practical reason, theoretical reason thus naturally and necessarily becomes subject to the will; it humbly enters the service of the moral ideal. The dualism of the "two reasons" disappears; *the understanding simply becomes a phase in the development of* FREEDOM;[1] knowledge is a means, a secondary thing; action is the principle and final goal of being. The non-ego is, in the language of Aristotle, the matter which the form needs in order to realize itself as supreme energy; it is the limit which the ego sets itself in order to overcome it, and thus to realize its essence, freedom. Self-assertion or self-realization means struggle; struggle presupposes an obstacle; this obstacle is the phenomenal world, the world of sense and its temptations.

Liberty, we said, realizes itself in time and by means of thought, i. e., by distinguishing between a subject which perceives and thinks, and an object which is perceived and thought. But this object, which the magician Reason shows to the ego, the external world, the non-ego, is in turn composed of a multitude of egos, of personalities apart from mine. Hence, freedom does not realize itself in the separate individual (the empirical ego), but in human society. In order to become a reality, the ideal ego divides itself into a plurality of historical subjects, and realizes itself in the moral relations established between them, and these relations are the source of natural, penal, and political rights.

Considered apart from the individuals which realize it, the absolute or ideal ego is a mere abstraction. The real God is a living God, or the God-man. "I abhor all religious conceptions," says Fichte, "which personify God, and regard them as unworthy of a reasonable being." And why? Because a personal being, or a subject, does not exist without an object that limits it. True, this limitation is the work of the subject

---

[1] Read *will*, and you have, word for word, the teaching of Schopenhauer minus his pessimism.

itself; but whether limited by itself or by something else, the subject is a limited being, and God cannot be conceived as such. God is the moral order of the world, the freedom which gradually realizes itself in it: he is nothing but that.

Fichte's opposition to the idea of a personal God is the criticism of his own system, or, at least, of the subjectivistic form which it assumed under the influence of Kant, and of which it gradually divested itself under the influence of Spinoza. By denying the personality of God, he condemns both the notion of an absolute ego, as the creator of the non-ego, and the method of *a priori* construction.

Schelling, Fichte's most brilliant disciple, turns his attention to this contradiction.

§ 65. Schelling[1]

Friedrich Wilhelm Joseph SCHELLING, born 1775, at Leonberg, in Würtemberg, received the master's degree from the University of Tübingen, when seventeen years old, and continued his studies at Leipsic. In 1798 he was made professor of philosophy at Jena, where he became acquainted with Fichte and renewed his friendship with his fellow-countryman Hegel. In 1803 we find him at the University of Würzburg; then he becomes the General Secretary of the Munich Academy of Plastic Arts (1806–1820). After serving as a professor in the Universities of Erlangen, Munich, and Berlin, he died (1854) in the seventy-ninth year of his age. A precocious and fruitful[2] writer, but an inconsistent thinker, Schelling passed from Fichte to Spinoza, from Spinoza to Neo-Platonism, from Neo-Platonism to J. Böhme, with whom his friend and colleague Franz Baader[3] had made him acquainted. The following works[4] belong to his Spinozistic and Neo-Platonic phase, which he calls his "negative philosophy": *Philosophy of Nature*[5] (1797);

---

[1] See Watson, *Schelling's Transcendental Idealism*, Chicago, 1882.
[2] At least during his earlier stage.   [3] See § 71.
[4] We mention only the most important.
[5] In this work he cuts loose from Fichte.

The World-Soul (1798); *Transcendental Idealism*[1] (1800);
Bruno (1802); *The Method of Academic Study* (1803); *Philosophy and Religion* (1804). To his "positive" period, which is
characterized by the influence of Böhme and a more or less
pronounced tendency to orthodoxy, belong: *The Essence of
Human Freedom* (1809); *On the Divinity of Samothrace* (1816);
Philosophy of Mythology and Revelation, published by his son.

1. The non-ego, Fichte had said, is the unconscious product
of the ego, or, what amounts to the same thing, the product of
the unconscious ego. But, Schelling objects, the unconscious
ego is not really the ego; what is unconscious is not yet ego or
subject, but both subject and object, or, rather, neither one nor
the other. Since the ego does not exist without the non-ego, we
cannot say that it produces the non-ego, without adding, conversely: the non-ego produces the ego. There is no object without a subject, — as Berkeley had previously declared, — and
in this sense Fichte truly says that the subject makes the object; but neither can there be a subject without an object.
Hence the existence of the objective world is as much the condition *sine qua non* of the existence of the ego, as conversely.
Fichte, who implicitly recognized this in his profession of pantheistic faith, regards the distinction between the empirical
ego and the absolute ego as fundamental to his thought. But
what right has he to speak of an absolute ego, when it is certain
that the ego, or the subject, is *never* absolute, but limited, as
it necessarily is, by an object? Hence we must abandon the
attempt to make an absolute of the ego.

Is the non-ego absolute? Not at all, for it does not exist unconditionally; it is nothing without the thinking subject. Hence
we must either deny the absolute or seek it *beyond the ego and
the non-ego*, or beyond all opposition. If the absolute exists, —
and how can it be otherwise! — it can merely be the synthesis
of all contraries, it can only be *outside of and beyond* all conditions of existence,[2] since it is itself the highest and first condi-

---

[1] The most consistent and systematic of his writings.
[2] Cf. §§ 25 and 31.

tion, the source and end of all subjective as well as of all objective existence.

Consequently, we can neither say that the ego produces the non-ego (subjective idealism), nor that the non-ego produces the ego (sensationalism); *the ego and the non-ego, thought and being, are both derived from a higher principle which is neither one nor the other*, although it is the cause of both: a neutral principle, the indifference and identity of contraries. This brings us to Spinoza's point of view; though different terms are used, we find ourselves face to face with the infinite substance and the parallelism of things emanating from it: thought (the ego) and extension (the non-ego).

Philosophy is the science of the absolute in its double manifestation: nature and mind. It is philosophy of nature and transcendental philosophy, or philosophy of mind. By adding the science of nature to the science of mind, Schelling fills the great gap in Fichte's system. His method does not essentially differ from that of his predecessor. Schelling, it is true, recognizes that the universe is not, strictly speaking, the creation of the ego, and, consequently, has an existence relatively distinct from the thinking subject. To think is not to produce, but *to reproduce*. Nature is, according to him, what it is not for Fichte: a datum or a fact. He cannot, therefore, escape the necessity of partially recognizing experience and observation; he even goes so far as to call them the *source* of knowledge.

But, the reader will please observe, though Schelling denies that the ego makes the non-ego, he denies, with equal emphasis, that the non-ego makes the ego, that sense-perception constitutes thought (Locke, Hume, Condillac). Thought, knowledge, science, cannot be derived from the non-ego and outer or inner perception; they have their source and principle in that which also constitutes the source and principle of the non-ego, in the absolute. Experience is but the starting-point of speculation, the point of *departure* in the literal sense of the term: *a priori* speculation continues to be the philosophical method. Speculation operates with the facts of experience, but these facts cannot contradict *a priori* thought; they must, therefore, conform to its laws, because the world of facts (the real order) and the world of thoughts (the ideal order) have a common source, the absolute, and cannot contradict each other. Nature is *existing* reason, mind is *thinking* reason. Thought must accustom itself to separating the notion of reason from the idea of mind; it must conceive an *impersonal reason*, and no longer regard this formula as a contradiction in terms. We must conceive the substance of Spinoza as impersonal reason embracing the ego and the non-ego; we must look upon things as the images of thought, and thought as the twin brother of things. There is a thoroughgoing parallelism between nature and thought, and they have a common origin: *the one develops according to the same law as the other*.

Thought, as Fichte, inspired by Kant, had said, is invariably thesis, antithesis, and synthesis. Nature, the image of thought, is (1) matter or gravity (thesis: brutal affirmation of matter); (2) form or light (antithesis: negation of matter, principle of organization and individuation, ideal principle); (3) organized matter (synthesis of matter and form). The three stages of material evolution are not separated in nature; no more so than the three original acts of thought. The whole of nature is organized even in its smallest details (Leibniz), and the so-called inorganic world, the earth itself, and the heavenly bodies, are living organisms. If nature were not alive, it could not produce life. The so-called inorganic kingdom is the vegetable kingdom in germ; the animal kingdom is the vegetable kingdom raised to a higher power. The human brain is the climax of universal organization, the last stage of organic evolution.[1] Magnetism, electricity, irritability, and sensibility are manifestations of the same force, in different degrees (correlation and equivalence of forces). Nothing is dead, nothing is stationary in nature; everything is life, movement, becoming, perpetual oscillation between two extremes, *productivity*[2] and

---

[1] Giordano Bruno.   [2] The *Will* of Schopenhauer.

product, polarity (electricity, magnetism, and intellectual life), expansion and contraction, action and reaction, struggle between two contrary and (at the same time) correlative principles,[1] the synthesis of which is the soul of the world.[2]

The philosophy of mind or transcendental philosophy has for its subject-matter the evolution of psychical life, the genesis of the ego, and aims to demonstrate the parallelism of the physical and moral orders.

The stages in the evolution of mind are: sensation, outer and inner perception (by means of the *a priori* intuitions and the categories), and rational abstraction. Sensation, perception, and abstraction constitute the theoretical ego, the different degrees of the understanding. Through absolute abstraction, i. e., the absolute distinction which the intelligence draws between itself and what it produces, the understanding becomes will: the theoretical ego becomes the practical ego. Like magnetism and the principle of sensibility, intelligence and will are different degrees of the same thing.[3] They are merged in the notion of *productivity*, or creative activity. The intellect is creative without knowing it; its productivity is unconscious and necessary; will is conscious of itself; it produces with the consciousness of being the source of what it produces: hence the feeling of freedom accompanying its manifestations.

Just as life in nature is the result of two contrary forces, so the life of the mind springs from the reciprocal action of the intellect, which posits the non-ego, and of the will, which overcomes it. These are not new forces; they are the same forces which, after having been gravity and light, magnetism and electricity, irritability and sensibility, manifest themselves, in the sphere of mind, as intelligence and will. Their antagonism constitutes the life of the race: *history*.

History unfolds itself in three ages which run parallel with the three stages of organic evolution, corresponding to the three kingdoms. The primitive age is characterized by the predomi-

---

[1] The "strife" of Heraclitus.   [2] Plato and the Stoics.
[3] Spinoza and Fichte.

nance of the fatalistic element (thesis: matter, gravity, intelligence without will); the second, which was inaugurated by the Roman people and still continues, is the reaction of the active and voluntary element against the ancient *fatum;* the third, finally, which belongs to the future, will be the synthesis of these two principles. Mind and nature will gradually be blended into a harmonious and living unity. The idea will become more and more real; reality will become more and more ideal. In other words: the absolute, which is the identity of the ideal and the real, will manifest and realize itself more and more.

However, as history is developed in time, and as time has no limits, history necessarily consists in *infinite* progress, and the realized absolute remains an ideal which cannot be definitively and completely realized. Hence if the ego were merely theoretical and practical, it could never realize the absolute; for, reflection as well as action is necessarily subject to the law of the dualism of subject and object, of the ideal and the real. Thought, it is true, can and must rise beyond reflection and its dualism; through the *intellectual intuition* [1] we deny the dualism of the ideal and the real, we affirm that the ego and the non-ego spring from a higher unity in which all antitheses are blended; we rise, in a measure, beyond personal thought and ourselves; we identify ourselves with impersonal reason, which becomes objectified in the world and is personified in the ego. In a word, we partially return into the absolute whence we came.

But even this intuition cannot completely free itself from the law of opposition; consequently it is still a polarity, forming, on the one hand, a perceiving subject, on the other, an object perceived from without. The ego is on one side, God on the other; the dualism continues; the absolute is not a reality possessed or assimilated by the mind. The mind does not attain or realize the absolute, either as intelligence or action, but as the feeling of the beautiful in nature and in art. [2] Art, religion, and revelation are one and the same thing, superior even to philosophy.

[1] Plato, Plotinus, St. Augustine, and the Mystics. [2] Kant.

Philosophy *conceives* God; art *is* God. Knowledge is the ideal presence, art the real presence of the Deity.[1]

2. Schelling's "positive" philosophy, inaugurated in 1809 by the dissertation on human freedom, accentuates the mystical element contained in the foregoing sentences. Under the influence of Böhme, the philosopher becomes a theosophist; the pantheist, a monotheist. He insists on the *reality* of the divine idea, on the personality of God, on the cardinal importance of the Trinity. However, when we peer beneath the strange forms enveloping his romanticism, we find that there is less change in the essence of his thought than one would suppose: this essence is monism, a form of monism, however, which, under the influence of Böhme, is clearly defined as *voluntarism*.[2] The absolute, the absolute indifference or identity, of "negative" philosophy exists, but it now receives the name applied to it by the Saxon theosophist: *primitive will*. The foundation or first principle of the divine being, and of all being, is not thought or reason, but will striving for being and individual and personal existence, or the *desire-to-be*. *Before* being, every being, God included, desires to be. This desire or unconscious will precedes all intelligence and all conscious will. For God, the evolution by which he realizes himself, personifies himself, or *makes himself God*, is eternal, and the stages through which this evolution passes (the persons or hypostases of the Trinity) are merged into each other; but they are distinguished from each other in the human consciousness, appearing successively and forming stages in the religious development of humanity. The evil in the world has its source, not in God considered as a person, but in what precedes his personality, in that which,

---

[1] Neo-Platonism.

[2] The voluntaristic conception is, it is true, already found in the *Abhandlungen zur Erläuterung des Idealismus der Wissenschaftslehre*, published by Schelling in the *Philosophisches Journal* (1796 and 1797), as well as in numerous passages in Fichte, whose philosophy is entirely impregnated with it. But he clearly and consciously affirms the principle in his treatise on liberty. In the last analysis there is nothing but will, which is the original reality. Only to will could be ascribed such attributes as that of being unconditioned, of eternity, and of self-affirmation. (*Works*, first series, vol. VII, p. 350.)

in God, is not God himself, i. e., in the *desiderium essendi* (desire for existence) which we have just recognized as the first cause of all things, and which Schelling does not hesitate to call the divine egoism. In God, this principle is eternally merged in his love; in man, it becomes an independent principle and the source of moral evil. But however great the latter may be, it serves the purposes of the absolute, no less than the good.

We shall not here consider the *philosophy of mythology and revelation*, which we have set forth in another work,[1] and which interests the historian of religion rather than the historian of philosophy. Our main purpose was to outline the contents of the principal treatises written by Schelling from 1795 to 1809, and to elucidate: (1) his masterly critique of Fichte's *egoism;* (2) his conception of the absolute as will, the common ground of the object and subject (Kant), of the ego and non-ego (Fichte), of thought and extension (Spinoza); (3) his philosophy of nature, which, though abandoned by positive science, produced such naturalists as Burdach, Oken, Carus, Oersted, Steffens, G. H. Schubert, and, by carrying speculation into a field from which ideological investigations had banished it, prepared the way for the fusion of metaphysics and science, which we are now endeavoring to bring about; (4) his philosophy of history, a happy prelude to Hegel's philosophy of mind.

The philosophy of Schelling, the influence of which was partially counteracted and obscured by the Hegelian school,[2] really consists of two very distinct systems, which are connected by a common principle:[3] according to the first, which forms its starting-point, thought precedes being (idealism); according to the second, (potential) being is the antecedent

---

[1] *Examen critique de la philosophie religieuse de Schelling*, Strasburg, 1860.

[2] Nevertheless, this influence was considerable. Even omitting the disciples properly so called, we can detect it in most of the thinkers mentioned in § 71. Observe that the most celebrated among contemporaneous German philosophers, Eduard von Hartmann, is as much a disciple of Schelling as of Schopenhauer, and that the most original of our French metaphysicians, Charles Secrétan, is an avowed adherent of the "positive philosophy."

[3] We noticed the same dualism in Plotinus.

of thought (realism). Under the influence of the former, he speaks of intellectual intuition and conceives his *Transcendental Philosophy*, while the latter exalts experience and the philosophy of nature. The one leads to Hegel and the *a priori* construction of the universe and of history, the other, to Schopenhauer and contemporaneous empiricism.

§ 66. Hegel

Georg Wilhelm Friedrich HEGEL was born at Stuttgart, 1770, and died as a professor in the University of Berlin, 1831. Like his friend Schelling, he attended the theological seminary at Tübingen. Jena, where he renewed and then dissolved the friendship with his fellow-countryman, who was five years his junior, Nuremberg, where he had charge of the Gymnasium, Heidelberg, and the Prussian capital, mark the different stages in his academic career. We mention the following works: (1) *Phenomenology of Mind*[1] (1807); (2) *Science of Logic*,[2] in three volumes (1812–1816); (3) *Encyclopedia of the Philosophical Sciences*[3] (1817); (4) *Philosophy of Right*[4] (1821); also, *Philosophy of History*,[5] *Esthetics*,[6] *Philosophy of Religion*,[7] *History of Philosophy*,[8] published after his death.

According to Fichte, the *thing-in-itself* (the absolute) is the ego itself, which produces the phenomenal world by an unconscious and involuntary creation, and then overcomes it by a free and conscious effort. According to Schelling, the absolute is neither the ego nor the non-ego, but their common root, in

---

[1] Tr. by Baillie, London, 1910.   [2] Vol. II, tr. by Harris.

[3] Tr. by Wallace, *The Logic of Hegel*, Oxford, 1892.

[4] Tr. by Dyde, London, 1896.

[5] Tr. by Sibree, Bohn's Library, 1860.

[6] Tr. by Bosanquet (*Philosophy of Art*), London, 1886.

[7] Tr. by Speirs and Sanderson, 3 vols., London, 1895.

[8] Tr. by Haldane, 3 vols., London, 1892. Works on Hegel: Stirling, *The Secret of Hegel*, 2 vols., London, 1865; McTaggart, *Studies in the Hegelian Dialectic*, 1896, *Studies in Hegelian Cosmology*, 1901, *Commentary on Hegel's Logic*, 1910, Cambridge (Eng.); E. Caird, *Hegel*, Philadelphia; Hibben, *Hegel's Logic*, New York, 1902; Croce, *What is Living and What is Dead in the Philosophy of Hegel* (tr. by Ainslie), London, 1915.

which the opposition between a thinking subject and a thought object disappears in a perfect indifference; it is the neutral principle, anterior and superior to all contrasts, the identity of contraries. Fichte's absolute is one of the terms of the opposition, that of Schelling is the transcendent, mysterious, impenetrable source of the same. Fichte's conception errs in reducing the absolute to what is but one of its aspects: the absolute of Fichte is the ego limited by a theoretically inexplicable non-ego; it is a prisoner, it is not really the absolute. Schelling's absolute is a transcendent entity, which does not explain anything, since we do not know either how or why to deduce from it the oppositions constituting the real world. The absolute indifference, far from being the highest and most concrete reality, is, at bottom, nothing but an abstraction.

According to Hegel, the common source of the ego and of nature does not transcend reality; it is immanent in it. Mind and nature are not aspects of the absolute, or a kind of screen, behind which an indifferent and lifeless God lies concealed, but its successive modes. The absolute is not immovable, but active; it is not the principle of nature and of mind, but is itself successively nature and mind. This succession, this process, this perpetual generation of things, is the absolute itself. In Schelling, things *proceed from the absolute*, which, for that very reason, remains outside of them. In Hegel, the *absolute is the process itself;* it does not produce movement and life, it *is* movement and life. It does not exceed the things, but is wholly in them; nor does it, in any way, exceed the intellectual capacity of man. If we mean by God the *being transcending human reason*, then Hegel is the most atheistic of philosophers, since no one is more emphatic in affirming the immanency and perfect knowableness of the absolute. Spinoza himself, *the philosopher of immanency*, does not seem to go so far; for, although he concedes that the intellect has an adequate idea of God, he assumes that the Substance has *infinite attributes*.

While modifying the Schellingian idea of the absolute, Hegel at the same time subjects the extravagant imagination of his friend to a merciless intellectual discipline. In order to arrive at a knowledge of the principle and logical connection of things, we must, of course, think, but we must think logically and methodically. Only on that condition will the result tally with that of infinite thought in nature and history. The absolute, let us say, is movement, process, evolution. This movement has its law and its goal. Its law and its goal are not imposed upon the absolute from without; they are immanent in it, they are the absolute itself. Now the law which governs both human thought and unconscious nature is *reason;* the end at which things aim is, likewise, reason, but self-conscious reason. Hence the terms *absolute* and *reason* are synonymous. The absolute is reason, which becomes personified in man, after passing through the successive stages of inorganic and living nature.

But reason is not, as Kant conceives it, the human understanding, a faculty of the soul, a combination of principles, forms, or rules according to which we think things. It is the law according to which being is produced, constituted, or unfolded; or, rather, it is both a subjective faculty and an objective reality: it is *in me* as the essence and norm of my thought, and it is *in the things* as the essence and law of their evolution. It follows that its categories have a much greater significance than Kantianism supposed. They are not only modes of *thinking* things; they are the modes of *being* of the things themselves. They are not empty frames, which receive their contents from without; they are *substantial forms*, as the Middle Ages used to say; they give themselves their own content; they are creative acts of divine and human reason. They are both the forms which mould my thought and the stages of eternal creation.

Hence it is of essential importance to metaphysics that we make a more thorough study of the categories, their nature and, above all, their connection. Kant had already observed that the categories are not separate from and indifferent to each other, ranged alongside of each other in our intelligence like drawers in a piece of furniture, but intimately connected with each other. They are, in short, nothing but transformations of one and the same fundamental category, the idea of being. Hence it will not suffice to discuss them at random; we must consider them in their connection, surprise them, as it were, in the very act of their mutual production. Kant saw the importance of such an *a priori* deduction of the categories, and attempted it, but his deduction is, in reality, a merely empirical enumeration (incomplete at that) of pure concepts. We must return to Kant's notion, but we must substitute for his table of categories a real deduction, a true genealogical table.

This is the most exalted and withal the most arduous task of metaphysics. In order to succeed in it, we must eradicate our prejudices, all our sensible ideas, and trust to reason alone; we must let it unfold its own contents, and do nothing ourselves but follow it in its development, or record its oracles, as it were, at the very time of their production. To leave thought to itself, to abandon it to its spontaneous self-activity: that is the true philosophical method, the *immanent* or *dialectical* method.

The science which does all this is *logic*, i. e., in the sense of Hegel, the genealogy of pure concepts. But since, in the panlogistic hypothesis, the *logos*, the object of logic, is both the principle which thinks the things in us, and the objective cause which produces them, or the *thing-in-itself;* the genealogy of its concepts is at the same time the genealogy of the things, the explanation of the universe, or metaphysics. Hegel's speculative logic is both what the school calls logic and what it calls metaphysics or ontology. It is called *speculative*, in order to distinguish it from the former and to include the latter. It is metaphysical, for it speaks of mechanical, chemical, and organic processes, and likewise embraces ethics, since it treats of the good. In this it is consistent with its panlogistic premises: if reason not only *conceives*, but *produces* being, if it is the creator of things, if it is everything; the science of reason (λογική) must be the universal science, which includes all the particular sciences.

It is an inconsistency[1] in Hegel, as we have shown elsewhere,[2] to have his *Logic* followed by a *Philosophy of Nature* and a *Philosophy of Mind*. Logic treats of reason *in abstracto*, the philosophy of nature and of mind reveals it to us as it realizes itself in the universe and in history.

I. Logic, or Genealogy of Pure Concepts

1. *Quality, Quantity, Measure*[3]

The common root of the categories or pure concepts is the notion of *being*, the emptiest and at the same time the most comprehensive, the most abstract and the most real, the most elementary and the most exalted notion. It is the identical substance, and the material of all our notions, the fundamental theme which runs through them all. Indeed, quality is a mode of *being*, quantity, a mode of *being*, proportion, phenomenon, action, modes of *being*. All our concepts express modes of being, and hence are merely transformations of the idea of being.

But how shall we explain these transformations? How does *being*, which is everything, become *anything else*? In virtue of what principle or inner force is it modified? The *contradiction* which it contains is this principle or force. Being is the most universal notion, and for that very reason, also the poorest and emptiest. To be white, to be black, to be extended, to be good, is to be something: being without any determination is nonbeing. Hence, being pure and simple is equal to non-being. It is both itself and its opposite. If it were only itself, it would remain immovable and barren; if it were only nothing, it would be equal to zero, and, in this case, perfectly powerless and fruitless. Because it is *both* it *becomes* something, a different

---

[1] The philosophy of nature and the philosophy of mind are already implicitly contained, the former in the first and second, the latter in the third, part of the logic.

[2] *Introduction historique à la philosophie hégélienne*, Paris and Strasburg, 1866, p. 16.

[3] *Logic*, vol. I.; *Encyclopedia*, §§ 84 ff.

thing, everything. The contradiction contained in being is resolved in the notion of *becoming*, or development. Becoming is both being and non-being (that which will be). The two contraries which engender it, being and nothing, are contained and reconciled in it. A new contradiction results, which is resolved by a new synthesis, and so on, until we reach the absolute idea.

This, then, is the moving principle in the Hegelian logic: a contradiction is reconciled in a unity, reappears in a new form, only to disappear and reappear again, until it is resolved in the final unity. By repudiating the *principle of contradiction* of Aristotle and Leibniz, according to which a thing cannot both be and not be, it takes sides with the Sophists, without, however, falling into their scepticism. The contradiction does not, according to Hegel, exist in thought alone, but also in the things themselves; existence itself is contradictory. When, with the realistic and dualistic systems, we separate thought from its object and concede to each an independent existence, the antinomies of thought necessarily become a source of discouragement and scepticism. However, when we regard nature as the self-development of thought, and thought as nature becoming conscious of itself, when we recognize that the world, being thought objectified, contains nothing but thought; the contradiction in which the philosopher is involved ceases to be an obstacle to the understanding of things, and appears to him as their very essence reflecting itself in the antinomies of his thought.

Now that we know the moving principle and the unchanging form of the Hegelian dialectics, we need not follow out the unvarying and monotonous mechanism of its deductions. It will be sufficient to emphasize the most salient points of his metaphysics as set forth in the *Logic*.

The contradiction found in the idea of being is resolved in the notion of *becoming*. Being becomes, i. e., determines itself, limits itself, defines itself. But determinate or *finite* being continues *ad infinitum;* the finite is infinite; nothing compels thought to assign limits to it. Here we have a new contradiction, which is resolved in the notion of *individuality* (being-for-self). The individual is the unity of the finite and the infinite. To consider these two terms as excluding each other is to forget that the infinite, excluded by the finite, would be limited by the finite, or would be finite itself. If the infinite begins where the finite ends, and if the finite begins where the infinite ends, so that the infinite is *beyond* the finite, or the finite *on this side of* the infinite, it would not really be the infinite. The infinite is the essence of the finite, and the finite is the manifestation of the infinite, the infinite existing. Infinity determines itself, limits itself, sets boundaries to itself; in a word, it becomes the finite by the very fact that it gives itself existence. Existence is possible only under certain conditions, in certain modes, or within certain limits. Existence is self-limitation. Existence is finite being.[1] Finite being, the individual, the atom, is infinity existing in a certain manner, limited infinity: quality becomes *quantity*.

Quantity is *extensive* quantity (*number*) or *intensive* quantity (*degree*). Number, which is quantity broken up, so to speak, and degree, which is concentrated quantity, are reconciled in the notion of *measure* and *proportion*.

Measure is being becoming *essence*.

2. *Essence and Appearance. Substantiality and Causality. Reciprocity*[2]

Essence is being, unfolded or expanded so that its aspects reflect each other. Hence the categories which follow come in pairs: essence and appearance, force and expression, matter and form, substance and accident, cause and effect, ground and consequence, action and reaction. This reflection-into-itself, or, if we prefer, this reflex, is the *phenomenon*. Essence and phenomenon (appearance) are inseparable; indeed, the phenomenon is the very essence of essence; or, in other terms, it is as *essential* to essence to appear (φαίνεσθαι), to life to manifest

---

[1] Cf. § 50.   [2] *Logic*, vol. II; *Encycl.*, §§ 112 ff.

itself, to the principle to produce its consequences, as it is essential to the phenomenon to imply an essence. Phenomenon without essence is *mere show*, or *mere appearance*.

The essential is opposed by the *accidental* or contingent, which in turn becomes essential in the sense that the idea of the essential needs it in order to be produced. No category, we see, is independent of its neighbors. Although excluding each other, the categories need and mutually engender each other.

Essence expresses itself in a series of phenomena, and constitutes the *thing* or *object*, which is a totality of characteristics connected by one and the same essence. Considered in their relation to the object, these characteristics or phenomena are called *properties*. Just as there is no essence without a phenomenon, there is no thing apart from its properties. A thing is what its properties are; *nothing else*. Separate the thing from its essential properties, and nothing is left; its qualities *are* the thing itself.

As the generative principle of the phenomenon, the essence is the *force* or *agent* of which the phenomenon is the *act* or *expression*. Since a force is nothing but a totality of phenomena considered in their identity, and its expression merely the acting force itself, in so far as it *exerts itself*, it is a mere tautology to explain an act by an agent. As the matter, so its form; as the agent, so the act; as the character, so its manifestations; as the tree, so its fruits.

The dualism: essence and phenomenon, ground and consequence, force and expression, agent and act, matter and form, is resolved in the notion of *activity*, the synthesis and summary of the preceding notions. This logical category corresponds to what is called nature in metaphysics.[1] In short, nature is action, production, creation. All the treasures lying in her fruitful lap, she manifests, produces, and then takes back, only to reproduce and take back again, and reproduce eternally.

Activity is synonymous with *reality*. Nothing is active

---

[1] It must not be forgotten that Hegel identifies logic and metaphysics.

except what is real, and nothing is real except what is active.[1] Absolute rest does not exist.[2] Reality, compared with mere *possibility*, becomes *necessity*. What is real is *necessarily* active. Activity, reality, and necessity are synonymous. A being exists in so far as it acts, and acts in so far as it exists.

Essence or reality, considered as a necessary principle of activity, becomes *substance*. Substance is not a substratum in the proper sense of the word, but the sum of its *modes*. Hence we must abandon: in theology, the idea of a God existing *outside* of the universe; in psychology, the idea of a soul existing independently of the phenomena constituting the ego; in physics, the assumption of a kind of mysterious substratum of phenomena, of an unqualified and unqualifiable something, I-know-not-what, without extension, without color, without form, and yet supposed to be something real. A *substance* so constituted as to escape scientific observation would be a pure chimera. It was owing to an illusion peculiar to dualism that the poet could say: "No mere created mind e'er penetrates the heart of nature." Nature *has no heart* or inner part; the outside of matter is matter itself; it belongs to its essence to unfold itself, to have no inner life.

Substance is the totality of its modes. But it is not, on that account, as Spinozism conceives it, a purely mechanical aggregate, a mere sum; it is a *living* totality, united with its modes by an organic tie: it is the *cause* of its modes, and its modes are the *effects* of the substance. These notions are not indifferent to each other; they are correlative pairs. The cause is inseparable from its effect; the effect indissolubly connected with its efficient cause. The latter is immanent in the former, as the soul in the body. Modes are unfolded, revealed, expressed substance; the effect is the cause effected, explicated, manifested. There is nothing in the effect which is not also in the cause; nor is there anything in the cause that does not effect, assert,

---

[1] Since "reason alone is real," Hegel concludes that *what is real is rational* (p. 524).

[2] Πάντα χωρεῖ καὶ οὐδὲν μένει (Everything moves and nothing remains) (§ 8).

or realize itself. The idea of the effect cannot be separated from the idea of the cause; nay, every effect is, in turn, a cause, and every cause, the effect of a preceding cause. In any series of causes and effects, A, B, C, D . . ., the effect B is nothing but the cause A asserting itself as a cause, and becoming in B the cause of C, in C the cause of D, and so on.

The causal series is not, as formal logic maintains, an indefinite series, a *progressus in infinitum*, in which each effect produces a new effect without reacting upon the cause that produced it. The truth is, the effect B is not only the cause of C, but also the cause of A. In short, A would not be a *cause* unless it effected B; hence it is owing to B, or *because* of B, that A is a cause; hence B is not only the effect, but also the cause of the cause A. By a necessary reaction, every effect is the cause of its cause, and every cause the effect of its effect. Rain, for example, is a cause of moisture, and moisture, in turn, a cause of rain; or again: The character of a people depends on their form of government, but the form of their government also depends on the character of the people. Hence, since the effect is not fatally pre-determined by its cause, but reacts on it, the causal series in nature is not a straight line prolonged to infinity, but a curved line which returns to its starting-point, i. e., a *circle*. The notion of a rectilinear series is a vague and indefinite conception; the idea of the circle is exact and clearly defined, a finished whole.

This reaction of the effect upon the cause (*reciprocal action*) enhances the importance of the effect, and gives it the character of freedom, which it lacks in the system of Spinoza. According to this philosopher, the effect necessarily depends upon the pre-existing cause: in reality, however, it is an effect only *in a certain measure*, and is but *relatively* determined. There is neither in the beginning, nor in the middle, nor in the end of the causal series, a cause distinct from all the rest, and absolute with reference to the others. The absolute is not to be found in any particular part of the causal chain; it resides in the sum-total of the particular and relative causes. The latter are not so many slaves following the triumphal chariot of a first cause which excludes all other causality, and with regard to which the relative causes are as nothing; but each cause takes part in the absolute. Each is relatively absolute, none is absolutely absolute. *No one* has an exclusive claim to omnipotence; the sum of individual energies, or, to express it still more clearly, everything that exists through causal power, constitutes *all existing power*.

In reciprocal action, the two spheres into which being is divided when it becomes essence and phenomenon, are re-united and thus become logical totality.

3. *The Notion, or Subjective, Objective, and Absolute Totality* [1]

Outside of totality, none of the ideas thus far evolved has reality. A quality, a quantity, a force, or a cause, is nothing apart from the whole in which it is produced. Nothing in nature exists in isolation; nor can anything in the domain of thought lay claim to autonomy. This belongs only to the categories taken in their totality. Liberty is found in the whole alone. Hence in *logical totality* or the *notion (Begriff)*,[2] being and essence return into themselves.

The idea of totality is divided into *subjective* totality (the notion proper) and *objective* totality.

The essential elements of the idea of life: essence, phenomenon, and reciprocal action, reappear in the concept of subjective totality or notion, as *universality, particularity*, and *individuality*. In the *judgment*, which is thought or the subject in action, universality and individuality, generality and particularity, have the appearance of being distinct and separate, while in reality the judgment is merely the affirmation of their identity. When I say that man is mortal, or that Paul is mortal, I affirm that the characteristic common to all created beings, mortality, belongs to the particular being (man), and

---

[1] *Logic*, vol. III; *Encycl.*, §§ 160 ff.
[2] Hegel regards *Begriff* (notion) as synonymous with *Inbegriff*, whole, totality.

that the individual Paul, in turn, as a mortal being, is identical with the universality of creatures. In so far as the judgment affirms the identity of the universal and the individual, of the general and the particular, it is contradictory. The solution of the contradiction is found in reasoning, or the *syllogism*. The universal or general notion is unfolded in the major premise, the individual notion in the conclusion; and the minor premise, which is the connecting link between the major premise and the conclusion, expresses their identity.

The *subjective notion* is a form without matter, a container without a content. It exists, in principle, as a *goal* or *final cause*, but does not exist in reality. Hence its tendency to objectify itself; it is the eternal source of life in nature and of progress in history. The objectified notion is the universe, the *objective whole*, or *objects*. The general, the particular, and the individual are successively objectified in *mechanism* (simple external juxtaposition of objects), in *chemism* (mutual penetration of objects), and in *organism* (totality-unity).

However, a notion which is no longer a notion, thought which has become body, is again contradictory. Just as thought is not made to remain empty, but to be filled with an objective content; so, too, the world, or the whole of things, is not made to remain a stranger to consciousness, but to be thought or understood. The subjective notion is a container with a content; the universe which is unconscious of itself is a content without a container. The latter contradiction is abolished by the interpenetration of the two spheres in the *absolute Idea*, which, from the theoretical standpoint, is called *Truth*, and from the practical standpoint, the *Good :* this is the highest category and the last term in the development of being.

To sum up: Being is becoming, development. The contradiction inherent in being is the principle or impulsive force of development. Being, self-expansion (self-unfolding), and self-concentration (the understanding of self) constitute the unchanging stages in the process. Quality, quantity, measure;

essence and phenomenon, substantiality and causality, reciprocal action; subjectivity, objectivity, absolute: these are the serial stages of being.

Knowing this principle, this process, and these stages, we know *a priori* the order followed in the creations of *nature* (expanded reason) and of *mind* (concentrated and comprehended reason).

II. PHILOSOPHY OF NATURE[1]

1. *The Inorganic World*

Creative thought, like the reproductive thought of man, begins with the most abstract, the most vague, and the most intangible: with *space* and *matter*. After passing through a long line of development it culminates in the most concrete, the most perfect, the most accomplished: the human organism.

Like *being*, the first notion in logic, space exists and does not exist; matter is something and nothing. This contradiction is the very principle of physical evolution, the spring which sets it in motion; it is reconciled in *movement*, which divides matter into separate unities and forms the heavenly system of them. The formation of heavenly bodies is, as it were, the first step taken by nature on the path of individuation. The individualizing tendency, which runs through nature like a mighty desire, manifests itself as *attraction*. Universal gravitation is the ideal unity whence all things spring and whither they tend, affirming itself in the midst of their separation. It is the individuality, the soul, the cement of the world; it makes an organism, a living unity of the world.

Primitive and formless matter, the common source of the heavenly bodies, corresponds to what logic calls indeterminate being. The distribution of this matter, its organization into

---

[1] *Encyclopedia*, §§ 245 ff. — We shall consider, in the following *résumé* of the *Philosophy of Nature*, the changes (which were not very important) to which it was subjected by the school.

a sidereal world, corresponds to the categories of quantity. Gravitation, at last, realizes the idea of proportion.

The astronomical cosmos is an elementary society which anticipates human society. But the laws which govern it are, as yet, merely mechanical laws; the relations which the stars sustain to each other are summed up in the law of attraction. Hence the science which considers this primary phase of being, astronomy, deals with the dimensions of the stars, their distances, their external relations, rather than with their essential qualities, their composition, and their physiology.

2. *Chemism*

A second evolution leads to the qualitative differentiation of matter. The original state of indifference is followed by a variety of agencies (light, electricity, heat), by the reciprocal action of elements, by the inner process of opposition and reconciliation, separation and combination, polarity and union, which form the subject-matter of physics and chemistry.

Sidereal motion affects only the surface of bodies; chemism is an inner transformation, a change not only of place, but of essence, a prelude to that ultimate transformation of "substance" into "subject," of matter into mind, of being into consciousness, of necessity into freedom, which is the final goal of creation.

Nothing in the original flow of things resembles individuality; nothing is stable, fixed, or concentrated. But nature soon returns into itself. Just as in logic pure thought returns into itself and forms a circle or totality, so in nature, *the realization of logic*, the chemical process returns into itself at a certain point and forms those centralized wholes which we call organisms, living beings.

3. *The Organic World*

The appearance of life is wholly spontaneous, and needs no *deus ex machina* to explain it. It is the effect of the same higher and immanent power which, as attraction and affinity, separated the stellar groups and the elements of chemism. Surely, mechanism alone cannot produce it; and if matter were nothing but matter, the course of its transformations would forever be in the straight line and centrifugal. But beneath the physical process the evolution of the Idea takes place, which is the final goal of things, only because it is also their creative principle.

The earth itself is a kind of organism, a crude outline of the masterpiece which nature tends to realize. In this sense, Schelling and his school have a right to speak of the *soul* of the celestial bodies, of the *life* of the earth. This life has its vicissitudes, its revolutions, and its history, the subject-matter of geology, and though it gradually diminishes, it does so merely to become the inexhaustible source of new, truly organic and individual life.

From the ashes of the terrestrial organism arises the vegetable kingdom. But the plant itself is, as yet, merely an imperfect organism, a kind of association or federation, the members of which are more or less autonomous individuals. Individuality proper is realized only in the animal kingdom. The animal is, decidedly, an indivisible whole, whose parts are really *members*, i. e., servants of the central unity. It asserts its individuality by constant assimilation, respiration, and locomotion. It is endowed with sensibility, nay, even with inner heat and voice in its most perfect representatives. However, there are insensible transitions here. As the inorganic kingdom is connected with the vegetable kingdom by astral individualities and crystallizations; so the vegetable kingdom passes into the animal kingdom in the zoöphyte. Animals are developed by degrees. The same idea, the same fundamental plan, more and more perfectly executed, runs through crustaceans, mollusks, insects, fishes, reptiles, and mammals. Finally, in the human organism, the most perfect animal form, the creative idea is reflected in all its fulness. Here it stops. In the material realm it produces nothing more perfect. We say, in the material realm, for instead of being exhausted in the creation of man, the creative idea saves its most precious treasures until it reaches the sphere of *mind*, i. e., humanity.

III.   PHILOSOPHY OF MIND

1.   *The Subjective Mind, or the Individual*

Man is essentially mind, i. e., consciousness and freedom. But on emerging from the hands of nature he is so only in principle. The mind, like nature, is subject to the law of development. Consciousness and freedom do not exist at the dawn of individual or generic life; they are the products of the evolution called *history*.

The individual in the state of nature is governed by blind instinct, by brutal passions, and by that egoism which characterizes animal life. But as reason develops, he recognizes others as his equals; he becomes persuaded that reason, freedom, spirituality — these terms are synonymous — are not his exclusive property, but the common possession of all; he henceforth ceases to claim them as his exclusive privilege. The freedom of his fellow-creatures becomes the law, the bridle, the limit, of his own freedom. By giving way to this power, which is higher than the individual, the subjective mind yields to —

2.   *The Objective Mind, or Society*[1]

The blind forces manifested in the state of nature, e. g., the instinct for the propagation of species and the instinct for revenge, continue, but change their form. Henceforth they become marriage and legal punishment: regulated, disciplined instincts, ennobled by the law.

The objective mind first manifests itself in the form of *right*, which is freedom conceded and guaranteed to all. The individual who is recognized as free is a *person*. The personality realizes and asserts itself through *property*. Each legal per-

---

[1] *Encyclopedia*, §§ 482 ff.

son has, by virtue of his free activity, the right to possess, and, consequently, also the right to transfer his property. This transference takes place in the form of a *contract*. The contract is the *State* in embryo.

Right appears in the fulness of its power, only when individual caprice opposes the general or legal will (the objective mind).

The conflict between the individual will and the legal will gives rise to wrong (i. e., the un-right, *Unrecht*, the negation of right). But though denied by the individual, right remains right, the will of all. Temporarily defeated, it triumphs in the form of *penalty*. Injustice, wrong-doing, and crime thus merely serve to bring out the power of justice, and to prove that reason and right are superior to individual caprice. Punishment inflicted by law is not a chastisement or correction, but a just retribution; it is not a means, but an end. Right rights itself, justice justifies itself, and the penitent is the involuntary instrument of its glorification. Capital punishment is no more than just, and should be maintained. But is it not absurd to attempt to correct an evil-doer by killing him? This objection, which is too common in our times, rests, as Hegel holds, upon a false notion of legal punishment, the object of which is not the reform of the individual but the solemn affirmation of the violated principle.[1]

There is truth in the objection that the juridical view is one-sided and extreme. The jurist considers only the law and its fulfilment, without regard to the inner motive of the legal act. Now the individual may, in all respects, conform to the prescriptions of the law, he may be perfectly honorable in his outer life, and yet the general will may not be *his* will and the true motive of his acts. Hence, in spite of the semblance of conformity, we find a hidden but quite real antagonism between the subjective mind and the objective mind.

This antagonism must disappear, this impersonal will, which

---

[1] It was as a consistent Hegelian that the late M. Véra, in his capacity as a *député*, defended capital punishment.

called right, justice, must become the personal will of the individual, the inner law of his acts; legality must become *morality;* or, rather, to use a Hegelian phrase, the objective mind must become a subject.

Morality is the legality of the heart, the law which is identified with the will of the individual. In the moral sphere the code becomes *moral law, conscience, the idea of the good.* Morality inquires not only into the act as such, but into the spirit which dictates it. The legal sphere regulates the material interests of life, without reaching the conscience; it fashions the will according to a certain type; material interest is its highest goal. Morality aims higher: it subordinates the useful to the good.

Morality is realized in a number of institutions, which aim to unite the individual wills in the common service of the idea.

The fundamental moral institution, the basis of all the rest, is *marriage,* the *family.* On this institution rest *civil society* and the *State.* Since the State cannot exist without the family, it follows that marriage is a sacred duty and should be primarily and chiefly based on the consciousness of duty, or reason. It is a moral act, only in case it is contracted with a view to society and the State. Otherwise it is almost equivalent to concubinage. From this standpoint also we must consider the question of *divorce.* Divorce would be justifiable, only in case matrimony were merely a matter of sentiment. Rational morality condemns it in principle, and cannot tolerate it in practice except in exceptional cases provided for by the law. The holiness of marriage and the honor of corporations constitute the indispensable basis of society and the State, and the source of a people's prosperity; prostitution and individual egoism are an infallible cause of decadence.

Civil society, grounded on the family, is not yet the State. Its aim is the protection of individual interests. Hence the particularism which prevails in smaller countries where civil society and the State are identical, and which disappears with the formation of great united States. The State differs from civil society in that it no longer solely pursues the good of the individuals, but aims at the realization of the idea, for which it does not hesitate to sacrifice private interests. The egoism and particularism which prevail in the community are here counterbalanced and corrected. The State is the kingdom of the idea, of the universal, of the *objective* mind, the goal, of which the family and civil society are merely the means.

The *republic* is not, according to Hegel, the most perfect form of government. Ultimately resting upon the confusion of civil society and the State, it exaggerates the importance and the rôle of the individual. The republics of antiquity were superseded by dictatorships, because they sacrificed the idea to the individual, the family, and the caste. In the Greek Tyranny and Roman Cæsarism sovereign reason itself condemns the radical vice of the republican, democratic, and aristocratic forms of government.

The monarchy is the normal political form. In the free and sovereign action of a unipersonal ruler the national idea finds its adequate expression. The State is nothing but an abstraction unless personified in a monarch, — the depositary of its power, its political traditions, and the idea which it is called upon to realize. The prince is the State made man, impersonal reason become conscious reason, the general will become personal will. That is, according to our philosopher, the true meaning of the motto of Louis XIV: *l'État c'est moi* (I am the State).

Though Hegel condemns political liberalism, he favors *national* liberalism and the principle of nationality. From the Utilitarian standpoint of civil society, there may be, at best, a union or confederation of heterogeneous elements. Switzerland is an example of such a federation. But State means nationality, and nationality means unity of language, religion, customs, and ideas. The State which incorporates a people absolutely different from its own, and, against their will, fastens upon them an odious yoke, commits a crime against nature. In such a case, and only then, is opposition, or even rebellion, legitimate. A political community is impossible without a communion of ideas.

Here, however, a distinction must be made. Annexation is not a crime that justifies rebellion unless the annexed nation represents an idea which is as great, fruitful, and viable as the idea represented by the conquering people. There are nationalities which represent no idea and have lost their *raison d'être*. Such nations are to be condemned. The Bretons in France and the Basques in France and Spain belong to this class.

In spite of appearances to the contrary, the most vigorous people, the State representing the most viable idea, always succeeds in gaining the mastery. History is merely an incessant struggle between States of the past and those of the future. The idea of the State is gradually realized by means of such defeats and victories. The historical States are the temporary forms in which it appears, and which it discards when time has worn them out, only to assume new forms. Since the absolute is not restricted to a particular existence, but is always found in the whole, we cannot say that the ideal State is anywhere. The ideal State is everywhere and nowhere: everywhere, because it tends to realize itself in historical States; nowhere, for as an ideal, it is a problem to be solved by the future. History is the progressive solution of the political problem. Every nation adds its stone to the building of the ideal State, but each people also has its original sin, which brings it into opposition with the idea, and sooner or later compasses its ruin. Each State represents the ideal from a certain side; none realizes it in its fulness; none, therefore, is immortal. Like the logical notions, which are absorbed by a more powerful rival, and by virtue of the same law, the nations, one after another, succumb to each other, and transmit to their successors, in a more developed and enlarged form, the political idea of which they have been the depositaries, the civilization of which they have been the guardians.

This passing of the civilization of one people to another constitutes the *dialectics of history*: an expression which is not taken figuratively by Hegel. Logic or dialectics is the evolution of reason in individual thought; the dialectics of history is the development of the same reason on the world's stage. One and the same principle is unfolded in different environments, but according to an identical law. In pure logic, abstract ideas succeeded each other on the stage of thought and then disappeared, only to be followed by more comprehensive and concrete ideas. In the logic of nature, objectified ideas, material organisms, succeeded each other and formed an ascending scale, thereby realizing, with increasing perfection, the ideal type of physical creations. In the logic of history, ideas, again, become incarnated in nature, and invisibly weave the web of human destinies. Whether these ideas unfold themselves beneath the spiritual gaze of the philosopher, or whether they succeed each other in the form of bodies, or become incorporated in historical nations, they are always the same, and their order of succession is invariable. Reason is the innermost substance of history, which is a logic in action. In the eyes of the superficial historian, empires rise, flourish, and decline, peoples struggle, and armies destroy each other. But behind these nations and their armies are the principles they represent; behind the ramparts and the batteries ideas antagonize each other.

War, like the death penalty, has changed in aspect. With the advance of military art and civilization its cruelties are lessened. But in a tempered and modified form, it will continue as one of the indispensable means of political progress. It is the boast of our times that we see it in its true light, and no longer regard it as the passing satisfaction of the caprice of a sovereign, but as an inevitable crisis in the development of the idea. True, legitimate, necessary war is the war for ideas, war in the service of reason, as the nineteenth century has learned to wage it. Not that antiquity and the Middle Ages did not battle for ideas; but they were not yet conscious of the moral essence of war. The ideas formerly collided with each other, like blind forces; the modern world is conscious of the cause for which it is shedding its blood. Formerly the conflict was one between passions; now it is a battle for principle.

The victorious State is truer, nearer to the ideal State, better, in a word, than the vanquished State. The very fact that it has triumphed proves this: its triumph is the condemnation of the principle represented by the vanquished; it is the judgment of God. Thus interpreted, history resembles a series of divine reprisals directed against everything that is finite, one-sided, and incomplete; it is an eternal divine wrath, which nothing earthly can escape.

There is, in every epoch, a people in whom mind is more completely incarnated than in the rest, and who march in the front rank of universal civilization. That is, the God of history has successively "chosen" the Egyptians, the Assyrians, the Greeks, the Romans, and the French. The *national minds* are grouped around the infinite Mind of which history is the temple, and, one after another, become its privileged organs. So the archangels surround the throne of the Eternal.

The three phases of every evolution: being, expansion, and concentration, recur in the three great epochs of history.

In the Oriental monarchies, the State personified in the sovereign dominates the individual to the extent of annihilating him. What does the Ocean care for the waves playing on its surface?

In the States of Greece, Asiatic sluggishness is followed by political life and its fruitful conflicts; the absolute monarchy is superseded by the republic. Here individuals are no longer mere modes with which the *substance* of the State has nothing to do, but integral parts of a whole, which exists only through them; as such they have a feeling of their importance, and appreciate that the State needs their co-operation. The classical republics last as long as the individual elements and the State remain in equilibrium. They are imperilled as soon as the demagogue's *régime* substitutes for the national interest the selfish interests of individual ambition. The Cæsarean reaction forces the rebellious individual into obedience; the habitable world is conquered; the most diverse nations are thrown into one and the same mould and reduced to an inert and powerless mass.

The equilibrium between the State and the individual is restored in the Christian and parliamentary monarchy, as the best example of which Hegel regards the English constitution.[1]

3. *The Absolute Mind* [2]

However perfect the moral edifice called the State may be, it is not the highest goal whither the evolution of the Idea tends; and political life, though full of passion and intelligence, is not the climax of spiritual activity. Freedom is the essence of mind; independence is its life. Now, in spite of the contrary assertions of political liberalism, even the most perfect State cannot realize this. Whether it be a republic, a constitutional or an absolute monarchy, an aristocracy or a democracy, it does not cease to be a State, an external, armed, armored power, a kind of prison in which what is essentially infinite is deprived of its vital element. *Mind cannot unconditionally subject itself to anything but mind.* Not finding in political life the supreme satisfaction which it seeks, it rises beyond it into the free realms of *art, religion,* and *science.*

Does that mean that the mind, in order to realize its destiny, shall destroy the ladder by which it rose; shall it overturn the State, society, and the family? Far from it. Indeed, the creations of art, the religious institutions, the works of science, are possible only under the auspices of a strong State and under the protection of a firmly established government. The artist, the Christian, and the philosopher can no more do without society and the State than the vegetable and animal can exist without the mineral kingdom. So, too, the Idea,

[1] We ought to add that what influenced Hegel's judgment was not the parliamentarism, but the conservatism of the English constitution.

[2] *Encyclopedia*, §§ 553 ff. See also Hegel's lectures on *Æsthetics*, the *Philosophy of Religion*, and the *History of Philosophy*.

whether it operates in the form of nature or of mind, never destroys its creations; it develops and perfects them, and even though their preservation may seem useless to us, it keeps the first-fruits of its labors intact. Nature, in which everything appears to be in a state of endless destruction and revolution, is eminently preservative: the mineral kingdom continues to exist alongside of the vegetable kingdom; the vegetable kingdom, alongside of the animal kingdom; and in the animal kingdom the most elementary and most unfinished types exist alongside of the most perfect types: nature preserves them and uses them as a kind of pedestal for her masterpiece. Moreover, the higher creations are possible only because those which precede them endure. The mineral kingdom gives life to the vegetable kingdom; the animal lives on the vegetable or on the animal inferior to it; finally, plants and animals nourish man, who cannot live without them. The same is true of the creations of the mind: from the depths of the soul arises the demand for liberty; from the fact that liberty is claimed by all, grow right, property, and the penal law; upon the solid foundation of right the moral institutions, the family, society, and the State, are established. All these developments are closely connected with each other, and each exists only through the instrumentality of the others. Take away one of the foundation-stones, and the entire universal edifice crumbles to pieces. The higher stories of this structure presuppose the perfect stability of the lower ones.

Man was, first of all, an individual (subjective mind) shut up in his native egoism; then, emerging from himself and recognizing himself in other men, he formed a community, society, and State (objective mind); finally, returning into himself, he finds at the bottom of his being the ideal of art or the beautiful, the religious ideal or God, the philosophical ideal or truth, and in the realization of this threefold ideal, the supreme independence to which he aspires: he becomes *absolute mind.*

In *art*, the mind enjoys by anticipation the victory over the external world which science reserves for it. The thought of the artist and his object, the human soul and the infinite, become identified; heaven descends into the soul, and the soul is carried heavenward. Genius is the breath of God, *afflatus divinus*.

Religion reacts against the pantheism anticipated by art, and shows us in God the transcendent Being, whom the genius of man cannot reach. By proclaiming the dualism of the infinite and the finite, religion is, in appearance, a relapse, a kind of return of the mind to the external yoke; in reality, however, it is a necessary crisis of the mind, which develops its forces and brings it nearer to God, in struggling beneath the yoke. That it is an evolution may be seen from the fact that Christianity itself, its most perfect form, proclaims the unity of the finite and the infinite in Jesus Christ, and thus anticipates the highest development of the mind: *philosophy*.

Philosophy realizes what art and the Christian dogma foreshadow. Art and religious faith spring from feeling and imagination; science is the triumph of pure reason, the apotheosis of mind. By understanding the world, the mind frees itself from it. Nature and its forces, the State and its institutions, which but lately seemed like a pitiless Fate, change in appearance so soon as the mind recognizes in nature the works of reason, i. e., its own works, and regards social and political institutions as the reflection of the moral authority dwelling in itself. If nature, law, right, State, represent different forms of mind (*objective* mind), all these barriers fall away; if everything that is real is found to be rational, reason has no other law except itself. On this summit of universal life, the ego and the world are forever united.

In conclusion, we shall summarize Hegel's philosophy of art, religion, and philosophy, especially the first, which has not been surpassed.

1. Art is the anticipated triumph of mind over matter; it is the idea penetrating matter and transforming it after its image. But the matter which the idea employs to incorporate

itself is a more or less docile or rebellious servant; hence the different forms of art, the *fine arts*.

In *architecture*, the elementary stage of art, idea and form are quite distinct; the idea cannot as yet wholly conquer the matter which it employs, and the matter remains rebellious. Architecture is merely a symbolic art, in which the form *suggests* the idea without directly expressing it. The pyramid, the pagoda, the Greek temple, the Christian cathedral, are admirable symbols, but the distance between these edifices and the idea which they symbolize is as great "as that between heaven and earth." Moreover, the materials of architecture are the most *material* in the physical world. This art is to sculpture, painting, and music, what minerals are to vegetables and animals. Resembling the astronomical universe in its gigantic proportions and overwhelming majesty, it expresses solemnity, austerity, mute grandeur, the unalterable repose of force, the immovable *statu quo* of the infinite; but it is incapable of expressing the thousand shades of life, the infinitely varied beauties of reality.

The dualism of form and idea, which characterizes architecture, tends to disappear in *sculpture*. The art of the sculptor has this in common with architecture: like its elder sister, it employs gross matter, marble, brass; but it is much more capable of transforming and spiritualizing them. In the purely symbolical work of the architect, there are details and accessories which in no wise assist in expressing the idea; in the statue, nothing is indifferent, everything is in the service of the idea of which it is the direct expression, the immediate revelation. But the statue is incapable of representing the soul itself as revealed in the eye. This advance is made in *painting*.

The matter employed by painting is somewhat less material than that of sculpture and architecture; it is no longer the three-dimensional body, but the plane surface. Depth is reduced to a mere appearance, produced by perspective, spiritualized. However, painting can express only a moment of life, a moment which it is obliged to stereotype and consequently to materialize; the idea is still bound to matter and extension. Owing to this common characteristic, architecture, sculpture, and painting, together form *objective art*. Hence, they are inseparable; they are combined in a thousand different ways. These first three external, visible, material forms of art are superseded by *subjective*, invisible, immaterial art, or *music*.

Music is a spiritualistic art, the art which can, with thrilling truth, reproduce the innermost essence of the human soul, the infinite shades of feeling. The direct opposite of architecture, sculpture, and painting, it, too, is an incomplete art. There can be nothing extreme in perfect art; it is the synthesis of all contraries, the harmonious union of the world of music and the world of objective art. This art of arts is *poetry*.

Poetry is art endowed with speech, the art which can say everything, express everything, and create everything anew, the universal art. Sculpture, like architecture, employs matter in its grossest form, but it spiritualizes marble; it gives life and intelligence to this block of which architecture can merely make a more or less eloquent symbol. So, too, poetry and music both employ sound, but in music this is vague and indefinite, like the feeling which expresses it. In the service of the poet it becomes articulate and definite sound, a word, language. Music makes a symbol of sound, — a piece of music, like an edifice, is susceptible of the most diverse interpretations, — poetry wholly subordinates it to the idea. Architecture contents itself with suggesting the Divinity who reigns beyond the stars; sculpture brings him down upon the earth. Music localizes the infinite in feeling; poetry assigns to it the boundless realm which of right belongs to it: nature and history. It is all-powerful and inexhaustible, like the God who inspires the poet.

Sculpture and poetry, on the one hand, architecture and music, on the other, are to art what pantheism and theism are to religious thought. Architecture and music show the traces of the theistic idea; sculpture and poetry, which make the ideal descend into the real, are pantheistic arts. Hence it comes that architecture and music are the faithful followers of religion; while sculpture, painting, and poetry, which are also enrolled in the service of religious faith, do not serve it so submissively. Sculpture is pagan; and it was owing to its pantheism that images of God were condemned by Mosaism and rigorous Protestantism. Poetry, on the other hand, celebrated its great triumphs outside of the domain of religion. Shakespeare, Molière, Goethe, and Byron are no more Christians than Sophocles, Pindar, and Euripides. Modern religious poetry seems to be afflicted with barrenness. It is because great poetry is so intimate a union of divine and human elements that the dogma of divine transcendency is actually cancelled by it.

The epitome and quintessence of all the arts, poetry constructs, sculptures, designs, paints, sings; it is architecture, sculpture, painting, and music, and these diverse forms which it can successively assume are again found in what we call its *genres*.

Corresponding to objective art, represented by architecture, sculpture, and painting, we have *epic poetry*, which is to poetry what the pyramid is to art. The epic represents the childhood of poetry. It is garrulous, ornate, full of the marvellous, like the imagination of the child, indefinitely long, like the first years of life.

Lyric poetry corresponds to music. The epic, like the objective arts, loves to paint nature and its wonders, history and its glories; lyric poetry falls back upon the invisible world, no less vast than the other, called the human soul. It is, therefore, an extreme and incomplete class.

The perfect *genre*, which reconciles the two worlds, the poetry of poetry, is *dramatic poetry*. The drama, which flourishes only among the most civilized peoples, reproduces history, nature, and the human soul with its passions, emotions, and conflicts.

Art has not only its different forms, it has also, like each of its forms, its historical development in three epochs.

Oriental art is essentially symbolical. It delights in allegory and parables. Unlike the Greek masterpieces, which are self-explanatory, its products must be interpreted, and may be interpreted differently. It is still powerless to overcome matter, and the feeling of this weakness reveals itself in all its works. Despising form, finish, and detail, it is fond of caricature, exaggerations, and the colossal, and, in all its creations, betrays its predilection for the infinite and incommensurable.

In Greek art, symbolism is superseded by direct expression; the whole idea descends into the form. But even the sublime and almost superhuman perfection of this art is extreme and imperfect. The idea so completely penetrates the matter as to be, ultimately, indistinguishable from it; it is sacrificed to outward form and physical beauty.

This defect, which is no less signal than the formless spiritualism of Asiatic art, is corrected in Christian art. Christianity recalls art from the visible world, in which it had lost itself, to the ideal sphere, its true home. Under the influence of the Gospel, the idea of the beautiful is spiritualized, the adoration of physical beauty makes way for the worship of moral beauty, purity, and holiness; the worship of the Virgin follows the cultus of Venus. Christian or romantic art does not exclude physical beauty, but subordinates it to transcendent beauty.

Now, the material form is inadequate to the moral ideal. The most finished masterpieces cannot satisfy the Christian artist. The Virgin of whom he dreams, the eternal dwelling-places which his spiritual eye perceives, the heavenly music whose harmonies his soul enjoys, the divine life which he desires to portray, his ideal, in a word, is still more beautiful; so beautiful, indeed, that neither burin, nor brush, nor bow, nor pen, nor anything material can express it. Hence Christian art, despairing of its powers, finally relapses into that contempt for form and that excessive spiritualism which is both the characteristic feature and the failing of romanticism.

2. Though man may, in his inspired moments, regard himself as identical with the God who inspires him, he very soon discovers his insignificance when it comes to giving his ideal a material form. Thus *religion* springs from art. Primitive art is essentially religious; natural religion, essentially artistic. Idolatry is the connecting link between religion and art.

Religion becomes conscious of itself, and emancipates itself from art by abolishing idols. This advance is made in Mosaism. The Bible condemns idolatry because it recognizes man's inability to express the infinite by means of matter; it forbids stone images because the idea has no adequate form except itself. But though it prohibits us from *picturing* the invisible, it does not hinder us from picturing it *to ourselves;* it forbids the outward image, but it does not forbid the imagination itself and the ideas with which it peoples the mind. Far from it. The fact is, religion is essentially representation. Art represents the infinite; religion represents it *to itself* as a personal and extra-mundane being. Anthropomorphism is its characteristic feature. In religious thought, the finite and the infinite, earth and heaven, which are united in the feeling of the beautiful, are again disjoined. Man is *down below*, God is *up above*, so high and so far that he needs the ministry of angels in order to communicate with the world. Religion is dualistic, but there is nothing final in its dualism. It separates heaven and earth, only to unite them; it separates God and humanity, only to reconcile them.

The essential elements of the religious idea: infinite God, mortal man, and their relation, successively prevail in the history of religion.

In the religions of the Orient the idea of infinity predominates. Their salient feature is pantheism; an ultra-religious pantheism, however, which is synonymous with acosmism and may be summed up in these words: God is everything, man is nothing. Brahmanism is the most complete expression of Asiatic pantheism. Mosaic monotheism, though otherwise differing from Indian religions, shows the same characteristics. The God of the Orient bears the same relation to man as the princes of the Orient bear to their subjects. He is the Creator, and men are his *creatures;* hence he can dispose of them, he can make them live and die, exalt them and debase them, just as he pleases. Man is to God what the earthen vase is to the potter; no more, no less. Human liberty and spontaneity are out of the question. Not only the act, but also the will comes from God; he enlightens and hardens the hearts; he predestines everything, be it for good or for evil. Since *omnipotence* belongs to God, there is nothing left for man but total impotence and mournful resignation. The infinite as such cannot tolerate an independent existence by its side; Siva, Moloch, and Saturn devour their own children, and where this does not happen, the latter, knowing that their existence is displeasing to God, destroy themselves, or suffer a slow martyrdom, or absolutely relinquish their personality.

Greece is as fond of finitude and form, nature and the things of the earth, as Asia is religious. Its religion is as serene as its skies, as radiant and transparent as the atmosphere surrounding it; the clouds which elsewhere hide God from the eye of man, vanish at the first effort of the mind; the divine and the human are blended and united; religion is identified with art, and art with the worship of humanity. The riddle of the Sphinx is the riddle of Hellenic polytheism. Man is the solution of the riddle. The God whom the Greek adores under the form of Zeus, Apollo, Athene, Aphrodite, is man and his power, intelligence, and beauty. His divinities are relative beings. Nay, this mythological heaven, radiant with eternal youth, is in reality subject to Fate, the mysterious power which rules over gods and mortals alike. This Destiny, the supreme power of which the poets eagerly strive to exalt, is like a conscience which antiquity cannot silence; it is the infinite of the Oriental religions, which, like a Shakespearean ghost, haunts the sensuous environment of the polytheistic cultus.

The Orient professes the religion of the infinite and abstract; Greece worships at the shrine of the finite. These two extremes of religion are reconciled in Christianity, in which the spirit of the Orient and the Greek genius are united. For the Hindoo, God is everything, man nothing; for the Greek, God is nothing or very little, man, everything; for the Christian, the important thing is neither God considered in the abstract, the Father, nor man in the abstract, but the concrete unity of the divine and the human as realized in Jesus Christ. The God whom Jesus reveals to us is the same as the God who reveals him; he is neither an infinite being like the God of Oriental religions, nor a finite one, like the pagan divinities, but a Being who is both God and man, the God-Man. The distance between the Christian heaven and the earth, between the God of the Gospel and humanity, is not insuperable; nay, this God comes down from his throne, enters the sphere of finity, lives our life, suffers and dies like us, then rises from the dead and enters into his glory. Christianity is to the preceding religions what poetry is to the fine arts; it embraces them and at the same time purifies and completes them. It is the synthesis of all religions, the absolute religion.

3. The Christian dogma is truth in the form of *representation*. The three stages in the evolution of immanent reason, idea, nature, and mind, become three persons. The union of the infinite and finite in human consciousness, i. e., a process embracing the whole of universal history, is regarded as an event that happened once for all times in Palestine, eighteen hundred years ago. In this form the dogma is an inadequate expression of the truth which it contains. Moreover, it is imposed as an external authority, whereas the mind, which is free in essence, can only be realized as free. In order to reach the climax of its evolution, it has simply to divest the religious doctrine of its *representative* form, and to give it the *rational* form. This advance is made by *philosophy*. The

Gospel and true philosophy have the same *content.* But the *container* is not the same; with the Christian it is the *imagination*, with the philosopher, *reason.* Philosophical truth is religious truth in the form of a *concept;* it is comprehended truth. The absolute idea becomes absolute mind, absolute self-consciousness.

The history of philosophy, like all history, is a regular development, reproducing the entire series of categories: Eleatism is the philosophy of being; Heraclitus is the philosopher of becoming; Democritus and atomism correspond to the idea of individuality, and so on. It attains to its fullest expansion in absolute idealism, i. e., in the system which we have just outlined.

What truth is there in this final claim? How much of it is illusory?

Hegelianism is, without doubt, the most comprehensive and complete synthesis ever attempted by the human mind, — a veritable encyclopædia, animated by a central idea, and supported by a method that has implicit confidence in itself. Hence, if philosophy is what our opening paragraph defined it to be, we must give Hegel the credit of having come nearer to the ideal of science than any of his predecessors. Furthermore, no one, after Kant, gave to modern thought so powerful an impetus, — no one more completely dominated and fascinated it. Jurisprudence, politics, ethics, theology, and æsthetics, — all have suffered his influence. Nor is that all. By demonstrating that being is becoming, logical development, history, that history is not only a science among others, but the science of sciences, he ably seconded, if he did not create, the historical movement of the nineteenth century, and impressed upon it the stamp of impartial objectivity which characterizes it, and which was foreign to the eighteenth century. David Strauss and his *Leben Jesu*, Baur, the celebrated historian of primitive Christianity and the founder of the historical school of Tübingen, Michelet, Rosenkranz,

ERDMANN, PRANTL, ZELLER, KUNO FISCHER, the brilliant interpreters of ancient and modern thought, come from Hegel. The conception that philosophies and religions are different stages of one and the same development; the hypothesis that an unconscious reason creates and transforms languages; the ideas of, and even the expressions, *genesis, evolution, process,* the *logic of history,* and many others, which have become common-places in the political, religious, and scientific press, are products of the Hegelian movement.

What discredited Hegelianism and philosophy itself — for there was a time when the two terms were employed synonymously — was the material errors which necessarily followed from its exclusively a-prioristic method; was the authoritative tone which it assumed towards the leaders of modern science, Copernicus, Newton, and Lavoisier; was its presumptuous attempt to withdraw the hypotheses of metaphysics from the supreme jurisdiction of facts. If the philosophical mind perceives truth by an immediate and instinctive intuition, whereas experience discovers it step by step only, then its oracles, precisely because they are *immediate,* i. e., unproved, and wholly unaccounted for, need the counter-signature of experience in order to have the force of laws in the scientific sphere. The immediate and spontaneous, as Hegel himself declares, is never definitive, but the starting-point of an evolution. Hence, *a priori* speculation, as he conceives and pursues it, cannot be the final form of science, but should, at the very least, be verified by experience, and, in case of need, be corrected by criticism. Moreover, the defects of the Hegelian method and the errors of fact following from it are due to the rationalistic prejudice of which the system is the classical expression. According to Hegel, the absolute is idea, thought, reason, and *nothing but that;* whence he concludes that the idea, or, as the School says, the *form,* is also the content, the *matter,* of things. When he assumes that the *ideal world of science* can be deduced from reason alone, it is because, according to him, the *real world,* the *world of beings,* is derived from reason and reason alone. Now the absolute, or at least — since the absolute is unknowable as such — the primary phenomenon is not thought, intelligence, reason, but will.[1] Thought is a *mode* of the creative activity of things; it is not their *principle*.[2] It follows that the *knowledge of things* does not come from pure thought, but from thought supported and governed by experience.

§ 67. Herbart [3]

Kant, the master, protested against the absolute idealism of his "false disciples," and opposed to it his ideo-realism, which distinguishes between the form and the matter of our knowledge, considering the form alone as given *a priori*, and the content, the matter, as solely and necessarily furnished by the outer and inner sense. Reason produces *a priori* the categories of quality, quantity, causality, and measure, which are indispensable to the knowledge of nature; but it cannot produce *a priori* the ideas of iron, light, pleasure, and pain, which experience alone supplies. Experience has its *a priori* conditions, which pure sensationalism erroneously denies; but experience alone gives us complete and concrete ideas properly so called, while the categories, which reason produces *a priori*, are not, strictly speaking, ideas, but mere frames for our ideas: which is an entirely different thing. Schelling himself concedes that, in the last analysis, everything comes from experience, although experience presupposes *a priori* conditions without which it would be impossible. That is, in truth, the real teaching of Kant.

A number of thinkers, and particularly JOHANN FRIEDRICH HERBART (1776–1841), professor at Königsberg and Göttingen, followed the master. They occupied a position between Hegel, whose star sank in 1830, and Locke, whose empiricism, which

[1] See § 68.

[2] According to the Christian dogma itself, which Hegel professes to translate into philosophical language, the *logos* is *created* and is not the "Father."

[3] *A Text-Book in Psychology*, tr. by Smith, New York, 1891; Davidson, *Herbart's Psychology and Educational Theory*, London, 1906.

had been temporarily checked by the idealism of the Restoration, only to reappear, more powerful than ever, as positivism, after the setting of the Hegelian sun. The most important philosophical writings of Herbart are: *General Metaphysics* and *Psychology as Science, based upon Experience, Metaphysics, and Mathematics*. What especially characterizes them is their systematic opposition to the principles, method, and conclusions of Hegel. Things are not merely our thoughts, as idealism holds; they exist *really* and independently of the reason which thinks them (realism in the modern sense). Hence, the problem of philosophy is not to construct the universe, but to accept it as it exists, and to explain its mechanism, so far as that can be done. Observation and experience form the indispensable foundation of speculation. A philosophy not based on the positive data of science is hollow. It has merely the import of a poem, and we cannot concede to it any scientific value. Herbart restores to philosophy the boundaries which Kantian criticism had declared impassable.

Philosophy is defined as the elaboration of the concepts which underlie the different sciences. Such general ideas[1] are not free from contradictions, and should therefore be revised. This work is the real business of the metaphysician.

The contradictions which philosophy is asked to resolve have been ascertained by the Eleatics, the Sceptics, and Hegel. But Zeno of Elea, instead of resolving them, considered them insoluble, and hence inferred that nothing real corresponds to them. The Sceptics saw in this a reason for repudiating metaphysics. Hegel, at last, does not deny that our ideas are contradictory, but by a *tour de force* unheard of in the history of philosophy, accepts the contradiction without reserve, and declares that it forms the very essence of thought and being. That is, he pretends to dispense with the *principle of contradiction*. But we cannot, with impunity, violate the law which has governed human thought from the very beginning, and we shall have to reckon with it as long as reason is reason

[1] For example, the ideas of cause, space, and the ego.

The Hegelian paradox is not a solution. Scepticism has its *raison d'être;* it is even necessary, in a certain measure; it forms the starting-point, in the history of thought, of the great philosophies (Socrates, Descartes, Kant). But to remain sceptical is to give proof of the incompetence of speculation. Doubt in its most absolute form, scepticism extended even to the existence of things, is refuted by one of the most simple reflections. Though it may be doubted that things exist, it is *beyond doubt* that they *appear* to exist. This appearance (*phe-nomenon*) is absolutely certain, and the most obstinate sceptic cannot doubt it. The phenomenon exists. If nothing existed, nothing could appear to exist. But, though we assume what is evident, namely, the existence of things, it is not so certain that they are what we think they are, that they exist as they are thought (Ænesidemus, Sextus), that they are in time and space, connected by the tie of causality (Hume, Kant). This doubt, founded, as it is, on the contradictions and obscurities which even the most superficial reflection can discover in our ideas, is perfectly legitimate, provided it provokes philosophical thought.

The business of philosophy, as we have said, consists essentially in revising and correcting our general ideas, in freeing them from the contradictions which they contain. The ideas of *extension, duration, matter, movement, inherence, causality,* and *egoity*, particularly, require elaboration. The idea of extension, duration, matter, is the idea of *multiple unity* (hence the supposed antinomies of rational cosmology). To change, to become, and to move means to be and not to be. By the notion of inherence we assign manifold properties to the same substance; i. e., we affirm that *one* thing is *several* things (colored, odorous, sapid, liquid), that unity is not one. The notion of cause, likewise, is contradictory from every point of view. We both affirm that the thing modified by an external cause is the same as before, and that it is not the same. When we speak of the self-determination of the subject (Leibniz), we become involved in the no less flagrant contradiction that a being is both active and passive, i. e., that it is not one but two. Finally, the notion of the ego with its diverse faculties is as contradictory as the idea of inherence, of which it is an application. In all these notions there is a confusion of being and non-being, the one and the many, affirmation and negation, i. e., of two things which exclude each other, and which thought should clearly separate, Hegel to the contrary notwithstanding.

From the confusion of two contraries arises the idea of limited and relative being. This conception Herbart unconditionally rejects. Being, according to him, admits of neither negation nor limitation. It is absolute position, wholly excluding diversity of properties, divisibility, limitation, and negation. It cannot be conceived either as quantity or continuous magnitude, or as being in space and time (Kant). It is what Plato and Parmenides called the One, what Spinoza named Substance; but it differs from the Eleatic principle in that it exists independently of thought, and from Spinoza's Substance in that it is not *one*. There are, according to Herbart, a plurality of *real beings* or *realities*, and, since each reality is absolute position, a plurality of absolute beings; which seems contradictory, but is not so because extended beings alone limit each other, and the realities are supposed to be inextended. The realities of Herbart, therefore, closely resemble Leibniz's monads; but they differ from them in an essential respect: the "monads" are complex unities endowed with many properties, having their inner states, their modifications, and their immanent development; the realities of Herbart are absolutely simple; they have only one single property; they suffer no internal change, they are immutable.

Real being, then, is not what the senses show us; for the objects perceived by the senses have many properties. What follows? Why, the sensible object (iron, silver, oxygen) contains as many realities as it has distinct properties.

Thus the difficulty involved in the notion of inherence is resolved. This idea is contradictory only when applied to the real being (Kant's *thing-in-itself*); it is not so when applied to the phenomenal being, or the thing presented by the senses. The latter is always an *integration of real beings* in greater or smaller numbers, never a unitary real being.

The ideas of causality and change are explained in the same way. The relation of causality cannot obtain either between two real beings (external causality), or between a real being and its supposed characteristics (immanent causality); for each real being exists *absolutely* (by itself), while immanent causality (for example, iron considered as the cause of its properties) divides the one into many, i. e., contradicts the notion of real being. Hence, causality cannot signify anything but reality and, at the utmost, *self-preservation*.[1]

Change cannot be assumed except under certain reservations. Change as affecting the real beings is out of the question in metaphysics. Not the substances, but only their mutual relations, are incessantly modified. Geometry shows that a thing can change relatively to another thing without changing itself: the tangent of a circle A B C becomes the radius of another circle D E F. The same is true of music: the same note is true or false, according to its relation to other notes. In pharmacy we observe the same fact: one and the same plant is both a poison and a remedy.

But though the substances themselves do not change, their mutual relations change. The real beings, *though absolute*, are related to each other. In order to understand this, we must imagine them to exist in a space which is not phenomenal space, but which Herbart calls intelligible space. In this space two monads can occupy different points, and then there is no relation between them; but they can also, by means of a movement of whose laws we are ignorant, occupy the same point. Nothing can hinder us from assuming this, since we

---

[1] Here Herbart contradicts himself; for self-preservation is a reflective act, which divides the monad in two, — namely, into a subject which preserves, and an object which is preserved. Now, does Herbart believe that he can in no case contradict himself, because that would be a reflective act, a division in the monad, an impossibility?

are not here dealing with material atoms. Two or more substances which occupy the same point interpenetrate (as though penetration did not presuppose extension). Substances which thus interpenetrate may be of the same quality; they may differ in quality, or, finally, they may be opposite in quality (difference between Herbart and the Greek atomists). If they are identical in quality, their interpenetration produces no change in their respective modes of being; but if the substance B, which comes to occupy the place of the substance A, is of a different or opposite quality, there will be a conflict between the two monads, since two contraries cannot coexist in one and the same point. Each will tend to preserve itself; it will resist its rival, and affirm its indestructible individuality.

Thus we may explain phenomena in general, and the phenomenon of *thought* in particular. The ego ceases to be a contradictory idea when we give up regarding it as a unity composed of different faculties, — a multiple unity, i. e., a unity which is not a unity. The ego has not *many* functions, but *one single* function: it tends to preserve itself in its indestructible originality. That is its only function, but it varies under the influence of the surroundings; its only faculty manifests itself in a number of apparently different faculties, according as the soul is solicited by similar, different, or contrary monads. From such a conflict thought arises. Thought is the act by which the subject affirms itself, preserves itself, in opposition to the object which solicits it. It is infinitely modified, according to the nature of the object. Hence, the infinite variety of our perceptions. The psychological consciousness is the sum of relations which the real being called ego sustains to other real beings.

Hence, inner perception is not essential to the soul; it is a mere phenomenon, produced by the *coming together* of the ego and other realities, — a resultant of the combined actions of the subject and the object, a relation. If the soul were isolated from all other beings, it would not think, feel, or will. Feeling is a thought arrested by other more energetic thoughts; but this, in turn, may overcome the latter, and become thought when the ego is solicited by other objects. Similarly, will is nothing but thought (Spinoza); moral freedom is the permanent domination of reflected thought over feeling, i. e., a matter of equilibrium. Psychical life is a mechanism, the laws of which are the same as those of statics and dynamics. Psychology, properly understood, is a true mechanism, an application of arithmetic, an exact science.

The scientific bent of Herbart's philosophy, and particularly his application of mathematics to the science of the soul, — a bold and original attempt, — could not but make him the centre of a large school. Hegel's attitude towards the pioneers of modern science prejudiced serious thinkers against idealism and drove them into the camp of *exact metaphysics*. They entered this school for want of a better; for the philosophy of Herbart, which undertook to free thought from all contradictions, was itself full of the most glaring contrasts. While Herbart's ontology declares real being to be simple and inextended, his psychology is based on the opposite hypothesis. His theodicy, which is perfectly conservative, and his teleology, which is wholly spiritualistic, seriously clash with his paradoxical theory of the multiple absolute, which logically culminates in polytheism, and his mechanism, which is closely akin to the materialistic theories. Moreover, his metaphysics contains the strangest contradictions. *Real being* excludes the plurality of properties, change, and movement, i. e., in brief, life, and, ultimately, *reality*. *Real reality*, life, activity, is excluded from the sphere of beings, and Herbart's *Real Beings*, instead of being realities, are lifeless abstractions, scholastic entities, and nothing more. Furthermore, his monadology shares all the disadvantages of the Leibnizian theory, which serves as his model. Like the "pulverized universe" with which he presents us, his philosophy possesses neither the unity nor the homogeneity which we have a right to demand from a doctrine claiming to be a metaphysic. It is, in every respect, the antipode of Hegelian philosophy, and, provoked by the logicism of its powerful rival, affects to ignore the monistic tendency.

The latter reasserts itself in Schopenhauer, whose philosophy, a happy mean between speculation and positive knowledge, exercises a preponderating influence on modern German thought.

§ 68. Schopenhauer. Will as the Fundamental Reality

ARTHUR SCHOPENHAUER, the son of a banker in Danzic, and Johanna Schopenhauer, an authoress formerly well-known in Germany, was born 1788. He studied at Göttingen (1809–1811) and Berlin (1811–1813), taught philosophy at the latter institution as a *Privatdocent* from 1820 to 1831, then abandoned the university career, and spent the remainder of his life at Frankfort on the Main, where he died in 1860. The writings which established his reputation are: (1) his inaugural dissertation, *The Fourfold Root of the Principle of Sufficient Reason;*[1] (2) *The World as Will and Idea;*[2] (3) *The Will in Nature;*[3] (4) *The Two Fundamental Problems of Ethics.*[4] He heard the lectures of Schulze[5] at Göttingen and of Fichte in Berlin, and devoted himself, particularly, to the study of Kant, Plato, and Buddhism, so far as this was known in Europe. To Kant, Fichte, and Schelling he owes his cardinal doctrine, which conceives the will as the absolute, to Plato, his theory of Ideas or stages of the voluntary phenomenon, to Buddhism his pessimistic bent and his doctrine of the negation of the will.

His chief work, *The World as Will and Idea*, opens with a glowing tribute to criticism. In asserting, with Kant, that

---

[1] Tr. by Hillebrand in *Bohn's* Library, 1891.
[2] Tr. by Haldane and Kemp, London, 1909.
[3] Tr. by Hillebrand in *Bohn's* Library, 1891.
[4] *Popular Essays*, tr. by Saunders, New York, 1915. Works on Schopenhauer: Wallace, *Schopenhauer*, London, 1890; Caldwell, *Schopenhauer's System*, London, 1896; Whittaker, *Schopenhauer* (*Philosophies Ancient and Modern*).
[5] See § 63.

the world is *my idea*, he does not deny the reality of the world; he distinguishes between the world as it is in itself, apart from my senses and my intelligence, and the world as I see and conceive it, i. e., the phenomenal world. The phenomenal world is *my* perception, *my* idea, the product of *my* intellectual organization. Indeed, if I were differently organized, the world would be different, or, at least, would seem different; it would consist (*for me*) of different phenomena. As a *reality*, it exists independently of me, but as an *object* of sensibility and the understanding, or, in a word, as a *phenomenon*, it depends on the *subject* which perceives it: it is a wholly relative thing, created by the ego and the *a priori* conditions of thought.

On the other hand, consciousness emphatically declares that behind this phenomenal world, the product of our organization, there is a higher reality, which does not depend on us, an absolute, a *thing-in-itself*. Kant acknowledges the existence of the thing-in-itself; but what he gives with one hand he takes back with the other. He denies to the understanding the right to apply to this *thing* any of its categories, maintains that reason is incapable of knowing it, and, consequently, regards the phenomenal world, i. e., in the last analysis, the thinking subject, as alone knowable; for the phenomenon is *my* thought, nothing but *my* thought. It is true, the subject cannot get beyond itself, identify itself with what it is not, assimilate things as they are in themselves. But it is equally true that the belief in the existence of the world irresistibly forces itself upon us; it is, consequently, true that the perception which we have of ourselves gives us, at the very least, an *image* of what the things outside of us are. It would, undoubtedly, be impossible for me to know anything of the essence of *objects* if I were merely a *subject*. But I am both the subject and the object of my thought, as I am the object of the thought of others. I am conscious of being an *object* among other objects. Thus the chasm made by criticism between the thinking subject and the things themselves is partly bridged. I have the right to convert the proposition: I (the

subject) am an object, and to say: most probably — Schopenhauer, the pupil of Schulze the sceptic, does not lay claim to
absolute knowledge — the object (all objects, the entire objective world) is what I am; its essence is analogous to mine.

This *analogy* of all beings, which dogmatism affirmed in
Leibniz, we must assume even from the standpoint of criticism. We have the right, even as Kantians, to judge things
according to what we find in ourselves. Only, we must make
sure of what in us is truly essential, original, and fundamental.
According to Descartes, Spinoza, Leibniz, Hegel, and all the
rationalists, this essential thing is *thought*, intellect. Hence,
inasmuch as all existing things are analogous, Leibniz concludes that all beings perceive and think in a certain degree;
but experience does not confirm this hypothesis. Hegel, likewise, regards thought as the universal typical phenomenon.
According to Schopenhauer, *the essential and fundamental thing
in us is the* WILL, whereas thought is but a derived or secondary phenomenon, an accident of will. Now, we have every
reason to believe, and experience strikingly proves, that what
is essential and fundamental to us is also the essence, the ultimate principle of the nature of all other beings. We are essentially will, and the entire universe, considered in its essence,
is a will that *objectifies itself*, gives itself a body or a real existence.

In the first place, my body is the product of will; it is my
will become phenomenon, my desire-to-be made visible. And.
the objects which I perceive through it are like my body: all
are phenomena, manifestations, products of a will analogous
to mine. The will, the principle of everything that exists, is
sometimes pure, i. e., not connected with an intellect. In this
case it is identical with *irritability*, the mysterious force which
governs the circulation of the blood, the digestion, and the
secretions. Sometimes it is connected with the intellectual
phenomenon; it is conscious, and in this case it is what we
commonly call will and free-will. Will, in this special sense, is
irritability acting knowingly, and according to motives, as,

for example, when I raise my arm. Sometimes, again, our acts are both the result of irritability and motived will: the pupil is contracted when it is excited by too much light; this is the effect of irritability, a *reflex* act; but it is also voluntarily contracted when we will to observe a very small object. The power of conscious will is immense. We may cite the cases of negroes who committed suicide by arresting their respiration. But, whether it be conscious or unconscious, irritability or free activity, and however diverse and innumerable its manifestations may be, will as such is *one*.

Whether it is conscious or not, the will acts in us without interruption. The body and the intellect grow tired and need rest; the will alone is indefatigable; it acts even during sleep and causes dreams. It acts in the body not only during its formation, but exists prior to the body. The will forms and organizes it according to its needs; the will, in the embryo, transforms a part of the cerebral substance into a retina *in order* to receive optical phenomena. The mucous membrane of the thoracic canal is transformed into lungs, because the body *wills* to assimilate the oxygen of the atmosphere. The capillary system produces genital organs, because the individual in process of formation *wills* to propagate the species.

Consider the organization of animals, and you will always find that it conforms to their mode of life. It seems, indeed, at first sight, as though their mode of life, their habits, depended on their organization; in the order of time the organization precedes the mode of life. It seems that the bird flies because it has wings, that the ox butts because it has horns. But intelligent observation shows the contrary. We observe that many animals manifest the will to use organs which they do not yet possess. The goat and the ox butt before they have horns; the wild-boar attacks with that part of his snout where tusks are going to be; he does not, as might be done, fight with his teeth. Hence, the will is the principle of organization, the centre of creative evolution. Wild beasts that *desire* to tear their prey to pieces, to live on plunder and on blood, have teeth and huge claws, strong muscles, piercing eyes (eagles, condors); such, on the other hand, as, by instinct, do not desire to fight, but to seek safety in flight, develop, instead of organs of defense, a fine sense of hearing, slender and agile legs (stags, roe-bucks, gazelles). The bird of the moor, which *desires* to feed on reptiles, has particularly well-developed legs, neck, and beak (stork, pelican); owls *desire* to see in the dark, and so have enormous pupils, soft, silken down, in order not to awaken the animal *desired* for prey. The porcupine, the hedge-hog, and the tortoise cover themselves with a shell, because they do not *desire* to flee. The cuttlefish conceals itself in a brownish liquid; the ai, in order to hide from its enemies, assumes the appearance of a tree-trunk covered with moss. As a rule, especially in the desert, the animal assumes the color which least distinguishes it from the surroundings in which it lives, because it *desires* to escape the pursuit of the hunter. In all these cases, the will, or, more correctly, the will-to-be, the *will-to-exist*, is the principal agent.

Where none of these means suffices, the will provides itself with a still more efficient safeguard, the most efficient of all, *intelligence*, which, in man, supersedes all the others. The intellect is all the more powerful a weapon because it can conceal the will under false appearances, while, in the case of animals, the intent is always manifest and always of a definite character.

The will plays the same part, although this is not so apparent, in the vegetable kingdom. Here, too, everything is *striving, desire, unconscious appetition*. The tree-top, *desiring* light, invariably *tends* to assume a vertical position unless it finds it elsewhere. The root, which *desires* moisture, often seeks for it in the most roundabout manner. The seed planted in the ground will invariably push its stem upward, its roots downward, in whatever position it may be placed. The toadstool performs real feats of strength, wonderful acts of will, breaking through walls, splitting stones, in order to reach the light. Potatoes growing in a cellar infallibly turn their sprouts

to the light. Climbing plants seek supports and make visible
efforts to reach and catch hold of them. Hence, here, as in the
animal kingdom, everything is reduced to will, to that elementary will which we call irritability. There is no essential
difference between irritability and the faculty of being determined by motives; for the motive regularly produces an irritation which sets the will in motion. The plant turns to the sun
by irritation; the animal likewise; only, the animal is endowed with intelligence, and knows what effect the sun produces on the body.

Considering its manifestations, it is hardest to recognize
the will in the two extremes of creation, i. e., on the one hand,
in man, on the other, in the mineral kingdom. Every animal,
every vegetable, has its fixed character; indeed, we can tell
in advance what to expect of it. When we are dealing with a
dog, or a cat, or a fox, we know at once that the dog will be
faithful, the cat treacherous, and the fox cunning. We can
predict with certainty that a cactus *will desire* dry surroundings, and a myosotis moist soil. We know at what time a
particular plant will bud, when it will bloom, and bear fruit.
But in man and in the minerals, at the summit and at the base
of creation, the character is full of mysteries. We cannot
discover it by direct observation, and we can know it only after
prolonged experience. This is a difficult procedure, especially
in the case of man, who can conceal his character, and disguise
the particular tendency of his will. Nevertheless, we find in
man clearly marked tendencies, inclinations, and propensities,
while the mineral kingdom has its constant tendencies also.
The magnetic needle invariably points to the north. Bodies
always fall in a vertical line, and we call this the law of weight
or gravitation. Liquid matter obeys the same law in following
the descending plane. Certain substances invariably expand
under the influence of heat, and contract under the influence
of cold; certain ones form crystals when acted upon by other
substances with which they come in contact. Particularly
in chemistry do we observe striking examples of such constant

wills, sympathies, and antipathies.[1] Moreover, this truth
that the will lies at the basis of all things is instinctively proclaimed in a number of characteristic expressions. Thus we
say: the fire *will* not burn; the water *wants* to get out; iron
desires oxygen. These are not mere figures of speech, but must
be taken literally.

Hence, that which the Eleatics call the One and the All;
Spinoza, substance; Schelling, the absolute; Schopenhauer
calls will. But he denies, with pantheism, that this principle
is a person. He regards will as the unconscious force which
produces specific beings, individuals living in space and in
time. It is that which, not being, strives to be, becomes life,
objectifies itself in individual existence; it is, in a word, the
will-to-be. In itself, will is neither subject to the laws of space
and time, nor capable of being known. But its manifestations
occur in time and in space, which together form the principle
of individuation. At least, the intellect conceives its manifestations as alongside of and following each other.

The phenomena of universal will succeed each other in time
according to uniform laws, and according to the immutable
types which Plato calls Ideas. These ideas or constant forms
in which the will objectifies itself in the same species, form an
ascending scale, from the most elementary being to man.
They are independent of time and of space, eternal and immutable, like the will itself, while individuals *become* and
never *are*. The inferior Ideas, or elementary stages of the
manifestation of will, are: weight, impenetrability, solidity,
fluidity, elasticity, electricity, magnetism, chemism. The
higher stages appear in the organic world, and the series is
completed in man. Inasmuch as the different stages of the
voluntary phenomenon contend with each other for the matter,
space, and time which they need, the *struggle for existence* arises
which characterizes nature. Each organism represents the
idea of which it is the copy, minus the amount of force expended

---

[1] The objection is made that this is equivalent to anthropomorphizing nature;
but if nature produced man, did it not create him in its own image?

to overcome the inferior ideas which oppose it. The more the organism succeeds in overcoming the natural forces constituting the lower stages of life, the more perfect an expression is it of the idea which it represents, and the nearer it comes to what, in the species, is called beauty.

The will is a perpetual desire to be, the never-ending source of the phenomenal world. As long as there is a will, there will be a universe. Individuals come and go, but the will, the desire which produces them, is eternal, like the specific types according to which it produces them. Birth and death do not apply to the will, but only to its manifestations. Our innermost essence, the will, never dies. The religion of the Hindoos, Greeks, and Romans evidently aims to give expression to this truth in the joyful themes, feasts, and dances depicted on its sarcophagi.

Death is not a subject for grief. On the contrary; it is, like birth, the consequence of the universal order. But though the fact that we have in ourselves a part of the universal will, a principle that cannot die, is consoling, because it guarantees us a certain measure of immortality, it is a source of sorrow to those who desire to free themselves from the pains of existence by committing suicide. Since death merely destroys the phenomenon, that is, the body and never the soul, or the universal will, suicide can deliver me from my phenomenal existence only and not from myself.

The will is the endless source of all life, and hence also the origin of all evil. The world which it produces, instead of being the "best possible world," is the worst of all. In spite of what the poets may say, animals are constantly preying upon each other, and we have simply to balance the sufferings of the victims against the pleasures of the victors, to be convinced that the amount of pain exceeds the pleasure. History, in turn, is merely an interminable series of murders, robberies, intrigues, and lies, and if you know one page of it, you know them all. The alleged human virtues, the love of labor, perseverance, temperance, frugality, are nothing but refined

egoism, splendid vices. There is no virtue worthy of the
name except *pity* or sympathy, the principle of Buddhistic
morality, and, Spinoza to the contrary, the basis of all true
morality. All other virtues are grounded on the will-to-live-
and-to-enjoy. And what is the use of this mighty effort, this
merciless, never-ending struggle? Life is its goal, and life is
necessary, irremediable suffering. The more life is perfected,
i. e., advanced in the scale of intelligence, the unhappier it
becomes. Man who is capable of conceiving ideas suffers
infinitely more than the ignorant brute. Laughter and tears
are peculiarly human phenomena.

Since being is synonymous with suffering, positive happiness is an eternal Utopia. Only negative well-being, consisting
in the cessation of suffering, is possible, and this can be realized
only when the will, enlightened as to the inanity of life and its
pleasures by the intelligence, turns against itself, negates
itself, renounces being, life, and enjoyment. This doctrine of
salvation by the *negation of the will* is the common essence of
the Gospel and of Buddhism. Both Christianity and Buddha
hold that man enters the world as a sinner; he is the product
of two blind passions; for marriage, in the opinion of St. Paul,
is merely a concession to those whose will is not strong enough
to conquer itself. The propagation of the species is an evil,—
the feeling of shame proves it, — and it would be better not to
be born than to descend into this world of lust and pain: such
is, according to Schopenhauer, the meaning of the dogma of
original sin and of the miraculous conception of the Savior.
To recognize through the agency of the intellect that everything in our willing is vanity, is what Christianity calls the
effect of grace, whence spring the love of justice, charity towards neighbors, renunciation of self and our desires, finally,
the absolute negation of will (regeneration, conversion, sancti-
fication). Jesus is the type of man who understands his vocation. He sacrifices his body, which is the affirmation of his
will; he stifles the *will-to-be* in himself in order that the Holy
Ghost, i. e., the spirit of renunciation and charity, may take

its place in the world. Furthermore, it must be acknowledged that Catholicism, with its predilection for celibacy, its vows, its fasts, its alms, and other means of fettering the will, has remained more faithful to the spirit of the Gospel than Protestantism. Christianity is true in such of its teachings as are derived from the Aryan Orient, especially in its doctrine of the self-sacrifice of the will and universal charity; but the Jewish elements[1] which it contains are erroneous, particularly its dogma of a personal God, as the creator of the world.

To sum up, Schopenhauer concludes,[2] my philosophy does not presume to explain the ultimate causes of the world; nay, it confines itself to the facts of inner and outer experience, which are accessible to everybody, and points out the true and intimate connection existing between these facts, without, however, concerning itself with that which may transcend them. It refrains from drawing any conclusions concerning what lies beyond experience; it merely explains the data of sensibility and self-consciousness, and strives to understand only the *immanent* essence of the world. It is, in this respect, purely Kantian. Consequently, it leaves many questions unanswered, particularly the question, Why are the facts of experience just what they are and not different? All such questions, however, are transcendent, i. e., they cannot be explained by the forms and functions of our intellect. The intellect bears the same relation to them as our sensibility bears to such qualities of bodies as we have not the sense-organs to perceive. The mind is fatally dependent on the law of causality, and understands only what is subject to this law. The dogmatic metaphysicians and transcendentalists who keep on asking *why* and *whence*, forget that *why* means *by what cause*,

---

[1] Schopenhauer's antipathy to the Jews and Judaism is only equalled by his hatred of Hegel and "the professors of philosophy." His attitude is consistent with his Buddhistic principle of "renunciation," which constitutes the essence of morality. Israel seems to be more determined than any other race *not to renounce* existence; it is, therefore, in the eyes of our philosopher, the most "immoral" of peoples.

[2] *Die Welt als Wille und Vorstellung*, II, chap. L.

that there are no causes and effects outside of time-succession, and that, therefore, the *why* has no meaning in the sphere to which the forms of time and space cannot be applied, i. e., in the sphere of the transcendent, where there is no before or after. Everywhere the intellect strikes against insoluble problems, as against the walls of a prison-house. The essence of things not only transcends our knowledge, but, most probably, knowledge in general; it is both unintelligible and unintelligent,[1] and intelligence is but a form, an addition, an accident. With the Eleatics, Scotus Erigena, Bruno, Spinoza, and Schelling, I accept the one and the all, the doctrine of the unitary essence of all beings; only I am careful not to add: all is god, and so I differ essentially from the pantheists. The god of the pantheists is an *x*, an unknown quantity by means of which they aim to explain the known; my "will," on the other hand, is a fact of experience; I proceed, as all true science must proceed, from the known to the unknown. My method is empirical, analytic, inductive; that of the pantheistic metaphysicians, synthetic and deductive. Pantheism is synonymous with optimism; in my system, however, the evil in the world is frankly conceded and its significance fully recognized. In this respect, my system differs from most ancient and modern philosophies, especially from Spinoza, Leibniz, and Hegel. It is to Spinoza what the New Testament is to the Old.

Schopenhauer, therefore, offers us an *empirical metaphysics*, and because he stands on the ground of experience he is the first to call that which "constitutes the basis of being and its substance"[2] by its right name: *Will*. That is what constitutes his originality, his merit, the secret of his success in contemporary Germany, which has been surfeited with a-priorism. His philosophy reunited elements which but recently seemed forever irreconcilable: experience and specula-

[1] There is no difference here between Schopenhauer and materialism.

[2] Ch. Secrétan (*Revue philosophique*, VII, 3). True, the term is found in his predecessors, especially in Fichte and Schelling, but Schopenhauer gives it its final sanction as a technical term.

tion, realism and idealism, positivism and metaphysics. It is speculative, for it rises to the universal, and it is empirical, because it arrives at it by induction. It is an ontology, for it has for its object the essence, and, if we may venture to say so, the secret, of things, and it is positive, since it rests on the solid basis of facts. It is realistic because of the extreme concessions it makes to materialism; it is idealistic and critical in that it denies the absolute reality of the phenomenal world, and makes it depend entirely on our intellectual organization. It gives promise of the future reconciliation of metaphysics and science, and hence its disciples are willing to condone its theory of ideas, borrowed from Plato and contrary to the essentially nominalistic natural-science of the times; its extreme pessimism, which, though unquestionably superior to the self-satisfied optimism of Leibniz, rests on an imperfect knowledge of human nature, and evidently exaggerates the import of our personal experiences; and finally, the extreme bitterness of its diatribes against Fichte, Schelling, and Hegel, from whom, in spite of its protests, it derives the monistic idea, and whose chief wrong really consisted in having been professors of philosophy.

FOURTH PERIOD[1]

THE DEVELOPMENT OF EUROPEAN AND AMERICAN PHILOSOPHY SINCE 1860[2]

§ 69. The State of Philosophy in 1860

Schopenhauer, the last representative of the great metaphysical movement inspired directly by the critical philosophy of Kant, died in 1860. A cross-section of European and American philosophy in the years immediately before and after this date reveals both the diversity and diffusion of the post-Kantian metaphysics itself, and the rise of the great rival movement which was to dispute its control during the latter half of the nineteenth century.

The metaphysical impulse communicated by Kant took two forms. In his recognition of the thing-in-itself behind appearances, in his provision under the form of faith for God, freedom and immortality, and in his qualified assent to a purposive and æsthetic interpretation of nature, he encouraged the revival of a *spiritualistic realism* after the manner of Leibniz. In his doctrine of the organizing and creative activity of the knowing mind, through its forms of sensibility, its categories of understanding and its ideals of reason, he founded modern *idealism*. Each of these forms of post-Kantian metaphysics proved capable of great diversification in the course of their later history both in Germany and abroad. The rival movement

[1] The remainder of the text, unless otherwise indicated, is added or rewritten by the present Editor.

[2] Cf. H. Höffding, *History of Modern Philosophy*, English translation, 1908, vol. II (European philosophy from Kant to 1880); W. Moog, *Die Deutsche Philosophie des 20. Jahrhunderts*, 1922 (recent German philosophy); H. K. Schjelderup, *Hauptlinien der Entwicklung der Philosophie von Mitte des 19. Jahrhunderts bis zur Gegenwart*, 1920 (European and American philosophy from 1860 through James); D. Parodi, *La Philosophie Contemporaine en France*, 1920 (French philosophy from 1860 to the present); A. K. Rogers, *English and American Philosophy since 1800*, 1923; R. Piccoli, *Benedetto Croce*, 1922 (recent Italian philosophy).

was *naturalism*, or the philosophy inspired by the progress of the physical sciences. This influence of science on philosophy took two forms, according as attention was directed to the content of science or to its form. *Materialism* adapted the content of physics to the purposes of metaphysics, or employed particular scientific theories, such as the conservation of matter and force, or evolution, as an account of reality. *Positivism*, on the other hand, held that science alone provided knowledge. This unique cognitive success of science was attributed by some to its dealing with the facts of experience, and by others to its experimental technique and manner of formulating laws. The first of these interpretations of scientific knowledge furnished the motive of *empirical* positivism, and was peculiarly congenial to the tradition of English thought; the second constituted the motive of *methodological* positivism and was relatively characteristic of Germany and France. Naturalism of both varieties turned human hope and aspiration away from the supernatural world and focussed them upon man and *society*. Hence the growth of naturalism was accompanied by the scientific study of society (sociology), and by the formulation of programs of social reform.

Turning to the state of German philosophy in or about the year 1860, its most notable characteristic was undoubtedly the rise of naturalism. This was in part a development within the reigning metaphysical schools. The internal controversy among the Hegelians arose from the general prominence at this time of the issue between philosophy and established religion. DAVID STRAUSS,[1] the leader of the "left" or liberal wing of the Hegelian school, reduced the orthodox dogmas to myths, and contended that the only religion consistent with a strict interpretation of Hegel's teachings was a naturalistic pan-

---

[1] In his famous *Leben Jesu* (1835). His most important later writings were *Die christliche Glaubenslehre* (1840–1841), and *Der alte und der neue Glaube* (1872). He has an important place in the history of the philosophy of religion and of biblical criticism.

theism. LUDWIG FEUERBACH[1] contended that in view of Hegel's rejection of creation, providence, immortality, and free-will, it could not be justly claimed that he gave philosophical support to popular spiritualism and religious orthodoxy. As his thought developed Feuerbach identified himself closely with the scientific view of the world, and construed religion as only the imaginative projection of human needs and hopes.[2] This tendency of naturalism to substitute human and social for supernatural values is most conspicuously represented among Hegelians by KARL MARX,[3] whose famous book on *Capital* (*Das Kapital*) was published in 1867, and became the bible of modern socialism. Marx adopted Hegel's historical method and his emphasis on dialectic, construing the former in terms of economic development and the latter in terms of class conflict.

Strauss, Feuerbach, and Marx illustrate the materialistic trend, toward 1860, of Hegelianism, the greatest of the post-Kantian metaphysical schools. But there was also a strong naturalistic motive in Kant himself which had been overruled by his idealistic followers, and which was now revived. Although Kant gave no encouragement to materialism, his *Critique of Pure Reason*, strictly construed, and separated from the *Critique of Practical Reason* and the *Critique of Judgment*, could be cited as an indorsement of positivism; since it set forth the view that science alone fulfils the requirements of knowledge, as uniting the forms of intuition and the cate-

---

[1] 1804–1872. The greatest of his works is the *Wesen des Christenthums*, 1841. His *Grundsätze der Philosophie der Zukunft* appeared in 1843, the *Theogonie* in 1857, and the *Gott, Freiheit und Unsterblichkeit* in 1866.

The other important representatives of this group were Arnold Ruge (1802–1880) and Bruno Bauer (1809–1882). The extreme development of Feuerbach's anthropological ethics and religion is represented by the revolutionary individualism of Caspar Schmidt (1806–1856), commonly known under his pseudonym of Max Stirner. His *Der Einzige und sein Eigenthum* (1845) has had great popular vogue.

[2] Feuerbach was the author of the famous dictum, cited at this time as the quintessence of the crassest materialism, that "man is what he eats" (*Man ist was er isst*).

[3] 1818–1883.

gories of the understanding with the data of experience. Hence, in the 1860's, German positivism, as represented by Albert Lange and OTTO LIEBMANN, adopted the shibboleth "Back to Kant," [1] and appealed to the master against his disciples. These thinkers regarded Kant as untrue to his own insight in so far as by his recognition of the thing-in-itself he encouraged the revival of dogmatic metaphysics, and they proposed to limit philosophy to the critical examination of the presuppositions of science. They thus furnished a connecting link between a positivistic naturalism, and the strict Kantianism which came to be known as *Neo-criticism* or *critical idealism*.[2]

But while German naturalism may be said to have sprung in part from within the Kantian movement itself, it received its chief impetus at this time from the achievements of science. Although naturalism is inspired by science, it undertakes to satisfy the philosophical demand for a comprehensive view of the world, and is therefore influenced by the *generalizations* of science, rather than by its particular items. Modern naturalism had up to this time appealed mainly in the *mechanical theory* originated by Galileo and perfected by Newton. But in the middle of the nineteenth century the most impressive scientific generalization was that of *conservation*, or the quantitative constancy of both matter and force (or energy) in all their diverse qualitative manifestations. The principle of the conservation of matter had been established by LAVOISIER, the founder of modern chemistry.[3] The principle of the conservation of energy was not generally accepted until the year 1860, as a result of the work of MAYER, JOULE, and HELM-

---

[1] This exhortation (*Also muss auf Kant zurückgegangen werden!*) appeared at the close of each chapter of Liebmann's *Kant und die Epigonen* (1865). Liebmann was born in 1840 and died in 1912. Lange (§ 72) published his important *History of Materialism* in 1866. With the name of Lange should be associated that of Eugen Dühring (1833–1921), whose *Natürliche Dialektik* appeared in 1865.

[2] § 79.

[3] Antoine Laurent Lavoisier (1743–1794) was a Frenchman and a victim of the Revolution.

HOLZ.[1] The combination of these two principles suggested a new type of philosophical monism, in which nature was regarded as a fixed amount of energized matter proceeding in a ceaseless and circular round of change. Life and mind were regarded as parts of this closed system, the organism being one of the forms assumed by matter, and consciousness one of the forms assumed by energy. The most important exposition of this thesis was contained in MOLESCHOTT'S *Circulation of Life* (*Der Kreislauf des Lebens*), published in 1852, and it acquired great popular vogue through BÜCHNER'S *Force and Matter* (*Kraft und Stoff*), of which sixteen editions appeared in Germany between 1855 and 1889.[2] The bitter controversy to which this movement gave rise was due to its uncompromising denial both of Christian orthodoxy and of common-sense spiritualism.[3]

The counterclaims of spiritualism were championed in Germany at this time by the "right" wing of the Hegelian School, and by the so-called "semi-Hegelians" who sought to correct Hegel and to develop a philosophical basis for theism.[4] But it

[1] Julius Robert Mayer (1814–1874) announced his conclusions in 1842. In his *Die organische Bewegung in ihrem Zusammenhange mit dem Stoffwechsel* (1845) he combined the principle of the conservation of energy with that of matter, in their application to vital processes. James Prescott Joule (1818–1889), an Englishman, announced his conclusions in 1843. Hermann L. F. von Helmholz (1821–1895) published his *Über die Erhaltung der Kraft* in 1847. These scientists together with the Danish physicist Colding and the German physicist Mohr appear to have reached their conclusions independently, and their rival claims to priority are still a matter of controversy. The English physicist based his conclusions on experimental research, while the Continental physicists were more influenced by general philosophical considerations, such as the axiom of the equality of cause and effect (*causa æquat effectum*). The new principle must also be viewed as the logical outcome of earlier developments in physics. It is peculiarly an idea of the *times*, rather than of any single individual.

[2] Jacob Moleschott (1822–1893); Louis Büchner (1824–1899). Other leading members of this school were Karl Vogt (1817–1895) and Heinrich Czolbe (1819–1873). Ernst Haeckel (§ 70) continued this tradition, but was distinguished as belonging to a later period by the shift of emphasis from the principle of conservation to that of evolution, resulting from the influence of Darwin.

[3] As illustrated, for example, by Moleschott's famous saying: "No phosphorus, no thought" (*Ohne Phosphor kein Gedanke*).

[4] To this latter group belonged Christian Hermann WEISSE (1801–1866), Karl Philipp Fischer (1807–1885), and Immanuel Hermann Fichte (1797–1879).

is a striking fact that the great leaders of the anti-naturalistic movement did not draw their inspiration mainly from Kantian idealism. They were not primarily concerned with the ideality of nature, or its dependence on mind through the act of knowledge, but rather with the immanence of mind *in* nature. They were, in short, spiritual realists, who revived the Aristotelian and Leibnizian tradition. They were alienated even from Schopenhauer and Schelling, because, having felt the influence of science, they could not be wholly in sympathy with the romantic and *a priori* method of dealing with nature. Fechner, whose *Zenda Vesta* appeared in 1851, and Lotze, whose *Microcosmos* appeared in 1856, were not only spiritualistic in their metaphysics, but were among the founders of experimental and physiological psychology. The third of the great representatives of this movement[1] was von Hartmann, whose *Philosophy of the Unconscious (Philosophie des Unbewussten)* was published in 1869.

The currents of thought which were characteristic of German philosophy in 1860 were reproduced in Italy, France, England, and America. In these countries as well as in Germany, one finds two major and conflicting tendencies, on the one hand naturalism, either materialistic or positivistic, and on the other hand the anti-naturalistic movement inclining either to idealism or to a spiritualistic realism.

Italian thought, outside of orthodox Catholicism, was dominated at the opening of the century by the sensationalism and naturalism of the French Revolution. Later influences of the same type were received from Comte, and stimulated the work of ARDIGÒ, the leader of Italian positivism.[2]

Italian spiritualism and idealism was represented towards

---

[1] § 74.

[2] Roberto Ardigò, 1828–1918. His *La Psigologia come Scienza positiva* appeared in 1871. Giuseppe Ferrari (1811–1876) and Ausonio Franchi (1821–1895) represent the critical and sceptical reaction against both Catholic orthodoxy and the spiritualistic metaphysics.

the middle of the century by ROSMINI and GIOBERTI,[1] who were churchmen and patriots as well as philosophers; and sought, on the one hand, to reconcile Catholicism with modern philosophy by emphasizing the Platonic-idealistic element in Christian thought, and on the other hand, to give a philosophical and spiritual meaning to Italian national aspirations. They borrowed something of the letter of Kantianism and some of the extravagances of romanticism, but the critical spirit was inconsistent with the theological and dogmatic tradition which as yet dominated Italian thought. As after 1848 the nationalistic movement became increasingly secular and anti-traditional, Italian thought became more receptive to the German, and in particular to the Hegelian, influence. This influence was spread after 1860 by the teaching of VERA and SPAVENTA at Naples.[2]

The philosophical situation in France in 1860 differed profoundly from that of Germany owing to the fact that naturalism, so remarkably developed in the closing decades of the eighteenth century, was here the indigenous and established, rather than the innovating, tendency. The naturalism of the Revolutionary period[3] had been carried over into the nineteenth century in two forms. The so-called "idealogues," represented by DESTUTT DE TRACY,[4] continued to psychologize concerning the origin of ideas after the manner of Condillac and Cabanis. SAINT-SIMON,[5] on the other hand, gave his

---

[1] Antonio Rosmini-Serbati (1797–1855); Vincenzo Gioberti (1801–1852) These are the first Italian philosophers of importance after Vico (cf. p. 235). Pasquale Gallupi (1770–1846), who slightly preceded them, was influenced by the Scottish school, and in particular by Reid. Their successor was Terenzio Mamiani, a Christian Platonist like themselves, but more free from the influence of dogma and authority.

[2] Augusto Vera (1813–1885) was primarily a translator and expositor of Hegel: cf. his *l'Hégélianisme et la Philosophie*, 1861. Bertrando Spaventa (1817–1883) attempted to free Hegelianism from the odium of a foreign importation and to assimilate it to the Italian tradition; cf. his *La Filosofia di Gioberti*, 1863.

[3] Cf. above, pp. 326–338.

[4] 1754–1836. *Œuvres Complètes*, 1824.

[5] Claude Henri de Rouvroy, Comte de Saint-Simon, 1760–1825, *Œuvres Choisis*, 1859–1861. With Charles Fourier (1772–1837), Pierre Joseph Prou-

attention to a naturalistic philosophy of history, to the classification of the sciences, and to social reform. From these sources sprang the French positivistic system of Auguste Comte.[1] This great philosopher had himself passed from the scene in 1857, but his influence, as manifested in LITTRÉ, TAINE, and RENAN,[2] was paramount at the time of the Second Empire in secular and unofficial circles, and has maintained itself steadily down to the present date.

This naturalistic tendency within philosophy proper was reinforced, as in other countries, by the influence of science. Cuvier and Laplace had given France a position of ascendency in science at the opening of the century. The eminent physicist AMPÈRE laid the foundations of modern electromagnetism in 1820,[3] and in the 1860's BERNARD, BERTHELOT, and PASTEUR were continuing this brilliant tradition.[4] But the devotion of French science to the experimental and mathematical method,

dhon (1809–1865), and the Englishman Robert Owen (1771–1858) he belongs to the group of "utopian" or "humanitarian" socialists, with which the history of modern socialism begins.

[1] § 71.

[2] Maximilien Paul Émile Littré (1801–1881) was an expositor of Comte, though a dissenter from the strict Comtean orthodoxy. Hippolyte Adolphe Taine (1828–1893; Les Philosophes français au XIX Siècle, 1857; De l'Intelligence, 1870) and Ernest Renan (1823–1892; L'Avenir de Science, written in 1848, but not published until 1890) were versatile and widely influential thinkers, who developed away from their earlier positivistic position. Taine was a historian and critic of literature and art, while Renan (like his contemporary David Strauss) was one of the founders of modern biblical criticism. To these names should be added that of Étienne VACHEROT (1809–1897), who emphasized the gulf between the reality revealed in science and the ideal conceived and pursued by man. He was closely related to the "left" of the Hegelian group.

[3] André Marie Ampère (1775–1836) is characteristic of the close relation between French science and philosophy in the nineteenth century. Ampère was an intimate associate of the "Idealogues" and of Maine de Biran, and wrote himself both acutely and voluminously on the origin of ideas and theory of knowledge.

[4] Claude Bernard (1813–1878) and Louis Pasteur (1822–1895) were biologists and physiologists. Pierre Eugène Marcellin Berthelot (1827–1907) was one of the founders of modern physical chemistry. The influence of Lamarck (1744–1829) did not make itself felt in French philosophy until the principles of evolution had been given prominence by Darwin and Spencer. Comte and his followers, holding to the discontinuity of nature, rejected the Lamarckian theory of the development of species.

together with the pervasive spirit of positivism, prevented the
appearance in France of the dogmatic materialism which
characterized this period in Germany.

Turning to spiritualism and idealism, the extreme reaction,
in the name of religious faith and authority, to the excesses of
the Revolution, had run its course;[1] and had been superseded
by the official and academic philosophy of Cousin, whose
famous lectures on *The True, the Beautiful, and the Good* had
created a furore in 1818, and who reached the height of his
power in the middle of the century. His philosophy was an
eclectic spiritualism, derived in part from Scotch realism,[2] in
part from Schelling and Hegel, and in part from earlier seventeenth and eighteenth century sources.[3] To Cousin was also
due the rediscovery of Maine de Biran,[4] who had exercised
little influence during his life (1766–1824), but now assumed
a position of steadily growing importance in French thought.

As the school of Cousin lost prestige it was superseded in
the 1860's by two new movements. The first of these was
identified with the name of Renouvier,[5] who began the publication of his *Essais de Critique Générale* in 1854, and who, like
his German contemporary Lotze, represented not only the
Kantian and spiritualistic motives, but the influence of science
as well.[6] The second of the new movements was inaugurated
by Ravaisson[7] and in particular by his famous *Report on
Philosophy in France* (*Rapport sur la Philosophie en France au
XIX* *Siècle*), prepared in 1867. This work was a résumé

[1] The most important philosophical representatives of this reactionary tendency were Joseph de MAISTRE (1754–1821) and Louis Gabriel Ambroise de
BONALD (1754–1840).

[2] Through Roger Collard, who introduced Reid in his lectures at the Sorbonne, 1811–1814. Cf. § 75.

[3] Other members of this so-called "Eclectic School" were Théodore Simon
JOUFFROY (1796–1842) and Paul JANET (1823–1899).

[4] § 75. [5] § 76.

[6] A similar position is occupied by the mathematician Antoine Augustin
COURNOT (1801–1877), who like Renouvier approached philosophy through an
examination of the limits of science, but stood closer to Comte. Cf. his *Essai
sur les Fondements de nos Connaissances*, 1851, and *Traité de l'Enchainement des
Idées fondamentales*, 1861.

[7] § 75.

and critique of the past, in which the author rejected both positivism and eclecticism; and also an appeal for a new spiritualism, which should be both rigorous in its methods and boldly metaphysical in its results.

Turning to the state of British philosophy in 1860, we find the naturalistic tendency broadly represented by BUCKLE, whose famous *History of Civilization*,[1] founded on the premise of inflexible natural law, was an attempt to interpret history in terms of the physical environment, and progress in terms of the advancement of science. The positivistic movement in Great Britain was represented in 1860 most notably by the positivism of John Stuart Mill, who, following his father, JAMES MILL,[2] continued the empirical tradition of the eighteenth century, and was at the same time related to Comte. Other representatives of this empirical type of positivism were the psychologist and moralist Alexander BAIN,[3] and George Henry LEWES, who interested himself especially in the problem of the relations of mind and body, and who, like J. S. Mill, was influenced by Comte.[4] Somewhat later CLIFFORD,[5] beginning as a zealous and uncompromising advocate of the scientific method, sought in *panpsychism* a method of construing physical nature in terms of experience and thus of overcoming the dualism of mind and matter.

From the side of science the greatest stimulus to naturalism in England came from the new conception of evolution. If the discoveries of physics were not philosophically fruitful in England at this time it was not for lack of eminent men. DAVY,

[1] Henry Thomas Buckle, 1821–1862. The *History of Civilization* was published in 1857 and 1861.

[2] 1773–1836. He is known as one of the founders of the "associationist" school in psychology (*Analysis of the Phenomena of the Human Mind*, 1829), and as, after Bentham, the leader of the "utilitarian" school in ethics. Cf. § 71.

[3] 1818–1903: *The Senses and the Intellect*, 1855; *The Emotions and the Will*, 1859.

[4] 1817–1878. *Comte's Philosophy of the Positive Sciences*, 1853; *Problems of Life and Mind*, 1874–1879.

[5] William Kingdon Clifford, 1845–1879: *Lectures and Essays*, 1879.

FARADAY, KELVIN, and MAXWELL,[1] as well as Joule, stood in the foremost ranks of science, and contributed largely to that unified view of nature as a physico-chemical system which had excited the speculative imagination of the German materialists. But whether because of the anti-metaphysical temper of British thought, or because the conception of evolution appealed more strongly to the spirit of the age and touched human interests more nearly, in any case, the influence of physics was at the time almost wholly eclipsed by that of the biological sciences as represented by Darwin and Spencer.[2] The former's epoch-making work on the *Origin of Species* appeared in 1859. Spencer, to be sure, made much of the principle of the conservation of force and matter, as well as of the results of the new geology,[3] but his own scientific competence lay within the field of the biological and social sciences, and his final synthesis, formulated in 1862 in his *First Principles*, was a law of evolution. In the controversy which the theory of evolution at once precipitated, the most redoubtable controversial champion was HUXLEY,[4] who not only played an important part in the dissemination of the theory, but sought to work out its philosophical presuppositions and moral applications. Associated in the same cause was TYNDALL, and afterwards ROMANES,[5] who devoted himself to a study of the evolution of mind, and hoped to reconcile Darwinism with religion.

The indigenous spiritualistic movement of the Scotch real-

---

[1] Sir Humphry Davy, 1778–1829; Michael Faraday, 1791–1867; Lord Kelvin (William Thomson), 1824–1907; James Clerk Maxwell, 1831–1879.

[2] § 70.

[3] The so-called "uniformitarian" geology, founded on the work of the mineralogist James Hutton (1726–1797), and developed at this time by Sir Charles Lyell (1797–1875).

[4] Cf. his famous essay on *Man's Place in Nature*, 1863; and his volume on *Hume*, 1878. Thomas Henry Huxley was born in 1825 and died in 1895.

[5] John Tyndall, 1820–1893: *Fragments of Science*, 1871. George John Romanes, 1848–1894: *A Candid Examination of Theism*, 1878; *Mental Evolution in Man*, 1888. Alfred Russel Wallace (1823–1913) arrived independently at conclusions similar to Darwin's in 1858.

ists, provoked by the sceptical conclusions of Hume,[1] was brought to a close by Sir William HAMILTON and Henry MANSEL,[2] who argued the relativity of all knowledge and hence the impossibility of knowing the "unconditioned"; and who, having thus disposed of every rationalistic metaphysics (including naturalism), defended a spiritualistic and religious belief founded on analogy and faith. The negative or agnostic portion of their thought was absorbed by Spencer; while their qualified support of spiritualistic and religious belief was rapidly superseded by the rising influence of the Kantian and post-Kantian thought, for whose introduction into England Hamilton was himself partly responsible, and against which his polemic had been largely directed. This new and transforming influence had already permeated literature and popular thought through the medium of COLERIDGE and CARLYLE.[3] It now established itself in academic and scholarly circles through STIRLING'S[4] Secret of Hegel, which appeared in 1865, and marks the beginning of the idealistic movement which, through Caird, Green, Bradley, and others, came to dominate English philosophy at the close of the century.[5]

America produced no eminent representatives of the naturalistic movement during the nineteenth century, but was influenced by contemporary English thought, as well as, to a

---

[1] Cf. above, pp. 350–352.

[2] Hamilton was born in 1788, and died in 1856. His Discussions on Philosophy and Literature were published in 1852, and his Lectures on Metaphysics (posthumously) in 1859. Henry Longueville Mansel (1820–1871) is chiefly famous for his lectures on the Limits of Religious Thought, delivered and published in 1858.

[3] In particular through Coleridge's Aids to Reflection, published in 1825, in which the author invokes the Kantian conception of an intuitive "reason" to escape the metaphysical shortcomings of the "understanding." Samuel Taylor Coleridge was born in 1772, and died in 1834. Thomas Carlyle (1795–1881) was the great English apostle of romanticism, deriving his inspiration mainly from Fichte and Goethe. His Sartor Resartus appeared in 1833, his French Revolution in 1837, and in 1860 he was at work on his History of Frederick II.

[4] James Hutchinson Stirling (1820–1909).   [5] § 77.

lesser degree, by Comte. Mill was widely read, as Locke had
been in the previous century, and his leadership was followed
in circles of economic and political liberalism. Here, as in
England, the scientific conception that most affected philosophical thinking was that of evolution.[1] The publication of
Darwin's *Origin of Species* precipitated in America in 1860 a
lively controversy both among scientists themselves and
between the party of science and the party of religion. AGAS-
SIZ, an eminent biologist and geologist, and a distinguished
exponent of the spirit and method of science, resisted the
Darwinian teachings, and defended both the immutability of
species and the older hierarchical philosophy of nature.[2] The
principal champion of Darwin was the botanist Asa GRAY.[3]
These first American Darwinians did not find evolution to be
in conflict with the traditional religious view of the world; but
the teaching of Darwin, combined with that of Spencer,
whose works were read in America almost as promptly and as
widely as in England, exerted a powerful and growing influence
in the direction of naturalism, and soon gave rise to an evolutionary philosophical cult, of which the most conspicuous
leader was John FISKE.[4]

---

[1] The most eminent representative in America at this time of the new physics
was Joseph HENRY (1797–1878). As Secretary of the Smithsonian Institute,
and as first president of the National Academy of Sciences, founded in 1863, he
accomplished much for the development of experimental science and of tech-
nology in America, but this movement appears to have exerted little or no influence in the direction of positivism or materialism. Josiah Willard GIBBS
(1839–1903), one of the founders of physical chemistry, and perhaps the greatest of American scientists, was scarcely known outside the circle of his col-
laborators. The general standpoint of naturalism, especially in its opposition
to religion, was represented by John William Draper (1811–1882) in his *History
of the Intellectual Development of Europe* (1862) and his *Conflict between Religion
and Science* (1874).

[2] Jean Louis Rodolphe Agassiz (1807–1873) had originally derived his zoölogi-
cal principles from Cuvier and his philosophy of nature from the teachings of
Schelling. His chief disciple in America was Joseph Le Conte (1823–1901), whose
Evolution, its Evidences and its Relation to Religious Thought appeared in 1891.

[3] 1810–1888; afterwards supported by the geologist James Dwight Dana
(1813–1895).

[4] 1842–1901. Fiske lectured on "The Positive Philosophy" in 1869; and
published his *Outline of Cosmic Philosophy* in 1874.

The academic philosophy of the time, providing a rational ground for the Protestant faith, was the Scottish realism, introduced in earlier days by WITHERSPOON, and now represented by McCOSH and PORTER.[1] The Scottish realism was not without a tincture of Kantianism, but this latter current came mainly, as in England, from two sources and in two successive waves. EMERSON[2] was at this time in the full vigor of his genius. While drawing inspiration from many sources, his "transcendentalism" was influenced largely by Coleridge's *Aids to Reflection*, and thus indirectly by Schelling. Like Coleridge and Carlyle in England, Emerson and the Transcendentalists represented post-Kantian thought in its romantic form and in its literary and popular manifestations. Transcendentalism was also linked with Scottish realism through the influence of Cousin, whose works were translated and widely read in the second quarter of the century. The second wave of Kantian influence came in America, as in England, in the form of the introduction of Hegel. The study and translation of this philosopher, inaugurated in 1867 by HARRIS,[3] marked the beginning in America of the idealistic movement, which numbered Howison and Royce among its more conspicuous leaders, and which rapidly rose to a position of ascendency in the second half of the nineteenth century.[4]

[1] John Witherspoon (1723–1794) came from Scotland in 1768 to be president of the College of New Jersey (now Princeton University). James McCosh (1811–1894), a pupil of Hamilton, came from Scotland to the same institution just one hundred years later. Noah Porter (1811–1892) was president of Yale College from 1871 to 1886.

[2] Ralph Waldo Emerson (1803–1882). *The Conduct of Life* appeared in 1860, the *Essays* having been published in 1842.

[3] William Torrey Harris (1835–1909) founded in 1867 the *Journal of Speculative Philosophy* and was the leader of the so-called "St. Louis School." Owing to the influence upon Harris of a German pioneer named H. C. Brockmeyer, this movement may be said to have been in part a direct importation from Germany to the American Middle West.

[4] § 78.

A. Naturalism, Materialism, and Positivism

§ 70. The Philosophy of Evolution. Darwin. Spencer. Haeckel. Ostwald

Just after the middle of the nineteenth century naturalism recovered an influence upon European thought similar to that which it had possessed at the close of the eighteenth century.[1] It assumed both the *positivistic* form of the cult of scientific empiricism and technique, and also the *materialistic* form of the scientific view of the universe. It is the naturalism of this latter or materialistic type to which we now turn.

Materialism attempted so to extend and unify the physical sciences as to provide for those conscious, moral, and spiritual aspects of life which were commonly supposed to transcend science.[2] Its alliance with political and religious radicalism gained for it the sympathies of the public, and it received support from a number of recent discoveries and scientific theories. It appealed to the transformistic theory of Lamarck[3] and Charles Darwin against the miracle of creation; to the anatomical study of anthropoid apes, against the view that there is an insurpassable gulf between animals and man, matter and mind;[4] to the advance of chemical synthesis, against the phantom of the *vital principle;*[5] to the theory of the equivalence and transformation of forces[6] and electrological discoveries,[7] against the hypothesis of a separate force for the explanation of thought; to the geological theory of gradual evolutions and imperceptible changes,[8] against the theory of cataclysms,[9] behind which, according to materialism, lurks the belief in the arbitrary intervention of a supernatural

---

[1] Cf. § 60.

[2] The following account of Darwin up to page 480 is taken from the original text of the English translation of Weber, save for minor verbal and bibliographical changes.

[3] Jean Baptiste Pierre Antoine de Monet, Chevalier de Lamarck, 1744–1829; *Philosophie zoologique,* 1809.

[4] T. H. Huxley, *Man's Place in Nature,* 1863.

[5] R. Virchow, 1821–1902.   [6] Cf. § 69.

[7] E. Du Bois-Reymond, 1818–1896.

[8] C. Lyell, *Principles of Geology,* 1830.   [9] Georges Cuvier, 1769–1832.

power; finally, to the many conclusive facts which prove, beyond the shadow of a doubt, that a relation exists between the
brain and thought, against the spiritualistic distinction between soul and body.

Of all these innovations, the Darwinian theory is the one
which materialism appropriated most readily, and to which
it is most indebted. This theory answers the following cardinal
question, which had remained unsolved until the days of Darwin: How can the purposiveness which is revealed in the
structure and arrangement of our organs be produced without
the intervention of an intelligent creative cause, and through
the purely mechanical action of unconscious forces? or, rather:
How can we explain finality [purposiveness, teleology] without
final causes? Darwinism provides materialism with a satisfactory answer to the main objection of theistic spiritualism,
and thereby becomes its indispensable ally. So close is this
alliance that Darwinism and materialism have been regarded
as synonymous terms.

Ever since the eighteenth century two systems have been
opposing each other.[1] According to the one, which rests on the
supposed immutability of species, every animal and vegetable
species has been created independently of all its congeners
(the *creationism* of Linnæus and Cuvier); according to the
other, whose principles were formulated by Diderot and Robinet, species are merely varieties, more pronounced and more
stable than the forms which we commonly call varieties, and
descend from each other by generation (*transformism*, or *evolutionism*). The theory of transformation opposes to the *dogma*
of the immutability of species the *fact* of their variability. The
parent form and its offspring always resemble each other; they
are never identical. That is to say, there are differences
between them. Moreover, — and that is important, — these
differences may be transmitted by heredity. But how and
by what causes are these endless variations and progressive
metamorphoses produced? How and by what causes could

[1] See § 60.

the tiger and the gazelle, the mouse and the elephant, spring from one and the same source? According to Lamarck and Geoffroy Saint-Hilaire, this is explained by the influence of the environment upon the organism, and by the gradual adaptation of the organism to its conditions of existence. This explanation, which sufficed for a certain number of cases, but left a still larger number unexplained, was completed by Charles Darwin, the most celebrated naturalist of the last century, in his monumental work: *On the Origin of Species by Means of Natural Selection.*

Darwin was born in Shrewsbury, England, in 1809. Led by his scientific interests to join the *Beagle* in its voyage around the world (1831–1836), he became interested in a comparative study of flora and fauna, in relation to their environment. Led by these early observations to conjecture that the correspondence of life to its environment could be explained only by supposing the environment itself to exercise a selective rôle by determining survival, he devoted himself, until his death in 1882, to the patient accumulation of evidence in support of this hypothesis. His eminence was due not less to the rigor of his method than to the fruitfulness of his idea. In addition to that named above, which was published in 1859, his most important works were: *Variation of Plants and Animals under Domestication*, 1868; *Descent of Man*, 1871; *Expressions of Emotions in Man and in Animals*, 1872.[1]

The transformation of organized beings and the diversity of their specific types is, according to Darwin, brought about by the natural *competition* between them, by the *struggle for life*.[2] This struggle for existence results in a *selection* wholly

---

[1] Cf. also: Francis Darwin, *Life and Letters of Charles Darwin*, 1887; E. Haeckel, *Natural History of Creation*, 1875; Oscar Schmidt, *The Doctrine of Descent and Darwinism (International Scientific Series)*; T. Huxley, *Man's Place in Nature*, 1863; same author, *Lectures on the Origin of Species*, 1892; H. Spencer, *Principles of Biology*, 1863–1867; A. R. Wallace, *Darwinism*, 1889; G. Romanes, *Darwin and after Darwin:* I, *The Darwinian Theory*, 1892; II, *Post-Darwinian Questions* (edited by Lloyd Morgan), 1895.

[2] Darwin's attention was attracted to the tendency and the effects of over-

similar to the artificial selection by means of which the horti-
culturist and breeder obtain their varieties. What, for instance, does the breeder of pigeons do?[1] He observes that one
of his pigeons has one more tail-feather than the others. He
finds a female possessing the same peculiarity, and this pair
produce offspring having two, three, or four more tail-feathers
than the original stock: the fantail. By a similar process he
obtains the pouter, the Jacobin, the tumbler, the carrier, and
other varieties. The same principles are followed by horti-
culturists and breeders of horses, dogs, and cattle: by selecting
their pairs and seeds according to certain qualities, these
artists succeed in infinitely modifying the types. They realize
their purpose by methodical selection and with a distinct
object in view; nature obtains the same results (modification
of types) unintentionally, by means of the competition or
struggle for existence. As a result of this struggle, a selection,
or kind of choice, is made among beings; some, i. e., the
strongest, or the most clever, or such as, for some reason or
other, are best fitted to survive, are reproduced [*survival of
the fittest*]; others perish. The latter are the *outcasts*, the
former the *elect* of nature, the *select* of the competition, which
is not only the principle of all social progress, but also the first
cause of all development in nature.

Let us imagine, says Strauss, commenting on Darwin,[2] a
herd of cattle, at a time when these animals had no horns.
The herd is attacked by wild beasts. It is evident that in
the ensuing struggle for existence, those which have the
strongest heads will stand a better chance of surviving than
the others, and it is also evident that if there be in the
attacked herd an individual possessing rudimentary horns,
it will have more chances of survival than the rest of the
herd. Great numbers of the latter will perish; the favored

---

population by the important *Essay on the Principle of Population*, published
by Thomas Robert Malthus (1766–1834) in 1798.

[1] *Origin of Species*, 6th ed., pp. 14 ff.

[2] *Der alte und neue Glaube*, 2d ed., pp. 190 ff.

animal, however, will escape; it will produce offspring and (what is important in this connection) transmit to its descendants the peculiarity which saved its life and enabled it to be reproduced: its rudimentary weapons of defense. Its descendants will possess the same peculiar characteristic in greater or less degree. The better equipped they are in this regard, the greater will be their chances of conquering in the renewed struggle for existence, and of transmitting their organs of protection to the succeeding generations. And thus the organ, which, in the first animal possessing it, was nothing but a freak of nature, and which, without the struggle for existence, would have disappeared with its owner, without leaving a trace in the bovine species, goes on developing and perfecting itself from generation to generation. What was at first a purely individual characteristic becomes a generic characteristic, in consequence of the never-ending struggle for existence and the accumulated effects of the constantly renewed process of selection.

In the foregoing example, the selection is determined by a positive advantage, a surplus, but there are cases in which a defect may have the same effect, in which an imperfection may be an advantage and a cause of selection. Let us suppose, with Haeckel,[1] that a swarm of winged insects on an oceanic island are overtaken by a storm, blown to sea, and destroyed. Let us also suppose that one of these insects is wingless; it will not be able to follow the swarm in their flight, and to this very defect it will owe its safety. It will survive its winged congeners and transmit its defect to some of its offspring, which will, consequently, possess the same advantage (that of being "selected"); and so on, until, from selection to selection, the complete absence of wings comes to constitute the characteristic of the species.[2] In this case, undoubtedly, the process of natural selection is really a retrogression, for

[1] *History of Creation.*
[2] [See Darwin's explanation of the wingless condition of the Madeira beetle, *Origin of Species*, ch. V, pp. 101 ff. — Tr.]

here we have to deal with a deformity, with a gradual weakening; but evolution in nature is retrogressive as well as progressive.

Selection by means of the struggle for life sufficiently explains every teleological characteristic in organisms. It even explains the formation of the sense-organs, the eye and the ear, these wonderful works of art, which have always been appealed to as the most conclusive evidences of finalistic and creationistic doctrines. The first eye produced in the evolution of the animal kingdom was, like the first horn of the bovine genus, a mere rudimentary organ, differing as much from the eyes of higher species now existing as the fin of the fish differs from the arm of man. But in so far as it refracted light and aroused a luminous sensation, however weak, it gave the individual endowed with it an immense advantage in the struggle for existence, and made him the "elect of nature." His blind congeners necessarily disappeared, leaving it to him to preserve the species and to transmit this visual organ, in a more pronounced form perhaps, to the descendants. The same causes continued to act, and to accumulate their effects, from generation to generation, until, after thousands of centuries of progressive evolution, the eye at last attained to its present perfection, surpassing the most consummate products of art and the wisest combinations of intelligence; and it attained to it, not through intelligent intervention, but by natural selection.[1]

It was, as we have said, owing to this mechanical explanation of finality — an explanation which, in Darwin, does not exclude the idea of creation — that contemporary materialism at once enthusiastically adopted the theory of natural selection. What we attribute to "the wisdom of Providence," or to "the kindness of Mother Nature," appeared, in the Darwinian hypothesis, as the product of the natural competition of beings and the selection resulting therefrom. Animals that can live in warm climates without any covering are pro-

[1] *Origin of Species*, chap. VI, pp. 139 ff.

tected by warm fur in Northern regions; most of those inhabiting the desert resemble their surroundings in color, and are thereby concealed from their enemies; finally, the existence of every living being is, in a certain measure, "assured." But there is no charitable design nor supernatural and providential arrangement in all this. The animals of the North do not have fur *in order to* protect them from the cold; they do not suffer from the cold, *because* they have fur. And they have fur, *because* their progenitors, whom chance clothed with a thicker skin, were, on that account, better fitted to carry on the struggle for existence than their less favored congeners; and were able, in consequence of this natural selection, to reproduce themselves and to transmit their peculiarities to their offspring, whereas the others perished, and their type disappeared. The same may be said of the animals of the desert, and of all animals and plants enjoying some advantage apparently due to final causes.[1]

The principle of selection applies not only to anatomy and physiology, but also to animal psychology. The instincts of spiders, ants, bees, beavers, and birds, which, even according to Hartmann's[2] belief, can only be explained by means of a *deus ex machina* (the unconscious), are, in Darwin's opinion, nothing but inherited habits, which have become a second nature through the effects of the struggle for life and natural selection. That which is *innate* in the present generation was not so in the original ancestors, and the wonderful art manifested in the instincts of certain animals is merely the result of an evolution lasting countless ages, and of a gradual perfection, beginning with the very earliest origin of these species. Our intellectual habits originated in the same way. The ideas which spiritualism considers as innate, and which, according to Kant, belong to the very constitution of the intelligence, are, undoubtedly, a part of our *present* mental organization, but they were not native to our first progenitors. The latter acquired them by experience; they were transmitted to us, as

[1] Haeckel, *History of Creation*, chap. XI.   [2] Cf. § 74.

intellectual habits or dispositions, by heredity aided by selection, and thus eventually became innate.

An inevitable corollary of the principle of transformation
and selection is the simian origin of man. Darwin advances it
in his second main work: *The Descent of Man* (1871). Man
is the descendant of a variety of apes, more favored than the
rest. The false pride which hinders us from accepting this view
arises from the fact that the ape has a comical demeanor which
gives him the appearance of a *crétin*, an idiot, a caricature of a
man. We should not feel so, if it were held that we descended
from the lion or the rose-bush. Strange to say, we do not even
experience this feeling when we read the Biblical story, according to which our species sprang from a clod of earth: a still more
humiliating origin, considering the enormous distance between
a clod of earth and an organized being, and an organized being
as advanced as the ape. The objection is made that a Cæsar,
a Kant, a Goethe, could not have descended from an animal, —
that there is an insuperable distance between them and the
ape. But this objection falls to the ground when we take into
account, on the one hand, the intermediate links between the
anthropoid ape and Cæsar (Papuans, New Zealanders, Caffirs,
etc.), and, on the other, the immense period of time which
nature, i. e., the struggle for existence and selection, needed to
effect the evolution from the man-ape to Cæsar and Goethe. It
is true, the six thousand years, which, according to the Bible,
is the age of the world, would not have sufficed. But the
palæontological discoveries of our century (lacustrine deposits,
flint tools, cave-dwellers, the kjökken-möddings on the Danish
coasts, etc.) unquestionably prove that the human race is much
older, and that even Egyptian civilization, which is prodig-
iously ancient, is *relatively modern*.[1] Infinitely short steps and
infinitely long periods: these, says Strauss,[2] are the two keys
which open the gates hitherto accessible to miracle only.
Well! Does not Christianity teach that God became man?
Then why cannot an animal become man? The non-Christian

[1] Strauss, *Der alte und neue Glaube*, p. 202.   [2] *Id.*

religions do not believe it to be impossible, as the doctrine of the transmigration of souls, taught by ancient Egypt, Brahmanism, and Buddhism, shows. In truth, there is no gulf between man and the animal. We cannot deny the latter sensibility, memory, and intelligence. The facts which prove it would fill volumes. The moral sense is not foreign to animals; it may, as Strauss adds,[1] be aroused in the dog by the whip; but can we not say the same for many men? The animal has feelings of motherly love, attachment, and devotion. It differs from us in degree only; its "soul" is to ours what the bud is to the flower and the fruit.

What characterizes Darwinian materialism is not its mechanical explanation of the world, nor its absolute negation of final causes, — in this respect as well as in all the others, materialistic principles have not changed since the times of Democritus, — but solely the fact that it found, as its adherents claim, a ready answer to the constantly reiterated and never refuted objection of the teleologists: Every work adapted to an end presupposes a workman, an intelligence, a design, and shall not the most admirable product of all, the most perfect camera obscura, the human eye, presuppose one?

Although Darwin contributed an important link to the materialistic argument, and thus added greatly to its force and vogue, it must not be forgotten that Darwin himself possessed the cautious temper of the scientist. He did not profess either to explain evolution exclusively in terms of natural selection, or to explain the universe wholly in terms of evolution. The principle of evolution dealt with the *effects* of variations rather than with their causes. Darwin undoubtedly supposed these to be physico-chemical in nature, but the fact that he left them unexplained suggested the possibility of reconciling his specifically biological teachings with a spiritualistic or teleological metaphysics. While Darwin made fruitful applications of the genetic method to psychology, and

[1] *Der alte und neue Glaube*, p. 207.

especially in relation to the instincts and emotions, he did not commit himself as to the origin of either life or mind. Nor was the principle of natural selection, as Darwin employed it, necessarily a progressive principle. It explained survival in terms of adaptation to existing conditions, and might under the proper conditions lead to the development of a more rudimentary rather than a more highly organized form of life.[1] Hence Darwin cannot be said to have himself presented any rounded view of the world, or any complete philosophical system, as was claimed by Spencer and Haeckel.

There were, however, certain moral and religious implications which he drew himself, or which his teachings suggested to others. What is, in the broad sense, known as "evolutionary ethics," assumed three quite distinct forms. Darwin himself proposed to reconcile evolution with traditional ethics through the conception of adaptation. Some degree of sociality, or of mutual aid and sympathy, is a condition of the survival of a race, and is therefore as "natural" as the self-seeking propensities. Conscience may be construed in this sense as a set of favorable variations. This is the form of evolutionary ethics which was further developed by Spencer. The second and third forms take the conception of struggle, rather than that of adaptation, as their point of departure. According to the second view, developed by Huxley,[2] the natural life presents the antithesis of the moral life. In the natural life the individual exploits his superiority, and the weak are allowed to suffer the fatal consequences of their weakness; whereas in the moral life the weak are protected by the self-sacrifice or assistance of others. The third view would propose to accept capacity to survive as its criterion of good, and would reject the traditional ethics as interfering with the operation of the law of natural selection. Let the strong man assert his strength, and in this way guarantee the future of the race. It is this idea that links the teachings of Darwin with the

[1] *Variation of Animals*, etc., ch. I.
[2] In his *Evolution and Ethics*.

ethics of *Nietzsche*.[1] The extension of the same idea to social groups has been used by the Marxian socialists as a justification of class-struggle, and by extreme nationalists as a justification of war and aggrandizement.

As regards the religious implications of his teachings, Darwin began as a theist, but was led more and more to the rejection of the traditional conception of a creative and providential God. Not only did the law of natural selection, in his judgment, destroy the force of the argument from design, but it revealed nature in a light that was wholly incompatible with the supposition of benevolent authorship.

HERBERT SPENCER was born in Derby, England, in 1820. Declining the opportunity of a university education, he found employment from 1837 first as an engineer and afterwards, until 1853, as sub-editor of the *Economist*. By the latter date his central ideas were fixed and he was ready to devote the remainder of his life to their systematic elaboration. In 1860 he announced the plan of his *Synthetic Philosophy* in ten volumes. To the fulfilment of this program he devoted himself unrelentingly until his death in 1902.[2]

Spencer belongs to the naturalistic school in a double sense. In the first place, he is associated with positivism in that he limited knowledge to the field of experience, and held that science alone fulfils this requirement. In the second place, he is associated with materialism in that he constructs a cosmic

---

[1] § 81. From the idea that the moral practice of civilized societies interferes with the law of natural selection and permits the weak to survive and reproduce themselves, has sprung the modern cult of *eugenics*. Cf. Karl Pearson, *Groundwork of Eugenics*, 1909.

[2] The parts of his system and the dates of their completion are as follows: *First Principles*, 1862; *Principles of Biology* (two volumes), 1864–1867; *Principles of Psychology* (2d ed., two volumes), 1870–1872; *Principles of Sociology* (three volumes), 1876–1896; *Principles of Ethics* (two volumes), 1879–1892. Among the more important of his smaller works are *Education* (1861) and *The Man versus The State* (1884). In addition he wrote many articles and pamphlets and an *Autobiography*, published two years after his death, which occurred in 1902. On Spencer, cf. B. P. Bowne, *The Philosophy of H. Spencer*, 1874; J. Watson, *Comte, Mill and Spencer;* and T. H. Green, *Works*, vol. I.

philosophy in which the unifying idea of evolution is borrowed from science, and in which man and society are assimilated to physical nature. Spencer's philosophy thus falls into two main divisions, which are very unequally represented in his written works, his agnostic realism, defended in parts of the *First Principles* and *Psychology*, and his evolutionary survey of nature and man. The former constitutes the definition of his fundamental philosophical position, and its reconciliation to the claims both of faith and of reason; the latter, his résumé and unification of the content of science.

With Hamilton and Mansel, Spencer subscribed to the doctrine of the "relativity of knowledge," and the consequent impossibility of knowing that non-relative or Absolute which has been the dream of metaphysicians.[1] To know a thing is to relate it to other things and to ourselves, or to introduce qualifying conditions; what the thing is unconditionally, must, therefore, escape us. But it does not follow, as Hamilton had supposed, that the unconditioned plays a wholly negative part in our thought. In the very recognition of our limits we refer beyond them to that Force which thrusts phenomena upon us. In calling it the Unknowable, therefore, Spencer did not imply doubt as to its existence. In fact, the Unknowable is in a sense the most familiar of objects. Science, in reaching out towards a first cause, or a final goal, or a supreme generalization, is perpetually forced to acknowledge it; the religious of all the ages have stood awe-struck in its presence. It thus furnishes the bond and the means of reconciliation between science and religion.

Over and above the dialectical proof of the Unknowable, there is a more empirical proof, derived from the examination of the data of experience. After the manner of Locke and Hume, Spencer distinguished between the relatively "vivid," constant, and uncontrollable impressions of sense, and the relatively "faint" and controllable series of ideas.[2] Our

---

[1] *First Principles*, part I.
[2] *First Principles*, part II, ch. II; *Principles of Psychology*, part VII, ch. XVI.

"vivid" experiences give us knowledge of an external world through a sense of resistance, which is most unmistakable in the case of muscular sensation. We are thus led to represent the external reality to ourselves as a sort of power, acting on us in a manner analogous to that in which we act on ourselves, as when, for example, we press one hand upon another. But this representation is purely symbolic. Strictly speaking all that we know of external reality through sensation is that there is a *something* which is thus manifesting itself to us, — a something whose existence is undeniable but whose nature is unknowable.

What is or is not inconceivable to us depends on certain established connections among our ideas, and therefore reflects the constitution of our minds. So much in general terms Spencer conceded to Kant. But as an associationist Spencer contended that this order among our ideas is an effect of the persistence or frequency of the vivid connections. The more often we experience things together, the more impossible it is for us to think them apart. To every new experience we thus bring certain habits of thought that reflect the experiences of the past, and that constitute our preformed and ingrained intelligence. This reflects not only the past experience of the individual, but ancestral experience as well, and may therefore be regarded, relatively to the individual, as *a priori*.[1] But it is justified because in its ultimate origin, or relatively to the racial experience, it is *a posteriori*, being a correspondence of internal to external relations. This was Spencer's proposed reconciliation of Kantian transcendentalism with British empiricism.

While Spencer's philosophy will be judged by critical historians in terms of its theory of knowledge, the powerful influence which it exerted in the latter half of the nineteenth century was due rather to its imposing architecture than to the solidity of its foundations. In English-speaking countries it stood for several decades as the most imposing monument of

[1] *Principles of Psychology*, § 208.

science, in which the extensive but scattered results of research were so conjoined as to afford a unified picture of the total cosmos. The materials were drawn from all the special sciences, inorganic as well as organic, but they received their structural and pictorial unity from the principle of development or evolution. The conservation of energy, or as Spencer preferred to call it, "the persistence of force," [1] was accepted as the universal law governing physical changes, and defended on *a priori* as well as on experimental grounds. But this law applies to life and mind only when these are first reduced to physico-chemical terms. The only "synthetic" law, which is directly applicable to phenomena of every level, — which unites them all concretely, and which reveals their historical trend, — is the law of increasing organization, or of correlative differentiation and unification. "Evolution is an integration of matter and concomitant dissipation of motion; during which the matter passes from an indefinite incoherent homogeneity to a definite coherent heterogeneity; and during which the retained motion undergoes a parallel transformation." [2] This principle Spencer both illustrated from existing science and extended into new fields. He found it in the evolution of the sidereal universe out of the primitive nebula, in the history and development of the earth; in the origin of life and of new and more complex species of organism; in the formation of complex ideas out of the primitive manifold of sensory "shocks"; in the building of an integrated will out of elementary reflexes; and in the progressive complication and organization of society. The application of this principle thus served the double purpose of exhibiting the fruitfulness of the genetic method, and of presenting nature as a totality with a majestic sweep of outline, and a clearly recognizable meaning and direction.

Finally, Spencer exerted a strong influence upon the moral and social philosophy of his times, and was a powerful ex-

[1] *First Principles*, part II, ch. VII.
[2] *First Principles*, part II, ch. XVII.

ponent of the prevailing tendencies to individualism and liberalism in economic and political thought. Good consists fundamentally in pleasurable activity.[1] Life and happiness are its inseparable aspects, since life would not be deemed good if it were not pleasant, and pleasure is essentially a sign of successful or well-adapted life. The course of evolution is a change for the better; the evolved society and the good life are one and the same thing. For as life evolves it is both differentiated and integrated, — both increased in amount and harmoniously adjusted, within and without. The evolved society represents both the maximum amount of life and its maximum smoothness and facility, thus doubly implying a maximum of happiness. "Absolute ethics" defines the conduct proper to such a perfected society, and "relative ethics" the conduct characteristic of the imperfect stages through which it is approached.

In the evolved society men will have many interests, but these interests will be tempered by the exigencies of social relations; so that men will be prompted by interest, and especially by sympathy and benevolence, to do that which is at the same time conducive to the interests of others. The advance towards this happy state takes place through the *gradual alteration of human nature as a consequence of experience.* Spencer was thus led to attach great importance to "the inheritance of acquired characters," and defended this view in a prolonged controversy with Weismann.[2] For the same reason he emphasized (in his treatise on *Education*) the importance of allowing the individual to learn for himself the natural consequences of his own behavior. He also favored a political and economic policy of *laissez-faire*, in which there should be the minimum of artificial interference with that interaction of individuals in which each learns to adapt himself to the other. Spencer found an even more fundamental reason for his individualism and libertarianism in his belief

---

[1] *Principles of Ethics*, part I, ch. III.
[2] Aug. Weismann, 1834–1914. *Studien zur Descendenztheorie*, 1875–1876.

that the individual, through being the seat of conscious happiness, is the end for which society exists.[1]

ERNST HAECKEL, who was born in 1834, and died in 1919, and who was professor of zoölogy at the University of Jena from 1862, represents, like Spencer, the philosophical generalization of science in terms of the conception of evolution. He was the most influential exponent of naturalism in Germany during the last decades of the nineteenth century, his popularity culminating in the extraordinary vogue of his *Riddle of the Universe* (Die Welträtsel) published in 1899. Unlike Spencer, Haeckel had some claims to be regarded as a biologist on his own account, and in promulgating his philosophy he did not hesitate to invoke the personal authority of the scientist as well as the impersonal authority of science.[2]

According to Haeckel we know external nature through sense-impressions, and through "presentations" of which "we are convinced that their content corresponds to the knowable aspect of things." "We do not know 'the thing in itself' that lies behind these knowable phenomena," nor do we even "clearly know whether it exists or not." He left "the fruitless brooding over this ideal phantom to the 'pure metaphysician,' " and turned eagerly to his "monistic philosophy of nature." [3] He was not troubled, as was Spencer, by the fact that the very conceptions of "phenomena" and "correspondence" have ulterior implications, or by the fact that his philosophy of nature itself transcends both phenomena and the experimental results of science.

Nor was Haeckel seriously disturbed by the outstanding problems of science itself. In addresses delivered in 1872 in

---

[1] *Principles of Sociology,* § 322.

[2] His most important writings, in addition to the above, were his *Generelle Morphologie* (1866), *Natürliche Schöpfungsgeschichte* (1868), and *Anthropogenie* (1874). The *Schöpfungsgeschichte* has been translated into English under the title of *The History of Creation,* 1883, and the *Anthropogenie* under the titles of *The Evolution of Man* (1879) and *The Pedigree of Man* (1880).

[3] *Riddle of the Universe,* pp. 292, 380–381. References are to the English translation by J. M. McCabe, 1902.

Leipzig and in 1880 before the Berlin Academy of Science, the physiologist Emil DuBois Reymond[1] had pronounced his famous "Ignorabimus!". We do not as yet, thought this cautious scientist, know the origin of life, the explanation of the orderly arrangement of nature, the origin of reason and of speech, or the truth about the freedom of the will; while on certain points, namely, the nature of matter and force, the origin of motion, and the origin of consciousness, we shall always remain in ignorance. But Haeckel had solutions of all these "seven riddles" in terms of two fundamental[2] laws.

Of these two great solvents the first was "the law of substance" — "the fundamental law of the constancy of matter and force." Although experimentally demonstrated by science, this law is "in the ultimate analysis," "a necessary consequence of the principle of causality."[3] The constancy of matter and of force are fundamentally the same thing, because matter and force are two aspects of one substance, the one its space-filling or extensional aspect, the other its energetic aspect. Under the material aspect may be brought all corporeal forms, ponderable mass and imponderable ether, the first being only a condensation of the second, and the two occupying "infinite space" continuously; under the energetic aspect may be brought not only every variety of inorganic force, but the vital, psychic, and conscious "affinities" as well.

The second great solvent is "the universal law of evolution," by which life emerges from physico-chemical conditions, "psychoplasm" from protoplasm, and "neuroplasm" from psychoplasm. Life is the energetic aspect of protoplasm, unconscious mind of psychoplasm, and consciousness of the associative centres of the brain. Both cognition and will rise in brute and man through a series of "psychic gradations," from irritability and reflex action to conscious thought and purpose. All is one and continuous, and one can read either from above

---

[1] 1818–1896. *Ueber die Grenzen des Naturerkennens* (1872); *Die sieben Welträtsel* (1882).

[2] *Riddle of the Universe*, pp. 15–16.   [3] *Ibid.*, pp. 381, 215.

down, and endow the atom with a soul, or from below up, and declare that the mind is nothing but force.

The "monism of the cosmos" which is established on the basis of these two basic principles, of substance and of evolution, "proclaims the absolute dominion of 'the great eternal iron laws' throughout the universe. It thus shatters, at the same time, the three central dogmas of the dualistic philosophy — the personality of God, the immortality of the soul, and the freedom of the will."[1] The emancipated mind will worship Nature itself, or "the Goddess of truth" that "dwells in the temple of nature."[2] With this new "natural religion," which Haeckel proclaimed in opposition to the other-worldliness and asceticism of Christianity, was allied a new æsthetic cult inspired by the wealth of natural forms which modern science has disclosed to the human eye; a new education, based on the teaching of science; and the new "monistic ethics," credited to Herbert Spencer, in which egoism and altruism are reconciled through the development of the social instincts in successive generations of the race.

In two respects the evolutionary materialism which has just been expounded shows a tendency to pass over into its philosophical opposite, — in its emphasis on force and in its emphasis on life.

Spencer believed the experience of force to afford the most adequate possible representation of the unknowable reality. Haeckel, like Büchner before him, while preserving the conception of matter, regarded force as its inseparable attribute. A step further in this direction was later taken by OSTWALD,[3] a prominent exponent of "energetics" both in physics and chemistry, and in the philosophy of nature. This

---

[1] *Ibid.*, p. 381. [2] *Ibid.*, p. 337.
[3] Wilhelm Ostwald, 1853–   . The systematic presentation of his views is to be found in his *Vorlesungen über Naturphilosophie*, 1902. Ostwald also approached closely to the position of Mach (§ 72), both in his conception of an experience prior to the distinction of subject and object, and in his use of the norm of "economy" in scientific method.

philosopher defined ponderable or tangible matter as a colloca-
tion of energies, its form being construed in terms of elasticity,
its volume in terms of compressibility, and its mass in terms
of work and velocity. Heat, electricity, sound, and light are
readily subsumed under the same concept. Life itself is a
peculiar combination of physico-chemical energies. Nature
having been reduced to energy, the antithesis of body and
mind disappears, for what is mind but energy? Instead of
regarding psychical energy as parallel to physical energy, Ostwald proposed the bold hypothesis that it is convertible from
and into physico-chemical energies through the intermediate
form of nervous energy, in accordance with the law of the
conservation.[1] Thus energy becomes the universal substance and its constancy the universal law. But if physical
energy and felt energy are thus interchangeable it is as true
to say that body has been reduced to mind, as to say that
mind has been reduced to body. From a naturalism of this
type it is not difficult to find a way across to the spiritualism of
Hartmann and Fechner.[2]

A bridge from evolutionary naturalism to spiritualism and
idealism is afforded also by its biological emphasis.

One[3] difference between the materialistic monism of the
evolutionary type of Spencer and Haeckel and the idealistic
monism of Fichte, Schelling, and Hegel, may be expressed
as follows: The former emphatically denied all finality or
purpose; whereas the latter, inspired by Kant's *Critique of
Judgment*, recognized in nature, if not the designs of a transcendent Creator, at least an *immanent* finality. The Idea of
Hegel is the highest end of nature realizing itself by means of
an evolution that is both physical and logical: physical, in so
far as it is unconscious; logical, in so far as it excludes chance.
Hence, it is closely related to what Schelling and, above all,
Schopenhauer, called *Will*.

---

[1] *Vorlesungen*, pp. 377 ff.   [2] § 74.
[3] The two following paragraphs are retained with slight modifications from
the text of Weber.

Those who sought to reconcile these two monisms reflected as follows: Does not the Darwinian principle, which materialism invokes with such absolute confidence, corroborate, rather than overturn, the hypothesis of immanent teleology? Is it really true that the *struggle for existence* is a *first* cause and exclusively mechanical? Does not the struggle for life, in turn, presuppose Schopenhauer's *will-to-live, will* or *effort*, without which, according to the profound remark of Leibniz, *there can be no substance?* [1] Does it not, therefore, presuppose an anterior, superior, and immaterial cause? What can the formula: struggle *for* existence, mean, except: struggle *in order to* exist? But this carries us directly into teleology. Besides, the entire Darwinian terminology is derived from the teleological theory: the terms, *selection, choice*, seem to introduce an intellectual element into nature.[2] These are mere images, it is said, or figures of speech. But does not the very impossibility of avoiding them prove the impossibility of explaining nature by pure mechanism?

Thus the biological form of materialism suggested the transition, through a vitalistic or voluntaristic conception of life, to spiritualism, its philosophical opposite. This tendency we shall resume below.[3]

§ 71. Empirical Positivism. Comte. J. S. Mill

Positivism is the critical rather than the dogmatic or systematic form of naturalism. Although the difference is one of degree rather than of kind, we may distinguish the *empirical* positivists, like Comte and Mill, who proclaimed the standpoint of experience, and regarded the descriptive law as a reproduction of the constant connections among observed facts;

---

[1] Haeckel himself says: In the last analysis, the impulses which determine (*bedingen, condition*) the struggle and its diverse forms, are merely those of self-preservation (*Selbsterhaltung*). See his *History of Creation*. Here we no longer have materialism, but pure voluntarism.

[2] [See Darwin's answer to such objections. *Origin of Species*. 6th ed.; chap. IV, pp. 58 ff. — Tr.]

[3] § 74.

and the *methodological* positivists, like Lange, Mach, and Poincaré, who emphasized the factor of technique which is introduced by the scientific mind.

AUGUSTE COMTE[1] was born at Montpellier in 1789. He was identified as student, tutor, and examiner with the *École Polytechnique*, which under the Restoration continued the scientific traditions of the eighteenth century. His *Cours de Philosophie positive*,[2] containing his defense of the positive method, his famous *three stages*, and an extensive summary and classification of the sciences, placed him at once in the first rank of the thinkers of his time. Having from his earliest years a strong humanitarian and reforming impulse, and being an intimate associate of Saint-Simon,[3] he sought to find in positivism the basis for a social reconstruction which should serve as a safeguard against the disintegrating tendencies of revolution. This phase of his development culminated in the *Politique positive* (1851–1854) in which he introduced the "religion of humanity." In his last years he devoted himself with piety and zeal to the development of this new cult, which strongly colored both his thought and his personal life.[4] Positivism is

---

[1] [The account of Comte follows the Weber text, with slight changes up to p. 499. — ED.]

[2] 0 vols., Paris, 1830–1842; 2d ed., with a *Preface* by Littré, 1864 [English version freely translated and condensed by Harriet Martineau, 1853. Later writings: *Discours sur l'Esprit positive*, 1844; *Système de Politique positive*, 4 vols., 1851–1854 (Engl. tr., 1875–1877); *Catéchisme positiviste*, 1853 (Engl. tr. by Congreve, 1858). See Littré, *Comte et la Philosophie positiviste*, 1863; J. S. Mill, *Comte and Positivism*, 1865; B. Pünjer, *Der Positivismus*, etc. (*Jahrbücher f. Protestantische Theologie*), 1878; E. Caird, *The Social Philosophy and Religion of Comte*, 1885; H. Gruber, *Comte und der Positivismus*, 1890; and *Der Positivismus vom Tode Comte's*, etc., 1891; J. Watson, *Comte, Mill, and Spencer*, 1895. — TR.]; L. Lévy-Bruhl, *La Philosophie d'Auguste Comte*, 3d ed., 1913.

[3] § 69.

[4] Comte's most distinguished followers were John Stuart Mill and Emil LITTRÉ (1801–1881). The latter's works were: *Analyse raisonnée du Cours de Philosophie positive de M. A. Comte*, 1845; *Application de la Philosophie positive au Gouvernement des Sociétés*, 1849; *Conservation, Révolution et Positivisme*, 1852; *Paroles de Philosophie positive*, 1859; *Auguste Comte et la Philosophie positive*, 1863; *Fragments de Philosophie positive et de Sociologie contemporaine*, 1876. Littré is also the founder of the *Revue positive* (1867–1883). His *Dictionnaire de la Langue française* constitutes his chief claim to glory.

John Stuart Mill and Littré, however, disavowed Auguste Comte's socialistic

not a mere negation, — otherwise it could not have formed a school, — it is a system whose central teaching, the theory of the history of thought, is the realistic counterpart, so to speak, of Hegel's philosophy of mind.

According to Comte, the human mind successively passes through three stages of thinking or philosophizing: the *theological* stage, which is elementary and represents the period of childhood, the *metaphysical* stage, and the *positive* stage.

From the *theological* or anthropomorphic point of view, cosmical phenomena are governed, not by immutable laws, but by wills like ours. This primitive form of thought has three stages. First, the objects themselves are regarded as animated, living, intelligent (fetichism). On the next stage, invisible beings are imagined, each of them governing a certain group of objects or events (polytheism). In a higher form, at last, all these particular divinities are merged into the conception of one God, who created the world and now governs it either directly or through the medium of supernatural agents of the second order (monotheism).

Metaphysical thought no longer explains phenomena by conscious wills, but by abstractions considered as real beings. Nature is no longer governed by an anthropomorphous God, but by a force, a power, a principle. We repudiate the divinities with which the ancients peopled nature, only to replace them by *souls*, mysterious *essences*. We pretend to explain facts by the *tendencies* of nature, which we regard as a kind of intelligent rather than impersonal being. We invest it with a *tendency* towards perfection, a *horror* of a vacuum, a curative *virtue* (*vis medicatrix*), occult qualities. The metaphysical view errs in that it takes abstractions for realities.

Utopias, which proceeded from Saint-Simon, and his positivistic church. The latter was organized in England under the leadership of Frederic Harrison (1831–1923). To these positivists, properly so called, we must add, as closely associated with the positivistic movement, two gifted mathematicians: Sophie Germain [1776–1831], who anticipated the system of Comte in her *Considérations générales sur l'Etat des Sciences et des Lettres aux différentes Epoques de ieur Culture* [posthumous work, published by L'Herbette, Paris, 1833], and Cournot (§ 69).

The dominion of metaphysics, more or less influenced by the theological spirit, lasted until the end of the Middle Ages, when the controversy between the nominalists and the realists, the first struggle of modern thought to rid itself of verbal abstractions, inaugurated the *positive* epoch (Descartes, Bacon, Hobbes, Galileo, Gassendi, Newton). Ever since the advent of this period, the positive explanation of facts is gradually superseding the theological and metaphysical explanations, in proportion as the advance of scientific research brings to light an increasing number of invariable laws.

Like philosophy in general, each science in particular passes through these three consecutive stages: the theological state, the metaphysical state, and the positive state. Now, the various branches of human knowledge have developed with unequal rapidity, and cannot simultaneously pass from one phase to the other. The order of succession in which they enter upon the metaphysical stage and the positive stage is indicated by the logical order in which they follow each other. Thus, the search for the order in which the special sciences pass from one phase of thought to the other leads Comte to construct his remarkable *classification of the sciences*.

In surveying the different sciences he observes that they are naturally arranged in an order of increasing complexity and diminishing generality: so that *each one depends on the truths of all the sciences which precede it, plus such truths as properly belong to it.*

The science of number (*arithmetic* and *algebra*) deals with the most simple, and, at the same time, most general phenomena; the truths which it formulates hold for all things, and depend only upon themselves. We can study it independently of all other sciences; hence it is the fundamental science, and, in a certain sense, the first philosophy. Then comes *geometry*, which presupposes the laws of number, and can be studied without previous knowledge of any other science except arithmetic. Then comes *rational mechanics*, which depends on the science of number and geometry, to which it adds the laws of equilibrium and movement. The truths of algebra and geometry would be true even if those of mechanics were not; arithmetic, algebra, and geometry, therefore, do not depend on mechanics, whereas the latter essentially depends on the science of number and extension. The science of number (arithmetic and algebra), geometry, and rational mechanics together constitute the science of mathematics, the universal science and sole basis of all natural philosophy.[1]

Astronomy is directly connected with mathematics. Its truths rest on arithmetical, geometrical, and mechanical truths, upon which it exercises no influence, but to which it adds a group of new facts: the laws of gravitation.[2]

Astronomy is followed by *physics*, which depends not only on the mathematical sciences, but also on astronomy, for terrestrial phenomena are influenced by the motion of the earth and of celestial bodies. It embraces *barology*, or the science of weight, a transition-state between astronomy and physics; *thermology*, or the science of heat; *acoustics*, *optics*, and *electrology*, a connecting-link between physics and the science which immediately follows it in the scale of our knowledge: *chemistry*.

Chemistry adds its own truths to the laws of physics, especially to those of thermology and electrology, on which it essentially depends.[3]

Biology (physiology) adds to the laws of the preceding sciences a group of special laws.

Finally, at the top of the scale, we have *social physics* or *sociology*,[4] which, in turn, depends on all the preceding sciences, and adds new data to them. In fact, the laws of organic and animal life, as well as those of inorganic nature, influence human society, either by directly acting upon life, or by determining the physical conditions under which society is developed.

With the sciences which Comte calls *abstract* are connected

[1] *Cours de Philosophie positive*, vol. I. Cf. Pythagoras, Plato, Descartes.
[2] *Id.*, vol. II.   [3] *Id.*, vol. III.   [4] *Id.*, vols. IV–V.

the respective *concrete* sciences: with physics and chemistry, abstract sciences, mineralogy, a concrete science; with physiology, an abstract science, zoölogy and botany, concrete sciences. The latter are concerned with existing beings and objects; the former, with the general laws of occurrence. The concrete sciences necessarily advance more slowly than the abstract sciences, since they depend on these. Hence they have not yet passed beyond the descriptive stage.

The abstract sciences (mathematics, astronomy, physics, chemistry, biology, sociology) pass from the theological phase to the metaphysical and positive phase, in the order of their simplicity. The more complex a science is, the more obstacles it throws in the way of the human mind in general as well as of the individual in particular. Thus, mathematics, the simplest of the sciences, has, for thousands of years, been almost positive. Forsooth, it never was theological in the sense that any man of common-sense ever prayed to God to make three times three ten, or the sum of the angles of a triangle exceed two right-angles. It was understood, from the very beginning, that in these matters there can be no intervention of freedom whatsoever.

We cannot say the same for astronomy. It had its theological period, during which the stars were conceived either as divinities, or as moved by many divine wills (polytheism), or by one divine will (monotheism). To this phase belongs the miracle of Joshua. It had its metaphysical epoch, during which the regular motion of the heavenly bodies was explained by their *tendency towards perfection*. Aristotle is almost a theologian in astronomy; even Copernicus and Kepler are still metaphysicians, and this science does not attain to its positive phase until the days of Newton. In our age positive astronomy has become a part of the popular consciousness. True, we still pray to God for rain and good weather, but we no longer ask him to arrest the apparent motion of the sun, or to change the celestial orbits. We are still theologians in meteorology, because, in this field, the uniformity of phenomena is less marked,

and because their apparent irregularity, joined with our ignorance of their true laws, favors the superstitious belief that
they are governed by a free will. Astronomy, however, has
abandoned this view.

Physics and chemistry were theologico-metaphysical sciences longer than the science of celestial bodies. They abound
in occult qualities, horrors, sympathies, and other abstractions
assumed to be realities. Chemistry was *alchemy* down to the
eighteenth century, and did not become a positive science
until the days of Lavoisier. It took physiology still longer to
reach the threshold of positivism. Until recently (think of
Stahl's animism, of vitalism, Schelling and Oken) it was right
in the midst of metaphysics, and positive biology does not go
back farther than to Bichat. Finally, sociology (moral and
political science) has not yet surmounted the barriers which
separate metaphysics from positivism. Many of its thinkers
have not even passed the theological stage (De Maistre, De
Bonald, the theological school).[1] It is true, attempts at political positivism were made by Hobbes and Spinoza, who treated
of man "as though he were dealing with lines, surfaces, and
bodies"; but their efforts met with no response. The eighteenth
century and the Revolution prepared the way for positive
social science, without, however, establishing it. Positivism
claims the honor of having founded it.

Political and social ideas succeed each other according to a
fixed law. As soon as this law is known, history will cease to
be a chaos, and become a *science* like physics and astronomy.
Historical facts follow each other and are connected with the
same necessity as biological phenomena. Formerly, one might
have believed that crimes and offenses vary considerably
from year to year, that chance and free-will are more prevalent
in this field than anywhere else. But the statistics published

---

[1] The *theological* school, chiefly represented by De Bonald and Joseph de
Maistre (§ 69), opposed to individual reason the "universal reason," to human
philosophy "divine philosophy" as set forth in the revealed dogma, to the
theories of political and religious liberalism the theocratic system now called
ultra-montanism.

by our governments prove the contrary. We must therefore insist upon the essential notion that historical events, i. e., social phenomena, are, like everything else, subject to fixed laws, and that supernatural interventions play no part in the development of societies.

When social ethics will have been raised to the rank of positive science, that is, of science, — for positive science alone is true science, — the totality of sciences, i. e., philosophy, will be *positive*. Positive philosophy is no longer a separate science, it is the synthesis, the systematic co-ordination of human knowledge. Emanating from the sciences, it does not differ from them in method: it employs the method of experience, supplemented by induction and deduction. Positive philosophy, moreover, is philosophy in the true sense of the word, since it has for its object the *whole of phenomena, the universe.* It is the business of positivism to study this totality, to unify the entire field of human knowledge, to make the sciences philosophical and philosophy scientific, to give the former the unity they need, and the latter the prestige which it lost in consequence of its recent indiscretions.

The reign of metaphysics is nearing its end. The reason why the serious thinkers of the day are abandoning it is plain: it never was a real science; all it did, in ancient as well as in modern times, was to turn out hypotheses after hypotheses, having no stability whatsoever. The systems which it brought forth antagonize each other in their very principles. The history of the sciences represents a continuous advance: what is once acquired is retained forever. In metaphysics, on the other hand, everything is in a state of perpetual agitation and endless revolution. Metaphysics has, undoubtedly, had its historical mission, and has creditably discharged its task. It has demolished the religions, and prepared the field for positive science. In Greece, it overthrew the polytheistic faith and substituted monotheism for it; in the Christian world, it produced the heresies which, little by little, weakened and disorganized the Catholic system. But this essentially negative and critical task is now fulfilled, and the futility of its efforts of two thousand years, when compared with the rapid and continuous advance of the sciences, clearly proves that it is merely a transitory form in the history of the human mind.[1]

So far the general position of Comte may be said to be that of empirical realism. There are, however, motives in Comte's thought which tend in a different direction, towards a methodological positivism, and even towards idealism. Positive science is relative to the "organization" and "situation of man";[2] it is a historic and social product which reflects the stage of human development. In the last analysis science will be what man makes it. Thus Comte tended unmistakably in his later years to a sociological theory of knowledge,[3] and a humanistic theory of nature. The laws of nature can be unified only by taking humanity as the centre. Science is an instrument of the will, and the will is governed by love. Mankind, which is the proper object of worship, is also the key to the understanding of the world; and the logic of the heart takes precedence of the logic of the mind.[4]

JOHN STUART MILL[5] became interested in Comte when his own general philosophical attitude was already fixed, and in his work on *Auguste Comte and Positivism*, published in 1865, he acknowledged him as an ally rather than as a master. With the Comte of the Positive Philosophy he found himself in fun-

---

[1] *Cours de la Philosophie positive*, vol. VI, pp. 645 ff. Littré, *Analyse raisonnée*, pp. 55 ff.

[2] *Discours sur l'Esprit positif*, p. 15.

[3] Cf. Durkheim, § 73.

[4] *Politique positif*, I, 447; II, 101–102.

[5] His principal works, other than those mentioned in the text, were the *Principles of Political Economy*, 1848; *Essay on Liberty*, 1859; *Considerations on Representative Government*, 1860; and the *Autobiography*, 1873. Cf. Jevon's criticism, reprinted in *Pure Logic*, 1890; A. Bain, *John Stuart Mill, a Criticism*, 1882; H. Lauret, *Philosophie de St. Mill*, 1886; C. Douglas, *J. S. Mill: a Study of his Philosophy*, 1895; J. Watson, *Comte, Mill and Spencer*, 1895; H. Taine, *Le Positivisme anglais, Étude sur J. S. Mill*, 1864; Th. Ribot, *Le Psychologie anglaise contemporaine*, 2d ed., 1875 (English translation, 1891).

damental agreement, while he deemed this author's "subsequent speculations false and misleading." [1]

Born in London in 1806, and being the son of James Mill, he was reared in the tradition of the introspective associationist psychology, of which his father was so eminent a representative.[2] His early studies of logic brought him to see the importance of the problem of *induction;* and his profound and original study of this problem resulted in the publication, in 1843, of his *System of Logic,*[3] generally regarded as the greatest of his works. The *Logic* is the application of empiricism to the method of science. In his *Examination of the Philosophy of Sir William Hamilton* (1865) Mill examined the other outstanding problem of empiricism, namely that of the relation between perception and the external world.

Meanwhile Mill's ethical, economic, and political views had been developing, first under the influence of the utilitarian school, of which he was a hereditary member. The founder of this school was JEREMY BENTHAM,[4] and James Mill was his most authoritative successor. This influence was, however, crossed and modified by two others. On the one hand, Mill was brought by a reaction against his early education, and by the cultural and romantic movement led by Coleridge and Carlyle,[5] to recognize the insufficiency of a purely quantitative and individualistic theory of value. On the other hand, he was led by his studies of political economy[6] to believe that the

---

[1] Edition of 1907, p. 5. Mill first became acquainted with Comte's philosophy in 1837; cf. *Autobiography,* 1873, pp. 207–213.

[2] § 69. After Locke the most important forerunner of James Mill in this line of development was David Hartley (§ 60).

[3] This work underwent much revision in successive editions, of which the most important were those of 1850 and 1872. Mill acknowledged his indebtedness, as regards his logic and philosophy of science, not only to Comte, but to William Whewell (1794–1866), whose *History of the Inductive Sciences* appeared in 1837; and to Sir John F. W. Herschel (1792–1871), whose *Discourse on the Study of Natural Philosophy* had appeared in 1830.

[4] 1748–1832. His most important work was his *Introduction to the Principles of Morals and Legislation,* published in 1789. The doctrines of this school can be traced to Hume and to Richard Cumberland (1631–1718).

[5] § 69.

[6] After Adam Smith (1723–1790) and David Ricardo (1772–1823), Mill was the most important founder of this modern science.

condition of the individual could be bettered only by a profound reconstruction of the foundations of society. Thus despite his individualism he was attracted to the program of socialism. The fundamental principles of his ethics were set forth in his essay on *Utilitarianism*, published in 1863. His views on religion, which were partially developed in his studies of Comte and Hamilton, were summarily but fragmentarily expressed in the three essays on *Nature, The Utility of Religion*, and *Theism*, published shortly after their author's death, which occurred in 1873.

As an empiricist, Mill held that all knowledge appeals in the last analysis to the test of experience. Deductive thinking draws conclusions by inference from a major premise, but this major premise itself, such as "all men are mortal," is a universal statement of fact which must be obtained by induction. The fundamental topic of logic is therefore the question how such universal statements of fact can be justified. They appeal to the connections found in experience, and the first step is to distinguish the connections that are "unconditional" from those that are due to accidental circumstances. This distinction is facilitated by experiment, which can vary conditions *ad libitum;* and to perfect this procedure, Mill formulated his "four methods of experimental inquiry." [1] By the method of "agreement" we compare situations having only one common antecedent A, and if we then find only one common consequent a, we may say that a is related to A unconditionally, that is, independently of the other varying conditions. By the method of "difference" and its combination with the method of agreement, we compare situations in which a occurs with situations in which it fails to occur, and find that they differ only in that A is present in the one case and absent in the other. By the method of "residues" we eliminate the connections already known, and conclude that there is a connection between the A left over and the a not yet accounted for. Finally, by the method of "concomitant

[1] *Logic*, book III, ch. VIII.

variation" we conclude that there is a connection between A and a because for every change of A there is a corresponding change of a.

But there remains a more fundamental and a more difficult question. Suppose it to be proved by the four methods that A and a are unconditionally connected, both in experience and in experiment, does this justify the *generalization* of this connection? If there were a limited number of cases and one had exhausted all of them, then one's induction could be said to be complete. But the number of A's and a's is supposed to be unlimited. Am I justified because of their unconditional connection *thus far*, or within experience *up to date*, in concluding that they are connected always and everywhere? The fact is, says Mill, that our reasoning thus far has assumed the principle of "the uniformity of nature." The proof of this principle he believes that he discovers in its very generality.[1] Inasmuch as it is presupposed as an underlying hypothesis in every particular hypothesis, the verification of every particular hypothesis adds evidence in its support. Inasmuch as all laws exemplify it, it cannot be overthrown, but must always be confirmed, by the discovery of any particular law; whereas one particular law may be overthrown by another. Furthermore, its universal application adds force to the fact that no breach of it has yet been detected. In other words, if it did not hold we should be peculiarly likely to know it.

Mill followed his predecessors of the empirical and nominalistic school in holding that our ideas are all reducible to sensations, and that these are given to us severally, being united by association. The virtue of Mill's theory of knowledge lies in the persistence with which he attempted to reduce both the external world and the mind to these terms. All that experience strictly verifies is the belief that, given certain sensations, others will follow. Matter, interpreted in terms of actual experience, means nothing but these constant uniformities, or these "permanent possibilities of sensation."[2] Mind is a set

[1] *Logic*, book III, ch. XXI.
[2] *Examination of the Philosophy of Sir Wm. Hamilton*, ch. XI.

of possibilities of another order, differing in their arrangement, in their inclusion of thoughts, emotions, and volitions as well as sensations, and in their being possibilities for one individual alone.

In ethics, Mill, like Bentham, takes his stand on the principle that actions are to be judged by their consequences, and "are right in proportion as they tend to promote happiness, wrong as they tend to produce the reverse of happiness." [1] He also holds, with Bentham, that the happiness by which the rightness of acts is to be judged is the general happiness, or happiness of the community, or greatest happiness of the greatest number. The proof of this principle, according to Mill, lies in the fact that each person desires his own happiness, so that each person's happiness being a good to that person, the general happiness is "a good to the aggregate of all persons." [2]

Mill differed from Bentham in two important respects. In the first place, he greatly softened the latter's selfish and pleasure-seeking psychology. According to Mill, man comes, owing to his original sympathy and his acquired education, to desire virtue for its own sake. Instead of valuing it as a means to his pleasure, he values it for itself, and takes his pleasure *in* it. In the second place, he adds a qualitative to Bentham's purely quantitative scale of values. Some pleasures, and particularly those which involve reason and virtue, are "higher" pleasures, not because they are greater, in respect of intensity or duration, but because they are *preferred*.[3] Thus Mill sought to free utilitarianism from the odium which attached to it as a sordid and base philosophy that justifies the appetites and material comforts in opposition to the cultural and spiritual values.

In his practical ethics Mill was a strong champion of personal liberty. Through his recognition of the higher pleasures, through his individualism, and through the provision made in his political philosophy for the representation of minority

[1] *Utilitarianism*, ch. I. [2] *Ibid.*, ch. IV. [3] *Ibid.*, ch. II.

opinion, he hoped to save democracy from vulgarity and the tyranny of the masses.

As against Hamilton and Mansel, he contended that the relativity of knowledge does not prove the inconceivability of God, but only the futility of conceiving God abstractly as the *Absolute* and *Infinite*. We cannot know anything except in its relations to ourselves, but it is as possible to know God relatively as it is to know nature relatively. He is especially vigorous in his rejection of Mansel's view that we must accept and worship a God whose nature violates both reason and conscience.[1] There is another alternative, which is to conceive God as finite, imputing to him only so much of the world as testifies to his goodness. Belief in a God who is the champion of righteousness gives to man a sense of partnership and reinforcement, and is thus morally fruitful even though it be incapable of proof by the strict standards of the intellect. Religion, in the end, is an invigorating and comforting hope, rather than a reasoned conviction.[2]

§ 72. Methodological Positivism. Lange. Mach. Poincaré

Empirical positivism may be termed "critical" in the sense that it limits knowledge to the field of experience. It is, on the other hand, deemed uncritical by those who believe that it ignores the part played in knowledge by the knowing mind. Empiricism is disposed to construe the subject as the passive recipient of sensations, and to interpret knowledge as reflecting an order which is *given* in experience. The knowing mind must frame hypotheses, but these are in the end tested and verified by their correspondence with experience; the knowing mind possesses its ingrained modes of thought, but these are habits built up by association, and traceable to the routine of individual or ancestral experience. Methodological positivism, on the other hand, denies the possibility of this reduction of

---

[1] *Examination of the Philos. of Sir Wm. Hamilton*, ch. VII.
[2] *Three Essays on Religion.*

knowledge to what is given, and insists that knowledge is always, even in the last resort, a product of the knowing mind. The positivist of this type will, like all positivists, hold that natural science is the supreme example of knowledge, and will be interested in it *as knowledge* rather than as offering an account of the world we live in; but unlike the empirical positivist, he will be primarily concerned with its "categories," or with that part of scientific knowledge which is supplied not by experience but by the scientific activity itself.

The German philosopher ALBERT LANGE,[1] professor at Zurich and Marburg, and author of the famous *History of Materialism* (*Geschichte des Materialismus*, 1866), serves through the very ambiguity and instability of his position, as the best starting-point for the study of this type of positivism. Being the source of diverging tendencies he has been universally criticised by those who have followed some one of these tendencies to the exclusion of the rest. Lange took as his point of departure Kant's *Critique of Pure Reason*, which he believed to have proved once and for all that instead of our concepts being determined by objects, objects are determined by our concepts.[2] Our knowledge, in other words, reflects the organization of our minds. He also held, in accordance with the strict interpretation of Kant, that the categories or forms of mental organization apply only within the realm of human experience; that the natural sciences afford the sole instance of their application, and hence the sole instance of knowledge; and that the only valid categories of science, and hence of knowledge, are those categories, such as space, time, and causality, which serve to provide an exact mechanical explanation of nature. While he thus supported the method of science, he denied the pretensions of a materialistic metaphysics, on the ground that, like all metaphysics, it illegitimately extends the categories beyond experience, and on the ground that it must necessarily fail in its attempt to

---

[1] 1828–1875. (Cf. § 69.)
[2] *Geschichte des Materialismus*, 6th edition, vol. II, p. 3.

reduce mind to physical terms.[1] So far he might, with justice, hold himself to be no more than a rigorous Kantian.

He clearly departed from Kant, however, in construing the organization of the mind in *physico-psychological* terms, as a fact of human nature proved by such evidence as was in Lange's time supplied by the new physiology of the senses. Here the orthodox neo-Kantians[2] refuse to follow him, contending that categories which are employed to construct our knowledge of nature cannot be a part of nature, but must be "transcendental," as Kant himself supposed them to be. Those who like Lange attempt to provide a naturalistic account of the categories (Mach, Avenarius, Poincaré, Durkheim) definitely break at this point with the Kantian tradition, and cease to be affiliated with idealism.

The second part of Lange's philosophy was not less suggestive and prophetic than the first. Nature, or the world of knowledge, is common to all, expressing, as it does, the mental organization of the species. Over and above this realm of actuality there is the ideal realm, which is the free creation of the inventive or poetic imagination (*Dichtung*) of the individual.[3] When ideals are mistaken for actualities error arises, but ideals are the legitimate expression of the moral, æsthetic, and religious nature, and as such may be compared with one another in respect of their *value*. This view that the claims of ideals are to be judged by their own peculiar standards, independently of their reference to fact, relates Lange to Lotze and Ritschl,[4] and to the later development of the philosophy of value.[5] From this position is but a short step to the view that truth itself is a value, and that even scientific judgments are justified, not solely by their conformity to outer fact, but by their satisfaction of the will. Here again there is a division between those philosophers who interpret the will naturalisti-

---

[1] It can go no further in this direction than to establish a parallelism of aspects between the physical and mental (*op. cit.*, 2d edition, vol. II, pp. 374 ff.). Lange's view here approaches that of Fechner (§ 74).

[2] § 79.   [3] *Op. cit.*, vol. II, p. 540.   [4] § 74.   [5] § 79.

cally and are the forerunners of pragmatism;[1] and those philosophers who, adhering more closely to the Kantian teaching, interpret the will in transcendental and *a priori* terms.[2] The former group comprises the same philosophers that construe the categories of science in naturalistic terms, and to these we now turn.

For the purpose of illustrating that widely diffused methodological positivism which rejects the Kantian deduction of the categories, but which nevertheless admits a subjective or voluntary factor in knowledge, it will be most instructive to select two thinkers who approached philosophy through science.[3] This philosophy expresses the desire, on the one hand, to reduce the objects of science to the terms of experience, and, on the other hand, to reduce its categories to the actual technique of experimentation. It seeks to avoid, on the one hand, speculative excursions beyond the given facts, and on the other hand, logical schematisms and assumptions. It represents the positivistic motive of science in its greatest purity.

ERNST MACH, born in 1838, was for many years professor of physics at the University of Prague, and afterwards, until his death in 1916, professor of philosophy in Vienna. His *Die Mechanik in ihrer Entwicklung*, published in 1883,[4] is a historical and critical study of scientific method, in which the author shows that in the course of its development mechanics has come more and more clearly to see that its purpose is "the abstract quantitative expression of facts." It does not seek to "explain" phenomena by referring them to purposes or hidden causes, but gives a simple and comprehensive account

---

[1] §§ 81–83. [2] § 79.

[3] Among the scientists who exhibited the same general tendency of thought are the physicists Maxwell (§ 69), H. Hertz (1857–1894), G. Kirchhoff (1824–1887), the physiologist M. Verworn (1863–1921). The most important of the philosophers affiliated with this tendency are Richard AVENARIUS (1843–1896; *Kritik der reinen Erfahrung*, 1888); his follower, J. Petzoldt (b. 1862); H. Cornelius (b. 1863); and Karl Pearson (b. 1853; *Grammar of Science*, 1892).

[4] Translated into English under the title of *The Science of Mechanics*, 1893.

of the relations of dependence *among* phenomena.[1] His most notable philosophical work, the *Analysis of Sensations,* first published in 1886,[2] attacks the question of the relations of physics and psychology, reducing their content to common terms, and defining scientific method in such terms as to be applicable equally to both branches of investigation. Mach spoke as a scientist and disclaimed any intention of solving "riddles of the universe." He was only clearing the ground for science by eliminating problems with which the scientist is not concerned. But he clearly implied by the ironical tone in which he referred to "sure foundations" and "unshakable axioms," that what is good for the scientist is good also for the philosopher.[3]

Mach's boldest step was his resolution of body and mind into common elements. Here the way had been prepared for him by Berkeley, Hume, Mill, and others of the sensationalistic school, who had taught that physical things in their *knowable* aspect may be reduced to the sum of their sensible properties. Many of these philosophers had also proposed to reduce mind to a similar congeries of feelings. But, save for a suggestion of Hume,[4] these philosophers had regarded the members of both complexes as mental. The physical object still lurked behind the scenes as a duplicate of its sensible appearances, or as the activity of God, or as the unknowable, or as a permanent possibility of sensation. Mach took the radical step of *identifying* the physical object with its sensible appearances. There is then no difference between the physical and the mental save the type of dependence among elements which in themselves are *neither* physical nor mental. The visible color, for example, is intrinsically neither physical nor mental; but in so far as

---

[1] *Ibid.*, p. 502.

[2] *Beiträgen zur Analyse der Empfindungen.* The 5th edition of 1906 contains important additions. Both editions have been translated into English under the title of *The Analysis of Sensation.* His other important philosophical works are *Populär-wissenschaftliche Vorlesungen,* 3d ed., 1903 (English trans., *Popular Scientific Essays,* 1910), and *Erkenntnis und Irrtum,* 1905.

[3] *Erkenntnis u. Irrtum,* Preface, and ch. I.

[4] *Treatise of Human Nature,* Selby-Bigge's edition, p. 207.

dependent upon its luminous source it is physical, while in so far as dependent on the retina (as proved by its disappearance when the eyes are closed) it is mental. "Physical" and "mental," in other words, signify different *systems* of homogeneous elements.[1]

Mach was far from supposing that science is the mere observation or reproduction of the data of experience. Its purpose is to "save experiences," by achieving ideas in which these are summarized and anticipated.[2] It is governed by the purpose of *economy*. It is therefore primarily concerned not with the elements of experience, but with the "functional relations"[3] by which they are controlled. How far these functional relations, which appear as concepts and theories in the finished product of knowledge, subsist among the elements themselves, and how far they are the creation of science, is not clear. They are observed in phenomena, abstracted from phenomena, and verified by phenomena. On the other hand, they are tested subjectively by their congruence with one another, and possess a precision and a logical structure which is approximated but never fully realized in experience. Their very convenience as working tools is due to their being freely fashioned to the use to which they are put. In any case they owe their form to the necessity of *restricting expectation* to that which is vitally important. They are a "product of the *psychological* need of finding our way in nature," and their growing refinement expresses the demand for a more *methodical adaptation* that shall keep pace with the increasing complexities of life.[4]

The tendency of recent French philosophy of science has been to give greater emphasis to this subjective element which is recognized by Mach. The most important influence in this

---

[1] *Analysis of Sensations*, English translation, 1914, pp. 8–17. The aggregate of these homogeneous elements in their bare qualitative differences constitutes the "pure experience" of Avenarius.

[2] *Science of Mechanics*, pp. 481, 490.

[3] *Analysis of Sensations*, 1914, p. 363.

[4] *Erkenntnis und Irrtum*, ch. XXIII.

direction from the side of positivism was that exercised by the great mathematician and physicist HENRI POINCARÉ,[1] who at the opening of the century published a series of books dealing with the method and value of science.[2] He was born at Nancy in 1854, was a student and lecturer at the École Polytechnique in Paris, — and afterwards, from 1886 until his death in 1912, a professor of the Faculty of Sciences at the Sorbonne.

In addition to the fact that Poincaré was a creative scientist of great theoretical acumen, and qualified to speak with authority of scientific motives and scientific procedure, the interest of Poincaré's philosophy lies in his attempt to combine three aspects of science, the rational, the conventional, and the experimental; each of which has had its partisans, but none of which in Poincaré's judgment affords an adequate picture of science as a whole.

As a pure mathematician who is himself to be credited with important contributions to the theory of functions, Poincaré could scarcely fail to make a place in science for the element of universal and *a priori* truth. This he provided for in his account of "reasoning by recurrence" [3] which he believed to lie at the basis of the simplest branch of mathematics, namely, arithmetic. That which is true of the number 1, and which when true of $n-1$ is true of n, is true of all numbers. This general theorem can be verified in the case of any given number by showing that if the truth in question holds of 1 it holds of 2, and if of 2, then of 3, and so on until the given number is reached. To establish the law for *all* numbers by this procedure would re-

---

[1] The tendency is further represented by Gaston Milhaud (1858–1918), *Essai sur les Conditions et les Limites de la Certitude logique* (1894), and Pierre Duhem (1861–1916), *La Théorie physique* (1906).

[2] These books, constituting only the philosophical part of his numerous publications, were *La Science et l'Hypothèse*, 1902 (English trans., *Science and Hypothesis*, 1914); *La Valeur de la Science*, 1905 (English trans., *The Value of Science*, 1907); *Science et Méthode*, 1909 (English trans., *Science and Method*, 1914); *Dernières pensées*, posthumous.

[3] *La Science et l'Hypothèse*, part I, ch. I. This principle is sometimes known as "mathematical induction."

quire an interminable, and therefore psychologically impossible, series of syllogisms. The generalization of the law is possible only because the mind can see, once and for all, the possibility of this interminable series. We are forced to rely on a "direct intuition of the mind," which "knows itself capable of conceiving the indefinite repetition of the same act when once this act is possible." [1] From this intuition, and neither from the principle of contradiction, nor from experience, is derived all generalization and universality.

When we pass from arithmetic and analysis, or the sciences of pure order, to geometry and to physics, the principle of recurrence no longer suffices. There now appears the factor of *convention* or arbitrary definition. Poincaré was here influenced by the newer developments of mathematics, and in particular by non-Euclidean geometry. [2] The three-dimensional homogeneous space of Euclid and of common-sense has ceased to possess any unique validity for mathematics, but is seen to rest upon certain assumptions which are, from the point of view of mathematics, quite arbitrary. By changing the assumptions mathematics can with equal truth develop a system of four-dimensional space. A similar range of possibilities exists in mechanics, in which the Newtonian system, for example, is only one alternative; or in mathematical physics, as exemplified by the theory of energy.

How, then, is one to choose among these alternatives? To find a criterion we must consider the relations of science to experience. Here enters the third, or empirical, aspect of science. Poincaré firmly opposed the extreme position of those who hold that science as a whole is "artificial," or controlled exclusively by subjective principles, whether logical or æsthetic. [3] The physical sciences have in the end to submit to experimental verification or the test of prediction. Only experience can es-

---

[1] *Science and Hypothesis*, English translation, 1905, p. 13.

[2] As developed by G. R. B. Riemann (1826–1866) and N. I. Lobatchewsky (1793–1856).

[3] Cf. his refutation of Le Roy, *La Valeur de la Science*, part III.

tablish their truth. "Empirical" laws and hypotheses are determined altogether by the "brute facts" of sensation. Exact theories, such as those of mechanics and mathematical physics, are not to be proved or disproved in the same decisive manner, but choice is made among them according to their *simplicity* and *convenience*. Theories upon this level are always subject to change, while empirical laws remain relatively constant. Theories are like languages or standards of measurement, alternative modes of representing the facts, which are all true so far as they *do* represent the facts; and supersede one another according as they prove better capable of representing these facts, and of assimilating new facts, without devious and unnecessary complications.

We thus find in Poincaré a not wholly consistent combination of two views of the relation of knowledge to reality. On the one hand, science conforms itself to given facts, and rests on an experimental basis; while on the other hand, it rests on an intuition of the inherent power of the mind, and expresses a taste for simplicity and harmony.

§ 73. Sociological Positivism. Durkheim

It has been remarked that naturalism tends by rejecting the divine to exalt the human. A desire to find some substitute for the ideals and absolutes of the opposite philosophy leads to a special emphasis on society, because this provides some human sanction of truths or of values beyond the individual. This tendency culminated in the nineteenth century in the sociological positivism of "sociologism" of France, and its most important representative was ÉMILE DURKHEIM,[1] who was

---

[1] This movement is continuously related to Comte. The forerunner of Durkheim was Alfred Espinas (1844–1922; *Les Sociétés animales*, 1876). While Espinas anticipated Durkheim in his emphasis on the organic unity of society, Gabriel Tarde (1843–1904; *Les Lois d'Imitation*, 1890) proposed to explain society in terms of "inter-psychology," or the influence of mind on mind through the force of imitation. The racial factor in sociology, together with the social application of Darwinian conceptions, was emphasized by Joseph Arthur Comte de Gobineau (1816–1882), and the psychology of the crowd by Gustave Le Bon (b. 1841; *La Psychologie des Foules*, 1895).

born in Paris in 1858, inaugurated university instruction in sociology in Bordeaux in 1887, and was called in 1902 to the Sorbonne, where he was "professor of the science of education" from 1906 until his death in 1917. Durkheim's[1] teachings have led to the creation of a school which constitutes one of the major tendencies of contemporary French thought.[2] His influence was due in part to his commanding personality, in part to the bold and constructive character of his doctrines, and in part to their fertility for sociological research.

Of the genuinely philosophical character of these doctrines there can be no doubt. Society for Durkheim is not a mere incident of evolution, to be assimilated to more fundamental laws of nature, but a being *sui generis*, which is to be taken as the centre and point of departure for human knowledge. Truth owes its objective and authoritative quality to the fact that it is an expression of collective, as distinguished from individual, thought. The fundamental concepts of science, such as space and time, are "collective representations," or products of social experience arising as the necessary conditions of religious rites and other forms of concerted action. Even the fundamental principles of logic, such as those of contradiction and identity, reflect the peculiar needs of civilized society, as is proved by their absence in the "prelogical" and "mystical" mentality of primitive man.[3] That difference which rationalists have emphasized between the universality of the principles of knowledge and the particularity and relativity of sense, is thus to be accounted for in terms of the difference between the common, impersonal mind,

---

[1] His most important writings were: *De la Division du Travail social*, 1893; *Les Régles de la Méthode sociologique*, 1894; *Les Formes élémentaires de la Vie religieuse*, 1912 (English translation, *The Elementary Forms of the Religious Life*, 1915).

[2] Its most eminent representative on the philosophical, as distinguished from the strictly sociological, side is Lucien Lévy-Bruhl (1857–   ): *Morale et la Science des Mœurs*, 4th ed., 1910 (English trans., *Ethics and Moral Science*, 1905); *Fonctions mentales dans les sociétés inferieures* (1910); *La Mentalité primitive*, 1922.

[3] *Formes élémentaires de la Vie religieuse*, p. 18. Cf. Lévy-Bruhl, *op. cit.*

and the private, capricious mind of the individual. Nor is the content of the collective mind to be reduced to that of individual minds, either through their psychological interaction, or through the accumulation of ancestral habits. Societies are irreducible entities, which have to be studied in their own terms and can be compared only with one another. It is true that societies embrace and are composed of individuals; but once constituted, they behave in a manner peculiar to themselves. They have a property, which like those of chemical substances, is irreducible to the properties of their component elements.

This unique property of a social fact, by which it is distinguished from every other fact, is *constraint*, or *obligation*. In other words, society is primarily a moral or religious (and not, as is sometimes supposed, a biological or economic) entity. Hence the importance for Durkheim of ethics and comparative religion. Morality consists of certain established rules or customs, peculiar to a given historical group, and having a peculiar coercive power upon its members, who feel it to be at one and the same time both *of* them and *over* them. It is not a wholly external restraint, but rather the object of disinterested devotion. The moral good which the individual acknowledges is neither his own private good, nor the private good of any other man, but something which he feels to be both immanent and transcendent, the very essence of himself and yet lying on a plane wholly different from that of any merely individual life. Morality is, therefore, not a calculation of individual interests, as the utilitarian would have it, nor an ideal formulation of what ought to be, but a social force and social fact that is capable, like other facts, of scientific description.[1] In other words the group is a law to its members, and the standard of value is the genius of the group. Although this view evidently has conservative implications, it does not, Durkheim thought, cut off the possibility of criticism and reform. For there are aberrations and abnormalities which the group conscience will

[1] Cf. Lévy-Bruhl, *Morale et la Science des Mœurs*.

condemn; and there is a manifest destiny for each society, which its enlightened members will perceive, and which by the light of reason they will confirm and promote.[1]

The most profound manifestation of social life is religion. This does not consist of beliefs, traceable, as Spencer and others had proposed, to the individual's experience of nature or to his ghostly dreams; but of the force which men feel in the exaltation of the collective religious experience. The most primitive religious idea is the distinction between the *sacred* and the *profane*. Sacred objects, like the totem, are symbols of the group, and are invested with the power and awfulness which the group possesses for its members. Religion like morality rests on the postulate that "*society can be considered as a personality qualitatively different from the individual personalities which compose it.*"[2]

B. SPIRITUALISM AND IDEALISM

§ 74. Spiritualism in Germany. Fechner. Lotze. Hartmann

Although naturalism[3] of either the materialistic or the positivistic variety was the dominant feature of German philosophy just after the middle of the nineteenth century, spiritualism had been struggling valiantly to hold its own. Kant, who pitilessly destroyed it in his *Critique of Pure Reason*, had called it back to life in his moral postulates, and, ultimately, rendered it a signal service. F. H. Jacobi,[4] whom we found among the opponents of the *Critique*, defended spiritualism against the pantheism of Spinoza, Schelling, and Hegel, by appealing to the *inner sense*. The theologian and philosopher FRIEDRICH SCHLEIERMACHER,[5] although an enthusiastic Spi-

---

[1] Durkheim's most important pronouncement on moral questions is his paper on "La Determination du Fait moral," in *Bulletin de la Société française de Philosophie*, 1906.

[2] *Op. cit.*, p. 115.

[3] The present paragraph is retained with minor changes from the Weber translation, pp. 587–588.

[4] See § 63.

[5] 1768–1834. Complete works, Berlin, 1835–1864. *Reden über die Religion*, etc., 1799; Eng. tr. by J. Oman, 1893; *Monologen*, 1800; *Grundriss der philosophischen Ethik*, 1841.

nozist, indirectly advanced the spiritualistic cause by his appeal to religious feeling (*das fromme Gefühl*) and the "awakening" which it tends to produce. A disciple of Spinoza (though an original disciple, like Herder), Schleiermacher attempted, especially in his ethics, to reconcile the monism of the master with the principle of individual spontaneity, by substituting for the abstract idea of *unity* the concrete principle of *harmony*. His theory of knowledge is likewise an attempt to reconcile sensationalism with the intellectualism of Fichte and Hegel. He is most famous for his definition of religion, as consisting essentially in the feeling of dependence on the infinite. CHRISTIAN F. KRAUSE,[1] a thinker of great merit, but unappreciated in his own country, substituted for pantheism *panentheism*, or the doctrine of the immanency of things in God, considered as a transcendent personality and yet united in substance with the creature. The so-called "semi-Hegelians," such as Weisse, opposed to this doctrine the system of *speculative theism*. A. TRENDELENBURG[2] created a system of metaphysics whose leading thought is the idea of *movement*, the common essence of thought and being.

The last of these philosophers already exhibited the tendency, which had been so strong with Schelling in his later phases, and now became generally characteristic of the spiritualistic philosophy in Germany, to overcome the duality of mind and body by providing a spiritual interpretation of nature, in a manner reminiscent of Aristotle and Leibniz. Nature, according to this view, does not derive its relation to mind from the fact that it is an object of knowledge, but to the fact that it is inherently spiritual in substance, and is governed by purposes and ends, rather than by merely me-

[1] 1781–1832. *Grundlage des Naturrechts*, 1803; *Entwurf des Systems der Philosophie*, 1804; *System der Sittenlehre*, 1810 [2d ed., 1887]; etc. His principal adherent was the German Heinrich Ahrens (1808–1874), author of *Cours de philosophie*, 1836–1838; *Cours de droit naturel ou philosophie du droit*, 1838; *Cours de philosophie de l'histoire*, 1840. He had numerous disciples also in France, Belgium, and Spain.

[2] 1802–1872. Professor at Berlin, and author of *Logische Untersuchungen*, 2 vols., 3d ed., 1870; etc.

chanical laws. This method of attack, in which philosophy begins with nature, and construes nature objectively, rather than in terms of its relation to the knowing subject, signified the influence of the cult of science even on philosophers of the spiritualistic school. Just as materialism offered compromises with spiritualism, through its emphasis on force and life, so spiritualism made concessions to materialism by acknowledging the existence of an external and independent natural order.

GUSTAV THEODORE FECHNER, who was born in 1801 in Lauwitz, Germany, was a student of physics and of medicine, and in 1835 became professor of physics in Leipsic. His failing eyesight forced him eventually to abandon this professorship, and was one of the motives inducing him to turn in the direction of psychology and eventually of metaphysical speculation. As a scientist his most important achievement was the so-called "Weber-Fechner Law,"[1] according to which the intensity of sensation, instead of increasing in direct proportion to the strength of the stimulus, increases by diminishing increments; in other words, the stronger the existing stimulus the less will be the increase of sensation caused by an additional unit of stimulus.[2] This law marks the foundation of the branch of knowledge known as "psycho-physics," and the exact, quantitative method which he used to establish it gives its author an important place in the history of experimental psychology.[3] His doctrine of psycho-physical idealism or

---

[1] Named "Weber's Law" by Fechner himself, in honor of his teacher, the physiologist, E. H. Weber. It can be most simply expressed by saying that the intensity of sensation increases as the logarithm of the stimulus.

[2] Cf. the *Elemente der Psychophysik* (1860). The more important of his other works are: *Zendavesta* (1851), *Über die Seelenfrage* (1861), *Die drei Motive des Glaubens* (1863), *Über die physikalische und die philosophische Atomenlehre* (1855), *Vorschule der Æsthetik* (1876), *Die Tagesansicht gegenüber der Nachtansicht* (1879), *Das Büchlein vom Leben nach dem Tode*, 1836 (English trans., *The Little Book of Life After Death*, 1912).

[3] Among the pioneers of this general movement, leading to the establishment of psychological laboratories in Europe and America, the following, in addition to Fechner, are especially worthy of mention: H. Helmholtz (§ 69) and Wilhelm Wundt (1832–1920), in Germany; W. James (§ 82) and G. Stanley Hall (1846–1924), in America.

"panpsychism," and the companion doctrine of the plurality and hierarchy of souls, were developed with great eloquence and speculative ingenuity in the most famous of his works, the *Zendavesta*, and their religious and moral implications absorbed his attention up to the time of his death in 1887.

The difference between the physical and the psychical, according to Fechner, is a difference of point of view. That which *to itself* is psychical, is *to others* physical. In other words, the physical is the phenomenal or extrinsic appearance of things. Behind the phenomenon lies not a dark unknowable, or an inert matter, but a psychical life like our own. All things are inwardly or intrinsically psychical. The physical and psychical are not, as in the "identity theory" of Spinoza, two aspects of a third and substantial principle, but the psychical is the substance and the physical is the aspect. This relation is in philosophical speculation extended by analogy to all of nature, and all bodily phenomena may be assumed to be or belong to the outward aspect of some soul.

But Fechner was no more a Leibnizian monadist than he was a Spinozistic monist. Souls are possessed not by each distinguishable physical element or phenomenon, but only by such systems or organizations of phenomena as form organic wholes, like the bodies of plants and animals. Fechner believed, however, that not only plants and animals, but also the earth, the stars, and the total cosmos, are "bodies" of this type, and that one may therefore properly speak of an "earth-soul," and of a "soul of the world." God is this soul of the world, or the all-inclusive system of nature as it is to itself.

The relation of these souls to one another is a relation of inclusion. Just as the bodily man is a part of the physical system of the earth, so the soul of man is a part of the earth-soul, and the earth-soul in turn is a part of the soul of the world. As the soul of man embraces its diverse sensations and ideas within one synthetic unity, so the souls of all creatures are enveloped and unified within the soul of God. This may be otherwise expressed by saying that the soul of God is re-

lated to the soul of man as the ground swell to the waves
which it carries. Because of its comparatively high threshold,[1]
man's consciousness contains only fragments of the soul of
God, the rest possessing to man only the aspect of externality,
or body. God not only embraces the intermittent and isolated
consciousnesses of all creatures, but gives organic unity and
inward psychical nature to the dead past and to the inorganic
stretches of nature. All of nature belongs to God's body, and
is the outward manifestation of one psychical continuum,
which is God's soul.[2]

RUDOLPH HERMANN LOTZE, the most distinguished and
widely influential German philosopher during the latter half
of the nineteenth century, was born in Bautzen, in 1817.
Like Fechner, his early training as well as his mature interests
were divided between science and philosophy. At Leipsic he
studied medicine and physics, and in philosophy came under
the influence of Weisse. His numerous writings reflect the
wide range of his studies. In his *Medical Psychology* (*Medizinische Psychologie*, 1852) he made important contributions,
both physiological and speculative, to this new branch of
science. His most popular book was the *Microcosmus* (*Mikrokosmus*, 1856–1864), a work notable for its brilliancy of exposition and moral eloquence, in which the author dealt broadly
with man,—his natural constitution, his culture, and his destiny. His *History of Æsthetics* (*Geschichte der Æsthetik in
Deutschland*, 1868) was also widely read, and has exercised a
notable influence in this field, especially through his anticipation of the theory of "empathy" (Einfühlung), according to
which the enjoyment of æsthetic forms, such as symmetry, is
occasioned by the perception of corresponding movements and
tensions in the organism.[3] The most mature formulation of

---

[1] As proved by Weber's Law, which shows that there are intensities of physical stimulation which induce no psychical changes.

[2] *Elemente der Psychophysik*, II, p. 529.

[3] *Geschichte der Æsthetik*, pp. 76–79. Cf. *Medizinische Psychologie*, p. 293.

his system is to be found in the *Logic* (*Logik*, 1874), and in the *Metaphysics* (*Metaphysik*, 1879), written while the author was a professor at Göttingen. A third volume was to have dealt with æsthetics, ethics, and philosophy of religion, but its completion was prevented by the author's death in 1881, a year after having been called to the University of Berlin.[1]

All of our knowledge, said Lotze, reposes in the last analysis on a faith in reason. There is nothing by which reason can be corrected save itself. Even the sceptic, in the affirmation of his doubts, betrays some ultimate and indemonstrable conviction.[2] Ultimate convictions assume one of three forms. "All our analysis of the cosmic order ends in leading our thought back to a consciousness of necessarily valid *truths*, our perception to the intuition of immediately given *facts* of reality, our conscience to the recognition of an absolute standard of all *determinations of worth*." [3] These convictions are independent of one another. Necessary truths do not yield facts, nor facts necessity; and neither necessity nor fact follows from the apprehension of value. The synthesis of these three forms of knowledge, in the conception of a *universe which embraces the acts under necessary laws and realizes the norms of value*, is again an act of faith. Philosophy cannot be expected to do more than to elaborate this conception, and to remove objections that stand in the way of its acceptance.

Lotze's metaphysics starts with the mechanical conception of nature, as a system of interacting corporeal units. These units, or atoms, as ultimate and indivisible, have to be considered as active rather than as extended. Nor is their plurality to be regarded as a final view of their relations. For action and reaction are inconceivable if the interacting elements are independent. That one element should change in consequence of

---

[1] His other important philosophical works were: *Metaphysik*, 1841, and *Logik*, 1843 (not to be confused with the works of 1874 and 1879); *Kleine Schriften*, composed of shorter articles and reviews, published posthumously. Works mentioned in the text have been translated into English as follows: *Microcosmus*, 1884; *Logic*, 1884; *Metaphysics*, 1884.

[2] *Logik* of 1874, § 305.   [3] *Microcosmus*, English translation, book IX, § 2.

changes in another element implies that they are in reality only phases of one underlying substance, so unitary in nature that its several states are all reciprocal and compensatory. Since all of the elements of reality react to one another in a way that is determined, we must conclude that the nature of each is implicated in the nature of the rest, or that all are parts of one substance or vitally connected whole. Thus Lotze's ultimate view of nature was *monistic* rather than *monadistic*.

Having concluded that reality is a single substance within which all changes are reciprocally determined, Lotze had now to establish its spiritual constitution. To be real in the physical sense is to stand in dynamic relations, that is, to maintain identity, while inducing or suffering change. But we cannot grasp the meaning of these characters save in terms of actual feeling, and in terms of the unity of consciousness. To say of anything that *it* acts or suffers, implies something more than a change of state antecedent or subsequent to changes of state in other things. It implies that it *itself* recognizes such changes as its own, — as modes of its self-affirmation or of self-preservation. Only spiritual subjects exercise this function, and can be regarded as ultimately real.[1] Two such realities we are forced to recognize, namely, our finite selves, and God, or the universal being which is the ground of nature. Whether there be over and above these realities a third order of natural substances, cannot, Lotze thinks, be absolutely determined; but he accepted this view, with some hesitation, as affording the best explanation of sense-perception and of the facts of science. He was primarily concerned to show if nature is real, it must be thought as consisting of spiritual beings below the level of man, and, like man, grounded in the universal substance of God. "Either only minds exist, and the whole world of things is a phenomenon in minds, or things which appear to us as permanent yet selfless points of departure, intersection and termination of action, are beings which share with minds in various degrees the general characteristic of mentality, namely self-

[1] *Microcosmus*, bk. IX, ch. III; *Metaphysics* (1879), bk. I, ch. VII.

existence." Adopting the latter alternative, Lotze thought of nature as composed of beings which, while dependent on God in the sense of being modes of his activity, nevertheless exist themselves, as having both feeling and will, and in some measure that capacity for self-identification more fully manifested in the self-conscious ego.[1]

Lotze's philosophy of religion rests in part upon his spiritualistic metaphysics, which reveals God as the ultimate substance of things, and as possessing in a superlative degree that character of self-conscious personality which is the essential qualification for reality. But religion is primarily an expression of feeling rather than of intellect. It reflects, on the one hand, the feeling of dependence, and on the other hand, the acknowledgment of beauty and goodness. It cannot, therefore, be judged in the last analysis by canons of theoretical truth. It embodies judgments of value (the "indemonstrable but irreversible declarations" of "conscience and feeling"), which are irreducible to judgments of fact or of logical necessity.[2] It expresses, furthermore, a faith in the ultimate synthesis of fact, necessity, and value. According to the view with which Lotze concluded his *Microcosmus*, and which he offers as a "confession of his philosophic faith," God is a single power, "appearing to us under a threefold image" — "namely, first some definite and desired Good, then on account of the definiteness of this, a formed and developing Reality, and finally in this activity an unvarying reign of Law."[3]

Thus Lotze represented a regard for scientific fact, a recogni-

---

[1] *Microcosmus*, bk. IX, ch. III. English translation, edition of 1887, vol. II, p. 657.

[2] *Op. cit.*, p. 719. Through his insistence on the irreducibility of judgments of value to judgments of theoretic truth, Lotze is affiliated with that later form of idealism which would *reduce* the latter to the former (§ 79). Indeed, Lotze himself concluded his *Metaphysics* with the dictum that "the true beginning of Metaphysics lies in Ethics." Through his identification of religion with judgments of value, and his interpretation of dogmas in terms of their expression of religious experience, Lotze is related to the important movement in philosophy of religion of which the most distinguished leader was A. Ritschl (1822–1889).

[3] *Op. cit.*, p. 716.

tion of the universal necessities of thought, and beyond these, a speculative zeal for a metaphysical view which should satisfy not only the strictly intellectual demands, but the aspirations of man's moral, æsthetic, and religious nature.

The characteristics which are common to Fechner and Lotze appear again in EDUARD VON HARTMANN,[1] the most original among the disciples of Schopenhauer. Again we find a receptivity to science, combined with a willingness to supplement or reinterpret it by free speculation, and by the argument from analogy; again we find a general tendency to metaphysical realism, and the more specific tendency to overcome the dualism of the physical and mental worlds by construing nature as of the same substance with spirit.

In his famous *Philosophy of the Unconscious*,[2] Hartmann attempted to reconcile Schopenhauer and Hegel, by adding to the will a second principle, which serves as its guide: *idea (die Vorstellung)*. The will, he reasons, reaches its ends *as though* it were intelligent. It works through the mechanisms of inorganic nature, and creates the forms which (according to Darwinism) nature "selects." In the form of soul, it communicates to the human body such movements as it desires, as though perfectly conscious of the means necessary to realize its purpose. In animals it acts instinctively, like the most consummate intelligence. As the curative power in nature, it heals wounds

[1] 1842–1906.
[2] *Philosophie des Unbewussten*, 1869 [English trans., 1886]. Among his other works are: *Kritische Grundlegung des transcendentalen Realismus* (1875); *Phänomenologie des sittlichen Bewusstseins* (1879); *Das religiöse Bewusstsein der Menschheit* (1881). Among the prominent disciples of Schopenhauer was J. Frauenstädt (1813–1878; *Briefe über die Schopenhauersche Philosophie*, 1854; *Neue Briefe, etc.*, 1876). Frauenstädt is not a servile imitator: he criticises and corrects the master in several important respects. Not only does he distinguish between the *higher* or human will and the *inferior* will of the animal, thereby opposing Schopenhauer, who identifies them, but also substitutes for his pessimism a system which aims to reconcile pessimism and optimism. Cf. also Paul Deussen (1845–1919; *Elemente der Metaphysik*, 1877, English trans., 1894); Richard Wagner, the great composer (1813–1883; collected writings, 9 vols., 2d ed., 1887–1888); and Friedrich Nietzsche (§ 81). [The exposition of Hartmann is retained from the Weber translation. — ED.]

and fractures, like the most skilful physician. Hence it is *intelligent*, but *unconscious;* it knows without knowing that it knows.

This distinction between intelligence and consciousness is not new; we find it in Leibniz and in Schelling. But Hartmann was the first to formulate it with perfect clearness, and to support it by a great mass of facts. It would, however, be a mistake to regard the doctrine that ideas guide the will as creating an essential difference between Hartmann and Schopenhauer; for Schopenhauer, too, has his Platonic *ideas*, which serve as stages in the evolution of the will. Besides, Hartmann's *idea* cannot hinder the absolute from *willing*, i. e., from realizing itself in a world in which the evil necessarily and infinitely exceeds the good, and to which, though it be the best *possible* world, nothingness would be preferable. All that it can do is to guide the cosmical evolution, and to influence the absolute (by producing a more profound feeling of the universal misery and a more complete knowledge of the secret of things — in a word, by developing consciousness) not to will to be: which would mean the end of the world. Here, then, the difference between disciple and master is more apparent than real. According to Hartmann as well as according to Schopenhauer, the existence of the world is an evil, since it is synonymous with pain, sorrow, and anguish, — feelings which recur, in different degrees, in myriads of sensible creatures. But, in Schopenhauer's opinion, the evil is irreparable: the world and, consequently, the pains are eternal, and only the individuals that die are relatively redeemed. According to Hartmann, on the other hand, who rests on the principle that *no development is without beginning or end*, and assumes a creation and an end of the world, the evil is reparable: redemption is universal, and even the absolute is ultimately redeemed.[1] Only, this redemp-

---

[1] Hartmann calls this his *evolutionistic* optimism in opposition to Schopenhauer's absolute pessimism; i. e., he makes the historical evolution culminate at least in the negative happiness of nothingness, while Schopenhauer recognizes in reality neither history, nor evolution, nor progress of any sort.

tion is not *final*, for we have no assurance that the latent state to which the will returns is final, that it will not be re-aroused, and so create a new world.

§ 75. **Spiritualism in France. Maine de Biran. Cousin. Ravaisson. Boutroux**

The patron saint of French spiritualism in the nineteenth century is MAINE DE BIRAN, who, although he lived at the opening of the century, did not assume a place of high importance until fifty years later. He was born at Bergerac in 1766, and died in 1824, his life thus embracing both the Revolutionary and the Napoleonic eras. But he maintained a certain detachment from all the revolutionary changes of his time. He compared himself to a miner whose real life was spent in the subterranean depths of his own inner consciousness. His vocation was that of self-examination, in which he displayed that extraordinary delicacy of observation, and power to detect the nuance of a passing mood, which marked Rousseau, and is characteristic generally of modern French literature and psychology. He held no academic post, constructed no system of philosophy, published little, and owed his influence to his friendships, and to his rediscovery by a more sympathetic posterity.[1]

Maine de Biran's point of departure was the doctrine of the "idealogues,"[2] Cabanis and Destutt de Tracy, with whom he was intimately associated in the circle of Madame Helvetius at Auteuil in 1797. These thinkers had begun already to modify the traditional sensationalism of their school. Cabanis accepted instinct and unconscious dispositions as predetermining the mind's reception of impressions from without, while de Tracy insisted on the felt activity of will, as the source of the idea of an external world. Maine de Biran de-

---

[1] His only important publication during his life was *The Influence of Habit* (*L'Influence de l'Habitude*, 1802). His posthumous works are: *Nouvelles Considerations sur les Rapports du Physique et du Moral*, 1834; *Œuvres philosophiques*, 1841; *Œuvres inédites*, 1859; *Science et Psychologie*, 1887; *Œuvres*, 1920–1922.
[2] § 69.

veloped both of these ideas. Impressed with the power of temperament and uncontrollable moods to alter the whole current of the mental life, he conceived of a level of "pure affection," underlying conscious personality and intimately dependent on organic conditions. Self-consciousness emerges from these physiological depths, which can never be penetrated by clear introspection, but manifest themselves in somnambulism, or in the transition from the sleeping to the waking state, or in the twilight zone which surrounds the focus of attention. With the passivity of this sub-conscious mind is contrasted the essential *activity* of consciousness itself. We know ourselves only as active: "the same reflexive act by which the subject knows himself and calls himself 'I,' reveals him to himself as an acting force." This free and self-identifying activity is the first principle not only of all psychology, but of all philosophy as well. As the basic certainty of knowledge Maine de Biran proposed to substitute for Descartes's famous *cogito ergo sum*, "*I feel or perceive myself free cause*, therefore I am really cause." ("*Je me sens ou m'aperçois cause libre, donc je suis réelement cause.*" [1]) This same self-activity furnishes the bridge to the external world, since the subject as acting force is known as exerting itself against resistance.[2] It is also the source of the categories, such as force, cause, unity, and identity, by which we understand the world. It preserves the individual existences from being merged in a unity of substance, and establishes a polar relation between the personality of man the created and God the creative force.[3]

Unlike Maine de Biran, VICTOR COUSIN exercised a profound influence upon his times, but has been more lightly esteemed by posterity. His influence was due as much to the circumstances of his career, and his relation to his times, as to the quality of his genius. Born in 1792 he became professor at the Sorbonne in 1815, and from 1830 to 1851, as director of

---

[1] *Ibid.*, p. 249.   [2] *Œuvres inédites*, vol. I, pp. 47–48.
[3] *Œuvres philosophiques*, vol. III, p. 20.

the École Normale Supérieure and minister of state, he became a sort of educational dictator, being thus enabled to give to his teachings an official sanction and prestige of orthodoxy. To the influence of position was added an eloquence and enthusiasm which made the delivery of his famous lectures on *The True, the Beautiful and the Good* in 1818 a memorable event in the lives of his contemporaries.[1] His learning and keen interest in the history of philosophy, and his acquaintance with the thought of Germany, gained through his studies and travels in that country, greatly broadened the outlook of French philosophy. Above all he satisfied the need, so keenly felt in his epoch, after years of disillusionment and narrow empiricism, for an edifying and inspiring creed, and for a philosophy on the grand scale.

The school of Cousin is commonly known as "eclecticism," signifying an acceptance of the essential truths contained in all the great systems of the past, and their union in one all-embracing system. In opposition to the destructive temper of scepticism and the cautious temper of empiricism, the term implies a disposition to credit as at least partially true all of the ideas which have obtained a strong hold upon human belief. In opposition to original speculation it implies that the office of philosophy is architectonic rather than creative.

But Cousin saw, nevertheless, that the true historic doctrines cannot be distinguished from the false without some independent criterion, and that they cannot be combined without being re-thought. He preferred, therefore, to regard himself as the exponent of "spiritualism," the philosophy which is "the natural ally of all good causes."[2] This philosophy he

---

[1] This work (*Du Vrai, du Beau, du Bien*) was first published in 1837, and later reissued in a succession of revised editions. It was translated into English in 1853. His *Œuvres complètes* were published in 22 volumes, 1846–1847. Other works translated into English: *Elements of Psychology*, 1856; *History of Modern Philosophy*, 1852; *Philosophy of the Beautiful*, 1849. Cousin's thought exerted a powerful influence in England and America, where it combined with German influences (especially that of Schelling) to provoke the romanticist tendency. He died in 1867, after his influence had already begun to wane.

[2] *Du Vrai, du Beau et du Bien*, edition of 1881, p. iv.

sought to establish by the study of the mind, or by psychology, which he regarded as the "grand method of modern philosophy," [1] inaugurated by Descartes. The empiricists, Locke and Condillac, who have followed the psychological method are to be preferred to those who, like Spinoza, have departed from it; but while they are to be praised for their psychology they are to be condemned for their empiricism. They have construed the mind too narrowly in terms of sensibility and have neglected the reason. Among those who have by a deepening of the psychological method brought to light the universal and necessary principles on which science and metaphysics, religion and common-sense alike repose, Reid was "the most irreproachable," and Kant "the most systematic." [2] Cousin had made the acquaintance of Reid [3] through his teacher and acknowledged master, Roger Collard, and with the former's cast of mind, as well as with his doctrines, he always felt a peculiar affinity.

To Kant, Cousin devoted considerable attention. He credited him with having shown by the psychological method that space, time, causality, substance, and the other categories are necessary principles of reason underived from sense. He condemned him, however, for having attached these principles to the human mind and limited their application to the sphere of sensation. The outcome of Kant's view is a scepticism even more destructive than that scepticism of Hume which he had undertaken to overthrow. The principles of reason are not mere subjective necessities. They appear to be so only when in *reflection* the mind finds itself incapable of rejecting them. Reflection is a secondary process of mind, which implies a direct and positive apprehension of principles, a "spontaneous intuition," "a sphere of light and of peace where reason perceives the truth . . . because God has made reason to perceive it as he has made the eye to see." [4] This spontaneous intuition is the true logic of nature, which is revealed, as Reid had rightly maintained, to common-sense,

[1] *Ibid.*, p. 3.   [2] *Ibid.*, p. 13.   [3] § 61.   [4] *Ibid.*, pp. 40, 41, 61.

and which neither needs nor is capable of any proof. These
same principles lead us to God,[1] for they cannot be thought
either to exist by themselves, or to reside in particular existences, or in the human mind. They are the thoughts of God,
reflected in the laws of nature, and serving as a link between
man and God.[2]

Although Cousin represented the romantic reaction against
the eighteenth century, and regarded himself as the champion
of the spiritualistic revival, he was promptly repudiated by the
more advanced exponents of these very tendencies. His chief
critic was FÉLIX RAVAISSON-MOLLIEN, whose *Report on Philosophy in France in the Nineteenth Century* (1867) contained
a vigorous attack upon both eclecticism and positivism, and a
new spiritualistic confession of faith. Ravaisson was born in
1813, and in his early youth came under the influence both of
Cousin and of Schelling, whose lectures he attended at Munich.[3] He found his chief philosophical inspiration, however,
in Aristotle, Leibniz, and, above all, in Maine de Biran, for
whose canonization he was chiefly responsible. He was a man
of profound erudition and wide experience, not only steeped
in the history of philosophical and religious thought, but, as
Curator of the Department of Antiquities in the Louvre from
1874 to his death in 1900, both a learned archæologist and an
appreciative connoisseur in the field of the fine arts. His
strictly philosophical writings were few, and like his German
contemporaries of the romantic era he sought in philosophy
not a technical solution of its own traditional problems, but
rather a unified interpretation of all culture[4].

[1] As do conscience and the sense of beauty, by other routes.
[2] *Ibid.*, pp. 67–102.
[3] He here formed the acquaintance of CHARLES SECRÉTAN (1815–1895; *Philosophie de la Liberté*, 1848–1849), whose development was in many respects parallel to his own, and who became the most distinguished Swiss philosopher of
the second half of the century.
[4] Besides the above-mentioned *Report* (*Rapport sur la Philosophie en France*,
1867) his chief philosophical writings were: *De l'Habitude*, 1838 (*Revue de Métaphysique et de Morale*, 1894); *Essai sur la Métaphysique d'Aristote*, vol. I, 1837,
vol. II, 1846; *Métaphysique et Morale*, in *Revue des deux Mondes*, 1893.

To Ravaisson, Cousin's philosophy was only a "half-spiritualism" (demi-spiritualisme).[1] Cousin had, it is true, taken a step beyond empiricism by introducing the principles of reason, and by paying homage to the supremacy of spirit. But he had still proceeded after the manner of the eighteenth century, to observe and analyze *ideas*. To sensations he had added abstract conceptions, but these bore no intelligible relation either to the soul, or to nature, or to God. Ideas conceived as passive states of the mind, whether of sensation or of reason, remained but external and disconnected appearances of some underlying reality whose nature remained unknown, and whose existence had to be dogmatically affirmed. What was needed was a metaphysical *insight* that should, on the one hand, reveal the essential nature of reality, and, on the other hand, serve as an explanatory key to the universe. This Ravaisson found neither in the inductive, observational method of the British and French schools of the eighteenth century, nor in the dialectic and intellectual intuition of the German schools of the nineteenth century, but in Maine de Biran. This writer, however, had not realized the full significance of his own discovery. He had pointed to the mind's immediate awareness of itself as will, but by unduly stressing the experience of effort, he had failed to see that the essence of will is desire, and that desire is essentially aspiration or love, — a striving toward perfection.

Spirit so construed furnishes the desired key by which the diverse aspects of reality and experience can be united. Spiritual activity is not an attribute of substance, it *is* substance: to be is to act.[2] To will and to think are the same thing, since thought is an *operation*, which aims to complete and unify experience: to be is to think.[3] When thought is thus construed as creative synthesis, there is no longer any division between knowledge and art.[4] Spirit, so conceived, is seen to be the essence of nature. The organic sciences have always found it

---

[1] *Rapport sur la Philosophie en France*, p. 19.   [2] *Ibid.*, p. 241.
[3] *Ibid.*, p. 259.   [4] *Ibid.*, p. 236.

necessary to employ the conception of finality, or to construe the parts in terms of the whole.[1] But even the inorganic sciences must in the end resort to the same spiritual categories. Inanimate nature differs from life and consciousness only in the *degree* of its spirituality. All movement is at bottom a *tendency;* inertia is a tendency to maintain or conserve motion.[2] This tendency for any activity to persist gives rise to habit; and the aspect of automatism presented by inorganic nature is to be construed, after the analogy of habit, as a degraded or fossilized will.[3] Only active and self-identical spirits can form habits, and nature can only be understood as a by-product of God. Physical nature is "a refraction or dispersion" of the divine spirit.[4]

Ravaisson having designed and constructed the new spiritualism, ÉMILE BOUTROUX undertook to defend it against the rising tide of naturalism. Born in 1845, at Montrouge, he entered upon his career in that decade of the 60's when (despite the reign of eclecticism in official and academic circles) materialism and positivism were gaining many adherents in France as well as abroad. Science spoke with an authority that could not be ignored; it was necessary to take cognizance of it and meet it on its own grounds. This Boutroux undertook to do in the most important of his books, *On the Contingency of the Laws of Nature,* published in 1874.[5] He exerted a direct personal influence upon his younger contemporaries through his teaching at the École Normale Supérieure and Sorbonne, and through his directorship (from 1902 until his death in 1922) of the Fondation Thiers.

---

[1] Referring to the ideas of Claude Bernard (§ 69).

[2] *Rapport*, pp. 249, 250, 254.

[3] Cf. the author's work, *Sur l'Habitude.*   [4] *Ibid.*, p. 255.

[5] Translated into English in 1916, the French title being *De la Contingence des Lois de la Nature.* His other important works (all of which have been translated into English) were *De l'Idée de Loi naturelle dans la Science et la Philosophie contemporaines,* 1895; *Questions de Morale et d'Éducation,* 1895; *La Science et la Religion dans la Philosophie contemporaine,* 1908; and various studies in the history of philosophy.

There are, according to Boutroux, three types of necessity and determination that seem to exclude the reality of spirit, with its prerogative of freedom: logico-mathematical or deductive necessity, of the Cartesian type; categorical necessity, of the Kantian type; and empirical inductive uniformities, of the Humian type.[1] In each case, however, something is left *un*necessitated, or "contingent." Deductive necessity leaves existence itself contingent, since it deals only with abstract possibilities, which may or may not be realized, and which if they *are* realized are never realized exactly.[2] Furthermore, even mathematics starts from unproved postulates, and as physics is not deducible from mathematics, so each successive science in the scale of complexity presents novelties which are underivable from the last.[3] In the second place, Kant is correct in denying that nature imposes her laws upon our minds, but mistaken in supposing that our minds impose a set of predetermined categories upon nature. The categories themselves are both an adaptation of nature to mind and of mind to nature, an "accord" or "compromise" between the two.[4] There remains the empirical sequence of events, the routine of nature, in which an object is determined by the sum of its actual conditions. But here there is no necessity at all. The facts being given, we can grasp their relations and predict their recurrence; but we do not see why they must be so, nor could we have predicted their original occurrence. Our knowledge is of concrete existences, but it is experimental and *a posteriori*.

The element of contingency in science opens the way for metaphysics and invites its aid. From this point Boutroux restates and amplifies the thought of Ravaisson. That which from the standpoint of science is negative, a mere failure to complete its program, is from the standpoint of metaphysics a positive and explanatory principle. Science admits contingency as a limiting factor, metaphysics construes it in terms of the free, creative activity of spirit. Spirit is that which is at

---

[1] *De la Contingence, etc.*, ch. I. [2] *Ibid.*, ch. II.
[3] *Ibid.*, ch. III–VII.   [4] *L'Idée de Loi naturelle*, pp. 137–139.

once most concrete and most free. The failure of logic and the plasticity of the categories may now be seen as due to their failure to express the whole of spirit, which is not mere intellect, but also feeling and will, having æsthetic and moral, as well as scientific, aspirations.[1] Thus science, instead of being opposed to spirit, appears as one of its creative activities; expressing, together with art and morality, that aspiration towards perfection which, as a community of wills and an organized, historic institution, constitutes religion.[2]

§ 76. Idealism in France. Renouvier. Lachelier

Spiritualism, both in Germany and in France, owed its force to the fact that it offered a positive account of reality. It transcended the relativities of phenomenal appearance not by affirming an opaque (unknown or material) underlying substance, but by depicting the inwardness of things luminously, as well as auspiciously, in terms of the intuition of spiritual activity. But in projecting this spiritual inwardness beyond phenomena and attributing it to nature and to God, it was necessary to make use of the argument from analogy. In the last analysis it was *interpretation*, plausible and meaningful, but highly speculative. The tendency from spiritualism to idealism expressed the desire to be more *rigorous*, or to carry over into the metaphysics of the nineteenth century the critical temper of the eighteenth, especially as exemplified by Kant.

In France this tendency found its most notable exponent in CHARLES RENOUVIER, who stood somewhat apart from contemporary schools and currents of thought, as well as from

---

[1] *Science et Religion*, p. 357.

[2] To the spiritualist school belong also Alfred FOUILLÉE (1838–1912; *La Liberté et le Déterminisme*, 1872; *L'Évolutionnisme des Idées-forces*, 1890), who sought to reconcile spiritualism and positivism through the conception of the tendency of ideas to realize themselves in action; and Jean Marie GUYAU (1854–1888; *Esquisse d'une Morale sans Obligation ni Sanction*, 1885), who took "life," or the will to live, as his ultimate and reconciling conception, thus anticipating Nietzsche and Bergson (§§ 81, 82).

academic circles, and struggled indefatigably during his long career to reconcile his moral and religious faith with his intellectual conscience. He did not limit himself to indubitable fact or intellectual certainty, but he sought scrupulously to define their limits, and to acknowledge explicitly the excursions he felt justified in making beyond them. The systematic works on which his fame chiefly rests were not published until he reached middle age. Born in 1815, his first period was spent in assimilating the philosophy of his age, especially that of Comte and Saint-Simon, and in mastering Descartes. His early publications expressed his historical interests together with a republican and socialistic enthusiasm inspired by the stirring events of 1848. His middle period, which coincided with the Second Empire and the defeat of his political hopes, was devoted to the writing and publication of his *Essais de Critique générale*, of which the first edition appeared in the years 1854–1869, and a second and revised edition in the years 1875–1886. This, his so-called "neocriticism," was inspired by Kant. His last period, from 1886 until his death in 1903, was devoted to the restatement of his earlier doctrines, to the philosophy of history, and to the further development of his thought in the direction of a "personalistic" metaphysics.[1]

That which sets Renouvier's philosophy apart from the spiritualistic metaphysics of his time, and relates him both to positivism and idealism,—both to Hume and to Kant, is his "phenomenism." Philosophy, like science, must eschew substances and begin with the appearances themselves. All that we immediately know (*connaître*) is the particular phenomenon,

---

[1] The second edition of the *Essais de Critique générale* embraced a *Treatise of General Logic* (*Traité de Logique générale*, 3 vols.), a *Treatise of Rational Psychology* (*Traité de Psychologie rationelle*, 3 vols.), and *The Principles of Nature* (*Les Principes de la Nature*, 2 vols.). Among his other works the following are the most important: *Science de la Morale*, 2 vols., 1869; *Esquisse d'une Classification systématique des Doctrines philosophiques*, 2 vols., 1885–1886; *Philosophie analytique de l'Histoire*, 4 vols., 1896–1897; *La Nouvelle Monadoiogie*, 1899; *Les Dilemmes de la Métaphysique pure*, 1901; *Le Personnalisme*, 1903; and numerous articles in the reviews which he founded, the *Année philosophique*, and the *Critique philosophique*.

— the "representation." This must not be construed at the outset as either inside or outside of ourselves, since it is prior to any such division of the world, and provides the datum in terms of which alone such a division can be justified. The representation does, however, possess a double character. It is both a "representing" and a "represented" (*representatif* and *representé*). These are the two inseparable aspects of the least unit of experience: it is an experience *of* something; and it is something *experienced*. Realism makes the mistake of supposing that objects can be divorced from the representation of them; idealism makes the mistake of supposing that there can be representation with nothing to represent.[1] These errors can be escaped only by taking experience, thus doubly qualified, to be self-sufficient and to constitute the very stuff of reality. The notion of a thing-in-itself or substance of things, divorced from this positive content, is utterly meaningless and vain. The true philosophy will be a "critique" of knowledge, which takes *experience* in the above sense as the sole realm of fact, discovers the principles or categories which it involves, and by employing it as a norm, judges the legitimacy of the beliefs by which it is rounded into a metaphysics and philosophy of life.

Kant's error lay in his failure to construe the realm of experience in its own terms. He converted its two *aspects* into two realms lying outside it: the transcendental subject within, and the transcendent object beyond. The effect is to make the knowable unreal, and the real unknowable. It is true that provision must be made for a permanence and order of things (as distinguished from the individual's passing states), but this is to be found in the representations themselves. For representations have their own laws, or mutual relations of functional dependence. Over and above the particular laws or functions which the sciences discover, there are certain general laws which all representations obey, or which appertain to them generally *as representations*. These constitute the cate-

[1] *Les Principes de la Nature*, edition of 1912, pp. 8–17.

gories, of which Renouvier enumerated nine: relation, number, extent, duration, quality, becoming, causality, finality, and personality.[1] Of these the category of relation is the most abstract and universal, for to assert *anything* of a representation, is to predicate a relation of it. This category is also the most objective, belonging to the representation as represented, rather than as representing. As we pass on there is a progression towards concreteness and subjectivity, the category of personality reflecting the fact that all representations are conscious; so that even when they are conceived by any consciousness as independent of itself, or as its "represented" rather than its "representing," they have to be conceived at the same time as representing something *to themselves*, or as having a personality of their own.

None of these categories, nor all of them together, permit of a total synthesis of the world.[2] They suffice for the limited purposes of science, but they carry us on from next to next, and never yield an absolute or whole. To pass beyond this relativity and indefiniteness of science we have to employ two deeper principles, the negative principle of contradiction, and the positive principle of belief. Representations and their own immanent laws and categories give us knowledge of reality as far as they go, but they leave open the great issues or dilemmas of metaphysics, morality and religion. Is the world infinite or finite? Is man free or determined? Is there or is there not a supreme moral order? The facts themselves yield no answer to these questions; and there is no escape from doubt unless we can find it by reflecting upon thought itself.

The principle of contradiction has to be accepted unless thought is to destroy itself. It proves a decisive consideration only in its application to the category of *number*. As distinct and multiple, representations can be counted; if they can be counted, then there is a number which corresponds to every multiplicity. But numbers are finite. To avoid contradiction

---

[1] Summarized in *Logique générale*, edition of 1912, vol. I, pp. 117–123.
[2] *Op. cit.*, vol. II, pp. 199–351.

we must therefore suppose the world to be of finite extent in time and space; and to be composed of a finite number of indivisible units or monads. God, if there be a God, must also be finite. Since there are first beginnings and discontinuities in the causal series, a place is made for freedom; not as Kant would have it, in some "noumenal" world, but in the world of fact and experience.

The metaphysical consequences of the principle of contradiction are largely negative and permissive. *Belief* is something more positive and more fundamental. For in order to apply even the principle of contradiction it is necessary first to believe or *accept* it. The same holds of the positive knowledge of science. This has a relatively high degree of certitude, and is *universally* accepted. But it has to be *accepted*, none the less, before it constitutes knowledge; and acceptance is an act of will. The truth does not force itself on us. Certainty is subjective; it means that we evaluate evidence, cease to think further, and come to a decision. Freedom is thus a postulate of knowledge, but it is also, as Kant had contended, a postulate of morality. Indeed to conceive knowledge as belief, freely adopted by the will, is to recognize that knowledge and morality are indivisible. From this position the transition is easily made to a doctrine of immortality and of God, justified on moral grounds.

Although Renouvier thus traces belief to will, he does not in the least suppose it to be a matter of caprice. Justifiable belief is that which satisfies the demands of the *total personality*.[1] These demands qualify one another: will is as much bound to satisfy the intellect, as intellect to satisfy will. There is a coherent demand which constitutes the ultimate standard of "reasonableness." And man is entitled to demand that the universe shall satisfy *his* demands only in so far as he on his side accepts the demands of the universe, as revealed in his moral nature. There is a sort of fundamental compact between man and the universe, according to which the universe

[1] Cf. *Esquisse d'une Classification*, etc., vol. II, ch. 3 and *passim*.

engages itself to correspond with the requirements of right-eousness.[1]

Renouvier's philosophy represents the attempt to construct a world out of phenomena and their laws. The phenomenon, the given fact of experience, is qualified to exist, as it is. It is true that there are ultimate metaphysical questions which can be answered only in terms of unverifiable beliefs, and which take us beyond the limits of actual phenomena, but this is not because there is anything inherently unreal in the phenomenon as such. Instead of being as the term "phenomenon" suggests, the mere appearance *of* something *to* the mind, it takes up these two modes of reference into itself as its own aspects. Thus Renouvier may be said to have converted criticism into a metaphysics, or to have converted appearance into reality by removing its disparaging implications. This view is to be contrasted with agnosticism, which conceives reality to lie inaccessibly behind phenomena; with dogmatism or eclecti-cism, which supposes that this reality beyond phenomena can be brought into view by the peculiar rays of the intellect; and with intuitionism, which supposes that it may be interpreted by analogy in terms of the subject's direct acquaintance with himself as a free, voluntary activity. There is a fourth alter-native to Renouvier's phenomenism, which in German thought appeared in the Hegelian interpretation of Kant, and in French thought in the philosophy of Lachelier. According to this view phenomena are construed not as the appearance of something to something, but as *products of thought*. The metaphysical reality is then creative thought, together with the inherent principles which govern its activity.

JULES LACHELIER (1832–1918), like Ravaisson, has an importance in French philosophy out of proportion to the extent of his written works. Of these there are only two of

---

[1] The most important of the followers of Renouvier (excepting James, § 82) was Octave HAMELIN (1856–1907; *Essais sur les Éléments principaux de la Représentation*, 1907), who adopted a position close to that of Hegel.

importance, the doctoral dissertation on *The Foundation of Induction*[1] and the article on *Psychology and Metaphysics*. With the conciseness and rigor of thought which characterized his writings were united remarkable personal qualities, through which he exerted a powerful influence both on his students at the École Normale Supèrieure, where he taught from 1864 to 1875, and on his colleagues and friends during the later years of his life.

Lachelier diverged from the prevailing French spiritualism both in demanding rigorous proofs in place of intuition and analogy, and in construing spirit in terms of thought rather than of will. These two points are closely connected, since the alleged datum of inner intuition is will, while spirit, *argued as a necessity*, assumes the form of thought. Lachelier's point of departure was the Kantian view (which Lachelier accepted as against Hume) that the empirical world of science derives its organization from the mind, and the universality of its laws from the fact that, being the product of the mind, it cannot fail to agree with the mind's constitution. As with Kant, the categories are essentially modes of synthesis by which thought constructs its world. Lachelier went beyond Kant, however, in affirming that the world of organized experience instead of representing an adjustment of thought to externally given data, is through and through the product of thought; determined wholly by the inner requirements of thought, and revealing thought as the only substantive reality.

Lachelier was not content to base the existence of thought on anything so dubious as the existent world; and he attempted by a bold use of the dialectical method to establish the reality of thought independently, and to evolve the existent world out of it.[2] Thought begins with the idea of *being*, a truth which proves itself, since to doubt it is to affirm that it

---

[1] *Du Fondament de l'Induction*, 1871. This, together with the *Psychologie et Métaphysique* (which originally appeared in 1885, in the *Revue de Métaphysique et de Morale*), and (in later editions) the *Notes sur le Pari de Pascal*, appeared in a single volume in 1896.

[2] *Psychologie et Métaphysique*, edition of 1924, pp. 158 *sq.*

is true that it either is or is not. But thought is not content
with this condition of mere abstract being. In order to think
itself as a something which *has* being, as an attribute, it invokes sensibility, which gives a material content to space and
time. This step is not deducible from abstract being, but is
an act of will, in which thought shows itself to be something
more than pure intellect. The last and highest stage is that of
self-conscious reflection, in which thought distinguishes itself
as pure act or freedom from objects projected outside itself.
Thus thought appears on three levels: it is first, thought of
being in general; second, of something in particular; and third,
of itself. Or: it is first, intellectual and abstract; second, desiderative, pictorial and concrete; third, active and real.
These three levels of thought also signify to Lachelier the progression from science to art, and from art to religion. The
mechanical system of science is complete in its own terms, and
permits of no exceptions. But thought can rise to a higher
view in which the world assumes the form of realized and harmonious ends. Finally, in morality thought achieves the
higher level of freedom. But since freedom attaches to *thought*,
and since thought is *universal*, morality passes over into religion, in which the individual recognizes his dependence on the
universal thought, or God.

§ 77. Idealism in England. Green. Bradley

In England it was idealism rather than spiritualism which
was the champion of the moral and religious tradition against
the naturalistic tendencies of the middle of the last century.
The Kantian and post-Kantian doctrines, first unqualifiedly
adopted by Stirling,[1] found their most influential exponent
among English philosophers in THOMAS HILL GREEN. He
was born in 1836, and his career was identified with Oxford
University, where he was first an undergraduate, afterwards a
fellow and tutor of Balliol College, and finally, from 1878
until his death in 1882, professor of moral philosophy. His

[1] § 69.

most important works were originally delivered in the form of lectures, and the power exerted by his teaching was as far-reaching as that exerted by his writings. He was the accepted leader of the reaction against the cult of Buckle, Darwin, and Spencer; but in combating naturalism he went back to its roots in empiricism, and thus repudiated the whole British philosophical tradition, the essential errors of which he believed to be most perfectly exemplified in the work of Hume. Indeed the only expression of his views which was published during his life consisted in Introductions appended to an edition of Hume's *Treatises*.[1] But Green was not less interested in combating the utilitarian moral philosophy, which he believed to be as untenable as the empiricism in which it was rooted; and the most systematic and important of his works, in which he derived the principle of self-realization from an idealistic theory of knowledge, bears the title of *Prolegomena to Ethics*.

Green took as his point of departure "that analysis of the conditions of knowledge which forms the basis of all Critical Philosophy, whether called by the name of Kant or no." The beginning of knowledge is "the experience of connected matters of fact." Empiricism (as exemplified by Hume) makes the mistake of supposing that the "connection" can itself be one of the matters of fact,[2] whereas it has to be supplied by thought. The Kantian forms and categories become for Green the *connective* tissue of the known world. Things do not unite *themselves* into a relation, but require the intervention *ab extra* of some "combining agency." Since nothing can enter into knowledge that is unrelated to consciousness, this combining agency must be an activity of consciousness. "With such a combining agency we are familiar as our intelligence," our "thinking or self-distinguishing consciousness."[3] The unity

---

[1] *A Treatise on Human Nature*, by David Hume, edited by T. H. Green and T. H. Grose, 2 vols., 1874. The *Prolegomena to Ethics* appeared in 1883, and the *Works*, 3 vols. (including his important *Principles of Political Obligation* and miscellaneous historical writings), in the years 1885–1888.

[2] *Prolegomena*, § 8.   [3] *Ibid.*, §§ 28, 10, 29, 46.

of nature is explicable only as an expression of the unity of
the self.

But Green would not have us suppose that this explanation
of nature in terms of our "combining intelligence" is, as Kant
thought, prejudicial to its reality. This would be so if, in the
first place, there were another reality which lay beyond this
combining intelligence, whether of things-in-themselves, or of
bare sensations produced by things-in-themselves. Sensations
are nothing, according to Green, except in so far as they are
brought into systematic relations, and their dependence on
things-in-themselves could mean nothing except in terms of
such relations extended illegitimately beyond experience. To
know anything, whether sensations or things-in-themselves,
is to relate; and to relate is to confer on the terms related
whatever meaning, reality, and "objectivity" they possess.

The product of a relating consciousness would be unreal, in
the second place, if it were the work of the private, individual
mind, with its own particular and limited field of experience, —
with its place in nature, and its moment in history. We must
suppose, therefore, that the combining intelligence which
creates the real system of nature, as distinguished from that of
our private and limited selves, is an "eternal intelligence,"
which determines nature in advance of our individual human
acquaintance with it, and "partially and gradually reproduces
itself in us." [1]

Because man can *know*, or participate in that "combining
intelligence" which constitutes nature, he cannot be himself
merely a part of nature. But man transcends nature not only
cognitively in respect of his intelligence, but also morally in
respect of his will. Will is distinguishable from mere desire not
as the strongest desire, but as that desire with which the agent
identifies himself.[2] Thus all voluntary action is directed to
the end of realizing a certain idea of one's self. The object of
desire or will is *ipso facto* good, in the generic sense; but it is
morally good only when it is the object of a *moral* will.[3] What,

---

[1] *Ibid.*, § 36 and ff.   [2] *Ibid.*, § 143.   [3] *Ibid.*, § 171.

then, is this moral will which is in each one of us? The answer is to be found again in the implication of an eternal mind, which "reproduces" itself in man as that aspiration to perfection or to the absolutely best, which is characteristic of our moral consciousness.[1] The moral will is the willing by man of God's will.

But how does man know the divine will? For answer, Green had to employ the assumption that history and organized society are its embodiments. The state, which is an expression of will rather than of force, owes its authority to its being the expression of a "collective will."[2] Thus Green, although he did not adopt the dialectical method of Hegel, and was both nationally and temperamentally inclined to individualism, found himself forced by the exigencies of his philosophical premises towards the universalism and authoritarianism which are the characteristic developments of idealism in Germany.[3]

FRANCIS HERBERT BRADLEY (1846-1924), like Green, who was his teacher, waged war on contemporary naturalism, and on the British empirical and utilitarian tradition. Like Green, he drew his inspiration from Kantian sources, and in particular from Hegel. Otherwise there is a marked contrast between these leaders of the British idealistic movement. Although resident at Oxford, Bradley was prevented by ill-health from assuming the duties of an academic career, and spent the greater part of his life in seclusion, as a research fellow of Merton College. Profiting by his leisure and despite his ill-health, Bradley, unlike Green, developed his views systematically, and defended them against attack. His first book, entitled *Ethical Studies* (1876), was both a critique of hedonism and a development of the thesis that the good lies in the realization

---

[1] *Ibid.*, §§ 173, 174.   [2] *Principles of Moral Obligation, passim.*
[3] Cf. § 79. A closer approach to the position of Hegel is to be found in the Cairds. EDWARD CAIRD (1835-1908) is notable for his personal influence as Master of Balliol College, and for his *Critical Account of the Philosophy of Kant* (1877); JOHN CAIRD (1820-1898) for his *Introduction to the Philosophy of Religion* (1880).

of a harmonious and unified self in organic relations with society. In *The Principles of Logic* (1883)[1] he developed two important theses. As against the psychological method he asserted that the subject of judgment is not an idea, but is *reality*, which is qualified by the total ideal content of the judgment. Thus judgment takes us at once beyond the judging mind, and so beyond the jurisdiction of psychology. As against empiricism, he asserted that the act of judgment, instead of being a reproduction of data given in sense-perception, is grounded in ulterior *judgments* as part of a coherent and rational system of thought.

The *Appearance and Reality*, which was published in 1891,[2] revealed most clearly the qualities of Bradley's mind. An acute dialectician, and committed to the thesis that the real is the rational, he here turned the intellect against itself and held the traditional idealistic categories, especially that category of relation which Green had accepted as fundamental, to be contradictory and untenable. Although more intellectualistic than Green in his method, he found his ultimate solution in immediacy and feeling. In the controversy stimulated by this famous work Bradley took an active part through a series of articles, many of which were brought together in the last of his books, *Truth and Reality*, which was published in 1914.

The root of Bradley's metaphysics and theory of knowledge lies in the distinction already alluded to, between reality as the subject of judgment, and the ideal content which judgment ascribes to it; or in the distinction between the "that" and the "what." Reality is somehow indicated in experience as *that* which we think about; but reality is also *what* we think about it. That we should be compelled to think about it, and hold it to be what we think, proves that it is not real as it is given. Thought is the effort to supplement the evident inadequacy of immediate experience, by introducing distinctions and qualifi-

---

[1] 2 vols., second edition published in 1914.

[2] Second enlarged edition, 1897.

cations both within and without. But thought finds it impossible to complete this task. Its affirmations always point beyond themselves, so that as soon as they are made they have to be denied. There is no escape from the difficulty. We can neither accept experience without thinking it, nor can we think it successfully; thought is both necessary and self-contradictory. This characteristic pervades all of the categories, but is seen most clearly in the fundamental category of relation. A relation does not succeed in uniting its terms, because it has, in turn, to be related to these terms: and so on *ad infinitum*.[1] By a similar method Bradley disposes of the traditional conceptions of primary and secondary qualities, space and time, motion and change, causation, activity, self, and things-in-themselves, and thus by implication refutes materialism, phenomenalism, agnosticism, and monadic spiritualism.

But although this critique discredits most of the categories of common-sense and of philosophy, and compels us to relegate them to "appearance" as distinguished from reality, the results are by no means wholly negative. In the first place, we have discovered a *criterion*. "Ultimate reality is such that it does not contradict itself";[2] it must be self-consistent. Secondly, it must contain the appearances, for there is no other disposition that can be made of them. Combining these two affirmations we conclude that in reality appearance must be "concordant and other than it seems." Thirdly, reality must be one, for whether we perceive them together or think them together, different reals must *qualify* one another; and in accordance with our fundamental criterion they must be supposed to qualify one another as parts of a *harmonious whole*.[3] Fourthly, reality is sentient experience. "There is no being or fact outside of that which is commonly called psychical existence."[4] It follows from all of these conclusions that

---

[1] *Appearance and Reality*, ch. II, III. Cf. also *Truth and Reality*, ch. VIII.
[2] *Op. cit.*, edition of 1908, p. 136. [3] *Ibid.*, pp. 140–143.
[4] *Ibid.*, p. 144. Cf. *Truth and Reality*, p. 315. This does not mean, Bradley points out, that reality is subjective, for the conception of sentient experience is prior to the distinction between subject and object.

reality is an individual experience, in which all appearances are harmoniously resolved. This reality is henceforth referred to as the Absolute.

The Absolute is, however, not a mere construction. We cannot, it is true, enter into the Absolute's experience, but its "main features" are within our own. "Complex wholes are felt as single experiences." Mere feeling or "immediate presentation" is the experience of a whole containing diversity "not parted by relations"; it fails to satisfy us only because of its incompleteness.[1] Furthermore, the process of advancing to higher immediacies through intermediate stages of discursive thought is known to us in our æsthetic, cognitive, and moral experiences. From the standpoint of the higher levels the lower levels are seen to be partial "appearances" or "degrees" of the same reality. Thus "truth and life, beauty and goodness" are all revelations of an Absolute which must be all that *they* are, and yet pass beyond the defects which mar even these reconciling harmonies. No appearances fall outside the Absolute, and all must, in the Absolute, be in some measure other than they appear, in order that their contradictions may be overcome; but while some will undergo a "rearrangement" so radical as to be unrecognizable, others, which we commonly call "higher," afford us genuine premonitions of the Absolute perfection.[2]

§ 78. Idealism in America. Royce. Howison. Bowne

The idealism of JOSIAH ROYCE differed profoundly from that of Green and Bradley. Born in 1855 in California, when that

---

[1] *Ibid.*, pp. 159, 521.

[2] After Green and Bradley the most important member of the British idealistic school was BERNARD BOSANQUET (1848–1923), author of *Logic*, 1888; *History of Æsthetic*, 1892; *Philosophical Theory of the State*, 1899; *The Principle of Individuality and Value*, 1912; *The Value and Destiny of the Individual*, 1913; and numerous other works. He differed from Bradley in that he emphasized the success of thought (in reconciling immediacy and logic) rather than its failures. His leading ideas are the *concrete individual*, or *whole*, revealed in the higher synthetic experiences, and the "collective will" (cf. Green) which furnishes the basis for his political and social philosophy.

state was still a remote frontier community; influenced in his early youth by the evolutionary teachings of Le Conte,[1] and by his studies of Mill and Spencer; afterwards intimately associated with James:[2] his thought always retained a naturalistic and empirical flavor. As an American he was predisposed to individualism, and sought earnestly to reconcile this motive with the absolutistic trend of his philosophy. He acquired a strong interest in symbolic logic and the philosophy of mathematics, and employed them in his conception of the infinite and in his studies of methodology. Finally, he was led through his early religious training and his social interests to attempt a philosophical interpretation of Christianity. Nevertheless the influences which most profoundly moulded his thought were those received in Germany from his studies of Lotze, Schopenhauer, Kant, and Schelling. Romanticism made a strong appeal to him because of his interest in literature and music, and it is this influence which is most clearly reflected in his first book, *The Religious Aspect of Philosophy*, published in 1885. His most important work was *The World and the Individual* (1900–1901), which reveals a profound study of Hegel, of Indian philosophy, and of scholasticism.[3] He taught philosophy at Harvard University from 1882 until his death in 1916.

Starting (after the manner of British empiricism) with "finite ideas," Royce finds that they possess an "internal" and an "external" meaning.[4] Over and above its content, the judging thought carries a reference beyond itself to its object. This object cannot be regarded as an "independent real," for then it could never be known; nor as a mystical immediacy which "quenches" thought, for then it would be unintelligible; nor as a possibility of experience determined by valid ideas, for

---

[1] § 69. [2] § 83.

[3] The more important of his other writings were: *The Spirit of Modern Philosophy*, 1892; *The Conception of God* (in collaboration with Le Conte, Howison, and S. E. Mezes), 1897; *The Philosophy of Loyalty*, 1908; *The Problem of Christianity* (2 vols.), 1913.

[4] *World and the Individual*, vol. I, Lect. VII.

a *mere* possibility is nothing at all. Realism, mysticism, and "critical rationalism" being thus disposed of, idealism is introduced as the view which defines reality as the *fulfilment of ideas*, in which the purpose embodied in their internal meaning is realized in the experience of their external meaning. Only the idea itself can recognize its own object, as that which it intended, and thus testify authoritatively to its own fulfilment. The object can be "individual" only when the idea chooses it, claims it, and refuses otherwise to be satisfied.[1] Both the specificity of objective reference and the uniqueness of particular facts depend on thus construing ideas as having wills of their own. Thought is a conscious "life," in which ideas find satisfaction in their objects. "To be, in the final sense, means to be just such a life, complete, present to experience, and conclusive of the search for perfection which every finite idea in its own measure undertakes when it seeks for any object." [2]

The "Absolute" appears in Royce's philosophy in response to two demands. In the first place, reality must fulfil *all* ideas. In order to escape the relativity and conflict of finite ideas, it is necessary to suppose that they are taken up into one self-consistent system of ideas, or one individual purpose and will, which finds its satisfaction in the total realm of existence. In the second place, there can be no facts that are not experienced; and the Absolute experience is thus invoked to provide for such facts as are implied in finite experience, but fall outside it. The very possibility of truth and error, which attaches to all finite ideas, compels us to assume that there is a more inclusive experience which comprehends both the purposes of finite ideas and also the facts in which these purposes are fulfilled or thwarted.[3]

With this monistic metaphysics Royce sought earnestly to reconcile the distinctive peculiarities of human experience. He was not satisfied to declare them to be mere appearances, but

---

[1] *Conception of God*, pp. 217–272.
[2] *World and the Individual*, vol. I, pp. 341–342.
[3] *Religious Aspect of Philosophy*, ch. XI.

sought to provide for them in reality. Thus time is not an unreality to be superseded by the eternal, but is a peculiar sequence which in the Absolute is grasped all at once, as human perception grasps a melody.[1] Evil is not transmuted into good, and therefore condoned, but remains as that which even in the Absolute has to be resisted and overcome.[2] Human individuals are not swallowed up in the Absolute, but each is a unique part of the unique whole, contributing through its own expression of the divine will that which is both indispensable to the whole and peculiar to itself.[3]

Royce's thought tended to a greater and greater emphasis on the conception of society. In his theory of knowledge he came to define thought in terms of "interpretation," rather than in terms of the meaning of ideas. The latter was a direct relation of idea and object; the former is a social relation, in which one mind's idea becomes a sign of the object to a second mind.[4] His ethics centred in the principle of "loyalty," or of the individual's devotion to a "cause" greater than himself. The ultimate moral principle is that of "loyalty to loyalty" in which the individual, while serving his own cause, respects and co-operates with the spirit of loyalty wherever he finds it. It was this spirit to which Royce looked for a solution of racial and international problems through the idea of "The Great Community."[5] Finally, he found the essence of Christianity to consist in a "community of the faithful," "hopefully and practically devoted to the cause of the still invisible, but perfectly real and divine Universal Community."[6]

The tendency which was so marked in Royce's philosophy, to emphasize the human individual and to conceive values in terms of society, found a bolder expression in the "personal

---

[1] *World and the Individual*, vol. II, Lect. III.
[2] *Religious Aspect of Philosophy*, pp. 452, 465.
[3] *Conception of God*, pp. 272–275.
[4] *Problem of Christianity*, vol. II, Lect. XIII, XIV.
[5] *Philosophy of Loyalty*, and *The Hope of the Great Community* (1916).
[6] *Problem of Christianity*, vol. II, p. 425.

idealism" of GEORGE H. HOWISON (1825–1916), professor at the University of California. In a public discussion with Royce and others held at the University of California in 1895,[1] Howison attacked Royce's "Monistic Idealism," or conception of the Absolute, and defended a *"Pluralistic Idealism,"* on the ground that an "Infinite Inclusive Self" would not only swallow up and annihilate all human selves, but lose its own selfhood; since selfhood is essentially a *moral* consciousness, implying the recognition of *other* selves.

In a later book, entitled *The Limits of Evolution,*[2] Howison developed this thesis more systematically, against monism both of the naturalistic type, as exemplified by Spencer and Haeckel, and of the idealistic type, as exemplified by the Hegelian school. Having refuted naturalism on Kantian grounds, Howison's main purpose was to save Kantianism from destroying itself through the internal conflict between its cognitive and its practical principles. Nature is the product of the cognitive mind, and the systematic unity of nature suggests that it is the product of *one absolute* mind, of which the human mind is only a mode or vehicle. The practical or moral consciousness, on the other hand, implies that the human individual is one of a circle or kingdom of free, immortal, and autonomous persons. How reconcile these counter-claims of universality and personality? Only, thinks Howison, by construing cognition in terms of a "social logic," in which objectivity and truth are held to consist in a "universal social recognition."[3] Nature is the creation of our several personal selves, but nature is one, because we are like-minded and guided by the same rational purpose.

This unifying purpose finds its supreme expression in God. As a reality, God is one person among others. Only by recog-

---

[1] This discussion was published in 1897, under the title of *The Conception of God* (cf. above, p. 547, note 3).

[2] The full title was *The Limits of Evolution and Other Essays Illustrating the Metaphysical Theory of Personal Idealism,* 1901; second and revised edition, 1904.

[3] *Op. cit.,* edition of 1904, pp. xxxvi–xxxviii.

nizing persons other than himself who have rights, and towards whom he has duties, can God be a moral person at all. He does not include human individuals within himself, nor does he coerce them, but he acts upon them by attraction (by "final" or "moral" causation), as the *ideal* which they adopt of their own free will.[1] The realm of nature, or the world of sense, also falls outside of God, as being the product of the human mind. So God is not responsible for evil, but may be worshipped as the embodiment of perfection. He is the "Supreme Instance" in the "eternal circle of Persons," the first "citizen" in "the all-founding, all-governing Realm of Spirits."[2]

"Personal" idealism manifests three characteristic tendencies. In the first place, it tends through its desire to save the individual and his moral attributes, to emphasize the will and the practical consciousness, at the expense of the theoretical reason. Although Howison himself resisted this tendency, it resulted among British idealists in a movement towards voluntarism and pragmatism.[3] In the second place, personal idealism tends to an emphasis on *society* as a means of saving itself from the relativistic and sceptical consequences of an unqualified individualism. Finally, personal idealism tends to emphasize the substantive reality of persons, as known immediately in self-consciousness, and thus moves towards a spiritualism of the Lotzean type. The most influential exponent in America of this last tendency was BORDEN PARKER BOWNE.[4] This philosopher's interests were primarily meta-

---

[1] *Ibid.*, pp. 65, 328.　　　　[2] *Ibid.*, p. 355; *Conception of God*, p. 113.

[3] That is, towards the type of philosophy discussed below, §§ 81–83. This transition in British thought is best exemplified by the volume of essays entitled *Personal Idealism*, which appeared in 1902, and in which idealists, voluntarists, and pragmatists united on the common ground of pluralism. Exponents of the same tendency, but standing nearer to the centre of idealism, were Thomas Davidson (1840–1900), in America; and in England, James Ward (1843–1925; *Naturalism and Agnosticism*, 1899; *The Realm of Ends*, 1911) and J. M. E. McTaggart (1866–1925; *Studies in Hegelian Cosmology*, 1901).

[4] 1847–1910. His most important writings were *Studies in Theism*, 1879, and *Metaphysics*, 1882 (second edition, 1898). A brief popular summary of his position was contained in *Personalism*, 1908.

physical and religious. As for his teacher Lotze, so for Bowne, the real is that which can act and be acted upon, of which spirit is the only known case. The real meaning of the categories is to be found not in their conceptual or formal rôle, as modes of connection among phenomena, but "through our living experience of intelligence itself." In this "active self-experience" is to be found a revelation of causality, of substance, of unity-in-manyness, and of identity in change. The categories so construed in terms of the real mind which creates phenomena, may then be assigned to the reality beyond phenomena, — a step which all philosophers have virtually taken in the acknowledging the reality of other selves. This doctrine Bowne called his "transcendental empiricism." It leads to a spiritualistic metaphysics, which defines "a world of persons with a Supreme Person at the head," of which nature is the expression and means of communication, and which, despite their ultimate substantial and causal unity, nevertheless as persons preserve a "mutual otherness" and "relative independence."[1]

§ 79.   Critical Idealism in Germany.   The Marburg School.
Windelband.   Rickert.   Dilthey.   Eucken.   Simmel

The revival of Kant in Germany in the 1860's was followed by a revival of those very post-Kantian tendencies against which the Kantian revival had itself protested. Although neo-Kantianism sprang from a desire to purge Kantianism of the alien elements introduced by Hegel, Fichte, and Romanticism, it was promptly followed by neo-Hegelianism, neo-Fichteanism, and neo-Romanticism. There appears, in other words, to be an inevitable and recurrent cycle through which the thought of Kant passes, inspired by the intellectualistic Kant of the *Critique of Pure Reason*, the voluntaristic and moralistic Kant of the *Critique of Practical Reason*, and the æsthetic and intuitionist Kant of the *Critique of Judgment*.[2] Reject the conception of the thing-in-itself, as all later Kant-

---

[1] *Ibid.*, part I, ch. II; *Personalism*, p. 277.   [2] Cf. above, § 62.

ians proceed promptly to do, and mind and its creations are left in possession of the field. There then arises a rivalry of emphasis among the several modes of the mind's activity, thought, will, and feeling. Each, after absorbing the other two, may claim to be the original and generative principle of experience and reality.

There was nevertheless a marked difference between the new post-Kantianism and the old. While the original followers of Kant rejected the thing-in-itself, they rejected it as un-unknowable, rather than as a symbol of metaphysical reality. They found through thought or will or feeling a *knowable* thing-in-itself, and hence abandoned the critical method for speculative metaphysics. In this they were followed as a rule by the British and American idealists whom they influenced. The new German post-Kantians, on the other hand, not only rejected the thing-in-itself, but renounced the metaphysical aspiration which it symbolized. They endeavored to remain faithful to the critical method. They conceived philosophy, in other words, to be the study of the presuppositions of the sciences. Hence it was not so much a question of the relative reality of thought, will, or feeling, as of the relative priority of the categories of physics, ethics, and æsthetics.

The so-called "Marburg school" arose as an attempt to purify the Kantianism of Lange.[1] It derived its name from the fact that its members, including Lange, were professors at the University of Marburg. Its principal representatives were HERMANN COHEN (1842–1918) and his pupil and associate PAUL NATORP (1854–1924).[2] Their systems were symmetrical and closely similar, and followed the order of the Kantian critiques of which Cohen was a leading commentator.[3] In

---

[1] § 72.

[2] The most eminent living representative of this school is Ernst Cassirer (b. 1874; *Substanzbegriff und Funktionsbegriff*, 1910; English trans., *Substance and Function*, 1923).

[3] In his *Kant's Theorie der Erfahrung*, 1871; *Kant's Begründung der Ethik*, 1877; and *Kant's Begründung der Æsthetik*, 1899.

developing his own thought Cohen began with a *Logic of Pure Knowledge* and added an *Ethics of Pure Will* and an *Æsthetic of Pure Feeling*.[1]   To the first of these corresponds Natorp's *Logical Foundations of the Exact Sciences,* while the latter's ethical teachings are developed in his *Social Pedagogy*.[2]   Both writers also paid their respects to religion, and both recognized the need of some unifying conception by which natural science, ethics, and art should be united.   Cohen found such a conception in a general "cultural consciousness" (*Kulturbewusstsein*), while Natorp found it in that "subjectivity" of consciousness which, being transcended in natural science, ethics, and art, has afterwards to be restored and taken account of in a general or philosophical psychology.[3]

Kant's thing-in-itself being left out of the account, there was no longer for Cohen any occasion for retaining the distinction between the receptivity of intuition and the spontaneity of the understanding.   Thought is no longer an organization of the given, but a purely creative process.   To be and to be thought (the act and the product) are one and the same thing.[4]   Instead of nature as object (*Gegenstand*) there is only science and its task (*Aufgabe*).   The most distinctive feature of Cohen's doctrine of the categories is the fundamental place which he assigns to that of "origin" (*Ursprung*).   This category signifies the power of thought to construct by a synthesis of undecomposable elements.   Such elements Cohen thought to be provided by the "infinitesimal" of calculus.   The same idea appears among the categories of mathematics as the category of "reality."   Mathematics is essentially quantitative or numerical, and assumes an element to be measured or counted.   This

---

[1] *Logik der reinen Erkenntnis,* 1902; *Ethik des reinen Willens,* 1904; *Æsthethik des reinen Gefühls,* 1912.

[2] *Die logischen Grundlagen der exakten Wissenschaften,* 1910; *Sozialpädagogik,* 1899.

[3] *Allgemeine Psychologie nach kritischer methode,* 1912. Natorp also published historical studies of Plato and of Pestalozzi (*Plato's Ideenlehre,* 1903; *Der Idealismus Pestalozzi's,* 1919), which exercised a considerable influence on his own thought, especially his ethics.

[4] *Logik der reinen Erkenntnis,* p. 18.

element by which quantities can be generated, and which is not itself quantitative, but individual and "real," is again the infinitesimal.

While in the logic of natural science Natorp differed from Cohen in many points of detail, it is in ethics that the former displayed his own peculiar bent and genius. He found a transition from logic to ethics in the fact that the last word of science is an unfinished task (*Aufgabe*) pointing beyond experience, an *ought*-to-be (*Seinsollen*), over and above the world of being (*Sein*). Ethics is the science of this ideal of reason, which, as essentially shared and objective, is the bond that unites human wills into a community. Like Plato, Natorp thought of individuals as having their true interest and *rationale* in an organized society, and arranged the practical activities and corresponding virtues in three stages: desire and temperance; regulated will (*Willensregelung*) and courage; reason and truth. These moral levels are represented in society in economic, governmental, and creative (cultural) activities. To establish the ascendency of the creative reason over both industry and politics, and thus to unite individuals into a community of cultural aspiration, is the object of education, and the program of Natorp's "idealistic socialism."

On the whole it is characteristic of the Marburg school to retain intact the three-fold structure of the Kantian critiques. The data of philosophy are the three great systems, natural science, ethics, and art, and the task of philosophy is to bring to light their presuppositions or implicit reason. But there are two suggestions looking toward a further unification. In the first place, although both Cohen and Natorp manifested a rationalistic and even positivistic temper in giving first place in their systems to the logic of natural science, there was (notably in Natorp) a recognition of the fact that even the logical reason is a practical or moral activity, directed to an end. In the second place, both philosophers suggested that there is a mode of consciousness embracing logic, morality, and art: for Cohen it was the "cultural consciousness" which embraces them all, and for Natorp it was their common and unifying aspect of subjectivity or immediacy. These suggestions point in the direction of the schools of Windelband and Rickert, and Dilthey and Eucken.

WILHELM WINDELBAND, who was born in 1848, was the founder of a school which because of his connection with Freiburg, Strassburg, and finally (until his death in 1915) with Heidelberg, is commonly called the "Southwest German School," or "School of Baden." Although Windelband proceeded in the main directly from Kant, he owed much to Lotze's doctrine of "validity" (*Geltung*).[1] Influenced also by Kuno Fischer,[2] he gave special attention to the history of philosophy, which he treated not as a succession of distinct systems, but as a continuous development of ideas, forming part of the general process of human culture.[3] His own thought was set forth in a series of addresses and articles, and in an *Introduction to Philosophy*, published in 1914.[4]

Starting with the Kantian view of knowledge as consisting in the formative and synthetic act of judgment, Windelband contended that there is a deeper reflexive act in which the judgment itself is claimed to be true or false. Over and above "the intellectual element of bringing contents together in a certain relation," there is an act of *assent* or *dissent* on the part of the will,[5] which defines a realm of *validity* (*Geltung*). Truth is not a correspondence of ideas to facts, but a satisfaction of the fundamental demands of the subject. Since, however, it is assumed that truth is *universally* valid, the subject which truth satisfies cannot be the particular empirical subject, but

---

[1] § 74. [2] § 66.

[3] The most important of his numerous historical writings is the *Geschichte der Philosophie*, 1878–1880; second edition, 1892; English translation, *History of Philosophy*, 1893.

[4] *Einleitung in die Philosophie;* second edition, 1920; English trans., 1921. The *Präludien*, 1884 (sixth edition, 1919), was a compilation of his shorter writings. Cf. also his *Principien der Logik* in vol. I of the *Enzyklopädie der philosophischen Wissenschaften*, 1912.

[5] *Introduction to Philosophy*, pp. 170–171.

must be a "logical consciousness in general" (*logisches Bewusstsein überhaupt*). The sciences which realize the demands of this subject are both rational (like mathematics) and empirical. Among the empirical sciences there is an important difference between the "natural" and the "historical" sciences (*Naturwissenschaften* and *Geschichtswissenschaften*). Both are synthetic and selective, in accordance with the demands of the subject; but while the former is "nomothetic," seeking generalization, uniformity, and order, and expressing itself in types and laws, the latter is "idiographic," dealing with concrete individuals in so far as these possess some moral, æsthetic, or cultural value.[1]

Over and above logical value, or validity, there are ethical and æsthetic values, which in their universality again imply the claims of a transcendental subject. The moral consciousness, or consciousness of duty, is interpreted as the demand upon the individual of a communal will, which is in turn a manifestation of "the idea of humanity" or "the moral order of the world." [2] This universal life expresses itself historically as successive systems of culture,[3] in whose realization it is the duty of the individual actively to participate. Æsthetic values rise above moral values in their freedom from that sense of need and incompleteness which accompanies desire and will, and express themselves most perfectly in the unself-conscious inspiration of genius.

Religion does not signify a fourth realm of value, but only the super-sensuous aspect or reference of logical, ethical, or æsthetic values. Common to all three realms is the implication of a normative consciousness (*Normalbewusstsein*), whose demands remain in human experience as an unfulfilled aspiration. Religion is the demand for their complete realization in the perfect or "holy," or for the overcoming of that duality between value and reality which is both the impenetrable mystery and the essential characteristic of human life.[4]

[1] *Ibid.*, pp. 201–208. [2] *Ibid.*, p. 291.
[3] *Präludien*, edition of 1916, vol. II, p. 191. [4] *Ibid.*, p. 358.

Windelband's thought has been further developed by HEIN-
RICH RICKERT, who succeeded him at Heidelberg in 1916.[1]
Rickert differs from Windelband in a more explicit and
thorough-going reduction of the "is" (Sein) to the "ought"
(Sollen). Being is known to us only as an object of *judgment*,
but "the peculiar logical essence of judgment is affirmation
and denial, approval or disapproval, or an attitude to a value."[2]
In other words, the knowing subject pronounces judgment in
obedience to the requirements of an "ought," which it recognizes as *binding* upon it, and therefore as independent of its
private inclinations. This ideal objectivity transcends all
actuality and all subjectivity, not as being unrelated to them,
but as being a standard to which they are obliged to conform.
Taken in the context of knowledge at least, there is no meaning
in the "is," without an ulterior reference to what is valid
(*gilt*) or true. "It is valid or true or good *that a should be b*,"
underlies the simple "*a* is *b*" of the empirical consciousness.
Thus Rickert's philosophy centres in the Kantian "primacy
of the practical reason," and has been characterized as "neo-
Fichteanism."

Rickert was first concerned to *distinguish* between the
"ought" and the "is," or between value and actuality (*Wert*
and *Wirklichkeit*), but felt also the need of reconciling them, as
two aspects of the same being, or original felt immediacy, which
he characterized as "immanent meaning" (*immanent Sinn*).[3]
A problem of unification arose also within the realm of values
itself. The logical consciousness has its own peculiar duty to
perform, and its own peculiar norms or categories. In obedience

---

[1] He was born in 1863. His most important writings are *Der Gegenstand der
Erkenntnis*, 1892, and *Die Grenzen der naturwissenschaftliche Begriffsbildung*,
1896. Other prominent members of the school were Hugo Münsterberg (1863–
1916), called to America as professor at Harvard University in 1892, and eminent in psychology (*Grundzüge der Psychologie*, 1900) as well as in philosophy
(*Philosophie der Werte*, 1908; English translation, *The Eternal Values*, 1909);
and Max Weber (1864–1920), whose *Gesammelten Aufsätze zur Religionssoziolo-
gie* (1920–1922) and other writings are of importance in the field of the philosophy of the social sciences, especially of economics.

[2] *Der Gegenstand der Erkenntnis*, 1904, p. 108.

[3] *System der Philosophie*, 1921, I, pp. 235–255.

to these norms the cognitive subject develops two groups of sciences: the natural sciences, which generalize and explain in terms of laws; and the cultural and historical sciences,[1] which deal with concrete individuals and activities. The sciences of culture are thus governed by the norms of the logical subject. But, on the other hand, science is itself a branch of culture, having its historical development. It belongs, along with æsthetics and the mystical experience (*der Mystik*), to the "contemplative" and asocial branch of culture, which is contrasted with the "active" branch; the latter embracing ethics, the pursuit of happiness (*die Erotik*), and religion (the pursuit of perfection). There is thus a rivalry in Rickert between a tendency to subject culture to the demands of the theoretical consciousness as being the content of a special branch of science, and a tendency to subject science to the demands of a more general consciousness as being a special branch of culture.

This latter tendency, so pronounced in Windelband and Rickert, to accept *the history of culture* as the ultimate object of philosophy, or to view reality as the progressive unfolding of a universal life, whose norms are embodied with equal authority in science, morality, and art, found its most radical and consistent expression in WILHELM DILTHEY (1833–1912). This philosopher, who succeeded Lotze at Berlin in 1882, distinguished himself as a biographer of Schleiermacher and Hegel, and as a critic and historian of literature.[2] Owing to his broad cultural interests, he was many-sided both in his sources and in his influence; and his philosophy, being essentially unsystematic, never found any unified expression.[3]

---

[1] *Kulturwissenschaften* or *Geschichtswissenschaften*. Rickert rejects the conception of "spiritual sciences" (*Geisteswissenschaften*) because he regards psychology as one of the natural sciences.

[2] *Leben Schleiermachers*, 1870; *Die Jugendgeschichte Hegels*, 1905; *Die Einbildungskraft des Dichters*, 1887; *Das Erlebnis und die Dichtung*, 1905.

[3] The most important writings for the purpose of understanding Dilthey's fundamental position are the *Einleitung in die Geisteswissenschaften*, 1883; *Der*

Dilthey's central doctrine was the immediately apprehended "coherence of life" (*Lebenszusammenhang*) which expresses or objectifies itself in a "world-view" (*Weltanschauung*).[1] In his doctrine of an inner revelation or active, personal experience (*Erlebnis*) of life, he approximated the position of spiritualism. The difference between the natural and spiritual sciences for Dilthey is the difference between objective cognition (*Erkennen*), and the sympathetic insight (*Verstehen*) by which we grasp the inwardness of life.[2] This sympathetic insight extends beyond ourselves, and enables us to realize the unity of the great cultural manifestations of life. Here Dilthey turned, as did Windelband and Rickert, to a philosophy of history. We cannot deduce the course of history from any set of first principles, but we learn the rich possibilities of life from its progressive unfolding in modes of general outlook or world-view, each of which is relative to special social and natural conditions. Every such world-view is at one and the same time a conception of reality, an order of values, and a governing purpose.[3] Of such world-views Dilthey recognized three general types: *naturalism*, which is materialistic, utilitarian, and deterministic; *idealism* of the *subjective* or active type, in which mind is conceived as free and creative; and *objective idealism*, which expresses itself in a contemplation of the universal harmony. The first is exemplified by Hobbes and Hume; the second by Plato and the post-Kantians; the third by Spinoza and Goethe.

Dilthey's philosophy points in two directions, towards a spiritualistic-idealistic metaphysics, and towards a historical relativism. The former direction of thought is represented by RUDOLPH EUCKEN (b. 1846), pupil of Trendelenburg, professor of philosophy at Basel and Jena, and a writer of wide popularity

---

Aufbau der geschichtlichen Welt in den Geisteswissenschaften, 1910; *Weltanschauung, Philosophie und Religion*, 1911.

[1] *Weltanschauung*, etc., pp. 7, 29.

[2] *Der Aufbau der geschichtlichen Welt*, etc., p. 10.

[3] *Weltanschauung*, etc., p. 28.

both in Germany and abroad.[1] Eucken is an eloquent partisan of spiritualism and idealism against both the naturalistic philosophy, and what he deemed to be the deadening and confusing influences of modern life. Like Dilthey he finds in the history of philosophy the record of a spiritual movement to be interpreted in terms of an immediate revelation of the inwardness of life. But his philosophy, like that of Fichte, which it resembles throughout, is a call to arms rather than a historical survey. Spirit is essentially action and struggle, in which there is resistance to be overcome and a victory to be won. Life is a *deed*, and there is no deed without a duality of agent and object (*Keine Tat ohne Zweiheit*).[2] The world is to be construed in terms of the demands of the fullest and most active personal life. This method of taking as the principle of truth the requirements of the whole of life, rather than of the mere intellect, he calls the "noological" method.[3] The world is in a sense what we make it. Although Eucken's philosophy is thus a philosophy of faith and of action, it does not employ these categories in any limiting sense. All knowledge is faith in the sense that it springs from the exigencies of action, but the activity whose urge is thus obeyed is that of a universally immanent spirit.

While Eucken thus represents the bolder metaphysical implications of Dilthey's thought, GEORG SIMMEL (1858–1918) construed in more empirical terms Dilthey's view that philosophies and other cultural manifestations are relative to the special circumstances under which they arise. His interest lay not in metaphysical, nor even in historical, generalizations,

---

[1] His principal writings are: *Die Einheit des Geisteslebens in Bewusstsein und Tat der Menschheit*, 1888; *Die Lebensanschauungen der grossen Denker*, 1890 (English trans., *The Problem of Human Life*, etc., 1909); *Der Wahrheitsgehalt der Religion*, 1901 (English trans., *The Truth of Religion*, 1901); *Das Wesen der Religion*, 1901; *Grundlinien einer neuen Lebensanschauung*, 1907 (English trans., *Life's Basis and Life's Ideal*, 1912); *Geistige Strömungen der Gegenwart*, 3d ed., 1904 (English trans., *Main Currents of Modern Thought*, 1912).

[2] *Die Einheit des Geisteslebens*, etc., p. 354 and *passim*.

[3] *Grundlinien*, etc., pp. 119 ff.

but in the detailed study of the way in which ideas and ideals arise in response to specific human needs, and in relation to concrete human situations. Assuming, in common with the whole neo-Kantian school, that the spirit constructs its own world, he recognized no universal *a priori* principles by which this construction is determined and rationalized, but *described* it in psychological and sociological terms. Thus in his famous *Philosophy of Money*[1] he traced the change in the meaning or function of money, from a qualitatively distinct thing, having a value in itself, to a symbol and measure of power. Similarly in his ethics, he claimed no final and valid standard, but devoted himself to a study of the genesis of such typical concepts as "ought," or "egoism" and "altruism," and the particular contexts from which they derive their meaning.[2] All categories are for Simmel evolved in a certain setting and possessed of a limited and relative truth, in so far as they fit that setting. This relativity is itself the only possible philosophical generalization. A tendency always to transcend its own achievements, or to pass from a relative truth to an absolute which in turn becomes relative in the light of an ulterior absolute, is the very essence of life.[3]

Eucken's emphasis on the *deed*, and Simmel's interpretation of truth in terms of a life-process which refuses to be embraced under any fixed system of categories, represent a transition from idealism of the orthodox Kantian type to the new movement variously known as neo-vitalism, activism, or pragmatism.[4]

§ 80. Idealism in Italy. Croce

BENEDETTO CROCE may be considered as an exponent both of German idealism of the post-Kantian type, and also of the

---

[1] *Philosophie des Geldes*, 1900. Simmel has an important place in the development of modern sociology. Cf. his *Soziologie*, 1908.

[2] *Einleitung in der Moralwissenschaft*, 1892–1893.

[3] This characteristic *self-transcendence* of life (*Über-sichselbsthinausgehen, Sich-selbst-überwinden*) is developed in the author's *Lebensanschauung*, 1918, and *Philosophie des Lebens*, 1920.

[4] §§ 81–83.

Italian national tradition. The emphasis on history and universal culture, which was characteristic of German thought in the nineteenth century, had in Italy found a much earlier expression in Vico, the philosopher of the Renaissance whom Croce himself did much to rehabilitate;[1] and was also represented among Croce's early contemporaries by notable men of letters, such as De Sanctis and Carducci.[2] Croce, like Vico, came to philosophy by way of historical and linguistic interests. Born in 1866, in the province of Aquila, of a Neapolitan family, he settled in Naples, after his university studies in Rome, and adopted the career of a private scholar. This career has been interrupted only by occasional periods of service in public office, as senator and as minister of public instruction.

Beginning as a student of Neapolitan history, he first widened the range of his erudition and then deepened his reflection upon it. As his philosophy grew out of his brooding upon history, so it culminated in the doctrine that philosophy *is* history: meaning that events are only what they signify in that perpetual and progressive reinterpretation which they undergo in the thinking mind; or that history *is* as the historian conceives it, and that the historian in conceiving it in its universal aspects is the philosopher.[3] But although in construing reality as the rationalized historical process Croce approaches the view of Hegel, he does not believe that either history or nature can be subsumed under any general dialectic law that renders it predictable *a priori*.[4] His own system, while as a "Philosophy of Spirit" it is based on the idealistic principle of the identity of consciousness and being, is notable less for its unity than for the autonomy which it accords to the several realms of spirit. It is unfolded in three works, the *Æsthetic*, the

---

[1] § 50. Cf. Croce's *La Filosofia di Giambattista Vico*, 1911.

[2] Francesco De Sanctis, 1817–1883; Giosuè Carducci, 1835–1907.

[3] *Logic*, English trans., p. 494. Cf. *Teoria e Storia della Storiographia*, 1920; English trans., *History, Its Theory and Practice*, 1921.

[4] *Saggio sullo Hegel*, 1913; English trans., *What is Living and What is Dead in the Philosophy of Hegel*, 1915.

Logic, and the *Philosophy of the Practical,* the last embracing *Economics* and *Ethics,* and the whole setting forth the four fundamental forms of human activity.[1]

Rejecting every sort of transcendence, there will be as many aspects of reality as there are modes of conscious life. The latter is divisible into the theoretic and the practical consciousness, of which the first is again divisible into *intuition* and *intellect.* Intuition is genuine knowledge, distinguished by its immediacy and by the concrete individuality of its objects. It embraces not only the field of perception but also that of imagination and feeling, since it is prior to the distinction between existence and non-existence. It embraces spatial and temporal characters as parts of its content, but it is not a spatio-temporal system, as in Kant's *Æsthetic.* It has, in fact, no universal forms, save only that of consciousness itself. Nor is it passive and meaningless like pure sensation. The most original feature of Croce's view of intuition is his contention that it is essentially communicative or *expressive.* This does not mean that all intuition must be outwardly expressed in words or in *works* of art, but that the intuition itself is already an expression. Intuition is itself creative art, the artist in the usual and narrower sense being simply the man whose intuitions are extraordinarily clear and vivid, and who knows how to give them physical embodiment. The distinction between form and content in art is therefore a false one, since there is no content that is not already intuitively formed.

The intellectual mode of consciousness is that in which concepts are employed in acts of judgment claiming a universal validity. But all judgments are in the last analysis individual

---

[1] The work on History, mentioned above, constitutes the fourth volume of the *Filosofia dello Spirito.* The other volumes appeared as follows: *Estetica come scienza dell' espresione e linguistica generale,* 1902 (English trans., *Æsthetic,* 1909); *Logica come scienza del concetto puro,* 1905 (English trans., *Logic,* 1917); *Filosofia della Pratica: Economica ed Etica,* 1909 (English trans., *The Philosophy of the Practical,* 1913). His writings include, in addition to the above, a large number of essays (many contributed to his review called *La Critica*) and of works in literary and political history.

judgments, arising in a particular context and applied to concrete objects. Thus while intuition is possible without conceptual knowledge, the latter implies intuition as an antecedent stage. There is, for Croce, no thinking save that which occurs in the actual historical process.

"Man understands things with the theoretical form, with the practical form he changes them." [1] This form, also, appears in two grades, the *useful* or economical activity, and the *moral* activity. "Economy is, as it were, the Æsthetic of practical life; Morality its Logic." [2] Both are manifestations of will; in both cases to will is to intend or to adopt an end, whether or no this proceeds to overt action; and both presuppose knowledge. The difference lies in that the economic activity is directed to individual, and the moral to universal, ends. As in the case of theoretic activity, so here also, the second grade presupposes the first. There may be utility without morality, but there can be no actions having moral value without being also economic or useful.

Such unity as is retained by Croce's system as a whole is to be sought in his conceptions of "distinction" and "opposition," [3] as applied to the four fundamental divisions of the conscious life. Beauty, Truth, Utility, and Goodness are not opposed, and there is no dialectical relation between them by which (after the manner of Hegel) one generates the other as its contradictory opposite. Their unity lies in the fact that they cannot be understood except as *distinguished* from one another, and as having an orderly interdependence. They form a whole whose parts are reciprocally and integrally intelligible, — not a regress, but a circle or closed system all of which is virtually present in every reality. The relation of opposition holds not *between* values, but *within* each value, as the relation between its affirmation and its negation; that is, between beauty and ugliness, truth and error, utility and disutility, good and evil. While there is thus a negative im-

---

[1] *Æsthetic*, English translation, p. 78.   [2] *Ibid.*, p. 89.
[3] *Logic*, English trans., pp. 99 ff.

plication in each value, nothing is or can be wholly without value. Thus the "unreal" must have intuitive value, or beauty; while error and moral evil must have economic value, or utility. Opposition is nevertheless significant in that it reveals the fundamental dynamic quality of reality as a spiritual activity which both succeeds and fails, or which succeeds only by struggle and overcoming.[1]

C. VITALISM, VOLUNTARISM, AND PRAGMATISM

§ 81. The Will to Power. Nietzsche

Both idealism and spiritualism affirm the priority of mind to physical reality, the former in respect of knowledge, the latter in respect of being. The essential nature of mind being revealed on the plane of human self-consciousness, its categories are accordingly those of thought, moral will, æsthetic feeling, or artistic genius. But it is possible to hold that its essential nature is revealed upon a more primitive plane, in irrational desire, sense-perception, blind will, instinct, or life. These possibilities provide a gradation of views in which spiritualism approximates naturalism. According to a strict spiritualism, the key to reality is to be found in logic, ethics, or æsthetics. According to an intermediate view, widely held in the eighteenth century, this key is to be found in psychology. Progression in this direction leads finally to the view that the key is to be found in biology. If we conceive the sciences to form an order from physics through biology to logic, ethics, and æsthetics (the so-called "normative sciences"), we may say that naturalism reduces to physics, spiritualism to the normative sciences, while the third view reduces both ends to the middle, or conceives both physics and the normative sciences in terms of biology.

---

[1] The most important of Croce's disciples is Giovanni Gentile (b. 1875), who, like Croce, identifies reality with history, and history with the creative activity of spirit; but who seeks to discover a greater unity among the several modes of spirit, in terms of a dialectic of self-consciousness. Cf. his *L'atto del pensare come atto puro*, 1912 (English trans., *The Theory of Mind as Pure Act*, 1922).

This third view is known as *vitalism*, when the intention is to affirm the irreducibility of life to physico-chemical terms;[1] it is known as *voluntarism* (or *activism*), when the intention is to identify life and will, and so to obtain a biological interpretation of the content of psychology; it is known as *pragmatism* or *instrumentalism*, when the intention is to extend biological categories to the normative sciences, and in particular to logic. An exponent of this general type of philosophy may emphasize one of these aspects, but can scarcely fail to manifest all three.

FREDERICH NIETZSCHE represents this general tendency in its cultural and moral applications, and in the manner of the poet and reformer rather than of the systematic philosopher. The individualistic emphasis of this tendency, which is always marked, finds in Nietzsche its most extreme and powerful exponent. He was born in 1844, and the earliest formative influences on his thought were received from the teachings of Schopenhauer, from his personal friendship with the great composer Richard Wagner,[2] and from his studies of classical antiquity, this last interest leading to his appointment as professor of philology at Basel in 1869. His first important work, *The Birth of Tragedy*,[3] was an interpretation of history as a conflict between the principles of Dionysius and of Apollo, the first representing the blind but rich and inexhaustible force of life, the latter the balance, repose, and harmony of form. Diverging from his earlier masters he came under the influence of naturalism both in its positive and in its negative aspects. Positively, he adopted the standpoint of scientific biology; negatively, he accepted the gospel

---

[1] A movement known as "neo-vitalism" began in Germany with Johannes Reinke (b. 1849; *Die Welt als Tat*, 1899). Its most eminent representative is Hans Driesch (b. 1867): *Der Vitalismus als Geschichte und Lehre*, 1905 (English trans., *History and Theory of Vitalism*, 1914); *Philosophie des Organischen*, 1908; *Wirklichkeitslehre*, 1917. Two works published in English, *Science and Philosophy of the Organism*, 1908, and *The Problems of Individuality*, 1914, contain translations from several German originals together with added matter.

[2] 1813–1883. Wagner was influenced by Feuerbach and Hartmann, as well as by Schopenhauer.

[3] *Die Geburt der Tragödie aus dem Geist der Musik*, 1872; English trans., 1910.

of disillusionment;[1] in both he sought refuge from the too easy and too edifying enthusiasms of romanticism. To this naturalistic stage of his development belong his *Human, All Too Human*, and his *Joyful Wisdom*.[2] Finally, in his *Zarathustra* and later works[3] he found a unity of his own in the philosophy of "the will to power," which is both the Dionysian principle in culture and the vital principle in nature. Meanwhile a progressive disease, which he contracted during his service as nurse in the Franco-Prussian War, and which had compelled him to abandon his professorship in 1879, aggravated his extreme sensitiveness and emotional instability; and finally brought him, in 1888, to a state of entire mental collapse which lasted until his death in 1900.

In the naturalistic phase of his thought Nietzsche abandoned his earlier leanings towards a spiritualistic metaphysics, and adopted the standpoint of biology. But while in so doing he was greatly influenced by Darwin, he was a Darwinian only in a limited sense.[4] Life is essentially a force of self-assertion ("a living thing seeks above all to *discharge* its strength"), and evolution, or the "ascent of the line of life,"[5] is the triumph of strength over weakness. Adaptation, or a passive submission to the environment, is the very opposite of life. The course of evolution is determined by the will: those survive who *will* survive. This is both a description of fact, a practical appeal, and a standard of value. The good life is the life which by the might of its superiority both *can* survive and *deserves* to survive. There is but one obligation upon man, which is to stretch his powers to their limit, and thus to become "super-man."

---

[1] It was this which attracted him to Voltaire.

[2] *Menschliches, Allzumenschliches*, 1878 (English trans., 1909–1911); *Die fröhliche Wissenschaft*, 1882 (English trans., 1910).

[3] *Also sprach Zarathustra*, 1882 (English trans., *Thus Spake Zarathustra*, 1909); *Jenseits von Gut und Böse*, 1886 (English trans., *Beyond Good and Evil*, 1907); *Zur Genealogie der Moral*, 1887 (English trans., *The Genealogy of Morals*, 1910); *Der Wille zur Macht* (incomplete), 1888 (English trans., *The Will to Power*, 1909–1910).

[4] § 70.

[5] *Beyond Good and Evil*, § 13; *Will to Power*, p. 674. Cf. §§ 491–492.

"The Superman is the meaning of the earth. Let your will say: The Superman *shall* be the meaning of the earth." [1]

In terms of this central vitalistic and voluntaristic conception Nietzsche interpreted knowledge, ethics, and religion. He was not interested in proofs, but rather in the psychology of that which calls itself knowledge. Psychology is "the path to the fundamental problems." [2] Behind all logic there are "physiological demands for the maintenance of a definite mode of life." Man could not live without "logical fictions," errors, falsity, foolishness, — the only question being "how far an opinion is life-furthering, life-preserving, species-preserving, perhaps species-rearing." All philosophy is a "confession, a sort of ʹinvoluntary and unconscious auto-biography.ʹ " [3] The deeper truth of the disillusioned will to power is revealed only to the initiated, or to a sort of intellectual aristocracy. It would be cheapened and vulgarized by general agreement. It is not attested by its contributions to "happiness and virtue," but rather by its dangerousness, or by the fact that only the strong can endure it. [4] The supreme test of the strong man is his ability to endure the vision of that "eternal recurrence" which is the fundamental law of nature. He will endure it because his very strength ennobles existence and makes tolerable the thought of its eternity. [5]

Turning to "the genealogy of our moral prejudices," Nietzsche finds that the root of all value is to be found in the superior man's sense of his own nobility. [6] The true ethics, which serves as the norm by which to judge the diversity of moral codes, is this aristocratic ethics of self-affirmation and mastery. Any moral code is to be condemned which does not promote "*the maximum potentiality of the power and splendor of the human species.*" Judged by this standard the traditional code of self-denial and commiseration, "the morality of pity,"

---

[1] *Thus Spake Zarathustra*, Prologue, § 3.
[2] *Beyond Good and Evil*, § 23.
[3] *Beyond Good and Evil*, §§ 3, 4, 6.   [4] *Ibid.*, §§ 39, 43.
[5] *Thus Spake Zarathustra*, part III, ch. LX.
[6] *Genealogy of Morals*, Preface, § 2, and *First Essay*, § 2.

— is "the most sinister symptom of our modern European civilization."[1] It is the code of the slavish herd, a code of envy and helplessness, which since it disparages nobility and idealizes weakness is the very inverse of true morality.

Christianity itself is judged and condemned by the same standard. It is not a question of proving or disproving God's existence, but of determining the ennobling or degrading effect of the Christian cult. The Christian God is to be rejected because as conceived by Christianity he is not divine. The "Christian God" is "the poor people's God," "one of the most corrupt concepts of God ever arrived at on earth," because "everything strong, brave, domineering, and proud has been eliminated" out of it; it is "God degenerated to the contradiction of life, instead of being its transfiguration and its eternal *yea!*"[2]

§ 82. The Impulse to Life. Bergson

HENRI BERGSON is affiliated with the French spiritualistic movement represented by Ravaisson, Lachelier, and Boutroux, but he is none the less sharply distinguished by his naturalistic leanings. While French spiritualism proclaims the fundamental reality of the creative will, this reality is held to reveal itself most profoundly in its higher flights, — in thought, morality, art, and religion.[3] While will as active and free is prior to reason construed as passive necessity, this is only because will is itself essentially rational, in the sense of being governed by its own inherent ends of truth, goodness, beauty, and universality. With Bergson, on the other hand, the essential nature

---

[1] *Ibid.*, Preface, §§ 5, 6.

[2] *The Antichrist*, §§ 17, 18; English trans., *The Case of Wagner*, etc., 1896, pp. 257–258.

[3] The most distinguished contemporary exponent of this French tradition is Maurice Blondel (b. 1861; *L'Action*, 1893; *Le Procès de l'Intelligence*, 1922). Blondel affirms the primacy of will. His method, however, is that of rigorous proof (adapted to the circumstance that in the knowledge of the will the knower and the known are one); and he distinguishes over and above the empirical will of biology and psychology a deeper metaphysical will, which is universal, and which expresses itself in the ideals of ethics and religion.

of metaphysical reality is revealed in the natural life and consciousness. Philosophy takes as its point of departure not the standards and ideals of the normative sciences, but the empirical content of biology and psychology.

Bergson was born in 1859 and was for twenty years (1901–1921) professor at the Collège de France. His brilliancy of style, the cosmopolitan and versatile quality of his genius, and the daring and novelty of his ideas have given him an influence greater than that of any other living philosopher. His three principal works all adopt a psychological or biological point of departure. The *Immediate Data of Consciousness*[1] distinguishes between the fundamental self whose states are inseparably fused and "interpenetrating," and the "spatialized" self of discrete states; ascribing freedom to the former and determinism to the latter. *Matter and Memory*[2] investigates the relation of mind and body, and affirms that consciousness in the form of "pure memory" is independent of the brain, which is an instrument of action. Finally, *Creative Evolution*[3] traces the course of this same active reality in the physical cosmos, where, assuming the forms of plant and animal life, it opposes and overcomes the resistance of inert matter.

Bergson's entire philosophy is pervaded by a fundamental duality that appears in many forms, such as spirit and matter, life and mechanism, time and space, freedom and determinism, interpenetration and juxtaposition, spontaneity and rigidity, intuition and intellect. This duality can best be approached through the last of these oppositions, as being the most radical and distinctive.

[1] *Essai sur les Données immédiates de la Conscience*, 1889 (English trans., *Time and Free Will*, 1910).

[2] *Matière et Mémoire: essai sur la relation du corps avec l'esprit*, 1896 (English trans., 1911).

[3] *L'Évolution créatrice*, 1907 (English trans., 1911). The most important of his other writings are: *Le Rire*, 1900 (English trans., *Laughter*, 1911); *Introduction à la Métaphysique*, in *Revue de Métaphysique et de Morale*, 1903 (English trans., 1912); *L'Energie spirituelle*, 1920 (English trans., *Mind-Energy*, 1920); *Durée et Simultanéité*, 1922.

Bergson's view of knowledge begins with a distinction between perception and memory in their *purity* — a distinction of kind and not of degree.[1] Pure perception coincides with ever-changing present existence; it participates in the immediately given reality, following its movements, prolonging them in bodily movements, and having an intimation of their infinite spread and continuity. Pure memory, on the other hand, is the whole past preserved in the shape of unconscious psychical states, unlocalized, and irrelevant to the present moment of action.

But perception and memory in their purity are thus distinguished only in order to trace their interaction on one another. That which merges them or qualifies the one by the other is the body, which is a "centre of action," employing both perception and memory, and binding the two together for *practical* purposes. Ordinary perception is not, like pure perception, preoccupied with the object, but introduces memory, which evokes from the remoter past "those former perceptions which are analogous to the present perception," and so suggests "that decision which is the most useful." Similarly, ordinary memory is restricted to those images which are relevant to the present. Pure memory is the whole past indiscriminately preserved, the deep reservoir of spiritual energy which in the interest of present action has to be held below the threshold of waking consciousness, and allowed to manifest itself only in so far as it is appropriate and useful. In dreams, delirium, hallucination, false recognition, insanity, or revery the flood gates are inadvertently opened, and consciousness, though enriched, loses touch with actualities. Normally this under-mind is drawn upon only so far as it can be brought to bear on the present practical situation, and it is only memory in this limited sense of vigilant and economical recall, that is dependent on the body.[2]

Thus ordinary perception is not a theoretic contemplation

---

[1] *Matter and Memory*, English trans., p. 72.
[2] *Mind-Energy*, English trans., II, IV, V.

of reality, but a plan of action. The object is reduced to that which is to be done about it. The very cleavages that divide one object from another are an effect of artificial isolation. The corporeal aspects of the world,—its static, orderly, spatial, and quantitative characters, are an effect of fixation and abridgment; while its qualitative characters are an effect of the "condensation" of the immediate past. Science is only the elaboration and refinement of this same tendency, already manifested in perception and in common-sense. The most exact sciences, such as physics, mathematics, and logic, are not, as is commonly supposed, the most theoretical, the most purely cognitive; but, on the contrary, are the most conventional, schematic, and therefore practical. The intellect reaches the acme of artificiality and of utility in conceptual thinking. "To try to fit a concept on an object is simply to ask what we can do with the object, and what it can do with us. To label a certain object with a certain concept is to mark in precise terms the kind of action or attitude the object should suggest to us." [1]

Reality is to be known as it is only by "intuition"; and to obtain this metaphysical insight it is necessary to recognize and discount the bias of our practical needs. "By unmaking that which these needs have made, we may restore to intuition its original purity and so recover contact with the real." As regards our own inner life and freedom, instead of objectifying ourselves, and so bringing ourselves under the spatializing, decomposing, and deterministic categories of science, we can, by changing the point of view, become immediately aware of that "duration *wherein we act*" (*durée réele*) and wherein "our states melt into each other." [2] We may obtain a similar immediate knowledge or intuition of material reality by relaxing the tension of practical effort, and restoring the wealth of content which our practical effort has contracted into instantaneous and abbreviated summaries. Then the qualities

[1] *Introduction to Metaphysics*, English trans., p. 41.
[2] *Matter and Memory*, English trans., pp. 241, 243–244.

of perception dissolve into a myriad of little movements, and the minor differences which were negligible for practical purposes emerge again in all their multiplicity.

It is evident that the dualism of intellect and intuition is by no means unreconciled. In the first place, while the intellect falsifies reality in the interest of practice, it does so not by fabrication, but by *selection*. Of the lower or purely material aspect of nature it renders an approximately adequate account, and even in the sphere of life and mind it fails through insufficiency or partiality, rather than through any absolute contrariety to fact. Intellect does not create out of whole cloth, but isolates, arrests, and over-simplifies, through dwelling exclusively on something which *is* there, but which is only a small *fragment* of what is there. Furthermore, it has to be recognized that this very falsification is achieved in the interest of practice. Intellect is an indispensable adjunct of life where, as in man, this reaches the highest degree of emancipation from matter. When thought is construed as a plan of action, science becomes an infinite multiplication of the possibilities of action, which through its very extension of the range of determination in the object, increases the indeterminateness or freedom of the agent.

As Bergson's cognitive dualism is reconciled through conceiving intellect in terms of selection and the requirements of action, so his metaphysical dualism is reconciled through conceiving life and matter as only the inverse and complementary aspects of the same process, the one being its "making" and the other its "unmaking." Reality is movement or activity which has different degrees of intensity, and two opposite tendencies. Positively it tends to be gathered all at once into a moment of creation, or focussed to a point of pure activity; negatively it tends to relax and dissolve, and thus to become more repetitive, homogeneous, and stagnant.

Evolution reveals a struggle of the positive or active tendency, the vital impulse (*élan vital*), against the resistance offered by the negative or passive tendency. Life is everywhere endeavoring to maintain and increase itself amidst the drag and inertia of materiality. When it succumbs it lapses into mechanism, as in the case of habit. Its first victory is the accumulation and storage of energies which can be explosively released. This is the achievement of plant life. Profiting by this achievement, animal or mobile life diverges in two directions, culminating in the "instinct" of the arthropods and the "intelligence" of the vertebrates. Instinct is capacity to deal directly and infallibly with the object, an adaptation of the organism itself to its immediate environment. Intelligence is a capacity to deal indirectly and experimentally with the object by the fabrication and use of mechanical tools, which are external both to the organism and to the object on which it acts. Instinct tends to be unconscious through the fact that its knowledge is a perfect adaptation translated instantly into action: its knowledge consists in a capacity to *do* the right thing in the given circumstances. Intellect, on the other hand, has more projects than it can fulfil; and it is just this multiplication of possibilities which makes human life so highly conscious, and so unpredictable.

The value of life lies in its intensity and activity; and here again the duality of life and matter is softened by the reflection that effort would be impossible without matter. "By the resistance matter offers and by the docility with which we endow it, it is at one and the same time obstacle, instrument, and stimulus." [1] Matter also divides spirit, and individuates it, thus setting the task of the achievement and growth of personality. But Bergson, unlike Nietzsche, never loses sight of the *unity* of life. There appears to have been "some original and essential aspiration of life which could find full satisfaction only in society." "It is the moral man who is a creator in the highest degree, — the man whose action, itself intense, is also capable of intensifying the action of other men, and, itself generous, can kindle fires on the hearths of generosity." [2] Bergson's religious imagination is fired by the same idea. With

---

[1] *Mind-Energy*, English trans., p. 29.   [2] *Ibid.*, pp. 32–34.

this doctrine of life as a single immense wave spreading outward from the same centre, "we feel ourselves no longer isolated in humanity, humanity no longer seems isolated in the nature that it dominates. . . . All the living hold together, and all yield together to the same push." God is this central radiation of life. "God thus defined, has nothing of the already made: He is unceasing life, action, freedom." [1]

§ 83. Pragmatism and the Will to Believe. James

The difference between Bergson and WILLIAM JAMES is the difference between a psychological biology and a biological psychology. Both oppose materialism and mechanism in that they find the centre of reality in the field of life and mind, and both oppose spiritualism of the traditional type in that they interpret life and mind in terms of their observed or felt existence, rather than in terms of their standards or "norms." Both might be described by such phrases as "naturalistic spiritualism" or "spiritualistic naturalism." Both, furthermore, tend to reduce life and mind to common terms. The difference is that while for Bergson these common terms retain a stronger flavor of life, for James they retain a stronger flavor of mind. For Bergson's reality the most adequate term is "activity," for that of James "experience."

This difference arises, on the part of James, from the influence of the British empirical school, in which he takes his place in the line of succession after Hume and Mill; and from his lifelong preoccupation with psychology. This latter interest sprang both from the psychological emphasis of British empiricism, and from his own early training in the biological sciences. In experimental and physiological psychology he found a fruitful contact between the scientific method and the larger human problems. Through his wide reading and culture, and owing to a profound antipathy to what he took to be the dogmatic negations of science, his philosophical interests took root early in his career and never ceased to dominate him;

[1] *Creative Evolution*, English trans., pp. 265–266, 270–271, 248.

but it was through his contributions to psychology that they found their first important expression. *The Principles of Psychology,* his greatest work, and of epoch-making importance in the history of this science, appeared in 1890. The volume of essays entitled *The Will to Believe,* published in 1897, brought more clearly to light the broad philosophical implications of his psychology. His theory of truth was published under the title of *Pragmatism* in 1907, and gave its name to the school of which he was now the accepted leader. *The Varieties of Religious Experience* (1902) and *A Pluralistic Universe* (1909) contained his speculations in the field of religion and metaphysics.[1] From 1880 until 1907, three years before his death in 1910, James was a teacher of psychology and philosophy at Harvard University. His numerous contacts with European scholars, his cosmopolitan outlook and cast of mind, and his extreme versatility combined to spread his influence more widely than that of any American thinker of his day.

James's psychology contains, over and above a wealth of empirical detail, two central ideas that governed his later philosophical thought. Although disposed to construe consciousness, after the manner of the British tradition, as a manifold of distinguishable states traceable to sense-experience, he insisted upon its *activity* and *unity*. The activity of consciousness is selective, interested, teleological. It attends to this or that within a "theatre of simultaneous possibilities," and thus "carves out" its own world from "the jointless continuity of space and moving clouds of swarming atoms."[2] Especially is this true of the higher faculties of will and intellect, of which the former, by dwelling upon one idea to the exclusion of others, causes it to fill the mind and thus to express itself in outward action; while the latter isolates and integrates "things," imputes reality to them in so far as they are re-

---

[1] Among the more important of his other philosophical writings are, *The Meaning of Truth,* 1909, and the posthumous publications, *Some Problems of Philosophy,* 1911, and *Essays in Radical Empiricism,* 1912.

[2] *Principles of Psychology,* vol. I, pp. 288–289.

lated "to our emotional and active life," and conceives them under whatever aspect may prove most significant and fruitful.[1] The unity of consciousness consists in its through and through connectedness. It is a flowing stream, of which the "substantive" parts shade into one another through the "transitive" parts, and in which every object is surrounded by a "fringe," or accompanied by a "feeling of tendency" through which it passes over into another.[2]

James's theory of knowledge was developed from this psychological standpoint, and is throughout dominated by its two main characteristics: its emphasis on the categories of interest and practice; and its reduction of relations, substances, activities, and other alleged transcendent elements to the continuities of sense-experience. The former motive in James's thought led to his voluntarism and pragmatism, the latter to his "radical empiricism."

The voluntaristic or pragmatic[3] theory of knowledge begins with a distinction between knowledge *by acquaintance* and knowledge *about*. In the former the object is immediately presented, in the latter it is known mediately, or by means of ideas. The function of the idea in knowledge is not to reproduce the object, but to prepare for or lead the way to it. Pragmatism consists, in the first place, in the "method" which interprets our idea of an object as "what conceivable effects of a practical kind the object may involve — what sensations we are to expect from it, and what reactions we must prepare."[4] The truth of an idea will therefore consist in the satisfaction which it affords, either through the fulfilment of the sensory expecta-

---

[1] *Op. cit.*, vol. II, p. 295; ch. XIX, XXI, XXII, XXVI.

[2] *Op. cit.*, vol. I, ch. IX.

[3] James attributed this theory and its name to Charles S. Peirce (1839–1914), a scholar of great erudition and originality, who distinguished himself in physics as well as philosophy, and was one of the founders of "symbolic logic." Some of his scattered writings were published in 1923, under the title of *Chance, Love and Logic*. The article to which James referred as the original source of pragmatism was entitled "How to Make Our Ideas Clear," and appeared in *Popular Science Monthly* in 1878. James's reference to Peirce is in *Pragmatism*, p. 46.

[4] *Ibid.*, pp. 46–47.

tion or the success of the reaction. But since we form expectations only for the purposeso f action, their fulfilment is only
an incident of practical success, and we may say of truth as
a whole that it consists in the utility or "working" of ideas;
or that "the true . . . is only the expedient in our way of
thinking." [1] It is the will which accounts for our having ideas
at all, and it is the will to which in the last analysis they are
accountable.

This being the case, moral or æsthetic demands may properly
be decisive where ideas are not verifiable in the limited sense
of the fulfilment of sensory expectations. This is James's
famous doctrine of the "will to believe," which, following
Renouvier, he argues against the scruples of positivists such as
Clifford.[2] Since science itself arises in response to practical
demands, it cannot overrule such demands. He who from
scientific scruples declines to believe in God is in effect *dis*-
believing in God; and sense-experience does not support the
negation any more than it supports the affirmation. Since
one cannot remain non-committal, — since, in other words,
there is a "forced option," "our passional nature not only law-
fully may, but must decide." [3]

James's doctrine of "radical empiricism" is closely related
to the "phenomenism" of Renouvier. It means not only that
reality in order to be "debatable" at all shall be "definable in
terms drawn from experience," but that experience is coherent
and self-sufficient *in its own terms*. There is no need of invoking
any non-empirical type of unity, such as a transcendent substance, or a pure activity, or an *a priori* synthetic consciousness,
since experience contains its own bonds, in the shape of "conjunctive relations," which "are just as much matters of direct
particular experience, neither more so nor less so, than the
things themselves." [4] The most remarkable application of this
thesis is to consciousness itself, which is not an entity outside
its own experience, but only one type of conjunctive relation

---

[1] *Ibid.*, p. 222. [2] §§ 71, 76. [3] *Will to Believe*, p. 11.
[4] *Meaning of Truth*, pp. xii, xiii.

among these experiences. The same identical terms of "pure experience" taken in one (the causal or energetic) type of relationship constitute "the system of external realities," while taken in another type of relationship they constitute "the stream of our internal thinking." [1]

James's metaphysics, like his theory of knowledge, has both its empirical and its practical mode of approach. Empirically we must take reality to be just what it seems to be, as it is given to us in direct acquaintance: "that distributed and strung-along and flowing sort of reality which we finite beings swim in." [2] Its most characteristic features are those which the ordinary logic rejects. Logical difficulties are, however, created by that very intellectualism which is baffled by them. For intellect deals with things by abstraction and then proceeds as though there were nothing to the thing but what is abstracted. The solution lies not in making more abstractions, but in a return to the original concreteness. It is in this appeal from the self-limiting and self-defeating processes of the intellect to the illumination of intuitive immediacy that James found himself confirmed by Bergson.[3] It enabled him not only to adhere to the empirical standpoint in metaphysics, or to identify reality with experience, but also to accept as a probable hypothesis Fechner's doctrine of a superhuman consciousness, compounded of the experiences of human and infra-human minds. This hypothesis acquires plausibility from the "abnormal or super-normal phenomena" of multiple personality, automatic writing, and mediumship; but above all from the *religious experience*, with its conviction "that we inhabit an invisible spiritual environment from which help comes, our soul being mysteriously one with a larger soul whose instruments we are." [4] The mystical intuition would then be "only very sudden and great extensions of the ordinary 'field of consciousness,'" — "an immense spreading of the margin of the field." [5]

[1] *Essays in Radical Empiricism*, p. 22. Cf. Mach, § 72.
[2] *Pluralistic Universe*, p. 213. [3] *Ibid.*, Lect. VI.
[4] *Ibid.*, pp. 298–299, 308–309. Cf. *Varieties of Religious Experience*, Lect. XX.
[5] *Collected Essays and Reviews*, 1920, p. 500.

In this sense a metaphysics which is pluralistic and yet religious obtains a certain "direct empirical verification." [1] But this same view is supported also by the demands of the moral and emotional life. Theism is "the most practically rational solution it is possible to conceive." Only the supposition of a finite God of limited responsibility, and an undetermined world, in which what ought to be is genuinely possible, can make the existence of evil tolerable to the moral will.[2] Only the sense of being under God a "faithful fighter" in the cause of righteousness, together with faith in an ultimate victory to which one will one's self have furnished a genuine contribution, can make "life worth living."[3] Thus the pragmatic theory of knowledge and the empirical-pluralistic metaphysics converge in a militant moralism and theistic faith.

After James the most distinguished American representative of the vitalistic, voluntaristic, pragmatic school is JOHN DEWEY (b. 1859). His philosophy is commonly referred to as "instrumentalism," in so far as it affirms that cognition consists in forging ideal tools or instruments by which to cope with a given situation in which activity has been thwarted. Dewey's thought is distinguished by its emphasis on *social philosophy* and *progress*, thought consisting in the perpetual reconstruction of ends or purposes by which life is liberalized and expanded.[4]

In England the leading exponent of this school is F. C. S. SCHILLER (b. 1864). He calls his philosophy "humanism," in order to emphasize the dependence of knowledge and truth on human nature and on the moral and religious demands. His emphasis on the creative and authoritative rôle of the concrete individual gives him a certain affinity with "personal idealism" (§ 78).[5]

---

[1] *Pluralistic Universe*, p. 308.
[2] *Ibid.*, essay on "The Dilemma of Determinism."
[3] *Ibid.*, essay on "Is Life Worth Living?"
[4] Cf. his *Studies in Logical Theory*, 1903; *Essays on Experimental Logic*, 1916; *Democracy and Education*, 1916; *Experience and Nature*, 1925.
[5] Cf. his *Riddles of the Sphinx*, 1891; *Humanism*, 1903; *Studies in Humanism*, 1907.

In Germany HANS VAIHINGER (b. 1852) has emphasized the
biological and economic nature of thought, and construed the
concepts of science, ethics, jurisprudence, and religion as useful "fictions." It is convenient or fruitful to treat objects "as
if" they were what in fact and in logic they are not.[1]

D. THE REVIVAL OF REALISM

§ 84. Realism in Germany. Meinong. Husserl

The term "idealism" is used in modern philosophy to indicate the view that to be and to be known are one and the same;
or that the act by which anything comes into mind is the same
as the act by which it comes into being. "Realism," as the
opposite to this view, will then mean that some or all known
objects owe their being to conditions different from those to
which they owe their being known; or that it is possible that
objects should be without being known. It is evident that one
may take either the idealistic or the realistic view of *all* objects,
and thus be pan-idealistic or pan-realistic; or that one may
take the idealistic view of some objects, and the realistic view
of others. In the latter case, one may stress either the real or
the ideal objects as being the more fundamental.

During the nineteenth century half-realisms were very
common, but they had great difficulty in maintaining themselves because of an inherent drift toward idealism. Thus
materialism, for example, was idealistic as regards the content
of both sense-perception and thought, since the former was
conceived as the effect on the mind or sentient organism of
external physical stimuli, and the latter as a secondary and
still more subjective reproduction of sense-perception. Sense-
qualities and ideas were thus conceived as owing their existence and nature to the same causal act which brought them
into consciousness. The original physical cause itself, on
the other hand, was supposed to exist independently of being

[1] Cf. his *Philosophie des Als Ob*, 1911 (English trans., *The Philosophy of "As
If,"* 1924).

known, and was regarded as the more fundamental reality. But a double difficulty arose. All sense-qualities and ideas being construed as subjective effects, there was nothing left in terms of which to characterize the alleged external object; and there being no specified act of knowledge which did not create its own content, it was inconceivable that one should even know that there *was* such an object. The external object was reduced to an *x*, of which one could neither know *what* it was nor *that* it was.

Spiritualism also was commonly idealistic as regards both sense-perception and thought, and also, like materialism, held a realistic view of the world lying beyond them. But spiritualism introduced a new type of content in terms of which to characterize this outlying reality, a content derived from the immediate self-experience of the subject, or what the knowing mind is to itself. This content, also, must be construed idealistically, since it *is* the very character of being *to* or *for* itself. By what act, then, is this character ascribed by any human self to *another* self, human or divine? If by perception or thought, as these are employed in the argument from analogy, then the other self is annexed to the knowing self; for sense-qualities belong to the subject that perceives them, and ideas to the subject that thinks them. There remains only the supposition of a kind of sympathetic insight, in which the knower projects himself into the known, and grasps it as it is to itself. In other words, one knows the other self by *becoming* the other self. But in that case the other self ceases to be *another* self, and one is reduced again to the case of the immediate experience of the active self, in which being and being known are one and the same thing.

Thus the realisms of the nineteenth century tended to gravitate towards idealism of one or the other of two types: either of the relatively intellectual type, in which reality is the organization of sense-perception by thought; or of the relatively irrational type, in which reality is the pure activity of spirit. Of these types the former tended to prevail over the latter because it embraced both experience and logic, while the latter rested its case on a more elusive and doubtful intuition.

The first two decades of the twentieth century have witnessed a widespread reaction against this victorious idealism, and the revival of realism in a more circumspect and stable form. This new movement is yet in its beginnings, and embraces a wide diversity of doctrine. Its unity, apart from its common polemic against idealism, lies in its endeavor to escape the essential weakness of the earlier realisms. This weakness lay in its virtually abandoning its case at the outset in conceding the idealistic interpretation of sense-perception, or of thought, or of both. Instead of construing sense-perception as an effect induced in the mind by the action of external objects, and capable, therefore, of revealing only the momentary state of the mind itself, the newer realism construes sense-perception as an act in which the existent object is *given* or *disclosed*. Instead of construing thought as a creative activity, in which the laws of the mind itself are exhibited and expressed, the newer realism construes thought as an act which *refers to* or *intends* objects of a non-existent or subsistent realm, such as logical entities or relations. There is thus in the current realistic theory of knowledge a general insistence that knowledge is a way of *taking* rather than of *making* objects; and there is a division or alternation of emphasis between empirical, existent objects, and logical, non-existent objects.

The German branch of this movement was influenced by the psychologist FRANZ BRENTANO,[1] who derived from his studies of Aristotle and scholasticism a view of mind as "intentional." It is characteristic of psychical activity to be directed primarily upon *òbjects*, which may either exist or not exist; and only secondarily, in retrospect, upon itself. ALEXIUS MEINONG,[2] student of Brentano at Vienna in 1874, and after 1882

[1] 1838–1917. *Psychologie vom empirischen Standpunkte*, 1874.

[2] 1853–1920. Among his more important writings are the following: *Psychologisch-ethische-Untersuchungen zur Wert-Theorie*, 1894; *Über Annahmen*, 1902,

professor at the University of Graz, developed a branch of philosophical investigation which he called "theory of objects" (*Gegenstandstheorie*); which differs from psychology and theory of knowledge in abstracting from the relation to the empirical subject, and from metaphysics in transcending the realm of existence. "Object" in this generalized sense includes not only that which exists, like a physical thing, and that which merely "subsists" (*Bestehen*), such as qualities, numbers, or propositions, but even that which like the "round square" can neither exist nor subsist, although it can be referred to and thought about. It is peculiarly characteristic of Meinong to distinguish between judging (with conviction) and merely considering or "assuming" (*annahmen*); and to insist that even this latter act, tentative and non-committal as it is, nevertheless addresses itself to a peculiar kind of complex object, which can be verbally expressed only by a clause beginning with the conjunction "that." Thus "a white horse" is an object (*Objekt*) in the narrower sense of that which may be perceived, or of which I may form an idea; while "*that* the horse is white" is an "objective," which can be an object (in the broader sense of *Gegenstand*) only when one judges or assumes "that" such is the case. Objects stand to one another, furthermore, in a relation of "superior" to "inferior," or of higher to lower order, the former being "founded" upon or presupposing the latter, as "the difference between red and green" presupposes "red" and "green." Although the object of a mental act is "immanent," in the sense of being within range of, or *before*, the mind, it has to be distinguished from the content (*Inhalt*), which is *in* the mind. This latter is always existent, present and psychical, like the mental act itself; while the object may be non-existent, past or future, or physical.

Meinong has also been largely influential in securing recog-

1910; "*Über Gegenstandstheorie*" in *Untersuchungen zur Gegenstandstheorie und Psychologie*, 1904; *Über emotionale Präsentation*, 1917; *Zur Grundlegung der allgemeinen Werttheorie*, 1923.

nition for a new branch of philosophy known as "theory of value," [1] which deals with the general principles applicable to all the senses in which things can be good or bad. His own peculiar doctrines appear in his view that value appertains only to "objectives"; or is the content of feeling when this is mediated by judgments or assumptions. The measure of the value of an object is the pleasure and pain felt on the assumption of its existence or non-existence. This particular kind of objective, or what one feels *should* exist, he calls a "dignitative"; just as he terms what one desires *to* exist, a "desiderative." Values have, in other words, that peculiar *nonexistent objectivity* which is so basic a feature of Meinong's whole philosophy.

EDMUND HUSSERL,[2] like Meinong, was influenced by Brentano, and, like Meinong, he has formulated a new branch of philosophical investigation, which he calls "phenomenology" (*phänomenologie*). This is a descriptive study of consciousness, or (since it is essentially characteristic of consciousness to have objects), a study of consciousness-of-objects. It is distinguished from ordinary science, including psychology, by its attitude (*Einstellung*). This peculiar phenomenological attitude is contrasted with the primary or "natural" conscious act, which is directed upon the object, and takes it to be real. By reflection the naïve, dogmatic attitude may be "reduced," or devitalized. One now no longer *lives* in the perceiving act, or views the object *through* it, but takes a detached position from which the object appears as simply the objective aspect of the act. It is like the difference between *believing* in God and thinking of myself as believing in God. In the latter case

---

[1] Cf. also Ch. von Ehrenfels, *System der Werttheorie*, 1897, and W. M. Urban, *Valuation*, 1909.

[2] Born 1859. His principal work is his *Logische Untersuchungen*, originally published in 1900–1901. His later views have appeared in revisions of this work (1913–1921) and in his *Ideen zu einer reinen Phänomenologie und phänomenologischen Philosophie*, 1914. He is professor at the University of Freiburg.

the belief is not asserted, but simply noted — God becoming only the objective component of the act.

Assuming the phenomenological attitude, what do we find? First of all that consciousness consists of acts directed to objects. But this is only a small part of the story. It is characteristic of Husserl's genius to multiply and refine distinctions rather than to reduce them to systematic unity. Consciousness may be viewed as lying between two poles, the ego and the object. On the side of the ego lies the subjective attitude with its various qualitative forms, such as believing, doubting, considering, or willing; and its modes of apprehension, such as presentation, representation, or symbolism. On the side of the object lies the object itself, and its "sense" (*Sinn*) or ideal character. Midway between the two lies the datum or content, such as images or sensory experience.

Whether this view is to be deemed realistic or idealistic is largely a matter of emphasis. The analysis of the cognitive process contains many realistic suggestions. The relation of the subject to the object is essentially one of seeing and intending, and implies that the object is approached or addressed, rather than constituted, by knowledge. Thus the physical object cannot be presented except in partial aspects or in perspective, so that there is a large element of uncertainty and error in perception; but what *is* presented is a part of the object, and the residual parts are such as may in turn be presented. Universals, on the other hand, can be wholly given, in a sort of intellectual vision or intuition of essences (*Wesenserschauung*). Similarly, the certainty of phenomenology lies in the fact that it does not "intend" any more than is given. Here even the perceptual object may be absolutely known, because it is "reduced" to what is immanent in the act of perception. All of these considerations suggest that objects are both independent of consciousness, and also capable of being more or less adequately brought within it.

On the other hand, Husserl's growing tendency to identify phenomenology and metaphysics is suggestive of idealism.

For the subject-matter of phenomenology is consciousness. In phenomenology all objects of consciousness assume the character of being objects-of-consciousness. From this point of view we are compelled to say not that the relation of the object to consciousness is that of being intended or seen — a relation to which the object is prior, and into which it may enter without prejudice to its independence; but that it is of the very nature of objects that they *should* be intended or seen, or that the complex operation of conscious objectification creates reality in the act of knowing it.

§ 85.   Realism in England and America

BERTRAND RUSSELL[1] forms the connecting link between Meinong and the realism which emerged on English soil as a reaction against the sceptical outcome of empiricism in Hume, and of intellectualism in Bradley. Russell believes that philosophy can be rescued from this predicament, and at the same time reconciled with science, only by the adoption of a reformed logic. His treatment of logic resembles Meinong's "theory of objects" (*Gegenstandstheorie*) in that it provides for a realm of entities which are neither physical nor psychical existences, — neither things nor thoughts — but which may be referred to, meant, and described. The subject-matter of mathematics belongs to this realm, and one of Russell's most signal contributions to contemporary thought is his unification of logic and mathematics; logic borrowing from mathematics its symbolic method, and mathematics borrowing from logic its fundamental premises.[2]

---

[1] Born 1872, and for some years fellow of Trinity College, Cambridge University. His most important philosophical works are: *Critical Exposition of the Philosophy of Leibniz*, 1900; *Principles of Mathematics*, 1903; *Principia Mathematica* (with A. N. Whitehead), 1910–1913; *Our Knowledge of the External World*, 1914; *Analysis of Mind*, 1921.

[2] Mathematics and logic thus merge into one branch of knowledge, which may be called (according to differences of emphasis) "mathematical" or "symbolic logic," or "the philosophy of mathematics." The most important contributions to this branch of knowledge (in addition to those of Russell and his

Russell describes his philosophy as a "logical atomism," in order to indicate his acceptance of the fundamental multiplicity of things, as revealed in analysis. He does not mean that the world is composed of corporeal atoms which are physically divisible from one another, but of relations, facts, and particular items which are *distinguishable* from one another without losing their meaning. Logic itself is atomistic in that it deals with propositions, which are essentially *relational* in structure and hence analyzable into simpler components. As between any two expressions of the same logical form the corresponding parts are interchangeable. Thus in the proposition "John is mortal," "James" may be substituted for "John" without altering the meaning of the remainder of the proposition. This Russell argues against the view that a proposition is an indivisible unity such that if any of it is changed, all of it is changed.

The confusions and contradictions of thought (including the so-called "paradoxes" and "antinomies") which have brought discredit on the intellect can all be avoided by a more scrupulous logic, which recognizes its essentially relational character, and observes the requirements of logical form. Most of the traditional difficulties are due to talking nonsense, that is, to combining words in ways which grammar permits but which logic forbids. Modern mathematics, escaping by the use of symbols the confusions arising from language, has already cleared up the most important of the traditional intellectualistic difficulties, those, namely, connected with infinity and continuity.

The intellect, being thus purified, is capable of providing the necessary support to sense-experience. The factual world is constituted of systems of particulars: the particulars are sensed, the systematic relations are logically conceived or judged. A fact is known by "description," when it is known

collaborator, Whitehead) have been made by G. Boole (1815–1864), G. Frege (b. 1848), G. Peano (b. 1858), L. Couturat (1868–1914), E. Schroeder (1841–1902), and C. S. Peirce (§ 83).

only by its systematic relations as judged; it is known by acquaintance, or in perception, when to this knowledge of its logical structure there is added the sensible presence of its constituent particulars.

Following James,[1] Russell construes the particular existences of sense as ground common to the physical and the psychical realms. The sense-datum is either physical or psychical according to the causal relations in which it is viewed. Hence the physical world, or the world of science, is composed of the same stuff as our sensory consciousness. Matter and "things," and all the entities of physical science (such as electrons), are only highly complex systems or "constructions" of the same experiential data which in other types of systematic unity make up minds.

Through all of the numerous representatives of the realistic tendency in England and in America there runs this same doctrine that knowledge (whether sense-perception or thought) addresses itself to reality, and at some point embraces it, but without compromising its independence. G. E. MOORE[2] presses the distinction between the object (such as the sense-quality) *of* which one is aware, and the *act* of awareness; insisting that it is essentially characteristic of such an act of awareness that "its object, when we are aware of it, is precisely what it would be, if we were not aware."[3] S. ALEXANDER[4] construes knowledge as an act of contemplation whose object is "compresent," the act itself being experienced immediately or "enjoyed." American realists fall, for the most part, into one or the other of two groups, known as "neo-realists" and "critical realists."[5] The former group has argued for the

---

[1] § 83.

[2] Cf. his "Refutation of Idealism," published together with other essays in his *Philosophical Studies*, 1922.

[3] *Op. cit.*, p. 29.

[4] Cf. his *Space, Time and Deity*, 1920.

[5] Each of these schools has published a co-operative volume, the former *The New Realism* (1912), by E. B. Holt, W. T. Marvin, W. P. Montague, R. B.

immediate presence both of physical existence in perception and of logical (or mathematical) subsistence in thought. The latter group, represented by G. SANTAYANA,[1] has distinguished between the general natures or "essences" which are immediately given, and the transcendent "existences" to which these are referred. According to this view, all that one can directly grasp in intuition is *what* the object is, if there is such an object; while *whether* there is such an object or not, can only be taken on "faith," or ascertained pragmatically. Both of these groups affirm that there is knowledge of an extramental reality, and that the character of this reality is conveyed by the content of our conscious experience.

While all contemporary realists agree that in cognition the mind somehow reveals reality rather than constitutes it, there are wide differences of opinion as to the nature of mind. At least three views are distinguishable. Moore, like Meinong and Husserl, is disposed to construe mind in terms of acts having a unique and irreducible character of intentional awareness. Others, like Russell and F. J. E. WOODBRIDGE,[2] are disposed to agree with James[3] in construing mind as a peculiar type of relationship (such as "meaning") whose terms are the same as those which, when otherwise related, compose the physical world. A third group, including Alexander and the American neo-realists, conceive mind in terms of the functional peculiarities of an organism endowed with a nervous system; or as an activity of the organism which, however, lies upon a different plane from those activities ordinarily construed as biological.[4]

Perry, W. B. Pitkin, and E. G. Spaulding; the latter *Essays in Critical Realism* (1920), by D. Drake, A. O. Lovejoy, J. B. Pratt, A. K. Rogers, G. Santayana, R. W. Sellars, and G. A. Strong.

[1] Cf. his *Life of Reason*, 1905; and *Scepticism and Animal Faith*, 1923.

[2] Cf. his "Nature of Consciousness," *Jour. of Philos.*, vol. II, 1905.

[3] § 83.

[4] This view is closely related to the contemporary psychological movement known as "behaviorism" according to which the *mind is* what, in its higher and more complex developments, the *body does*.

Realism is disposed to a metaphysical "pluralism"[1] through emphasis on the category of relation, whether of the empirical or logical variety. Materialism and spiritualism tend to a monism of substance: idealism to a monism of the cognitive act, or to the embracing of all reality within a single knowing mind. But through the realistic conception of relations, the differences of the world may compose an orderly structure without becoming inseparably one. Otherwise, realism is divided, in respect of metaphysics, between a tendency to "neutralism" and a tendency to naturalism. By the former is meant the view that reality cannot properly be characterized either in physical or in mental terms, but only in more primitive terms which underlie this distinction. Thus sense-qualities and relations, for example, are regarded as intrinsically neither physical nor mental, but as possessing a character common to these two realms. The naturalistic tendency, on the other hand, arises from the view that while, as regards their composition as revealed in analysis, physical and mental reality are both secondary, the order and history of existence is determined by physical laws, so that mind can be said to be a product of physical nature. This does not, however,[2] mean that mind is a product of ponderable matter, or of "merely" mechanical causes; for physical nature, as reinterpreted in terms of the content of perception and thought, assumes a character which reduces its difference from mind to one of degree rather than of kind. Alexander and L. T. HOBHOUSE[3] maintain that an emergence of purposiveness in life and mind is entirely consistent with a physico-chemical view of the lower levels of nature; while Alexander, Russell, and A. N. WHITEHEAD,[4] influenced by the current theory of relativity,

[1] Realists like Meinong and Husserl in his earlier stages of development represent a tendency in realism to avoid metaphysics, in a manner analogous to the "critical" method in idealism.

[2] Except in the case of Santayana, who inclines to a materialistic view of existence and a mechanical view of causation.

[3] *Development and Purpose*, 1913.

[4] *An Inquiry Concerning the Principles of Natural Knowledge*, 1919; *The Concept of Nature*, 1920.

conceive physical nature in terms of "events" occurring in "space-time," and thus relieve it of that aspect of inertness in which it once appeared as the very antithesis of mind.

As regards their practical philosophy, there is no agreement among contemporary realists, although their disagreements illuminate their realistic premises. Somewhat similar to Meinong's view of value as an "objective" is Santayana's view that value attaches to "essences" rather than to either physical or psychical existences. Values are immediably objective, but to mistake them for existences is to suffer illusion: to enjoy them one must intuit them without imputing existence to them. Moore, on the other hand, regards value ("intrinsic goodness") as an indefinable quality, which attaches to existent objects in the same sense as the color "yellow"; while Alexander and the American neo-realists incline to the view that value is a psychological character, which the object acquires only by relation to the liking or aversion of a sentient subject. Despite this marked diversity, all realists agree in being "realistic" in the popular sense. Realists of all schools reject the view commonly held by idealists, that value is a universal condition of existence. This idealistic thesis is based on the assumption that reality of every type arises from an act of mind, and is supported by the argument that since mind is essentially purposive or directed to the good, reality as the creation of mind will necessarily be an embodiment of perfection. Realism denies both the assumption and the argument. The nature of the world is judged by facts rather than by ideals. But though the world is not *necessarily* good, neither is it necessarily evil or indifferent to good. The degree of its goodness is a question of experience, or of practical endeavor, or of faith.

Realism is now sufficiently extended and developed to justify its being ranked among the major currents of modern philosophy. A survey of contemporary European and American philosophy reveals four strands: naturalism, both materialistic and positivistic; idealism and spiritualism; pragmatism, voluntarism, and vitalism; and realism. Though these strands are interwoven and interpenetrating, they can nevertheless be unmistakably distinguished as having each a characteristic color of its own.

INDEX